JOURNAL
of the
American Research Center in Egypt

VOLUME 58

2022

Published by

THE AMERICAN RESEARCH CENTER IN EGYPT

Contents

A Wooden Panel Inscribed for Amasis

Robert Steven Bianchi
The Ancient Egyptian Museum, Shibuya-ku, Tokyo, Japan

Abstract

A wooden, openwork panel inscribed for Amasis and embellished with secondary glass inlays and gilding was discovered in 2018 by the Franco-Swiss Archaeological Mission at South Saqqara in a disturbed, archaeological context littered with bovine skeletal remains in the southern section of the pyramid complex of queen Ankhnespepy II. The panel's openwork design finds its closest parallels in two-dimensional representations of funerary furnishing that suggest that this particular object formed part of the panoply of a sacred animal, suggested to have been a bull, the cults of which were supported by Amasis at Saqqara. Those comparisons call into question the function of all of the wooden panels embellished with glass inlays dated to the Late Period (given in Appendix) and whether the term, naos, is an appropriate designation for all such objects.

الملخص

تم اكتشاف لوحة خشبية مخرمة منقوشة لأمازيس مزينة بتطعيمات زجاجية ومذهبة في عام 2018 من قبل البعثة الأثرية الفرنسية-السويسرية في جنوب سقارة في سياق أثري مضطرب مليء ببقايا الهياكل العظمية البقرية في القسم الجنوبي من مجمع هرم الملكة عنخ-نس-بيبي الثانية. يعد تصميم اللوحة المخرمة قريب من التمثيلات ثنائية الأبعاد للأثاث الجنائزي التي تشير إلى أن هذه اللوحة كانت تشكل جزءًا من لوحة حيوان مقدس، يُقترح أنه كان ثورًا، وهي الطائفة التي دعمها أمازيس في سقارة. هذه المقارنات تثير التساؤل حول وظيفة جميع الألواح الخشبية المزخرفة بتطعيمات زجاجية التي تعود إلى العصر المتأخر (الواردة في الملحق) وما إذا كان المصطلح ناووس هو تسمية مناسبة لجميع هذه القطع.

The Mission archéologique franco-suisse de Saqqâra,[1] financially supported in part by the Fondation Gandur pour l'Art, Genève, excavated a remarkably well-preserved wooden panel exhibiting secondary inlays of glass with traces of gilding in a disturbed context in the southern section of the pyramid complex of Queen Ankhnespepy II (fig. 1).

[1] I wish to recognize the following members of the Mission archéologique franco-suisse de Saqqâra: Philippe Collombert, Director, for entrusting the publication of this object to me: Alain Charron, conservateur en chef du musée départemental de l'eArles antique, for his profitable discussions; and Jérôme Rizzo, Université Paul-Valéry, Montpellier 3, the mission's photographer. I am indebted to Jean Claude Gandur of the Fondation Gandur pour l'Art, Genève, for introducing me to Philippe and supporting my research during my tenure at the Fondation, during which time part of the research for this essay was completed. In particular I owe a debt of gratitude to Mervat Seif el-Din for providing me with offprints, and to Paola Davoli for several publications that feature prominently in the notes and for her continuing discussions with me about figural glass inlays in general. The acquisition of photographs used as figures in this essay was facilitated by Sylvia Schoske, Dietrich Wildung, and Jan Dahms in Munich; Yekaterina Barbash and Kathy Zurek-Doule in Brooklyn; Gloria R. Lopez, Kristen N. Qarles, Felicia Pickering, Barbara Watanabe, and James Krakker in Washington, D.C; Vincent Rondot and Audrey Viger in Paris; and François Maresquier of Meretseger Books. I thank the anonymous reviewers for their helpful comments. As always, I am indebted to Kyria Marcella Osborne for her copy-editing.

Journal of the American Research Center in Egypt 58 (2022), 5–17
http://dx.doi.org/10.5913/jarce.58.2022.a001

Fig. 1. Gilded wooden panel with inlays. Photo © Franco-suisse mission archéologique de Saqqara, Field Number 18-6; photographer, Jérôme Rizzo.

Franco-suisse mission archéologique de Saqqara Field Number 18-6
Wood, with glass inlays, gilded, and stuccoed
30 cm. greatest width
26.5 cm. greatest height, tang to tang
2.5 cm. greatest thickness
2.5 cm. greatest width of the smaller wooden panel

The preserved panel, almost square in format, is designed as an openwork composition. The panel is composed of two separately crafted pieces of wood with their joint running vertically just to the (spectator's) left of the cartouche (fig. 2). The two pieces have been fastened together without pegs or tenons. There is a single vertically aligned tang at approximately each of the four corners of the panel. The bottom left one is more fragmentary than the others. The skill of the fine joiners is evident in the manner in which the recesses into which the inlays were subsequently set have been designed so that they seamlessly span the joint with the result that the completed panel gives the impression that it had been cut from a single piece of wood.

The congruence between the design of each of the sockets and that of their corresponding inlays is so accurate as to suggest that each glass inlay was custom cast to fit into one and only one socket (fig. 3). Such precision

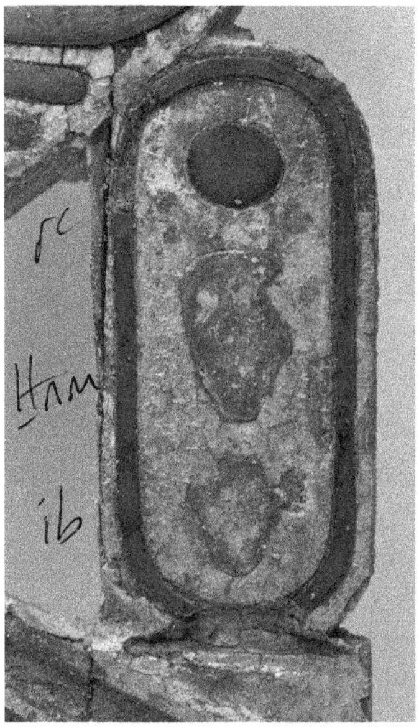

Fig. 2. The join of the two pieces of wood (left). Photo © Franco-suisse mission archéologique de Saqqara, Field Number 18-6; photographer, Jérôme Rizzo.

Fig. 3. View of the inlays in their sockets. Photo © Franco-suisse mission archéologique de Saqqara, Field Number 18-6; photographer, Jérôme Rizzo.

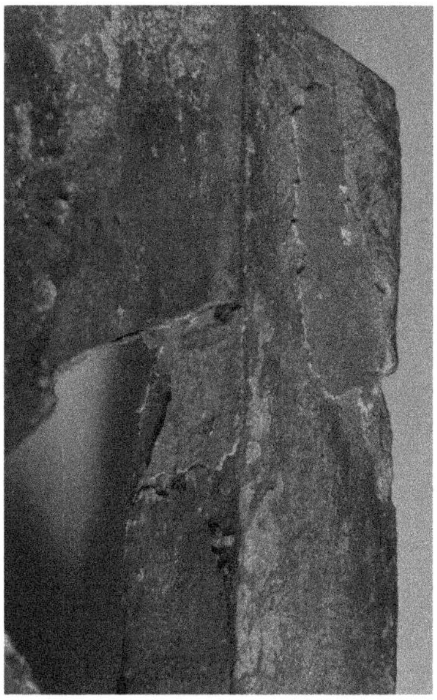

Fig. 4. Gilding on the vertical surfaces. Photo © Franco-suisse mission archéologique de Saqqara, Field Number 18-6; photographer, Jérôme Rizzo.

recalls that of the consummately crafted inlays so characteristic of the finest jewelry created during the Middle Kingdom, as a comparison with a pectoral from the tomb of Sithathoriunet so graphically reveals.[2] More remarkable still is the observation that the surfaces of the wood on the face of the panel have been gilded as have the vertical surfaces on the interiors of all of the cutouts (fig. 4). The vertical, exterior surface of the smaller wooden panel is completely gilded suggesting that it was intended to remain exposed and was never intended to be concealed by a door closing over it (fig. 5). The entire back of the panel, where the joint of the two pieces of wood is particularly evident, has been coated with a thin layer of plaster that does not appear to have been painted (fig. 6). Several of the glass inlays in the form of individual feathers exhibit an extraordinary technique that can best be compared to a human finger with its nail (fig. 7). The "finger" itself is either of blue or green glass on to which a red glass "nail" appears to have been fused. Such a technique appears to have been introduced for the first time during the Amarna Period as seen in the design of some of the feathers inlaid into the anthropoid, wooden sarcophagus discovered in KV 55[3] and in the design of the feathers on some of the jewels discovered in the tomb of Tutankhamun.[4] The design seems to have been favored for glass inlays created during the reign of Amasis because this same technique is exhibited by the glass inlays in a second panel that is likewise inscribed for him.[5] Isolated examples of such glass inlays were also discovered at Bacchias.[6] The bichrome appearance of such inlays is achieved either by simply adhering one element to the other or by fusing both together.[7]

---

[2] New York, The Metropolitan Museum of Art 16.1.3 in C. Andrews, *Ancient Egyptian Jewellery* (London, 1990), 24, fig. 15.

[3] Cairo, The Egyptian Museum JE 39627: A Grimm, "Das Münchner Konvolut aus "KV 55," in A. Grimm and S. Schoske (eds.), *Das Geheimnis des goldenen Sarges* (Munich, 2001), 68–77 with fig. 34 in particular.

[4] Carter 267a (Cairo, The Egyptian Museum JE 61666; GEM 159) in K. El Mallakh and A. C. Brackman, *The Gold of Tutankhamun* (New York, 1978), no. 114.

[5] Paris, Musée du Louvre E 605 (N 504). See Appendix, no. 3, below.

[6] V. Gasperini, G. Paolucci, and M. Tocci, *Catalogo dei frammenti lignei e degli intarsi in pasta vitrea da Bakchias (1996–2002)* (Bologna, 2008), 101–2.

[7] M.-D. Nenna, "Le mobilier religieux en bois incrusté de verre des temples égyptiens: nouvelles données (VIIe siècle av. J.-C. - Ier siècle apr. J-C.)," *Annales de l'Association Internationale pour l'Histoire du Verre 19* (2015), 30–32.

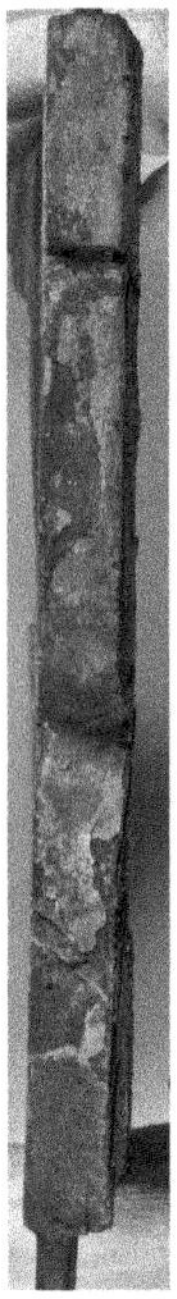

Fig. 7 (above). Bi-chrome inlays. Photo © Franco-suisse mission archéologique de Saqqara, Field Number 18-6; photographer, Jérôme Rizzo.

Fig. 6 (left). Reverse of panel with seam (left). The surface has a thin layer of plaster. Photo © Franco-suisse mission archéologique de Saqqara, Field Number 18-6; photographer, Jérôme Rizzo.

Fig. 5 (above left). Gilding on vertical exterior face of the panel. Photo © Franco-suisse mission archéologique de Saqqara, Field Number 18-6; photographer, Jérôme Rizzo.

Fig. 8. Detail of the goddess Khuit with her accompanying inscription. Photo © Franco-suisse mission archéologique de Saqqara, Field Number 18-6; photographer, Jérôme Rizzo.

The principal figure on the panel under discussion is that of a winged goddess facing right, kneeling upon a ground line. All of her flesh has been gilded, the layer appears to have been applied directly over a reddish-colored adhesive layer. Of her physiognomic features, only her eyebrow had originally been inlaid. Her accessories include a broad collar consisting of several strands of darker and lighter light blue glass inlays to which are attached green glass inlaid floral (?) elements. Her costume, assumed to have been a tightly fitting sheath, appears to have been designed with green colored glass inlays. Her upraised hand holds a green glass inlay of a maat-feather, its perimeter accented by a thin blue glass border.

The rectangular panel adjoined to the right side of the sun disc contains a hieroglyphic inscription of blue glass inlays oriented to the right and vertically bordered on each side by a thin framing band of blue glass. It reads:

ḏd mdw in Ḫwi

Recitation by Khuit

This goddess appears to be a personification of protection because the etymology of her name as based upon the root, *ḫwi* "to protect." She is principally regarded as a protectress, not only of the deceased but also of newly born child gods. The motif of a goddess with winged arms spread in a gesture of protection is a time-honored motif with variations that developed in ancient Egyptian art over time.[8] The image is found on pectorals from the tomb of Tutankhamun,[9] in vignettes within the tomb of Nefertari,[10] and on numerous representations on the sides of shrines on processional barques.[11] Often the winged arms of those goddesses embrace a cartouche. In this instance, the image of Khuit in conjunction with the cartouche between her wings, serves as a rebus, or visual pun, "the one who protects pharaoh," who is specifically named in hieroglyphs of blue inlays within a blue glass inlayed cartouche: *Ḫnm-ib-Rʿ*... Fig 2

Khnum-ib-Re is the prenomen of Amasis (570–526 BC), the fifth pharaoh of Dynasty 26. The association of Khuit and Amasis may not be coincidental because her function as a protectress is reinforced by the recurrence of her epithet, *ḥbs.t nṯr* "the one who envelops the god," particularly at Athribis, her principal cult center where Amasis appears to have been particularly active.[12] A wife of Psametik II whose tomb was discovered at Athribis was named Ta-[net]-Khuit,[13] and Amasis himself appears to have been particularly active there as well.

Although this panel is inscribed for Amasis, the object to which it belonged may not necessarily have been originally part of the funerary panoply of that pharaoh. The presence of his cartouche on this object resonates with numerous wooden receptacles containing the mummified remains of animals from the catacombs at Tuna el-Gebel that have panels that depict pharaohs in adoration.[14] These examples may not even have been commissioned by the pharaohs depicted on them,[15] although one must always keep in mind that the numerous animal cults of the Late Period have been associated with the cults of individual divinized rulers.[16] The presence of Khuit protecting Amasis represented by his cartouche must be understood within this general context, religiously

[8] R. Shonkwiler, "Sheltering Wings: Birds as Symbols of Protection in Ancient Egypt," in R. Bailleul-LeSeur (ed.), *Between Heaven and Earth: Birds in Ancient Egypt*, OIMP 36 (Chicago, 2012), 49–57.

[9] El Mallakh and Brackman, *The Gold of Tutankhamun*, nos. 89 and 91.

[10] G. Thausing and H. Goedicke, *Nofretari: Eine Dokumentation der Wandgemälde ihres Grabes* (Graz, 1971), figs. 46, 47, 52, and 53.

[11] C. Traunecker, F. Le Saout, and O. Masson, *La chapelle d'Achôris à Karnak II, Texte*, RGCS 5.1 (Paris, 1981), 83.

[12] P. Vernus, "Athribis," *LÄ* I, col. 522.

[13] R. B. Gozzoli, *Psammetichus II: Reign, Documents and Officials* (London, 2017), 20–22.

[14] Mallawi, Mallawi Antiquities Museum 200, in H. Messiha and M. A. Elhitta, *Mallawi Antiquities Museum: A Brief Description* (Cairo, 1979), 15 with pl. XVI.

[15] H. P. Colburn, *Archaeology of Empire in Achaemenid Egypt* (Edinburgh, 2020), 164–66, who opines that inscribed representations of pharaohs on such objects do not automatically imply that the pharaoh depicted was the object's commissioner.

[16] S. Davies and H. S. Smith, "Sacred Animal Temples at Saqqara," in S. Quirke (ed.), *The Temple in ancient Egypt: new discoveries and recent research* (London, 1997) 112–31, furthering the comments made earlier in that same volume by B. M. Bryan, "The Statue Program for the Mortuary Temple of Amenhotep III," (in Quirke, *The Temple in Ancient Egypt*, 57–81); and A. Monson, "Political and Sacred Animals: Religious Associations in Greco-Roman Egypt," in B. Eckhardt (ed.), *Private Associations and Jewish Communities in the Hellenistic and Roman Cities*, Supplements to the Journal of the Study of Judiasm 191 (Leiden, 2019), 37–57.

protecting and adoring the targeted animal mummy, which we suggest was contained within the piece of furniture of which this panel was a part.

It is interesting to note that there are a handful of other fragments of wooden objects inscribed with the name of Amasis discovered at Saqqara. In addition to the panel under discussion, there is a door leaf in London inscribed with the prenomen of Amasis in black ink,[17] and a fragment of a painted and gilded wooded cavetto cornice now in Toronto.[18] Although discovered in unstratified contexts, each of those two objects was found in loci associated with animal cults. Such objects have almost universally been described as elements belonging to naoi, from the Greek noun ναός, the extended meaning of which is a receptacle.[19] The term is generically applied to any box-like structure, but is principally understood as a term referring to a "shrine" that served as an eternal abode for any deity and by extension for any royal or elite member of society whose image was placed within it.[20] The ancient Egyptian nouns that are often considered to be synonyms for "naos" are much more nuanced in their connotative meanings that encompass concepts not only traditionally understood as naoi in stone, wood, and other media, but which extend to any number of box-like containers such as a palanquin and even a cabinet.[21] The continued use of the term naos within the context of these panels prejudices one's understanding of their function(s) because the default meaning of that term excludes other functional possibilities. Arguably, they may have originally been components of reliquaries used to house the mummified remains of animals, rather than of naoi, shrines in the strictest sense, for housing either divine, royal, or elite images.

The wooden panel under discussion must be taken into consideration with a second object[22] discovered in 2016, that consists of a painted wooden receptacle housing a bundle designed as a pseudo-mummy of a recumbent bovine to which a head of a real cow was attached (fig. 9).[23] Both the wooden panel (2018-6) and the pseudo-mummy within its painted wooden receptacle (2016-MASF) are best understood within the context of a series of two-dimensional representations discovered at Memphis that have been identified as images of the Apis Bull placed within a receptacle resting on a processional barque transported by a wagon,[24] of which a relief in Paris serves as an exemplar.[25] The pseudo-mummy discovered by the Franco-Swiss mission demonstrates that the relief in Paris is based on reality and is not the product of artistic license. The relief in Paris also suggests that the wooden panel under discussion may have been an element of a larger composition in which a series of panels was inserted into horizontal registers by means of tenons secured in place by rails, and that those horizontal registers may have been stacked one on top of another to form a series of registers not unlike those depicted on the relief in Paris.

Such a suggestion gains support from the fact that the two pieces of wood from which the panel under discussion was constructed are seamlessly joined. Such fine joinery suggests that it could easily have been added to similar panels in the same register, as perhaps illustrated in the representation of a funerary bier in a vignette from the pronaos of the tomb of Petosiris in Tuna el-Gebel, which clearly is intended to represent an openwork

[17] British Museum EA 68168 in G. T. Martin, *The Tomb of Ḥetepka and Other Reliefs and Inscriptions from the Sacred Animal Necropolis, North Saqqâra, 1964–1973,* TFE 4 (London, 1979), 50, no. 161.

[18] Toronto, The Royal Ontario Museum 969.137.2 in Martin, *Tomb of Ḥetepka*, 50, no. 160, and see Appendix, no. 2, below.

[19] H. G. Liddell and R. Scott, *Greek-English Lexicon* (Salt Lake City, 2019), 457, "... the shrine in which the image of the god was placed."

[20] M. Müller, "Schrein," *LÄ* V, cols. 709–12.

[21] A. Falk, *Ritual processional furniture: a material and religious phenomenon in Egypt* - The University of Liverpool Repository (Dissertation, University of Liverpool, 2015), 100–109 [https://livrepository.liverpool.ac.uk/2012561/ <viewed 2021.11.25>]. See, too, the comments by both Müller in *LÄ* V, cols. 709–12 and D. Arnold, *Lexikon der ägyptischen Baukunst* (Zürich, 1994), 124 and 171, for how imprecise the discipline's terminology for these types of receptacles really is.

[22] Franco-suisse mission archéologique de Saqqara Field Number 2016-MASF: Mission archéologique franco-suisse de Saqqâra (Égypte), *Rapport 2016*, 6–8 and figs. 3–4. I thank Alain Charron, who is entrusted with the publication of this object, for sharing data about it with me.

[23] This discussion has been abstracted from the unpublished report of M. Luret, "Rapport préliminaire: étude de l'accumulation de restes de bovinés au mur Ouest de la pyramide d'Ânkhnespépy II (2019)," kindly made available to me by Philippe Collombert.

[24] Hildesheim, Roemer-und Pelizaeus Museum 1876: in H. Köpp-Junk, "Wagons and Their Significance in Ancient Egypt," *Journal of Ancient Egyptian Interconnections* 9 (2016), 33–34, for discussion of wheeled vehicles, to which Musée du Louvre E 3887 belongs, see C. Boutantin, "Quelques documents de la région memphite relatifs au taureau Apis," *BIFAO* 113 (2013), 82–83, no. 3.

[25] Musée du Louvre E 3887 in Boutantin, "Quelques documents de la région Memphite," 86, no. 11.

Fig. 9. A representation identified as a depiction of an Apis Bull within a receptacle resting on a sacred barque being transported by a wheeled conveyance. Photo Paris, Musée du Louvre E 3887, © 2000 Musée du Louvre, dist. RMN-Grand Palais/Georges Poncet.

frieze (fig. 10).[26] Such a technique is clearly documented in the archaeological record.[27] The relative dimensions of the panel under discussion and the presence of its tangs suggest that it was a component element of such a receptacle. These observations suggest that the animal associated with this object would have been relatively large and heavy, such as a bovine.

That such a constructed housing may have contained a bovine mummy with its head protruding from an open side seems to be confirmed by the observation that one side of the panel under discussion exhibits a finished, gilded, vertical edge that reveals no signs of wear which the presence of a repeatedly opened and closed door would have caused. The appearance of such a mummified bovine within the suggested receptacle to which this panel may have belonged would recall the appearance of the pseudo-mummy within its housing and the similar subject depicted in two-dimensional representations.

C. Boutantin opines that the representation of the bovine in its housing on the relief in Paris, and the others in her corpus, are to be understood as containers in which mummified animals were placed so that they could be transported to the place of their interment.[28] She had earlier suggested that such depictions are also to be understood as "snapshots" of actual funerary processions.[29] Her comments can, perhaps, be furthered. After the procession and interment, the head of such bovines would still be visible and arguably accessible as an interme-

[26] N. Cherpion, J.-P. Corteggiani, and J.-F. Gout, *Le tombeau de Pétosiris à Touna el-Gebel: relevé photographique* (Cairo, 2007), 50, scene 50 [GL.39], embellishing a state bier = G. Lefebvre, *Le tombeau de Petosiris: 1: Description* (Cairo, 1924 [reedition 2007]), 57, inscription 39; and G. Lefebvre, *Le tombeau de Petosiris, vol. 2: Les textes* (Cairo,1924 [reedition 2007]), pl. XI [bottom].

[27] C. A. Hope, "Objects from the Temple of Tutu," in W. Clarysse, A. Schoors, and H. Willems (eds.), *Egyptian Religion: The Last Thousand Years; Studies Dedicated to the Memory of Jan Quaegebeur: part II*, OLA 85 (Louvain, 1998), 803–58, and D. Kessler and P. Brose, *Ägyptens letzte Pyramide: das Grab des Seuta(s) in Tuna el-Gebel* (Munich, 2008), 24–36.

[28] Boutantin, "Quelques documents de la région Memphite," 81, 89, 97–98.

[29] C. Boutantin, "Les terres cuites d'Héracléopolis Magna—État de la question," *CdE* 85 (2010), 300–301, and S. Cauville, "Entre exi-

Fig. 10. A vignette of fine joiners constructing a funerary bier in the pronaos of the tomb of Petosiris at Tuna el-Gebel. Photo © François Maresquier, www.meretsegerbooks.com.

diary[30] for private devotion[31] on every level of society[32] because such objects functioned as important foci of daily life from possible incubation to dream interpretation and oracular pronouncements.[33] Such participatory events were not solely restricted to the cultic praxis associated with the principal sacred animal at any given site,[34] but are also documented by officials at animal cemeteries in general.[35]

Within such cultic practices, the importance of confronting the face of the divinity is of paramount importance.[36] Such a praxis is amply demonstrated by the oracular pronouncements delivered by simians at both Tuna

---

gence décorative et significations multiples: les graphies suggestives du temple d'Hathor à Dendara," *BIFAO* 102 (2002), 90, for a discussion of such processions at Dendera.

[30] H. te Velde, "A few remarks upon the religious significance of animals in ancient Egypt," *Numen* 27.1 (1980), 76–82.

[31] Davies and Smith, "Sacred Animal Temples at Saqqara," 113–31; M. Hill, "Small divine statuettes: outfitting religion," in A. Masson-Berghoff (ed.), *Statues in Context: Production, meaning and (re)uses*, BMPES 10 (Louvain, 1997), 36, points out that oftentimes the participation of the non-elite members of society in these practices is difficult to document, but see D. Kessler, "Tierische Missverständnisse: Grundsätzliches zu Fragen des Tierkultes," in M. Fitzenreiter (ed.), *Tierkulte im pharaonischen Ägypten und im Kulturvergleich*. IBAES 4 (2005), 33–67, who argues against the wholesale participation of non-elite members of society in these animal cults.

[32] D. Meeks, "Zoomorphie et image des dieux dans l'Égypte ancienne," in C. Malamoud and J-P. Vernant (eds.), *Corps des dieux* (Paris, 1986), 190, for a concise description of the suggested interaction between the worshipper and the mummified animal at moment when the one confronts the other.

[33] D. Kessler, "Zur Funktion der Horusstelen und Heilstatuen vor den Sanktuaren und Kapellen," in K. Daoud, S. Bedier, and S. Abd El-Fattah (eds.), *Studies in Honor of Ali Radwan* vol. 2, SASAE 34.2 (Cairo, 2005), 81–94, for the performance of such oracular practices at night within the context of an animal necropolis.

[34] G. Gorre, *Les relations du clergé égyptien et des Lagides d'après les sources privées*, STH 45 (Louvain, 2009), 141–56, no. 30; and 194–97, no. 40.

[35] J. D. Ray, *Texts from the Baboon and Falcon Galleries: Demotic, Hieroglyphic and Greek Inscriptions from the Sacred Animal Necropolis, North Saqqara*, TFE 15 (London, 2011).

[36] Y. Volokhine, "Une désignation de la 'face divine' *ḥ3wt, ḥ3wty*," *BIFAO* 101 (2001), 381–83.

el-Gebel[37] and Saqqara,[38] and by ibises at Thebes.[39] Significantly, this practice is also attested in the performance of oracular pronouncements in which the petitioner interacts face-to-face with a sacred bull.[40] It is within such a cultic praxis that one is to understand the function of the panel under discussion. Moreover, this face-to-face interaction between a petitioner and the divine must be integrated into the wider arena of such ancient Egyptian cultic praxis that includes the opening of shutters to reveal cultic reliefs[41] and the opening and closing of other types of receptacles housing animal mummies.[42] The practice was extended to include such interactions with the deceased as seen in the moveable mechanism exhibited by a painted, wooden box coffin now in Malibu[43] as well as in the design of two vertically aligned receptacles, termed *schreinartigen Särgen*, in Berlin[44] in which the praxis involved communication, perhaps not oracular in nature, with the deceased by the living. To these examples must be added representations on stelae in which a bust of the divine entity is represented within such an open doorless receptacle in order to be accessible for petitioners seeking oracular consultations[45] in keeping with the liminal function of all such openings in such receptacles.[46]

As already stated, the wooden panel was discovered by the Franco-Swiss Archaeological Mission at Saqqara in 2018 in a disturbed, archaeological contexts littered with bovine skeletal[47] remains on two sides of the pyramid complex of queen Ankhnespepy II (fig. 11). The southern locus measured approximately 25 square meters and appears to have been continued along the western side of the precinct.[48] The jumbled state of the remains of these bovines suggests that the deposits were both secondary[49] and helter-skelter, resulting, as has been suggested, by a pillaging of one or more sacred sites because several of the remains exhibit clear signs of having been mummified.[50] Numerous bovine skeletal remains, both male and female, have been found at the site. Provisional forensic analysis suggests that the population ranged in date from newly born calves to very aged adults.[51]

---

37 Kessler and Brose, *Ägyptens letzte Pyramide*, 11.

38 Ray, *Texts from the Baboon and Falcon Galleries*, 39.

39 D. Klotz, *Caesar in the City of Amun: Egyptian Temple Construction and Theology in Roman Thebes*, MRE 15 (Turnhout, 2012), 216.

40 D. Klotz, "Two Overlooked Oracles," *JEA* 96 (2010), 252.

41 J. D. Preisigke-Borsian, *Bittplätze an ägyptischen Tempeln vom 7. Jahrhundert v. Chr. bis zum 4. Jahrhundert n. Chr.: ihre Architektur, Zugänglichkeit, Ausstattung und Bedeutung*, ÄAT 102 (Münster, 2021).

42 Mallawi Antiquities Museum 200 in Messiha and Elhitta, *Mallawi Antiquities Museum*, 15 with plate XVI, although Colburn, *Archaeology of Empire in Achaemenid Egypt*, 162–67, suggests that this particular object may have been repurposed.

43 Malibu, The J. Paul Getty Museum 82.AP.75 in K. Parlasca, "Ein spätrömischer bemalter Sarg aus Ägypten im J. Paul Getty Museum," in Anonymous (ed.), *Alexandria and Alexandrianism: Papers Delivered at a Symposium Organized by the J. Paul Getty Museum and the Getty Center for the History of Art and the Humanities and Held at the Museum April 22–25, 1993* (Malibu, 1996), 155–69.

44 Berlin, Ägyptische Museum und Papyrussammlung 17039/40 and 17126/7 in K. Parlasca and H.Seemann (eds.), *Augenblicke: Mumienporträts und ägyptische Grabkunst aus römischer Zeit; Eine Ausstellung der Schirn-Kunsthalle Frankfurt, 30. Januar bis 11. April 1999* (Frankfurt-Munich, 1999), 25–26; and K. Parlasca, *Mumienporträts und verwandte Denkmäler* (Wiesbaden, 1999), 107.

45 Cairo, The Egyptian Museum JE 40720, among the publications: É. Bernand, *Recueil des inscriptions grecques du Fayoum. Tome I: la "Méris" d'Herakleidés*, AEG 57 (Leiden, 1975), 45, no. 14, although the suggestion that this monument is to be associated with Julius Caesar has been challenged by both H. Heinen (*Kleopatra-Studien: gesammelte Schriften zur ausgehenden Ptolemäerzeit, Xenia* 49 (2009), 244–47) and Y. Volokhine ("Tithoès et Lamarès," *BSdEG* 27 (2005–2007), 81–92).

46 M.-C. Bruwier, "Présence et action d'Anubis sur le coffret d'un prêtre héracléopolitain," in W. Clarysse, A. Schoors, and H. Willems (eds.), *Egyptian Religion: The Last Thousand Years, part I*, OLA 84 (Louvain, 1998), 72–73, furthering the comments of H. Brunner, "Die Rolle von Tür und Tor im alten Ägypten," *Symbolon: Jahrbuch für Symbolforschung, Neue Folge* 6 (1982), 37–59.

47 I thank both Mathieu Luret and Alain Charron for sharing this information with me, which will appear in the forthcoming publication, M. Luret, A. Charron, and L. Chaix, "A case of fluorosis in a bull (Bas taurus) linked to Apis worship at Saqqara (Egypt)."

48 The following information has been extracted from the unpublished report prepared by Luret 2019.

49 Compare the animal bones discovered in the repurposing of Abusir Mastaba AS 33 in M. Verner, "Leben für den Tod: die Texte der Abusir-Papyri," in V. Brinkmann (ed.), *Sahure: Tod und Leben eines großen Pharao. Eine Ausstellung der Liebieghaus Skulpturensammlung, Frankfurt am Main, 24. Juni bis 28. November 2010* (Frankfurt-Munich, 2010), 250–63.

50 The extraordinarily large number of bovine skeletal remains found within these two areas are indicative of the enormous economic impact such endeavors must have had upon the royal economies at the time of their original interments, for which see M. C. Flossmann-Schütze, "Études sur le cadre de vie d'une association religieuse dans l'Égypte gréco-romaine: l'exemple de Touna el-Gebel," in G. Rosati and M. C. Guidotti (eds.), *Proceedings of the XI International Congress of Egyptologists, Florence Egyptian Museum, Florence, 23–30 August 2015* (Oxford, 2017), 203–08, and S. Ikram, "Speculations on the role of animal cults in the economy of ancient Egypt," in M. Massiera, B. Mathieu, and F. Rouffet (eds.), *Apprivoiser le sauvage / Taming the wild* (Montpellier, 2015), 211–27.

51 A. Łukaszewicz, "La stèle de Patoubasthis et les vaches sacrées à Edfou," *The Journal of Juristic Papyrology* 29 (1999), 75–78, for the suggestion that the bovine remains (βους) may actually be those of cows.

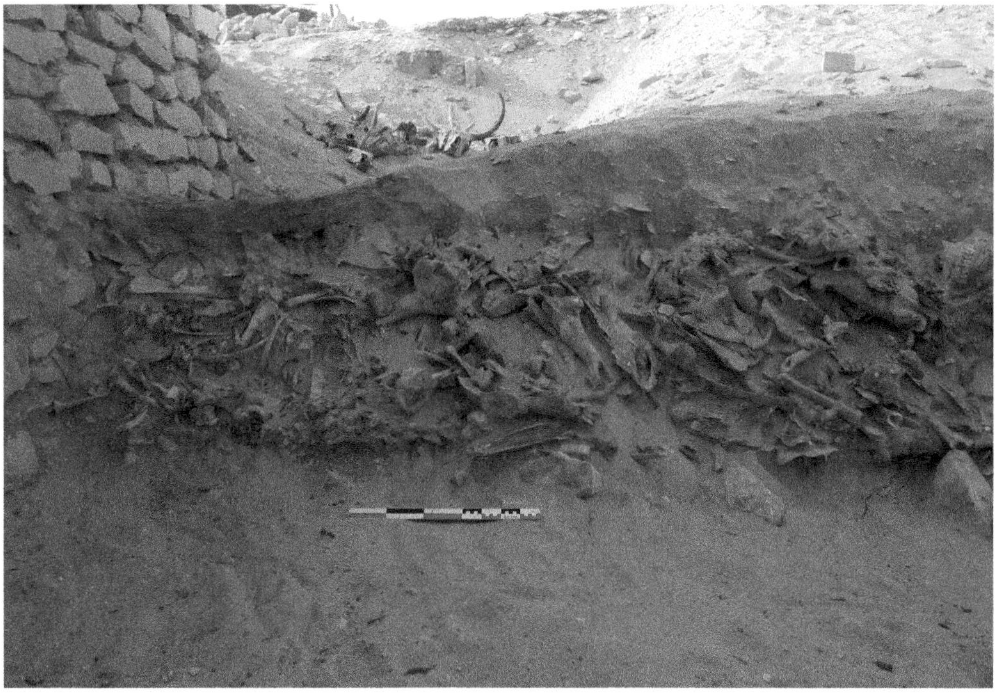

Fig. 11. The bovine deposit along the western side of the pyramid complex of Ankhespepy II at Saqqara in which Franco-suisse mission archéologique de Saqqara Field Number 2016-MASF was found. Photo © Franco-suisse mission archéologique de Saqqara; photographer Philippe Collombert.

One has yet to identify the location(s) of the original archaeological site(s) from which those bovine remains found at the pyramid complex of queen Ankhnespepy II may have come. That such a suggested locus did in fact exist is reinforced by the observation that somewhere in Saqqara, perhaps even in the proximity the pyramid complex of Queen Ankhnespepy II, may lie a bovine animal necropolis,[52] separate and distinct[53] from the famed Apis bull burials in the Memphite Serapeum. Such a necropolis is mentioned in the papyrological documentation.[54] That locus may have been situated anywhere within the zone stretching from North Saqqara to Abu Roash, to judge from the known animal necropolises that litter that area and from reports about the provenances of bovine mummies in Cairo.[55] In antiquity, there was no strictly defined geographical border between the areas now designated as southern Saqqara and northern Abusir so that Miroslav Verner's observation that there may have been several other bull cults at Saqqara—the *gm*-steers, members of the Apis bull's entourage, his children—which are mentioned in the preserved documentation may in fact still wait to be discovered in this area.

[52] Mission archéologique franco-suisse de Saqqâra (Égypte), *Rapport 2018,* 7–8; and Mission archéologique franco-suisse de Saqqâra (Égypte), *Rapport 2016*, 6–7, citing the remains of 252 heads of bovines.

[53] G. Martin, *The Sacred Animal Necropolis at North Saqqara: The Southern Dependencies of the Main Temple Complex*, EM 50 (London, 1981), 8, for the distinction between cemeteries reserved for sacred animals and those used for animal mummies in general.

[54] S. Davies, "Uncharted Saqqara: a postscript." *JEA* 84 (1998), 45–56; S. Ikram, "Nile currents," *KMT* 13.3 (2002), 5.

[55] Cairo, The Egyptian Museum CG 29516 in C. Gaillard and G. Daressy, *La faune momifiée de l'antique Égypte* (Cairo 1905), 16–18.

Fig. 12. The mummified ox in Munich, Staatliches Museum Ägyptischer Kunst ÄS 60. Reproduced with the kind permission of the Museum from Gerfried Ziegemayer, "Müncher Mumien," Schriften aus der Ägyptischen Sammlung 2 *(Munich, 1985) =Dietrich Wilding, "Keine Leichen in Keller: Das Münchner Mumienprojekt," in Sylvia Schoske (ed.),* Staatliche Sammlung Ägyptischer Kunst München *(Mainz, 1995), 88, fig. 101.*

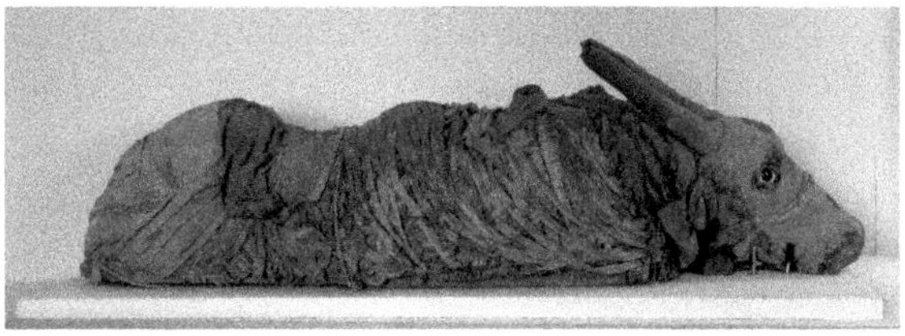

Fig. 13. One of the three bull mummies acquired by Dr. Henry Abbott. Photo © Smithsonian Institution, National Museum of Natural History, Department of Anthropology Catalogue Number A413941; photographer Kim Nielsen.

Consider for a moment that some of the bovine mummies, reportedly found in the 19th century,[56] one of which now in Munich has been identified as an ox (fig. 12),[57] and two more now in Washington, D.C. (fig. 13),[58] would seem to confirm the existence of one or more of these bovine cemeteries in the Saqqara-Abusir zone. It is, therefore, tempting to ask whether the bull mummies discovered by Dr. Henry Abbott[59] (the one in Munich and those in Cairo[60]), may have originally come from one and the same necropolis. Furthermore, the involvement of Amasis with animal cults at Saqqara is well-attested not only in relation to that of the Apis Bull, but also with that of the cult of the Mother of the Apis, which he is suggested to have initiated.[61] In light of these observations, it is entirely plausible to suggest that the inlaid, gilded wooden panel discovered by the Mission archéologique franco-suisse de Saqqâra in a disturbed context in the southern section of the pyramid complex of queen Ankhnespepy II can be associated with one or more bovine cults, perhaps even that of one of the bulls, promoted by pharaoh Amasis. The presence of these bovine remains should, therefore, caution one

---

[56] Gaillard and Daressy, *La faune momifiée*, 16–18.

[57] Munich, Staatliche Sammlung Ägyptischer Kunst ÄS 90 in D. Wildung, "Keine Leichen im Keller," in S. Schoske (ed.), *Staatliche Sammlung Ägyptischer Kunst München* (Mainz am Rhein, 1995), 88 with fig. 101; and J. Boessneck (ed.), *Die Münchner Ochsenmummien* (Hildesheim, 1987). The skeletal remains of this bovine, identified as an ox, have been removed from their bandages and reassembled, for which see https://smaek.de/ausstellungen/voll-ent-wickelt/ <accessed 14 November 2021>. Gerfried Ziegelmayer, *Münchner Mumien* (Munich, 1985) who confirms that the specimen in Munich is probably from Saqqara and not from Armant; and Charron 2014, 229–47.

[58] The example in Munich can be compared with three bovine mummies formerly in New York, Collection of Henry Abbott, *Catalogue of a Collection of Egyptian Antiquities, The Property of Henry Abbott, M.D* (New York, 1854) 15–16, no. 152; and E. A. Powell, "Messengers to the Gods," *Archaeology* (March-April 2014), 48–52. These entered the collections of The Brooklyn Museum of Art. Two were ultimately deaccessioned and entered the collections of the Smithsonian National Museum of Natural History under inventory numbers 209589 [USNM A413941-0 and A413942, respectively: https://collections.nmnh.si.edu/search/anth/ <viewed 2020.07.27>. For the third bovine mummy, The Brooklyn Museum of Art 37.1381E (https://www.brooklynmuseum.org/opencollection/objects/117932 <viewed on 14 November 2021>) judged too fragile to transfer to Washington, DC, is currently represented in that collection by a single one of its bones. Abbott simply records their provenance as "Dashour," without providing details, although a backstory is provided by J. V. C. Smith, *A Pilgrimage to Egypt: Embracing a Diary of Explorations on the Nile; with Observations Illustrative of the Manners, Customs, and Institutions of the People and of the Present Condition of the Antiquities and Ruins* (Boston, 1959), 242–43.

[59] These three bull mummies should not be confused with an ancient and authentic model of a mummified bull in the collections of The Brooklyn Museum of Art 37.1381E in E. Bleiberg, Y. Barbash, L. Bruno, *Soulful Creatures. Animal Mummies in Ancient Egypt* (Brooklyn-London, 2013), 134–35. [https://www.brooklynmuseum.org/opencollection/objects/117932 <viewed on 2-21.11.26>].

[60] Gaillard and Daressy *La faune momifiée*, 16–18. There appears to have been some confusion between the plates and the text in the publication by Gaillard and Daressy, because the "chat gante" described on page 8 does not appear to be the mummy illustrated on plate V, the caption of which identifies the mummy in that illustration as CG 29511, identified on page 12 as a gazelle.

[61] A. Leahy, "Beer for the gods of Memphis in the reign of Amasis," in Clarysse, Schoors, and Willems (eds.), *Egyptian Religion: the Last Thousand Years, part I*, 392; and D. Devauchelle, "La XXVIe dynastie au Sérapéum de Memphis," in D. Devauchelle (ed.), *La XXVIe dynastie, continuités et ruptures: actes du Colloque international organisé les 26 et 27 novembre 2004 à l'Université Charles-de-Gaulle – Lille 3; promenade saïte avec Jean Yoyotte* (Paris, 2011), 139–52.

against identifying any bovine depiction from the Memphite area as an Apis Bull, unless there is supporting, corroborative evidence.

APPENDIX

Inlays in both glass and faience either as isolated objects,[62] or as parts of complete figures, designed as body parts of both divine and human beings together with wigs and accessories such as collars,[63] have been discovered in abundance among fragmentary pieces of wood, admittedly in disturbed archaeological contexts dated to the Late and Roman Imperial Periods, most recently at the Faiyumic sites of Bacchias[64] and Dime (Soknopaiou Nesos).[65] Inlays correctly identified as feathers[66] can now be more properly understood on the basis of those on the wings of Khuit on the panel from Saqqara. It has been tacitly assumed that all of these wooden panels that are sometimes embellished with the types of inlays under discussion and are often gilded were component elements of objects putatively identified as naoi, at least one hypothetical reconstruction of which has been proposed using a papyrus in London as a didactic, architectural pattern-book of sorts on to which some of the secondary inlays from Dime have been theoretically superimposed.[67] The use of such inlays continued into the early Christian Period.[68]

The majority of glass inlays that are suggested to date to the Late Period have not been found in association with wood.[69] Since that is the case, the following list is provisional and includes only those wooden objects that are embellished with such glass inlays or that have been found with wooden fragments. The default interpretation of virtually all of these wooden panels incrusted with glass inlays is that they formed parts of naoi in which images of either deities or royals were housed. Several wooden receptacles from the animal cemeteries at Tuna el-Gebel are designed with moveable front panels that could be opened and closed to reveal the mummified animal within.[70] That design suggests the object may have been used in a performance ritual, discussed above, as perhaps was the pseudo-mummy within a painted, wooden shrine (Field Number 2016-MASF). The finished edge of the wooden panel under discussion suggests that its "front" was open, doubtless to reveal its contents, suggested to have been a mummified bull. Consequently one should revisit each of the other objects listed in this Appendix in order to reassess their possible function(s).

1. Mission archéologique franco-suisse de Saqqara Field Number 18-6 inscribed for Amasis. This and the following two objects are the earliest datable examples of such wooden panels exhibiting glass inlays from the Late Period.[71]
2. Toronto, Royal Ontario Museum 969.137.2 discovered at Saqqara and inscribed for Amasis.[72]
3. Paris, Musée du Louvre N 504 (=E 605),[73] also inscribed for Amasis.

---

[62] Gasperini, Paolucci, and Tocci, *Catalogo dei frammenti*, 85–99; A.Cervi, "L'arredo ligneo del tempio di Soknopaio," in M. Capasso, Mario and P. Davoli (ed.), *Soknopaiou Nesos Project I (2003–2009)* (Pisa, 2012), 293–95.

[63] Gasperini, Paolucci, and Tocci, *Catalogo dei frammenti*, 84–99; Cervi "L'arredo ligneo del tempio di Soknopaio," particularly page 293.

[64] Gasperini, Paolucci, and Tocci *Catalogo dei frammenti.*

[65] Cervi, "L'arredo ligneo del tempio di Soknopaio."

[66] Gasperini, Paolucci, and Tocci *Catalogo dei frammenti*, 100–102; and Cervi, "L'arredo ligneo del tempio di Soknopaio," 290.

[67] London, University College 27934: Cervi,"L'arredo ligneo del tempio di Soknopaio," 274–314.

[68] Dakhleh Oasis, Kellis, the East Church, for fragments of figural glass inlays associated with a screen of wood dated to the late Constantinian period in E. S. Bolman, "Veiling Sanctity in Christian Egypt: Visual and Spatial Solutions," in S. E. J. Gerstel (ed.), *Thresholds of the Sacred* (Washington, D.C. 2006) 77–78.

[69] Nenna, "Le mobilier religieux en bois," 30–38.

[70] Mallawi, Mallawi Antiquities Museum 200 in Messiha and Elhitta, *Mallawi Antiquities Museum*, 15 with pl. XVI.

[71] Nenna, "Le mobilier religieux en bois," 30.

[72] C. I. Green, *The Temple Furniture from the Sacred Animal Necropolis at North Saqqâra 1964–1976,* EM 53 (London, 1987), 10, no. 8; and Nenna, "Le mobilier religieux en bois," 31.

[73] Paris, Musee du Louvre N 504 (=E 605) in Cervi, "L'arredo ligneo del tempio di Soknopaio," 282; Nenna, "Le mobilier religieux en bois," 30, and T. Mathews and N. Muller, T*he Dawn of Christian Art in Panel Paintings and Icons* (Los Angeles, 2016), 115.

4. Bologna, Museo Civico di Bologna KS 289[74] inscribed for Shr-ib-ra, one of the names of Petobastis-son-of-Bastet,[75] a petty prince suggested to have led an insurrection against Aryandes, the Persian satrap of Egypt, in 522–520 BC.[76]
5. Paris, Musée du Louvre N 503[77] inscribed for the same individual and ostensibly from the same object.
6. Paris, Musee du Louvre N 874[78] inscribed for the same individual and ostensibly from the same object.
7. London, The British Museum 37496[79] inscribed for Darius I of Dynasty 27.
8. Cairo, The Egyptian Museum JE 91103,[80] suggested to date to the same reign.
9. Brooklyn, The Brooklyn Museum of Art 37.258E, 37.259E, and 37.260E[81] inscribed for Nectanebo II of Dynasty 30. The earliest appearance of mosaic glass are not those exhibited by these panels,[82] but are those found at Ain Manawir dated according to their archaeological context to the fifth century BC.[83] Nevertheless, the glass inlays on the panels in Brooklyn are the earliest dated attestations for the appearance of new colors for that glass.[84]
10. Cairo, The Egyptian Museum JE 91103 from Saqqara (Green, *Temple Furniture*, 10–11, no. 9, and Nenna, "Le mobilier religieux en bois," 34).
11. Bacchias, a jumbled find consisting of a reported 60 kgs of wood and 530 examples of glass inlays.[85]
12. Turin, Museo Egizio, Supplement 18155m[86] excavated by Carlo Anti at Tebtunis in the Faiyum in 1931, and now in Turin, after having been transferred there from the Museo Nazionale Romano, suggested to date to the late Ptolemaic Period.

Examples suggested to have been associated with wooden naoi:

13. Fragments from Tebtunis.[87]
14. Tell e-Herr, 167 examples of glass inlays.[88]

To which one should perhaps add this example with faux-inlays:

15. Art Market, an openwork, painted, not inlaid, wooden panel which features a standing, winged goddess facing right.[89]

---

[74] Museo Civico di Bologna KS 289 in J. D. Cooney, "Glass Sculpture in Ancient Egypt" *Journal of Glass Studies* 2 (1960), 29, note 22; E. Bresciani, *La collezione egizia nel Museo Civico di Bologna* (Ravenna, 1975), 65–66, plate 41; and V. Cortese, "II.16 Elemento decorativo," [incorrectly dated to the Third Intermediate Period] in E. A. Arslan, F. Tiradritti, M. Abbiatri Brida, and A. Magni (eds.), *Iside: il mito, il mistero, la magia* (Milan, 1997), 54.

[75] Bresciani, *La collezione egizia nel Museo Civico di Bologna*, 65.

[76] J. Yoyotte, "Pétoubastis III," *RdE* 24 (1972), 216–23, revisited by O. Kaper, "Petubastis IV in the Dakhla Oasis: new evidence about an early rebellion against Persian rule and its suppression in political memory," in J. M. Silverman and C. Waerzeggers (eds.), *Political Memory in and after the Persian Empire* (Atlanta, 2015), 125–49.

[77] Paris, Musée du Louvre N 503: https://collections.louvre.fr/ark:/53355/cl010009552 <accessed 14 November 2021>

[78] Paris, Musee du Louvre N 874 in Cooney, "Glass Sculpture in Ancient Egypt," 29, note 22.

[79] London, The British Museum 37496 in Cervi, "L'arredo ligneo del tempio di Soknopaio," 282; Nenna, "Le mobilier religieux en bois," 31; and L. Martzolff, "La pratique du rituel dans le temple égyptien, *Archimède* 1 (2014), 23, who identifies this panel as a door leaf.

[80] Cairo, The Egyptian Museum JE 91103 in Cervi, "L'arredo ligneo del tempio di Soknopaio," 282 and Green, *Temple Furniture*, 10–12.

[81] R. S. Bianchi, "Fragment of a naos, or shrine," in R. A. Fazzini, R. S. Bianchi, J. F. Romano, and D. B. Spanel, *Ancient Egyptian art in the Brooklyn Museum* (New York-London 1989), no. 79; and N. Spencer, *A Naos of Nekhthorheb from Bubastis: Religious Iconography and Temple Building in the 30th Dynasty*, BMRP 156 (London, 2006), 4.

[82] S. H. Auth,"Mosaic glass mask plaques and the ancient theater," *Journal of Glass Studies* 41 (1999), 56.

[83] Nenna comma "Le mobilier religieux en bois," 34.

[84] Nenna, "Le mobilier religieux en bois," 34.

[85] Nenna, "Le mobilier religieux en bois," 35.

[86] Turin, Museo Egizio, Supplement 18155 in Cervi, "L'arredo ligneo del tempio di Soknopaio," 282; Anonymous (ed.) 1988. *Le vie del vetro: Egitto e Sudan. Convegno, mostra* (Pisa, 1988), 93, no. 8; and V. Rondot, *Tebtynis II: Le temple de Soknebtynis et son dromos*. Relevés et encrages Ramez Boutros - Georges Soukiassian. Fouilles de l'Institut Français d'Archéologie Orientale 50 (Cairo, 2004), 33–36, who adduces figural parallels in Cairo, The Egyptian Museum JE 55943–55951.

[87] Nenna, "Le mobilier religieux en bois," 34, citing V. Rondot, *Tebtynis II: Le temple de Soknebtynis et son dromos* (Cairo 2004), 259–61.

[88] Nenna, "Le mobilier religieux en bois," 35–36.

[89] Bonhams, London, *Antiquities* (Thursday, 5 July 2018), lot 218.

From Fiend to Friend: The Serpent Sata in Ancient Egyptian Funerary Art and Literature

Abir Enany
Misr University for Science and Technology, Giza, Egypt

Abstract

Ancient Egyptian funerary books are rich with incantations and depictions of an array of snakes. While some were considered evil creatures, others were deified. In this paper we are particularly interested in studying the serpent Sata, a serpent that appears in ancient Egyptian texts and representations from the Old Kingdom onwards. The serpent's presence is predominant in the funerary context with its zenith in the Book of the Dead, where one of the Transformation Spells is dedicated to ensuring the transformation of the deceased into Sata. The material related to the serpent is studied and analyzed to reach an understanding of the perception of the creature in the eyes of the ancient Egyptians with a focus on dynastic Egypt. The material includes a corpus of 38 representations of Sata that has been classified according to shape into four categories and is included in the appendix attached to the current work.

الملخص

تذخر النصوص الجنائزية المصرية القديمة بالصور والتعاويذ المتعلقة بالعديد من أنواع الثعابين. وبينما أعتبر المصري القديم بعض هذه الثعابين مخلوقات ضارة إلا أنه قام بتأليه البعض الأخر. ويعني هذا البحث بدراسة أحد هذه الثعابين، وهو الثعبان ساتا أبن الأرض والذي ظهر في النصوص ثم المناظر المصرية القديمة ابتداً من عصر الدولة القديمة. ويظهر هذا الثعبان بصورة أساسية في سياق جنائزي ويعتبر أبرز ظهور له في كتاب الموتي حيث يكرس أحد فصول التحولات وهو الفصل ٧٨ لضمان تحول المتوفي الي الثعبان ساتا كما يظهر الثعبان في نصوص ومناظر أخري. وفي هذا البحث تم دراسة وتحليل النصوص والمناظر المتعلقة بالثعبان ساتا للوصول الي فهم وتحديد طبيعة هذا المخلوق في أعين قدماء المصريين منذ عصر الدولة القديمة وحتى نهاية عصر الأسرات. وقد تم حصر ٨٣ صورة للثعبان ساتا تم تصنيفها حسب الشكل الي أربع فئات وتضمينها في قائمة ملحقة بالبحث.

Serpents have always intrigued the ancient Egyptians due to their dual nature and character. The creatures could simultaneously inflict harm yet also be useful, as from the same harmful venom of the snakes, the ancient Egyptians extracted the very cure to their ailment. The legless creatures that crawled above the ground and hid within also shared other auspicious traits. Their ability to shed their old skin and replace it with new skin offered a blend of symbolism, simultaneously representing destruction and creation through the shedding and regrowing of the skin, respectively. This contradiction emphasized the idea of the cycle of life and transformation into a new form, thus suggesting survival and life renewal.[1] In addition, the serpents' ability to hide under the desert sand and rocks led the ancient Egyptians to associate them with the underworld,[2] and their ability to hibernate

[1] A. Colazilli, "Skin in Ancient Egyptian Belief: Sacred Texts and Rituals," In T. Lekov, and E. Buzov (eds.), *Cult and Belief in Ancient Egypt: Proceedings of the Fourth International Congress for Young Egyptologists 25–27 September 2012* (Sofia, 2014), 121.

[2] G. Pinch, *Magic in Ancient Egypt* (London, 1994), 35.

Journal of the American Research Center in Egypt 58 (2022), 19–44
http://dx.doi.org/10.5913/jarce.58.2022.a002

and wake up anew further enforced the notion of renewal and resurrection. The serpents' contradicting characteristics led to their overall categorization into two groups, namely harmful serpents, and beneficial serpents.[3]

The ancient Egyptians' mixed perceptions of serpents are reflected in the serpent named *sꜣ-tꜣ* (hereafter referred to as "Sata"), the "ground's son," a serpent whose character shifted from evil to benevolent as it appeared in ancient Egyptian texts and representations from the Old Kingdom until the Greco-Roman Period.

The naming of this serpent as the "ground's son" is meant to emphasize its strong bond with earth. The snakes' connection with earth inspired the ancient Egyptians to develop an array of magical and funerary concepts. In the Book of the Heavenly Cow, the god Re appointed the god Geb to watch over the snakes that lived within him as the earth god and to control their destructive magical powers,[4] thus preventing them from inflicting harm on humans.[5] This reflects the ancient Egyptians' view of the serpents as mysterious primaeval beings representing the suppressed forces lying within the ground.[6] Nevertheless, the Egyptians related the serpents to the world of the gods,[7] a view that further mirrored the dual nature of the creatures.

The Nature of Sata in Old and Middle Kingdom Texts

The serpent Sata was not, to my knowledge, depicted before the New Kingdom. During the Old and Middle Kingdoms, it appeared exclusively in funerary texts. In the Pyramid of Teti, it appeared in Pyramid Texts Utterances 393 and 395 in a group of spells against hostile beings, mostly venomous serpents. The texts read as follows:

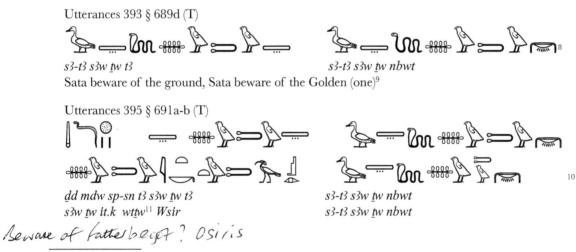

Utterances 393 § 689d (T)

 [8]

sꜣ-tꜣ sꜣw ṯw tꜣ *sꜣ-tꜣ sꜣw ṯw nbwt*

Sata beware of the ground, Sata beware of the Golden (one)[9]

Utterances 395 § 691a-b (T)

 [10]

ḏd mdw sp-sn tꜣ sꜣw ṯw tꜣ *sꜣ-tꜣ sꜣw ṯw nbwt*

sꜣw ṯw it.k wtṯw[11] *Wsir* *sꜣ-tꜣ sꜣw ṯw nbwt*

Beware of father begot? Osiris

[3] T. Rundle Clark, *Myth and Symbol in Ancient Egypt* (London 1959), 239–40.

[4] E. Hornung, *Der ägyptische Mythos von der Himmelskuh Eine Ätiologie des Unvollkommenen*, OBO 46 (Freiburg, 1982), 18–21, 44–5, 64, and verses 202–25; W. K. Simpson (ed.), *The Literature of Ancient Egypt: An Anthology of Stories, Stelae, Autobiographies, and Poetry* (New Haven-London, 2003), 294–95.

[5] Pinch, *Magic*, 26; W. Golding, *The Brooklyn Papyrus (47.218.48 And 47.218.85) and its Snakebite Treatments* (PhD diss., University of South Africa, 2020), 99, 155.

[6] Rundle Clark, *Myth and Symbol*, 243.

[7] Rundle Clark, *Myth and Symbol*, 243.

[8] K. Sethe, *Die altägyptischen Pyramidentexte: nach den Papierabdrücken und Photographien des Berliner Museums*, I (Leipzig, 1908), 375 (hereafter, Sethe, *PT* I).

[9] J. Allen, *The Ancient Egyptian Pyramid Texts*, WAW 23 (Atlanta, 2005), 91. Allen gives the translation gold for *nbw* but we used the Golden One as it is likely to indicate Hathor, see Allen, *Pyramid Texts*, 96, n. 42. Mercer translates the texts as "*sꜣ-tꜣ*-serpent, protect thyself against the earth; *sꜣ-tꜣ*-serpent, protect thyself against Geb," S. Mercer, *The Pyramid Texts in Translation and Commentary* (New York, 1952), 210. However, we prefer Allen's translation as it fits with the warning tone used in the context.

[10] Sethe, *PT* I, 375.

[11] For the word *wtṯw* here translates as "producer" or "who begot," see *Wb* I, 382, 10; R. Faulkner, *A Concise Dictionary of Middle Egyptian* (Oxford, 1988), 72. However, the use of the word written with the determinative of the bird (Gardiner Sign List G15), *wtṯ* is a bird associated

To be recited twice, "Ground, beware of the Ground, Sata beware of the Golden (one)."
Beware of your father (Geb),[12] who begot Osiris, Sata beware of the Golden (one).[13]
s3w tw it.k wtṯw wsir s3-t3 s3w tw nbwt

The text indicates that the serpent is considered an enemy and sends it a warning to ward it off. However, Sata is referred to as an evil son of the god Geb.[14] One might find here a connection with another unfavorable son of Geb, namely Seth, the enemy of Osiris and subsequently of the deceased. However, an intriguing spell of the Pyramid Texts refers to Osiris as an evil being that needs to be expelled to protect the pyramid.[15] This notion might allow us to consider the probability that Sata, as a son of Geb and despite his apparent evil association might have had some connection with the god Osiris rather than Seth, a notion that will find supporting grounds during the New Kingdom.

Another text that mentions Sata is found at the Pyramid of Queen Neith, Utterance 727 that is another collection of spells directed against inimical beings:

 [16]

ẖr r.f s3-t3 ṯs.f ẖr.f
Sata has fallen with his vertebrae under him.[17]

Utterance 727 § 2255b (Nt)

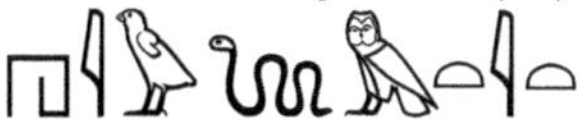

hiw[18] *mtit*
Monster snake, be dead.[19]

These extracts of the same utterance take a more aggressive approach and doom the serpent Sata to fall on its back, a posture mostly taken by dead reptiles. The use of the word *ṯs* that refers to the vulnerable body part of the vertebra[20] is intentional to magically weaken the serpent thus annihilating it. The text of the utterance continues in the same aggressive tone only to end with a damnation and a clear wish of death for the snake. As they were not suitable for recitation, it is likely that these spells were part of silent rituals intended to protect the corpse from real snakes and prevent their bites.[21] In his analysis of the snake utterances of the Pyramid Texts, Christian Leitz concluded that they were of a preventive nature, serving the king when he resurrects as a young Horus in case he encounters serpents or other poisonous beings. In such instance, the king recites the necessary words to convince those creatures to turn around.[22]

The same hostile attitude towards Sata continued through the Middle Kingdom, where it was still used solely in a funerary context. Sata is mentioned in CT 885, a collection of sentences against serpents that were collected from earlier sources.[23]

---

with Osiris, see *Wb* I, 381.9. This determinative might have been used by mistake instead of Gardiner Sign List D53 used with the word in its sense of "who begot," *Wb* I, 381.10; 382.10.

12 Mercer, *Pyramid Texts*, 211.

13 Allen, *Pyramid Texts*, 91.

14 In another PT utterance, the term *s3-t3* is used without the determinative of a snake to indicate a guardian of earth who reports to Geb. See Sethe, *PT* II, 150 § 1163; B. Mathieu, *Les textes de la pyramide de Pépy Ier*, MIFAO 142 (Cairo, 2018), 448.

15 Utterance 534, spell 1267, Mercer, *Pyramid Texts*, 330.

16 R. Faulkner, *The Ancient Egyptian Pyramid Texts: Translated into English, Supplement of Hieroglyphic Texts* (Oxford, 1969), 77.

17 Allen, *Pyramid Texts*, 145.

18 A snake, used in magic spells for destroying snakes: *Wb* II, 483.20–22.

19 Allen, *Pyramid Texts*, 330.

20 C. Leitz, "Die Schlangensprüche in den Pyramidentexten," *Orientalia* 65 (1996), 388.

21 Leitz, "Die Schlangensprüche," 384–85.

22 Leitz, "Die Schlangensprüche," 385.

23 R. Faulkner, *The Ancient Egyptian Coffin Texts*, III (Warminster, 1978), 49, n. 1. For a discussion regarding the *nʿw*-snake that shares

CT 885

[24]

ẖr r.f s3-t3 hr ṯs/// ẖr hiw ẖr

Fall, Sata on [your] back(?),[25] monster, fall.[26]

The text refers to Sata, among other snakes, as a demon—an enemy who should be annihilated.[27] It repeats similar notions towards other serpents that represent harm to the sun god Re and similarly to the deceased. The similarity of the text with the abovementioned Pyramid Text Utterance 727 is unmistakable. The utterance concerning Sata in the Pyramid Texts mentions the serpent within groups of snake repelling spells that were often grouped together[28] as an epithet for the *sḏḥ*-snake.[29] The same concepts continued through the Middle Kingdom as one reads almost the same annihilation spells, mostly copied into the Coffin Texts, with Sata being a designation for the *sḏḥ* -snake as well.[30] In these texts, Sata was clearly associated with harmful venomous snakes that the ancient Egyptians wished to magically control in order to prevent them from harming the deceased.

However, the term *s3-t3* is mentioned in a contradictory sense in other spells of the Coffin Texts, where it appears as an epithet of the deceased Osiris.[31] The epithet here is not followed by a determinative of a serpent but rather the determinative of a god, A40 of Gardiner's List.[32] The use of this epithet finds explanation in the nature of the god Osiris as a chthonic deity, a nature that will lead to further association of Osiris with Sata in the following periods of Egyptian history.

The Nature of Sata in New Kingdom Texts and Representations

Attitudes towards Sata shifted significantly during the New Kingdom. There are more references to the serpent, although most are still funerary in character. Chapter 87 of the Book of the Dead was focused exclusively on Sata, funerary hymns were dedicated to Osiris associating him with Sata, the Book of Caverns texts referred to Sata, and even a book of dream interpretation mentioned the serpent in an unusual non-funerary context. For the first time in ancient Egyptian history, we find a variety of illustrations of the serpent Sata on papyri, in tomb decorations, and on linen shrouds. These texts and representations are discussed below:

1. Sata in BD Spell 87

BD Spell 87 is entitled Spell for Assuming the Forms of Sata. The text of this chapter ensures that the deceased should take the form of Sata. The text is presented in several variations. We take the text of the Papyrus of Yuya as an exemplar and will comment on the variations of this text as needed.

---

characteristics with Sata see, H. Willems, *The Coffin of Heqata (Cairo JdE 36418): A Case Study of Egyptian Funerary Culture of the Early Middle Kingdom* (Leuven, 1996), 353, n. 2176.

24 A. de Buck, *The Egyptian Coffin Texts, VII. Texts of Spells 787–1185*, OIP 87 (Chicago, 1961), 98.

25 For "vertebra," see Faulkner, *Dictionary*, 307.

26 Faulkner, *Coffin Texts*, III, 49.

27 Faulkner, *Coffin Texts*, III, 49.

28 Golding, *Brooklyn Papyrus*, 45.

29 Faulkner, *Supplement*, 77; Allen, *Pyramid Texts*, 145, 330.

30 De Buck, *Coffin Texts*, VII, 98; Faulkner, *Coffin Texts*, III, 49.

31 Spell 557: A. de Buck, *The Egyptian Coffin Texts, VI. Texts of Spells 472–786,* OIP 81 (Chicago, 1956), 158, and Spell 609: De Buck, *Coffin Texts*, VI, 222.

32 Coffins B4B0 and S11C.

ỉrt ḫprw m sꜣ-tꜣ ḏd-mdw ỉn ỉt-nṯr Ywỉw mꜣꜥ-ḫrw
ỉnk sꜣ-tꜣ ꜣw rnpwt sḏr ms rꜥ nb
ỉnk sꜣ-tꜣ ỉmy ḏrw
sḏr.ỉ ms.kwỉ rnp.kwỉ rꜥ nb
Assuming the forms of a Sata serpent, words spoken by the Divine Father Yuya, True of Voice:
"I am Sata, extended of years, I lie down, I am born, every day.
I am Sata, who is in the boundaries[33] [of earth].[34]
I lie down, I am born, I am young every day."

As in other transformation spells, the deceased becomes Sata (*ḫprw m sꜣ-tꜣ*) with the help of magical utterances and metaphors that get him into a state of analogue enabling him to act as Sata.[35] The deceased in this chapter is identified with the double-natured Sata. On one hand, he is sleeping like a hibernating serpent, thus reflecting the ancient Egyptian belief that the dead are sleepers who needed beds and headrests and that the underworld is the place where the dead repose.[36] On the other hand, this repose should not last eternally, as the deceased is identified with Sata who is bestowed with an extended lifespan in the regions of the underworld.[37]

However, one may notice contradictory concepts in the text. Despite the strong association of the text with the daily birth of the sun, the connection with the earth is unmistakable. The name of the creature and the notion of lying down is challenged by the confirmation of rebirth. The identification of the deceased with Sata is in accordance with the notion that the deceased identified himself "with everything in which the principle of resurrection dwells."[38] This principle is present in the awakening after hibernation that the text implies, and in the renewal connected to it.

The perpetuality of Sata is expressed in the text by the expression *ỉnk sꜣ-tꜣ ỉmy ḏrw,* "I am Sata, who is in the boundaries," implying that Sata is the serpent encircling earth as interpreted by Rundle Clark,[39] who further suggested that Sata himself is the Primeval Ocean surrounding earth, and at the same time is its protector against the waters of that same ocean.[40]

The vignette accompanying the text of BD Spell 87 represents Sata in various forms. The specimens studied here consist of thirty-eight representations that we classified into three groups as follows:

---

33 Faulkner, *Dictionary*, 323.

34 Used instead of *ỉmy ḏrw tꜣ,* similar to Papyrus Berlin P. 3002 a-z of Nakht-Imn: I. Munro, *Das Totenbuch des Nacht-Amun aus der Ramessidenzeit (pBerlin P. 3002)*, HAT 4 (Wiesbaden, 1997), 10, n. c. and Pls 7, 10. In the majority of specimens of BD 87, this text is found in the form *ỉmy ḏrw tꜣ.* See for example the text of the Papyrus of Ani EA10470,3 in B. Lüscher, Die Verwandlungssprüche (Tb 76-88), Totenbuchtexte Synoptische Textausgabe nach Quellen des Neuen Reiches 2 (Basel, 2006), 401; the text of the Papyrus of Nakht P. London BM EA 10471, the text of TT 6, the tomb of Neferhotep discussed below, and *Wb* V, 586.8.

35 F. Servajean, *Les formules des transformations du Livre des Morts à la lumière d'une théorie de la performativité: XVIIIe–XXe dynasties*, Bibliothèque d'Étude 137 (Cairo, 2003), 48.

36 Pinch, *Magic*, 156–57.

37 E. Hornung, *Das Totenbuch Der Ägypter* (Zurich, 1979), 469.

38 J. Griffith, *The Origins of Osiris and his Cult*, Studies in the History of Religions 40 (Leiden, 1980), 68.

39 Rundle Clark, *Myth and Symbol*, 241.

40 Rundle Clark, *Myth and Symbol*, 241.

a. Sata as a Winding Serpent

This group is represented by twelve specimens in our study. These include the papyri of Nebseni (fig. 1a);[41] Neferwebwnef (fig. 1b);[42] and the linen shroud of Hapi (fig. 1c),[43] all of which date to the Eighteenth Dynasty. Additionally, Ramesside Period representations of Sata are found in the papyri of Nakhtamun (fig. 1d);[44] as well as the Twenty-First Dynasty papyrus of Maatkare[45] (fig. 2). This group also includes other examples discussed elsewhere within the current work.[46]

The serpent Sata may be represented with one, two, three or four bends and may be black, yellow, or with colored stripes. In the twelve examples of this group, the vignette follows the more widely used style of being depicted in a square. In four examples of this group, the serpent shares the square with another vignette of the Transformation Chapters, in figures 1b, 7, and 9 with a crocodile of BD Spell 88, and in figure 2 with a swallow of BD Spell 86. The windings of Sata in this group of representations led to the suggestion that the serpent represents the primordial serpent that has no beginning.[47] A likely reason for this association is the multiple bends of the serpent that accentuate the notion of repetition. It is worth mentioning that within this group we find only one example of Sata represented as a hooded cobra.

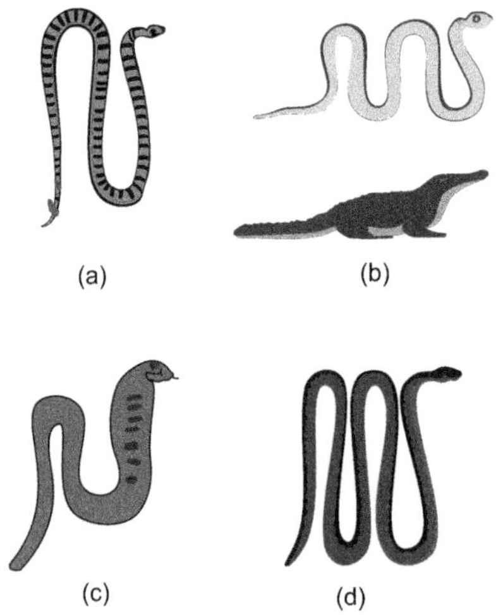

Fig. 1. Sata as a Winding Serpent: (a) Papyrus of Nebseni, BM EA 9900; (b) Papyrus of Neferwebwnef, Louvre N. 3092 [III 93]; (c) Linen shroud of Hapi, Swansea W 869; (d) Papyrus of Nakhtamun, Berlin P. 3002 a-z. Drawings by Iman Elsaid.

Fig. 2. Sata as a Winding Serpent. Papyrus of Maatkare, SR IV/980 = JE 26229. Photo by Sameh Abdel-Mohsen. Courtesy of The Egyptian Museum, Cairo.

[41] P. BM EA 9900.

[42] P. Louvre N. 3092 [III 93].

[43] L. Swansea W 869.

[44] P. Berlin P. 3002 a-z.

[45] SR IV/980 = JE 26229.

[46] These are the Eighteenth Dynasty papyri of Nu (P. BM EA 10477) fig. 10a; Kha (P. Turin 8438) fig. 10c; Yuya (CGC 51189) fig. 18a; and Nebqed (P. Louvre AE/N 3068) fig. 19a; and the Ramesside Period examples of the papyrus of Neferrenpet (P. Brüssel MRAH E. 5043) fig. 7, and the tombs of Irinefer (TT 290) fig. 9, and Inherkhoui (TT 359) fig. 20a.

[47] G. Thausing and T. Kerszt-Kratschmann, *Das Grosse Ägyptische Totenbuch (Papyrus Reinisch) der Papyrussammlung der Österreichischen Nationalbibliothek*, Schriften des Österreichischen Kulturinstituts Kairo, Archäologisch-Historische Abteilung 1 (Cairo, 1969), 23, n. 3.

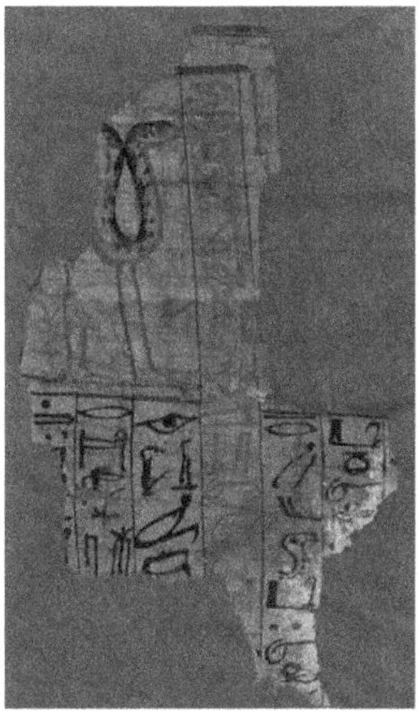

Fig. 3. Sata as a Human-legged Serpent: Papyrus of Nakht B, Cairo JE 95720 [1]. Photo by Daniel Méndez-Rodríguez Courtesy of Egyptian Museum, Cairo.

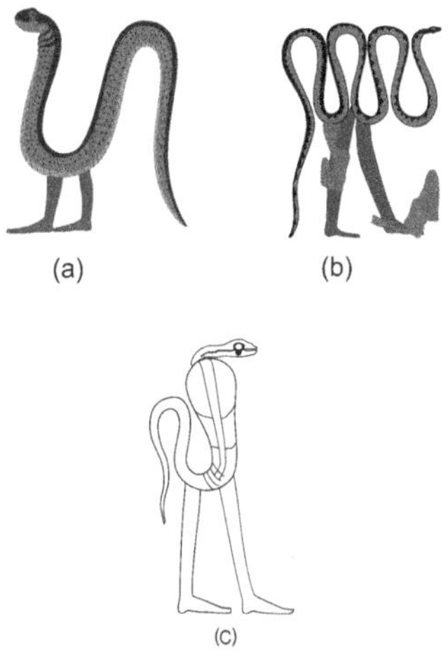

Fig. 4. Sata as a Human-legged Serpent: (a) Papyrus of Nakht A, London BM EA 10471; (b) Papyrus of Rames, Cambridge E.2a.1922; (c) Papyrus of Nesitanebtawy B, London BM EA 10554. Drawings by Iman Elsaid.

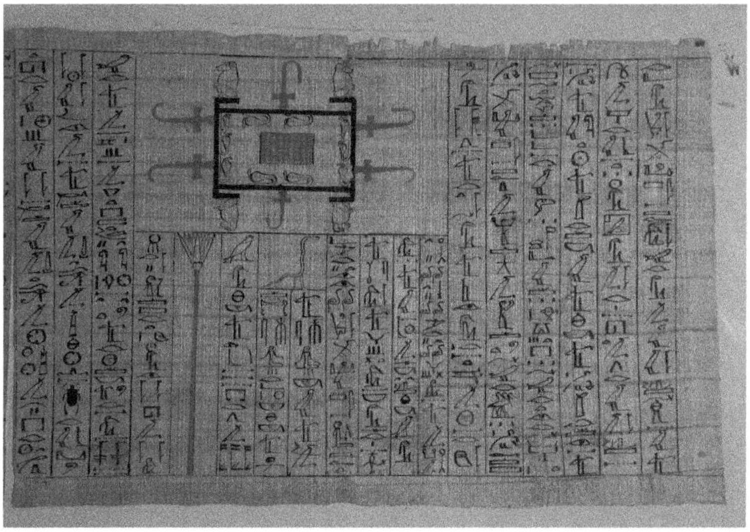

Fig. 5. Sata as a Human-legged Serpent Pap Padiamun B, SR VII 10653 (TR 23/4/40/1). Photo by Abir Enany.

b. Sata as a Human-Legged Serpent

This group is represented with nineteen representations found in the Eighteenth Dynasty Papyrus of Nakht A (fig. 4a);[48] and the Ramesside papyri of Nakht B (fig. 3);[49] and Rames (fig. 4b),[50] as well as the Twenty-First

48 P. London BM EA 10471, referred to herewith as Nakht A to avoid confusion with the Cairo papyrus of his namesake referred to herewith as Nakht B.

49 P. Cairo JE 95720 [1], referred to herewith as Nakht B.

50 P. Cambridge E.2a.1922.

Dynasty papyri of Nesitanebtawy B (fig. 4c);[51] and Padiamun B (fig. 5).[52] In addition, our specimen includes other examples referred to below.[53]

The serpents of this group are represented as either black, spotted, or striped. The winding bends are generally fewer in number, with a higher occurrence of serpents with one or no bends. The walking legs of Sata in this group are used to indicate the deity's mobility.[54] The legs also indicate the fields that should be walked in order for the deceased to complete his transformation. In addition, the human feet reflect the notion of the human being as an eternal wanderer.[55] In this group, only three examples carry the depiction of Sata as a hooded cobra.

c. Sata as a Human-Headed Hooded Cobra

This group is represented in this work by seven representations. These are the shroud of Hrw (fig. 6a);[56] the tomb of Padiherresnet (TT196, fig. 6b); papyri of Pasndjemibnakht (fig. 6c);[57] Iahtaisnakht[58] (fig. 6d), as well as other examples referred to in the course of the paper.[59] All specimens of this group are dated to the Late Period except for the shroud of Hrw that is dated to the Eighteenth Dynasty.

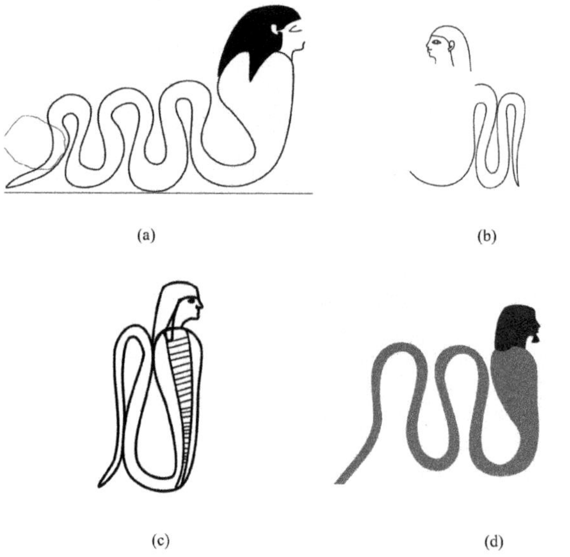

Fig. 6. Human-headed Hooded Cobras: (a) Shroud of Hrw, Uppsala VM MB 2; (b) Tomb of Padiherresnet, TT 196; (c) Papyrus of Pasndjemibnakht, Paris Louvre E. 11078; (d) Papyrus of Iahtaisnakht, Colon. Aeg. 10207. Drawing by Iman Elsaid.

These mostly Late Period representations of Sata as a human headed hooded cobra recall earlier depictions of the New Kingdom funerary representations. In the Seventh Hour of the Amduat a human headed cobra called *ʿnḫwyt*, the Living One, is requested by Re to open up her coils for Osiris' benefit.[60] Additionally, a human headed serpent on four human legs called *Tpy* appeared in the Fourth Hour of Amduat where it acted as a guard of the way,[61] and in an enigmatic text on the second chapel of Tutankhamun where he was represented

[51] P. London BM EA 10554 (P. Greenfield), here referred to as Nesitanebtawy B.

[52] P. Cairo SR VII/10653 (TR 23/4/40/1), here referred to as Padiamun B.

[53] These are the Eighteenth Dynasty papyri of Kha and Merit (P. Paris BN 826, Luynes B) fig. 10b, Tjanena (P. Paris Louvre N. 3074) fig. 21a, and Senusert (P. Wien Vindob. Aeg. 10.994–10.997, P. Reinisch) fig. 21b, and the Ramesside Period examples of the papyri of Qenna (P. Leiden T 2, SR) fig. 21c, Ani (P. London BM EA 10470) fig. 21d, and Paqerer (P. Leiden T 4, AMS 14) fig. 21e, and the tombs of Khawi (TT214) fig. 11 and Neferhotep (TT6) fig. 8, H. Wild, *La tombe de Néferḥotep (I) et Neb.néfer à Deir el-Médîna [No 6] et autres documents les concernant*, II, MIFAO 103.2 (Cairo, 1979), pl. V; as well as the Twenty-First Dynasty examples of the papyri of Nesikhonsu (P. Paris BN 170–173) fig. 10d, Padiamun A (P. Cairo SR I/10654, referred to herewith as Padiamun A to avoid confusion with the papyrus here referred to as Padiamun B) fig. 13, Nesitanebtawy A (P. Cairo CG 40017, referred to herewith as Nesitanebtawy A to avoid confusion with the papyrus here referred to as Nesitanebtawy B) fig. 14, Tamniwt (P. London BM EA 10002) fig. 15a, and Tawyherit (P. Leiden T 3, AMS 40) fig. 21f, and the sarcophagus of Tantwenmether (JE 29660=CG 6214, CG 6183), *Totenbuchprojekt Bonn, TM 135483*. Accessed May 30, 2021.totenbuch.awk.nrw.de/objekt/tm135483, fig. 15b.

[54] Hornung, *Das Totenbuch Der Ägypter*, 469.

[55] Thausing, and Kerszt-Kratschmann, *Das grosse ägyptische Totenbuch*, 23, n. 3.

[56] Uppsala VM MB 2.

[57] P. Paris Louvre E. 11078, *Totenbuchprojekt Bonn, TM 56856*. Accessed May 30, 2021. totenbuch.awk.nrw.de/objekt/tm56856.

[58] P. Colon. Aeg. 10207.

[59] Late Period papyri of Ankhwahibre (P. London BM EA 10558), *Totenbuchprojekt Bonn, TM 57267*. Accessed May 30, 2021.totenbuch.awk.nrw.de/objekt/tm57267) fig. 12b; Thaihepimw (P. Paris Louvre N. 3094), *Totenbuchprojekt Bonn, TM 56604*. Accessed May 30, 2021. totenbuch.awk.nrw.de/objekt/tm56604, fig. 12c, and that of Iptweret (P. Cortona 3186, *Totenbuchprojekt Bonn, TM 57169*. Accessed May 30, 2021.totenbuch.awk.nrw.de/objekt/tm57169), fig. 12d.

[60] E. Hornung, *The Egyptian Amduat*, Translated from German by D. Warburton (Zurich, 2007), 214, 220.

[61] Hornung, *Amduat*, 110, 119. Similar depictions are found in the Book of Gates, the Book of the Creation of the Solar Disk, and in

encircling an oval representing the sarcophagus of Osiris.[62] These examples reflect the notions of protection as well as resurrection and perpetuality, all of which may easily resonate with the characteristics of Sata.

We find that the choice of depicting Sata as a human-headed cobra in this group best expresses the personification of the deceased with Sata. The deceased, represented by the human head, and the serpent Sata, are indeed one creature. The transformation is fully achieved to further confirm the notion of rebirth and rejuvenation of the deceased.

2. Sata in the Hymn to Osiris Outstretched in Earth

A hieratic Ramesside text written on an ostracon that was found in KV 9 has been labelled "Hymne à Osiris étendu à terre" by George Daressy.[63] However, we would rather use the translation "Hymn to Osiris outstretched in Earth" based on the context that describes the god's actions within the ground not above it. The text, which has been studied and translated by Adolf Erman,[64] includes the following passage:

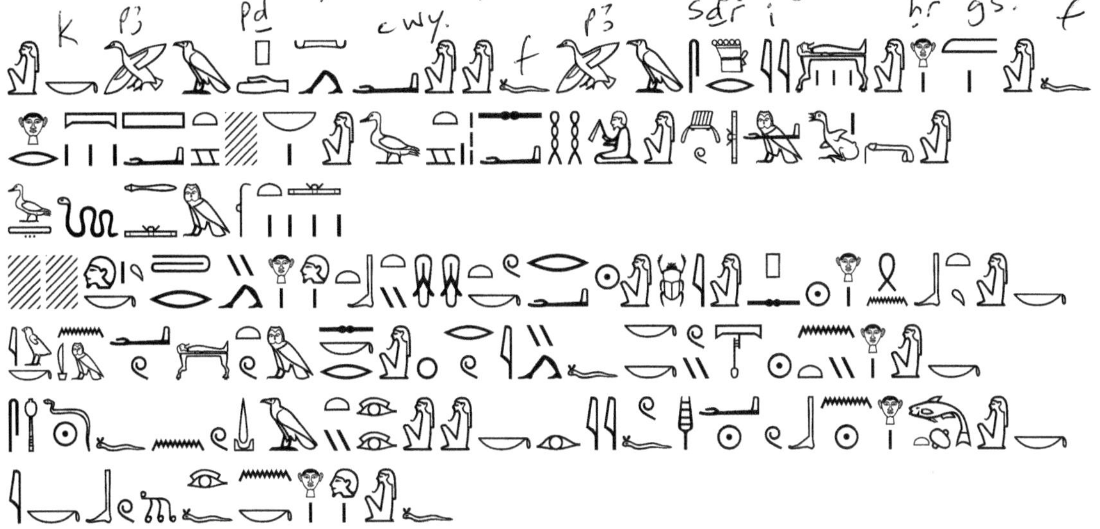

[///].k p3j pḏ ꜥwy.f p3j sḏrj ḥr gs.f
ḥrj šꜥjt /// nb s3w.t sꜥḥḥ 3w m ṯ3j
s3-t3 ꜥ3 m rnpwt
//// tp.k pẖr ḥr-tp tb(w).ty tw.k rꜥ ḫpri ps ḥr šnbt.k
iw.k nmꜥ.tw m skr rwi.f kkw ntj ḥr.k
sḥḏ.f n wḏ3.ty.k irj.f ꜥḥꜥw wbn ḥr ẖ3t.k
i3kb.f n.k ḥr-tp.f
/ / / you, who stretches his arms, who sleeps on his side,
Who is on the sandbank, lord of the ground, you mummy with long phallus [lit. manhood],
Sata, long of years.
Your head[65] turn around your soles [lit. your sandals]. Re-Kheperi shines on your breast.[66]
When you are sleeping like Sokar, so that he prevents the darkness that is upon you

enigmatic texts, see: J. Darnell, *The Enigmatic Netherworld Books of the Solar-Osirian Unity: Cryptographic Compositions in the Tombs of Tutankhamun, Ramesses VI and Ramesses IX*, OBO 198 (Fribourg, 2004), 90–91.

[62] A. Piankoff, *The Shrines of Tut-Ankh-Amon* (Princeton, 1977), fig. 41; Darnell, *The Enigmatic Netherworld Books*, 90.

[63] Ramesside Ostracon oCG 25209 found in KV 9, G. Daressy, *Ostraca* (CGC Nos 25001–25385), (Cairo, 1901), 41, pl. XXXVII.

[64] A. Erman, "Gebete eines ungerecht Verfolgten und andere Ostraka aus den Königsgräbern," *ZÄS* 38 (1900), 30–31.

[65] The sign used here as a determinative for *tp* is likely mistaken instead of Gardiner's sign F51 which we used instead.

[66] Faulkner, *Dictionary*, 269. The sign used here as a determinative for *šnbt* is likely mistaken instead of Gardiner sign F51 which we used instead.

> and gives light to your eyes. He spends a lifetime shining over your corpse
> and mourns for you over himself.

There are numerous aspects of the identification of Sata and Osiris in this text. Osiris is referred to as the Lord of Earth , an epithet that Erman believed had been used only twice for Osiris.[67] The beginning of this text describes how Osiris would awaken from death, stretch his arms, and lie on his side in similarity to the scenes of the Awakening of Osiris. He becomes the master of the ground in which he is buried. He is the one who is still fertile even in death. Here, the resurrection takes place with the help of Re who, during his nightly journey, shines over the deceased Osiris. The text echoes that of BD 87 where the serpent Sata falls asleep every night and is reborn every day at the border of earth.

Erman suggested that the reference to Osiris' fertility in the text is a way of associating him with the long-lived rejuvenating Sata,[68] thus connecting the resurrection of Sata with that of Osiris. Representations of the dead Osiris with an erect phallus were often associated with the production of his heir Horus,[69] thus symbolizing continuity of life according to the notion that Osiris resurrected, or rather continued, in the form of his son Horus.[70] Moreover, the concept of renewal and perpetuality is expressed in the text with the request of Sata turning his head towards his soles, a notion that is inferred in the BD 87 text discussed above, mentioning the presence of Sata at the boundaries of earth.[71] In other words, this hymn to Osiris is a mere confirmation of renewable eternal life for the deceased.

3. Sata in the First Division of the Book of Caverns

The text starts with Re addressing the gods of the Ennead of Osiris as he enters the first cavern of the West. Sata is the third of three serpents represented in front of an ennead of Serpents.

Text of the first register of the First Division:

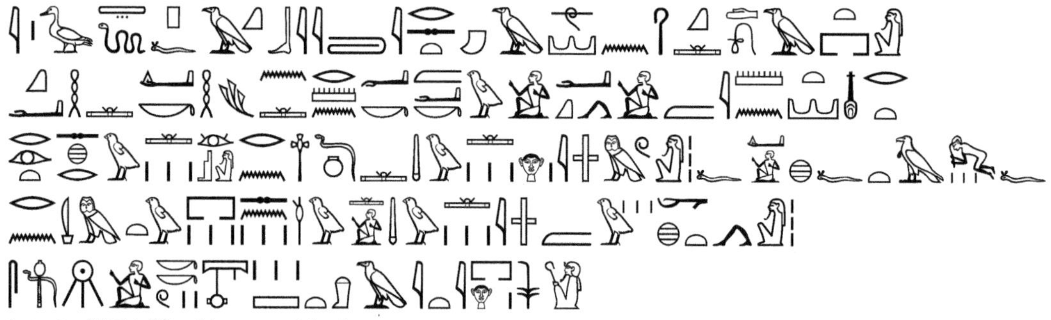

ỉ sꜣ-tꜣ pf ḳꜣbj {ỉ} r(ꜣ)-sṯꜣw n ḥḳꜣ dwꜣt
ḳꜥḥ ꜥ.k ḥn rmn.k mk.wi ꜥḳ.i m imnt nfrt
r irt sḫrw Wsir r nḏ-mdw ḥr imyw.f di.i ḫftw.f
r nmwt.sn wḏ.i mdw ⸢n-⸣ imyw ḫt
sḥḏ.i kkw štꜣyt ḥr nsw

[67] Erman, "Gebete eines ungerecht," 31.

[68] Erman, "Gebete eines ungerecht," 31–32.

[69] H. S. K. Bakry, *The main elements of the Osiris legend with reference to Plutarch and certain folk-tales*, (PhD dissertation, Durham University, 1955), 101, Available at *Durham E-Theses Online*. Accessed June 10, 2021. http://etheses.dur.ac.uk/9519/; R. David, *A Guide to Religious Ritual at Abydos* (Warminster, 1981), 104–5; Darnell, *The Enigmatic Netherworld Books*, 337 and n. 273.

[70] Griffith, *Origins*, 169.

[71] The connection between the encircling serpent, fertility, and creation is also found in other texts: R. Landgráfová, F. Coppens, J. Janák et al., "Myth and Ritual in the Burial Chamber of the Shaft Tomb of Iufaa at Abusir: Snakes and Snake-like Beings," in M. Bárta, F. Coppens, and J. Krejčí (eds.), *Abusir and Saqqara in the Year 2015* (Prague, 2017), 618–19; J. Janak, "The Book of Snakes from the Tomb of Iufaa at Abusir," in K. A. Kóthay, *Burial and Mortuary Practices in Late Period and Graeco-Roman Egypt* (Budapest 2017), 118–19.

O, Sata, who curl in Ro-Setau for the ruler of the Duat.
Bend your hand, restrain your arm. Behold me, I enter into the beautiful West.
To take care of Osiris, to protect those who are in him.
To put his enemies in their place of execution. I command words to those in his suite,
I light the darkness of the secret chamber for the king.[72]

Text of the third register of the First Division:

i psḏt nt Wsir wḏʿt-mdw ḥr dw3t Wsir ḫnty imnti
imyw-ḫt.f ḥtpw m k3r s3 t3 {n?} ʿ3
O, Ennead of Osiris, judging in the Duat of Osiris Khenty-Imenty,
those who follow him rest in the chapel of the great Sata.[73]

These texts indicate that Sata is one of the guardians of the Netherworld whom Re instructs to protect the deceased king and not inflict him with harm.[74] Frankfort suggests that ***rmn*** here is used to indicate the "fang" of a serpent rather than an "arm," signifying a restraining fang rather than being a metaphor of bending the arm in homage, an interpretation that he believes matches the magical context of the text that is meant to protect the king from the venomous snakes of the underworld.[75] In this case, the text acknowledges the harmful side of the serpent Sata as well as the protective one in order to protect the deceased king and ensure that he achieves resurrection, a concept that mirrors the double character of creation, represented in its two aspects of ***m3ʿt*** and ***isft,***[76] and that resonates with the earlier texts of the Old and Middle Kingdoms discussed above.

In the third register of the First Division, the text further defines the role of Sata. The passage that describes the approach of Re through the Netherworld addresses a group of divinities requesting their help through the journey. One of those divinities is the great Sata, who is said to guard the chapel of the companions of Osiris. The connection of Sata with Osiris is likewise indicated in the text in the mention that Sata curls in Ro-Setau, the mythical Memphite birthplace of Osiris that developed to signify the realm of the dead.[77] Once again, the text reflects that the resurrection of Osiris will happen with the help of the sun god bringing life to Osiris and likewise to the deceased.[78]

4. Sata in a Text from the Dream Book

On the recto of the Papyrus Chester Beatty III is found this Nineteenth Dynasty text entitled the Dream Book:

[72] A. Piankoff, "Le Livre des Quererts I," *BIFAO* 41 (1941), 8, pl. IV, col. 2. Also compare H. Frankfort, *The Cenotaph of Sety I at Abydos* (Oxford, 1933), vol. 1, 37, and vol. 2, pl. 23, and 24, col. 9; Darnell, *The Enigmatic Netherworld Books*, 347, pl. 29; D. A. Werning, *Das Höhlenbuch: Textkritische Edition und Textgrammatik*, vol. II, Textkritische Edition und Übersetzung, Göttinger Orientforschungen, Reihe 4, Ägypten 48 (Wiesbaden, 2011), 8–9.

[73] Piankoff, "Le Livre des Quererts I," 9, pl. VI, col. 4; also compare: Werning, *Das Höhlenbuch*, 24–25.

[74] Sata plays the same role as a protector of Osiris in J. Vandier, *Le Papyrus Jumilhac* (Paris, 1961), vignette VII, and 176, 242.

[75] Frankfort, *Cenotaph of Sety I*, I, 37, n. 1.

[76] Servajean, *Les formules des transformations*, 19.

[77] Griffith, *Origins*, 136.

[78] A. Piankoff, *The Tomb of Ramesses VI*, Bollingen Series XL.1 (New York, 1954), 36, 50.

Ỉr m33 sw.s m rswt
ḥr s3 t3 /////// nfr ḏf3 pw
If a man sees himself in a dream
Seeing Sata ….. good, this means food

In this magical context of dream interpretation, Sata holds a positive position. If a man sees himself in his dream seeing Sata, that is considered a good omen that will ensure nourishment for the deceased.[79] The dreams' interpretations are based on concepts related to the creatures or the object that the dreamer sees. For instance, if a man sees himself looking into a well, it is bad and it means that he is going to jail. One may see the connection between the depth and darkness of the well with that of jail, in addition to the similar difficulty of escaping them both. The same measure may be used in the case of seeing Sata in a dream. The serpent Sata was associated with the renewal of life, resurrection, and with Osiris, a god primarily associated with agriculture. This therefore represented a sensible sign of good fortune and nourishment for the authors of the Dream Book. This text is the only text from dynastic Egypt known to us that mentions Sata in a non-funerary context.

Manifestations of the Divinity of Sata

As noted above, the nature of the serpent Sata changed from being an enemy in the Old and Middle Kingdoms Texts to being deified in the texts and representations from the New Kingdom onwards. In addition to the aforementioned New Kingdom texts associating Sata with both Re and Osiris and BD Spell 87 implying the veneration of Sata, other texts and representations show more tangible signs of the divinity of the serpent.

Sata was depicted as a divinity worshipped by the deceased in four Ramesside Theban tombs,[80] on the Papyrus of Neferrenpet,[81] and on the Twenty-First Dynasty sarcophagus of Tantwenmether[82] (see figs. 7, 8, 9, 11,

Fig. 7. Sata as a Divinity. Papyrus of Neferrenpet, Brüssel MRAH E. 5043. Drawing by Iman Elsaid.

Fig. 8. Sata as a Divinity. Tomb of Neferhotep (TT 6). Drawing by Iman Elsaid.

[79] P. Chester Beatty III, 2, 15: A. Gardiner, *Hieratic Papyri in the British Museum: Third Series Chester Beatty Gift* (London, 1935), vol. 1, 12; vol. 2, pl. 5.
[80] TT 6 (fig. 6), TT 214 (fig. 11), TT 290 (fig. 9), and TT 359.
[81] P. Brüssel MRAH E. 5043.
[82] JE 29660 (CG 6214, CG 6183).

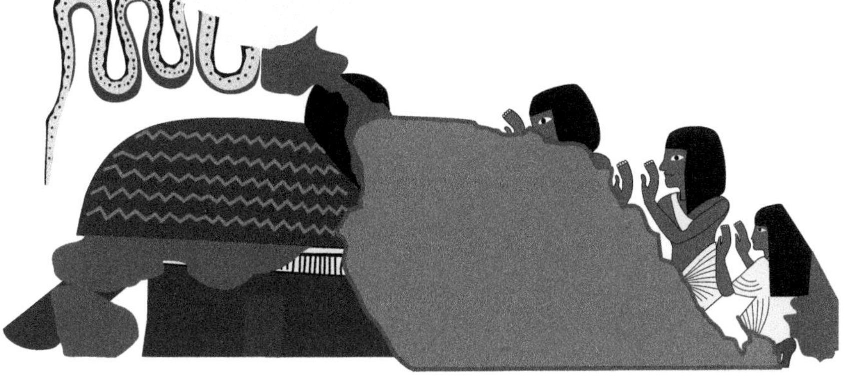

Fig. 9. Sata as a Divinity. Tomb of Irinefer, TT 290. Drawing by Iman Elsaid.

15b). The deceased in these scenes is portrayed either standing or kneeling in prayer with his arms raised towards Sata, and in some of these examples (figs. 11, 15b), he may present a pile of offerings to the serpent.

In TT 6, the deceased Neferhotep stands in the attitude of prayer in front of Sata (fig. 8). The accompanying text reads:

r sḥtp kꜣ n s n.f ḏd-mdw in wsir ḥry iswt m st-mꜣʿt[83] *nfr-ḥtp mꜣʿ-ḫrw*
ink ms.kwi rnp.kwi rʿ-nb
ms.k rʿ-nb ink sꜣ n tꜣ im//// ḏrw tꜣ
ḏd mdw in wsir nfr-ḥtp mꜣʿ-ḫrw ink sꜣ-tꜣ sḏri /// pr-wr
Spell for pleasing a man's ka: Words spoken by Osiris, the Foreman of the Place of Truth, Neferhotep, true of voice:
I am born, I am rejuvenated every day.
I am born every day, I am Sata, in the entire land.
Words spoken by Osiris-Neferhotep, True of Voice, I am Sata who lies down in the Chapel [of Upper Egypt].

In this version of BD 87, the name Sata is followed by the determinative Gardiner A40 (seated deity) used with the names of gods. The text accentuates that the rebirth and rejuvenation would be granted to Neferhotep via his identification with the divine Sata. The text emphasizes on the divinity of Sata by stating that the serpent lies down in Per-wer, the divine symbolic shrine of Upper Egypt that is strongly related to the Sed feast[84] and the rejuvenation associated with it.

[83] A. Al-Ayedi, *Index of Egyptian Administrative, Religious and Military Titles of the New Kingdom* (Ismailia, 2006), 389.
[84] A. Gardiner, "The Coronation of King Ḥaremḥab," *JEA* 39 (1953), 15, 24; D. Arnold, "Per-wer II," *LÄ* IV, cols. 934–35.

A similar concept is found in TT 290, where the deceased and his wife and son kneel in front of Sata and the crocodile, and the vignettes of BD 87–88 respectively[85] (fig. 9).

di.n[.i] n.k st m ḫrt-nṯr st ḥtp n iri mꜣꜥt

sꜣ ꜥnḫ nb ḥꜣ.f mi Rꜥ ḏt

I will give you a place in the realm of the dead, the resting place for those who do what is right."[86]

All protection and life are behind him like Re, eternally.

In this text, the deity Sata assures well being and eternal life to the deceased Irinefer. Sata is here rendered as one of the divinities of the underworld with crucial influence on the resurrection of the deceased. In spite of the absence of the name of Sata and the fact that the text is not what is typically found with BD Spell 87, the adjacent crocodile has the rubric of BD 88 "Transforming into a Crocodile" written above the scene, thus confirming the identity of the text and the serpent as those of BD Spell 87.

In the tomb of Inherkhoui (TT 359), the vignette and text of BD Spell 87 are both shown (fig. 20a).[87] The text presents a novel approach towards Sata:

inḏ ḥr.k sꜣ-tꜣ pr m nww iwꜥ pn nṯrw

wsir ḥry iswt m st mꜣꜥt In-ḥr-ḫꜥw mꜣꜥ ḫrw ḏd.f sn tꜣ nw nbw r ḥḥ

wrw n ꜣbḏw

Hail, Sata, who comes out of the primordial sea, the heir of the gods,

Osiris, the Foreman[88] of the Place of Truth, Inherkhoui, justified, he says: kiss the earth before the lords of the Eternity,

the great ones of Abydos.[89]

Once again, this text is not typical of the usual Transformation Chapter BD Spell 87, but rather an homage and prayer to Sata and other divinities. However, its proximity to Transformation Chapters BD Spell 82, Assuming the Form of Ptah, BD Spell 85 for Assuming the Form of a Ba-bird, and BD Spell 86 for Assuming the form of a swallow—all of which are part of the decoration of the northern section of the vault, confirms its character as BD 87.

This text mentions that Sata comes out of the primeval ocean. The serpent here is clearly marked as a primordial being and is welcomed by the deceased as being the son of earth who emerged from the primeval waters and as the heir of the gods.[90] The deceased lists other divinities that he made sacrifices to so that they would open

85 PM I, 1, 373.10. The snake is partly damaged.

86 M. Saleh, *Das Totenbuch in den Thebanischen Beamtengräbern des Neuen Reiches: Texts und Vignetten, AVDAIK* 46 (Mainz am Rhein, 1984), 49, 51, fig. 58.

87 B. Bruyère, *Rapport sur les fouilles de Deir El Médineh (1930)*, FIFAO 8.3 (Cairo, 1933), 52, pl. 15; PM I, 1, 423.

88 Chief Workman in the Place of Truth, in Al-Ayedi, *Index*, 389–90.

89 Saleh, *Totenbuch*, 49.

90 Hornung, *Das Totenbuch Der Ägypter*, 469.

a b c d

Fig. 10. Serpent Sata and Lotus: (a) Papyrus of Nu, BM EA 10477; (b) Papyrus of Kha and Merit, Paris BN 826 (Luynes B); (c) Papyrus of Kha, Turin 8438; (d) Papyrus of Nesikhonsu, Paris BN 170-173. Drawing by Iman Elsaid.

the realm of the dead for him. The text here differs from the usual text of the BD Spell 87 in that it emphasizes the other powers of Sata instead of the usual rebirth and rejuvenation powers,[91] because here the divinity of Sata is additionally associated with creation. The solar connection of Sata is stressed in his emergence from Nu.

This text recalls the image of the lotus emerging from the Primeval Ocean at the instant of creation. It is relevant to note that both the lotus and Sata, the vignettes representing Spells 81 and 87 respectively, are depicted in proximity of one another with both their figures stretching along the width of the scene in eight examples from our specimens (figs. 10a-d, 14, 15a-b, 18a). This connection between the serpent and the lotus is mentioned in the Brooklyn Papyrus where a serpent is described as having a body similar to that of a lotus, a description that relates to the rising action of a hooded cobra.[92] This association is also echoed in later texts found in the temple of Dendara, where the serpent is described as *sꜣ-tꜣ wr wbn m nḫb* "the great *sꜣ-tꜣ* who emerges from the lotus flower," and *sꜣ-tꜣ nṯry pr m Ỉwnw* "the divine *sꜣ-tꜣ* who comes from Heliopolis."[93] This connection reflects the association of both the serpent Sata and the lotus with creation as coming from beneath and of the notion that both the lotus and Sata wake up and rise after sleep. In addition, it is a manifestation of their shared solar liaison.

The link between Sata and the lotus is more clear on the Ptolemaic Period sarcophagus of Khaf[94] that shows the twelve forms that the sun god Re takes as he travels through the twelve hours of the day.[95] These forms are aligned with the twelve forms of the Transformation Chapters of the Book of the Dead.[96] Intriguingly, the form Sata is aligned with that of Nefertum, the newborn young sun god whose symbol and identity are the lotus flower.

Such an association may seem to contradict with the name of Sata that reflects its chthonic powers. Nevertheless, the stretch of the body of Sata throughout the breadth of the scene is intended to express the idea of coming from earth just like it is intended for the lotus to express the notion of coming out of the ocean. Furthermore, in

---

91 Saleh, *Totenbuch*, 49, n. 360.

92 S. Sauneron, *Un traité ÉgyptienneÉgyptien d'ophiologie : papyrus du Brooklyn Museum N° 47.218.48 et .85* (Cairo, 1989), 21–23; Golding, *Brooklyn Papyrus*, 105–06, 189.

93 S. Cauville, J. Hallof, and H. Van Den Berg, *Dendara: les chapelles osiriennes (Index)*, BdE 119 (Cairo, 1997), 459.

94 Cairo JE 49531.

95 G. Daressy, "Fragments de deux cercueils de Saqqara," *ASAE* 17 (1917), 16.

96 H. Brugsch, "Die Kapitel der Verwandlungen im Todtenbuch 76 bis 88," *ZÄS* 5 (1863), 23, and table facing 24; S. Quirke, *Going out in Daylight prt m hrw: The Ancient Egyptian Book of the Dead, Translation, Sources, Meanings*, GHP Egyptology 20 (London, 2013), 179.

the text here discussed, Sata is himself coming out of the primeval ocean, which is once again an emphasis on the symbolic association of Sata with creation.

The text reflects the double nature of the serpent. On one hand, the serpent lives on earth yet hibernates within, thus associating the reptile with earth and consequently with death and the god Osiris. On the other hand, the serpent wakes up from its hibernation as the weather gets warmer, thus associating it to the sun god Re and subsequently with resurrection and rejuvenation. This double nature of the serpent fits with the belief that spread from the New Kingdom onwards that both Re and Osiris unite into one during the nightly journey,[97] only to be born again like Re leaving Osiris in the realm of the dead, thus emphasizing on the cyclic perpetual correlation of life and death.[98] The notion of the sun god taking the form of a serpent while in the company of Osiris through the nightly journey is found in BD 175, "Spell for not Dying a Second Time."[99]

Two intriguing terms caught our attention in this regard. The reference to the deceased Osiris as *ỉmy-tꜣ*, "the one who is within earth"—a term also used to designate snakes[100]—and the reference to Re as *tꜣy,* "the one of Earth," also interpreted as "the chthonic sun."[101] The use of these terms adds more coherence to the connection of the three divinities. Sata may therefore be considered a nocturnal form of the sun god in his nightly journey as he unites with Osiris, the one who sleeps within earth, to renew and rejuvenate in order to be able to be born again, a fate that the deceased aspired to share.[102] In other words, Sata combines the Celestial Re and the Chthonic Osiris, two opposing powers[103] that were united during the nightly journey only to achieve perpetuality. Such duality is reflected in later texts of the temple of Dendara, where Sata is called *sꜣ-tꜣ nṯry pr m Ỉwnw* 'the divine *sꜣ-tꜣ* who comes from Heliopolis', and *sꜣ-tꜣ šps pr m Ndyt* 'the good *sꜣ-tꜣ* who comes from Nedyt',[104] two designations of significant relevance considering that *Ỉwnw* and *Ndyt* are two sites associated with Re and Osiris respectively.

Another unique feature is found in TT 214 (fig. 11), where the following text is found above a picture of a human-legged cobra:

 105

wꜥb sp-sn n kꜣ n tꜣ nbt-tꜣwy
Pure, pure, for the ka of the Lady of the Two Lands.

For the first time we find the reference to Sata as a female divinity, contrary to the masculinity of the deity as implied by its name and in textual evidence. This example is, to our knowledge, the only instance of a feminine Sata. The tomb owner, Khoui, who kneels on a Maat sign, offers to the human-legged hooded cobra. Although the name of the divinity is not stated, it has been identified as Sata.[106] This identification may be based on the feet and the parallel from TT 6 discussed above. It is likely that the widespread worship of Meretseger at Deir el Medineh, and the fact that both

Fig. 11. Sata as the Lady of the Two Lands. Tomb of Khawi (TT 214). Photo credit © IFAO.

[97] J. G. Griffith, "Osiris," *LÄ* IV, col. 629; Darnell, *The Enigmatic Netherworld Books*, 129–30, 190, 248, 359–73; M. Smith, *Following Osiris: Perspectives on the Osirian Afterlife from Four Millennia* (Oxford, 2017), 302–5.

[98] Piankoff, *Ramesses VI*, I, 34–35 and fig. 5.

[99] E. A. W. Budge, *Book of the Dead: The Chapters of Coming Forth by Day* (London, 1898), 326; Colazilli, "Skin," 121.

[100] P. Vernus and J. Yoyotte, *Bestiaire des pharaons* (Paris, 2005), 83, 293.

[101] Darnell, *The Enigmatic Netherworld Books*, 353.

[102] L. Žabkar, "Correlation of the Transformation Spells of the Book of the Dead and the Amulets of Tutankhamun Mummy," *Mélanges Offerts a Jean Vercoutter* (Paris, 1985), 380.

[103] Griffith, "Osiris," 629.

[104] Cauville, Hallof, and Van Den Berg, *Dendara*, 459. A parallel to the double natured Sata is the *nꜥw*-snake that plays a double role as a protector of Re and Osiris. See Willems, *Heqata*, 353, n. 2176.

[105] B. Bruyère, *Tombes thébaines de Deir el Médineh à décoration monochrome*, MIFAO 86 (Cairo, 1952), 97, pl. XXVIII.

[106] PM I, 1, 310–11; Saleh, *Totenbuch*, 50.

divinities were serpents, led to an association of Sata with Meretseger in this tomb, to the extent that it was given the feminine title of *nbt-t3wy*. Bernard Bruyère points out that the title *nbt-t3wy* is enough to designate the cobra as a formidable chthonic divinity analogous to the serpent Sata and to Meretseger.[107] It may be worth mentioning that of the four examples of Sata represented as a hooded cobra known from the New Kingdom, two are found in Deir el Medineh tombs.

In addition to the aforementioned signs of divinity, Sata is represented with a divine beard in the papyri of Nesitanebtawy[108] (fig. 14) and of Nesikhonsu A[109] (fig. 10d), and on the sarcophagus of Tantwenmether (fig. 15b), all of which are dated to the Twenty-First Dynasty. The feature that also appears on the Twenty-Sixth Dynasty Papyri of Ankhwahibre[110] (fig. 12a); Thaihepimw[111] (fig. 12b), and Iptweret (fig. 12c). Sata is also represented amongst a group of netherworld divinities attending the awakening of Osiris on the Papyrus of Padiamun A (fig. 13). The latter example has been identified based on the iconography of the feet associated with Sata.[112]

The divinity of Sata is also reflected in its association with symbols related to the sun god. For instance, some representations of the serpent Sata were linked to the east. In the tomb of Inherkhoui TT 359, Sata looks towards the east of the tomb facing the deceased who looks towards the west (fig. 20a).[113] In addition, in the papyrus of Tamniwt (fig. 15a),[114] Sata is represented above the sign of the east. A similar depiction is found in the papyrus of Nesitanebtawy A (fig. 14),[115] where the deified bearded human-legged Sata is placed on the sign of the east placed on a mountain.[116] Similarly, on the sarcophagus of Tantwenmether (fig. 15b) the deceased is

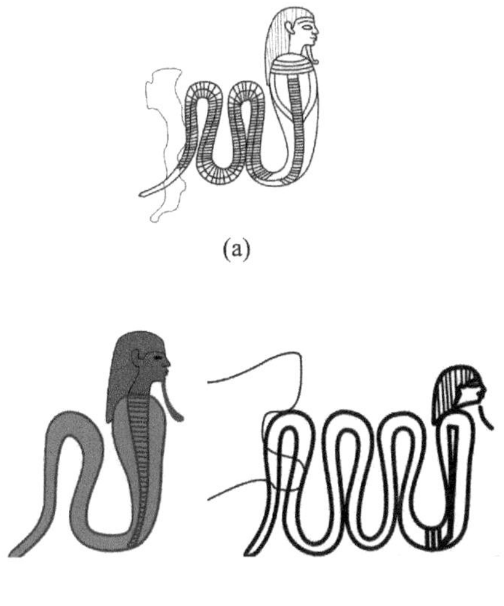

(a) (b) (c)

Fig. 12. Sata as a Serpent with Divine Beard: (a) Papyrus of Ankhwahibre, London BM EA 10558; (b) Papyrus of Thaihepimw, Paris Louvre N. 3094; (c) Papyrus of Iptweret, Cortona 3186. Drawing by Iman Elsaid.

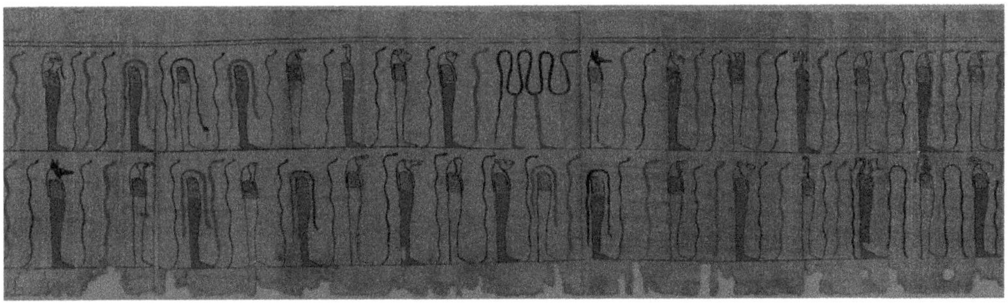

Fig. 13. Sata with other Divinities. Papyrus of Padiamun A, SR I/10654. Photo by Sameh Abdel-Mohsen courtesy of Egyptian Museum, Cairo.

[107] Bruyère, *Tombes thébaines*, 94.
[108] P. Cairo CGC 40017. *Totenbuchprojekt Bonn, TM 114109*. Accessed May 30, 2021.totenbuch.awk.nrw.de/objekt/tm114109.
[109] P. Paris BN 170-173, A. Piankoff, *Mythological Papyri*, vol. II, Plates, Bollingen Series XL.3 (New York, 1957), papyrus 4.
[110] P. London BM EA 10558
[111] P. Paris Louvre N. 3094.
[112] SR I/10654. A. Piankoff, *Mythological Papyri*, vol. I, *Texts*, 115; *Totenbuchprojekt Bonn, TM 134725*, Accessed June 13, 2021.
[113] Bruyère, *Rapport sur les fouilles de Deir El Médineh (1930)*, 52.
[114] P. London BM EA 10002.
[115] P. Cairo CGC 40017.
[116] JE 29660.

Fig. 14. Sata above the Sign of the East Papyrus of Nesitanebtawy A, Cairo CG 40017. Photo by Abir Enany.

(a) *(b)*

Fig. 15. Sata with the Sign of the East: (a) Papyrus of Tamniwt, London BM EA 10002; (b) Sarcophagus of Tantwenmether, JE 29660 (CG 6214, CG 6183). Drawing by Iman Elsaid.

represented with the sign of the west behind her, facing the bearded Sata who is depicted to the right with a table of offerings that resembles the sign of the east in front of the serpent and a lotus flower behind him.

Nevertheless, it might be worth noting that the divinity of Sata is different than that of Re and other gods. We note that in the headings of the Transformation Chapters of the Book of the Dead the names of Sata, Seshen, Menet, Bik, and Benu are usually written in red like the rest of the heading *ỉr ḫpr m*, while that of Ptah is written in black within the chapter heading that is in red (figs. 16a–b, 17). Examples of this are found in the papyri of Ani, Yuya, Senusert, Nu, Maatkare and others. The same observation is noticed for other divinities' names, for instance the name of Re that is found in black in the middle of a text written in red, such as in the Papyrus of Nu.[117] This is likely to avoid writing the name of a divinity in red, which was the color used to write the name of the god Seth and the names of enemies.[118] This indicates that Sata is more of a personification of a deity in the same way that the lotus, the swallow, the falcon, and the heron are. The divinity of Sata is therefore not absolute but is related to the powers that its form and character reflect.

The Nature of the Expression "Sata"

The available texts and representations of Sata are somehow ambiguous regarding the species of the serpent, which opens the door for some inquiries regarding the nature of the creature.

One finds that the depictions of the serpent Sata take an array of forms and colors. In the papyrus of Yuya (fig. 18a), the serpent resembles the species *Naja nubiae*, the Nubian Spitting Cobra or the Black Cobra, a venomous nocturnal serpent with limited diurnal activities,[119] or *Walterinnesia aegyptia*, the Black Desert Cobra, another nocturnal and venomous snake.[120] These two are the only black serpents known in Egypt.[121] However, we propose that our example belongs to the latter type as it is represented entirely in black similarly to the Black Desert

[117] *Totenbuchprojekt Bonn, TM 134299*. Accessed June 13, 2021. totenbuch.awk.nrw.de/objekt/tm134299.

[118] G. Pinch, "Red Things: The Symbolism of Colour in Magic," in W. Davies (ed.), *Colour and Painting in Ancient Egypt* (London, 2001), 184.

[119] S. Baha El Din, *A Guide to the Reptiles and Amphibians of Egypt* (Cairo, 2006), 557–58, fig. 110. https://www.scribd.com/read/384590055/A-Guide-to-Reptiles-Amphibians-of-Egypt#b_search-menu_486645_Accessed_May 25, 2021.

[120] Baha El Din, *A Guide to the Reptiles*, 560, figs. 111–12; Golding, *Brooklyn Papyrus*, 186, fig. 33.

[121] Golding, *Brooklyn Papyrus*, 186.

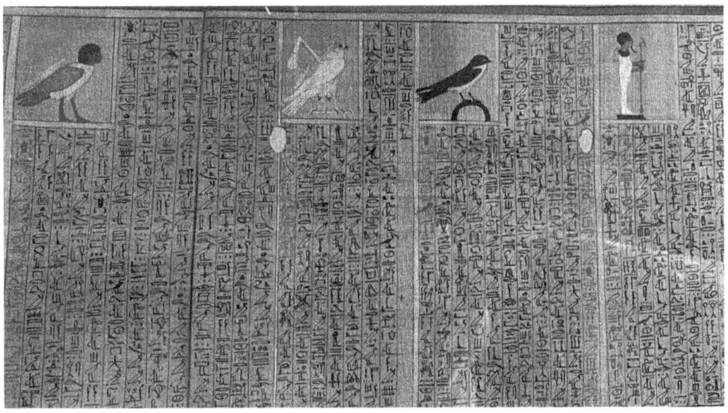

Fig. 16a-b. Variations of the Use of Black and Red in Transformation Chapters Headings. Papyrus Yuya, CGC 51189. Photos by Abir Enany.

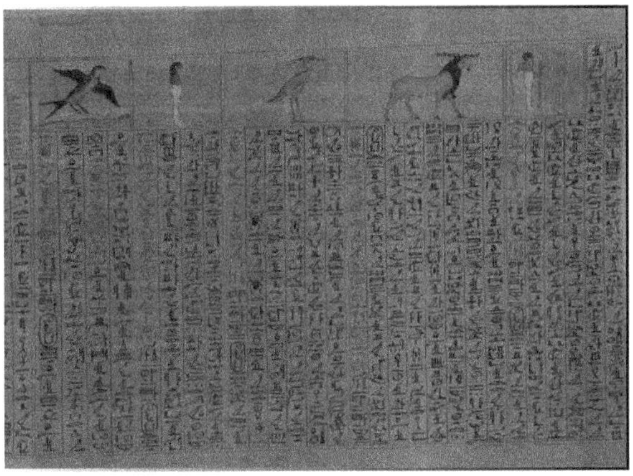

Fig. 17. The Name Sata written in Red and that of Ptah in Black within Transformation Chapters Headings Papyrus of Maatkare, SR IV/980 = JE 26229. Photo by Sameh Abdel-Mohsen courtesy of Egyptian Museum, Cairo.

Fig. 18a. Black Serpent on the Papyrus of Yuya, CGC 51189. Photo by Abir Enany.

Fig. 18b. Walterinnesia aegyptia, the Black Desert Cobra. Photo by Radhavar/Shutterstock.com, https://www.shutterstock.com/image-photo/black-cobra-snake-family-national-park-1670658253.

Cobra[122] (fig. 18b), whereas the Nubian Spitting Cobra has a buff color for the venter and its back is of brownish grey rather than pitch-black.[123]

Some of the representations of Sata discussed above show the serpent with striped skin (figs. 1a, 10c, 15a) similar to that of *Naja annulifera,* the Banded Cobra,[124] another venomous serpent.[125] However, as this species is not recorded in Egypt,[126] we suggest that the banded serpent in these documents might be *Platyceps sinai*, the Sinai Banded snake, a nocturnal non-venomous small snake[127] that bears much resemblance to our specimens.

Other examples resemble *Echis c. coloratus* and *Echis pyramidum*, both of which are subspecies of the *Genus Echis* species that belongs to the venomous *Viperidae* family.[128] The serpent on the papyrus of Nebqed (fig. 19a) bears notable resemblance to the *Echis c. coloratus*, a nocturnal snake that is also known as Burton's Carpet Viper, judging by the broad triangular head,[129] the light color of the serpent, and the side winding of the body indicating a side movement characteristic of this type of serpent (fig. 19b). The Egyptians recognized this side movement and recorded it.[130]

The serpent in the tomb of Inherkhoui (fig. 20a) resembles the *Echis pyramidum*, another nocturnal snake[131] known as the Carpet Viper[132] (fig. 20b). Serpents of the species were described as "Dorsum gray, with a mid-dorsal series of dark-edged, whitish, narrow saddles, interspersed with large dark brown-gray blotches; a lateral series of smaller dark spots; dorsal side of head with a dark arrow-like mark (often broken); indistinct dark, diagonal band below the eye. Venter white,"[133] a description that perfectly fits our example. To this species we may also suggest the serpents of our figures 21a-f as well as the snakes referred to earlier in our work (see figs. 3, 4b, 10b, 10d, 14, and 15b)

Other specimens are harder to identify. Nevertheless, judging by the bands on their necks, we may suggest that our figures 2, and 4a belong to the species *Naja nubiae*,[134] the Nubian Spitting Cobra. Our specimens also have a black back like the suggested species. However, the available data does not allow further confirmation.

Other specimens represent Sata as a hooded Egyptian cobra, *Naja haje*, (figs. 1c, 4c, 6, 8, 11, 12). However, it should be noted that the hooded cobra was widely associated with female goddesses.[135] All female serpent goddesses were represented in the form of a rearing cobra, while male serpent gods were represented with a divine beard.[136] Even though the ancient Egyptians rarely identified types of male serpent mythical creatures, modern researchers were able to identify some species based on the iconography, such as the serpent Apophis which was identified as the *Naja nubiae*, Nubian Spitting Cobra, or the red cobra based on the number of its fangs.[137] Only one male serpent god was represented as a rearing cobra, namely Netjer-ankh.[138] Due to the male identity of Sata, it was therefore a more natural choice to represent the deity as a serpent of another species than cobra,

---

122 Sauneron, *Un traité d'ophiologie*, 10; Golding, *Brooklyn Papyrus*, 186.

123 Baha El Din, *A Guide to the Reptiles*, 557–58, and compare 313, figs. 110–11.

124 Snouted Cobra. https://www.africansnakebiteinstitute.com/snake/snouted-cobra. Accessed May 25, 2021.

125 F. Silva-de-França, I. Villas-Boas, S. Serrano et al., "Naja annulifera Snake: New Insights into the Venom Components and Pathogenesis of Envenomation," PLoS Negl Trop Dis. 2019 Jan 18;13(1):e0007017. doi: 10.1371/journal.pntd.0007017. PMID: 30657756; PMCID: PMC6338361.

126 J.-F. Trape, L. Chirio, D. Broadley et al., "Phylogeography and Systematic Revision of the Egyptian Cobra (Serpentes: Elapidae: Naja haje) species complex, with the description of a new species from West Africa," *Zootaxa.* 2236 (1) (2009), 1–25, https://www.biotaxa.org/Zootaxa/article/download/zootaxa.2236.1.1/49807. Accessed May 25, 2021.

127 Baha El Din, *A Guide to the Reptiles*, 517, and fig. 99.

128 Baha El Din, *A Guide to the Reptiles*, 567–68, figs. 117–18.

129 Golding, *Brooklyn Papyrus*, 150.

130 Sauneron, *Un traité d'ophiologie*, 30; Golding, *Brooklyn Papyrus*, 128–29.

131 J. Anderson, *Zoology of Egypt*, I (London, 1898), 338. It must be noted that the names of some of the species given by Anderson have been modified by modern reptile researchers. We therefore used this reference based on the description and the Arabic names of the snakes.

132 Baha El Din, *A Guide to the Reptiles*, 579.

133 Baha El Din, *A Guide to the Reptiles*, 580.

134 Baha El Din, *A Guide to the Reptiles*, 556–58; Golding, *Brooklyn Papyrus*, 193.

135 Rundle Clark, *Myth and Symbol*, 249; W. Golding, *Perceptions of the Serpent in the Ancient Near East: Its Bronze Age Role in Apotropaic Magic, Healing and Protection* (MA diss., University of South Africa, 2013), 205, 211.

136 Rundle Clark, *Myth and Symbol*, 249

137 R. Andreozzi, "Categorizing Reptiles in Ancient Egypt: An Overview of Methods," *Anthropozoologica* 55 (9) (2020), 134.

138 Golding, *Perceptions of the Serpent*, 204–5.

Fig. 19a. Side-winding Snake Papyrus of Nebqed, Louvre AE/N 3068. Drawing by Iman Elsaid.

Fig. 19b. Echis c. coloratus, the Burton's Carpet Viper. Photo by AbuMazna/Shutterstock. com https://www.shutterstock.com/image-photo/snake-echis-coloratuswrithing-on-rocks-camouflaging-1824070781.

Fig. 20a. Snake with Dark Blotches. Tomb of Inherkhoui, TT 359. Photo by M. Y. Sedek.

Fig. 20b. Echis pyramidum, the Carpet Viper. Photo by Vladislav T. Jirousek/Shutterstock.com. https://www.shutterstock.com/image-photo/kenyan-carpet-viper-echis-pyramid-leakeyi-731584027.

or as a cobra in its crawling form rather than as a rearing cobra, a form mostly associated with goddesses. The influence of the worship of Meretseger at Deir el Medineh may have been given way to the representation of Sata as a hooded cobra as discussed above.

The diversity of shapes and colors of the Sata serpent indicates that Sata designates more than one species of snakes. Nevertheless, we noticed that within this array of snakes, two traits are shared between the proposed species. They are all nocturnal, and all venomous except for one, namely the *Platyceps sinai*, the Sinai Banded snake.

In spite of this variety of representations, the name of *s3-t3* is usually followed by the determinative of a winding snake (Gardiner's Sign List I14), used in a mythological context with words indicating snakes with no specific species specified.[139] Another point, already noted, is that the term *s3-t3* is used predominantly in

[139] Vernus and Yoyotte, *Bestiaire des pharaons*, 295. In some cases, the ancient Egyptians used a specific determinative to indicate the

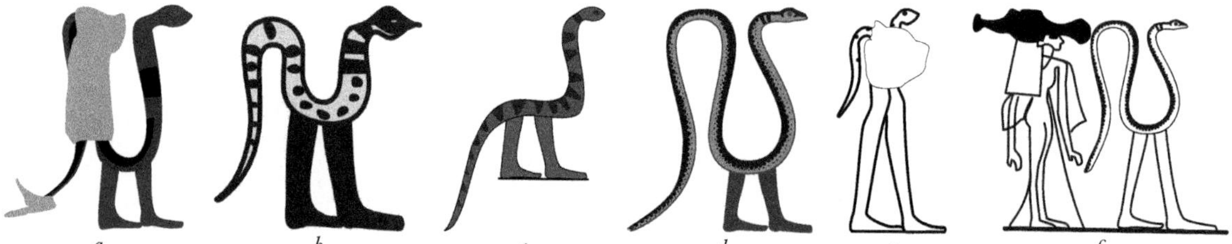

Fig. 21. Sata as Snakes with Dark Blotches: (a) Papyrus of Tjanena, Paris Louvre N. 3074; (b) Papyrus of Senusert, Wien Vindob. Aeg. 10.994-10.997; (c) Papyrus of Qenna, Leiden T 2 (SR); (d) Papyrus of Ani, London BM EA 10470; (e) Papyrus of Paqerer, Leiden T 4 (AMS 14); (f) Papyrus of Tawyherit, Leiden T 3 (AMS 40). Drawing by Iman Elsaid.

the funerary context,[140] with only one exception known to us from the dynastic period, in the aforementioned Dream Book text.[141]

This may be comprehensible in the light of the texts and representations discussed above, which are rich in connotations related to the journey through the afterlife and resurrection. We therefore propose that *s3-t3* was not a specific snake, but rather a personification of the chthonic powers that—in spite of being harmful—would serve a positive function of protection and renewal of the deceased from his nightly journey into a new life. This hypothesis explains why the name Sata is used mainly in the funerary context—to accentuate the underworld journey through the Duat. We find this to be in accordance with the view that *s3-t3* is a metaphor [142] or a designation[143] for an unspecified species of snake, likely inspired by several species. In later texts, the term was sometimes used as a general term for "snake."[144] The use of the term *s3-t3* is an illustration of the ancient Egyptian strategy to replace the name of a dangerous creature with an euphemistic anti-phrase such as Son of Earth to designate a "serpent."[145]

Concluding Comments

While examining the texts and representations of Sata, we noticed a gradual change in the character of the creature. During the Old Kingdom, as seen in the Pyramid Texts examples cited above, Sata was considered a fiend and an enemy of the sun, and consequently of the deceased. The utterances were therefore directed to neutralize its danger. This malevolent creature is one of the forces of earth and was therefore recognized as a son of Geb. These texts indicated that Sata was likely a designation for evil chthonic powers more than being a specific creature. The same view of Sata as a harmful being continued during the Middle Kingdom when spells of the Coffin Texts repeat the earlier concept. Nevertheless, we noticed that his name appeared in a different context as an epithet for the god Osiris.

By the Eighteenth Dynasty, this attitude towards Sata changed, and the serpent acquired a favorable nature to the extent that the deceased aspired to take the form of Sata in BD Spell 87, one of the Transformation Spells. From this period and more clearly later during the Late Period, Sata and the deceased would grow to be one and the same, as the former would be represented with a human head.

---

snake's type such as the use of the sign of a viper (Gardiner's Sign List I19), to indicate a viper: Golding, *Brooklyn Papyrus*, 15. However, this is not a strict rule as we notice that the sign I 64 of a hooded cobra was used as a determinative for other serpents that do not fit the description of cobras. See for example Sauneron, *Un traité d'ophiologie*, 31–32; Golding, *Brooklyn Papyrus*, 150, 155, 159, and 180.

140 Andreozzi, "Categorizing Reptiles," 139, 141.

141 In addition to two examples from the Greco-Roman Period, in the Temple of Horus at Edfu: É. Chassinat, *Le temple d'Edfou* VII, MIFAO 24 (Cairo, 1932), 108, and as an epithet for the god Horus Sema Tawy in the temple of Denderah: S. Cauville, R. Boutros, P. Deleuze et al., "La chapelle de la barque à Dendera," *BIFAO* 93 (1993), 127, and pl. XIV.

142 Allen, *Pyramid Texts*, 91, 92, and n. 42.

143 *LGG* VI, 96–97; Allen, *Pyramid Texts*, 432; Vernus and Yoyotte, *Bestiaire des pharaons*, 16, 88, 293.

144 P. Wilson, *A Ptolemaic Lexikon: A Lexicographical Study of the Texts in the Temple of Edfu*, OLA 78 (Leuven, 1997), 785.

145 Vernus and Yoyotte, *Bestiaire des pharaons*, 83.

Moreover, from the New Kingdom onwards evidence of the divinity of Sata is unmistakable. A text of the Book of the Caverns names a series of serpents including Sata, requesting them to protect the deceased Osiris and not to harm him. In addition, representations of Sata being worshiped by the deceased are found in tombs and on papyri.

The shared connection of both Sata and Osiris with the earth was a leading factor in the development of the former from being one of the evil creatures related to earth into an epithet of the latter, a change that led to their eventual identification with one another. In addition, their common transformational aspect led to their association with the god Re as is detected in a number of texts.

In this regard, we find that BD Spell 87 and the seemingly related texts are a reflection of the transformation not only of the deceased into Sata but also of Osiris into Re, thus transforming the deceased Osiris buried under the ground, personified as Sata, into the celestial Re who rejuvenates and is reborn into eternity.

Furthermore, the name Sata, that translates to the "ground's son" and its appearance almost exclusively in the funerary context, allows us to reach a better understanding of the being as a personification of the chthonic double natured powers of the underworld. Despite being dangerous, mysterious, and dwelling in the darkness of the underworld, these powers have a beneficial side that would help the deceased transform into a new being that endures forever and regenerates perpetually.

Appendix 1: Representations of Sata by Form

Representation Document	Location	Date	Fig. no.
Winding Snake			
Papyrus of Nebseni	BM EA 9900	18th Dyn	1a
Papyrus of Neferwebwnef	Louvre N. 3092 [III 93]	18th Dyn	1b
Linen shroud of Hapi	Swansea W 869	18th Dyn	1c
Papyrus of Nu	BM EA 10477	18th Dyn	10a
Papyrus of Kha	Turin 8438	18th Dyn	10c
Papyrus of Yuya	CGC 51189	18th Dyn	18a
Papyrus of Nebqed	Louvre AE/N 3068	18th Dyn	19a
Papyrus of Nakhtamun	Berlin P. 3002 a-z	Ramesside Period	1d
Papyrus of Neferrenpet	Brussels MRAH E. 5043	Ramesside Period	7
Tomb of Irinefer	TT 290	Ramesside Period	9
Tomb of Inherkhoui	TT 359	Ramesside Period	20a
Papyrus of Maatkare	SR IV/980=JE 26229	21st Dyn	2
Human-Legged Snake			
Papyrus of Nakht A	London BM EA 10471	18th Dyn	4a
Papyrus of Kha and Merit	Paris BN 826 (Luynes B)	18th Dyn	10b
Papyrus of Tjanena	Paris Louvre N. 3074	18th Dyn	21a

Representation Document	Location	Date	Fig. no.
Papyrus of Senusert	Wien Vindob. Aeg. 10.994-10.997 (P. Reinisch)	18th Dyn	21b
Papyrus of Nakht B	Cairo JE 95720 [1]	Ramesside Period	3
Papyrus of Rames	Cambridge E.2a.1922	Ramesside Period	4b
Tomb of Neferhotep	TT 6	Ramesside Period	8
Tomb of Khawi	TT 214	Ramesside Period	11
Papyrus of Qenna	Leiden T 2 (SR)	Ramesside Period	21c
Papyrus of Ani	London BM EA 10470	Ramesside Period	21d
Papyrus of Paqerer	Leiden T 4 (AMS 14)	Ramesside Period	21e
Papyrus of Nesitanebtawy B	London BM EA 10554 (P. Greenfield)	21st Dyn	4c
Papyrus of Padiamun B	SR VII 10653 (TR 23/4/40/1)	21st Dyn	5
Papyrus of Nesikhonsu	Paris BN 170-173	21st Dyn	10d
Papyrus of Padiamun A	SR I/10654	21st Dyn	13
Papyrus of Nesitanebtawy A	Cairo CG 40017	21st Dyn	14
Papyrus of Tamniwt	London BM EA 10002	21st Dyn	15a
Sarcophagus of Tantwenmether	JE 29660 (CG 6214, CG 6183)	21st Dyn	15b
Papyrus of Tawyherit	Leiden T 3 (AMS 40)	21st Dyn	21f
Human-Headed Hooded Cobra			
Shroud of Hrw	Uppsala VM MB 2	18th Dyn	6a
Tomb of Padiherresnet	TT 196	Late Period	6b
Papyrus of Pasndjemibnakht	Paris Louvre E. 11078	Late Period	6c
Papyrus of Iahtaisnakht	Colon. Aeg. 10207	Late Period	6d
Papyrus of Ankhwahibre	London BM EA 10558	Late Period	12b
Papyrus of Thaihepimw	Paris Louvre N. 3094	Late Period	12c
Papyrus of Iptweret	Cortona 3186	Late Period	12d

Appendix 2: Table of Figures

Representation Document	Location	Date	Fig. no.
Papyrus of Nebseni	BM EA 9900	18th Dyn	1a
Papyrus of Neferwebwnef	Louvre N. 3092 [III 93]	18th Dyn	1b
Linen shroud of Hapi	Swansea W 869	18th Dyn	1c
Papyrus of Nakhtamun	Berlin P. 3002 a-z	Ramesside Period	1d
Papyrus of Maatkare	SR IV/980=JE 26229	21st Dyn	2
Papyrus of Nakht B	Cairo JE 95720 [1]	Ramesside Period	3
Papyrus of Nakht A	London BM EA 10471	18th Dyn	4a
Papyrus of Rames	Cambridge E.2a.1922	Ramesside Period	4b
Papyrus of Nesitanebtawy B	London BM EA 10554 (P. Greenfield)	21st Dyn	4c
Papyrus of Padiamun B	SR VII 10653 (TR 23/4/40/1)	21st Dyn	5
Shroud of Hrw	Uppsala VM MB 2	18th Dyn	6a
Tomb of Padiherresnet	TT 196	Late Period	6b
Papyrus of Pasndjemibnakht	Paris Louvre E. 11078	Late Period	6c
Papyrus of Iahtaisnakht	Colon. Aeg. 10207	Late Period	6d
Papyrus of Neferrenpet	Brussels MRAH E. 5043	Ramesside Period	7
Tomb of Neferhotep	TT 6	Ramesside Period	8
Tomb of Irinefer	TT 290	Ramesside Period	9
Papyrus of Nu	BM EA 10477	18th Dyn	10a
Papyrus of Kha and Merit	Paris BN 826 (Luynes B)	18th Dyn	10b
Papyrus of Kha	Turin 8438	18th Dyn	10c
Papyrus of Nesikhonsu	Paris BN 170-173	21st Dyn	10d
Tomb of Khawi	TT 214	Ramesside Period	11
Papyrus of Ankhwahibre	London BM EA 10558	Late Period	12a
Papyrus of Thaihepimw	Paris Louvre N. 3094	Late Period	12b
Papyrus of Iptweret	Cortona 3186	Late Period	12c
Papyrus of Padiamun A	SR I/10654	21st Dyn	13
Papyrus of Nesitanebtawy A	Cairo CG 40017	21st Dyn	14
Papyrus of Tamniwt	London BM EA 10002	21st Dyn	15a
Sarcophagus of Tantwenmether	JE 29660 (CG 6214, CG 6183)	21st Dyn	15b

Representation Document	Location	Date	Fig. no.
Papyrus of Yuya	CGC 51189	18th Dyn	16a-b
Papyrus of Maatkare	SR IV/980 = JE 26229	21st Dyn	17
Papyrus of Yuya	CGC 51189	18th Dyn	18a
Walterinnesia aegyptia, the Black Desert Cobra			18b
Papyrus of Nebqed	Louvre AE/N 3068	18th Dyn	19a
Echis c. coloratus, the Burton's Carpet Viper			19b
Tomb of Inherkhoui	TT 359	Ramesside Period	20a
Echis pyramidum, the Carpet Viper			20b
Papyrus of Tjanena	Paris Louvre N. 3074	18th Dyn	21a
Papyrus of Senusert	Wien Vindob. Aeg. 10.994-10.997 (P. Reinisch)	18th Dyn	21b
Papyrus of Qenna	Leiden T 2 (SR)	Ramesside Period	21c
Papyrus of Ani	London BM EA 10470	Ramesside Period	21d
Papyrus of Paqerer	Leiden T 4 (AMS 14)	Ramesside Period	21e
Papyrus of Tawyherit	Leiden T 3 (AMS 40)	21st Dyn	21f

Ligature Style in the Middle Kingdom Hieratic Papyri

Marwa A. Ewais and Mohamed A. Nassar
Faculty of Archaeology, Fayoum University, Egypt

Abstract

This paper focuses on ligatures—one of the most typical features of hieratic script—through three of the most important sources of hieratic papyri in the Middle Kingdom: The Heqanakht papyri, the el-Lahun papyri and The Ramesseum papyri. This paper aims to respond to some questions raised about hieratic ligature signs, such as did the ancient Egyptian scribe have reasons and motives that made him choose either a connected or a separate spelling when writing a word, and was there a standard way to write ligature words rather than others? It also aims to study the different styles of ligature signs in Middle Kingdom hieratic papyri. In addition, a catalog is provided of one hundred and ninety ligature signs (Appendix).

الملخص

تركز هذه الورقة البحثية على العلامات المركبة التي تعد واحدة من أكثر السمات النموذجية للكتابة الهيراطيقية وذلك من خلال دراسة ثلاثة من أهم مصادر البرديات الهيراطيقية في الدولة الوسطى (برديات حقانخت - بردية اللاهون - بردية رامسيوم). تهدف هذه الورقة إلى الرد على بعض الأسئلة التي أثيرت حول العلامات الهيراطيقية المركبة ، مثل هل كان للناسخ المصري القديم أسباب ودوافع جعلته يختار العلامات المتصل أو المنفصل عند كتابة كلمة؟ وهل هناك طريقة معيارية لكتابة الكلمات المركبة؟. كما تهدف الدراسة أيضا إلى تصنيف الأنماط المختلفة للعلامات المركبة في البرديات الهيراطيقية خلال عصر الدولة الوسطى. هذا بالإضافة إلى توفير كتالوج مكون من مائة وتسعين علامة مركبة تعود الي فترة الدراسة (الملحق)

Introduction

Hieroglyphic was inscribed on religious and funerary monuments[1] with discrete signs characterized by a high degree of iconicity that generally decreased in cursive writing. The cursive form of hieroglyphic script is hieratic. It retained a significant amount of iconicity. Hieratic was mainly written with a rush brush and ink on papyri, writing boards, ostraca, textiles, etc., but it was also employed for graffiti or dipinti on walls of tombs and temples.[2]

According to Ilona Regulski, the first appearance of "proto-hieratic," that expresses the simplifications and abbreviations characteristic of later hieratic inscriptions, can be dated to the Second Dynasty.[3] Before the end of

We would like to thank Prof. Robert Demarée for his comments and English review of the paper draft, and Prof. Stefan Wimmer, Prof. Dr. Ursula Verhoeven, and Tabitha Kraus for their kind comments. Our gratitude also goes to the reviewers and the editor of *JARCE* for their valuable comments.

[1] Pascal Vernus, "Les espaces de l'ecrit clans l'Egypte pharaonique," *ESPE* 119 (1990), 35–56.

[2] Kathryn E. Bandy, "Hieratic," in Christopher Woods (ed.), *Visible Language: Inventions of Writing in the Ancient Middle East and Beyond*, OIMP 32 (Chicago, 2010), 159; Andreas Stauder, "Scripts," in Ian Shaw and Elizabeth Bloxam (eds.), *The Oxford Handbook of Egyptology* (Oxford, 2020), 1–37.

[3] Ilona Regulski,"The Beginning of Hieratic Writing in Egypt," *SÄK* 38 (2009), 265.

Journal of the American Research Center in Egypt 58 (2022), 45–81
http://dx.doi.org/10.5913/jarce.58.2022.a003

the Old Kingdom, it is difficult to distinguish between hieratic and cursive hieroglyphic scripts. The clear distinction between the two scripts can only be witnessed from the First Intermediate Period.[4]

The Middle Kingdom was a crucial period in the history of hieratic, as hieratic shows more significant changes in sign forms and a major change in practice by its transition from writing in columns to writing in lines during the reign of king Amenemhat III.[5]

In the late Middle Kingdom, a distinction was made between a book-script (unciale) and a business or administrative cursive script.[6] In the periods thereafter the hieratic characters gradually evolved towards more abstract, cursive, and linear forms. However, the hieratic script never lost its link with the iconic domain of hieroglyphs.[7]

By the mid-3rd millennium BCE, ligatures or sign-combinations appeared, and the characteristics of the cursive writing hieratic are distinguished as a separate type of script.[8] Using ligatures is a feature of cursive writing generally and one of the most typical features of hieratic script, because in rapid writing the emphasis is on speed of execution rather than neatness. Old Hieratic shows few ligatures, but Middle Hieratic and Late Hieratic in the New Kingdom demonstrate a frequent use of ligatures.[9]

The three volumes of Möller's *Hieratische Lesestücke* I–II (1927) and *Hieratische Paläographie* III (1936) indeed remain very important tools for both learning hieratic and studying hieratic texts. Paleographic tables covering thirty-two sources from the Fifth Dynasty to the Roman Period provide the hieratic forms corresponding to more than 700 individual hieroglyphic signs and seventy groups and ligatures. Schrauder and Laudenklos's book[10] (2014) contains the material from Möller, but in a new arrangement. Goedicke's *Old Hieratic Paleography* of 1988[11] explores the origin of the hieratic script and its features, documents changes in it, provides both the Gardiner and Möller codes for each sign, and provides the hieratic forms for more than 700 individual hieroglyphic signs and 150 groups and ligatures. Allen provides tables for the Heqanakht Papyri, listing seventy-five ligature signs.[12]

The Sources

The skill of the scribe and the type of script must have had an impact on ligature signs. It is deemed useful to study various sources from the Middle Kingdom in order to display the range of variations in the connected signs. There are many hieratic sources from the Middle Kingdom such as the Hekanakht papyri (Mentuhotep III, Eleventh Dynasty), p.Reisner (Senwosret I, Twelfth Dynasty),[13] the el-Lahun papyri (late Twelfth Dynasty (Senwosret III)- the early to mid-Thirteenth Dynasty), p.Boulaq 18 (Sobekhotep II, Thirteenth Dynasty),[14] p.Brooklyn 35.1446 (year 10 of king Amenemhat III and year 2 of King Sobekhotep III),[15] and the Ramesseum papyri (Twelfth to mid-Thirteenth Dynasties).

---

[4] Stéphane Polis,"Methods, Tools, and Perspectives of Hieratic Paleography," in Vanessa Davies and Dimitri Laboury (eds.), *The Oxford Handbook of Egyptian Epigraphy and Palaeography* (Oxford, 2020), 550–51.

[5] Polis, "Methods, Tools, and Perspectives of Hieratic Paleography," 555.

[6] Vivian W. Davies, "Egyptian hieroglyphs," in C. B. Walker and John Chadwick (eds.), *Reading the Past: Ancient Writing from Cuneiform to the Alphabet* (Berkeley-London, 1990), 95.

[7] Polis, "Methods, Tools, and Perspectives of Hieratic Paleography," 551.

[8] Ben Haring, "Identity marks in ancient Egypt: Scribal and non-scribal modes of visual communication," in Judith Weingarten, Anna Jasink, and Silvia Ferrara (eds.), *Non-Scribal Communication Media in the Bronze Age Aegean and Surrounding Areas*, Periploi 9 (Florence, 2017), 233–34; Hans Goedicke, *Old Hieratic Palaeography* (Baltimore, 1988), XXII.

[9] For more information about history of hieratic, see Hans W. Fischer-Elfert, *Grundzüge einer Geschichte des Hieratischen,* Einführungen und Quellentexte zur Ägyptologie 14 (Berlin, 2021).

[10] Julienne Schrauder and Frederic Laudenklos, *Neue Paläographie des Mittelägyptischen Hieratisch*, 3rd ed. (Heidelberg, 2014).

[11] Goedicke, *Old Hieratic Palaeography*.

[12] James P. Allen, *The Heqanakht Papyri,* PMMA 27 (New York, 2002), 217–22.

[13] William Simpson, *The Records of a Building Project in the Reign of Sesostris I: Pap. Reisner I* (Boston, 1963).

[14] Auguste Mariette, *Les Papyrus Egyptiens du Musee de Boulaq,* vol. II (Paris, 1872); Alexander Scharff, "Ein Rechnungsbuch des königlichen Hofes aus der aus der 13 Dynastie," *ZÄS 57* (1922), 51; Anthony Spalinger, "Foods in P.Boulaq 18," *SÄK 13* (1986), 207–47; Anthony Spalinger, "Notes on the Day Summary Accounts of P. Bulaq 18 and the Intradepartmental Transfers," *SÄK 12* (1985), 179–241.

[15] William C. Hayes, *A Papyrus of the Late Middle Kingdom in the Brooklyn Museum*, WM 5. (Brooklyn, 1955).

The authors focused on three categories of these texts for chronological diversity, as well as for displaying and comparing a personal "archive" to more "institutional" texts. It would be interesting to see the occurrence, shape, and density of the ligatures in different genres of these papyri. The following table shows the sources cited.

Table 1. Sources cited

Source	Genre	Source	Genre	Source	Genre
The Heqanakht papyri					
MMA 22.3.516	Letter	MMA 22.3.517	Letter	MMA 22.3.520	Account
MMA 22.3.518	Letter	MMA 22.3.519	Letter	MMA 22.3.522	Account
MMA 22.3.521	Account	P. Purches	Letter		
The el-Lahun papyri					
pUC 32037	Legal	pUC 32095	Account	pUC 32180	Letter
pUC 32148	Letter	pUC 32286	Account	pUC 32166	Legal
pUC 32174	Account	pUC 32134	Account	pUC 32055	Legal
pUC 32158	Account	pUC 32178	Account	pUC 32131	Letter
pUC 32167	Legal	pUC 32271	Literary	pUC 32149	Letter
pUC 32178	Account	pUC 32168	Account	pUC 32198	Letter
pUC 32180	Letter	pUC 32199	Letter	pUC 32170	Account
pUC 32147	Account	pUC 32175	Account	pUC 32201	Letter
pUC 32183	Account	pUC 32096	Account	pUC 32157	Literary
pUC 32185	Account	pUC 32269	Account	pUC 32122	Letter
pUC 32189	Account	pUC 32341	Fragment	pUC 32210	Letter
pUC 32163	Legal	pUC 32196	Letter	pUC 32179	Account
pUC 32109	Letter	pUC 32278	Fragment	pUC 32271	Letter
pUC 32143	Account	pUC 32107	Account	pUC 32353	Fragment
pUC 32119	Letter	pUC 32333	Fragment	pUC 32214	Letter
pUC 32186	Account	pUC 32139	Fragment	pUC 32190	Account
pUC 32113	Letter	pUC 32058	Legal	pUC 32092	Letter
pUC 32124	Letter	pUC 32117	Letter	pUC 32150	Letter
pUC 32359	Fragment	pUC 32271	Account	pUC 32178	Account
pUC 32057	Healing	pUC 32211	Letter	pUC 32359	Fragment
pUC 32194	Account	pUC 32179	Account	pUC 32284	Fragment
The Ramesseum papyri					
pRam. III.v	Account	pRam. XVIII	Account	pRam. VIII.8	Magic
pRam. IX	Magic	pRam. X	Magic	pRam. XI	Magic
pRam. XII	Magic	pRam. XV	Magic	pRam. XVI, 8	Magic
pRam. XVI, 14	Magic	pRam. XVI, 19	Magic	pRam. XVI, 20	Magic
pRam. XVI, 22	Magic	pRam. XVI, 23	Magic	pRam. XVI, 26	Magic
pRam. XVI, 27	Magic	pRam. XVI, 28	Magic	pRam. XVI, 29	Magic

The Heqanakht papyri[16] date to the early Middle Kingdom. They were found in the tomb of Meseh, within the funerary complex of the vizier Ipi (TT 315) at Deir el-Bahari,[17] and are now in the Metropolitan Museum of Art, New York. They consist of letters and accounts; all were written by and for a ka-servant named Heqanakht. The importance of these papyri is that they provide considerable insight into aspects of mundane life and family relationships in the early Middle Kingdom. T. G. H. James first published the Heqanakht papyri,[18] and later James Allen studied the handwriting by statistical study and re-examining each letter/account manuscript closely from various aspects.[19] In his methodological study, Allen listed the signs and tabulated the similarities and differences between them. He also made comments on the qualitative aspects of some particular signs. He listed seventy-five ligature signs that constitute from 5 to 11% of all the hieratic signs included in all the Heqanakht papyri.[20]

The el-Lahun papyri[21] form one of the most important hieratic papyri finds from the Late Twelfth and Early Thirteenth Dynasties. These papyri were discovered by William Matthew Flinders Petrie when he excavated the town during several years (1889, 1890, 1911, 1914 and 1920).[22] They are now in the Petrie Museum. They deal with a wide range of topics like administrative and business records, healing and veterinary texts, literary and religious compositions, and legal and personal issues. These papyri were first published by Griffith[23] and then repeatedly by Mark Collier and Stephen Quirke,[24] but without any palaeographical study for the signs of these papyri.

In June 1899, after the discovery of the Petrie papyri in 1898, Ludwig Borchardt obtained permission for a survey of el-Lahun. The excavations yielded three rubbish heaps located east, north, and west of the town. Borchardt's activities concentrated on the western rubbish heap that was situated outside of the town wall to the north of the Valley Temple of the Senwosret II pyramid complex.[25] He discovered the papyri that are now called the Berlin papyri or "The Temple Archive." These papyri deal with the administration of the temple and the cult for king Senwosret II. They are now in the Egyptian Museums of Berlin and Cairo, and they date to the reigns of Senwosret III and Amenemhat III.[26]

The hieratic script of the el-Lahun papyri is characterized by angular and rounded signs.[27] The small angular signs are typical of the temple manuscripts,[28] while the large, rounded signs are a feature of the town

---

16 See https://www.metmuseum.org/art/collection/search?q=Heqanakht

17 Herbert E. Winlock, *Excavations at Deir el Bahri, 1911–1931* (New York, 1942), 54–55, 58–59.

18 T. G. H. James, *The Hekanakht Papers and other Early Middle Kingdom Documents*, PMMA 19 (New York, 1962).

19 Allen, *The Heqanakht Papyri*.

20 Allen, *The Heqanakht Papyri*, 77.

21 see https://collections.ucl.ac.uk/results

22 William M. F. Petrie, *Kahun, Gurob and Hawara* (London, 1890); William M. F. Petrie, *Illahun, Kahun and Gurob* (London, 1891); Guy Brunton, *Lahun I: The Treasure*, ERA 27 (London, 1920); William M. F. Petrie, Guy Brunton and Margaret Murray, *Lahun II*, ERA 33 (London, 1923).

23 F. L. Griffith, *The Petrie Papyri: Hieratic Papyri from Kahun and Gurob* (London, 1898).

24 Mark Collier and Stephen Quirke, *The UCL Lahun Papyri: Letters*, BAR International Series 1083 (Oxford, 2002); Mark Collier and Stephen Quirke, *The UCL Lahun Papyri: Religious, Literary, Legal, Mathematical and Medical*. BAR International Series 1209 (Oxford, 2004); Mark Collier and Stephen Quirke, *The UCL Lahun Papyri: Accounts*, BAR International Series 1471 (Oxford, 2006).

25 Ludwig Borchardt, "Der zweite Papyrus fund von Kahun und die Zeitliche Festlegung des Mittleren Reiches der Ägyptischen Geschichte," *ZÄS* 37 (1899), 89–103.

26 The Berlin papyri, published by Borchardt, "Der zweite Papyrus fund von Kahun," 89–103, and Alexander Scharff, "Briefe aus Illahun," *ZÄS 59* (1924), 20–52; and retranslated here, form only a portion of a much larger corpus of still unpublished documents, catalogued by Kaplony-Heckel, *Ägyptische Handschriften I.* and republication by Ulrich Luft, *Das Archiv von Illahun: Briefe 1. (Hieratische Papyri aus den Staatlichen Museen zu Berlin, Preussischer Kulturbesitz, Lieferung 1)* (Berlin, 1992), followed by *Urkunden zur Chronologie der Späten 12. Dynastie. Briefe aus Illahun*, Contribution to the Chronology of the Eastern Mediterranean 7 (Vienna, 2006).

27 The authors are now preparing a research project regarding scheduling the el-Lahun papyri signs and make a detail paleographical study.

28 Ulrich Luft, *Die Chronologische Fixierung des Agyptischen Mittleren Reiches nach dem Tempel archiv von Illahun* (Berlin, 1992); Ulrich Luft, "The Ancient Town of El-Lâhûn," in Stephen Quirke (ed.), *Lahun Studies* (Reigate, 1993), 1–10.

manuscripts.[29] In this article, the focus will be on the town papyri only that display various abstract and linear administrative hand styles.

The Ramesseum papyri[30] date to the Late Twelfth to mid-Thirteenth Dynasties.[31] They were discovered during an excavation carried out in 1895–1896 by Petrie and James Edward Quibell in a shaft-tomb below the Ramesseum, the funerary temple of Ramses II at Thebes. [32] The papyri were found in a single box in poor condition. They consist of twenty-three manuscripts with a group of fragments. They are kept in the British Museum and the Berlin Museum.[33] They deal with various topics such as magical and theological matters, prescriptions and formulae for good health/protection, administrative accounts, literary compositions, and private notes.[34]

In 1955 A. H. Gardiner published most of the Ramesseum papyri, but they were not methodically analyzed and several magical texts were omitted due to their poor and fragmentary condition.[35] In 2019, Pierre Meyrat studied these papyri closely and he produced palaeographic tables for papyri IV–XIX.1.[36]

Types of Ligature Signs in the Middle Kingdom Sources

Ligatures are cursive groups derived from two or more individual hieratic signs that are combined to make larger groups. Various Middle Kingdom texts display a range of variations in the connected signs. Although there are principal ligatures that appear in most Middle Kingdom papyri, there are also irregular forms (called incidental[37] or pseudo). Some scribes developed their own types of ligatures. Some scribes elegantly composed and joined signs for more aesthetic purposes; their elaborate ligatures are sometimes called a "flourish' style" which is deliberately done to make the signs conspicuous.[38]

The range of typological study is characterized by the distinction between multiple different types of writing connected signs. This is divided into three types:

A) Real or Principal Ligatures.[39] A is subdivided into three main categories:
- A.I) incidental and A.II regular ligatures
- A.II.1 consists of two signs
- A.II.2 of three signs, and A.II.3 of four signs

B) Pseudo Ligatures

C) Overlapping Words

29 Stephen Quirke, "Agendas for Digital Paleography in an Archaeological Context: Egypt 1800 BC," in Franz Fischer, Christiane Fritze, and Georg Vogeler (eds.), *Codicolgy and Palaeography in the Digital Age 2* (Norderstedt, 2010), 286.

30 See https://www.britishmuseum.org/research/publications/online_research_catalogues/rp/the_ramesseum_papyri/the_catalogue.aspx.

31 Jean Yoyotte, "Compte rendu: Sir Alan Gardiner, The Ramesseum Papyri," *RdE* 11 (1957), 172.

32 James Quibell, *The Ramesseum/The Tomb of Ptah-Hetep*, ERA 2 (London, 1898); Alan Gardiner, *The Ramesseum Papyri* (Oxford, 1955); Richard Parkinson, *The Ramesseum Papyri* (on-line resource at the British Museum: (2011–) (https://webarchive.nationalarchives.gov.uk/ukgwa/20190801105848/https://www.britishmuseum.org/research/publications/online_research_catalogues/rp/the_ramesseum_papyri.aspx).

33 Bridget Leach,"Conservation History of the Ramesseum Papyri," *JEA 92* (2006), 225–40.

34 Gianluca Miniaci attempts to thoroughly reconstruct the archaeological context of the tomb and its contents in Gianluca Miniaci, *The Middle Kingdom Ramesseum Papyri Tomb and its Archaeological Context* (London, 2020), 22–30.

35 Gardiner, *The Ramesseum Papyri*.

36 Pierre Meyrat, *Les papyrus magiques du Ramesseum Recherches sur une bibliothèque privée de la fin du Moyen Empire*, vol. 1, BdÉ 172.1 (Cairo, 2019).

37 For this term, see Jac. J. Janssen, "Idiosyncrasies in Late Ramesside Hieratic Writing," *JEA 86* (2000), 52.

38 David Ellen, *Scientific Examination of Documents: Methods and Techniques*, 3rd ed. (Boca Raton FL, 2006), 20.

39 Allen differentiates between "typical" and "aberrant" or deviating from the rule character forms (and not only for ligatures), which he lists in his palaeography: Allen, *The Heqanakht Papyri*, 78, Appendix A.

Type A) Real or Principal Ligatures

The real or principal ligatures are certain groups of two or more signs that are written together by one or more stroke of the brush to link individual signs to create larger groups. It is not an easy distinction between the deliberate and incidental writing of a scribe. This can be a way to express the skill of the writer, who may enjoy using many different forms for the way he writes the ligatures. The deliberate choice of the writer consists of the frequency of occurrence of one special form that was consciously chosen as one of the established methods of writing the word, rather than other forms that are produced by accident. This is because the writer limited it to use it only once or randomly.

A.1) Incidental or Irregular Ligatures

We should distinguish one scribe's regular ligatures and incidental ligatures, and the extent of the prevalence of such unusual signs during the Middle Kingdom. Random or irregular ligatures are related to personalization and time period that tend to occur irregularly within a single hand[40] (Table 2).

Table 2. Examples of incidental ligatures in Middle Kingdom hieratic papyri

Hiero	Sign	Hiero	Sign	Hiero	Sign
	pUC 32037.7 pUC 32201.13		pUC 32190f.c.2.2		pUC 32271.c.1
	pUC 32179b.v.7		pUC 32186.5		pRam XVI.2.7
	pUC 32269.5		pUC 32158.c2.1		pUC 32148A.5
	pUC 32201.6		pUC 32167.2		pRam XV.4
	pRam XVI.27.3		pUC 32158f.9		

In some cases, such as of 32201.13, a shorter ligature type is utilized instead of the shorter forms or the articulated type.

40 This type, that could be called "principal," shows a completely different way of shaping a specific sign. See Janssen, "Idiosyncrasies in Late Ramesside Hieratic Writing," 52.

Table 3. Articulated, ligature, and briefer ligature types of the group .

Articulated Type		Ligature Type	Briefer Ligature Type

pUC 32184F.6	pUC 32058.V3	pUC 32037.7	pUC 32201.13

The same thing appears in  where the scribe used a brief form of the sign  ligatured with  so the ligatured  has the form of  rather than its normal shape 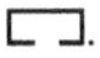.

Table 4. Articulated and ligature types of .

Articulated Type	Briefer Ligature Type

pUC 32058.5	pUC 32167.2

In the el-Lahun papyri, sometimes the scribe used a briefer ligature type. The ligature is made between the sun sign  and *ḫ3* sign  in the current type. The sun seems to be the familiar short horizontal line. The *ḫ3* sign is written in an unusual form where the horizontal line with a rounded curve:

Table 5. Articulated, ligature, and briefer ligature types of the group 

Articulated Type	Ligatured Type	Briefer Ligature Type

pUC 32115C.4	pUC 32115F.2	pUC 32186.5

A.II) Regular (Conventional Ligatures)

Conventional ligatures occur in all the hieratic papyri during the Middle Kingdom. They generally involve two, three, or four signs but may combine as many as six, as summarized on Table 6 and figure 1.

Table 6. Percentage of conventional ligatures in Heqanakht, el-Lahun, and Ramesseum papyri

	Heqanakht Papyri	el-Lahun Papyri	Ramesseum Papyri
2 signs	48	88	48
3 signs	14	42	11
4 signs	2	7	0
Total	64	137	58

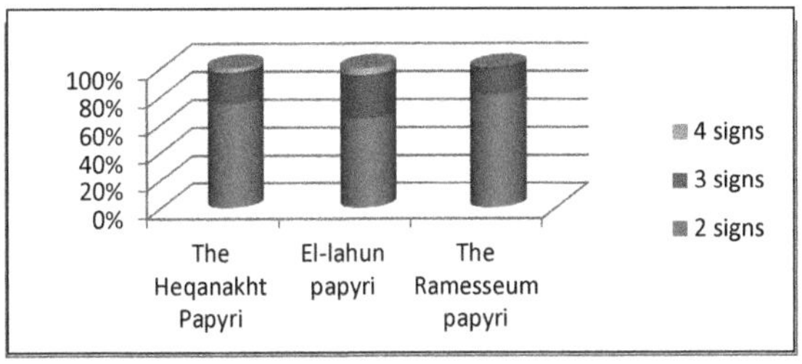

Fig. 1. Conventional ligatures in Heqanakht, el-Lahun, and Ramesseum papyri

A.II.1 Regular Ligatures Consisting of Two Signs

In Middle Kingdom manuscripts, we notice the high rate of recurrence of the combination of two signs. The shape and structural design of two compound signs with a regular ligatures can be specified when the two signs are always or often intentionally ligatured.

Comparing the number of Middle Kingdom ligatures attested in this paper, we notice that in the Heqanakht papyri, of the sixty-four ligatured signs, forty-eight (75%) are two-sign ligatures; in the el-Lahun papyri, of the 139 ligatured signs, eighty-eight (63.30%) are two-sign ligatures, while in the Ramesseum papyri of the fifty-eight ligatured signs, forty-eight (82.075%) are two signs ligatures.

Table 7. Examples of regular ligatures consisting of two signs

Hiero	Signs	Hiero	Signs
	pUC.32055.16		P. Heq 1v.5 P. Heq 3.8 P. Heq 4.3 P. Heq 5.43 pUC. 32134A.4 pUC. 32174.13 p.Ram.XVI.22.3
	P. Heq 1.3		pUC 32037.4 pUC 32163.3 pUC 32058.v.1 pUC 32201r.7
	pUC 32168f.8 pUC 32179b.2 pUC 32201.6		P. Heq 2.r.36 P. Heq 3.6
	P. Heq 2.r.1		P. Heq 2.r.38 P. Heq 3.r.1
	P. Heq 1v.13 P. Heq 2.r.9 P. Heq 2.r.11 P. Heq 3.r.1 pUC.32196.4		P. Heq 1v.8 P. Heq 2.r.39 P. Heq 3.r. 4 pUC.32163.2 pUC. 32201v.9 pUC. 32359.2 pUC. 32194f.4
	P. Heq 5.v.1		pUC.32119f.4
	pUC.32037.2 pUC.32055.14 pUC.32158.5		pUC.32037.1 pUC.32058.1 pUC.32167.1 pUC.32174.1 pUC.32180.1

A.II.2 Regular Ligatures Consisting of Three Signs

The higher the number of ligature signs, the more expressive the writing skill and technique of the scribe.[41] In some cases, we find that the scribe's skill is demonstrated by elegantly composing and joining more than two signs for aesthetic purposes. For instance, the signs 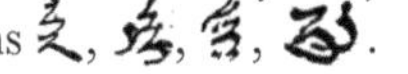.

In the Heqanakht papyri, of the sixty-four ligatured signs, fourteen are three-sign ligatures (21.87%); in el-Lahun papyri, of the 139 ligatured signs, forty-two are three-sign ligatures (30.21%); and in Ramesseum, of the fifty-eight ligatured signs, there are eleven three-sign ligatures (18.96%).

Table 8. Examples of regular ligatures consisting of three signs

Hiero	Signs	Hiero	Signs
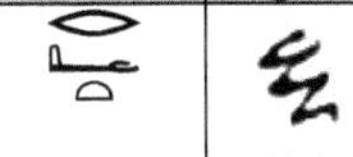	pUC.32055.6	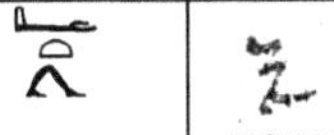	pUC.32158.c2.1
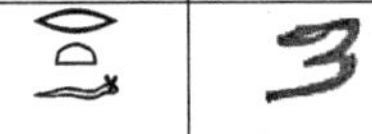	P. Heq 2.37	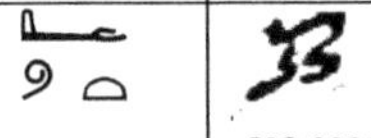	pUC.32214.11
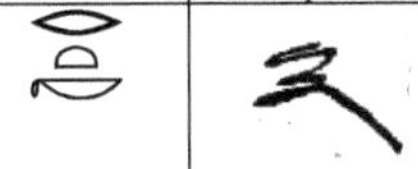	P.Heq 3.1		P. Heq 1v.1 P.Heq 3.r.3
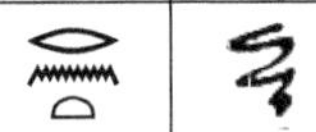	P.Heq 5.23	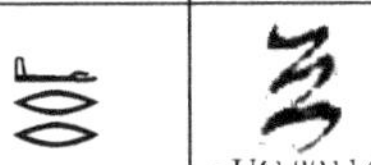	pUC.32114c
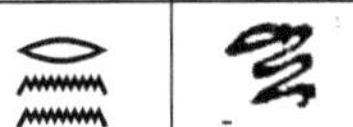	pRam XVI.8.c.3	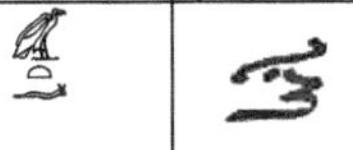	P. Heq 2.r.1
	pUC.32058v.1 pUC.32171.1  pUC. 32284b.2 pRam XV.9	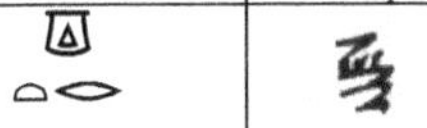	P. Heq 1.3
	pUC.32124.12 pUC.32148A.4		pRam XVI.26.1 pRam XVI.24.3 pRam X.1.5
	P.Heq 3.r.2 pUC.32149A.2	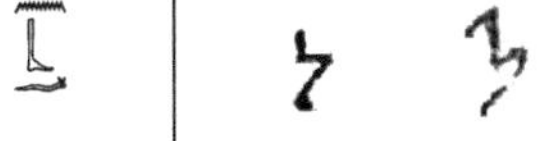	pUC.32163v.6 pUC. 32269.5
	pUC.32167.6 pUC.32143.10		P. Heq 3.r.3 pUC.32037.9
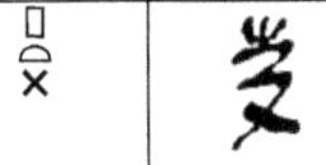	pUC.32134d	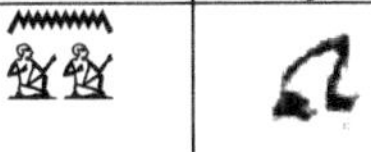	pUC 32163.v.5

[41] Ilona Regulski, "Writing habits as identity marker: On sign formation in Papyrus Gardiner II," in Ursula Verhoeven, Svenja A. Gülden, and Kyra Moezel (eds.), *Ägyptologische „Binsen"-Weisheiten III. Formen und Funktionen von Zeichenliste und Paläographie Akten der internationalen und interdisziplinären Tagung in der Akademie der Wissenschaften und der Literatur, Mainz im April 2016* (Mainz, 2018), 241.

A.II.3 Regular Ligatures consisting of Four Signs

Ligatures consisting of four signs are attested, for example, in the el-Lahun papyri where there are seven examples; two examples are attested in the Heqanakht papyri, while no such sign appears in the Ramesseum papyri.

Table 9. Examples of regular ligatures consisting of four signs

Hiero	Signs	Hiero	Signs
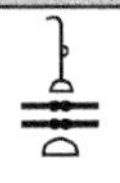	  pUC.32333		 pUC. 32199.1
	 P. Heq 3.1  P. Heq 3. 3		 pUC.32198.6
	 P. Heq 2.r.6		

Type B) Pseudo Ligatures

The pseudo-ligatures are those in which the signs overlap but are not written in the same brush flow, and therefore the signs are unintentionally connected.[42] One can usually notice that the scribe must have lifted his brush in order to write the next sign which then partly overlapped with the previous one, creating a pseudo-ligature[43] (Table 10). In some cases, the compositional structure of the ligatures is more complicated than in others. Especially when the text is written in vertical columns, where the overlapping appears unintentionally in many signs and words, such as the words 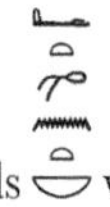 where the end of each sign was connected to the beginning of the next sign as a result of ink flow and vertical writing. The pseudo-ligatures are also noticed in words, 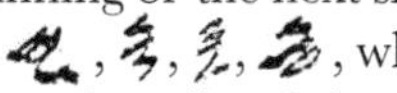, where all signs partly overlap, but are not written in a single brush movement, which may be merely a slip of the scribe's brush. The word  is written in a ligature but the determinative is written in pseudo-ligature touched the real ligature because the scribe used new ink to write it, therefore the ligature is attributed to the rapid movement of the scribe's hand. It is explained by the way of writing the *n*-sign, which is written with a little tick at its end. This is the result of the scribe's hand moving to the position where the *t*-sign begins before the brush completely left the surface of the manuscript when the scribe lifted his hand.

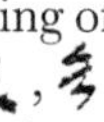

[42] Regulski, "Writing habits as identity marker," 255.

[43] Ilona Regulski, "Papyrus Fragments From Asyut: A Palaeographic Comparison," in Ursula Verhoeven (ed.), *Ägyptologische „Binsen" Weisheiten I–II. Neue Forschungen und Methoden der Hieratistik, Akten zweiter Tagungen in Mainz im April 2011 und März 2013* (Mainz, 2015), 307.

Table 10. Examples of pseudo ligatures in the Middle Kingdom hieratic papyri

Hiero.	Pseudo-ligatures	Hiero.	Pseudo-ligatures
	 pUC.32353		 pUC.32156
	 pUC.32341		 pUC.32150
	 pUC.32333		 pUC. 32149B
	 pUC. 32328		 pUC. 32146a
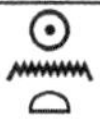	 pUC.32156		 pUC.32117b
	 pUC.32107		 pHeq.3.1
	 pRam. XVI.18.2		 pHeq. 2.r.39 pHeq. 3.r. 4
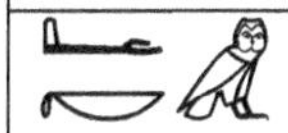	 UC.32124.13 UC.32119b.2 UC. 32157.9 UC.32201r.15 p.Ram.XVI.21.8  p.Ram XVI.14.5		

Type C) Overlapping Words

Overlapping of words means combining signs of a word, or more that one word. Overlapping is more common in horizontal than in vertical arrangements. Although the form gives the impression of a ligature, in reality, overlapping is not ligature. Overlapping is used not only within the individual signs of words, but also across word boundaries.

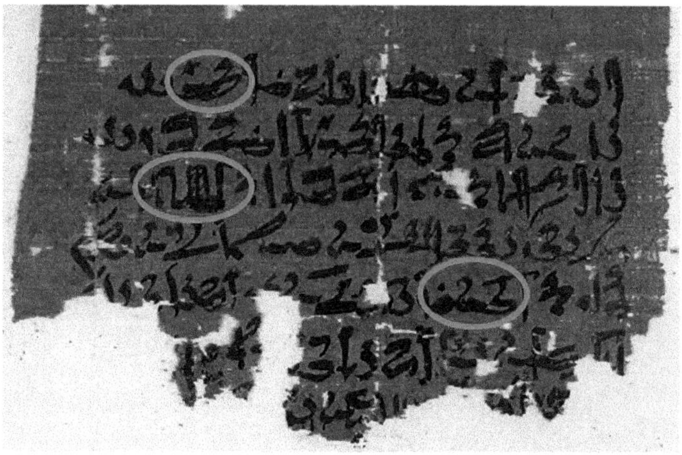

Fig. 2. pRam.XVI.28, the first category of overlapping words. From Meyrat, Les papyrus magiques du Ramesseum, *371.*

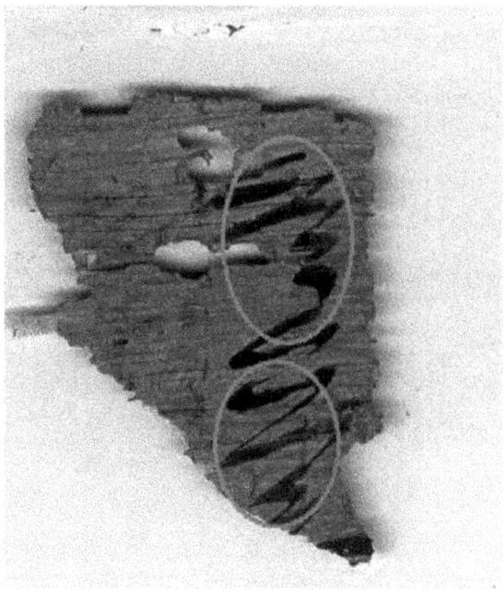

Fig. 3. pUC.32358, the second category of overlapping words. Collier and Quirke, The UCL Lahun Papyri: Accounts, *CD files.*

Fig 4. pUC.32212, the third categorie of overlapping words the signs in the line is overlapping. Collier and Quirke, The UCL Lahun Papyri: Letters, *CD files.*

We can divide word ligatures into three categories:
1) The signs of only one word overlap the signs during the writing (fig. 2)
2) The signs of more words are overlapped (fig. 3)
3) Sometimes, all of the signs in the line are overlapping (fig. 4)

Ligatures and Textual Content of the Papyri

There are many factors affecting the number and percentage of ligatures within the text. One of them is the content of the text itself, because the proportions of ligatures vary according to the content. We note in the Heqanakht papyri, the proportion of connected signs in the letters ranged between 6 to 9% while the proportion of ligatures in administrative texts is 7.5 to 8.5%.

Table 11. Ligatures and textual content in the Heqanakht papyri

Heqanakht papyri				
Letters				
	Letter I	Letter II	Letter III	Letter IV
Total of signs	1925	1523	536	222
Ligature sign	113	99	38	20
percentage	5.87%	6.50%	7.08%	9%
Account				
	Account V		Account VI	
Total of signs	773		235	
Ligature sign	67		17	
percentage	8.66%		7.23	

As for the el-Lahun papyri, we note that the percentage of ligatures in the letters ranged between 13% and 14%, with the exception of the letter UC32203 that is characterized by unusual handwriting that is accurate and more angular, and lacks ligature, perhaps because it was written by somebody who did not often write. It did not exceed thirty-four signs, and all of them were common signs in the ligatures. Also, the letter UC32212, where the percentage of ligatures represents 25.7%. This letter falls under the category overlapping words of the types of ligatures.

The matter differs with respect to administrative documents, as the percentage of ligatures range between 15% to 20%, for instance, p.UC32183 that contains a large percentage of accounts.

The percentage of ligatures in el-Lahun legal documents range between 12% to 14%, while literary texts have 10% to 12%.

Table 12. Ligatures and textual content in the el-Lahun papyri

el-Lahun papyri					
Letters					
	pUC 32198	pUC 32199	pUC 32201	pUC 32203	pUC 32212
Total of signs	405	307	983	396	229
Ligature sign	56	43	139	34	59
percentage	13.82%	14%	14.14%	8.58%	25.76%
Account					
	pUC 32121	pUC 32170	pUC 32183	pUC 32189	
Total of signs	133	510	372	192	
Ligature sign	26	105	27	30	
percentage	19.54%	20.58%	7.25%	15.62%	
Legal					
	pUC 32037	pUC 32163	pUC 32167		
Total of signs	387	314	214		
Ligature sign	50	47	31		

percentage	12.91%	14.96%	14.48%
Literature			
	pUC 32157	pUC 32271	
Total of signs	1219	292	
Ligature sign	131	34	
percentage	10.74%	11.64%	

The third category of texts is the Ramesseum papyri, where the percentage of ligatures in magical texts range between 8.5% to 11%, while the accounts are between 9% to 11%.

Table 13. Ligatures and textual content in the Ramesseum papyri

Ramesseum papyri			
Magic			
	pRam. IX	pRam. X	pRam. XI
Total of signs	694	376	257
Ligature sign	57	33	28
percentage	8.21%	8.77%	10.89%
Account			
	pRam. III.v	pRam. XVIII	
Total of signs	264	247	
Ligature sign	25	26	
percentage	9.46%	10.52%	

The contrast and difference in the percentage of ligature signs in papyri were not limited to the difference of the subjects (legal, letter, account, etc.) in one category, but this contrast also appeared between the same subject in the three different sources (Hekanakht, el-Lahun, Ramesseum).

Ligatures and the Layout of Papyri

The ligatured signs display great differences in terms of number or form depending upon whether the text is in horizontal lines or in vertical columns. Hence, the layout of the document is one of the important factors that affected the shape of the ligature signs.

In the Heqanakht papyri, the ligatures are attested in both vertical and horizontal text. Five papyri are recorded in vertical columns. These papyri yield sixty-three ligatures out of a total of seventy-four signs (85%). Twenty-nine of them appeared only in the vertical columns without the horizontal lines (Table 14).

Table 14. List of ligature signs attested only in columns

Hiero.	sign	Hiero.	sign	Hiero.	sign	Hiero.	sign
	3.3		2.r.6		2.v.3		1.v.15
	2.37		2.30		2.r.37		2.r.1
	3.1		3.r.1		2.r.35		3.r.3

The el-Lahun papyri include forty papyri arranged in vertical columns, or in a mixture of columns and rows. These display sixty-four ligatures, amounting to 46.37% of the total ligature signs of the el-Lahun papyri. Fourteen ligatures are attested only on the vertical columns while they are not in the papyri recorded in horizontal rows (Table 15).

Table 15. Examples of ligatures attested only in vertical columns

Hiero.	sign	Hiero.	sign	Hiero.	sign
	pUC.32150		32119A.3		pUC.32117b
	pUC.32174.1		pUC.32134d		pUC.32119f.4 pUC.32092a
	pUC. 32149B				

Papyrus UC32157 is one of the important examples that mixes horizontal lines and vertical columns. The importance here is that it shows the differences in the shape of the ligatured signs in the horizontal lines versus those in the vertical columns in a single document. Ligatures appear eighty-two times on the papyrus, sixteen times on the columns (19.52%), while ligatures appear sixty-six times on horizontal lines (80.48%). These ligatures are divided into two categories:

A) Similar signs. Most of ligature signs that appear in vertical columns are similar to the ligature signs on horizontal lines including: [hieroglyphs] and [hieroglyphs].

B) Signs that differ according to the different ways of writing and the method the word was executed, such as: mk (Table 16).

Table 16. The different ways of writing *mk*

	vertical columns		horizontal lines
	 pUC. 32157.col.9	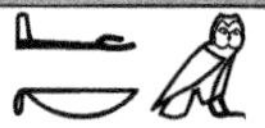	 pUC. 32157.9

In the Ramesseum papyri, six papyri are arranged in vertical columns; these papyri yield forty-seven ligatures (82.45%) of the total ligature signs of the Ramesseum papyri. It is noticeable that the total ligature signs in both layouts are similar

Why Were Ligatures Used?

It is certain that there were motives for the use of the different spellings of the signs and the way they were written—whether they were individual or connected signs—but until now these motives have not been discussed.[44]

In some cases, the ligature writing style was used to create an elegant and aesthetic form of the signs, and to make the ligature sign more conspicuous. Increasing the number of ligatures was also an expression of the scribe's superior skill that was thus displayed by the text. The level of the scribe, or the scribe's preferred style, may be the motives as well as the factors affecting the way of writing the ligatures.[45] Another reason may have been to express the personal and individual characteristics of the specific scribe through the shape, size, line quality, and positioning of the compound signs.

Writing economy and the writing direction are aspects that are also very likely to be reasons that ligatures were used. The higher degree of abstraction of the characters may also have motivated ligatures, since the link to the actual motif was lost in the effort to save time.

The Fixed Rules of the Ligatured Signs

The Egyptian scribe never wrote irrational or randomly. Rather, he adhered to fixed rules, even if the personality of each scribe allowed for some variation. One of the obvious, and essential ways of teaching the Egyptian scribe was to learn how to write ligatures, whether it was a link between two signs, or more, as a way to write hieratic signs. The scribe probably learned the regular ligatures when he was an apprentice scribe and he used ligatures that evolved with practice, reflecting some of his handwriting's characteristics.[46] During the Middle Kingdom, there are two different attestations that confirm this suggestion: A) scribal exercises and B) the standard way of writing these examples.

[44] Regulski made the same observation. See Regulski, "Writing Habits as Identity Marker," 258.

[45] Ellen, *Scientific Examination of Documents: Methods and Techniques*, 20–21.

[46] Janssen, "Idiosyncrasies in Late Ramesside Hieratic Writing," 55.

A) Scribal Exercises

pUC32196 (fig. 5) is part of a series of nine brief model letters found in el-Lahun,[47] all written on a single sheet of papyrus. These model letters are, by their content, tied to scribal training, and through their general form and way of writing, they are intended for didactic purposes.[48] One of the writing habits is expressed in these models by the use of ligatures. Out of the total of 764 hieroglyphs, there are seventy-two (9.42%) ligatures. A maximum of three signs are included in a ligature. In the nine model letters, there are repetitions of the same ligature with minor differences as a result of the content changing.

Fig. 5. pUC 32196, Scribal exercises as model letters. Collier and Quirke, The UCL Lahun Papyri: Letters, *CD files.*

B) The Standard Way of Writing the Ligatures

First of all, we must take into account that personalization was an important factor in the diversity of the forms of ligature signs between pseudo ligatures, real ligatures, and unconventional or random ligatures. Yet, scribes must have kept in mind that their writing, for instance, letters, had to be legible to others. This may have led to a limitation of the usage of ligatures.

In the Middle Kingdom papyri, there are many examples of a sign-combination that is almost always written in a ligature, which means that it became the standard way of writing those examples.

The following tables show the degree of similarity between the ligature signs in the letters. In the Heqanakht letters (Table 17) there are fifty-eight combinations, forty-five (77.58%) are used in all letters, while only thirteen (22.42%) show uncommon ligature.

[47] UC32196 in Collier and Quirke, *The UCL Lahun Papyri: Literature*, 48–49.

[48] Stephen Quirke, "Narrative Literature," in Antonio Loprieno (ed.), *Ancient Egyptian Literature: History and Forms*, PÄ 10 (Leiden-New York, 1996), 381; Fredrik Hagen, "Ostraca, Literature and Teaching at Dier el-Medina," in Alice Stevenson and Rachel Mairs (eds.), *Current Research in Egyptology (2005): Proceedings of the Sixth Annual Symposium* (Cambridge, 2005), 43.

Table 17. Similarity between ligature signs in the Heqanakht

		Letter I	Letter II	Letter III	Letter IV
Letter I	Similar	______	19 (86.4)	12 (54.5)	3 (43%)
Letter II	Similar	19 (61.3)	______	5 (16%)	5 (71.5%)
Letter III	Similar	12 (54.5)	13 (59.1)	______	7 (100%)
Letter IV	Similar	3 (43%)	5 (71.5%)	7 (100%)	______
Total of ligature		22	31	32	7

The major and complete letters in the el-Lahun papyri (Table 18) contain ninety-three combinations, fifty-one of which (54.83%) are regular, while forty-two (45.16%) are irregular.

Table 18. Similarity between ligature signs in el-Lahun letters

	pUC 32124	pUC 32198	pUC 32199	pUC 32201	pUC 32205	pUC 32212
pUC32124	______	6 (24%)	6 (31.57%)	9 (20.45%)	5 (27.77%)	5 (21.73%)
pUC32198	6 (31.57%)	______	10 (52.63%)	5 (11.36%)	3 (16.66%)	6 (26.08%)
pUC32199	6 (31.57%)	10 (40%)	______	9 (20.45%)	9 (50%)	7 (30.43)
pUC32201	9 (47.36%)	5 (20%)	9 (47.36%)	______	9 (50%)	6 (26.08%)
pUC32205	5 (26.31%)	3 (12%)	9 (47.36%)	9 (20.45%)	______	5 (27.77%)
pUC32212	5 (26.31%)	6 (24%)	7 (36.84%)	6 (13.63%)	5 (21.73%)	______
Total of ligature	19	25	19	44	18	23

Conclusion

Ligature signs are one of the distinguishing palaeographic features of hieratic texts, and comparing their form and subject provides an important means of clarifying a papyrus's chronological sequence and dating. Therefore, this article focuses on studying the different forms and types of ligatured signs through three Middle Kingdom corpuses, an effort that is part of a broader and comprehensive study of Middle Kingdom hieratic signs to access the epigraphic and thematic features characteristic of each category of texts of that era.

During the Middle Kingdom, ligatures are divided into three types: A) Real or principal ligatures; B) Pseudo ligatures; and C) Overlapping words. The differences in the form and style of writing ligatures varied according to the diversity of topics attested in the three groups of papyri in this study, and whether the text was in horizontal lines or in vertical columns, for layout was one of the most important factors that affected the shape of the ligature signs. However, comparing the method used to write these signs, it is clear to us that the ancient Egyptian scribe kept fixed rules in the implementation of ligatures, although they sometimes vary by different scribes.

Moreover, there are many motives behind the use of ligatures that can be deduced from the paleography and the form of the sign, although it is important to bear in mind that handwriting analysis and palaeographic study inevitably include a degree of subjective interpretation. These motives can be for aesthetic purposes, to express the skill and experience of the scribe, or to highlight the personal and individual characteristics of the scribe.

Appendix: The Forms of Ligature Signs in the Middle Kingdom

Gardiner nrs	Hieroglyphs	Heqanakht papyri	El-lahun papyri	Ramesseum papyri
A1+A1			 pUC 32055.2	
A1+N35		 1r.1	 pUC 32163.3 pUC 32167.3  pUC 32170.2.8	
A1+V31			 pUC 32055.16	
A1+Z2			 pUC 32037.4 pUC 32163.3  pUC 32058.v.1 pUC 32201r.7	 pRam XVI.18.4 pRam IX.1.6
A1+B1 +Z2			 pUC 32037.8 pUC 32170.2.11  pUC 32157.c.9	 pRam XVI.26.1  pRam XVI.24.3 pRam X.1.5
A2+V31			 pUC 32271RI.1	
D2+D22		 1v.10 2.32 2.v 3.v.1  4.13	 pUC 32055.16 pUC 32058.3  pUC 32156.8 pUC 32166.5  pUC 32194.8	 pRam XVI.28.5  pRam XVI.26.2

Gardiner nrs	Hieroglyphs	Heqanakht papyri	El-lahun papyri	Ramesseum papyri
D2+D2I +N37+I9		 3.1 3.3		
D21+D36 +X1			 pUC 32055.6	
D21+D21			 pUC 32179.8	 pRam XVI.23.3
D21+D46				 pRam X.1.7
D21+I9		 Frag.A.r.5		
D21+X1		 1v.5 3.8 4.3  5.43	 pUC 32134A.4 pUC 32166.5  pUC 32174.13	 pRam XVI.22.3  pRam XVI.9.1 pRam I.B1.2  pRam IV.13
D21+X1 +I9		 2.37		
D21+X1 +V31		 3.1		
D21+N35		 5.22 5.23	 pUC 32148A.1 pUC 32170.6  pUC 32201r.8	 pRam XVI.23.4  pRam XVI.8.c.3 pRam XV.4

Gardiner nrs	Hieroglyphs	Heqanakht papyri	El-lahun papyri	Ramesseum papyri
D21+N35 +I9			  pUC 32058v.1 pUC 32171.1  pUC 32284b.2	 pRam XV.9
D21+N35 +X1+X1			 pUC 32199.1	
D21+V31		 1.3	 pUC 32158f.5	 pRam XVI.22.1
D21+V13	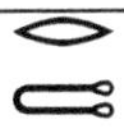		 pUC 32058v.1	 pRam X.1.5
D21+Aa1		 3.3	 pUC 32158f.4  pUC 32168.c.2.2  pUC 32179b.1	  pRam XVI.19.3 pRam I.B1.2
D28+X1			 pUC 32178.2	
D36+D36	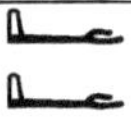		 pUC 32143.2	
D36+G43			 pUC 32057.2	

Gardiner nrs	Hieroglyphs	Heqanakht papyri	El-lahun papyri	Ramesseum papyri
D36+D21 +D21			 pUC 32114c	
D36+V31		 3.6	 pUC 32201.6	 pRam XVI.14.3
D36+N35			  pUC 32055.5 pUC 32157.5	
D36+N35 +I9			 pUC 32146a	
D36+Aa1			 pUC 32167.7	
D36+X1	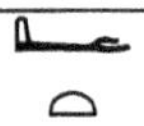		 pUC 32157.5  pUC 32272BO.1  pUC 32359.1	 pRam XII.6
D36+X1 +D54			 pUC 32158.c2.1	
D36+X1 +Z7	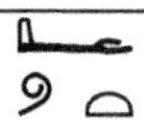		 pUC 32214.11	

Gardiner nrs	Hieroglyphs	Heqanakht papyri	El-lahun papyri	Ramesseum papyri
D36+X1+ V12+N35+ X1+V30	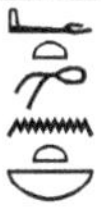		 pUC UC.32150	
D46+D58			 pUC 32055.14	
D46+X1			  pUC 32168f.8 pUC 32179b.2  pUC 32201.6	
D46+D21			 pUC 32131.12	 pRam XVI.20.1  pRam XVI.22.C.1
D50+D50 +D50+V31			 pUC 32158.7	
D54+V31				 pRam XVI.26.6
D54+Z2				 pRam XVI.18.2

Gardiner nrs	Hieroglyphs	Heqanakht papyri	El-lahun papyri	Ramesseum papyri
D58+D54			 pUC 32144b.7 pUC 32201.5	
D58+X1			 pUC 32119A.3  pUC 32190f.c.2.2	 pRam XVI.13.6
D58+W3			 pUC 32191f.6	
E34+N35 (N35)+(I9)		 1v.1 3.r. 3  2.r.6	 pUC 32211.2	 pRam IX.3.2 pRam IV.13
F4+X1 +Z1			 pUC 32037.6 pUC 32157.9	
F32+X1	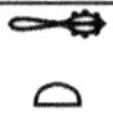		 pUC 32167.2	
G1+X1		 2.r.36 3.6		
G14+I9		 2.r.1		
G14+ X1+I9		 2.r.1		

Gardiner nrs	Hieroglyphs	Heqanakht papyri	El-lahun papyri	Ramesseum papyri
G17+D36			 pUC 32156.5	
G17+D36 +V31	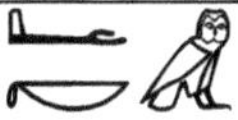		 pUC 32124.13 pUC 32119b.2  pUC 32157.9 pUC 32201r.15  pUC 32199.10	 pRam XVI.21.8  pRam XVI.14.5
G17+D21		 1v.11 3.r.7	 pUC 32055.5 pUC 32119f.1  pUC 32158.4 pUC 32163v.4  pUC 32199.c.1	 pRam IV.14
G17+X1		 3.r.6	 pUC 32037.2 pUC 32058.2  pUC 32157.5 pUC 32158f.6	 pRam XVI.27.5 pRam XV.5
G25+Aa1			 pUC 32109a.11	 pRam XVI.20.2
G29+U7		 2.30		

Gardiner nrs	Hieroglyphs	Heqanakht papyri	El-lahun papyri	Ramesseum papyri
G29+V31		 1v.13 2.r.9 2.r.11  3.r.1 3.r.3	 pUC 32117.c.3 pUC 32271.1  pUC 32201r.c.1 pUC 32363  pUC 32156.16 pUC 32196.4	
G29+V31 +A1			 pUC 32124.12 pUC 32148A.4	
G29+V31 +A1+M17 +G17			 pUC 32150B pUC 32271.c.1 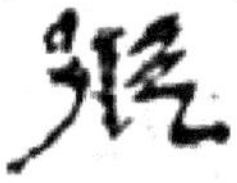 pUC 32198.13	
G36+Z2				 pRam XVI.18.1
G36+D21 +X1		 3.r.2	 pUC 32149A.2	 pRam XVI.22.C.2  pRam XVI.26.1
G39+I9			  pUC 32037.3 pUC 32055.2	
G39+X1		 2.r.22 4.r.1	  pUC 32166.18 pUC 32170.9	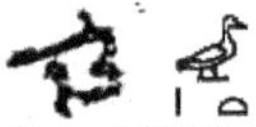 pRam XVI.20.4

Gardiner nrs	Hieroglyphs	Heqanakht papyri	El-lahun papyri	Ramesseum papyri
L1+D21 +X1	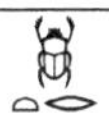		 pUC 32107a.7	
M2+N35 +N35			 pUC 32158.9	
M3+X1		 5.v.1		
M5+O35 +O35+X1			 pUC 32333	
M8+Aa1 +X1			 pUC 32037.1 pUC 32139A.3  pUC 32180.1 pUC 32193f.1	
M17+G17			 pUC 32119f.4 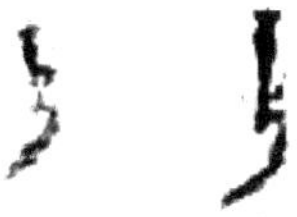 pUC 32124.v.1 pUC 32092a	
M36+D21		 1.v.16 2.r.2		
M36+D21 +I9		 3.r.25		
N5+N28			 pUC 32270.3 pUC 32186.5	
N5+V30			 pUC 32156	

Gardiner nrs	Hieroglyphs	Heqanakht papyri	El-lahun papyri	Ramesseum papyri
N35+W24		2.r.34 5.r.39		
N35+X1		1.2 1.5 2.r.32 3.r.1 5.r.41	pUC 32037.5 pUC 32156.10 pUC 32163.2	pRam XVI.20.4 pRam XV.2 pRam XIA.1 pRamIV.26
N35+X1 +X1		1.13	pUC 32037.5 pUC 32037.9 pUC 32124.8	pRam XVI.13.4
N35+X1 +F32		1.v.6 2.33		
N35+X1 +I9			pUC 32.37.2	
N35+X1 +V31			pUC 32201.5 pUC 32199.8	
N35+X1 +N35			pUC 32196.4	
N35+X1 +Z4			pUC 32055.8 pUC 32147.2 pUC 32156.5 pUC 32201v.11 pUC 32269.3	pRam XVI.22.4

Gardiner nrs	Hieroglyphs	Heqanakht papyri	El-lahun papyri	Ramesseum papyri
N35+Aa1	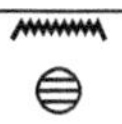	 2.r.38 3.r.1	 pUC 32148A.5 pUC 32170.6	 pRamXVI.24.4 pRam IV.19  pRam XVI.28.6
N35+Aa1 +X1	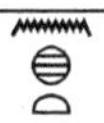		 pUC 32201.6	
N42+X1		 5.r.21		
N37+D21				 pRam IX.1.1
O1+D21 +X1	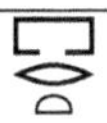	 1.r.2		
O1+N35			 pUC 32163v.3 pUC 32167.2	
O6+X1		 1.v.1 1.v.14 5.r.13		
O29+D36	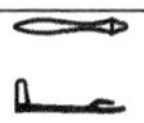		 pUC 32131.11  pUC 32156.18	 pRam XVI28.5
O34+A1 +Z1				 pRam XVI.23.6
O34+D54				 pRam XV.4

Gardiner nrs	Hieroglyphs	Heqanakht papyri	El-lahun papyri	Ramesseum papyri
O34+N35			  pUC 32147f.4 pUC 32166.5   pUC 32166. 6 pUC 32168.5	 pRam XVI.27.3
O34+O35 +X1			 pUC 32166.20	
O34+Q3 +O50		 1.v.15		
O38+X1 +Z4			 pUC 37037.8	
O49+X1 +Z1			  pUC 32216672 pUC 32167.6	
P1+D36			 pUC 32096A.2	
Q1+X1		 2.r.28		
Q3+A1			 pUC 32185.c.1.6	
Q3+D36			  pUC 32201r.5 pUC 32189f.4	
Q3+G43			 pUC 32055.7	
Q3+I9		 2.r.37		

Gardiner nrs	Hieroglyphs	Heqanakht papyri	El-lahun papyri	Ramesseum papyri
Q3+N5			 pUC 32157.Col.10	
Q3+N35			 pUC 32180.3	  pRam XVI.23.6 pRam XII.3  pRam X.1.3
Q3+O50		 2.r.35		
Q3+V31		 2.v.3		
Q3+X1		 3.r.2	  pUC 32167.6 pUC 32170.6  pUC 32275BO.5  pUC32179.13	  pRam XVI.22.4 pRam XIA.1
Q3+X1 +Z9			 pUC 32134d	
R4+X1	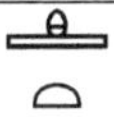	 3.r.2	  pUC 32158.c.1.6 pUC 32167.6	 pRam XVI.26.6
R8+R8 +R8			  pUC32149A.2 pUC 32198.6  pUC32199.4	 pRam X.1.5
S29+X1			 pUC 32158f.9	

Gardiner nrs	Hieroglyphs	Heqanakht papyri	El-lahun papyri	Ramesseum papyri
S34+U28 +S29			  pUC 32201r.5 pUC 32179bv.7   pUC32198.c.2 pUC 32199.c.1  pUC 32150B.c.2	
T21+D21			 pUC 32175.2	
T28+D21		 2.r.14	  pUC 32158.6 pUC 32166.3  pUC 32270.3	 pRam XII.3
T28+W3			 pUC 32278RI.1	
U2+D4			 pUC 32107	 pRam XVI.9.1
U2+X1		 V.r.5		
U2+Aa1			 pUC 32157.8	
U2+Aa11			 pUC 32174.1	 pRam XVI.28.4
V13+G43		 1v.17		

Gardiner nrs	Hieroglyphs	Heqanakht papyri	El-lahun papyri	Ramesseum papyri
V15+X1		1.6	pUC 32145D.2 pUC 32157.1 pUC 32179b.1	
V30+A1			pUC 32201r.5 pUC 32156.4 pUC 32275BO.5 pUC 32189f.8	
V30+N35			pUC 32199.2	
V30+X1			pUC 32037.9 pUC 32143A.3	pRam XVI.18.5
W12+D21		1.5 1v.17 1v.11	pUC 32095A.7	pRam XVI.13.1
W12+D21 +X1		1.3	pUC 32201v.co.2	
W24+V31			pUC 32170.5	pRam XVI.29.1 pRam XVI.28.2 pRam XVI.28.5
X1+D54				pRam IX.1.4
X1+I9		P.19	pUC 32201r.9 pUC 32286.2 pUC 32134.6	

Gardiner nrs	Hieroglyphs	Heqanakht papyri	El-lahun papyri	Ramesseum papyri
X1+N21			 pUC 32158 Col.2.3	
X1+N23			 pUC 32058.3 pUC 32163v.3	
X1+N35	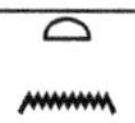		 pUC 32055.8	 pRam XVI.19.1 pRam XV.4
X1+O1	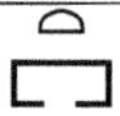		 pUC 32037.7	
X1+O34		 5.r.34	 pUC 32037.1 pUC 32058.1  pUC 32167.1 pUC 32174.1  pUC 32180.1	
X1+Q3			 pUC 32166.8	
X1+Z1			 pUC 37037.9	 pRam XVI.18.2
X1+X1			 pUC 32148A.1 pUC 32174.13  pUC 32180.4	
X1+X5	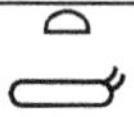		 pUC 32166.6	
Y1+Z2			 pUC 32055.2 pUC 32055.7  pUC 32178.3	 pRam XVI.18.3 pRam XVI.14.5

Gardiner nrs	Hieroglyphs	Heqanakht papyri	El-lahun papyri	Ramesseum papyri
Y5+N35	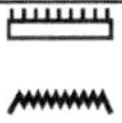	 2.r.1	 pUC 32166.9  pUC 32168.5  pUC 32180.2	
Aa1+X1		 2.r.12  3.v.1	 pUC 32055.3  pUC 32055.18  pUC 32147e.3  pUC 32189f.6	
Aa2+A1			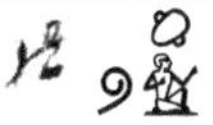 pUC 32170.c.2.15  pUC 32201v.c.2  pUC 32201.3  pUC 32168f.4	

Finding the Village: Qurna in the 1810s between Antiquities Collectors and Local Working Practice

Ikram Ghabriel
Helwan University, Egypt

Stephen Quirke
University College London, United Kingdom

Abstract

Historians and archaeologists tend to detach sites and objects in urban and rural settings from the people living there, as neglected treasures awaiting recognition and rescue by an outsider. In this paper, we consider the range of persons and institutions involved in accumulating material evidence for the Ramesside artists who worked on the tombs in the Valley of the Kings and lived in a village between the Theban desert cliffs and the fields. A first wave of extracting their monuments, in the late 1810s, offers an opportunity to investigate the processes involved in collecting antiquities, and the relations between the protagonists—local, international, and intermediary. We argue that a focus on questions of historical method and sources would increase precision on statements of provenance in collections and help to align a more self-critical history of archaeology with the primary aim of others to understand a past society.

الملخص

لقد اعتاد المؤرخون والاثريون على فصل المواقع الاثرية والقطع المكتشفة بها سواء بالريف او الحضر عن سكان هذه المناطق كما اعتادوا على تصوير هذه المواقع والقطع الاثرية بأنها كنوز مهملة عادة ما تحتاج إلى شخص من خارج هذه المناطق لتقديرها وانقاذها. تتناول هذه المقالة دراسة للأشخاص والمؤسسات التي قامت بتكوين مجموعات من آثار فناني عصر الرعامسة. هؤلاء الفنانون الذين عملوا بمقابر وادي الملوك وسكنوا بمدينة تقع بين تلال صحراء طيبة والحقول الزراعية. وتقدم لنا دراسة أولى عمليات تمت بهدف التنقيب عن آثار هؤلاء الفنانين بنهاية عام 1810 مثال لفهم أساليب تكوين مجموعات الآثار المصرية وما تتضمنه هذه الأساليب من علاقات مختلفة بين مستفيدين محليين وعالميين وما بينهما من وسطاء. وتسلط هذه المقالة الضوء على كيفية استخدام الأدلة التاريخية وطرق البحث المستخدمة في علم التأريخ لمعرفة أماكن اكتشاف المجموعات الاثرية على نحو أكثر دقة وتساعدنا هذه الدراسة على تقديم رؤية نقدية لنشأة وتاريخ علم الآثار المصرية مما يجعل فهم المجتمعات القديمة من أولويات البحث في علم الآثار.

On Funders and Finders in the History of Egyptian Archaeology

The primary aim of an archaeologist or ancient historian today may be to understand past human lives and practices.[1] The evidence may be analyzed at different scales on a spatial spectrum from region, to site, to find

[1] See G. Lucas, *Critical Approaches to Fieldwork: Contemporary and Historical Archaeological Practice* (London-New York, 2001), 62, noting changes in "the prevailing conception of the past" over the 19th and 20th centuries, "as the evolution of culture, as the history of cultural groups, and as cultural behaviour," such that, for current fieldwork archaeologists, "the site is a repository of behavioural patterns, structured activities revealed through close analysis of contextual association within or between assemblages."

Journal of the American Research Center in Egypt 58 (2022), 83–99
http://dx.doi.org/10.5913/jarce.58.2022.a004

context, to object.[2] Even at the level of the object, as the atom in this sequence of scales, the underlying target in research is likely the society that produced, used, and deposited it. However, our developing knowledge of ancient lives cannot be detached from the circumstances and process of finding. The starting point that enables any understanding is the modern life story of the objects. Therefore, precision on the circumstances of finding should be of acute importance, but a general practice of naming finds after modern sponsors of collections has come to distort our view, not only of the history of collecting but of the ancient society at the heart of the study. In this article, we assess the impact of this problem, and the possibilities of identifying the modern finders, through a paradigmatic case: monuments from the community of artists known to Egyptology as Deir al-Medina.[3]

Information on the early nineteenth-century collections of ancient Egyptian objects regularly connects them with names of a range of individuals, mainly from western European countries and never from Egypt. This practice continues in research writing and museum display text despite recent attention to a wider circle of participants, starting from the skilled foremen and workforce recruited for archaeological fieldwork since the mid-19th century.[4] Prominent in current histories of Egyptology are European funders directly involved in collecting activity, such as Henry Salt,[5] William John Bankes,[6] and Bernardino Drovetti.[7] Here we define the funder as the person who pays for others to organize collecting activities in the field. These funders may accumulate more than one name, as in the case of hereditary landowners whose legal title to an agricultural base changed, seen in the equations Lowry-Corry = Belmore[8] and Annesley = Valentia = Mountnorris.[9] A second category of protagonists in collection history comprises the paid agents who supervised collecting activity in the field, such as Athanasi,[10] Belzoni,[11] Passalacqua,[12] and Rifaud.[13] These sets of European names in the "acquisition history" field of a museum database for objects from Egypt raise two immediate questions: how did this material come to be in the hands of the named person? And where are the Egyptian names? In the public sphere of both the museum and archaeology, the modern personal name now attached to an ancient object involves a normative but one-sided claim: a collecting funder or agent or fieldwork director is made the primary point of contact between modern societies and the ancient objects and their societies.

Closer examination reveals a more complex tale. Beatrix Gessler-Löhr has outlined one particularly spectacular instance where the prize of contact name is contested between funder and field agent:[14] the rediscovery in autumn 1817 of the tomb of king Sety I in Biban al-Muluk the Valley of the Kings at Qurna on the West Bank of the Nile across from Luxor, ancient Thebes. In 1816, the London African Association agent Louis Burckhardt (1784–1817) and the English Consul in Cairo Henry Salt (1780–1827) had engaged a trained engineer Giovanni Battista Belzoni (1778-1823) to organize the removal of the detached upper part of a colossal statue of Ramses II from Qurna.[15] Following the success of the operation, Belzoni received further funding from Salt

2 On the difficulty of defining the breakpoints in this spectrum, see the history of use of the word "site" in J. Trampier, *Landscape Archaeology of the Western Nile Delta* (Atlanta, 2014), 7–23.

3 The site is also the focus of the excellent study, with comparable results, by J. Gee, "The Archaeological Context of the Late Ramesside Letters and Butehamun's archive," in S. Töpfer, P. Del Vesco, and F. Poole (eds.), *Deir El-Medina Through the Kaleidoscope: Proceedings of the International Workshop Turin 8th–10th October 2018* (Modena, 2022), 181–208.

4 W. Doyon, "On Archaeological Labor in Modern Egypt," in W. Carruthers (ed.), *Histories of Egyptology: Interdisciplinary Measures* (New York, 2015), 141–56; S. Quirke, *Hidden Hands: Egyptian Workforces in Petrie Excavation Archives, 1880–1924* (London, 2010).

5 M. Bierbrier, *Who Was Who in Egyptology*, 4th edition, (London, 2012), 484–85.

6 Bierbrier, *Who Was Who*, 38–39; P. Usick, "William John Bankes' Collection of Drawings of Egypt and Nubia," in P. Starkey and J. Starkey (eds.), *Travellers in Egypt* (London, 1998), 51–52.

7 Bierbrier, *Who Was Who*, 161–62.

8 Bierbrier, *Who Was Who*, 340–41.

9 Bierbrier, *Who Was Who*, 22.

10 Bierbrier, *Who Was Who*, 28.

11 Bierbrier, *Who Was Who*, 52–53.

12 Bierbrier, *Who Was Who*, 418.

13 Bierbrier, *Who Was Who*, 467.

14 B. Gessler-Löhr, "Who Discovered Belzoni's Tomb? A Glimpse behind the Scenes of Early Exploration and the Antiquities Trade," in M. Betrò and G. Miniaci (eds.), *Talking along the Nile: Ippolito Rosellini, Travellers and Scholars of the 19th Century in Egypt* (Pisa, 2013), 101–23.

15 E. Colla, *Conflicted Antiquities: Egyptology, Egyptomania, Egyptian Modernity* (Durham, NC, 2007), 24–71.

to continue forming a collection of antiquities on the model set by the ex-Consul of France Bernardino Drovetti (1776–1852).[16] In the following two years, Belzoni established himself as one of the leaders in the extraction of large quantities of antiquities, most notably monumental sculpture, and their transport from Luxor to Cairo for passage onward to Alexandria and export to Europe. His later autobiographical account, as published in English, recounts the finding of the tomb of Sety I as his own single-handed act of genius, even against the advice of the workforce recruited from the *fellahin* "farmers" of Qurna:[17]

> (a) "I" (European travelogue author) = discoverer
> "On the 16th I recommenced my excavations in the valley of Beban el Malook, and pointed out the fortunate spot, which has paid me for all the trouble I took in my researches."
> (b) local inhabitants ≠ discoverers
> "...The Fellahs who were accustomed to dig were all of the opinion, that there was nothing in that spot, as the situation of this tomb differed from that of any other."
> (c) "I" (European travelogue author) = discoverer *despite local advice*
> "I continued the work however, and the next day, the 17th, in the evening, we perceived the part of the rock that was cut, and formed the entrance. On the 18th, early in the morning, the task was resumed, and about noon the workmen reached the entrance"
> (d) "I" discoverer roles: (a) organizer of finding; (b) first to see/enter
> "... I descended, examined the place, pointed out to them where they might dig, and in an hour there was room enough for me to enter through a passage ... I perceived immediately ... that this was the entrance into a large and magnificent tomb."

Belzoni had good reasons for insisting on his role in the narrative published in 1820. Within a year of the "find," he had to defend his version of events against rumors that he had simply bought the information on the tomb location from a Qurna inhabitant. Belzoni blamed the rumors on, and fought with, his main rival Joseph Rossignana[18] (also known as Yussef Cachef), an agent collecting for Drovetti. However, Gessler-Löhr identifies another source, Eduard Rüppell,[19] who in the 1840s, recorded his own 1817 Nile journey. According to this account, on his way from Cairo to Luxor in April 1817, Rüppell was treated for smallpox at Asyut by the surgeon Filiberto Marucchi. Marucchi had just returned from directing the retrieval of antiquities at Luxor on behalf of the Defterdar (Director General of Finance, an Ottoman office[20]) Muhammad, governor of Upper Egypt and son-in-law of the powerful governor of all Egypt Muhammad Ali (1769–1849).[21] European-language narratives have downplayed or dismissed this active involvement of a member of the Muhammad Ali family in these decisive early years of the Theban antiquities gold rush. Gessler-Löhr wonders whether the surgeon told his patient about struggles with Belzoni, who would claim in his autobiography to have started work in 1816 at the site explored by Marucchi, and that Marucchi even "went to the west side of Thebes, and forbade the Fellars with threats to sell any thing to the English."[22] Once cured, Rüppell sailed on to Luxor, where, in May 1817, he received on board "ein alter Araber, in der Umgegend der berühmten Königsgräber ansässig" ("an old Arab, living in the area of the famed Tombs of the Kings"). The man offered to reveal the location of a treasure for

---

[16] S. Guichard, *Lettres de Bernardino Drovetti consul de France à Alexandrie (1803–1830)* (Paris, 2003), 29 on how Drovetti, after receiving from the Bourbon authorities in Paris the letter terminating his position as consul in December 1814, began two projects, one being a small trading house at Alexandria, and the other, apparently separately, "la recherche des antiquités," "soutenu dans ces démarches par Méhémet Ali qui s'oppose à son départ et lui fait des propositions avantageueses." See 62–64 on the question "À quelle date Drovetti a-t-il commencé à collectionner?" noting the limited evidence for a first journey to Upper Egypt in 1811–1812 with Yves Boutin, agent of Napoleon, and concluding that antiquities collecting became a major activity for Drovetti only in 1815–1816, after losing the salaried position of consul.

[17] G. Belzoni, *Narrative of the Operations and Recent Discoveries Within the Pyramids, Temples, Tombs and Excavations in Egypt and Nubia; and of a Journey to the Coast of the Red Sea, in Search of the Ancient Berenice; and Another to the Oasis of Jupiter Ammon* (London, 1820), 230–32.

[18] S. Cincotti, "'Les fouilles dans le musée': La collection égyptienne de Turin et le fonds Rifaud," *Karnak* 14 (2013), 279–80.

[19] Bierbrier, *Who Was Who*, 479.

[20] N. Michel, *L'Égypte des villages autour du seizième siècle*. Collection Turcica XXIII (Leuven, 2013), 43.

[21] K. Fahmy, *Mehmed Ali: From Ottoman Governor to Ruler of Egypt* (Oxford, 2009).

[22] Belzoni, *Narrative of the Operations*, 149; Gessler-Löhr, "Who Discovered Belzoni's Tomb?," 108.

twenty Spanish piasters. Rüppell dismissed the idea, but later that month he met Belzoni at Kom Ombo and told him the story.[23] Four decades later, in 1862, Rüppell travelled to London to relate a more detailed version of the tale to Joseph Bonomi: "The Arab related that one day he had seen a fox or a jackal come out of a hole in the side of the mountain of Gorna, whereupon he went and enlarged the hole sufficiently to admit himself," returning the next day with candles to explore his find as far as the burial chamber with its "large box of a fine material like crystal."[24] Rüppell had dismissed the tale as fantasy but told it to Belzoni at dinner to which "Belzoni replied that he had heard of it but that he knew the man to be mad and that there was no truth in the story." In 1843, John Gardner Wilkinson, a traveler who had lived in Thebes in the 1820s, so several years after 1817, relayed a similar line of events, but with an anonymous collective in place of the single man: "The sinking of the ground at this part, from the water that had soaked into the tomb, led the peasants to suspect the secret of its position, which was first mentioned to Dr. Rüppell, and afterwards to Belzoni."[25]

Through the fog of the half-recollected English and German versions from Belzoni and Rüppell, the reader cannot readily judge who knows whom, or what, when in October or May 1817, or earlier. The status of the information in each part of the story seems equally unclear: what is at stake for either Belzoni or Rüppell, or for the one or more "anonymous *Gurnawi*"?[26]

From the African Great Lakes to Mount Everest, European history and science tend to narrate their overseas ventures in the terms of heroic exploration, but the paths turn out to be well trodden.[27] In the alternative version of the Sety I tomb "find," the first modern finders are those living closest to the site. The initial instinct in the biographical tradition might be to recover the names of anonymous finders. However, inquiry into historical sources may reveal different, equally fundamental factors, in the collective, multi-layered and multicentric dimensions to "finding." Even if we cannot identify key individual protagonists at Qurna by name, we may find evidence for the local organization of antiquities finders in the early 19th century. To test the possibilities, we offer here a further case-study from the West Bank at Luxor, with a focus on Deir el-Medina. This history of collecting may remind us how current research practice still prefers literary narrative to a search for new documentary sources in a way that strategically excludes local modern populations from the discipline. In the tangled relations of knowledge and power, researchers should be alert to the difficulty of changing the standard narrative or its litany of funder and agent names. Nevertheless, as a first move, we argue for a renewed focus on the documentary evidence for find-place, as a precondition also for understanding ancient Egypt.

(Re-)Constructing Context for Antiquities without Securely Documented Provenance: Finds Ascribed to Deir el-Medina

Most ancient makers are as anonymous to us as the modern local finders. However, through their own inscriptions on architecture and artefacts, one group within the archaeological record documented itself particularly vividly: the team comprising sculptors who prepared the limestone walls and artists who drafted and painted the scenes covering them in the corridor tombs cut for kings in the Ramesside Period (13th–11th century BC), including that of Sety I. These artists lived with their families in a purpose-built stone-walled village set apart from the fields, on the east side of the mountain from their main workplace in the Valley of the Kings.[28] For this settlement site, Egyptologists have adopted the Arabic name Deir el-Medina "Monastery of the Town," evoking

[23] Gessler-Löhr, "Who Discovered Belzoni's Tomb?," 111–13

[24] Gessler-Löhr, "Who Discovered Belzoni's Tomb?," 113–17.

[25] J. Wilkinson, *Modern Egypt and Thebes: Being a Description of Egypt; Including the Information Required for Travellers in That Country*, vol. 2 (London, 1843), 202; Gessler-Löhr, "Who Discovered Belzoni's Tomb?," 104.

[26] Gessler-Löhr, "Who Discovered Belzoni's Tomb?," 119.

[27] J. Fabian, *Out of Our Minds: Reason and Madness in the Exploration of Central Africa* (Berkeley, 2000).

[28] R. Demarée, "The Workmen who Created the Royal Tombs," in R. Wilkinson and K. Weeks (eds.), *The Oxford Handbook of the Valley of the Kings* (Oxford, 2016), 75–86.

the Christian community established in the earlier temple enclosure;[29] the 13th–11th century BC inhabitants had called their home *wḥyt* "the village."[30]

Several museums now have online access to images and provisional information from their inventories of Egyptian antiquities, including inscribed objects made by the Ramesside community of artists from Deir el-Medina. The examples from four major collections (Table 1) provide a useful starting point for research into the first period of extraction and export of the object collection. The museum accession dates span much of the 19th century, and Athanasi assembled collections in Luxor into the 1830s. However, the main collecting activity on the ground seems concentrated in the years 1815–1824. As noted above, Drovetti seems to have started in earnest on forming a major collection for sale in 1815–1816, followed in 1816–1817 by Salt. The British Museum and the Egyptian Museum in Turin received the largest number of Deir el-Medina items, respectively, from Salt in 1823 and Drovetti in 1824. William John Bankes travelled in Upper Egypt in 1815 and 1818–1819,[31] and Somerset Lowry-Corry, the 2nd Earl of Belmore, was there in 1817–1818.[32] A stela acquired by the British Museum from Samuel Rogers in 1856 may seem an isolated later find but is also already recorded in the 1820s.[33]

Table 1. Objects with hieroglyphic inscriptions related to the Deir el-Medina artist teams and accessible on the online collections databases for London, Liverpool, Kingston Lacey, and Turin.

British Museum acquisitions:	
Annesley 1854 (from Salt)	EA 810–12, 814–16, 818
Athanasi 1845	EA 807, 1388
Hay 1868 (in Egypt 1820s)	EA 916, 918, 1243, 36861
Somerset Lowry-Corry (2nd Earl of Belmore) 1843	EA 262, 264, 265, 267, 269, 273, 284, 286, 589, 597
Rogers 1856	EA 35630
Salt 1823 (received 1821)	EA 332, 342, 355, 359
Salt posthumous 1835 auction	EA 217, 291, 305, 345?
Sams 1834 (from Athanasi?)	EA 360, 371, 373, 381, 446, 8497
Wilkinson 1834	EA 8493
Unidentified before 1840- Birch slips	EA 144, 150, 186, 191, 270, 316–17, 320, 328, 341, 344, 369–70, 372, 444, 448, 8501
World Museum Liverpool:	
Mayer 1867 (in large part from Sams)	M13830, M13832
Kingston Lacey Dorset:	
Bankes (in Egypt 1815, 1818–1819)	NT 1257687-91, 1257693-701 (total 14 stelae)

[29] R. Coquin and M. Martin, "Dayr al-Madinah," in A. Atiya (ed.), *The Coptic Encyclopedia* 3 (New York-Toronto, 1991), 816–18; for the 6th–8th century AD Coptic graffiti, see C. Heurtel, *Les inscriptions coptes et grecques du temple d'Hathor à Deir al-Médîna: suivies de la publication des notes manuscrites de François Daumas, 1946–1947, Bibliothèque d'Etudes Coptes* 16 (Cairo, 2004).

[30] R. Ventura, *Living in a City of the Dead: a Selection of Topographical and Administrative Terms in the Documents of the Theban Necropolis*, OBO 69 (Freiburg, 1986), 184; J. Černý, *A Community of Workmen at Thebes in the Ramesside Period*, BdÉ 50 (Cairo, 1973), 92; A. Zingarelli, "Comments on the Egyptian term *wḥyt*: family or quasi-village?," in P. Kousoulis and N. Lazaridis (eds.), *Proceedings of the Tenth International Congress of Egyptologists: University of the Aegean, Rhodes. 22–29 May 2008,* OLA 241.2 (Leuven, 2015), 909–20.

[31] P. Usick, *Adventures in Egypt and Nubia. The Travels of William John Bankes (1786–1855)* (London, 2002), 32, 51, 98, 146–47.

[32] As narrated in R. Richardson, *Travels along the Mediterranean and Parts Adjacent in Company with the Earl of Belmore, during the Years 1816–17–18: extending as far as the Second Cataract of the Nile, Jerusalem, Damascus, Balbec, &c. &c.* Volumes 1–2 (London, 1822).

[33] J. Burton, *Excerpta Hieroglyphica* (Cairo, 1825–1828), pl. 37.15.

Egyptian Museum Turin:	
Drovetti 1824	Cat. 1372, 1450-3, 1455?, 1463, 1471, 1514, 1516, 1522, 1533, 1542, 1546, 1548-9, 1553, 1566, 1570, 1579-80, 1587, 1589-91, 1606-8, 1618, 1648, 1658, 1754, 3032, 3038-40, 7357-8
Unidentified before 1882 catalogue	Cat. 1521, 1593, 1603, 1619

From these 114 entries, we select as our case-study a pair of stelae in which one artist from Deir el-Medina, Neferaabet, repents for taking the name of a deity in vain.[34] Although the inscriptions on the stelae are often cited by researchers on ancient Egyptian religion, the lack of any documented provenance removes essential information about the object. This problem tends to be either overlooked, or replaced by assertions of an inferred provenance, that then becomes accepted as if an observation. On one stela, now in the Egyptian Museum Turin (fig. 1), Neferaabet prays to Meretseger, the goddess presiding over the Theban mountain; in the other, now in the British Museum (fig. 2), his hymn is to Ptah, the god of artistic creation. Their online databases currently provide the following fields and content:

Stela 1: Egyptian Museum Turin Cat. 1593[35] (fig. 1)
Provenance: Deir el-Medina
Acquisition history: Acquired before 1882

Stela 2: British Museum EA 589[36] (fig. 2)
Found/Acquired: Deir el-Medina (Thebes)
Acquisition name: Purchased from Somerset Lowry-Corry, 2nd Earl of Belmore.
Acquisition date: 1843

Egyptological researchers have tended to apply the toponym Deir el-Medina as a provenance for the objects whose owners are designated as ***sḏm ꜥš m st mꜣꜥt***, Servant in the Place of Truth or other titles ending with Place of Truth, as characteristic of artists living there.[37] However, while "made by X in the Place of Truth" may indicate that an object belongs to a member of the community of artists living in Deir el-Medina, it does not necessarily mean that it was deposited in their village. It seems misleading to extend our use of the place name to every location where the artists left their mark. Even the immediate site of their village valley contains buildings with a wide range of functions: houses, tombs (comprising offering-chapels above the ground and the underground burial spaces), chapels and small temples to deified rulers and deities, and a religious-administrative building called the *khenu* of Ramesses II. Beyond this inner circle of diverse buildings around the village, objects dedicated by the artists of Deir el-Medina have also been found in the nearby rock-cut chapels on the route from their village to the Valley of the Queens,[38] and in the West Bank royal temples (e.g., the stela of Ramose[39] from the Ramesseum and the stela of Nebamun[40] from Medinet Habu), besides the objects they left in their main work places, the Valley of the Kings and the Valley of the Queens.

34 M. Lichtheim, *Ancient Egyptian Literature*, vol. 2, *The New Kingdom* (Berkeley-Los Angeles-London, 1976), 107–9.

35 M. Tosi and A. Roccati, *Stele e altre epigrafi di Deir el Medina (n. 50001-50262)*, TCB 1 (Turin, 1972), 94–95, 286 (CGT 50058); The Egyptian Museum Turin database: https://collezioni.museoegizio.it/it-IT/material/Cat_1593/?description=&inventoryNumber=&title=&cgt=50058&yearFrom=&yearTo=&materials=&provenance=&acquisition=&epoch=&dynasty=&pharaoh= (accessed 3 October 2021).

36 The British Museum database: https://www.britishmuseum.org/collection/object/Y_EA589 (accessed 3 October 2021).

37 Demarée, "The Workmen who Created the Royal Tombs," 75–77.

38 B. Bruyère, *Mert Seger à Deir El-Médineh*, MIFAO 58 (Cairo, 1930).

39 J. Quibell, *The Ramesseum*, ERA 2 (London, 1898), 8, pl. 4.

40 Bruyère, *Mert Seger à Deir El-Médineh*, 299; Chicago OIM E4653A-B, documented as found "by the high gate in rubbish"; an example with a different location within Deir el-Medina is published in E. Teeter, "A Stela of the Family of Khaemtir (i) and the Scribe Qenherkhepshef (i) (Chicago OIM E14315)," *JARCE* 50 (2014), 147–60, documented in the Oriental Institute excavation records as "found in the precinct of the Small Amun Temple, north of the Achoris Porch" on 3 February 1928.

Fig. 1. Stela of Neferaabet with hymn to Meretseger, Egyptian Museum Turin Cat. 1593 © Museo Egizio Torino.

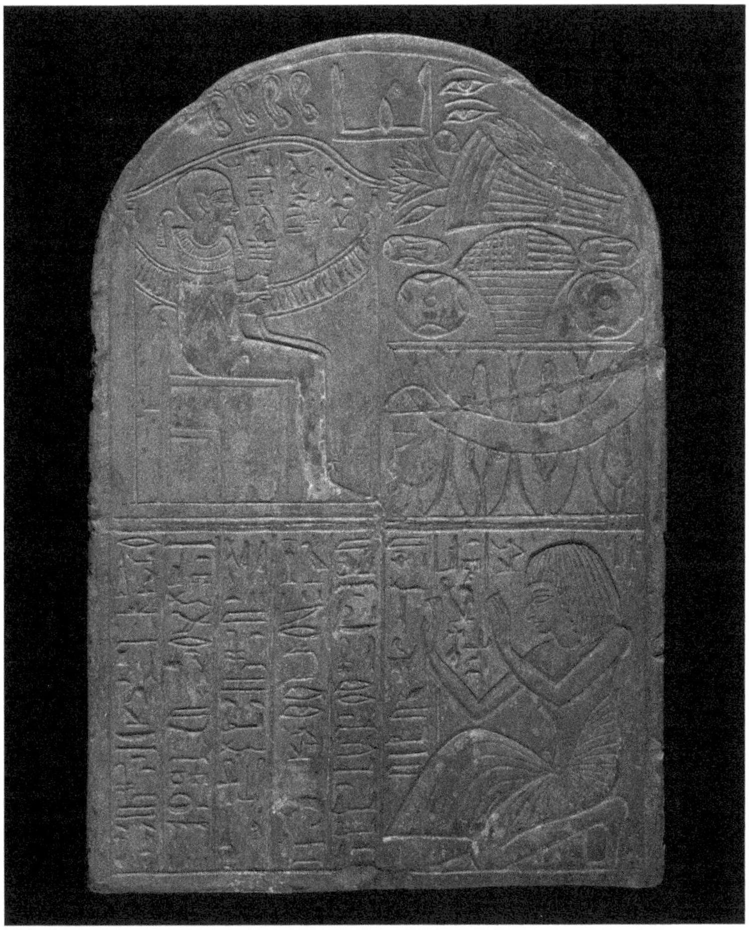

Fig. 2. Stela of Neferaabet with hymn to Ptah inscribed on both sides. British Museum EA 589. © The Trustees of the British Museum.

Table 2. Examples of European-language writers of published accounts of 1816–1819 antiquities extraction at Thebes.

Work supervisors	Draughtspeople	Other collectors	Short-term visitors	Companions
Athanasi	Linant de Bellefonds	Forbin	Fuller	Richardson
Belzoni	Ricci	Rüppell	Irby and Mangles	
Cailliaud				
Finati				

However influential these authors may be in our attempts to view Luxor in the 1810s, they constitute only one part of the overall foreign presence. Outside the list are those who wrote their own narratives but never managed to publish them, notably the architect Jean Nicolas Huyot.[57] The bias of selection is further exacerbated by the filter of translation into English from Greek (Athanasi) and Italian (Finati, and perhaps Belzoni). Overshadowing these issues is the relation to authors writing in Arabic and Turkish, whether scholars of the region or government officials or visitors, with their own diversity of views. One brief account by the Egyptian historian Abd al-Rahman al-Jabarti has entered discussions of antiquities collecting in this period. In his entry for 1817, Jabarti reported the frenetic activity by Europeans in Upper Egypt, and the collections: "They have sent the objects to their own land, to sell at many times the amount they had spent on them, these being for them a type of curio merchandise."[58] This succinct assessment is part of his description of a visit to the house of Henry Salt to view objects collected from Belzoni and other field agents. Elsewhere Europeans lay this charge at European rivals, as where two English military officers remark "Mr. Drovetti is not an amateur, but collects to sell."[59] However, the comment by Jabarti concerns the entire enterprise of foreigners forming collections in Egypt and exporting them to Europe. The accuracy of his observation is clear from views expressed by Salt himself after arriving in Egypt to take up his position as consul and settling in Cairo. On 28 December 1816, he wrote to his former employer and patron George Annesley (from 1793 titled Viscount Valentia, and then from July 1816 Earl of Mountnorris):

> I found that Monsieur Drovetti, the quondam French Consul, was in Upper Egypt, buying up everything there to complete a collection upon which he has been engaged some years. This collection, which I have lately had an opportunity of examining, contains a great variety of curious articles, and some of extraordinary value... The whole is intended for sale, and I have tried to persuade him to send proposals to the British Museum: but do not know whether it is rich enough to buy it. The collection, I imagine, will not be sold for less than three or four thousand pounds. Since our release from quarantine, I have taken every possible means to collect, and am glad to say that I have been very successful; so that I shall in spring have to send you a cargo of such thing as I believe you have not before seen. I must however inform you, that I am so bit with the prospect of what may still be done in Upper Egypt, as to feel unable to abstain from forming a collection myself...[60]

While Salt had promised to send antiquities, including coins and medals, to Annesley (recently elevated to Mountnorris) and his son (simultaneously elevated to Valentia), evidently the catalyst for his entry into the collecting business was the sight of the material amassed for Drovetti. In spring 1817, he employed a Mr. Riley to organize collecting in Upper Egypt,[61] and then Burckhardt introduced Belzoni for the single challenge of trans-

[57] P. Pinon, *Le voyage d'Orient de l'architecte Jean-Nicolas Huyot (1817–1820) et la découverte de la maison ottomane* (Leuven, 1994).

[58] C. Bosworth, "Al-Jabartī and the Frankish Archaeologists," *International Journal of Middle East Studies* 8 (1977), 229–36; Colla, *Conflicted Antiquities*, 73–74, 290–91 nn. 2–3.

[59] C. Irby and J. Mangles, *Travels in Egypt and Nubia, Syria, and Asia Minor, during the years 1817 and 1818* (London, 1823), 44.

[60] Halls, *The Life and Correspondence of Henry Salt*, vol. 1, 472.

[61] Halls, *The Life and Correspondence of Henry Salt*, vol. 1, 486.

porting the Ramses II colossus fragment from Qurna,[62] as outlined above. The dramatic success of this operation and subsequent collecting activity by Belzoni brought Salt some hope for his future, as he expressed already to Mountnorris in a letter from the Valley of the Kings dated 18 January 1818:

> In the way of antiquities I have been very fortunate; though my expenses have far exceeded what I had intended ... All that I wish is, to be reimbursed my expenses, as it breaks in seriously on the small patrimony which I have inherited, and which is all that I have to look to for support should I ever return to England, which, after a certain number of years, I cannot help, even upon that small pittance, looking forward to.[63]

With his direct financial interest and expenditure, Salt expected a substantial sum to cover his costs, but at the crucial moment the British Museum Trustees objected to paying for what they expected to be more of a gift to the nation. After several years of negotiation, a settlement at £2,000 in 1823 left out the prize of the collection, the translucent calcite sarcophagus of Sety I which would, in nationalist rhetoric, be "saved for the nation" only when the architect John Soane acquired it for his London house the following year. In 1826, Salt was happier to sell a second massive batch of material to the king of France.[64]

The modern history of the sarcophagus of Sety I brings to center stage both the financial calculations and the uncertainties over naming finders. For Egypt, as for many regions, archaeologists and historians of the modern period have not engaged with each other, and, partly as a result of this, the home language may still be excluded from scientific research in archaeology.[65] In these conditions, the inextricable tangle of economic and scientific factors in any fieldwork may remain beyond our capacity to analyze and to change. Accordingly, as Egyptologists, we seek in our concluding section to introduce some recent publications by colleagues in anthropology and history, inviting their comments and corrections on this question of finders in Qurna two centuries ago.

Anthropological Approaches to the History of Qurna

For present and recent past, Caroline Simpson has striven to document the changes of recent decades, including foremost the 2006–2009 demolition of Qurna houses and resettlement of villagers away from the central monument zone.[66] Kees van der Spek has charted from his own ethnographic fieldwork the contemporary patterns of life on the West Bank of Luxor governorate, incorporating the histories detectable through both the accounts by the Qurnawi themselves and the literary versions by Europeans who spent less or more time in the area.[67] For the settlements over the foothills at the low desert, van der Spek reports two groupings of communities, locally named from ancestral figures, particularly Harb, Ghaba, and 'Atya as three sons of Adman who settled at the area where the Sety I temple stands, near the point where the Theban mountains and foothills come closer to the river Nile.[68] One group name is al-Hurabat (from Harb), and relates to the zone south from Asasif, al-Khukha, and Sheikh abd al-Qurna to Qurnet Murai; to their north along Dra abu al-Naga are the groups al-Hasasna,[69] al-Ghabat, and al-Atyat.

---

62 Halls, *The Life and Correspondence of Henry Salt*, vol. 1, 490.

63 Halls, *The Life and Correspondence of Henry Salt*, vol. 2, 52–53.

64 Halls, *The Life and Correspondence of Henry Salt*, vol. 2, 295–386.

65 N. Hansen, "Arabic and its role in Egyptology and Egyptian archaeology" *Archaeologies: Journal of the World Archaeological Congress* 4.1 (2008), 171–74.

66 C. Simpson, "Qurna History Project," accessed 11 October 2021, http://www.qurna.org/index.html.

67 K. Van der Spek, *The Modern Neighbors of Tutankhamun. History, Life, and Work in the Villages of the Theban West Bank* (Cairo, 2011).

68 Van der Spek, *Modern Neighbors of Tutankhamun*, 49, 135–36.

69 Hasasna may relate to a further ancestral figure Hassan; note the comment by Van der Spek, *Modern Neighbors of Tutankhamun*, 131, on references to Qurnawi groups in 1820s–1830s English-language publications: "It is of interest that there is no group as yet that could be identified with present-day al-Hasasna in the northern foothills, possibly confirming the later arrival of Shaykh Tayyeb's ancestors."

Among his European-language historical sources, Van der Spek assigns a prominent place to the vivid and positive description published in London in 1836 by Athanasi.[70] As a field agent collecting in Thebes and other sites both for Henry Salt and for himself, Yanni Athanasi lived in the Qurna foothills from 1818 to around 1835.[71] In his narrative to accompany the posthumous 1835 sale of a last set of antiquities amassed for Henry Salt, Athanasi identifies in Qurna "six tribes, of which two together form one class, and each of the united classes form a third of the village," giving names that correspond in part to the southern Harabat and northern Ghabat-Atiyat zones in the anthropological investigation by Van der Spek: Ilhourabat, protecting a smaller group Ildigagat; Ilgabat-Oullatiat; Ilmassaah Oullovassa.[72] Athanasi also conveys an agricultural dimension of these divisions, stating that the "lands are also divided into three portions, for the occupancy of which the three classes draw lots, in order to avoid all complaint and dissension on the subject." This part of his description in turn echoes, in the opposite historical direction, the 16th century tribunal and land registers surviving from the first century of Ottoman Turkish rule over Egypt.

Legal and Economic Documentary Evidence: The Ottoman Period Tax Registers

According to the analyses by Nicolas Michel, the Ottoman Period administrators assigned everyone in the farming population of each district to a particular *ḥiṣṣa* "part" of the *ḫarāǧ* or amount due from a specified land.[73] In one detailed entry for 1586 for Abu Numrus, a village in Giza governorate, fourteen villagers declare that they have covered the sum due for a total of 125 feddan divided into two equal halves, each of six *ḥiṣṣa* "parts," with one or two individuals responding for each "part."[74] Unusually, this listing gives the names of the "parts" as well as the persons held accountable for them, enabling Michel to draw a social portrait of Abu Numrus village. One person emerges as a leading figure, some but not all "parts" are named after a lineage, and there is one Coptic "part." From this and other documents, he concludes that the assignment of responsibility across the village operated in a flexible way. While family ties might be a recurrent or dominant principle, other factors are also present, as indicated by references to associates and groups, though the records do not provide information on the nature of the association.

The 16th century registers provide Michel with crucial evidence to clarify the terms of village authority, above all in relation to the expression *shaykh al-balad* "the village shaykh" (with *naḥiya* a synonym for *balad*).[75] First, the tribunal registers indicate that each village had not one *shaykh* but several, and therefore contrasts with the later choice of English colonial power to impose a single official at the village level, the *ʿumda*. Secondly, to designate responsibility for collecting dues from village to center, the registers set the word *shaykh* after the personal name as a context-specific role, not in front of the name as would be the case for a religious title. Thus, *shaykh al-balad* is an administrative role, not a religious authority. The registers use the plural *mašāyiḫ*, as in the summary of villagers as *al-mašāyiḫ al-nāḥiya wa-l-fallāḥīn bi-nāḥiyat X*: "*shaykh*s and farmers of village X." Michel cites from the registers of the tribunal at Mit Ghamr (Sharqiya governorate) for 1613–1615 the extended phrasing *al-mašāyiḫ wa-l-fallāḥīn wa-ruʾūs al-ḥiṣaṣ wa-l-muzāriʿīn*, "the shaykhs and farmers, the heads of parts and cultivators." Here, "heads of parts" would identify the function of the shaykhs much as the word "cultivators" describes the *fallahin* "farmers."[76]

To this view of the village through a fiscal lens, the Athanasi description of Qurna would add a local method of assigning responsibility for the agricultural yield; there, allowing for translation from Arabic to Greek to English, three "classes" draw lots to decide on "the occupancy" of the "portions." Further research in the 19th

70 G. Athanasi, *A Brief Account of the Researches and Discoveries in Upper Egypt Made Under the Direction of Henry Salt* (London, 1836); Van der Spek, *Modern Neighbors of Tutankhamun*, 82, 101–2, 130–33.

71 Taylor, "The Collecting Activities of Giovanni d'Athanasi," 251–54.

72 Athanasi, *A Brief Account of the Researches*, 130–31.

73 N. Michel, *L'Égypte des villages autour du seizième siècle*, Collection Turcica 23 (Leuven, 2018), 291, 294–303.

74 Michel, *L'Égypte des villages*, 297–302.

75 Michel, *L'Égypte des villages*, 288–92.

76 Michel, *L'Égypte des villages*, 290–92.

century land and tribunal records might indicate whether this democratic procedure applied either outside the immediate aftermath of the state confiscation of large estates in Upper Egypt after 1811, or outside the singular ecology of Qurna. Here it is important to avoid exaggerating differences with other villages. While accepting the word of Athanasi, as he lived at Qurna for eighteen years, Van der Spek warns against too literal a reading of other European accounts, especially where they are most evocative, as in this vivid portrayal by Frédéric Cailliaud:[77]

> Aujourd'hui les hommes ne suffisent plus pour les fouilles; ils emploient leurs femmes à fouiller aussi les catacombes: elles parcourent sans cesse les plus grands et les moindres tombeaux; et, jusqu'à leurs enfans depuis l'âge de neuf ans, tous travaillent incessament à porter la terre au dehors. Cette manie est poussée à un tel point, que si les *kâchef* ou les *qâymaqâm* n'obligeoient avec rigueur les Arabes à travailler à la culture, ceux-ci abandonneroient entièrement leurs terres, pour se livrer uniquement à la recherche des antiquités.
>
> (Today the men no longer suffice for the digs; they employ their wives to dig the catacombs too: the women are ceaselessly scouring the tombs from largest to smallest; and, with even their children down to the age of nine, everyone works incessantly carrying out the earth. This mania is pushed to such a point that, if the *kashef* or *qaymaqam* were not forcing the Arabs rigorously to work the fields, they would abandon their lands entirely and devote themselves solely to the hunt for antiquities.)

However usefully Cailliaud raises questions of age and gender here, Van der Spek seeks to correct the extreme distortion from the outsider focus on an ancient past: "by and large, the reality of the Qurnawi preference for antiquities over agricultural work is one of western representation and portrayal, and a product of European single-minded antiquarian pursuit."[78] In our attempt to trace the local organization of antiquities finders in the late 1810s, the pattern of village authority in the earlier official Ottoman records may help towards decoding the partial information from European-language travelogues; the motives and stock motifs of the travelogue-writer may also become clearer, and therefore easier to filter out, from comparison with analyses of other ages of travel.[79] Future archival research in Egypt may be expected to add names for the officials most often identified in European travelogues only by their titles *kashif* and *qaymaqam.*[80] As is clear in the Belzoni narrative on the Ramesseum colossus, the role of both positions in the chain of authority was crucial for providing or refusing access to the labor for extracting and moving antiquities. The names and social networks of these officials would add another local dimension to the history of antiquities collecting at Qurna.[81] As Michel observed from the 16th century registers, the internal division of the village reflects a socially heterogeneous space, where prestige and economic power are unequally distributed.[82] A combination of historical and anthropological enquiry seems essential in any effort to identify the factors involved at any moment in this landscape.[83]

Re-Reading the European-Language Literary Evidence

Keeping in mind the essential warning above from Van der Spek, here it may be useful to cite again four of the references to labor organization in European publications from the early 19th century formation of antiquities

[77] F. Cailliaud, *Voyage dans l'oasis de Thèbes et dans les déserts situés à l'est et l'ouest de la Thébaïde* (Paris, 1821), 82.

[78] Van der Spek, *Modern Neighbors of Tutankhamun*, 48–51, 97–102.

[79] Discussions relevant to each side of the Egyptian-European encounter include H. Touati, *Islam et voyage au Moyen Âge: Histoire et anthropologie d'une pratique lettrée* (Paris, 2000), and Amin, *Ägyptomanie und Orientalismus*.

[80] Exceptions include Belzoni's visit to Soliman, *kashif* of Armant, south of Luxor, at his estate at Tahta, near Asyut, far to the north: Belzoni, *Narrative of the Operations*, 288–89.

[81] Colla, *Conflicted Antiquities*, 24–70.

[82] See also K. Cuno, *The Pasha's Peasants: Land, Society, and Economy in Lower Egypt, 1740–1858* (Cambridge, 1992).

[83] Van der Spek, *Modern Neighbors of Tutankhamun*, 171–217 and ch. 7 "Agriculture, Conflict and the Maintenance of Stable Social Relations."

collections, including passages where the local choice is represented as a choice by the "I" or, less often, "we" imposed by an outsider field agent:

(1) Athanasi: "…we determined on commencing our excavations into the Tombs of the Kings, having first divided our Arabs into companies, whom we appointed to work in different quarters."[84]

(2) Belzoni: "The Fellahs of Gournou who dig for antiquities are sometimes divided into parties, and have their chiefs over each; so that what is found by any of the party is sold, and the money divided among them all."[85]

(3) Belzoni: "The men were divided into two classes. The most knowing were making researches on their own account, employing eight or ten to assist them."[86]

(4) Irby and Mangles (August 1817 meeting Belzoni in Qurna, during disputes between field agents for Drovetti and Salt): "About a dozen of the leading characters of Gourna, that is, the greatest rogues in the place, have headed their comrades, and formed them into two distinct digging parties, or resurrection men, designating them the French and the English party; these are constantly occupied in searching for new tombs, stripping the mummies, and collecting antiquities. The directors have about three-fourths of the money, and the rest is given to the inferior labourers."[87]

These authors separate the finders into two groups: an undifferentiated mass of seekers, and their leaders. On its own, the statement by Belzoni on the "most knowing" is ambiguous, as it may just be a comment on relative success, rather than qualifying a "class" of leaders. The ambiguity in these brief descriptions perhaps reflects outsider ignorance about local modes of operation, which would likely be concealed in such a lucrative business. However, in specifying "eight or ten" assistants, Belzoni adds a useful point of detail where further research might find evidence to corroborate or revise his account. The aspect that seems least clear is the distribution of seekers, and the authority to seek, across the landscape. On the European side, the increasingly violent altercations in late 1817 to early 1818 between the rival field agents for Salt (Belzoni to December 1817, Athanasi from 1818) and Drovetti (Rifaud on the East Bank, Rossignana on the West Bank) led to an official settlement, described in spatial terms by Belzoni (finding no ground permitted for work on return to Thebes 10 May 1818)[88] and Cailliaud ("lignes de démarcation" across Karnak in January 1818).[89] On the ground, matters might have been more flexible, and it is not clear how long a demarcation was meant to last, or whether it was arranged between the European protagonists or imposed by the authority of Mohammed Ali. For archaeological enquiry in the field and in museums, we see this question of local authority over space as a priority for future research.

With the information on conditions of collecting in 1810s Qurna, we may return to the history of acquisition of the two monuments of Neferaabet. First, we can review what we can know of the way they were moved from their find-place to their present locations in separate west European cities. The Meretseger stela arrived in Turin at some point before 1882. From the history of the museum, it most plausibly left Egypt as part of the Drovetti collection, but no further detail can be given from present knowledge. The Ptah stela entered the British Museum as part of the Belmore collection, and again there is no precise record of the find for this individual item, though Belmore seems most likely to have acquired it during his Nile journey. According to Richardson, on 14 January 1818, Athanasi showed Belmore the material assembled in Thebes over the previous three months, when Belmore himself had been away on a journey into Nubia.[90] Two weeks later, Cailliaud recorded that, at least at Karnak, either the officials of Muhammad Ali, or Salt and Drovetti as the main rival funders of collecting, had demarcated the terrain allotted to the Drovetti field agents and the Salt field agents, in order to prevent further conflict between them. Were demarcation lines in force at the time that each stela was found, and, if so,

[84] Athanasi, *A Brief Account of the Researches*, 12.

[85] Belzoni, *Narrative of the Operations*, 159; Van der Spek, *Modern Neighbors of Tutankhamun*, 107.

[86] Belzoni, *Narrative of the Operations*, 165; Van der Spek, *Modern Neighbors of Tutankhamun*, 108.

[87] Irby and Mangles, *Travels in Egypt and Nubia*, 44.

[88] Belzoni, *Narrative of the Operations*, 289: "on my arrival at Thebes I found, that all the grounds on each side of the Nile were taken, partly by Mr. Drouetti's agents, and partly by Mr. Salt himself, who marked the grounds before his return to Cairo this last time" (presumably the January-February period in Thebes with the Belmore party).

[89] Cailliaud, *Voyage dans l'oasis de Thèbes*, 82, arriving at Thebes 29 January 1818, "tout l'espace occupé par les ruines de Karnak étoit couvert par des lignes de démarcation qui séparoient le terrain des Français, celui des Anglais, celui des Irlandais, celui des Italiens &c. " ("Irlandais" referring to the Belmore party, from his position as an Irish peer in the House of Lords in London).

[90] Richardson, *Travels along the Mediterranean* vol. 2, 2–3.

would they apply to local finders who sold to the field agents?[91] There are also limits to our knowledge of find-place, in relation to the type of object. As indicated above, a votive stela might be placed at any of the shrines at and around Deir el-Medina, or across the wider Theban West Bank. Alongside the absence of find-place, it is important to note the absence of a find date so far for either object. Finally, as yet there is no clear understanding of the local organization of finders and its interface with the outsider funders who were collecting on a large scale.

Qurna and the Outside World

In 1818, Upper Egypt hosted, perhaps for the first time, the director of a European institution of a fairly recent type, the national museum in its late 18th century revolutionary form. When the alliance against Napoleon restored the Bourbon monarchy in France, the director of the Louvre, Vivant Denon, seemed too close to the Napoleonic cause, and the government of the new king Louis XVIII replaced him in 1815 with the painter Count Auguste de Forbin. Two years later, Forbin sailed to the Ottoman territories in the Eastern Mediterranean to seek cheaper means of acquiring ancient Greek and Roman art for the French capital, bankrupted by war and defeat.[92] On return, he published an account of his journey including a call for national funding for the national museum in his charge, whenever that would become affordable again. As his dedicatory preface addresses the king directly, his aims in publishing the travelogue are clear enough. Forbin arrived in Egypt from Palestine, and travelled via Damietta to Cairo. There, like Salt two years earlier, he was impressed by the ex-consul Drovetti and the antiquities on display in his house. Drovetti was as closely tied to Napoleon as Denon had been, and Forbin needed to make an especially strong argument for buying his collection. At the time, despite the hopes of Drovetti and Salt, no European government considered ancient Egyptian antiquities worth large sums. The reports from the most influential travelers would slowly change this attitude, but it was only several years later that the government of Savoy, at Turin in Piedmont, agreed to purchase the collection amassed for Drovetti, himself Piedmontese, as the first instance of large-scale national expenditure on ancient Egyptian material.

Forbin travelled south in January 1818, and at Luxor he visited the Drovetti field agent Joseph Rossignana, briefly stating his views of the business of collecting: "Je voyais cette tribu d'Oulâd-Aly trafiquer des restes des morts, et défendre contre les prétentions des autres Arabes le privilège de ce commerce impie" ("I saw this tribe of Awlad Ali trafficking in the remains of the dead, and defending against the claims of other Arabs the privilege of this impious trade").[93] According to his narrative, Forbin had planned to travel on as far as Abu Simbel, but the lure of adventure and the unknown evaporated when Luxor filled with a large English group just returning from Elephantine: "Lord et lady Belmor avaient visité une partie de la Nubie: ils voyageaient avec un luxe extrême; trois ou quatre grands bateaux suivaient celui qui les portait. Maris, femmes, petits enfans, aumôniers, chirurgiens, nourrices, cuisiniers, tout cela parlait d'Eléphantine" ("Lord and Lady Belmore had visited part of Nubia; they were travelling in extreme luxury; three or four large boats followed the one carrying them. Husbands, wives, little children, chaplains, doctors, nurses, cooks, all spoke of Elephantine").[94] Fleeing the disenchanting wave of other Europeans, Forbin sailed back north to Cairo and then on to Alexandria where the governor of Egypt himself, Mohammad Ali received him in audience, interrupted by an episode curious enough for inclusion in the published narrative:[95]

> Au milieu de notre conversation, et lorsqu'il me parlait de la France avec un vif intérêt, en homme bien instruit de sa situation et de ses ressources, on introduisit des Arabes, des Bédouins de la tribu d'Oulâd Aly, qui lui offrirent une jeune panthère, une gazelle blanche et une petite autruche. Mohamed Aly souriait : les Bédouins prosternés se traînaient jusqu'au bas de sa robe pour la baiser, et demeuraient dans

[91] On the demarcation in practice, see the evidence presented by Gee, "Archaeological Context of the Late Ramesside Letters," 182, 195.

[92] P. Linant de Bellefonds, "The Journey of the Comte de Forbin in the Near East and Egypt, 1817–1818," in C. Foster (ed.), *Travellers in the Near East* (London, 2004), 107–33.

[93] A. Forbin, *Voyage dans le Levant en 1817 et 1818* (Paris, 1819), 262.

[94] Forbin, *Voyage dans le Levant*, 273.

[95] Forbin, *Voyage dans le Levant*, 303.

> cette position jusqu'à ce que des chiaoux les relevassent, en les faisant sortir du divan d'une manière assez dure.
>
> (In the middle of our conversation, while he was talking to me about France with keen interest, as a man well informed of his situation and his resources, some Arabs, Bedouin of the Awlad Ali tribe, were brought in and offered him a young panther, a white gazelle, and a little ostrich. Mohammad Ali smiled: the prostrated Bedouin dragged themselves to the edge of his garment to kiss it, and remained in that position until the attendants had them stand, removing them rather roughly from the audience chamber.)

Here, Forbin uses the same name that he had given to the Qurna finders. Yet Awlad Ali is not one of the Qurnawi terms in describing themselves to Athanasi or Van der Spek, whereas it appears for people in the northwestern desert of Egypt, up to the Fayum and Nile Delta.[96] Whether error or co-incidence in the Forbin narrative, the recurrence of this name at the point of his departure may prompt us to rethink the way our histories marginalize the rural and exclude it from the global stage.

The Saharan way-stations and oases connect with one another and with the Nile Valley through a network of roads that are becoming better documented now in archaeological fieldwork, including routes entering the Nile floodplain from the mountains at the west of Thebes.[97] Van der Spek has drawn attention already to the possible link between Qurna and long-distance trade centuries ago, through supplies of *mumiya*, a resinous material from the remains of ancient embalmed bodies, to city pharmacies.[98] He cites the report from the physician Abdallatif of Baghdad, around AD 1200, on the trade at Cairo, and suggests that the material was for export to western Europe though that was perhaps amply supplied from nearer sources at Saqqara and Giza.[99] His argument seems plausible with regard to the role of *mumiya* trade in the development of a wider practice of collecting other antiquities on an industrial scale. However, at the time of Abdallatif of Baghdad, and still in the 18th century, western Europe seems a minor participant in Egyptian trade, as compared with the lucrative Arab World and farther Asian markets. As the thriving metropolis of Ayyubid and Mamluk power, Cairo seems more likely to have generated its own interest in, and market in, the resinous matter from ancient burials. Therefore, any trade from Qurna sources would more plausibly have been directed for an internal Egyptian market, even if it was known to, and interesting also to, visitors from other lands, including the small number of traders from the Latin West. It might also be doubted whether Qurna played a large part in the internal Nile Valley trade. The larger Late Period to Roman Period cemeteries at sites closer to Cairo would presumably be the primary sources. Throughout the second millennium AD, the majority of sources for mining the *mumiya* might have been the large-scale multiple burials of the Late Period, not necessarily deposited with many objects.[100] In future research, it would be interesting to pursue the question of whether western Europe contributed substantially to the volume of any aspect of Cairo trade in proportion to the vast wealth circulating in the Islamic world before the mid to late 18th century.[101] In relation to trade in the opposite direction, from the Nile Valley towards Arabia and India, it is interesting that Van der Spek further notes the suggestion from Garcin on the commerce in *mumiya* going through Qus, 40 kilometers north of Luxor, at a juncture of Upper Egypt and the Red Sea trade.[102] Inhabitants

---

96 O. Bates, *The Eastern Libyans: An Essay* (London, 1914), maps; H.-D. Müller-Mahn, *Die Aulad 'Ali zwischen Stamm und Staat: Entwicklung und sozialer Wandel bei den Beduinen im nordwestlichen Ägypten* (Berlin, 1989).

97 F. Förster and H. Riemer (eds.), *Desert Road Archaeology in Ancient Egypt and Beyond* (Cologne, 2013); J. C. Darnell and D. Darnell, *Theban Desert Road Survey in the Egyptian Western Desert*, vol. 1: *Gebel Tjauti Rock Inscriptions 1–45 and Wadi el-Hôl Rock Inscriptions*, OIP 119 (Chicago, 2002); J. Darnell, *Theban Desert Road Survey*, vol. 2: *The Rock Shrine of Pahu, Gebel Akhenaton, and other Rock Inscriptions from the Western Hinterland of Naqada* (New Haven, CT, 2013).

98 Van der Spek, *Modern Neighbors of Tutankhamun*, 102–3.

99 Van der Spek, *Modern Neighbors of Tutankhamun*, 77.

100 Compare the brief report in W. M. F. Petrie, *Gizeh and Rifeh*, BSAE/ERA 13 (London, 1907), 29: "The later burials at Gizeh yielded very little that was worth note," with about 1,400 individuals from "a large number of tombs."

101 We did not succeed in identifying any immediate leads for this research in A. Raymond, *Artisans et commerçants au Caire au XVIIIe siècle* (Damascus, 1973–1974).

102 Van der Spek, *Modern Neighbors of Tutankhamun*, 76; J.-C. Garcin, *Un centre musulman de la Haute-Egypte médiévale: Qûs* (Cairo, 1976), 12 n. 3.

of rural and desert margins may participate visibly in long-distance circuits wherever and whenever the routes or the resources themselves are located there.

From the surge in attention that first drew Forbin into Qurna and Luxor, and then rudely propelled him away, it seems that the year 1818 cemented a short phase of transition (1815–1817) between two long timespans. In the pre-1815 history of Thebes, unearthing objects seems a marginal and sporadic activity. In contrast, the post-1818 age of its modernity, colored by increased European intrusion, normalized an industrial scale of antiquities extraction, to the extent that now we cannot imagine how any past inhabitant or traveler could fail to collect. The emergence of Neferaabet into the view of those collecting and then reading monuments is part of a larger movement with a precise modern history. We can trace the names of some of those who paid for and received payment for, the transfer of his monuments from Qurna to Cairo, Alexandria, Livorno, Turin, and London. We cannot yet name any of the people who made the first move of the object from its ground. A biographical instinct propels us to find out, as a matter of justice, giving credit where it is due. However, we might equally ask why anyone should give his name to a stranger—a foreigner or an official from outside. Athanasi reported at the Giza pyramids work "an Arab, named Argian, which in the Arab language means 'naked,' a man of gigantic height, but as thin as a stock-fish."[103] In 1828–1829, a decade after our tale of Neferaabet, Champollion and Rosellini directed an epigraphic expedition, and undertook limited excavations at select sites, including in Thebes.[104] Their expedition records give names for several leaders of finders for the expedition: Timsah, Abu Sakkarah, and the "two sheikhs Awad and Mohammed, ten men each."[105] These references take us close in time to the social networks in 1810s Qurna and Karnak. Yet the doubt remains, would AH 1230s /AD 1810s Qurnawi finders want us to ask for their names? Are Timsah and Abu Sakkarah the names they used in talking to foreigners, rather than the names they used in other settings? For resolving such questions, the disciplines of archaeology and Egyptology need help again from those living near the site, and from those studying the direct documentary evidence of the period in their languages.

103 Athanasi, *A Brief Account of the Researches*, 21.

104 M. Betrò, "Ippolito Rosellini, Egypt and Egyptology," in M. Betrò (ed.), *Ippolito Rosellini and the Dawn of Egyptology. Original Drawings and Manuscripts of the Franco-Tuscan Expedition to Egypt (1828–29) from the Biblioteca Universitaria di Pisa* (Cairo, 2010), 20–21.

105 M. Betrò, "Lost and (Sometimes) Found: Contexts and Objects from the Franco-Tuscan Excavations at Thebes West (1828–1829): The case of Tamutnefret," in A.-H. Perrot, R. Pietri, and J. Tanré-Szewczyk (eds.), *L'objet égyptien: source de la recherché* (Paris, 2020), 276–77.

Keeping It in the Family: The High Priesthood of Re and the Vizierate in Fifth Dynasty Egypt

Gemma F. P. Green
Macquarie University, Sydney, Australia

Abstract

The first half of Egypt's Fifth Dynasty saw a number of administrative and ideological changes. For the first time, officials of non-royal descent were able to hold positions within the higher levels of the administration, and Re became an integral part of the dogma of divine kingship. These occurrences may have caused some concern for the king, who seems to have taken profound measures to ensure that both his administration and Re's powerful priesthood remained under his control. The titulary of two successive officials, Seshathetep [G 5150] and Kanefer [Dahshur no. 28, EA 1324 and EA 1345], demonstrate that the vizierate and the High Priesthood of Re were held by the same royal official for much of the Fifth Dynasty. The concentration of these two titles into the hands of the same individual is previously unattested and may indicate some apprehension about the dispersion of these titles amongst the non-royal administration, and perhaps the need to keep the Re cult under the king's watchful eye. Using blood ties to ensure that these officials were loyal, trustworthy and reliable may have created a much-needed sense of security for the king, who may have been unsure about the integrity of his newly appointed court.

الملخص

شهد النصف الأول من الأسرة الخامسة في مصر القديمة عددًا من التغييرات الإدارية والعقائدية. وتمكن المسؤولون لأول مرة من أصل غير ملكي من شغل مناصب إدارية عليا، وأصبح رع جزءًا لا يتجزأ من عقيدة الملكية الإلهية. ربما تسببت هذه الأحداث في بعض القلق للملك، الذي يبدو أنه اتخذ إجراءات حاسمة لضمان بقاء إدارته وكهنة رع الأقوياء تحت سيطرته. يُظهر اللقب الخاص باثنين من المسؤولين المتعاقبين، سشات-حيب [G 5150] وكا-نفر [EA 1324 وEA 1345]، أن منصب الوزير والكهنوت الأعلى للإله رع كانا تحت حكم نفس المسؤول الملكي في معظم فترة الأسرة الخامسة. إن تركيز هذين المنصبين في أيدي نفس الشخص لم يتم التحقق منه من قبل وقد يشير إلى بعض التخوف من تشتت هذه الألقاب بين الإدارة الغير ملكية، وربما الحاجة إلى إبقاء عبادة رع تحت سيطرة الملك. ومن الممكن أن استخدام الصلات العائلية للتأكد من إخلاص وولاء المسؤولين وأنهم جديرين بالثقة ويمكن الاعتماد عليهم قد خلق إحساسًا بالأمن للملك، والذي ربما كان غير متأكد من نزاهة أفراد البلاط الملكي الذي تم تعيينه حديثًا.

The Fifth Dynasty of Egypt is often regarded as a period of prosperity. During this time, royal monuments were constructed on a grand scale, elite tombs became expansive, and foreign trade relations were thriving.[1] On the

I would like to express my sincere thanks to Prof. Naguib Kanawati for his invaluable feedback during the writing of this article.

[1] Although the royal monuments constructed during the Fifth Dynasty were less grandiose than those of the Fourth Dynasty, it is evident from both physical remains and contemporary texts that large-scale construction work was still undertaken. For more on Fifth Dynasty royal monuments, see M. Lehner, *The Complete Pyramids* (New York, 1997) and M. Nuzzolo, *The Fifth Dynasty Sun Temples: Kingship, Architecture and Religion in Third Millennium BC Egypt* (Prague, 2018). For examples of monumental elite tombs dating to the Fifth Dynasty, see J. Krejci, *Abusir XI: The Architecture of the Mastaba of Ptahshepses* (Prague, 2009); E. Brovarski, *The Senedjemib Complex, Part 1*, Giza Mastabas 7 (Boston, 2000); A. Moussa and H. Altenmüller, *Des Grab des Nianchchnum and Chnum-hotep*, AVDAK 21 (Mainz am Rhein, 1977); Y. Harpur and P. Scremin, *The Chapel of Niakhkhnum and Khnumhotep: Scene Details* (Oxford, 2010). For more on Egypt's foreign relations during the Fifth Dynasty, see

Journal of the American Research Center in Egypt 58 (2022), 101–11
http://dx.doi.org/10.5913/jarce.58.2022.a005

surface, the Fifth Dynasty appears unproblematic, and with the emphasis on secrecy that surrounded the monarchy, one should not expect to find direct evidence of instability.[2] However, given that both the administration and the royal ideology underwent significant changes during this time, it seems likely that at least some uncertainty occurred. This may be reflected in the titulary of two Fifth Dynasty officials, *Sšꜣt-ḥtp/Htj* [G 5150] and *Kꜣ-nfr* [Dahshur no. 28]. These two men are the only Fifth Dynasty officials to concurrently hold the titles *tꜣjtj sꜣb ṯꜣtj,* He of the Curtain, Chief Justice and Vizier,[3] and *wr-mꜣ,* Greatest of Seers,[4] the latter of which is usually considered to be the office of the High Priest of Re.[5] It is notable that these two powerful titles were concentrated into the hands of a *sꜣ nswt,* King's Son,[6] when major changes were occurring in the Egyptian state, as it may indicate some apprehension about the dispersion of these titles amongst the non-royal administration. Awarding these posts to members of the royal family presumably created a much-needed sense of security for the king by using blood ties to ensure that these officials were loyal, trustworthy and reliable.

Before the historical contexts of *Sšꜣt-ḥtp/Htj* and *Kꜣ-nfr* can be discussed, the relative date of each official should be established. The tomb of *Sšꜣt-ḥtp/Htj* is usually assigned to the end Fourth-early Fifth Dynasty, due to the location and decoration of his tomb.[7] According to Junker, the position of *Sšꜣt-ḥtp/Htj*'s mastaba indicates a date after the reign of Menkaure,[8] while Harpur suggested that the representation of the Journey to the West on the east wall of the tomb was a "Giza innovation" which dates to the end of the Fourth and beginning of the Fifth Dynasty.[9] Additionally, Baer noticed that the order of *Sšꜣt-ḥtp/Htj*'s title sequences violated the standardised systems used from the reign of Neferirkare onwards,[10] and Kanawati connected *Sšꜣt-ḥtp/Htj* with the *Htj* depicted on Sahure's funerary temple.[11] This date around the reign of Sahure seems to agree with the presence of the *sꜣ nswt n ẖt.f* title found in *Sšꜣt-ḥtp/Htj*'s tomb, indicating that he began his career before royal "sons" were phased out of the administration around the reign of Neferirkare.[12]

In contrast, Cherpion and Baud both suggest a date around the reigns of Khufu or Khafre by referencing Cherpion's dating system in which the latest cartouche found on the walls of a tomb is taken as its provisional

---

G. Mumford, "Tell Ras Budren (Site 345): Defining Egypt's Eastern Frontier and Mining Operations in South Sinai during the Late Old Kingdom (Early EB IV/MB I)," *BASOR* 342 (2006), 52–55 for Egypt's trade relations with the Levant.

[2] There is an unusual occurrence in the biography of the Sixth Dynasty vizier *Wnj* who recalls that he was allowed to hear a secret legal case against one of Pepy I's wives. However, texts that explicitly detail such sensitive matter are currently not attested for the Fifth Dynasty. See K. Sethe, *Urkunden I* (Leipzig, 1933), 98–110 for the biography of *Wnj.*

[3] D. Jones, *An Index of Ancient Egyptian Titles, Epithets and Phrases of the Old Kingdom* (Oxford, 2000), 1000–1001 [3706].

[4] Jones, *Ancient Egyptian Titles,* 386–87 [1428].

[5] For alternative views about this title, see W. Helck, *Untersuchungen zu den Beamtentiteln des ägyptischen alten Reiches,* ÄgF 18 (Glückstadt, 1954), 91–98 and R. Shalomi-Hen, "The Dawn of Osiris and the Dusk of the Sun Temples: Religious History at the end of the Fifth Dynasty," *Towards a New History of the Egyptian Old Kingdom: Perspectives on the Pyramid Age* (Leiden, 2015), 463–64 about this title's connection with the organisation of labour; see also S. Voß, "Untersuchungen zu den Sonnenheiligtümern der 5. Dynastie. Bedeutung und Funktion eines singulären Tempeltyps im Alten Reich" (PhD disseratation, University of Hamburg, 2004), 168–69 for the suggestion that the *wr-mꜣ* post was related to Atum until the beginning of the Sixth Dynasty, when it became the High Priesthood of Re title.

[6] Jones, *Ancient Egyptian Titles,* 799 [2911].

[7] Y. Harpur, *Decoration in Egyptian Tombs of the Old Kingdom: Studies in Orientation and Scene Content* (London-New York, 1987), 74 and 83; N. Kanawati, *Tombs at Giza, Vol II: Seshathetep/Heti [G 5150], Nesutnefer [G 4970] and Seshemnefer II [G 5080]* ACE Reports 18 (Warminster, 2002), 17–18; J. Swinton, *Dating the Tombs of the Egyptian Old Kingdom* (Oxford, 2014), 37 [88]; M. Nuzzolo, "Patterns of Tomb Placement in the Memphite Necropolis: Fifth Dynasty Saqqara in context," *Abusir and Saqqara in the Year 2015* (Prague, 2018), 275.

[8] H. Junker, *Giza II: Die Mastabas der Beginnenden der V. Dynastie auf dem Westfriedhof* (Vienna-Leipzig, 1934), 173–74.

[9] Harpur, *Decoration in Egyptian Tombs,* 83.

[10] K. Baer, *Rank and Title in the Old Kingdom: The Structure of the Egyptian Administration in the Fifth and Sixth Dynasties* (Chicago, 1960), 130–31 and 293 [473].

[11] Kanawati, *Tombs at Giza II,* 17–18.

[12] For discussions on the administrative elimination of royal family members and the appointment of non-royal officials to high positions for the first time, see B. Schmitz, *Untersuchungen zum Titel Sꜣ-NJSWT "Königssohn"* (Bonn, 1976), 165–69 and N. Strudwick, *The Administration of Egypt in the Old Kingdom: the Highest Titles and their Holders* (London, 1985), 312–13.

date and is then used to date other tombs with a similar decorative program.[13] As there are no royal names present in the tomb of *Sš3t-ḥtp/Ḥtj*, Cherpion's date for this tomb has evidently derived from a comparison with other tombs. Given that personal names and titles often incorporated royal cartouches from earlier periods, this dating method can be problematic, as it may attribute an unnecessarily early date to the tomb.

For example, it is highly likely that the tomb of *Sšm-nfr III* [G 5170] dates to the reign of Djedkare,[14] yet implementing Cherpion's dating method produces a date in the reign of Neferirkare, as this is the latest cartouche found on its walls.[15] This date is almost certainly too early, especially considering that the tomb of *Sšm-nfr III*'s father, *Sšm-nfr II* [G 5080], is usually dated to the reign of Niuserre.[16] Likewise, it appears that the Khufu date that Cherpion assigned to the tomb of *Sš3t-ḥtp/Ḥtj* is also too early, as the tomb's location, decoration and titulary as described above strongly indicates that it should be dated to the first part of the Fifth Dynasty. If Kanawati is correct in suggesting that *Sš3t-ḥtp/Ḥtj* was the same individual as the *Ḥtj* represented on Sahure's funerary temple, which seems likely given the rarity of this name and the probable date of both men, perhaps the tomb of *Sš3t-ḥtp/Ḥtj* should be dated more specifically to the reign of Sahure.[17]

Unlike *Sš3t-ḥtp/Ḥtj,* there is no general consensus about the date of *K3-nfr*'s tomb and administrative career, which largely stems from disagreements about the meaning of his *s3 Snfrw* inscription.[18] Schmitz suggested that *K3-nfr* should be dated to the late Old Kingdom and that he usurped the vizierate and *s3 Snfrw* title because of his connections to the cult of the dead king Sneferu,[19] but this hypothesis has been widely rejected. Reisner, Baer, Kanawati, and Baud, among others, viewed *K3-nfr*'s *s3 Snfrw* inscription as confirmation that he was a biological son of Sneferu and thus dated his tomb between the reigns of Sneferu and Radjedef.[20]

However, it appears that a date in the Fourth Dynasty is not consistent with the stylistic features of *K3-nfr*'s false door. Fischer suggested that the type of wig that adorns the large male figures was characteristic of the late Fifth Dynasty,[21] while Strudwick identified that the wide jambs, large figures of the deceased, and numerous columns of text found on the false door were typical of the mid-Fifth Dynasty.[22] Similarly, Helck observed that the presence of a man named *Ptḥ-špsj* on the false door indicated a date after the end of the Fourth Dynasty, as names formed with *Ptḥ* are found more frequently from the beginning of the Fifth Dynasty onwards.[23] The Old Kingdom tomb dating criteria established by Swinton has also been implemented, which more specifically proposed that *K3-nfr*'s stela may date to the reign of Niuserre.[24] Swinton's criteria has also been applied to the

---

[13] Cherpion suggests that *Sš3t-ḥtp* should be dated to the reign of Khufu, while Baud argues for a date during the reign of Khafre but considers that *Sš3t-ḥtp* may also have begun his tomb during the reigns of Khufu or Radjedef. N. Cherpion, *Mastabas et hypogées d'Ancien Empire: le problème de la datation* (Brussels, 1989), 225; M. Baud, *Famille royale et pouvoir sous l'ancien empire égyptien,* BdÉ 126 (Cairo, 1999), 576–77 [219].

[14] Baer, *Rank and Title,* 292 [297]; Reisner, *Giza Necropolis I,* 251; Harpur, *Decoration in Egyptian Tombs,* 270 [234]; Swinton, *Dating the Tombs,* 38 [92].

[15] Cherpion, *Mastabas et hypogées,* 227; E. Brunner-Traut, *Die altägyptische Grabkammer Seschemnofers III. aus Giza* (Mainz, 1982), supplement 2.

[16] Baer, *Rank and Title,* 132 [477]; Strudwick, *The Administration of Egypt,* 139 [130]; Harpur, *Decoration in Egyptian Tombs,* 270 [233]; Kanawati, *Tombs at Giza II,* 53; Swinton, *Dating the Tombs,* 38 [91].

[17] Kanawati, *Tombs at Giza II,* 17.

[18] J. de Morgan, *Fouilles à Dahchour II: 1894-1895* (Vienna, 1903), pl. 26; T. G. H. James, *Hieroglyphic Texts from Egyptian Stele, etc. Part 9* (London, 1961), pl. 10 [1].

[19] Schmitz, *Königssohn,* 145–49.

[20] G. Reisner, *Mycerinus: The Temples of the Third Pyramid at Giza* (Cambridge, 1931), 240; Junker, *Giza II,* 36; Helck, *Beamtentiteln,* 95 and 134; Baer, *Rank and Title,* 145 and 294 [534]; N. Kanawati, *The Egyptian Administration in the Old Kingdom: Evidence on its Economic Decline* (Warminster 1977), 11 and 123–24 [349]; Cherpion, *Mastabas et hypogées,* 106–08; Baud, *Famille royale,* 83–92.

[21] H. Fischer, "A Scribe of the Army in a Saqqara Mastaba of the Early Fifth Dynasty," *JNES* 18 (1959), 238–39.

[22] Strudwick, *The Administration of Egypt,* 152–53 [148].

[23] W. Helck, *Geschichte des alten Ägypten,* HdO 1 (Leiden-Köhn, 1981), 59–60. It may be worth noting that Harpur places *K3-nfr* in the reign of Sneferu but also recognises that his wig was dated by Fischer to the later Fifth Dynasty. Harpur, *Decoration in Egyptian Tombs,* 248; Fischer, *A Scribe of the Army,* 238–39.

[24] The criteria used here were criterion 10 (the broad collar down to the armpit, V.6–VI.E-M), criterion 14 (the animal skin with rear paws hanging down and worn over a kilt, IV.1–2–V.6) and criterion 21 (a belt is depicted over the animal skin, V.2–3-VI.2L-4E), which all intersected at the reign of Niuserre. See Swinton, *Dating the Tombs,* 55–59 and 81–83 for an outline and examples.

stela of *K3-nfr*'s wife, *Sw.n-sw*,[25] and has indicated that *Sw.n-sw*'s monument is probably not later than the reign of Djedkare.[26]

Although *K3-nfr* claimed that he was the son of Sneferu, the likelihood that his false door dates to the middle of the Fifth Dynasty may imply that this designation should not be taken literally. Rather, it may have conveyed his direct descendancy from this king. This seems plausible when one considers that *s3 nswt* titles were not just reserved for sons of the king but were also held by officials of royal dẹscent until the reign of Neferirkare. Although there were a limited number of non-royal officials who enjoyed the honorific *s3 nswt* title during the reigns of Niuserre and Djedkare,[27] it is unlikely that *K3-nfr* belonged to this group. There is no evidence for, nor clear purpose why, either of these kings would bestow an honorary *s3 Snfrw* title upon one of their own officials. As *K3-nfr* also held the title *s3 nswt n ẖt.f*, it seems that he probably began his career before royal sons were phased out of the administration in the early Fifth Dynasty.[28]

If *K3-nfr* began his bureaucratic career between the end of the Fourth Dynasty and the beginning of the Fifth Dynasty, his apparent mid Fifth Dynasty false door could indicate that he did not decorate his tomb until he felt that he had reached (or was about to reach) the apex of his long career.[29] This seems reasonable considering that there are numerous instances of delayed tomb construction and decoration from the Old Kingdom period. For example, an inscription in the early Fifth Dynasty tomb of the *s3 nswt n ẖt.f Sḫm-k3-Rꜥ* [G 8154] records that he was *jm3ḫw ḫr* Khafre, Menkaure, Shepseskaf, Userkaf and Sahure.[30] The presence of these successive royal names is a clear indication that while the tomb may have been constructed or at least planned during the reign of Khafre, the tomb's decoration could not have commenced much earlier than the reign of Sahure.

Another possibility is that *K3-nfr* died unexpectedly, and his tomb was posthumously decorated.[31] A dedicatory offering slab made by a son called *K3-nfr* was found at the foot of the false door,[32] which may indicate that the younger *K3-nfr* decorated the false door for his deceased father. On the other hand, as the main figures depicted on the false door are not the elder *K3-nfr* but his eldest son *K3-wꜥb*,[33] perhaps it was posthumously decorated by this son. If *K3-nfr* did not decorate his own false door, it may explain why its decoration is largely characteristic of the mid-late Fifth Dynasty and the unusual circumstance of a *s3 nswt* around the reign of Niuserre. The elder *K3-nfr* may have lived and died prior to the Niuserre period, but an untimely death meant that his false door was not decorated until this time. Although much of the detail remains uncertain, the evidence seems to suggest that the stela of *K3-nfr* should be dated to the middle of the Fifth Dynasty or slightly later, despite the likelihood that his career began much earlier.

Towards the end of the Fourth Dynasty and at the beginning of the Fifth Dynasty, officials outside of the immediate royal family began to hold positions within the higher levels of the administration for the first time.[34] Until this point, only officials described as *s3 nswt* or one of its variants were able to hold senior administrative

---

25 de Morgan, *Dahchour II,* 23 and fig. 53.

26 The criteria used here were criterion 1 (the single or double lines defining the "apron" of the flared kilt meet the hem of the kilt between the wearer's legs, IV.2–4–V.6L-8E), criterion 51 (priestly gesture: standing man holding a censer, IV.4–VI.4E-M) and criterion 71 (the choker is worn with the beaded collar by a female, IV.4–6–V.8). See Swinton, *Dating the Tombs,* 54–55, 67, 71–72, 80, 88, and 90 for an outline and examples.

27 Schmitz, *Königssohn,* 29–31. Only two viziers were granted *s3 nswt* titles during the mid-Fifth Dynasty, despite the likelihood that neither were blood relatives of the royal family: *Ptḥ-špss* of Abusir and *Sšm-nfr III* [G 5170]. The former was married to a daughter of Niuserre, while the latter received the *s3 nswt n ẖt.f* title with his promotion to the vizierate; both were evidently held in high favor by this king. See Strudwick, *The Administration of Egypt,* 308 [table 29] and 312–13.

28 Strudwick, *The Administration of Egypt,* 312–13.

29 Strudwick, *The Administration of Egypt,* 7–8.

30 S. Hassan, *Excavations at Giza 4: 1932–1933* (Cairo, 1943), fig. 64. Delayed tomb construction during the Sixth Dynasty may be exemplified by the officials *K3-gm-n.j* and *Ḥsj*. Both of these men were buried in the pyramid cemetery of Teti and attained the vizierate under this king, yet their biographies recounted their careers under Djedkare and Unis. See E. Edel, "Inschriften des Alten Reiches II: Die Biographie des *K3j-gmjnj*," *MIO* 1 (1953), 210–26 for the biography of *K3-gm-n.j* and N. Kanawati and M. Abder-Raziq, *The Teti Cemetery at Saqqara, vol. 5: the Tomb of Hesi*, ACER 13 (Warminster, 1999), 22–23 and pls. 7–8 for the biography of *Ḥsj*.

31 Kanawati, *The Egyptian Administration,* 11.

32 de Morgan, *Dahchour II,* 23, fig. 54 and pl. 26.

33 James, *Hieroglyphic Texts,* pl. 10 [1].

34 Schmitz, *Königssohn,* 165–67.

offices.[35] Schmitz suggested that true king's sons were removed from the administration at the end of the Fourth Dynasty and were replaced by "titular princes": officials who held *s3 nswt* titles but were not of royal blood.[36] Strudwick refuted the suggestion that royal officials were removed from the administration, and instead reasonably argued that it was more logical for true *s3 nswts* "to act out the remainder of their careers, but to appoint no further such officials."[37] According to both Schmitz and Strudwick, *Sš3t-ḥtp/Htj* was a "titular prince" and was not a true member of the royal family.[38]

However, there is compelling evidence to suggest that the so-called "titular princes" that Schmitz identified were indeed members of the royal family. For instance, the official *Ḥm-jwnw* [G 4000] held the title *s3 nswt n ẖt.f*, King's Son of his Body, even though the indirect evidence suggests that he was the son of *Nfr-m3ʿt* [Meidum no. 16],[39] who was probably the son of Sneferu. Likewise, another official named *Nfr-m3ʿt* [G 7060] is described as *s3 nswt n ẖt.f*, despite being the son of *Nfrt-k3w*, who was a daughter of Sneferu.[40] If these suggestions are correct, it is doubtful that *Ḥm-jwnw* and *Nfr-m3ʿt* of Giza were true king's sons;[41] rather, they were the king's grandsons, and thus direct royal descendants.

It is difficult to find an example from the Fourth Dynasty or the early Fifth Dynasty where an official with a *s3 nswt* title was unquestionably non-royal. This may indicate that *s3 nswt* titles were not solely held by sons of the king but could also be used to denote direct descendancy more generally. In the cases of *Ḥm-jwnw* [G 4000] and *Nfr-m3ʿt* [G 7060], it is only from indirect evidence that we know the parentage of these officials; otherwise, it would probably be assumed that they were true royal sons. Essentially, the evidence suggests that "titular princes," defined as non-royal officials who held the *s3 nswt* title during the Fourth and early Fifth dynasties, are not attested. Rather, it seems that this title was used as a more general designation to mean "descendant of the king." Given that both *Sš3t-ḥtp/Htj* and *K3-nfr* held *s3 nswt* titles and probably began their careers at a time when the administration comprised of royal family members, these men should be regarded as legitimate members of the royal family.

The allocation of the vizierate and the High Priesthood of Re to a single royal official during the early-mid Fifth Dynasty seems to have been a deliberate arrangement. A similar situation may be observed during the reign of Teti in the early Sixth Dynasty, when the vizierate and the High Priesthood of Re were held presumably in succession by Teti's sons-in-law, *K3-gm-n.j* and *Mrr.w-k3.j*.[42] Kanawati suggested that this policy was implemented in order to limit the independence of the Re cult and bring them under the direct control of the king.[43] In the case of the Sixth Dynasty, this may have been the result of a conflict with the Re cult, and as a consequence, a need to keep them under the watchful eye of the king.

This surveillance of the Re priesthood seems to have been essential for most of the Fifth Dynasty as well, perhaps due to their mounting significance over the course of the Fourth Dynasty. A study of the titles of *Rʿ-ḥtp*

---

[35] These variants include *s3 nswt smsw*, *s3 nswt n ẖt.f*, and *s3 nswt n ẖt.f smsw*.

[36] Schmitz, *Königssohn*, 168.

[37] Strudwick, *The Administration of Egypt*, 313.

[38] This was largely based on the argument that *Sš3t-ḥtp/Htj*'s approximate contemporaries *Dw3-n-Rʿ* [G 5110] and *B3-b3f* [G 5230] were not true members of the royal family, but the evidence for this suggestion remains circumstantial. In the case of *B3-b3f*, perhaps the clearest indication that he was directly related to the king is the use of the epithet *n jt.f*, "of his father," following his *smr wʿtj* title. This phrase is often used to argue for a genuine father/son relationship between a king and an official, which may also be true of *B3-b3f*. The presence of this epithet also seems to quash the suggestion that *Dw3-n-Rʿ* was *B3-b3f*'s father. Schmitz, *Königssohn*, 73–75; Strudwick, *The Administration of Egypt*, 312–13. See also H. Junker, *Gîza VII: Der Ostabschnitt des* Westfriedhofs (Vienna-Lepzig, 1944), 151–57 for the tomb and statues of *B3-b3f*.

[39] Y. Harpur, *The Tombs of Nefermaat and Rahotep at Meidum: Discovery, Destruction and Reconstruction* (Cheltonham, 2001), 31–33.

[40] G. Reisner, "Nefertkauw, the eldest daughter of Sneferuw," *ZÄS* 64 (1929), pl. 3; Strudwick, *The Administration of Egypt*, 110.

[41] According to Strudwick, there is no evidence to indicate that *Nfr-m3ʿt*'s father/*Nfrt-k3w*'s husband acquired the throne, as *Nfrt-k3w*'s children would have held titles with the epithet *n jt.f* "of his father" if she was married to Khufu, like Reisner suggested. This also appears to be true of *Ḥm-jwnw*'s mother/*Nfr-m3ʿt*'s wife, as *n it.f* is also unattested in *Ḥm-jwnw*'s titles. Strudwick, *The Administration of Egypt*, 110; Reisner, *Nefertkauw*, 98–99.

[42] C. Firth and B. Gunn, *Teti Pyramid Cemeteries, vol. 1*, ExSaq 7.1 (Cairo, 1926), 107 and 135, respectively.

[43] Kanawati, *Mereruka and King Teti*, 22.

(early Fourth Dynasty)[44] and *Mrj-jb* (late Fourth Dynasty),[45] two known *wr-m3* of the Fourth Dynasty,[46] reveals that the holder of this post had gained noticeably more authority between the beginning and the end of this period.[47] This heightened authority seems to agree with the emphasis on Re that had progressively increased during this time and which peaked at the beginning of the Fifth Dynasty. Given that Re was promoted to an unprecedented importance rather suddenly, these roles may have been entrusted to the same official to ensure that the king had direct control over the Re priesthood and their newfound significance. This direct control was apparently complemented by the appointment of a royal family member to these positions, whose bloodline may have represented a theoretical guarantee of their loyalty.

Sš3t-ḥtp/Htj's status as a member of the royal family may have been a key factor in his acquisition of the vizierate and the High Priesthood of Re, particularly if he was one of the last remaining royal officials amongst the newly appointed non-royal administration. Barta suggested that the conferral of important posts on non-royal officials may have occurred due to the growing complexity of the administration, which by this time required a greater workforce.[48] Alternatively, Schmitz posited that this may have reflected a change in the nature of the kingship.[49] Whatever the reason may have been, this policy of appointing non-royal officials was likely to have had a significant impact on the administration, as it probably caused the king to become more cautious about his court personnel. This may be corroborated by the appearance of the *ḫntj-š* title, translated here as "guard" based on *Wnj*'s description of this role in his Sixth Dynasty biography,[50] which is first attested during the reign of Sahure.[51]

Meanwhile, the elevation of Re to religious supremacy at the beginning of the Fifth Dynasty was likely to have caused the king to rely on both Re and his priesthood for support. If this suggestion is correct, the importance of the Re priesthood would certainly have increased. These factors seem to have concerned the king, which may have compelled him to award the vizierate and the High Priesthood of Re to *Sš3t-ḥtp/Htj* in order to limit the independence of the Re cult and bring them under his direct control. In all likelihood, *Sš3t-ḥtp/Htj* was a legitimate member of the royal family who seems to have been entrusted with both the vizierate and the High Priesthood of Re because of this association; perhaps in the king's eyes, this presumably guaranteed his loyalty and co-operation.

Likewise, there may be evidence that *K3-nfr*'s royal bloodline contributed to his appointment to these two posts. It was concluded above that the false door of *K3-nfr* may date to the reign of Niuserre or thereabouts. The

---

[44] *Rꜥ-ḥtp*'s tomb is generally considered to have been constructed and decorated under Sneferu, although he may have lived into the reign of Khufu. Baer, *Rank and Title,* 100 [307]; M. Moursi, *Die Hohenpriester des Sonnengottes von der Frühzeit Ägyptens bis zum Ende des Neuen Reichesm,* MÄS 26 (Munich, 1972), 16–17; Harpur, *Decoration in Egyptian Tombs*, 279 [620]; Baud, *Famille royale,* 512 [143]; Harpur, *Nefermaat and Rahotep,* 29; Swinton, *Dating the Tombs,* 32 [66].

[45] Scholarship usually favours a date between the late Fourth Dynasty and the beginning of the Fifth Dynasty for *Mrj-jb,* although Cherpion and Baud prefer to place him in the mid-Fourth Dynasty. Junker, *Giza II,* 122–24; Baer, *Rank and Title,* 79 [182]; Moursi, *Die Hohenpriester des Sonnengottes,* 20–22; Kanawati, *The Egyptian Administration,* 95–96 [122]; K-H. Priese, *Die Opferkammer des Merib* (Berlin, 1984), 28; Strudwick, *The Administration of Egypt,* 94 [59]; Harpur, *Decoration in Egyptian Tombs,* 74–75; Cherpion, *Mastabas et hypogées,* 224; Baud, *Famille royale,* 35–40; Swinton, *Dating the Tombs,* 23–24 [34].

[46] The only other attested holder of the *wr-m3* title during the Fourth Dynasty was *K3-mnj,* who is only known from the false door of his mother *Wnšt* [G 4840]. No additional titles are inscribed for him, although he doubtless would have held others. See H. Junker, *Giza I: Die Maṣṭabas der IV. Dynastie auf dem Westfriedhof* (Vienna-Leipzig, 1929), pl. 63 for the false door of *Wnšt.*

[47] Although *Rꜥ-ḥtp* and *Mrj-jb* held many of the same civil titles, *Mrj-jb* was able to acquire more religious responsibilities, both in number and significance, and held more prestigious honorific titles than his early Fourth Dynasty counterpart. See Table 1, below, for more.

[48] M. Barta, *Analysing Collapse: The Rise and Fall of the Old Kingdom* (Cairo-New York, 2019), 102.

[49] Schmitz, *Königssohn,* 166.

[50] According to *Wnj,* "His majesty promoted me to be sole companion and overseer of the *ḫntj-š*… I acted in accordance with what his majesty favoured when doing guard duty, preparing his way and standing in attendance." The description of "doing guard duty, preparing his way and standing in attendance" caused N. Kanawati, *Conspiracies in the Egyptian Palace: Unis to Pepy I* (London, 2003), 14–24 to suggest that the *ḫntj-š* were essentially bodyguards of the king. See N. Strudwick, *Texts from the Pyramid Age,* WAW16 (Atlanta, 2005), 353 for this translation of *Wnj*'s biography. For alternative translations of the *ḫntj-š* title, see H. Fischer, *Dendera in the Third Millennium BC, down to the Theban domination of Upper Egypt* (Locust Valley, NY, 1968), 170–71 for "land tenant"; P. Posener-Kriéger, *Les archives du temple funéraire de Néferirkarê-Kakaï (Les papyrus d'Abousir): traduction et commentaire II Traduction et Commentaire* BdÉ 65.2 (Cairo, 1976), 577–81 for "employé"; A. Roth, *A Cemetery of Palace Attendants,* Giza Mastabas 6 (Boston, 1995), 40–43 for "palace attendant."

[51] L. Borchardt, *Das Grabdenkmal des Königs Sahu-re II* (Lepizig, 1913), pl. 17; Roth, *Palace Attendants,* 40.

evidence suggests that there were some royal concerns about the administration during this period, as Niuserre married three of his daughters to some of his top officials to presumably guarantee their loyalty.[52] This was a rare occurrence at this time, as only two prior examples of a marriage between a royal daughter and a non-royal official are attested.[53] This seems to indicate that Niuserre was uncertain about the loyalty of his court, and sought to secure trust through political marriages. Although the reasons for this uncertainty largely elude us, the apparent wariness of the king about his officials could have contributed to *Kȝ-nfr*'s acquisition of both the vizierate and the High Priesthood of Re. If the king was unsure about the support of his officials, assigning these posts to a trusted member of the royal family probably provided assurance that this individual would act accordingly.

There may also have been an ongoing power struggle with the Re priesthood during this time. As Re himself had become fully ingrained into the dogma of divine kingship, the Re cult must have grown quite powerful, and thus the two had become inextricably linked.[54] With such an overwhelming dependency on Re, it seems plausible, and indeed likely, that this conflict continued throughout the Fifth Dynasty and plagued much of this period with uncertainty.[55] Barta even suggested that there was a rivalry between the sun temples and the Heliopolitan temple of Re.[56] These sources of conflict had evidently not been reconciled by the time that *Kȝ-nfr* held office, as the policy of appointing the same official to the vizierate and the High Priesthood of Re that was enforced in the early Fifth Dynasty was still in place during the mid-Fifth Dynasty. This may suggest that there was a continuing need for the king to keep a close eye on the Re cult, which was able to be enforced through *Kȝ-nfr*. It has already been recognised that it was unusual for a member of the royal family to be active in the administration in the mid-Fifth Dynasty, but it may be the case that *Kȝ-nfr* was appointed at the beginning of the Fifth Dynasty or at the end of the Fourth Dynasty and simply lived to an old age.[57] *Kȝ-nfr*'s longevity may have been advantageous to the king, as his royal ascendancy and perhaps his administrative experience was able to provide the king with reassurance of his loyalty to the crown.

Many of these issues were apparently resolved during the late Fifth Dynasty, as the next known *wr-mȝ*, *Ḥtp-ḥr-n-Ptḥ*, did not hold the vizierate or a *sȝ nswt* title. This seems to suggest that there was no longer a need for the Re priesthood to be under the direct control of the king, and that a peace may have been reached between the two parties.[58] However, if the dating of *Ḥtp-ḥr-n-Ptḥ* to the late Fifth Dynasty is correct,[59] his tenure of the *wr-mȝ* office may have coincided with the apparent demotion of Re as the supreme god. This may be evidenced by the removal of the Re element in the throne name of Menkauhor,[60] the cessation of sun temple construction during the reign of Djedkare, and the first equation of the king with Osiris during the reign of Unis.[61] As kings no longer relied on Re alone, his priesthood probably lost much of its influence during this time, which may also explain the reduction in *Ḥtp-ḥr-n-Ptḥ*'s status and responsibilities.[62]

---

[52] Barta, *Analysing Collapse*, 145–48.

[53] M. Barta and V. Dulikova, "Divine and Terrestrial: Power Rhetorics in Ancient Egypt (case of Nyuserra)," in F. Coppens, J. Janák, and H. Vymazalová (eds.), *7th Symposium on Egyptian Royal Ideology: Royal versus Divine Authority* (Weisbaden, 2015), 37–38.

[54] N. Kanawati and J. Swinton, *Egypt in the Sixth Dynasty: Challenges and Responses* (Wallesy, 2018), 1–2.

[55] See N. Kanawati, *Mereruka and King Teti: the power behind the throne* (Cairo, 2007), 17–19 for a succinct overview of the evidence.

[56] Barta, *Analysing Collapse*, 115–16.

[57] On *Kȝ-nfr*'s false door, the two large figures of *sȝ.f smsw Kȝ-wʿb*, "his Eldest Son, *Kȝ-wʿb*" are accompanied by two smaller figures, one who is identified as *sȝ.f jmj-r ḥm-kȝ Kȝ-nfr*, "his son, Overseer of *kȝ* Priests, *Kȝ-nfr*'. This *Kȝ-nfr* was presumably the son of *Kȝ-wʿb*, and thus a grandson of the elder *Kȝ-nfr*. If the elder *Kȝ-nfr* lived to see his grandson enjoy an administrative career, which seems likely given that the younger *Kȝ-nfr* was described as an Overseer of *kȝ* Priests, it seems to support the idea that he may have enjoyed a long career and died at a reasonably old age. See James, *Hieroglyphic Texts*, pl. 10 for the false door of *Kȝ-nfr*.

[58] If this suggestion is correct, it seems that this was only temporary, as the vizierate and the High Priesthood of Re were once again held by the same official during the early part of the Sixth Dynasty. See Kanawati, *Mereruka and King Teti*, 22.

[59] See N. Kloth, "Die Inschrift des Htp-hr-n(j)-Pth aus dem Alten Reich: Eine phraseologische Betrachtung," *Es werde niedergelegt als Schriftstuck: Festschrift fur Hartwig Altenmuller zum 65. Geburtstag* (Hamburg, 2003), 225–30 for the dating of *Ḥtp-ḥr-n-Ptḥ* to the late Fifth Dynasty.

[60] H. Gauthier, *Le Livre des Rois d'Égypte I, Des origines à la fin de la XIIe dynastie*, MIFAO 17 (Cairo, 1907), 130–32. Although Djedkare used the Re element in his throne name, it is interesting that there are also instances where his throne name is recorded as *Ḏd-kȝ-Ḥr*, (Djedkahor). Gauthier, *Le Livre des Rois I*, 133–38.

[61] See A. Piankoff, *The Pyramid of Unas* (Princeton, 1968) for the Pyramid Texts of Unis, where this king is called "Osiris Unis" in the burial chamber.

[62] Unlike his Fifth Dynasty predecessors, *Ḥtp-ḥr-n-Ptḥ* did not hold the vizierate or the highest rank-title of *jrj-pʿt*, Hereditary Prince.

Although the kings of the Fifth Dynasty projected an image of stability and prosperity, the evidence seems to suggest that this period experienced unique trials and tribulations. The appointment of non-royal officials to the top administrative positions for the first time was sure to have created some anxiety in the monarchy, which may have caused *Sš3t-ḥtp/Htj*'s concurrent tenure of the vizierate and the High Priesthood of Re in the early Fifth Dynasty. The concentration of these two titles into the hands of one royal official may indicate that the *wr-m3* office needed to be kept under the close eye of the king; this was easily accomplished when the *wr-m3* holder was also a vizier and reported directly to him. If this suggestion is correct, it may also imply that the king was already wary about the potential power of the Re cult and consequently saw that its highest office was entrusted to a member of the royal family. This concern does not appear to have been quashed by the mid-Fifth Dynasty during the time of *K3-nfr,* as he was also able to enjoy these two positions concurrently, and presumably as a result of his royal descendancy.

The support of his officials was crucial for the king, particularly at a time when the Egyptian administration was evolving into a mostly non-royal system. "Keeping it in the family" seems to have been a viable option to ensure that the most important posts were held by trustworthy officials and that the king was fully supported by these men. Assigning the vizierate and the High Priesthood of Re to a single blood relative probably provided the king with the reassurance that both the newly appointed non-royal administration and the Re cult was under his control—regardless of whether this was truly the case.

Table 1. Titles of the *wr-m3* during the Fourth and Fifth Dynasties

	Fourth Dynasty[63]		**Fifth Dynasty**		
	Rʿ-ḥtp	*Mrj-jb*	*Sš3t.Htp/Htj*	*K3-nfr*	*Ḥtp-ḥr-n-Ptḥ*
jwn knmwt				x	x
jmj-js titles				x	x
jmj-r jswt	x				x
jmj-r ʿḥ-nṯr Šmʿw				x	
jmj-r pḥ nb					x
jmj-r mstṯ(jw)	x				
jmj-r mšʿ	x	x			
jmj-r ḥmwt nbt					x
jmj-r of a king's pyramid				x1	
jmj-r k3t nbt nt nswt		x	x		x
jrj pʿt			x	x	
ʿ3 dw3w			x		x

Interestingly, *Ḥtp-ḥr-n-Ptḥ*'s titles were mainly concerned with the organisation of labour, much like his Fourth Dynasty *wr-m3* predecessors, *Rʿ-ḥtp* and *Mrj-jb.* For the titles of *Ḥtp-ḥr-n-Ptḥ*, see P. Newberry, "An Unpublished Monument of a "Priest of the Double Axe" named Hetepheren-ptah," *ASAE* 28 (1928), 138–40.

[63] The other known holder of the *wr-m3* title during the Fourth Dynasty named *K3-mnj* is not included here, as he is only attested with this single title on the false door of his mother *Wnšt* [G 4840].

	Fourth Dynasty		Fifth Dynasty		
	Rʿ-ḥtp	*Mrj-jb*	*Sšꜣt.Ḥtp/Ḥtj*	*Kꜣ-nfr*	*Ḥtp-ḥr-n-Ptḥ*
ʿḏ-mr wḥʿw	x	x			
ʿḏ-mr Ḥʿp (?)	x				
ʿḏ-mr dp					x
wʿ (m) wrw ḥb	x		x	x	
wʿ (m) wr šptjw	x				x
wn r			x		
wr npt	x			x	
wr 10 Šmʿ	x	x	x		x
wr 5 pr-ḏḥwtj				x	
wtj Jnpw		x	x		
wḏ(t)-mdw titles			x1	x1	
mnjw nḫn				x	
mdw rḫjt				x	
mḏḥ ꜣms	x				
mḏḥ Jnpw (ḫntj tꜣ-ḏsr)					x
mḏḥ bjtj					x
mḏḥ pr					x
mḏḥ nwd					x
mḏḥ nḫn					x
mḏḥ šn-tꜣ					x
r p nb		x		x	
rḫ nswt		x	x		
ḥꜣtj-ʿ				x	
ḥꜣtj-ʿ n jt.f				x	
ḥm titles				x2	
ḥm-nṯr titles		x1	x5	x7	x1
ḥrj-wḏb m ḥwt-ʿnḫ					x
ḥrj-sštꜣ titles			x1	x2	x1
ḥrj-tp nḫb				x	
ḥkꜣ nswt					x

	Fourth Dynasty		**Fifth Dynasty**		
	Rꜥ-ḥtp	*Mrj-jb*	*Sšꜣt.Ḥtp/Ḥtj*	*Kꜣ-nfr*	*Ḥtp-ḥr-n-Ptḥ*
ḥḳꜣ ḥwt	x				
ḥḳꜣ ḥwt-ꜥꜣt					x
ḥts Jnpw		x		x	
ḫrp jꜣt nbt nṯrt					x
ḫrp js(wj?) Jnpw					x
ḫrp ꜥpr.w nfr.w	x				
ḫrp ꜥḥ		x	x	x	
ḫrp wꜥb				x	
ḫrp m nṯrw					x
ḫrp mrwj pr-wr	x				
ḫrp mrt Šmꜥ Mḥw			x		
ḫrp ḥm-nṯr titles				x1	
ḫrp ḫntt nt mjtr	x				
ḫrp st ḏfꜣw					x
ḫrp tjst bjtj			x		
ḫrp tmꜣ(tjw)	x				
ḫt titles				x2	x1
ḫtmw-nṯr titles		x5			
ẖrj-ḥbt		x	x	x	
ẖrj-ḥbt ḥrj-tp					x
ẖrj-tp nswt				x	
sꜣ nswt titles	x2	x2	x2	x4	
sꜣb ꜥd mr				x	x
smꜣ titles					x1
smr		x	x	x	x
smr wꜥtj				x	
smr n it.f				x	
smk Jꜣ.t					x
smsw is.t	x			x	
smsw snwt			x		x

	Fourth Dynasty		**Fifth Dynasty**		
	Rꜥ-ḥtp	*Mrj-jb*	*Sšꜣt.Ḥtp/Ḥtj*	*Kꜣ-nfr*	*Ḥtp-ḥr-n-Ptḥ*
sḥḏ sš pr mḏꜣt					x
sš mḏꜣt-nṯr			x		
sš ẖrjt-ꜥ nswt					x
sḏꜣwtj bjtj				x	
sḏꜣwtj nṯr titles		x1		x1	
sḏtj nswt					x
ṯꜣjtj sꜣb ṯꜣtj			x	x	
Lost titles			x2		

A New Royal Woman of the Early New Kingdom

TOM HARDWICK
Cairo, Egypt

Abstract

Publication of a fragment of a faience menat naming Ahmose Sattjutji. It is suggested that Ahmose Sattjutji is a hitherto unknown member of the royal family of the Seventeenth and Eighteenth Dynasties.

الملخص

منشور علمي عن قِطْعة من حجرالفاينس "منات" حمل اسم أحمس ساتوتي. كان أحمس ساتوتي عضوغير معروف في العائلة المالكة في الأسرة المصرية السابعة عشر والأسرة المصرية الثامنة عشر.

A faience fragment now in a private collection (figs. 1–2) was acquired on the art market in the first decade of this century.[1] The fragment measures 3.8 cm high by 3.5 cm wide by 0.6 cm in thickness. It is made from a turquoise-blue faience with white, fine-grained core visible at the two broken ends, and is inscribed on both faces in a purplish black pigment applied before firing. The clear blue color of the faience and the rather ungainly paleography are consistent with a dating to the late Second Intermediate Period or early Eighteenth Dynasty.[2]

Fig. 1. Inscribed faience fragment, side 1. Private collection. Author's photograph.

Fig. 2. Inscribed faience fragment, side 2. Private collection. Author's photograph.

I am grateful to the owner of the object for access, and to Aidan Dodson, Marcel Marée, and the editor and anonymous reviewer at *JARCE* for useful comments on a draft.

[1] The fragment was acquired from a "runner" to the art trade who sourced material from private collections and minor sales on the south coast of the UK. The fragment was one of a group of small faience pieces acquired by them from the same source. These included a number of pastiche pieces bearing signs of old restoration (for one of these, see T. Hardwick, "Things of Threads and Patches," *CIPEG Journal* 5 (2021), 103–4), corroborating the suggestion that the pieces had spent some time on the British market. The fact that the fragment has no excavated findspot does not invalidate the information it can still provide, and it is presented here in the hope that publication may yet allow its ancient and more recent contexts to be recovered.

[2] For images and discussion of early New Kingdom faience, see most conveniently C. Roehrig (ed.), *Hatshepsut: From Queen to Pharaoh* (New York, 2005), 175–80. For an example of "ungainly paleography" on early New Kingdom faience, see most conveniently G. Pinch,

Journal of the American Research Center in Egypt 58 (2022), 113–17
http://dx.doi.org/10.5913/jarce.58.2022.a006

The shape of the fragment is similarly diagnostic. The two sides taper together slightly as they descend, and the thickness of the fragment is bisected by a groove running down each side. The fragment evidently derives from the counterpoise of a *menat*, the necklace of small beads with a flat, spoon-shaped counterpoise, associated especially with women and the cult of the goddess Hathor.[3]

The inscription is essentially identical on both faces, and consists of a name written right to left in two columns in a cartouche. Both faces lack the top part of the cartouche, but the name is otherwise complete. The name in the side illustrated in figure 1 is more complete, while the side illustrated in figure 2 has the remains of a sign below the cartouche: the square enclosure containing a raptor (Gardiner Sign List G5) which writes the name of the goddess Hathor. The inscription, reconstructed from both sides, can be read as follows:

([...] *ms ḏd*[*w*] *n=s* / [...] *sꜣt ṯwṯi*)| *ḥwt ḥr* [... *mry*][4]

Fig. 3. Reconstruction of inscription. Drawing by Ariel Singer.

sꜣt is usually the first element of a name (albeit sometimes pushed into second place after a divine name in honorific transposition, not the case here), so it seems likely that the name in the second column is complete. To begin at a level with the *sꜣ* goose, the first element of the first column must therefore be a flat sign that took up relatively little space above the *ms* sign. The *iꜥḥ* sign (Gardiner N12) is more likely than most,[5] and the inscription is thus restored

(*iꜥḥ.ms ḏd*[*w*] *n=s /sꜣt ṯwṯi*)| *ḥwt ḥr* [...? *mry*]
(Ahmose called Sattjutji)|, [beloved of] Hathor [?of ...] (fig. 3)

Yet another Ahmose can thus be added to the plethora of Ahmoses, male and female, that populate four generations of the royal family at the end of the Seventeenth Dynasty and the start of the Eighteenth Dynasty. Where precisely Ahmose called Sattjutji fits in the period that the object type and paleography suggest cannot be definitively established, but a little more information can be wrung from study of her name and the object itself.

Ahmose

The first royal Ahmose in the Seventeenth Dynasty is Senakhtenre Ahmose ("Ahmose the Elder"),[6] husband of Tetisheri and father of Seqenenre Tao. Among Seqenenre's children with his wife Ahhotep are his successor-but-two Ahmose I, and probably a number of daughters distinguished by their second names: Ahmose Nefertari; Ahmose Nebetta; Ahmose Henutempet; and Ahmose Tumerisi. With another other wife, Satdjehuty, Seqenenre fathered another princess Ahmose (no second name listed). Another likely daughter of Seqenenre is Ahmose

Votive Offerings to Hathor (Oxford, 1993), pl. 4 (a *menat* fragment of Ahmose Nefertari with poorly arranged signs and a cartouche base very close to the example discussed here).

[3] On *menats* see most conveniently Pinch, *Votive Offerings to Hathor*, 269–72, 278–81.

[4] I include *mry* as it is almost certain to follow a divine name in this context.

[5] The orientation of the proposed *iꜥḥ* sign is uncertain. There are no signs of the horns of the crescent moon dropping down to embrace the top of the *ms* sign, as might be expected if it faced down, so it is provisionally restored here with the horns pointing upwards. The missing sign cannot be a *rꜥ* (to consider a suggestion I owe to the reviewer). Not only is *rꜥ* fatter than *iꜥḥ*, and a less comfortable fit, but the name on the *menat* is self-evidently feminine (*ḏd*[*w*] *n=s* and *sꜣt*, not *ḏd*[*w*] *n=f* and *sꜣ*). No female Ramesseses are known to me or *PN*.

[6] S. Biston-Moulin, "Le roi Sénakht-en-Rê Ahmès de la XVIIe dynastie," *ENiM* 5 (2012), 61–71, identifying Senakhtenre's correct birth name, long believed to be "Tao." Some scholars now call him Ahmose I, renumbering Ahmose I and II as II and III.

Henuttamehu, who was probably a wife of Ahmose I. Ahmose I's own children included a son Ahmose Ankh, and daughters Ahmose Meritamun and Ahmose Sitamun.[7]

Even less securely placed in this list come Ahmose Inhapi, perhaps another wife of Seqenenre and probably mother of Ahmose Henuttamehu; Ahmose Sitkamose, presumably a daughter of Kamose and perhaps a wife of Ahmose I; and Ahmose Sapair, probably a brother or son of Ahmose I.

ḏdw n=s

The most unusual part of Ahmose Sattjutji's name is its use of the phrase *ḏdw n=s* "called" in the cartouche. A popular way to introduce a person's second name from the Middle Kingdom onwards,[8] *ḏdw n=f / ḏdw n=s* is exceptionally rare in royal contexts, even though several royal names from the Second Intermediate Period (e.g., Ameny Kemau, Seneb Kay, Amenemhat Sobekhotep) are clearly bipartite and one might expect *ḏdw n=f* to be used.

Kim Ryholt has identified these and other bipartite kings' names, however, as indicating not a second name but rather filiation to an earlier king.[9] Ryholt's thesis has alluring internal coherence but lacks evidence from other sources (i.e., independent attestations of their fathers' names) to support it, and has not received complete acceptance: it seems more likely that these are, instead, bipartite names.[10] Ryholt does not suggest that the other bipartite royal names from near this period—the profusion of male and female Ahmoses listed above—should conform to his proposed pattern of revealing filiation rather than being a second name. In many of these instances the bipartite Ahmoses are known to have parents with different names, further suggesting that Ryholt's theory should be reconsidered.

One other royal name written with *ḏdw n=s* is known to me: the "king's daughter and king's sister Satdjehuty called Satibu, born of the king's wife Tetisheri" (and Senakhtenre Ahmose the Elder), known from a fragment of her coffin lid, now in Munich.[11] On this, her name is not written in a cartouche, nor is Tetisheri's. Satdjehuty Satibu is also just called Satdjehuty (written, however, in a cartouche) on the mummy wrappings of her daughter Ahmose.[12]

It is impossible to draw firm conclusions from such a small sample, but it can be suggested that the use of *ḏdw n=f/s* was discouraged among members of the immediate royal family during the Second Intermediate Period and early New Kingdom, even though the royal families of this period were, like non-royals, fond of bipartite names. Did the two relatively unusual—and perhaps more "intimate"—contexts of Satdjehuty's coffin and Sattjutji's *menat* justify the use of the phrase; or were coffin and *menat* made in workshops that produced material for a variety of clients, and where scribes may have confused royal and non-royal protocols? Were these just mistakes? Or are the conventions for the use of this phrase entirely lost?

---

[7] Family relations adapted mostly from A. Dodson and D. Hilton, *The Complete Royal Families of Ancient Egypt* (London, 2004), 126–27, and D. Polz, Der *Beginn des Neuen Reiches. Zur Vorgeschichte einer Zeitenwende* (Berlin, 2007), 59.

[8] P. Vernus, *Le surnom au moyen empire* (Rome, 1986), 82–85.

[9] K. Ryholt, *The Political Situation in Egypt during the Second Intermediate Period*, CNI 20 (Copenhagen, 1997), 207–209.

[10] S. Quirke, "Royal Power in the 13th Dynasty," in S. Quirke (ed.), *Middle Kingdom Studies* (New Malden, 1991), 129–30. Doubt has been further cast on Ryholt's theory as epitomized by his King Seb-Kay (i.e., Kay-son-of-Seb). Ryholt places Seb-Kay as the 19th ruler of the 13th Dynasty (with Seb, otherwise completely unattested, as the 18th ruler), and as father of Amenemhat VII / Amenemhat-Kay, whose place in the middle of Dynasty 13 is relatively fixed by the Turin King List (Ryholt, *Political Situation*, 219, 340–41). However, the recent discovery of the tomb of King Senebkay at Abydos (J. Wegner, "A Royal Necropolis at South Abydos: New Light on Egypt's Second Intermediate Period," *NEA* 78.2 (2015) 68–78, especially page 71) now shows that Senebkay (the only attestation of his name known to Ryholt is ambiguously written, and was read by Ryholt as *sb* not *snb*; it is unequivocally *snb* in his tomb) reused fixtures from the tomb of Sobekhotep IV in his tomb. This automatically dates Senebkay considerably after the reign of Amenemhat-Kay, whom Ryholt's theory would place as his own son.

[11] Munich ÄS 7163: A. Grimm and S. Schoske, *Im Zeichen des Mondes: Ägypten zu Beginn des Neuen Reiches* (Munich, 1999), 2–33; 92, illustrated in color on the back cover and frontispiece.

[12] *PM* I, 755–56.

Sattjutji

Sattjutji is not listed in Ranke, *Personennamen*, although *ṯwṯi* is known from the Middle Kingdom and is also cited as a New Kingdom variant of *ṯt*.[13] It seems tempting to view the name Sattjutji as a hypochoristicon (contracted / pet name) of Satdjehuty, "Daughter of Thoth." There is apparently little phonetic justification for this, however, since *ḏ* does not change to *ṯ* in Demotic or Coptic,[14] but it has been suggested that the kingly name *tꜣ-ꜥꜣ* may conceal *ḏḥwty-nḫt*.[15] There can have been few unbreakable rules for making pet-names.

It is tempting to try to link both of Ahmose Sattjutji's names to the lunar devotion of the royal family, showcased in the names of Satdjehuty and the Ahhoteps, Ahmoses, and Thutmoses of this period. Ahmose Sattjutji could perhaps be the preexisting Ahmose, daughter of Satdjehuty Satibu (and thus sister / half-sister of Ahmose I and the numerous Ahmoses of that generation), who is listed without a second name on Satdjehuty's mummy wrappings. If this is the case, Sattjutji could perhaps be considered a diminutive variant of her mother's name Satdjehuty. Another hypothesis could see Ahmose Sattjutji as a new sister of Satdjehuty Satibu (and so a sister of Seqenenre Tao and aunt of Ahmose I). Both would be daughters of Tetisheri and Senakhtenre Ahmose the Elder; Sattjutji could then perhaps be viewed as a hypochoristicon of Sat-Teti(sheri).

The *menat* fragment cannot provide any firm conclusions, but it seems likely that Ahmose Sattjutji was either an aunt or sister of Ahmose I who lived through the end of the Seventeenth Dynasty and beginning of the Eighteenth Dynasty. Sattjutji's name is written in a cartouche, which Grajetzki suggests was the prerogative of kings' wives rather than kings' daughters in the Second Intermediate Period.[16] By the start of the Eighteenth Dynasty, however, the cartouche is occasionally used for kings' daughters too, and this may have started earlier than the first attested examples.[17] Sattjutji's titles—king's wife, sister, or daughter, or any combination thereof—are unknown.

The *Menat*, Its Context, and Conclusions

The *menat* was obtained on the art market, and its original findspot is unknown. Pinch cites *menats* inscribed for rulers of the early Eighteenth Dynasty, starting with Amenhotep I, as coming from Deir el-Bahri and Serabit el-Khadim.[18] The fragment is broken through the name of Hathor, so any following epithets are not preserved. She could have been Hathor *ḥry tp wꜣst*, from Thebes, *nbt mfkꜣt*, from Sinai, or *nbt iwnt*, from Dendera (found on New Kingdom examples from Deir el-Bahri). The fragment here does not have the distinctive weathering, greenish surface, and brown surface encrustation typical of material from Serabit, but is consistent with material from Deir el-Bahri.[19] One further point may hint that it came from Deir el-Bahri: the writing of Sattjutji's name in two columns within the cartouche. This format is otherwise unheard of in the early New Kingdom, but is vaguely reminiscent of the way in which some Middle Kingdom royal inscriptions—which would have been nearby at Deir el-Bahri—often have *sꜣ Rꜥ* written inside the cartouche, rather than atop it.[20] Did this local orthographic peculiarity influence the unusual treatment of the cartouche on the *menat*?

---

[13] *PN* I, 390.15; 395.21, 26.

[14] I am grateful to Roland Enmarch for a discussion of this topic.

[15] H. Jacquet-Gordon, "Two Stelae of King Seqenenre' Djehuty-aa of the Seventeenth Dynasty," in E. Teeter and J. Larson (eds.), *Gold of Praise: Studies on ancient Egypt in Honor of Edward F. Wente*, SAOC 58 (Chicago, 1999), 179–84.

[16] W. Grajetzki, *Ancient Egyptian Queens: A Hieroglyphic Dictionary* (London, 2005), 35.

[17] Louvre N496, seated figure of the king's daughter Ahmose Nebetta, her name in a cartouche: *PM* 801-675-210, to which add C. Barbotin, *Les Statues égyptiennes du Nouvel Empire 1: Statues royales et divines* (Paris, 2007), 35–36.

[18] Pinch, *Votive Offerings to Hathor*, 270.

[19] In this context, it is possible that the Sattjutji fragment may have been sold at Christie's London, *Egyptian and Classical Antiquities, the property of the most honourable the Marquess of Dufferin and Ava*, Monday May 31 1937, lot 26: "A blue faience menat 9 in. high; and eleven blue faience parts of menat amulets, with black line designs, cartouches of Aahmes Nefertari, Amen Hetep and Thothmes I – 1 ¼ in, to 4 ½ in. long – New Kingdom." The First Marquess of Dufferin and Ava carried out excavations at Deir el-Bahri in 1859: M. Bierbrier, *Who Was Who in Egyptology*, 5th edition (London, 2019), 54.

[20] Egyptian Museum JE 38655, stela of Senwosret III adoring Nebhepetre Mentuhotep with Senwosret's full title written inside a single

An unprovenanced *menat* fragment, suggested to come from Deir el-Bahri, not cited by Pinch, carries the name of Ahmose Nefertari in a cartouche.[21] The orientation of the *iꜥḥ* sign in this example, its horns turned down, indicates that it was made before the second half of the reign of Ahmose, when the crescent moon starts regularly to be written pointing upwards.[22] It therefore extends the documented use of *menats* back before the reign of Amenhotep I. The lack of the *iꜥḥ* sign on Sattjutji's fragment removes the one concrete dating criterion available for the piece.

If Ahmose Sattjutji was, as suggested, an aunt or sister of Ahmose I, then a shrine of Hathor already existed at Deir el-Bahri where she could have dedicated offerings. The *menat* discussed here may have been among them. Gratifying though it may be to add another individual to the royal prosopography of the early New Kingdom, Ahmose Sattjutji's resurrection is likely to remain limited to her *menat*.

---

cartouche; fragment of relief with cartouche of Mentuhotep, with *sꜣ Rꜥ* inside cartouche in E. Naville and H. Hall, *The XIth dynasty Temple at Deir el-Bahari Part III,* MEEF 32 (London, 1913), pl. XII [5].

[21] Munich ÄS 2929: Schoske, *Im Zeichen des Mondes*, 94. Her title is missing.

[22] C. Vandersleyen, *Les guerres d'Amosis, fondateur de la XVIIIe Dynastie,* MRE 1 (Brussels, 1971), 205–28; see also Ryholt, *Political Situation*, 187.

A Case Study of Polygamy in the Old Kingdom: *Mṯtj* and His Two Eldest Sons

KIM MCCORQUODALE
Macquarie University, Sydney, Australia

Abstract

The tomb of Metjetji, which was dismantled before 1947, depicts two "eldest sons" on the entrance doorway thicknesses. The presence of two eldest sons is usually an indicator of the premature death of the chronological eldest son with the second son taking over the role or an indicator that the tomb owner had more than one wife—either through death, divorce, or polygamy. Both Goedicke and Kaplony argued for the death of the eldest son, although they disagreed on which son died. Kaplony based his assumptions about the family on the groupings of the children on the entrance, but he incorrectly identified the left and right doorway thicknesses. Careful reexamination of the iconography of the children shows that Metjetji depicts two separate groups of children, as do many tomb owners who have more than one wife. He appears to have had two wives concurrently, practicing polygamy as his unidentified wife had both the eldest and the youngest of the children shown at the entrance to the tomb.

الملخص

تصور مقبرة مثتي، التي تم تفكيكها قبل عام 1947، الإبنين الكبيرين عند المدخل. عادة ما يكون وجود اثنين من الأبناء البكر مؤشرًا على الوفاة المبكرة للابن الأكبر حسب الترتيب الزمني مع تولي الابن الثاني الدور أو مؤشر على أن صاحب المقبرة كان لديه أكثر من زوجة - إما بسبب الوفاة أو الطلاق أو تعدد الزوجات. رجح كل من جوديكا وكابلوني فكرة موت الابن الأكبر، على الرغم من أنهما اختلفا حول الابن الذي توفى. بنى كابلوني افتراضاته عن عائلة مثتي على مناظر تجمعات الأطفال عند المدخل، لكنه حدد بشكل غير صحيح سماكة المدخل الأيمن والأيسر. تظهر إعادة الفحص الدقيق للمناظر التي تمثل الأطفال بالمقبرة أن مثتي يصور مجموعتين منفصلتين من الأطفال، كما يفعل العديد من أصحاب المقابر الذين لديهم أكثر من زوجة واحدة. يبدو أنه كان لديه زوجتان في نفس الوقت، مما يعني أن مثتي كان يمارس تعدد الزوجات لأن زوجته المجهولة الهوية هي أم كل من الأبن الأكبر والأصغر عند مدخل المقبرة.

Throughout Egyptian history, the king could have more than one wife,[1] and during the Old Kingdom polygamy was routinely practised by the pharaohs.[2] Analysis of the decoration of the tombs of Old Kingdom high officials shows that while they usually had one wife or sometimes two consecutive ones due to death or divorce, from the time of Niuserre, a small number of the highest officials increasingly adopted the practice of polygamy.[3] Polygamy was practised by a limited number of viziers, nomarchs, and high officials as a privilege of rank, influence, and wealth.[4] Polygamy, which had previously been exclusive to royalty, would have been a status symbol,[5]

[1] Z. Hawass, *Silent Images: Women in Pharaonic Egypt* (Cairo, 1998), 74.

[2] Teti had three wives, Pepy I had seven known and another two possible wives, Pepy II had eight wives; V. Callender, *In Hathor's Image I: The Wives and Mothers of Egyptian Kings from Dynasties I–VI* (Prague, 2011), 344.

[3] K. McCorquodale, *Representations of the Family in the Egyptian Old Kingdom: Women and Marriage* (Oxford, 2013), 67–85.

[4] N. Kanawati, "The Mentioning of more than one 'eldest' child in Old Kingdom inscriptions," *CdÉ* 51 (1976), 235–51; See also McCorquodale, *Representations of the Family*, 123.

[5] G. Robins, *Women in Ancient Egypt* (London, 1993), 64–65.

Journal of the American Research Center in Egypt 58 (2022), 119–28
http://dx.doi.org/10.5913/jarce.58.2022.a008

and the adoption of it may have been related to the fact that from the latter part of Dynasty 5, viziers had greater power, as did nomarchs who were now buried in their provinces with their titles increasingly becoming hereditary, thus giving them more authority and autonomy.[6] The examination of the Sixth Dynasty governors of Quseir el-Amarna and Meir in Middle Egypt, showed that these individuals were closely connected to the royal family and sometimes took on royal prerogatives.[7] The vizier Merefnebef, who shows his four wives playing the harp together in his tomb at Saqqara, also adopted royal prerogatives.[8] The two main indicators of polygamy are the representation of multiple wives in the same or complimentary scenes and the presence of two or more eldest children.[9] Two eldest sons are represented in the tomb of *Mṯṯj* (Metjetji).

The focus of this article is a re-examination of the available material from Metjetji's tomb to establish whether he had two eldest sons due to the death of the chronological eldest son, or due to remarriage after the death or divorce of his first wife, or because he practiced polygamy.

Metjetji: The Tomb and the Man

Metjetji's tomb was dismantled and a number of pieces were purchased by institutions in Europe and North America after they came on to the art market around 1947. In 1976, Kaplony published a monograph that examined all known pieces of the tomb that included stone, mud plaster fragments, and wooden statues.[10] Among them there was a broken lintel in the Louvre,[11] the two façades—the right in Berlin[12] and the left in Toronto,[13] the two entrance thicknesses (which each show an eldest son) in Kansas City,[14] the false door in New York,[15] and a block with a fowling scene in Switzerland.[16] Forty-three painted mud plaster fragments are in the Louvre,[17] and five wooden statues are in museums in Boston, New York, and Kansas City.[18] Three stone blocks that probably also came from this tomb are in Hanover, Toronto, and Richmond.[19] Subsequent to Kaplony's publication, Silverman identified a large relief fragment in the Denver Museum of Art as complementing the broken lintel in the Louvre.[20]

On the façade, the entrance thicknesses, and on the left part of the lintel in the Louvre, Metjetji's titles were listed as Noble of the King[21] and Overseer of the Department of *ḫnty(w)-š* of the Great House. This last title was held by the two polygamists Remni and the nomarch Qar/Meryre-nefer.[22] On the right part of the lintel, identified by Silverman, Metjetji had the additional titles of Royal Chamberlain, Overseer of the Department,

[6] N. Kanawati, "Interrelations of the Capital and the Provinces in the Sixth Dynasty," *BACE* 15 (2004), 51; M. Lashien, *The Nobles of el-Qusiya in the Sixth Dynasty: A Historical Study* (Wallasey, 2017), 2–3.

[7] N. Kanawati, "The Royal Governors of El-Qusiya in the Old and Middle Kingdom," *EDAL* 6 (2017), 250.

[8] Myśliwiec says he was "desperately trying to imitate royalty in its various aspects": K. Myśliwiec, *Saqqara I: The Tomb of Merefnebef Text* (Warsaw, 2004), 252. The vizier Ptahshepses' tomb at Abusir possessed several funerary attributes normally associated with the king alone; M. Verner, *Forgotten Pharaohs, Lost Pyramids* (Prague, 1994), 179.

[9] K. McCorquodale, "Multiple Marriages and Polygamy in the Old Kingdom," *EDAL* 6 (2017), 275.

[10] P. Kaplony, *Studien Zum Grab des Methethi*, Monographien de Abegg-Stiftung 8 (Bern, 1976).

[11] Louvre E 25 681.

[12] Ägyptisches Museum und Papyrussammlung, Staatliche Museen zu Berlin 32190 (Berlin Museum 5/70).

[13] Royal Ontario Museum, 953.116.1.

[14] Nelson-Atkins Museum, 52-7/1 and 52-7/2.

[15] Metropolitan Museum of Art, 64.100.

[16] Riggisberg Abegg-Stiftung 12.39.67.

[17] Louvre E 25507-49.

[18] Museum of Fine Arts, 47.1455, Brooklyn Museum, 50.77, 51.1 and 53.222, Nelson-Atkins Museum, 5-1.

[19] August-Kestner Museum, Hanover 1957.78, Royal Ontario Museum, 953.116.2, Virginia Museum of Fine Arts, Richmond VA 55.6.2.

[20] Denver Museum of Art, Marion Hendrie Fund, 1972.9; D. Silverman, "A Fragment of Relief Belonging to an Old Kingdom Tomb," in Z. Hawass, P. Der Manuelian, and R. Hussein (eds.), *Perspectives on Ancient Egypt: Studies in Honor of Edward Brovarski*, ASAE Cahier 40 (Cairo, 2010), 423–36.

[21] The translation of all titles follows D. Jones, *An Index of Ancient Egyptian Titles, Epithets and Phrases of the Old Kingdom*, BAR 886 (Oxford, 2000).

[22] McCorquodale, *Representations of the Family*, 76.

Companion of the House, Overseer of the Two Fields of Offerings and Overseer of *ḥwt-jḥwt*.[23] Jones says this last title refers to the capital of the third nome of Lower Egypt, while Silverman translates it as Overseer of the Cattle Estate.[24] On one of the painted mud plaster fragments, which must have been made later, Metjetji had the additional high titles of Royal Chamberlain of the Great House,[25] Juridical *ꜥḏ-mr* Official of the Great House, Supervisor of Linen, and Privy to the Secrets of the King in all his Cult Places.[26] The last title was held by the viziers Ptahshepses, Mereruka, Ankhmahor and Khentika.[27]

On the lintel and the false door he had the epithet Honoured by Unas, his Master. Due to this epithet, his tomb is thought to have come from Saqqara.[28] The tomb has been variously dated from the reign of Unas to the early Middle Kingdom.[29] The most comprehensive study, by Brovarski, convincingly dated the tomb from early Teti to the end of Teti or early Pepy 1.[30]

Two Eldest Sons

The doorway thicknesses of the tomb of Metjetji show two "eldest sons," *Ptḥ-ḥtp* (Ptah-hotep) and *Ḫwn-Sbk* (Khuen-Sobek); one on each thickness. The presence of two eldest sons in a tomb is generally accepted[31] as indicating either that the first-born son died prematurely and the chronological second son then had "eldest" added to his name, or they were the eldest sons of different wives through death, divorce, or polygamy.[32] When there were children of more than one wife, it was necessary to identify the eldest son of each wife (or daughter if there was no son) so that he/she could inherit from their respective mothers.[33] Another possibility for the presence of two eldest sons is the presence of twins but twins are usually shown together.[34]

23 Silverman, "A Fragment of Relief," fig. 3.

24 Jones, *Index of Ancient Egyptian Titles*, 161–62 [623]; Silverman, "A Fragment of Relief," 430.

25 Strudwick lists 144 men with the title King's Chamberlain, twenty-five of whom were also viziers; N. Strudwick, *The Administration of Egypt in the Old Kingdom: The Highest Titles and their Holders* (London, 1985), Table 30.

26 Louvre E 25 544.

27 Jones, *Index of Ancient Egyptian Titles*, 630–31 [2311].

28 Around the pyramid complex of Unas: PM III², 646; southeast of the Unas enclosure: P. Munro, "Berkungen zur Datierung *Mttj*, zu seinen Statuen Brooklyn 51.1 / Kansas City 51-1 und zu verwandten Rundbildern," in C. Berger, G. Clerc, and N. Grimal (eds.), *Hommages à Jean Leclant*, vol. 1, BdÉ 106.1 (Cairo, 1994), 248; west of the Step Pyramid: B. von Bothmer in *Egyptian Art in the Age of the Pyramids* (New York, 1999), 408 n. 1.

29 The reign of Teti: PM III², 646 and K. Baer, *Rank and Title in the Old Kingdom: The Structure of the Egyptian Administration in the Fifth and Sixth Dynasties* (Chicago, 1960), 83, 291 [203 B]. Slightly after the reign of Unas: C. Ziegler, *Catalogue des stèles, peintures et reliefs égyptiens de l'Ancien Empire et de la Première Période Intermédiaires vers 2686-2040 avant J.-C.* (Paris, 1990), 408, and E. Russman, "A Second Style in Egyptian Art of the Old Kingdom," *MDAIK* 51 (1995), 269–79. Dynasty 6: H. Altenmüller, "Zur Vergöttlichung des Königs Unas im Alten Reich," *SAK* 1 (1974), 1–18; the Heracleopolitan Period (Dynasty 9) or early Middle Kingdom: Munro, "Berkungen zur Datierung *Mttj*," 254, 266.

30 E. Brovarski, "The Date of Metjetji," in Z. Hawass and J. Wegner (eds.), *Millions of Jubilees: Studies in Honor of David P. Silverman*, vol. 1, ASAE Cahier 39 (Cairo, 2010), 107.

31 Allam, using Late Period evidence, suggested that any child could be designated as eldest; S. Allam, "Notes on the Designation 'Eldest Son/Daughter' (*z3/z3.t smsw: šri ꜥ3/šri.t ꜥ3*)," in Hawass, Der Manuelian, and Hussein, *Perspectives on Ancient Egyptian Studies*, 31–33. However, analysis of the iconography and titles of eldest sons proved that in the Old Kingdom the eldest child was the chronological oldest child; K. McCorquodale, "Reconsidering the Term 'Eldest Son / Eldest Daughter' and Inheritance in the Old Kingdom," *BACE* 23 (2012), 78–80.

32 Kanawati, "The Mentioning of more than one 'eldest' child," 235–51; K. Scheel-Schweitzer, "Zur Darstellung von mehr als einem ältesten Sohn in Gräbern des Altern Reiches," *GM* 213 (2007), 74. For examples of the various reasons for more than one eldest son see McCorquodale, "Multiple Marriages and Polygamy in the Old Kingdom," 275–79.

33 Women could own and bequeath property; J. Johnson, "The Legal Status of Women in Ancient Egypt," in A. Capel and G. Markoe (eds.), *Mistress of the House, Mistress of Heaven: Women in Ancient Egypt* (New York, 1966), 177–84. In the Old Kingdom, the eldest son inherited from his father and his mother unless an *jmyt-pr* document was witnessed and signed to bequeath property to someone else. See T. Logan, "The *Jmyt-pr* Document: Form, Function, and Significance," *JARCE* 37 (2000), 67.

34 J. Baines, "Egyptian Twins," *Orientalia* 54 (1988), 461–82.

Previous Explanations for Metjetji having Two Eldest Sons

Previous attempts have been made to explain the presence of the two eldest sons in the tomb of Metjetji. Goedicke suggested that Ptah-hotep died before his father because on the right thickness he is referred to as "his beloved eldest son, revered with his father."[35] Scheel-Schweitzer has suggested that this term is applied to an eldest son when he died prematurely and his sibling then became the eldest living male.[36] Helck suggested it was a relationship entailing provision for the funerary estate by the one with whom the deceased is *jm3ḫw*.[37] However, Allen pointed out that while this may have been true in many cases, it can hardly have applied to instances in which the person is described as "revered with those who are with him," or "revered with people" or even "revered with everyone."[38] He says the basic meaning is probably one of general association with the added connotation of worth, "worthy of being associated with his father."[39] Ptah-hotep does not appear to have died prematurely as he appears on the later mud plaster fragments where Metjetji has additional titles and children.

Kaplony used the sizes and placement of the children to account for the fact that two sons are described as eldest, concluding that the other eldest son, Khuen-Sobek, died prematurely, as he was not shown as a kȝ-priest or in the tomb, and the son Ptah-hotep then took over the position.[40] He surmised that all the children were born to one wife as the depictions of the two eldest sons were linked by the presence of a younger son *Jḥjj* (Ihy) on either side of the entrance pieces. However, his identification of the left and right doorway thicknesses had the tomb owner facing into the tomb, while Porter and Moss list the thicknesses in reverse, with the tomb owner facing out of the tomb.[41] The Nelson-Atkins Museum in Kansas City, where the entrance thicknesses are housed, has stated that they do not know which is the right or left.[42] It is crucial to try to establish which is the left thickness and which is the right for the groupings of the children and our understanding of the family of Metjetji.

Orientation of the Tomb Owner on Entrance Doorway Thicknesses

Referring to Metjetji's doorway thicknesses, Goedicke stated that it was easy to recognise the original layout as the tomb owner was directed outwards as if he had just left his tomb or wanted to greet the visitor at the entrance of his "House of Eternity."[43]

Harpur stated that major figures on entrance thicknesses "nearly always face outwards" but she lists eight exceptions.[44] Further examination revealed that five of these exceptions are incorrect and that the tomb owner actually faced out of the tomb.[45] The line drawing of another is probably reversed.[46] Only two instances defi-

---

[35] H. Goedicke, "Zwei inscriften aus dem Grabe des *Mttj* aus Sakkara," *ZAS* 83 (1958), 27.

[36] Scheel-Schweitzer, "Zur Darstellung von mehr als einem ältesten Sohn," 72–74.

[37] W. Helck, "Wirtschaftliche Bemerkungen zum privaten Grabbesitz im Alten Reiche," *MDIAK* 14 (1956), 69.

[38] P. Allen, "Some Aspects of the non-royal afterlife in the Old Kingdom," in M. Bárta (ed.), *Old Kingdom Art and Archaeology: Proceedings of the Conference held in Prague, May 31–June 4, 2004* (Prague, 2006), 16.

[39] Allen, "Some Aspects of the non-royal afterlife in the Old Kingdom," 16.

[40] Kaplony, *Studien Zum Grab des Methethi*, 82–85.

[41] PM III^2, 646.

[42] Personal correspondence with Dr. Robert Cohon, (then) Curator of Ancient Art, The Nelson-Atkins Museum of Art (August 15, 2014).

[43] Goedicke, "Zwei inscriften aus dem Grabe des *Mttj*," 19.

[44] Y. Harpur, *Decoration in Egyptian Tombs of the Old Kingdom: Studies in Orientation and Scene Content* (London, 1987), 53.

[45] The online publication of the Giza Archives by the Boston Museum of Fine Arts has made available previously unpublished photographs and documents that were invaluable in this investigation. Tomb owners face outwards in the tombs of Imisetka, Itti, Neferhotep, and Ipi. The double tomb of Kaunesut has two entrances for father and son, and it is the son who faces inwards on his father's entrance thickness. See K. McCorquodale, "The orientation of the tomb owner on entrance doorway thicknesses in Old Kingdom tombs," in C. Di Biase-Dyson and L. Donovan (eds.), *The Cultural Manifestations of Religious Experience: Studies in Honour of Boyo G. Ockinga*, ÄAT 85 (Münster, 2017), 146–47.

[46] Hassan's line drawing of the right doorway thickness of Inkaef's tomb, shows wear on the inner edge not the outer edge, as is normal. He reversed the line drawing of Niankhkhnum's left doorway thickness in the same volume. See McCorquodale, "The orientation of the tomb owner," 148.

nitely show the tomb owner facing into the tomb, and both of these are tombs for more than person and are in the G 8000 Cemetery in the Central Field at Giza.[47]

Considering that there are only two exceptions, which are tombs for multiple tomb owners at Giza, and given that Metjetji's tomb comes from Saqqara where the tomb owner never faces inward, the depictions of the children of Metjetji, and the two eldest sons in particular, needs to be re-examined considering that Metjetji is facing out of the tomb. That is, reversing the doorway thicknesses as they were shown in Kaplony's publication and placing them in accordance with Porter and Moss's recording. This places Metjetji with his eldest son Ptah-hotep and his son Ihy on the right thickness and with Ihy on the right façade. On the left of the entrance, Metjetji is shown with his other eldest son Khuen-Sobek and his daughter *Jrt-Sbk* (Iret-Sobek) on the left thickness and with his son *Ptḥ-sbw* (Ptah-sabu) on the left façade. This gives two distinct groups of children.

Table 1. Position of children at the entrance of the tomb.

	Children of Unknown Wife	**Children of Inti**
Lintel		his beloved eldest son Ptah-hotep
	Left	**Right**
Doorway Thickness	his beloved eldest son Khuen-Sobek	his [beloved] eldest son revered with his father [Ptah]-hotep
	his beloved daughter Jrt-Sobek	his [beloved son] Jhy
Façade	his beloved son Ptah-sabu	his beloved son Jhy

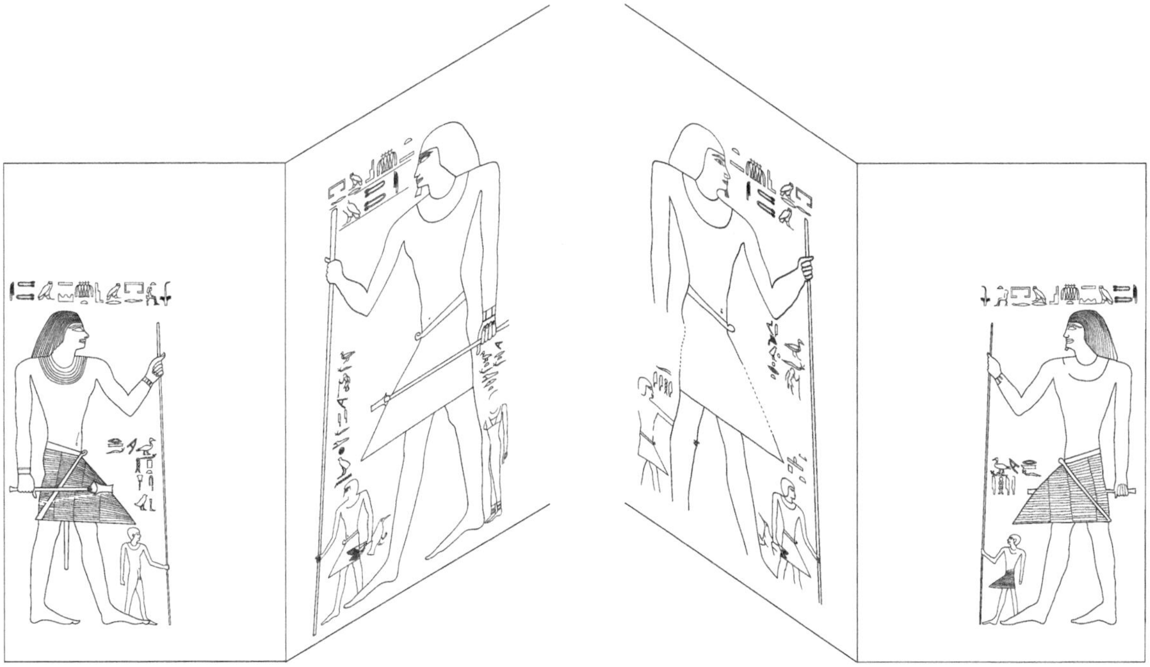

Fig. 1. Façades and doorway thicknesses reconstructed with tomb owner facing out of the tomb. Line drawings with relevant sections redrawn by Leonie Donovan after P. Kaplony, Studien zum Grab des Methethi, *figs. 5–8.*

[47] The tomb of Nimaatre and his female tomb partner Neferesres and the tomb of Sehkemankhptah and Nesutwesret; see McCorquodale, "The orientation of the tomb owner," 149.

Depictions of Children When There Is More Than One Wife

In order to determine whether Metjetji had more than one wife, analysis of the iconography in tombs where the tomb owner depicts more than one wife (irrespective of whether the multiple marriages were due to death, divorce, or polygamy) can help establish criteria of how children were depicted in this situation.

- The chronological eldest son (or daughter if there is no son) of different wives was identified as *s3/s3.t smsw*.[48]
- Children are shown in close contact with either the tomb owner and/or their mother, but not with other wives or with their father when he was with another wife.[49]
- When children were shown with a wife, other than their mother, they were separated from her by orientation—children being depicted facing her, or being in a different register, or on a separate baseline.[50]
- When in a separate register, children may be placed in chronological order or in family groupings.[51]
- Children who are full siblings or half siblings may have the same name.[52]
- The relative sizes of children and whether they were clothed or not is an indicator of their comparative ages. This was ascertained in a previous study of sixty-nine Old Kingdom scenes where only one child in a group of children was described as eldest.[53] The eldest son was always depicted as larger or of equal size, only younger siblings were shown smaller in size. A naked child was younger than a child wearing a kilt.[54] The eldest son was always shown wearing a kilt when other children wore kilts and was only shown as a naked child when all other children were naked.

Tomb owners go to great lengths to separate or identify children of different wives.[55] Using these criteria it is possible to re-examine the depictions of the children of Metjetji.

Reconsidering Metjetji's Tomb Decoration

Locating the left and right entrance thicknesses by placing the tomb owner facing out of the tomb, as was usual, reveals that there are two distinct groups of children on either side of the entrance (see Table 1).

The eldest son Ptah-hotep is shown standing with his father on the lintel as well as on the right doorway thickness with his brother Ihy. Ihy is also shown with his father on the right façade—either a second representation or possibly another brother with the same name.

On the left of the entrance there is a different group of children. On the left doorway thickness Metjetji stands with his eldest son Khuen-Sobek and his sister Iret-Sobek. The Sobek element in both their names is sugges-

[48] For example, Isi of Edfu identifies two wives, Seshseshet and her eldest son Qar, and Sautit and her eldest son Her-nebu-ef. See McCorquodale, "Multiple Marriages and Polygamy," 277–78.

[49] For example, Qar/Mery-Re-nefer shows three wives with their children in separate groups. Only on the lintel above the false door are two family groups shown, but the later addition of a wife and son is made obvious by them "floating" rather than being on a baseline; see M. el-Khadragy, "The Offering Niche of Qar in the Cairo Museum," *SAK* 30 (2002), fig. 6.

[50] For example, Mery-aa had six wives. When his children were shown with him and his wife Isi, who had no children of her own, they were positioned facing her and their father and do not have any physical contact; see N. Kanawati, *The Tombs of El-Hagarsa*, vol. 3, ACE Reports 7 (Sydney, 1995), pl. 42.

[51] For example, in the top register Mery-aa's three sons from different wives are shown in chronological order, but the daughters in the middle register are in family groupings; see Kanawati, *The Tombs of El-Hagarsa*, pl. 42.

[52] For example, Mery-aa had three sons named Nenu from different wives and three daughters named Shemat, two of whom had the same mother; see Kanawati, *The Tombs of El-Hagarsa*, pl. 42.

[53] McCorquodale, *Representations of the Family*, 88–89, Table P.

[54] In the Old Kingdom, children were shown naked only up until puberty. See R. Janssen and J. Janssen, *Growing up in Ancient Egypt* (London, 1990), 26.

[55] See for example the tombs of Mereruka, Mehu, and Merefnebef at Saqqara, Mery-aa at El-Hargasa, Qar/Mery-Re-nefer and Isi at Edfu. McCorquodale, *Representations of the Family*, 71–75.

tive of their close relationship. On the left façade, Metjetji is accompanied by their younger brother Ptah-sabu. He is the only one of the six children shown at the entrance who is naked; he is therefore the youngest of these children.

From inside the chapel, the fowling scene shows the eldest son Ptah-hotep as a naked child. Both he and the wife Inti are in close contact with the tomb owner, with an arm around one of his legs. Inti is therefore his mother, and by extension also the mother of the son (or possibly two sons) named Ihy. The daughter, Iret-Sobek, is shown standing on a separate baseline behind Metjetji, Inti, and Ptah-hotep. This may indicate that she had a different mother. While she is also naked except for a collar, she is taller than Ptah-hotep,[56] indicating that she is older than him. The representations of these two naked children show them at an earlier age than on the entrance where Ptah-hotep wears a kilt and Iret-Sobek wears a long sheath dress and where there are also additional children (another three or possibly four) so this relief represents an earlier stage in the life of Metjetji when only one son and one daughter were born.

The painted wall fragments provide further details regarding the familial relationships. They show Ptah-hotep censing before his father, Ptah-hotep and his brother Ihy offering birds in a top register, and Ptah-hotep as a seated scribe in a lower register.[57] Ihy stands in front of his father holding a dog on a leash, and he holds a *ḥs* jar containing the purification water for the funerary rites.[58] A narrow vertical inscription to the right of Metjetji's statue reads "his son whom he loves ..."[59] Three daughters are shown as harpists, with only the second's name being partially visible—she is named as Un[as]-merret.[60]

The painted wall fragments also show two more possible sons, Kai-pu and Metjetji (junior) presenting geese behind Ptah-hotep and Ihy.[61]

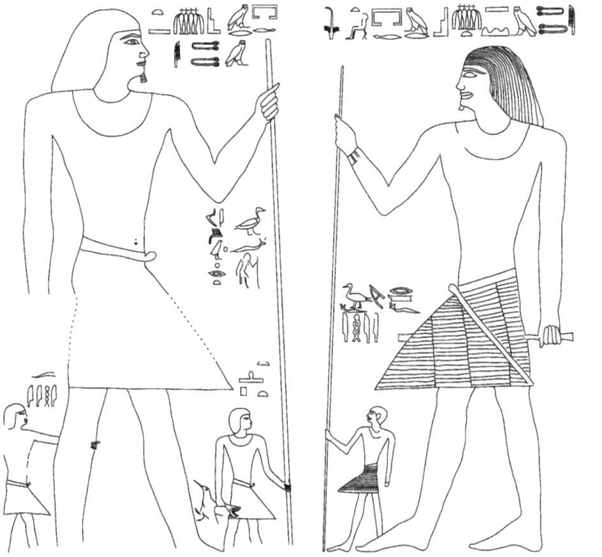

Fig. 2. Right doorway thickness and right façade with relevant sections redrawn by L. Donovan after Kaplony, Studien zum Grab des Methethi, *figs. 5 and 8.*

Fig. 3. Left façade and left doorway thickness with relevant sections redrawn by L. Donovan after Kaplony, Studien zum Grab des Methethi, *figs. 7 and 6.*

56 Estimating her complete height, using the size of the head of both Ptah-hotep and Jnti, she is 25% taller than Ptah-hotep.

57 Louvre E 25 507 and E 25 508.

58 Louvre E 25 524 and E 25 517.

59 Louvre E 25 525. Ziegler suggests that it is Ihy's name beneath but there is only the top of a curved hieroglyph remaining on the right and it does not look like the top of a feather for the *J* and in the other five instances where his name is written the *ḥ* is the same height and should therefore be visible; Ziegler, *Catalogue des stèles*, 136, 140 (drawing).

60 Louvre E 25 515.

61 Louvre E 25 508-9; Kaplony, *Studien des Methethi*, 84.

Conclusions

It would seem from the sequence of children, and the several consistent groupings of them, that it was very likely that Metjetji's household was a polygamous one. That he was not the only man who had such a family has been documented for several other high officials.[62]

The fowling scene, that shows only two children, represents an earlier stage in Metjetji's life as this is the only place where the eldest son Ptah-hotep is shown naked. Iret-Sobek is also naked but she is taller than Ptah-hotep—therefore older, making her the first-born child. The wife Inti is the mother of the eldest son Ptah-hotep as they are both in close contact with Metjetji. Iret-Sobek is on a separate baseline probably indicating that she had a different mother.

The entrance represents a later stage in Metjetji's life, showing five (or six) children. The lintel, the façades, and the entrance thicknesses form a cohesive unit but the lintel was usually decorated first.[63] Ptah-hotep is named as the eldest son on the lintel, which is consistent with him being the only son in the fowling scene. His depiction on the lintel gives him prominence over the eldest son Khuen-Sobek. He was born before Khuen-Sobek, as he is the only son shown in the fowling scene. The additional inscription of "revered with his father" on the right doorway thickness seems to indicate, as suggested by Helck, that he was responsible for the provisioning of his father, Metjetji's, funerary estate. This would be consistent with him being the first born of the two eldest sons.

The children shown on the entrance are in two distinct groups. The eldest son, Ptah-hotep, is shown on the right side of the entrance with his brother Ihy twice, or with two brothers with the same name. As Inti is his mother, which is established by their close proximity in the fowling scene, by extension she is also the mother of the son or sons named Ihy who are shown twice with Ptah-hotep, once on the doorway thickness, and again on the painted fragment where they offer geese—thus confirming their close relationship.

To the left of the entrance is another group of children. The eldest son Khuen-Sobek is shown on the left thickness with his sister Iret-Sobek, who is older than him due to her presence and his absence in the fowling scene. Their younger brother Ptah-sabu appears on the left façade. As he is the only one who is naked, he is the youngest of the six children on the entrance.

Khuen-Sobek is named as an eldest son on the left entrance thickness, a surface that was decorated after the lintel. If he was dead at the time the relief was carved he would not have been depicted holding Metjetji's staff, as the dead are not shown in close contact with the living.[64] This indicates that Khuen-Sobek did not die prematurely resulting in Ptah-hotep then being named as eldest, as the lintel was decorated prior to the thicknesses and façades. Khuen-Sobek is absent from the fowling scene that was executed earlier, so the reason he is named as eldest son on the thickness is because he was the eldest son of a different wife. This was necessary to identify eldest sons because they inherited from their respective mothers.

The painted fragments from the chapel were completed last because more children are shown and Metjetji bears additional titles. Three daughters are shown as harpists. The first may be Iret-Sobek, the second is Un[as]-merret, and the third's name is not given. There are also possibly two additional sons: Kai-pu and Metjetji.

Kaplony suggested that the eldest son Khuen-Sobek, and also probably the youngest son Ptah-sabu, died as they are not shown on the painted fragments. The scenes on the fragments preserve up to five registers, a minimum of one metre high. Ziegler states that they would have covered a wall area of at least seven meters in length.[65] The fragments constitute an area of 3.99 square metres, so it is possible that these two sons did not die but they were shown elsewhere in the decoration. As they were full brothers, we would expect them to be shown together. Fishing and fowling scenes are complimentary, and their unidentified mother, also the mother of Iret-

[62] Kanawati, "The Mentioning of More Than One 'Eldest' Child," 235–51; McCorquodale, *Representations of the Family*, 67–85.

[63] All eight tombs in the Teti Cemetery that were abruptly abandoned before completion have completed architraves. See G.-R. Harrington, "A Statistical Inquiry into the Titles from the Tomb of Hesi in Saqqara," *GM* 261 (2020), 29–30.

[64] In the Old Kingdom the dead are separated from the living by orientation, a line of hieroglyphs or an upright staff; N. Kanawati, "The Living and the Dead in Old Kingdom Tomb Scenes," *SAK* 9 (1981), 213–25.

[65] Ziegler, *Catalogue des stèles*, 123; https://www.louvre.fr/en/oeuvre-notices/paintings-tomb-metjetji, accessed June 2019.

Fig. 4. Fowling scene with relevant sections redrawn by L. Donovan after Kaplony, Studien zum Grab des Methethi, *fig. 1.*

Sobek, may have been shown in the fishing scene, much as Mehu shows one wife in the fishing scene and his other wife in the fowling scene.[66]

Kaplony concluded that all nine children belonged to Metjetji and one wife Inti.[67] However, this was based on the son Ihy linking all the children on the entrance. Given that, as has been shown, tomb owners always face out of the tomb on entrance doorway thicknesses at Saqqara, there are two distinct groups of children shown: the eldest son Ptah-hotep and his brother or brothers Ihy, and separately, the other eldest son Khuen-Sobek, his sister Iret-Sobek, and their younger brother Ptah-sabu.

Iret-Sobek was the first-born child to an unidentified wife, while the eldest son, Ptah-hotep, was the first-born child to the wife Inti and Metjetji's first son. This would explain why he was given the prominent position on the lintel and was responsible for the provisioning of Metjetji's funerary estate.

The unidentified wife had a second child, the eldest son Khuen-Sobek. The wife Inti had at least one, possibly two sons named Ihy. The unidentified wife then had the son Ptah-sabu who was the youngest of the children shown at the entrance, as he is the only child shown as naked there, a clear indicator that he was born later than Metjetji's other children shown at the entrance. At least two daughters, one called Un[as]-merret, were born after this and possibly two more sons, Kai-pu and Metjetji, all of whose maternity is unknown.

[66] Mehu and his wife Neferkawes/Jkw are shown in the fishing scene and on the west wall of Room 3 with his eldest son [Meri] (chipped out) and his daughter Merut with them in close contact. Mehu is shown in the fowling scene with his other wife Nebet with his sons [...] nesu [...r...] (chipped out) and Hetepka; See H. Altenmüller, *Die Wanddarstellungen im Grab des Mehu in Saqqara*, AVDAIK 42 (Mainz am Rhein, 1998), pls. 13, 53, and 11.

[67] Kaplony, *Studien des Methethi*, 80–85.

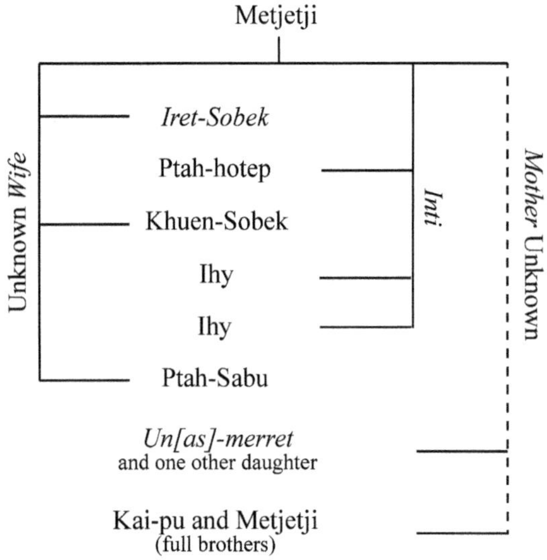

Fig. 5. Chronological family tree of Metjetji.

Of the children shown at the entrance of the tomb, the unidentified wife bore both the first child, the daughter Iret-Sobek, and the youngest child, the naked son Ptah-sabu. This means that Metjetji had two concurrent wives. The presence of two "eldest sons" was not due to the premature death of the chronological eldest son, nor did he divorce his first wife, nor did she die and he remarry. The evidence leads to the conclusion that Metjetji practised polygamy, and had two concurrent wives. This is consistent with him having high titles associated with the palace, administration, juridical and religious spheres, as well as his tomb dating from Teti to Pepy I, when other high officials increasingly began taking on royal prerogatives, such as polygamy.

The "Lost" Arabic Excavation Diaries of the Harvard University-Boston Museum of Fine Arts Expedition

Peter Der Manuelian
Harvard University, USA

Abstract

A new frontier has opened on Egyptian contributions to the Western expeditions of the early twentieth century, thanks to the 2006 (re)discovery in Egypt of more than seventy Harvard University-Boston Museum of Fine Arts Expedition Diaries written by the Diraz family of reises from Quft. Recent attempts to do justice to unnamed and unheralded Egyptian archaeologists have lacked such a treasure trove of written data: thousands of pages of Arabic text and sketches provided by Egyptian reises who were trained by George Reisner (1867–1942), director of the Expedition. A summary history is given of the main archaeological players of the Diraz family from el-Qal'a, Quft (Part 1), followed by the author's account of the discovery and recent history of the Arabic diary books in Egypt (Part 2). A brief discussion of their significance, with a few examples, is provided next (Part 3). The Arabic diaries form part of a new data-mining project since they offer us a reassessment of the role of Egyptians in what are usually described as Western excavations in Egypt.

الملخص

تم فتح حدود جديدة لفهم المساهمات المصرية في البعثات الاستكشافية الغربية في أوائل القرن العشرين، وذلك بفضل (إعادة) اكتشاف أكثر من 70 دفتر يوميات تابع لبعثة جامعة هارفارد - متحف بوسطن للفنون الجميلة عام 2006 في مصر، كتبها أفراد عائلة ديراز من رؤساء العمال من قفط. افتقرت المحاولات الأخيرة لإنصاف الآثاريين المصريين المجهولين وغير المعلنين إلى هذا الكنز الدفين من البيانات المكتوبة: وهو عبارة عن آلاف الصفحات من النصوص العربية والرسومات التي قام بها المصريون الذين دربهم مدير البعثة، جورج ريزنر (1867—1942). تم تقديم ملخص لتاريخ الأثريين الرئيسيين لعائلة ديراز من القلعة بقفط (الجزء الأول)، متبوعًا بشرح المؤلف للاكتشاف والتاريخ الحديث لدفتر اليوميات العربية في مصر (الجزء الثاني). يتم تقديم مناقشة موجزة لأهمية الاكتشاف، مع بعض الأمثلة (الجزء 3). يشكل دفتر اليوميات العربية جزءًا من مشروع جديد للتنقيب عن البيانات لأنها تقدم لنا إعادة تقييم لدور المصريين فيما يوصف عادة بالحفائر الغربية في مصر.

Egyptologists continue to reevaluate aspects of their field's history in light of recent social justice movements. Beyond the (particularly North American) Afrocentrist approaches that emphasize Egypt's place in Africa as opposed to the Mediterranean or even European worlds, there are equally important efforts to rediscover and explore the often-unsung contributions by Egyptians to the early twentieth century's Western-led expeditions. These men—and in the Delta, women—often went unidentified in contemporary expedition photographic metadata or excavation reports. They usually show up merely on paysheets, with little more than their names to flesh out their lives and personalities, but they contributed far more than just the "heavy lifting," in both the literal and figural sense, to the digs. Despite valiant efforts of recent years to redress this situation, the nature of these early expeditions' legacy data, now often exceeding a century in age, can defeat even the best efforts to credit native Egyptian achievements.[1]

This paper is dedicated to the memory of Ramadan Badry Hussein (1967–2022), a great scholar and dear friend.

[1] Stephen Quirke, *Hidden Hands. Egyptian Workforces in Petrie Excavation Archives, 1880–1924* (London, 2010); Wendy Doyon, "The History

http://dx.doi.org/10.5913/jarce.58.2022.a007

One shining exception to this unfortunate situation is provided by the Harvard University-Boston Museum of Fine Arts Expedition under George A. Reisner (1867–1942). Running from 1905—or more accurately from 1899 if we count its first incarnation as the Hearst Expedition—until 1947, the Expedition worked at twenty-three archaeological sites in Egypt, the Sudan, and even two seasons at Samaria, Palestine (1909–1910). Whatever one might think of Reisner's (mis)interpretations of Nubian cultures as anything but indigenous,[2] his expedition relationship with his Qufti workmen was progressive on many levels. He trained the Egyptian teams in the "skilled labor" positions of the expedition, not simply to act as basket carriers for debris removal. He delegated to them many of the most important aspects of the dig, from excavating fragile artifacts to keeping accounts, paying the men, and producing the professional documentation photography. But most impressive of all are the Arabic diaries kept by his Egyptian *reises,* often in tandem with Western, English-language diaries, but in the later years as the sole record of the team's daily progress. These diaries have survived and are invaluable for assessing the all-too-hidden contributions of Qufti *reises* and their teams to the success of what is usually seen as a Western undertaking.

Part 1 of the present article highlights the true "engine" of the HU-MFA Expedition, the Diraz family from el-Qal'a, Quft, as a contribution to our understanding of the labor relationships between Western archaeologists and their Egyptian counterparts in the early twentieth century.[3] The core of Reisner's original work force, beginning in late December 1899 with his first excavations at Quft (Coptos), were "Quftis," local men whom Flinders Petrie and James E. Quibell had trained, and it is well known that the tradition of hiring Quftis to supervise at Egyptian expeditions continues to this day.[4] Moreover, Reisner's impact, not just on the work in Egypt but on archaeology throughout the ancient Near East, can be traced back to the training these men received from him before they joined other expeditions in Egypt, Sudan, Palestine, and elsewhere. Part 2 of the present essay summarizes my (re)discovery and recovery of the Arabic diaries in Egypt, while Part 3 provides some selections of their content, along with plans for their future study and assessment.

The focus on this particular family of talented Qufti archaeologists originally derived from work on the Giza Project, established first at the Museum of Fine Arts, Boston (2000–2010), and then later at Harvard University (2011–present; http://giza.fas.harvard.edu). Established to assemble as much archaeological documentation on the Giza Plateau as possible, the Project highlighted many aspects of George Reisner's life that lay buried in archives at the MFA, at Harvard, and all over the world. This in turn convinced me to attempt a biography of Reisner himself, including his education at Harvard, his dramatic change of career from Semitic philology to archaeology, his choice of excavation sites, his rotating staff of Western assistants, and his constant and faithful

---

of Archaeology through the Eyes of Egyptians," in Bonnie Effros and Guolong Lai (eds.), *Unmasking Ideology in Imperial and Colonial Archaeology: Vocabulary, Symbols, and Legacy* (Los Angeles, 2018), 173–200; Wendy Doyon, "On Archaeological Labor in Modern Egypt," in William Carruthers (ed.), *Histories of Egyptology: Interdisciplinary Measures* (London, 2014), 141–56; Wendy Doyon, *Empire of Dust: Egyptian Archaeology and Archaeological Labor in Nineteenth-Century Egypt* (PhD dissertation, University of Pennsylvania, 2021); Allison Mickel, *Why Those Who Shovel Are Silent: A History of Local Archaeological Knowledge and Labor* (Louisville, 2021). For a recent homage to Reisner's chief photographer, Mohammedani Ibrahim, see Dianna Wray, "Egyptology's Eloquent Eye," *Aramco World* (September/October 2021), 26–33. An exhibition opened in January 2021 at the Misr Public Library in Luxor entitled "El-Reis;" see Wesam Mohamed (Aarhus University), "El-Reis: co-curated exhibition," *CIPEG e-News* 16 (2021), 5.

2 See for example, Elizabeth Minor, "Decolonizing Reisner: A Case Study of a Classic Kerma Female Burial for Reinterpreting early Nubian Archaeological Collections through Digital Archival Resources," in Matthieu Honegger (ed.), *Nubian Archaeology in the XXIst Century. Proceedings of the Thirteenth International Conference for Nubian Studies Neuchâtel, 1st–6th September 2014* (Leuven-Paris-Bristol, 2018), 345–52.

3 This paper uses the following abbreviations for archival repositories: DIR = Museum of Fine Arts, Boston, Director's Correspondence; BMNY = Brooklyn Museum Archives; EGP AC13 = HU-MFA Expedition Archives, Museum of Fine Arts, Boston; HMANE = Harvard Museum of the Ancient Near East Archives (formerly Harvard Semitic Museum); HUA JBC = Records of the President of Harvard University; James Bryant Conant, 1933–1955, UAI 5.168; HUS CLS = Harvard Radcliffe Institute, Schlesinger Library; Corinna Lindon Smith Papers; MFA DE = Museum of Fine Arts, Boston, Department of Ancient Egyptian, Nubian, and Near Eastern Art; UCBB = University of California, Berkeley, Bancroft Library.

4 Unfortunately, many of these individuals remain anonymous in the archaeological literature; see Quirke, *Hidden Hands;* Stephen Quirke, "Exclusion of Egyptians in English-directed archaeology 1882–1922 under British occupation of Egypt," in Susanne Bickel, Hans-Werner Fischer-Elfert, Antonio Loprieno, and Sebastian Richter (eds.), *Ägyptologen und Ägyptologien zwischen Kaiserreich und Gründung der beiden deutschen Staaten. Reflexionen zur Geschichte und Episteme eines altertumswissenschaftlichen Fachs im 150. Jahr der Zeitschrift für Ägyptische Sprache und Altertumskunde, ZÄS* Beiheft 1 (Berlin, 2014), 379–405, and Mickel, *Why Those Who Shovel Are Silent.*

teams of Egyptian workmen. Many of the accounts described below are treated, some in greater detail, other in less, in the aforementioned Reisner biography.[5]

Part 1. The Diraz Family of *Reises*

Table 1. Genealogy of the major archaeological contributors from the Diraz family.

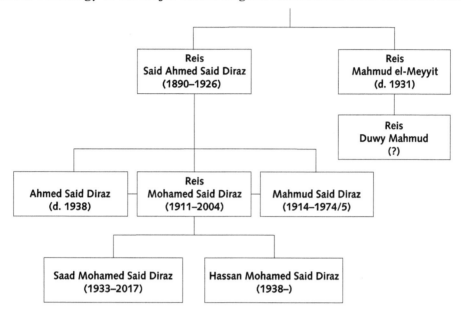

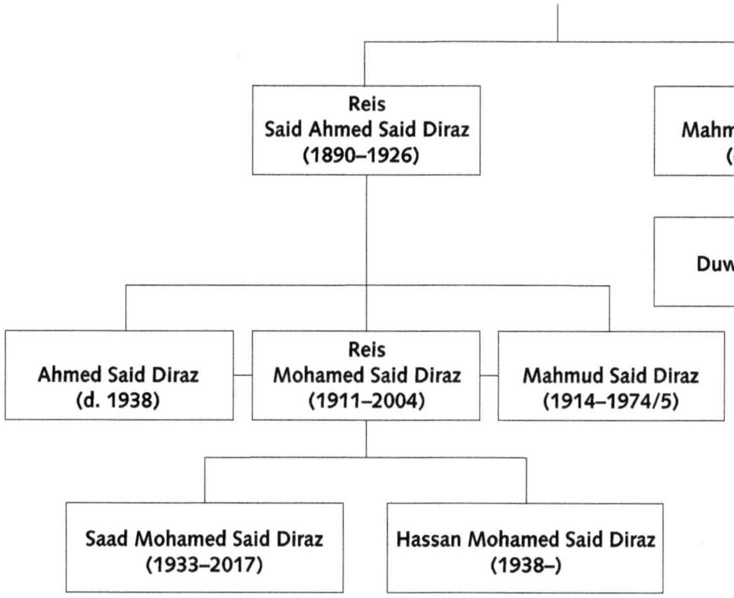

Said Ahmed Said Diraz

Mahmud Ahmed Said Diraz (1890–1926), known more simply as Said Ahmed or Said Ahmed Said, was a Qufti from the village of el-Qalʿa. Said Ahmed started with Reisner as a small boy back in 1899, first carrying his camera and notebooks (fig. 1). Already as a youth, it was clear that he possessed the integrity and ability to manage his fellow co-workers; more significantly, he picked up photographic skills. A series of images taken by Reisner at Deir el-Ballas in November 1900 shows Said and a man named Abdul Hadi running past the dig house as an exposure and speed test (shutter speed 1/400th and aperture 8 for the depth of field; fig. 2).[6] By 1901, Reisner had turned over his darkroom work to young Said Ahmed. Barely more than a decade old, Said learned to process and tone the photo prints. This left only the developing of the glass plate negatives to the Western staff.[7] Reisner once proudly wrote that Said was "doing the work to which Lythgoe and Mace gave over half their time last year, and *doing it fully as well.* This is the first time, I believe, that a *fellah* has been taught to do this work."[8]

By 1905 or 1906 he had taken over all the photographic responsibilities, even training several Egyptian assistants; his work is most prevalent during the excavation of the Menkaure temples at Giza. In an example of fore-

---

[5] Peter Der Manuelian, *Walking among Pharaohs: George Reisner and the Dawn of Modern Egyptology* (Oxford, 2022).

[6] I have experimented with colorizing several of the illustrations in this paper using artificial intelligence. I am aware that some feel this to be a distortion of history and the photographic record, for this reason I have included in all examples the original black-and-white image. I find that the colorized images, despite possibly misrepresenting an article of clothing, can reveal important details easily missed in the originals, in addition to their somewhat "romantic" use.

[7] For a summary of Reisner's photographic workflows, see Peter Der Manuelian, "George Andrew Reisner on Archaeological Photography," *JARCE* 29 (1992), 1–34.

[8] Reisner to Hearst, March 16, 1907; UCBB.

Fig. 1. Right to left: Young Said Ahmed Diraz (right) at Naga ed-Deir, along with Ashur, Ababdi, and Abdul Gawad, December 1901. Photo by David Gordon Lyon, Harvard Museum of the Ancient Near East.

shadowing the art of time-lapse photography, Reisner sent Said Ahmed one-third of the way up the pyramid of Menkaure's east face photograph the day's progress on the clearance of the Menkaure Pyramid Temple.[9] After taking about 1,246 images at many different sites, his last photograph is dated to April 1910 (at Mesaeed). His assistants eventually relieved Said Ahmed since in 1908 Reisner promoted him to head *reis*, replacing his brother Mahmud el-Meyyit (see below), who had held the post from 1905 to 1907. Reisner and Said Ahmed formed a partnership that endured more than twenty-five years, and their collaboration came to hold a very special place among all Reisner's relationships with his Egyptian staff.

Western expeditions at the time were generally set up to leave all practical control and decision-making to the Western staff. In the case of the Hearst, and later the HU-MFA Expedition, however, the situation was often reversed, with Said Ahmed training Reisner's young British and American assistants. They in turn were on site primarily to "provide cover"—as the "white men" ostensibly in charge of the excavations. For example, in April 1912 Reisner was comfortable sending Louis Earle Rowe (1882–1937) down to Mesheikh after only a month's training at Giza because Said Ahmed would be the one running the show. The First Intermediate Period stelae started turning up there as early as the

Fig. 2. Photographic exposure experiments at Deir el-Ballas with young Said Ahmed (shorter) and Abdul Hadi running past the dig house; November 1900. HU-MFA Expedition photos C1783_OS, C1784_OS, C1785_OS. Photo by George Reisner. Original print and colorized with artificial intelligence (colors may not be accurate).

[9] I have merged these images into a time-lapse movie as part of an Edx/2U/HarvardX online course on Giza: https://bit.ly/3dZFTyf.

first day of work. The following year, Said Ahmed supervised the Predynastic site excavations at Naga el-Hai (eleven km north of Wadi Hammamat), while Louis Caulton West (1882–1972) did the recording. After the two men excavated about 1,450 burials, the next task was to complete the excavations begun by Clarence Fisher and Reisner in 1910 at Mesaeed. Reisner left another assistant, Raymond W. Howe (1892–1965) "in charge" at Giza at the end of 1913, again because Said Ahmed ran the excavations, while Reisner himself headed south to join West at Kerma.

In February 1914, Dows Dunham arrived for the first time at Giza to join the expedition. Dunham met *reis* Said Ahmed, who "spoke little English, and in the beginning I did not know any Arabic, but I observed the men at work and was initiated into the methods of excavation and the well-organized system of recording."[10] Over the ensuing years Dunham and Said Ahmed worked together at several sites, including Gammai by the Second Cataract (December 18, 1915, to January 19, 1916), when Dunham was called in to finish the work started by Reisner's assistant Oric Bates (1883–1918). Dunham basically confessed about Said Ahmed: "He would have been quite capable of running the excavation by himself, but as he spoke little English, I went along primarily to keep the records and to be the white man ostensibly in charge (which was thought to be essential in relations with the largely British Sudan authorities)."[11] From the Second Cataract excavations at Semna fort, another Reisner assistant, George Vaillant (1901–1945), corroborated this scenario almost a decade later: "The *mudir* [Reisner] sets great store by him [Said Ahmed] and he conducts the excavations while the Europeans do paper work. For example, at Girga [= Sheikh Farag] neither Dunham nor Rowe had any particular orders while the *reis* was told where to dig and how. This habit of putting the *reis* in actuality over the whites annoyed the other two worthies considerably...."[12]

Said Ahmed enjoyed Reisner's confidence enough to work in tandem with MFA Registrar Hanford Lyman Story (1884–1939) in mid-1915 at the Middle Kingdom cliff site of Deir el-Bersha, while Reisner returned from Kerma to Giza. Said Ahmed oversaw the discovery and clearance of the famous tomb 10A of Djehutynakht, with its nested painted coffins and dozens of wooden models.[13] Reisner was particularly proud of Said Ahmed's Arabic diary, which he found "better than that kept by some Europeans."[14]

Reis Said Ahmed earned a sterling reputation, not only as a photographer and archaeologist, but as an administrator and manager of men as well. He was held in high esteem by both Egyptian and Sudanese workmen on Reisner's teams. Since so many of the workmen were related, and honor meant everything to entire family groups, the Expedition force was dissuaded from theft during the excavations.[15] At Deir el-Bersha, when the Expedition's tools mysteriously "disappeared" one day, Reisner and Said Ahmed played "good cop/bad cop" with the Coptic *omda* (village head), and the local Sheikh Mohamed. Said eventually learned that the two men were "partners in crime," and that the tools had been stolen because Sheikh Mohamed had been replaced as an antiquities guard, and because his own exorbitant price demands for supplying water-hauling donkeys to the Expedition had resulted in the hiring of a Copt instead. Once the Expedition discovered their tools, thrown down a burial shaft, the sheikh and the *omda* lost all their leverage.[16]

Said Ahmed could be clever as well, as he demonstrated for the benefit of the Expedition. At Gebel Barkal by the Fourth Cataract, when labor relations with the local population threatened to break down in 1916 due to a kickback scheme perpetrated by the local *omda*, it was Said Ahmed who strategically offered to hire a workforce from another region instead. This would have landed the *omda* in a difficult quandary as the man responsible for sabotaging lucrative employment opportunities for his fellow Barkal villagers.[17] At the pyramid field of Nuri, under cover of darkness Said Ahmed dismantled, moved, and rebuilt an entire modern Muslim monu-

---

[10] Dows Dunham, *Recollections of an Egyptologist* (Boston, 1972), 12.

[11] Dunham, *Recollections of an Egyptologist*, 16.

[12] Vaillant to his father, from Semna, January 31, 1924 (misdated 1923); private collection of Henry Vaillant. Note that Dunham sang a rather different tune about his deference to *reis* Said Ahmed in his memoir, *Recollections of an Egyptologist*, 16, and 23–24, 26–27.

[13] Rita E. Freed, Lawrence M. Berman, Denise M. Doxey, and Nicholas S. Picardo, *The Secrets of Tomb 10A: Egypt 2000 BC* (Boston, 2009).

[14] Reisner to Morris Gray, May 12, 1915; DIR.

[15] Dunham, *Recollections of an Egyptologist*, 24–26.

[16] Freed et al., *Secrets of Tomb 10A*, 96; Manuelian, *Walking Among Pharaohs*, 342–50.

[17] HU-MFA Expedition Diary, February 4, 1916; MFA DE.

ment (Reisner called it a "sheikh," but the reference is unclear whether it stood over an actual tomb) that happened to stand right over the entrance to Pyramid 10 where Reisner was keen to dig. The next morning, the local Sudanese never noticed the new location and the excavations could continue.[18] On a more serious note, later in 1916, when the wall flanking the staircase entrance to Nuri Pyramid 5 collapsed, killing several men, Said Ahmed (who was not on-site at the time) successfully coaxed 147 of the 260 local men back on the job, despite their fears; increased wages brought back the rest.[19]

Another skill Said Ahmed demonstrated concerned logistics: how to move massive stone objects, from colossal statue fragments in temple pits to huge sarcophagi located in buried chambers deep under Nubian pyramids. At Nuri, a British irrigation engineer once turned to Reisner wondering how on earth he would remove the sarcophagi of Kings Aspelta and Anlamani from their respective burial chambers. Estimated to weigh sixteen tons, the Aspelta sarcophagus had to pass through three cramped doorways, up seventy steps, and across a sandy mile to the expedition storehouse in the village. Reisner replied that all he had to do was task Said Ahmed with the job and then just requisition some beams, winches, and wire rope from the railway shops at Karima.[20] Said handled the rest; the sarcophagus of Anlamani was smaller but hardly less challenging (fig. 3). Said Ahmed often stayed behind after the close of the excavation season to pack and crate such large stone objects and transport them by river barge, train, or steamer via Port Sudan, Port Said, or Alexandria, off to Boston. Many years later, while attempting to raise several stone sarcophagi from the Eastern Cemetery at Giza, Expedition assistant Noel F. Wheeler (1894–1977) complained that Said's successor as *reis,* his brother Mahmud el-Meyyit, "knows about as much about lifting weights as my great-aunt,—which is not much."[21]

Fig. 3. Securing the sarcophagus of Anlamani at Nuri, with Pyramid 6 in the background, looking west, April 18, 1917. HU-MFA Expedition photo D386 NS. Photo by Mohammedani Ibrahim.

Inspecting the area of Kumma fort across from Semna on the east bank at the Second Cataract, Reisner found it filled with sixteen "modern" houses built of the mud bricks dating to the Middle Kingdom. He directed Said Ahmed to negotiate with the villagers to take immediate possession of the area. Reisner wanted this done soon as "our work may incite the owners to illicit excavations."[22] They bought all the villagers out with $300.[23] Back at Semna, Said Ahmed continued writing his own expedition diary in Arabic, while staff member Alan Rowe (1890–1968) wrote up his own daily entries in English.

18 Reisner, "The Adventures of an Archaeologist in the Valley of the Nile," Unpublished and unfinished autobiographical memoir (1939), 73–74, HUG 4737; Dunham, *Recollections of an Egyptologist,* 23–24; Manuelian, *Walking among Pharaohs,* 388.

19 HU-MFA Expedition Diary, November 28, 1916; MFA DE.

20 Reisner to MFA Director Arthur Fairbanks, July 11, 1918; EGP AC13.

21 Wheeler to Reisner, October 2, 1929; EGP AC13.

22 HU-MFA Expedition Diary, February 5, 1924; MFA DE.

23 HU-MFA Expedition Diary ($300), February 6, 1924, listing all sixteen names paid between LE1 and 4, totaling LE 40; MFA DE; compare Vaillant to his father ($200), February 7, 1924; private collection of Henry Vaillant.

Fig. 4. Said Ahmed and George Reisner supervise work at Nuri Pyramid 36, looking west, February 7, 1917. HU-MFA Expedition Paget photo D278 NS (negative lost). Photo by Mohammedani Ibrahim.

Fig. 5. To prepare for the Hetepheres excavation (G 7000 X), Said Ahmed poses for a one-minute exposure test with one 1000-candle power lamp using reflectors, Giza, December 7, 1925. HU-MFA Expedition photo C11064 NS. Photo by Badawi Ahmed.

As a small demonstration in 1921 of the, from a traditional Western perspective, perhaps unexpected social hierarchy of the Diraz family within the Expedition, Said Ahmed, now apparently an "ardent Zaghlulist"[24] (unlike Reisner), upbraided Dows Dunham on one occasion for the latter's mishandling an argument between his brother Mahmud el-Meyyit and talented Expedition photographer Mohammedani Ibrahim.[25] Needed in several locations at once, Said was moving large stones at Nuri while Dunham was struggling to maintain order up at Giza in Reisner's absence in Boston.[26]

A further testament to Said Ahmed's judgment portrays his sense of restraint, even in the face of gross injustice committed against him. In June 1924, he learned by telegram that someone had torn up all the young palm trees he had planted near the modern cemetery by his home, a considerable sum of about LE 25 worth of damage. He returned from Giza to Quft to find a full-blown investigation underway, with trackers following the perpetrators' footprints towards the village. A thousand men had gathered, armed with sticks, but Said Ahmed called off the investigation to avoid bloodshed. It turned out he had been pulled into a feud, falsely accused of having tipped off a European company that led to a family's dismissal from their employ. This gave a rival family, who had lost a member to murder at the hands of the first family, the opportunity to win Said Ahmed's family over to their side in the feud. Said chose to swallow the loss of his palm trees rather than embark on an endless three-way battle. The man's principles impressed all those around him.[27]

The Western Expedition staff were always welcome at the Diraz family's home village of el-Qalʿa, near Quft (fig. 6). Said Ahmed invited Dows Dunham and his wife Eveline Spencer Dunham to stop en route to the Sudan (fig. 7). Two days later, they were at Luxor visiting the Valley of the Kings, where Eveline was photographed sitting not a stone's throw from where Howard Carter would discover the tomb of Tutankhamun almost exactly one year later.[28] Others who visited the Diraz family at Said Ahmed's house, one of the grandest in the village, included, besides Reisner and his family of course, the American painter Joseph Lindon Smith and wife, the

[24] A follower of the Egyptian nationalist, statesman, and leader of the Wafd Party, Saad Zaghlul (1857–1927).

[25] For more on Mohammedani Ibrahim, see Wray, "Egyptology's Eloquent Eye," 26–33.

[26] Dunham to Reisner, October 21, 1921; EGP AC13.

[27] HU-MFA Expedition Diary, July 2, 1924; MFA DE.

[28] Peter Der Manuelian, "Six Feet from Tutankhamun—The Near Miss of 1914. What did Howard Carter know and when did he know it?" *Kmt* 32.4 (Winter 2021–22), 44–52.

a rough list of the objects found and a duplicate of the object-note is placed with the objects in the tray or basket. Our scribe or the office boy working with the man registering the objects, acts as store-keeper for all the ordinary run of antiquities, and reads to the Arabic notes in case the registrar does not read Arabic. Why not have Berberi and Labib try their hand at an Arabic Diary which Labeeb [sic] could put into English?[43]

Reisner called the Giza Arabic diary prepared by Duwy and Mohamed Said "the best we have ever had with scale drawings made by Mohamed Said. Duwy supervises the field work and guards from 6 A.M. to 6 P.M., and Mohammed Said supervises the guards from 6 P.M. to 6 A.M."[44] Duwy kept Reisner informed on the progress of the work with plans of the mastabas drawn in white lines on black paper. This is a reference to illustrations produced specifically for Reisner's benefit, as severe cataracts eventually claimed his eyesight.[45] The reversed contrast of white ink on black paper was just one of the methods the Expedition developed to assist him with his daily work. Mohamed Said used the same method for recording the burial shafts. Duwy even copied hieroglyphic inscriptions on occasion (see below, figs. 23–24).

Realizing Duwy's supervisory capabilities, Reisner was willing to send him to Gordon Loud (1900–1971), the third director of the Oriental Institute's Megiddo Expedition, after Clarence Fisher and P.L.O. Guy.[46] Loud had lost his Reisner-trained *reis* Hamid Ahmed to illness, so Duwy took over in January 1938. Unfortunately, the new environment and "tough unruly Palestine Arabs," stymied Duwy's effectiveness somewhat, but he continued for two seasons at Megiddo in between his Giza work.[47]

After Reisner's death in 1942, as the HU-MFA Expedition staff prepared to shut down, they were able to place Duwy Mahmud at Saqqara as *reis* for the excavations of Abdel Salam Mohammed Hussein.[48]

Fig. 11. Mohamed Said (left) and his brother Mahmud Said at Harvard Camp, Giza, March 1937; note the shadow of the (unlisted) photographer (likely Miss Mary Reisner), indicating a late afternoon shot (looking west). Harvard University Archives, Pusey Library, George Andrew Reisner Papers, HUG 4737.

---

[43] Reisner to Fisher, July 4, 1922, replying to June 29, 1922, letter of Fisher to Reisner; EGP AC13.

[44] Reisner, "Curriculum Vitae," unpublished manuscript, 1937, 17; EGP AC13.

[45] Reisner's oculist was Dr. Max Meyerhof; see Isolde Lehnert, "In the 'Land of the Blind': Dr Max Meyerhof and Friends," in Ernst Czerny (ed.), *In Search of the Orient. Proceedings of the Symposium held at Kunsthistorisches Museum Wien (September 20th to 24th, 2016),* Egypt and Austria XI (Krakow, 2018), 209–26, and Ernst Czerny, "Max Meyerhof (1874–1945). Augenarzt und Orientalist in Kairo," in T. L. Gertzen and J. H. Schoeps (eds.), *Grenzgänger. Jüdische Wissenschaftler, Träumer und Abenteurer zwischen Orient und Okzident* (Berlin, 2020), 334–59.

[46] Reisner to Corinna Lindon Smith, January 8, 1938; HUS CLS.

[47] Loud to Reisner, April 28, 1938; EGP AC13.

[48] For Reisner's proud description of Duwy's discovery of statuettes in mastabas G 2407 and G 2421, see Reisner to Corinna Lindon Smith, May 22, 1936; HUS CLS.

Mohamed Said Diraz (1911–2004), Son of Said Ahmed Diraz

Through the 1930s and 1940s, two sons of Said Ahmed Diraz, Mohamed Said Diraz and Mahmud Said Diraz, eventually took over almost every aspect of HU-MFA Expedition management (fig. 11). Living with the Expedition since about 1920, Mohamed Said attended private Egyptian school in Kafr el-Haram near the Giza Pyramids, and studied in a branch of el-Azhar in his Qufti village of el-Qal'a. He was then trained in the Expedition's archaeological methodology by his father Said Ahmed, by Expedition draftsman Alexander Floroff (1920–1979), and by Reisner himself.[49]

In 1926 Mohamed Said was a teenager at the death of his father. Reisner summoned him to Giza, and by 1936 he was promoted to head *reis*. That same year Reisner wrote his friend Corinna Lindon Smith that "Mohamed Said and Duwy have become excellent draughtsmen. Duwy reports to me the progress of the work with beautiful plans of the mastabas drawn in white lines on black. Mohamed is recording in the same way the shafts. He has done a shaft G 5210 A which I have wanted for months but Floroff (who is very busy) could not find time for it. Mohamed examined the mastaba and produced a full report (white on black) in one day. Mahmud is doing all the typing. These three boys are invaluable and I shall have to raise the wages of all three" (fig. 12).[50]

Along with his brother Mahmud, Mohamed Said became indispensable to the Expedition, not least because of the onset of Reisner's blindness, evident since 1931 (fig. 13). In addition to handling the men, keeping the Arabic diary, and supervising logistics, he kept the Expedition running through the difficult years of the Depression, Reisner's death in 1942, and the perils of the Second World War. Mohamed helped outfit "air raid shelters" in selected Giza tombs for Reisner and his staff during German bombing alarms, and he assisted with placing the men in other jobs once it became clear in the 1940s that the Expedition was nearing its end. His very final entry in the Arabic diary—on January 18, 1947—concerns packing the remaining glass plate negatives for shipment to Boston. Between the years 1900 and 1942 the Expedition photographers had taken about 45,000 photographs total at twenty-three sites.

Fig. 12. HU-MFA Expedition staff at Harvard Camp, Giza, celebrate the return of the Reisner family from their final trip to America. From left to right: Frank O. Allen, Mahmud Said, Nicholas Melnikoff, Mrs. Mary Reisner, George Reisner, Alexander Floroff, Miss Mary Reisner, Evelyn Perkins, Mohammed Said, looking west, July 25, 1939. HU-MFA Expedition photo A8286 NS. Photo by Mohammedani Ibrahim. Original print and colorized with artificial intelligence (colors may not be accurate).

---

[49] Reisner to Drioton, January 22, 1937; EGP AC13.

[50] Reisner to Corinna Lindon Smith, August 23, 1936; HUS CLS.

Fig. 13. George Reisner, Mohammed Said, and Frank Allen examining records at Harvard Camp (rephotograph from el-Mussawar Arabic magazine visit, but not used in issue no. 740, December 16, 1938); copy photograph, HU-MFA B9022 NS. Photo by Mohammedani Ibrahim. Original print and colorized with artificial intelligence (colors may not be accurate).

Mahmud Said (1914–1974/5), son of Said Ahmed Diraz

Finally, although never a head *reis* for the HU-MFA Expedition, Mahmud Said Ahmed Diraz, to use his full name, deserves listing here as well. Son of former head *reis* Said Ahmed, Mahmud Said obtained his primary school certificate in 1929, then spent four years in Secondary School, joining the Expedition in 1934. He was employed as an assistant secretary, trained by Reisner's chief clerical assistant Evelyn Perkins (1893–1951). A typist, Mahmud read and wrote English and French (fig. 14).[51] Most of his time was spent in the Harvard Camp dig house, assisting with manuscript preparation and Expedition correspondence. Reisner described the workflow in 1937: "I have the most efficient staff I have ever had... Mahmud Said Ahmed, assistant to Miss Perkins, translates the Arabic diary [written by Duwy Mahmud] into English and types all my mss. and letters from my original text. His brother Mohamed Said Ahmed is assistant surveyor. Their cousin Duwy Mahmud oversees the excavations. With such a staff, the work goes on steadily."[52] Like his brother Mohamed, Mahmud Said was the other "pillar" holding up the Expedition through the war years, and joining Evelyn Perkins in caring for Reisner, who was basically an invalid at Harvard Camp during the last year of his life.

The Reises after the HU-MFA Expedition

After George Reisner's death on June 6, 1942, Mahmud Said ended up assisting Expedition field director Frank Allen (1910–1991) in the Office of War Information in Cairo, while his brother Mohamed Said continued to manage affairs at the Camp along with Evelyn Perkins. The two Diraz brothers supported the remaining staff and held the Expedition together until 1946, when Dows Dunham and William Stevenson Smith were finally able to leave Boston for Cairo, assess the situation, and reach a decision about continuing or closing the HU-MFA Expedition (they chose the latter, shutting down on April 30, 1947).[53] Mahmud Said continued to work for the American Legation until September 13, 1947, when he was appointed as private secretary to the general di-

[51] Reisner to Drioton, January 22, 1937; EGP AC13.

[52] Reisner to J. W. Lowes, October 6, 1937; HUA JBC. See also Reisner to Corinna Lindon Smith, September 26, 1936; HUS CLS; and Reisner to Edgell, September 28, 1936; DIR.

[53] For a charming eulogy to the Expedition's headquarters, and a photograph of Mohamed Said and Mahmud Said playing chess on the terrace, see William Stevenson Smith, "Harvard Camp. The Earliest American Archaeological Center in Egypt," *Archaeology* 2.4 (Winter

Fig. 14. Mahmud Said recites a poem in Reisner's honor at his seventieth birthday party at Harvard Camp, Giza, November 5, 1937. Harvard University Archives, Pusey Library, George Andrew Reisner Papers, HUG 4737.

Fig. 15. Mohamed Said and Mahmud Said in undated photo. Hassan Diraz collection.

rector of the three primary (out of eight) bus companies owned by Mohamed Salem Salem (Upper Egypt, Lower Egypt, and Cairo). Mahmud lived until 1974 or 1975 (fig. 15). His brother, former *reis* Mohamed Said Ahmed Diraz, made the pilgrimage to Mecca in 1949, and worked for Mohamed Salem Salem in Misr Engineering and Car Company, later renamed to just the Misr Engineering and Car Co., until being laid off in 1954 for lack of funds. Both brothers kept in contact with most of their Boston colleagues (Dunham, Smith, etc.) until at least 1954, and both were instrumental in assisting MFA assistant curator Bernard Bothmer with travel and logistics when he visited Egypt for the first time in 1950.[54] Mohamed Said died on February 25, 2004, and was possibly the longest-living of all those in Reisner's immediate cohort; his wife Zohra lived for another four years, and I was privileged to meet her in Cairo in 2006 (see below).

The Post-Expedition Generation of the Diraz Family

The short summary above brings us to the next generation of the talented Diraz men from Quft, albeit long after Reisner's time. It is a pity, and a loss for archaeology, that neither Mohamed Said nor his brother Mahmud Said continued with other excavation work after the HU-MFA Expedition shut down in 1947. There were not many projects in operation during the late 1940s and 1950s, however, and the economics of earning a living with large-scale Western-backed expeditions had changed. As a result, none of the many Diraz children followed a career path as a *reis*. But two of Mohamed Said's children are worth mentioning here.

On Saturday, September 11, 1943, ten-year-old Saad Mohamed Said Ahmed Diraz (1933–2017), Reis Mohamed Said's eldest son, and six-year-old Sobhy Duwy Mahmud, the only son of Duwy Mahmud, discovered a

1949), 194–95. The American Research Center in Egypt was created upon the figurative ashes of Harvard Camp; see Manuelian, *Walking among Pharaohs*, 809–13.

[54] Bernard V. Bothmer, *Egypt 1950. My First Visit*, edited by Emma Swan Hall (Oxford, 2003), 8–9 with n. 19, and 12–13, 70–74, 110, 112–13, 115, 131–32, 154, 156.

Fig. 19. The HU-MFA Expedition Arabic diaries, kept safe by the Diraz family in el-Qal'a for about six decades, after arrival in Boston. November 20, 2006. Photo by the author.

company in Dokki to facilitate the shipping to Boston, incurring an expensive Fedex bill. I had already secured the necessary permissions from Zahi Hawass and the Ministry of Tourism and Antiquities, as it is called today, and I thank him and his staff once again. Since that time, several subsequent visits with Hassan Diraz have only deepened my appreciation for his keen memory and his interest in preserving the legacy of both his family and the HU-MFA Expedition.

One mystery remains, however, and that is why the Arabic diaries remained in Egypt all these years. We have already seen that George Reisner intended them to occupy shelves next to the Expedition's English language diaries in Boston. When Dows Dunham and William Stevenson Smith arrived in 1946 to inventory and eventually shut down Harvard Camp, they were meticulous in cataloguing everything. Even though they were of differing opinions on what to keep and what to discard (apparently every "letter, theatre program, social invitation or old calendar" had been retained,[58] and Dunham was ready for a purge while Smith was not), they would surely have realized the significance of the Arabic diaries. Perhaps the diaries were kept, not in Reisner's main work office but in the *reis*'s quarters. According to Hassan Diraz, Dunham felt they were not needed in Boston and apparently told Mohamed Said so.[59] We may never know why these books were not shipped home to Boston in 1947 along with the remaining antiquities, drawings, correspondence, notes, glass plate negatives, English diaries, and other register books.

After the Arabic diaries arrived without mishap in December 2006 at the Museum of Fine Arts, Boston, we performed a basic inventory, and then integrated the forty-two Giza Arabic diaries into the workflow of the Giza Project (fig. 19). Twenty Giza seminar students, supervised and organized by Project Archivist Catherine Pate, began scanning the books, a process which lasted from February 12 to June 22, 2007. At that point I hired Dr. Ramadan Hussein, then at Brown University, to translate all the Giza volumes over a period of several years, in between his other work. Dr. Hussein, who tragically passed away in Tübingen as this article went to press, was an excellent choice, being Egyptian, an Egyptologist, and a scholar familiar with the Upper Egyptian terminology used in the diaries. After translation, Giza Project staff, primarily Rachel Aronin, along with Nicholas Picardo and Jeremy Kisala, supervised Harvard PhD students including Katherine Rose, who began to parse out the text on the pages for database linking, by tomb number, personal name, etc. to the various records in our SQL Giza database and website. We expect all the Giza diaries to be viewable, with translations, and intelligent links to related media, on the Giza website (http://giza.fas.harvard.edu).

The overall inventory of the Arabic diaries, for all sites attested, is provided in Table 2.

[58] John D. Cooney to Elizabeth Riefstahl, January 28 and February 2, 1947; BMNY.
[59] Hassan Diraz, personal communication, May 31, 2022.

Table 2. Inventory list of Arabic diaries

Diary No.	Years	Pages assigned	Date range	Size (cm)	Site	Cover no.
1	1913–1914	1–100	16 Nov 1913–24 April 1914	20x27	Giza	A
2	1915	1–64	17 March 1915–30 May 1915	20x27	Deir el-Bersha	
		65–100	21 Oct 1915–18 Nov 1915		Giza	
3	1915	1–55	19 Nov 1915–22 Jan 1916	26x40	Giza	B
		55–102	23 Jan 1916–6 March 1916		Gebel Barkal	
4	1916	1–29	7 March 1916–15 April 1916	22.5x25	Gebel Barkal	
		30–100	21 March 1916–15 April 1916	22.5x25	Nuri	
5	1916	1–75	26 April 1916–17 Dec 1916	26x40	Gebel Barkal & Nuri	8
6	1916–1917	76–150	18 Dec 1916–7 Feb 1917	26x40	Nuri	9 (Nuri II)
7	1917	151–225	7 Feb 1917–30 March 1917	26x40	Nuri	10 (Nuri III)
8	1917	226–308	30 March 1917–8 May 1917	27x42	Nuri	11 (Nuri IV)
9	1917–1918	1–93	9 May 1917–26 Feb 1918	27x42	Nuri	12
10	1918–1919	94–161	27 Feb 1918–11 Jan 1919	26x40	Nuri & Gebel Barkal	13
11	1919	1–99	24 Jan 1919–20 March 1919	26x40	Kurru	I
12	1919	100–163	20 March 1919–10 May 1919	25x38.5	Kurru	II
13	1919	164–232	11 May 1919–29 Nov 1919	26x42	Kush	
14	1919–1921	233–319	30 Nov 1919–11 May 1920	26x40	Gebel Barkal	
		320–331	27 Dec 1920–19 Jan 1921		Meroe/Bega-rawiya/ Kabushiya	
15	1921	332–431	19 Jan 1921–2 March 1921	27x42	Meroe/Bega-rawiya/ Kabushiya	
16	1921	432–531	3 March 21–3 Dec 1921	27x42	Meroe/Bega-rawiya/ Kabushiya	
17	1921–1922	532–630	4 Dec 1921–26 Jan 1922	26x41	Meroe/Bega-rawiya/ Kabushiya	
18	1922	631–731	27 Jan 1922–12 March 1922	27x42	Meroe/Bega-rawiya/ Kabushiya	4
19	1922	732–828	12 March 1922–11 Jan 1923	26x40	Meroe/Bega-rawiya/ Kabushiya	

Diary No.	Years	Pages assigned	Date range	Size (cm)	Site	Cover no.
20	1923	829–946	12 Jan 1923–9 Feb 1923	29x42	Meroe/Bega-rawiya/ Kabushiya	
21	1923	947–1046	9 Feb 1923–3 March 1923	29x42	Meroe/Bega-rawiya/ Kabushiya	
22	1923	1047–1145	3 March 1923–24 March 23	29x42	Meroe/Bega-rawiya/ Kabushiya	
23	1923	1146–1191	24 March 1923–13 May 1923	21x29	Meroe/Bega-rawiya/ Kabushiya	
24	1923	1–13	28 May 1923–18 June 1923	26x39	Quft	
		13–21	5 July 1923–29 Sept 1923		Giza	
		22–100	9 Oct 1923–18 Nov 23		Girga & Sheikh Farag	
25	1923–1924	101–150	19 Nov 1923–29 Dec 1923	26x39	Girga	I
		150–152	30 Dec 1923–11 Jan 1924		Quft	
		152–201	17 Jan 1924–24 Feb 1924		Semna	
26	1924	202–302	25 Feb 1924–5 April 1924	26x39	Semna	II
27	1924	303–340	5 April 1924–19 May 1924	26x39	Semna	III
28	1924	1–67	8 Sept 1924–14 Dec 1924	26x39	Giza	I
29	1924–1925	68–164	15 Dec 1924–24 Jan 1925	26x39	Giza	II
30	1925	165–232	25 Jan 1925–13 Feb 1925	25x39	Giza	III
31	1925	233–300	14 Feb 1925–28 Feb 1925	25x38	Giza	IV
32	1925	301–400	1 March 1925–25 Nov 1925	25x39	Giza	V
33	1925–1926	401–500	26 Nov 1925–1 Jan 1926	26x39	Giza	VI
34	1926	501–598	1 Jan 1926–18 Feb 1926	26x39	Giza	VII
35	1926	599–697	19 Feb 1926–28 April 26	26x39	Giza	VIII
36	1926	698–796	29 April 1926–4 Feb 1927	26x39	Giza	IX
37	1927	797–895	5 Feb 1927–10 April 1927	26x39	Giza	X
38	1927–1928	896–994	11 April 1927–4 April 1928	26x39	Giza	XI
39	1928	995–1095	4 April 1928–5 May 1928	27x32	Giza	XII
40	1928–1929	1096–1192	6 May 1928–5 March 1929	27x32	Giza	XIII
41	1927–1928	1–99	14 Dec 1927–12 Feb 1928	26x39	Semna	IV
42	1928	100–129	12 Feb 1928–12 March 1928	26x39	Semna	II
		129–167	18 Oct 1928–12 Nov 1928		Semna	
		168–198	13 Nov 1928–30 Nov 1928		Uronarti	
43	1928–1929	199–297	1 Dec 1928–12 Jan 1929	27x32	Uronarti, Semna	Semna III

Diary No.	Years	Pages assigned	Date range	Size (cm)	Site	Cover no.
44	1929	298–301	13 Jan 1929–22 Jan 1929	27x32	Giza	Semna IV
	1930	302–376	28 Jan 1930–25 March 1930		Uronarti	
45	1929	1193–1292	6 March 1929–17 April 1929	27x32	Giza	XIV
46	1929	1293–1387	17 April 1929–18 Nov 1929	27x32	Giza	XV
47	1929	1388–1492	18 Nov 1929–15 Dec 1929	27x31	Giza	XVI
48	1929–1930	1493–1590	16 Dec 1929–18 Jan 1930	27x31	Giza	XVII
49	1930	1591–1342	19 Jan 1930–26 Dec 1930	27x31	Giza	XVIII
50	1930–1931	1343–1426	27 Dec 1930–25 Jan 1931	27x31	Giza	XIX
51	1931–1932	1427–1517	26 Jan 1931–12 March 1932	27x31	Giza	XX
52	1931	377–445	10 Feb 1931–31 March 1931	26x31	Saras/Shalfak	V
		446–470	9 Nov 1931–17 Dec 1931		Abka/Mirgissa	
53	1931–1932	471–543	18 Dec 1931–9 Feb 1932	26x31	Abka/Mirgissa	VI
54	1932	1518–1611	12 March 1932–22 April 1932	27x31	Giza	XXI
55	1932–1933	1612–1705	23 April 1932–30 Jan 1933	27x31	Giza	XXII
56	1933–1934	1706–1818	31 Jan 1933–29 Sept 1934	26x39	Giza	XXIII
57	1934	1819–1921	30 Sept 1934–10 April 1935	26x39	Giza	XXIV
58	1935	1922–2026	11 April 1935–22 Aug 1935	26x39	Giza	XXV
59	1935	2027–2131	23 Aug 1935–16 Nov 1935	26x39	Giza	XXVI
60	1935–1936	2132–2235	17 Nov 1935–9 Feb 1936	26x39	Giza	XXVII
61	1936	2236–2340	10 Feb 1936–19 April 1936	26x39	Giza	XXVIII
62	1936	2341–2463	20 April 1936–8 July 1936	26x39	Giza	XXIX
63	1936	2464–2567	9 July 1936–18 Nov 1936	26x39	Giza	XXX
64	1936–1937	2568–2657	18 Nov 1936–23 May 1937	26x39	Giza	XXXI
65	1937	2658–2757	24 May 1937–18 Oct 1937	26x39	Giza	XXXII
66	1937–1938	2758–2856	18 Oct 1937–28 Jan 1938	27x38	Giza	XXXIII
67	1938	2857–2955	29 Jan 1938–28 May 1938	27x38	Giza	XXXIV
68	1938–1939	2956–3055	29 May 1938–5 Jan 1939	26x39	Giza	XXXV
69	1939	3056–3153	6 Jan 1939–2 May 1939	26x39	Giza	XXXVI
70	1939–1940	3154–3252	3 May 1939–20 Jan 1940	27x38	Giza	XXXVII
71	1940	3253–3351	21 Jan 1940–3 April 1940	27x38	Giza	XXXVIII
72	1940	3352–3451	4 April 1940–31 May 1940	27x38	Giza	XXXIX
73	1940–1947	3452–3522	4 June 1940–18 Jan 1947	27x38	Giza	XL

Part 3. Significance of the Arabic Diaries and Selected Examples

Although the in-depth scholarly research on the diaries still lies ahead of us (see below) it is clear even at this preliminary stage that the texts provide an absolutely unique body of archaeological literature from early twentieth century Egyptian archaeology. They include details often missing from their English-language counterparts kept (primarily in the Expedition's earlier years) by Reisner's Western staff and missing even from some of Mahmud Said's English translations of the Arabic dating to the 1930s. For example, the Arabic versions are more complete in listing the Egyptians by name who were working in specific areas on a given day. The entries show a concern for detail and in many cases a meticulous approach to sketches and drawings. Below are just a few examples from the thousands of Arabic diary pages, which I have separated into three somewhat random categories: documentation of the Expedition's daily excavation progress (including drawings); archaeological interpretation and speculation by the Egyptian *reises;* and descriptions of "local color" and events concerning the Expedition staff. The examples in the first two categories are presented in chronological order, earlier to later.

Archaeological Documentation in the Arabic Diaries

The Arabic diaries generally follow the pattern Reisner laid out for daily recording in his own diaries. The site is named along with the day's date, and then a numbered table of contents usually listed all the monuments or areas worked on that day. Next come the individual descriptions of the progress made in each area. Illustrations range from rough sketches to fairly careful plans and sections, such as those showing the Nubian pyramid burial chamber from Nuri (fig. 20),[60] or the staircase entrance and two chambers of another one at el-Kurru (fig. 21).[61]

In Table 3 and figure 22 that compare the Expedition's English diary with the simultaneously kept Arabic diary at Giza in 1932, we find that the Arabic versions often contain lengthier descriptions of the clearance of individual Giza burial shafts; moreover, they name the Egyptians working in each shaft. The different texts complement each other well and give a fuller picture of the excavations.

The unusual dog stela of Abutiu, found reused at Giza in G 2188 shaft Y, caught Reisner's attention in 1936: "In the course of examining the list of objects to be presented for division...I came across an inscription in ten vertical lines which even from Duwy's copy I had seen was unusual...The ceremonial burial I think was intended to secure the future existence of the dog as a favorite animal associated with the kas of the king and his owner..."[62] Duwy Mahmud's hieroglyphic hand copy of the Abutiu dog inscription (fig. 23) is reproduced in fig. 24.[63] The caption above the drawing reads: "This is a copy of the text inscribed on the block found in shaft 2188 Y."[64]

For an in-depth description of a statue discovery at Giza, we may turn to Duwy Mahmud's account of work in shaft D of mastaba G 2420 in the Western Cemetery (fig. 25). In a letter home, Reisner informed his friend Corinna Lindon Smith of Duwy's successes, including the touching "joke" Duwy attempted that a lady he had met had greetings for Reisner, her name being "Mrs. Nedjemu," i.e., the wife of the owner of the first statue he found. With a team of only eight men, due to very limited excavation activity in 1936, Duwy Mahmud unearthed about eleven statuettes and a reserve head, mostly in Cemetery G 2400.[65]

---

60 Compare the plan to Dows Dunham, *Nuri,* Royal Cemeteries of Kush 2 (Boston, 1955), 6, fig. 1, 8, fig. 2b.

61 Compare the plan in Dows Dunham, *El Kurru,* Royal Cemeteries of Kush 1 (Cambridge, 1950), 38, fig. 12a.

62 Reisner to Dunham, September 29, 1936; EGP AC13. Reisner was being somewhat disingenuous here, for the relief had actually been discovered back in 1912, but he also wrote that "from the copy made by the reis Duwy, I could not understand the full purport;" Reisner to MFA director Edgell, September 28, 1936; DIR and EGP AC13.

63 George Reisner, "The Dog which was Honored by the King of Upper and Lower Egypt," *BMFA* 34, No. 206 (December 1936), 96–99; George Reisner, "Ancient King Gives Dog A Royal Burial," *The American Kennel Gazette* 55, No. 5 (May 1, 1938), 7–9, 180–82; Henry G. Fischer, "An Old Kingdom Monogram: ," *ZÄS* 93 (1966), 57–60, fig. 2; Orly Goldwasser, *Prophets, Lovers and Giraffes: Wor(l)d Classification in Ancient Egypt* (Wiesbaden, 2002), 93–94.

64 More on this stela, and the long delay between its initial discovery and its translation, may be found in Manuelian, *Walking among Pharaohs,* 697–98.

65 Reisner to Corinna Lindon Smith, May 22, 1936; HUS CLS.

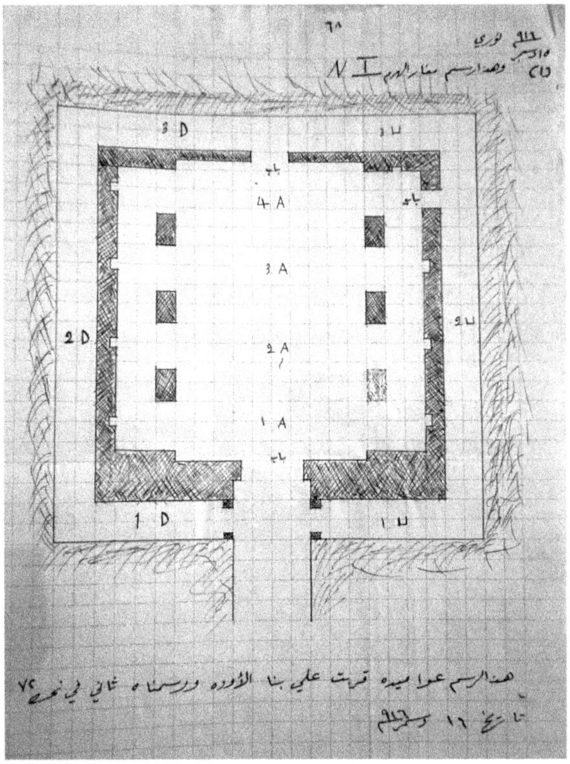

Fig. 20. Arabic Diary Book 5, October 25 to December 17, 1916, page 68, plan of Nuri Pyramid 1 (Taharqa). HU-MFA Expedition; MFA.

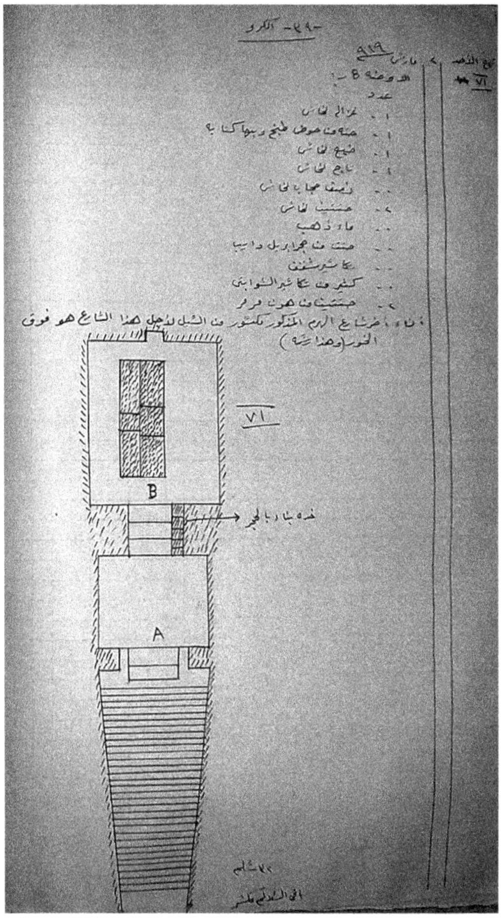

Fig. 21. Arabic Diary Book 11, page 39, El Kurru, January 24 to March 20, 1919, showing a plan of Ku. 6. HU-MFA Expedition; MFA.

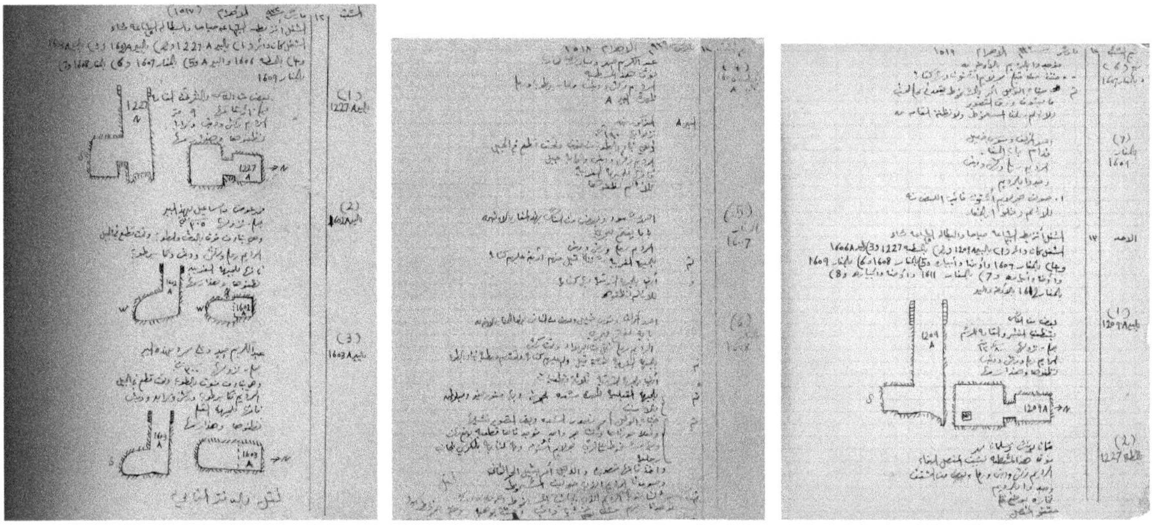

Fig. 22. Arabic Giza Diary Books 20–21, March 12, 1932, pages 1517–19. HU-MFA Expedition; MFA.

Table 3. Comparison of English (left) and Arabic (right) Giza Expedition diaries for March 12, 1932.

English Diary	Arabic Diary
Saturday, March 12, 1932 Sixth day of work. Times: 6:30–4:45 Work on:	[Diary Translation: begin page 1517] Saturday, March 12, 1932 Work started at 6.30 am and ended at 4.45 pm. Work was progressing on
(1) G 1227 A (2) G 1602 A (3) G 1603 A (4) G 1606 (5) G 1607 (6) G 1608 (7) G 1609	(1) shaft 1227 A (2) shaft 1602 A (3) shaft 1603 A (4) mastaba 1606 and shaft A (5) rock-cut tomb 1607 (6) rock-cut tomb 1608 (7) rock-cut tomb 1609
(1) G 1227 A. Cleared lower part of pit which is unfinished. Depth 9 meters. [ILLUSTRATION] The chamber has been cased, and most of the floor pavement remains. On the walls are the red lines of the builders, and also on the ceiling.	(1) Shaft 1227 A A crew of workmen was cleaning the shaft below the level of the burial chamber. This shaft is 9.00 m. deep. The fill is limestone chips, rubble, and dark soil. The workmen cleaned it. Here is its drawing. [ILLUSTRATION]
(2) G 1602 A. Depth 3.5 meters. Rubble above and roughly rock cut below. Chamber west. Cleared. [ILLUSTRATION]	(2) Shaft 1602 A Mohamed Awad and Ismail were working on this shaft. They cleaned it to a depth of 305 cm. The walls of the shaft are lined with rubble and mud bricks. The fill is limestone chips, rubble, sand and broken mud bricks. The burial chamber is on the west. The workmen cleaned it. Here is its drawing. [ILLUSTRATION]
(3) G 1603 A. Depth 3 meters like G 1602 A. Chamber south. [ILLUSTRATION] Cleared. End of page 1122 Begin page 1123	(3) Shaft 1603 A Abd Al-Karim Ahmed and Ali Mahmud were working on this shaft. They cleaned it to a depth of 300 cm. The walls of the shaft are lined with mud brick. The fill is limestone chips, rubble, dark soil and broken mud bricks. The burial chamber is on the south. The workmen cleaned it. Here is its drawing. [ILLUSTRATION] End of Page 1517 [End Book 20]
(4) G 1606 and A. Clearing rubble and mud mastaba. Found pit A. Pit A. Down 1.9 meters. Mud brick above, rock cut below. Chamber on west.	[Start Book 21] Begin page 1518 (4) Mastaba 1606 Abd El-Karim and Mubarak Mohareb are working above this Mastaba. The debris is rubble mixed with sand. Shaft A was uncovered. Shaft 1606 A The workmen Abd El-Karim and Mubarak Mohareb cleaned the shaft to the depth of 190 cm. Right above the bedrock, the shaft has walls built of mud bricks. The fill in the shaft is rubble and lime dust. The burial chamber is on the western side. They have not cleaned it yet.

(5) G 1607. Clearing rock cut tomb; clearing Room 'a'.	(5) Rock-cut Tomb 1607 Ahmed Mas'oud with a crew of men is working in this rock-cut tomb, in room "a". Its door opens to the north. The debris is rubble mixed with sand. In the western wall, there are six niches, only four of which bear inscriptions. Also the eastern wall is inscribed. They have not cleaned it yet.
(6) G 1608. Rock-cut tomb, east of G 1607. Clearing drift-sand and rubble from Room 'a'. Five niches in west wall, and a low mud mastaba beneath them as offering ledge. In the south wall is a cemented recess, closed with two slabs, one slab pierced, which is evidently the serdab and apparently undisturbed. Three responses in east wall, with pits descending from them. Opened serdab and found seated limestone statuette of owner, inscribed down front of seat at sides [GLYPHS] right hand open on right knee, left hand clenched on knee, wig covered ears (Dynasty 4). The sand in the floor of the serdab was over the feet. In sand found traces of wood, merely as discoloration of sand, with small scraps of color from its surface. Traces of at least two, and perhaps three wooden statuettes (?). [ILLUSTRATION] Found in debris of Room 'a', fragments of inscribed limestone reliefs - possibly from doorway inscription.	(6) Rock-cut Tomb 1608 Ahmed El-Mizlef and Mossa Khalil are working with a crew of men in this rock-cut tomb, in room "a". Its door opens to the north. The debris consists of a layer of rubble and wind-blown sand. Below this layer is another layer of limestone chips. There are five niches in the western wall. They bear no inscriptions. Below the niches there is a Mastaba [ledge] built of mud brick. There are three recesses in the eastern wall. In the southern side, they uncovered a blockage consisting of two stones, sealed with cement. The blockage has a hole in the middle. His Excellency, the Deputy Director, ordered that it should be photographed and then removed. Having photographed it, we removed the first stone. It appeared that it is a serdab with a seated limestone statuette in it. The statuette bears inscriptions on the chair, beside the feet. We photographed it, and then the Deputy Director ordered us to remove the second stone. We also photographed the debris around the statue. It was sand and small fragments of stones. It also contained small pieces of rotted wood, ..., and a small fragment of basalt. Moved [the word "moved" is an addendum written between lines 29 and 30]. End of Page 1518 Begin page 1519 (6) Rock-cut Tomb 1607: (continued) They found in the debris of room "a" fragments of an inscribed false door. His Excellency, the Deputy Director, decided to leave the statuette in the serdab until they find photo paper. We have not moved the statue yet. Nor have we cleaned room "a".
(7) G 1609. Rock-cut tomb, east of G 1608. The inscription over the door is almost entirely removed by salt, but traces remain: [GLYPHS]. Found in debris outside door, limestone libation basin, uninscribed.	(7) Rock-Cut Tomb 1609 The workmen Ahmed El-Mizlef and Moussa Khalil are working in front of the rock-cut tomb. The debris consists of rubble and sand. They found in the debris a limestone basin.... They have not entered the tomb yet.

Fig. 23. The Abutiu dog stela from G 2188 Y (35-10-22 = Egyptian Museum, Cairo JE 67573), October 18, 1935. HU-MFA Expedition photo B8518 NS. Photo by Mohammedani Ibrahim.

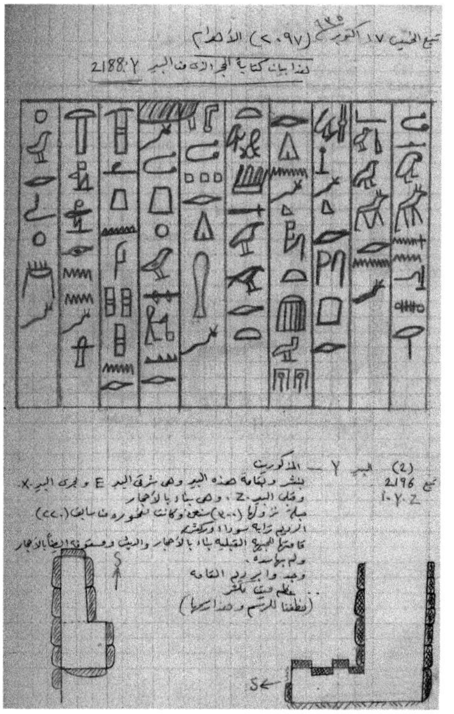

Fig. 24 (right). Arabic Giza Diary Book 26, page 2097, October 17, 1935, with drawing by Duwy Mahmud of the Abutiu dog stela from G 2188 Y. HU-MFA Expedition; MFA.

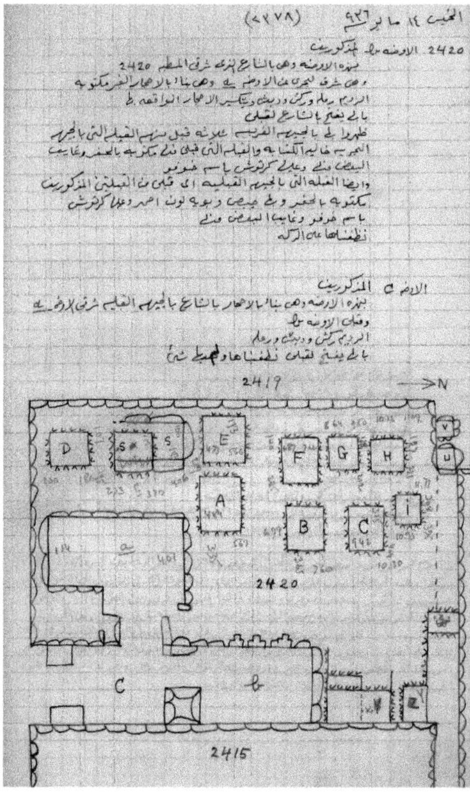

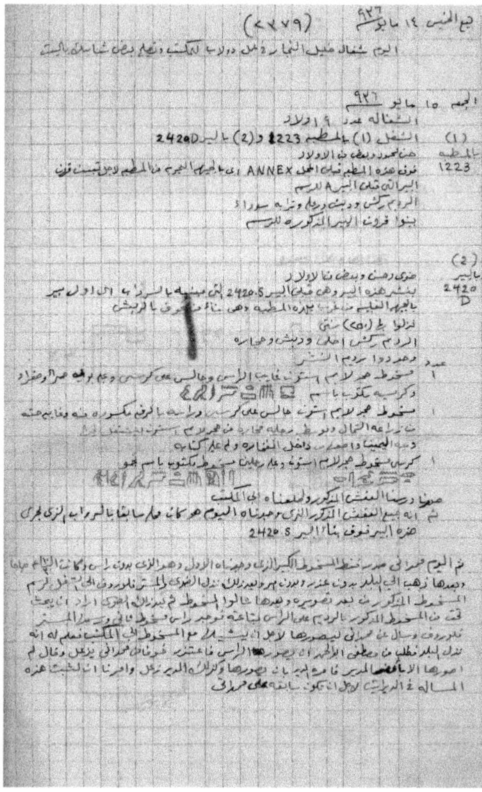

Fig. 25. Arabic Giza Diary Book 29, pages 2378–2379, May 14, 1936, describing the discovery of statues in the serdab *of mastaba G 2420. HU-MFA Expedition; MFA.*

The Arabic text includes an account of Expedition photographer Mohammedani Ibrahim apparently leaving work without permission for a trip home to Quft. A translation of the text written in figure 25 follows:

[Begin page 2378]
Thursday, May 14, 1936, the Pyramids
Chamber "b" of mastaba 2420
The above-mentioned workmen were in this chamber. It is on the street, east of mastaba 2420, i.e., it is northeast of chamber "a". It is built with stone blocks and is uninscribed. The debris is sand, limestone chips, rubble, and stone blocks. Its door opens onto the south. On the western wall of the chamber there are three niches. The northernmost niche is uninscribed, meanwhile the middle niche is inscribed with low reliefs, and its inscriptions include the cartouche of King Khufu. The southernmost niche is also inscribed with low reliefs. It is also painted with red color and bears the cartouche of King Khufu. We cleared the chamber on the floor of limestone chips.
Chamber "c"
The above-mentioned workmen were in this chamber. It is built with stone blocks. It is to the north of chamber "a", and south of chamber "b". The debris is limestone chips, rubble, and sand. Its door opens onto the south. We cleared it. There was nothing in it.
Illustrations:
[End of page 2378]
[Begin page 2379]
Thursday, May 14, 1936, the Pyramids (continued)
Today, Khalil, the carpenter, was working on the filing cabinets for the office. He was also working on fixing the windows of the House.
Friday, May 15, 1936, the Pyramids
The workforce was 9 workmen. Excavation was progressing on (1) mastaba 1223; (2) shaft 2420 D.
(1) Mastaba 1223
Hasan Mahmud and the workmen were on top of this mastaba, on the Annex area, i.e. on the area north of mastaba 1223. They are clearing the corners of the shaft to the south of shaft [1223] A for mapping. The debris is limestone chips, rubble, sand, and dark soil. We cleared the corners of the shaft for mapping.
(2) Shaft 2420 D
Duwy and Hasan were on this shaft. It is to the south of shaft 2420 S, i.e., it is the southernmost shaft on the mastaba. Its walls are rubble on top. They dug down a total of 250 cm. The debris is limestone chips, rubble and stone blocks. We found in the debris of the shaft:
1 seated limestone statue, missing the head. It is painted with red and yellow colors. The chair is inscribed with the owner's name and titles: illustration
1 seated [servant] limestone statuette, the head and the neck are broken. The left arm is also missing some part. He is making a stone vessel, placed between his legs. The right hand is shown inside the vessel. The statue is not inscribed.
1 lower part of a seated limestone statuette, only the legs and the chair remain. The chair is inscribed with the name of Nedjemu. [Illustration]
We photographed and drew the statuettes, and then moved them to the office. All the statuettes found today, in the shaft were originally in the serdab to the north of the shaft.
Today, Mohammedani photographed the statue, which is missing the head. It was already 10.30 am, and then he left for his hometown [Quft] with no excuse for that. He did not request permission [from the Director]. Duwy and Mr. Floroff had to go down the shaft in order to draw the statuettes. They moved the statuettes after photographing them. Duwy found the head of another statue. Mr. Floroff drew it. He also wanted Mohammedani to photograph it. We told him that Mohammedani left for his hometown. He then asked Mostafa Abu El-Hamd to photograph the discovered head. Mostafa apologized because he did not want to upset Mohammedani. Mostafa then asked for the Director's permission to photograph the head.

> The Director gave him the permission and, told us to keep this incident on record and to write in today's diary, in order to be a mistake in Mohammedani's file.
> [End of page 2379]

Archaeological Interpretation and Speculation by the *Reises*

Since the voices of the Egyptian staffs working for Western expeditions are so seldom heard in most early twentieth century expedition documentation, it is not known just how much archaeological interpretation the *reises* were producing on their own. The Arabic diaries provide us with some clues. On November 25, 1913, Said Ahmed recorded reaching the burial chamber of mastaba G 4440 at Giza. Finding a disturbed context containing two reserve heads (13-11-90 = MFA 14.718, and 13-11-91 = MFA 14.719), Said wrote the entry reproduced in figure 26 and translated below. Since there are no surviving examples of the original placement of Giza reserve heads, these comments are especially relevant.

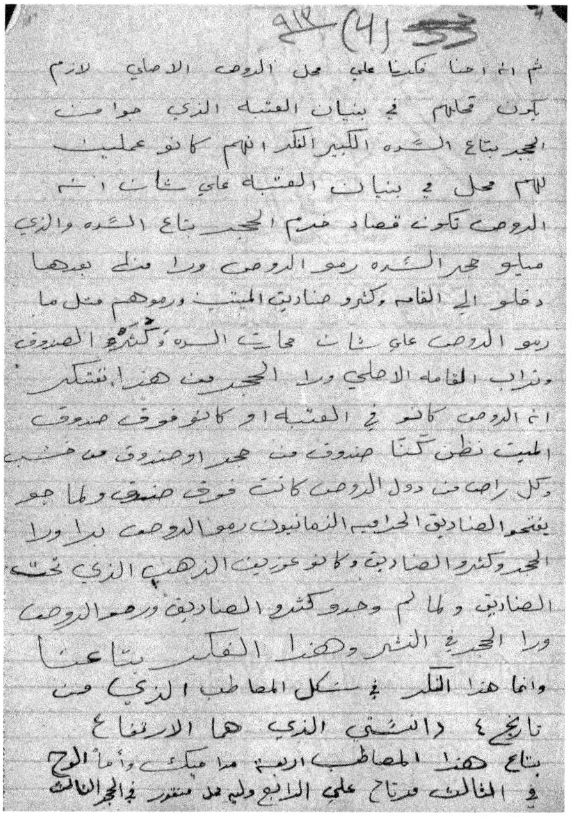

Fig. 26. Arabic Giza Diary Book A (November 17, 1913, to April 24, 1914), page 4, November 25, 1913, describing the excavation of mastaba G 4440. HU-MFA Expedition; MFA.

> We think that the head(s) must have been originally buried in the burial chamber behind the blocking stones. We think that whoever broke into the blocking stones tossed them outside of the burial chamber, then entered the burial chamber and destroyed the coffins and tossed them out, just as they did with the heads. The evidence for that is that the heads, the coffin fragments and the debris of the burial chamber are found right in front of the blocking stones.
>
> We think that the heads must have been on top of a coffin or a sarcophagus. When the ancient tomb robbers opened the coffins, they tossed the heads out, because they were looking for gold. But when they did not find gold they destroyed the coffins and tossed the heads outside the burial chamber. This is what I think.[66]

Two months later, Said Ahmed reported to Reisner on what he felt was a connection between reserve heads and sarcophagi: "I just realized that the shafts we excavated after your departure to Kerma do not have [reserve] heads. Nor do the two shafts we dug when you were still at the Pyramids. I think the reason for that is that there are no sarcophagi of white limestone in these shafts; we found [reserve] heads in all the shafts with a limestone sarcophagus or fragments of a sarcophagus. So, the shaft that does not have a limestone sarcophagus does not have a [reserve] head either. This is what I think; only Allah knows."[67]

[66] For discussion of one of the heads (MFA 14.719), and the in-situ photo, see *Egyptian Art in the Age of the Pyramids,* exhibition catalogue (New York, 1999), 238–39, with fig. 113; and George Reisner, *A History of the Giza Necropolis* 1 (Cambridge, 1942), pl. 49c.

[67] Arabic Giza Diary Book A, page 34, January 7, 1914.

Fig. 27. Mastaba of Setju, G 4710, with mud brick exterior chapel marked by the arrow, looking north, 1915. HU-MFA Expedition photo A6047 NS; photographer not listed.

Fig. 28. Mastaba of Setju, G 4710, with exterior chapel obscured, looking northwest, January 16, 2004. PDM_01231. Photo by the author.

Excavating in the former (Ernesto Schiaparelli) Italian concession of the Western Cemetery, the HU-MFA Expedition cleared the large mastaba of Setju, G 4710 (= Lepsius 49). The Arabic diary entry for November 23, 1915, reveals the *reis*'s analysis of the deterioration process of the mud brick chapel walls outside (east of) the limestone mastaba's entrance. This comment shows an appreciation for the stratigraphy, even more welcome since the chapel is all but invisible today (figs. 27–28). "These two chambers are part of the chapel of mastaba 4710. It seems that the walls and ceilings of these chambers caved in, because the walls are collapsed in big chunks, which still have plaster on them. What also corroborates this assumption is that the shaft of mastaba 4710 is filled with limestone chips with no sand."[68]

Work on the burial chamber of Queen Hetepheres (G 7000 X) in 1925 provides us with another rare example of Egyptian archaeological speculation. To explain the mysterious and highly unusual archaeological context that the burial chamber presented, prior to the discovery of the hieroglyphs that identified the owner, Said Ahmed recorded in the Arabic diary his theory of a dispute between Khufu and an unknown king. Khufu supposedly prevailed, destroyed his rival's pyramid complex, and buried him in G 7000 X.[69] Reisner did not bother to include this paragraph in his later English translation of Said's Arabic diary: "There follows half a page of

[68] Arabic Giza Diary Book B, page 4, November 23, 1915.

[69] Arabic Giza Diary, March 6, 1925, with the original text by Said Ahmed in Book 5, page 321: "This shaft is intact and has never been plundered. The potsherds, triangular stones and the limestone stone blocks we have found in the fill of the shaft were possibly thrown in the shaft by one of the kings of Dynasty Four. It seems that there was a family dispute between Khufu and an unknown king. It is also possible this unknown king once had a pyramid and shaft 7000 X belongs to him. When Khufu prevailed in this family dispute over the throne, he destroyed his rival's pyramid and buried him in shaft 7000 X. As an act of revenge, Khufu destroyed the temple of his rival's pyramid as well and used the stones of his rival's structures to fill shaft 7000 X. Khufu also made sure to completely hide the mouth of the shaft by sealing it with slabs of stones that match the bedrock. This kept the shaft unrecognizable during the Roman times and it remained intact."

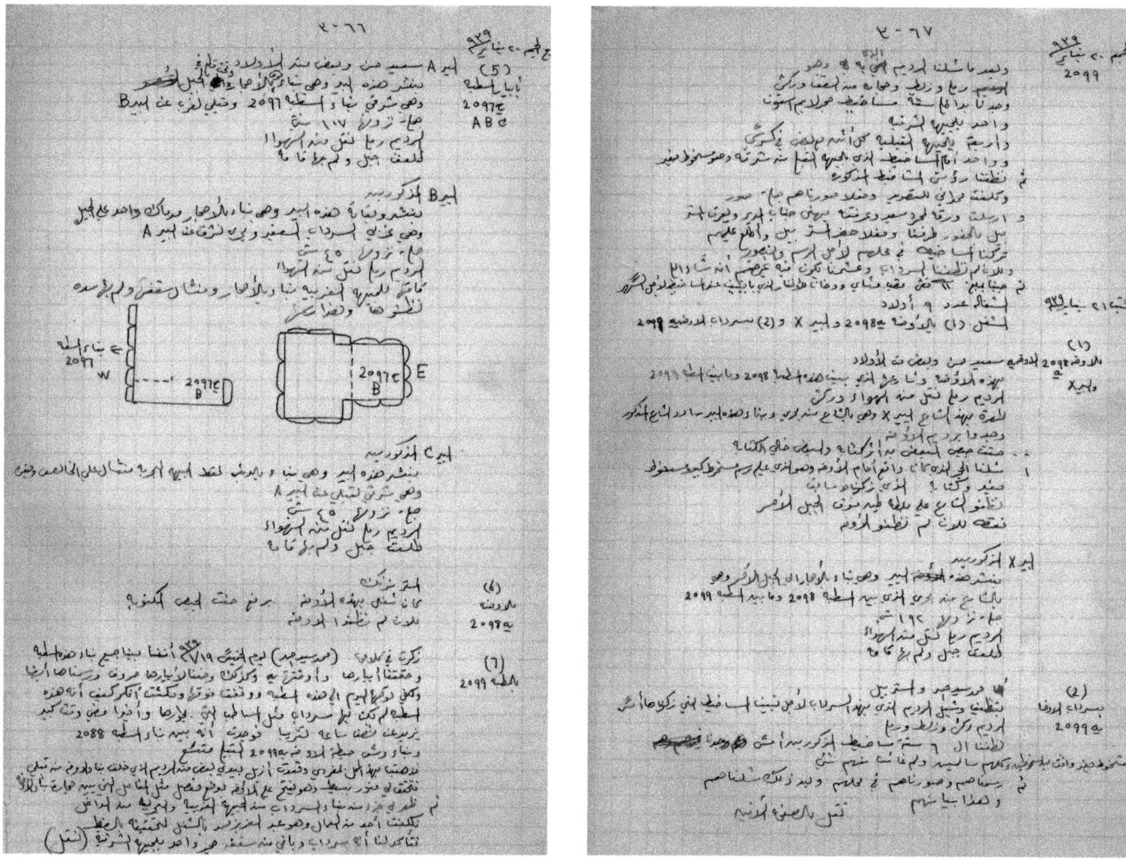

Fig. 29. Arabic Giza Diary Book 36, pages 3066–67, describing Mohamed Said's discovery of the serdab *in G 2099 on January 20, 1939. HU-MFA Expedition; MFA.*

Said's theories as to the person buried in the tomb; amusing but of no value."[70] Nevertheless, it is refreshing to gain a window into a native Egyptian attempt to interpret the data under investigation.

In 1939 Mohamed Said's men were excavating the Sixth Dynasty mastaba G 2099 (Raramu). The *reis* was perplexed over why the mastaba contained no *serdab*. His account of the discovery is provided in figure 29, with translation following. Reisner considered the find important enough to quote much of the passage in a report back to Harold Edgell, director of the Museum of Fine Arts, Boston (fig. 30).[71]

> [Begin page 3066]
> Friday, January 20, 1939, the Pyramids (continued)
> (7) Mastaba 2099
> I mentioned earlier (Mohamed Said Ahmed) that on Thursday 19/1/1939 we exposed the walls of this mastaba and found its shafts and chapel. We also numbered the shafts and drew the mastaba. But today I went to the mastaba and stood on top of it. I kept wondering why this mastaba does not have a serdab like the neighboring mastabas. I spent a little over 30 minutes, and then I found that there is a space between the wall of mastaba 2088 and the southern rubble wall of chapel 2099a. I walked to this spot and removed some of the debris behind the south wall of the chapel. I found a small window opening onto the chapel. I

[70] Reisner's English translation of Said Ahmed's Expedition Diary, March 6, 1925; MFA DE.

[71] Reisner to Edgell, February 7, 1939; DIR. The find is also described in Ann Macy Roth, *A Cemetery of Palace Attendants*, Giza Mastabas 6 (Boston, 1995), 150–52 and pls. 113–16.

Fig. 30. The serdab *of mastaba G 2099 during excavation, looking southeast, January 21, 1939. HU-MFA Expedition photo B9039 NS. Photo by Mohammedani Ibrahim.*

uncovered part of the serdab on the west and the north. I then ordered the workman Ahmed Abd Al-Aziz to clear this area. We uncovered the serdab. Only one stone of its ceiling remains in place.
[End of page 3066]

[Begin page 3067]
Friday, January 20, 1939, the Pyramids (continued)
Shaft [2099]
After we cleared out the debris in the serdab, we found six limestone statues: one on the east, two double seated statues on the south, and a statuette.[72] We cleared the heads of the statues. We also asked Mohammedani to photograph them. He did photograph them. I also send a note to Mahmud Said to let the Director know that we found the statues. Mr. Bill came to the site and looked at the statues. We left them in place for drawing and photography. We have not yet cleared the serdab. We hope to find more statues in the serdab. Because we have decided to ask the workmen to work late through the night, we bought for them tea and sugar: 11 piasters worth.

Saturday, January 21, 1939, the Pyramids
The workforce was 9 workmen. Excavation was progressing on (1) chapel 2098a and shaft X; (2) serdab of chapel 2099a.
(2) Serdab of chapel 2099a

[72] As Reisner noted in his letter to Edgell of February 7, 1939 (see above), the *reis* counted every figure as a "statue" hence six (actually seven, counting the son Kednes, perhaps not quite revealed yet at the time of writing) figures but contained within four statues.

Mohamed Said Ahmed and Mr. Bill were clearing the debris around the statues in the serdab. The debris is limestone chips, flint, and sand. We cleared the six statues. All the statues are intact. We drew and photographed them in situ. We then moved them. A list of the statues is on the next page.
[End of page 3067]

Local Color and Events Concerning the Expedition Staff

Our final category includes some miscellaneous notes that shed light on the daily events, mishaps, crises, and even some humorous moments during the excavations, all revealed in the Arabic diaries. Examples include:

—The wind ripped the roof off Reisner's office in 1933, requiring a small team to clear the sand and re-roof the mud brick building.[73]

—One day in September 1924, six faience objects from Naga ed-Deir that had been carefully arranged for photography in the Harvard Camp photo studio had all been displaced. The reason? Rats had helped themselves to the dough used to position the objects.[74]

—Years later, photographer Mohammedani Ibrahim's work in shaft J of mastaba G 2418 was ruined in 1934 after he accidentally broke his own glass plate negatives. If the documentation is correct, the burial was rephotographed a full two years later, when the skeleton was numbered 36-7-22. That the skeleton remained in the same position for photography in 1936 is curious, for two years earlier the diary mentions "moving" the same skeleton.[75]

On a more serious note, the dangers of expedition work are described on several occasions. Ahmed Maghrabi dropped a limestone block on himself and Mohamed Ali in 1935 while working in shaft A of mastabas G 1113. Head and hand injuries resulted in a trip to the hospital for X-rays, which fortunately showed no broken bones.[76] (The English translation makes no mention of this incident). Others were not so lucky. After the *reis* completed his diary entry for the evening on January 8, 1914, Ashur Mohamed el-Seleki fell unconscious, and no recitations or spells could revive him. He had put in a full day's work, dined with his co-workers, and even enjoyed conversation with "Mahmud Shadduf and Mahmud el-Khin until the angels of death took his soul. He was never sick."[77] And handling the heavy Decauville railway carts was no job for the uninitiated. One Ali Mahmud Ahmed Khayer Allah had no experience pushing the heavy carts on the tracks but took over without permission on November 8, 1924. Pushing too hard to the end of the track he derailed the cart and fell with it down to the bottom of the debris hill, breaking the wooden stairs, and suffering a head wound. He was sent to the hospital by car. A week later he seemed well on the way to recovery, correctly identifying his co-workers and declaring himself healthy; but he died the next day, and a police inquiry took place on November 17, 1924.[78]

The Expedition driver, Hassan Salem, welcomed a guest to Giza in 1941. Abd el-Satar Ibrahim Hussein was making his way back to camp in the early evening but lost his way west of Khafre's pyramid, falling down a shaft and breaking his hip and left arm. Appearing in stable condition, he nevertheless died a week later from his injuries at Qasr el-Aini hospital on December 2, 1941.[79] Another individual, Ibrahim el-Suefy, did not fall, but was thrown down a burial shaft off the northwest corner of the Great Pyramid, he claimed by his two sons, one of whom worked for the Giza police.[80]

---

73 Arabic Giza Diary Book 23, 1746, March 2, 1933.

74 Arabic Giza Diary Book 1, 2, September 19, 1924.

75 Arabic Giza Diary Book 30, July 11, 1934, 2469. Mohammedani Ibrahim's reshoots of the burial date to July 7 and 10, 1936 respectively (C13885_NS and B8721_NS).

76 Arabic Giza Diary Book 25, 1958, May 27, 1935.

77 Arabic Giza Diary Book A, 35, January 8, 1914.

78 Arabic Giza Diary Book 1, 21, 24, 27, 32; November 8, 14, 15, 17, 1924.

79 Arabic Giza Diary Book 40, 3489–90, November 21, and December 2, 1941.

80 Arabic Giza Diary Book 40, 3469, February 18, 1941.

Protecting the Giza cemeteries was always a major concern for the HU-MFA Expedition. On occasion some unique solutions were employed to stop tomb robbers and retrieve stolen objects. One day in July 1939, the southern doorjamb from mastaba G 7691 "disappeared." This Eastern Cemetery tomb originally lay within the Italian concession, before Reisner "inherited" it from Schiaparelli; his expedition had not excavated the tomb, hence the general lack of awareness of the area. The Arabic diaries describe fears that an "inside job" might lie behind the theft, even including some of the Antiquities Service guards, and some were concerned about how to "return" the stolen doorjamb and clear their names of any charges. I was surprised to read the name of a Giza *ghafir* caught up in the intrigue, Mohamed Abd el-Mawgood, whom I knew from my first seasons of work at Giza in 1977.[81]

Another theft of decorated limestone blocks occurred in January 1941, this time from the Western Cemetery mastaba G 1457. In this case footprints led to the modern Muslim cemetery by the Southern Mount and the (reburied) Menkaure Valley Temple, and freshly heaped dirt upon a new grave, covering up the stolen relief. From here the local police station got involved, and a footprint tracker determined there were three culprits, all of whom headed to the nearby village of Nazlet es-Samman, but he could make no further progress. Next, a sniffer dog named Nimr ("Tiger") arrived on the scene, and zeroed in on the house in the village, catching one of the thieves. He also identified the others in a lineup that took place near mastaba G 1457. One was an Antiquities Service guard.[82]

In addition to incidents in the Giza Necropolis, the *reises* also recorded events taking place at Harvard Camp. One was the annual exhibition of ancient Egyptian-themed paintings by Reisner's friend Joseph Lindon Smith, such as on April 16, 1939 (Smith's last exhibition prior to Reisner's death): "Today, we had our annual cocktail party in order to exhibit the pictures of Mr. Lindon Smith. We had 280 guests from the Egyptians and the foreign people. The Minister of the Interior, Nuqreshi Pasha, was among the Egyptian guests. Also, the English Ambassador, Sir [Miles] Lampson, was among the guests. The number of the guests' cars was 113. The party was very pleasant and went very well." All this took place after Mohamed Said recorded 600 Decauville carloads of debris removed during the day's work between 6:30 A.M. and 4:45 P.M.[83]

Another social event consisted of Mohamed Said's invitation to a tea party at his Harvard Camp house to celebrate Reisner's seventy-third birthday. In addition to the Expedition staff and friends (Frank Allen, Evelyn Perkins, Dorothy Ginger, Alexander Floroff, Nicholas Melnikoff, and Boris Lysenko), the *reis* was careful to list the external guests: "Those are Sir Robert Greg, Baron De Bildt, Mrs. Robert Greg, Mr. and Mrs. Perkins, Al-Arabi Bey, his wife and his children, Zaki Effendi Saad, and Nassim Effendi, the Antiquities Inspector. The party was very nice, thank God."[84] Reisner himself corroborated the successful event two days later in a letter home to Dows Dunham in Boston.[85]

Future Plans: The Arabic Diaries Project

Although the Giza diary books have been translated, serious academic analysis of this unique corpus has at this writing only just begun, and the non-Giza diaries still require full translation. A consortium of colleagues including myself, Wendy Doyon, Marleen De Meyer, and others hope to work with MFA curators Lawrence Berman and Denise Doxey to explore several research questions related to the Arabic texts. First, a general overview of the different hands (Said Ahmed, Duwy Mahmud, Mohamed Said, Mahmud Said, and others[?]) is necessary to comprehend the division of labor, and any possible use of dictation from "*reis*" to scribe during some of the field seasons (fig. 31). Exploring Duwy Mahmud's role further might improve our understanding of his impact as *reis* for the University of Chicago excavations at Megiddo in 1937–1939, and Mahmud el-Meyyit worked for several other expeditions during his career as well (Albert Lythgoe, Arthur Mace, Cecil Firth, Henry Wellcome,

---

[81] Arabic Giza Diary Book 37, 3189–90, August 6, 1939.
[82] Arabic Giza Diary Book 40, 3465–72, January 22–February 25, 1941.
[83] Arabic Giza Diary Book 36, 3217, April 16, 1939.
[84] Arabic Giza Diary Book 36, 3460, November 5, 1940.
[85] Reisner to Dunham, November 7, 1940; EGP AC13.

Fig. 31. George Reisner's seventieth birthday party in the courtyard of Harvard Camp, Giza, November 5, 1937, showing Mahmud Said (far left), Duwy Mahmud (behind Reisner's right shoulder), and Mohamed Said (second from right). Harvard University Archives, Pusey Library, George Andrew Reisner Papers, HUG 4737.

Clarence Fisher, etc.). Questions of literacy in early twentieth century Egypt will also come to the fore. In short, we hope to (re)create the context that made possible these unique archaeological documents deriving from an indigenous community in Upper Egypt. They are not merely the only Arabic diaries to survive but are the only ones covering such a substantial timespan, to my knowledge, that were ever produced.[86] Seen in this light, a social justice engagement with the diaries seems particularly appropriate for the current era.

The Arabic Expedition diaries written by Hassan Diraz's father, grandfather, uncle, and perhaps others, over so many years were carefully preserved since 1947 (or even earlier) in the family's village home at el-Qalʿa, Quft. Their pages throw the window wide open on not only the progress of the HU-MFA Expedition, but on one of the greatest unheralded contributions to Egyptian and Nubian archaeology—from a specifically Egyptian perspective.[87] We owe Hassan Diraz (and his illustrious family) a great debt, not just for his professionalism, but for his deep knowledge of family history, his willingness to share it, and his hospitality.[88]

86 Some of Reisner's Egyptian staff kept Arabic diaries for short periods while working for other projects, such as the 1915 Penn Expedition season under Clarence Fisher; I am grateful to Kevin Cahail for reminding me of this (missing) document.

87 Quirke, *Hidden Hands,* 303; Margaret Drower, *Flinders Petrie. A Life in Archaeology,* Second edition (Madison, 1995), 430–31.

88 I would also like to express my thanks to my Arabic Diary Project collaborators. Zahi Hawass assisted me with permissions and logistics. Mohamed Shiha and Mansour Boraik helped me locate the Diraz family descendants. Wendy Doyon clarified numerous Arabic translation questions. Marleen De Meyer joined me in recent years in the quest to meet and learn from the descendants of the HU-MFA Expedition reises. She also visited the ancestral home of the Diraz family, including their burial plot, at el-Qalʿa in 2018. My wife, Lauren Thomas, assisted in the negotiations and procurement of the books in Cairo, and William Kelly Simpson and David Pendlebury contributed financially. Catherine Pate managed the scanning of the Giza books by numerous student assistants, and the late Ramadan Hussein devoted considerable time over many years to translating the Giza diaries. Rachel Aronin, Nicholas Picardo, and Jeremy Kisala oversaw the processing and integration of the Giza diaries into the Giza Project database and website at Harvard. And my colleagues at the Museum of Fine Arts, Boston, Rita E. Freed, Lawrence Berman, Denise Doxey, and Susan Allen, have always been encouraging and welcoming partners in this ongoing research. Wendy Doyon, Donald Reid, and Marleen De Meyer suggested several corrections and improvements on a preliminary version of this paper, as did Emily Teeter, Kevin Cahail, and Eric Cline; all have my thanks.

Crossing the Gates of *t3-ḏsr*: The Sacred District Scenes in TT 123; Affecting and Being Affected

José Roberto Pellini
Universidade Federal de Minas Gerais, Belo Horizonte, Brazil

Abstract

The scenes of the Sacred District are characterized by the presence of a group of buildings that appear in a compact form and where there is no activity of human agents or of the deceased. According to some scholars, the scenes refer to the Butic funerary rituals. The purpose of this text is to present a study of the scenes of the Sacred District comparing those in Theban Tomb 123 to other Theban tombs. The article also proposes to think of images not as representations, but as alternative forms of existence that set in motion a series of affective flows. The affective flows generated by the encounters between bodies, allowed the dead person to leave his state of latency and become a manifest being.

الملخص

تتميز مشاهد الحي المقدس بوجود مجموعة من المباني التي تظهر بشكل مدمج ولا يوجد فيها نشاط للبشر أو للمتوفى. وبحسب بعض العلماء، تشير المشاهد إلى ما يعرف ب»الطقوس الجنائزية البوتية«. الغرض من هذا البحث هو تقديم دراسة لمشاهد الحي المقدس ومقارنة تلك الموجودة في مقبرة TT123 بمقابر أخرى في مدينة طيبة. تقترح الدراسة أيضًا التفكير في الصور ليس على أنها تمثيلات، ولكن كأشكال بديلة للوجود التي تطلق سلسلة من النتائج. سمحت تلك النتائج للميت أن يترك حالة الكمون ليصبح كائنًا له وجود واضح.

Theban Tomb 123

Theban Tomb 123 is in the plain of Sheikh Abdel Qurna, west of the Ramesseum, next to TT 55 (Ramose) and TT 56 (Userhat). In the pharaonic period, the tomb belonged to a scribe named Amenemhet and was built during the rule of pharaoh Thutmose III. Although the tomb has many structural problems, with several rock voids and cracks, the decoration is in good condition, and it is possible to observe the original coloring of the scenes in many places. The bas-relief is very detailed and of excellent quality. In the vestibule, the Offering List in its complete version, the Hunting in the Swamp scene and the scenes with oxen adorned with garlands stand out. In the transverse corridor, attention is drawn to the scene of Hunting in the Desert where Amenemhet is under a war chariot, a scene that possibly represents a pig farm, both located on the north wall and the scene of the funeral procession and the Journey to Sais and Abydos, both located on the south wall.[1] The Sacred District scene is located just below the funeral procession scene. The scene is in good condition and has some of the original coloring, especially the red tones (fig. 1). In the eastern part, a large void of rock can be seen that prevents the complete visualization of the scene. Signs of abrasion can be seen in various parts of the scene, as well as in other parts of the tomb, suggesting that in the past there was an attempt to erase and change the decorative program.

[1] José Pellini, "A Journey to the West: The Unpublished Scenes from Amenemhet's Funerary Ritual in TT 123," *Memnonia* (in press, 2022).

Journal of the American Research Center in Egypt 58 (2022), 163–70
http://dx.doi.org/10.5913/jarce.58.2022.a009

Fig. 1. View of the reliefs showing scenes from the Sacred District, TT 123. Transverse corridor, south wall. Photo: José Roberto Pellini.

Although most of the tomb scenes were never published, the inscriptions on the tomb's facade were included in Kampp's work,[2] Säve-Söderbergh did a study of the motive of the hippopotamus hunt,[3] and Settgast published sketches of the Sacred District scene, but without much detail.[4] These studies used photographs and sketches from TT 123 that were produced mainly between the 1920s and 1940s by the Oriental Institute of Chicago, Siegfried Schott, and Norman and Nina de Garis Davies.

The Sacred District in Theban Tombs

Popular in the days of Hatshepsut and Thutmose III, the scenes of the Sacred District are part of the scenes of the funerary ritual characterized by the presence of a series of buildings grouped in a compact way, where neither humans nor the dead person is shown. For Settgast,[5] this is because the intention of the scene is to highlight the complex of buildings, showing the places where rites took place during the funerary ritual. In TT 60, dated to the Middle Kingdom, the scene is accompanied by an inscription that identifies the set of buildings with an area called *tꜣ-ḏsr*.[6] Often found in the Coffins Texts, the word has been translated as Sacred District, Sacred Area, Sacred Temenos or Necropolis.[7] According to Diamond, the way in which the Sacred District is represented in the tombs gives the impression of a fenced area with clearly defined limits that functions as a transition zone within the structure of the scenes of the funerary ritual. In this way, we can think of the Sacred District as a liminal zone through which the dead person must pass before reaching the West.[8]

Settgast[9] divides the scenes from the Sacred District into eight different sections: 1) The *Muu* Dancers Hall; 2) The Women's Tent; 3) The Garden; 4) The Gods of the Great Gate; 5) The Divine Chapels; 6) The Sacred Lagoons; 7) The Slaughterhouse; 8) The Four Sacred Pools. There is no standard order of presentation of the

---

[2] Friederike Kampp, *Die Thebanische Nekropole, zum Wandel des Grabgedankens von der XVIII. Bis zur XX. Dynastie, teil 1*, Theben 13 (Mainz, 1996), 413.

[3] Torgny Säve-Söderbergh, *On Egyptian Representations of Hippopotamus Hunting as a Religious Motive*, Horae Soederblominae 3 (Uppsala 1953), 5–12.

[4] Settgast. *Untersuchungen zu altägyptischen Bestattungsdarstellungen,* ADAIK 3 (Hamburg, 1963), pls. 3, 5, 8, 11.

[5] Settgast, *Untersuchungen zu altägyptischen Bestattungsdarstellungen*, 48.

[6] Nina de Garis Davies and Alan Gardiner, *The Tomb of Antefoker, Vizier of Sesostris I and of his Wife Senet: (No. 60),* TTS 2 (London, 1920), 56.

[7] Siegfried Morenz, *Egyptian Religion* (Ithaca, 1992), 99; James Hoffmeier, *Sacred in the Vocabulary of Ancient Egypt: the Term* DSR, *with Special Reference to Dynasties I–XX,* OBO 59 (Freiburg-Göttingen, 1985), 85–87; Raymond Faulkner, *The Ancient Egyptian Coffin Texts* vol. 1 (Warminster, 1973), 30–31, Spell 38 (159, 160, 162, 163).

[8] Kelly-Anne Diamond, "An Investigation into the Sacred District as Depicted in New Kingdom Private Tombs," *ARCE Bulletin* 195 (2009), 23–27.

[9] Settgast, *Untersuchungen zu altägyptischnen Bestattungsdarstellungen, 48.*

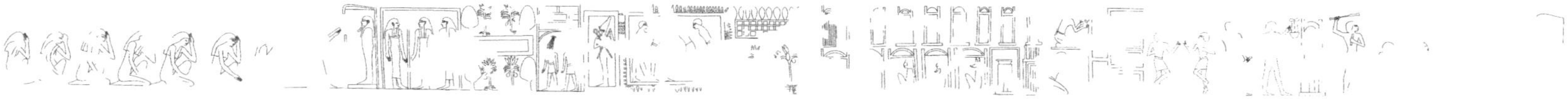

Fig. 2. The Sacred District in TT 123. Drawing: José Roberto Pellini.

Fig. 3. Reconstruction of the funeral scene in TT 123. Drawing: José Roberto Pellini and Lorrana Dauari.

scenes. The choice of scenes depended both on the owner's personal preference and the artist's choices, as well as on the space available for the scene and the time needed to make the drawings.

The Sacred District in TT 123

Although in general the Sacred District starts with the Muu Dancers Hall as it happens for example in TT 15, 21, 81, and 82, in TT 123, the first building shown is the Women's Tent that is represented as a simple structure with a roof and an internal division (fig. 2, left). Three women are depicted, two to the right of the internal division and one to the left. They are practically identical in costume and posture, which makes it difficult to identify them. Analyzing a similar structure in TT 82, Davies suggested that the woman on the left may represent the dead man's wife. This is complicated if we consider that one of the things that characterizes the Sacred District is precisely the absence of human beings.[10]

To the right is a garden with the pond with a rectangular lake surrounded by palm trees at both the top and at the bottom and sycamores on the sides. Settgast suggests that this scene represents the *wr.t* channel that connected Sais and Buto.[11] According to Junker,[12] while the *wr.t* channel was portrayed as a winding watercourse during the Old Kingdom, in the New Kingdom it came to be represented as a body of water in the shape of a lagoon surrounded by palm trees and sycamore trees, as seen in TT 123. In TT 15 (Tetiky), TT 21 (User), TT 81 (Ineni), and in the tomb of Reneni at el Kab, the same scene is accompanied by two obelisks, a clear association with the sacred city of Heliopolis. This reinforces the idea not only that the Sacred District has relations with the funerary Butic rituals,[13] but that the rituals are a journey that the deceased made, or should make, to the sacred cities of the Delta, especially to Sais, Heliopolis, and Buto.

Following the journey, the Hall of *Muu* appears.[14] The structure is rectangular, and the upper part shows an irregular division, perhaps an indication of other rooms behind. Two *Muu* dancers, wearing a crown made of reeds or papyrus, appear with their arms are their sides.

Following (right of) the Hall of *Muu*, Osiris is shown standing in a chapel, looking towards the entrance to the Holy District. If we think that the funeral procession scene in the above record is part of the total context, Osiris could be looking towards the procession that is approaching the Sacred District. It is interesting to note the presence of Osiris within the Sacred District, something that also happens in TT 15, 21, and 81, showing us the transformation of the Butic ritual into a ritual with characteristics linked to the cult of Osiris.[15]

After Osiris, we can see a large square structure decorated with *khekeru* friezes. Within are four individuals, two facing left and two facing right. As in the Women's Tent, they are identical in posture, in the clothes they wear, and in their faces. They have no arms and appear to bend slightly.[16] This is the largest and most conspicuous

[10] Nina de Garis Davies, "The Tomb of Tetaky at Thebes (No. 15)," *JEA* 11.1–2 (1925), 10–18.

[11] Settgast, *Untersuchungen zu altägyptischnen Bestattungsdarstellungen*, 51.

[12] Hermann Junker, "Der Tanz der *Mww* und das Butische Begrabnis im alten Reich," *MDAIK* 9 (1940), 38–39.

[13] Settgast associates the scenes of the Sacred District with the funerary rituals that took place in Buto between the Pre-Dynastic period and the beginning of the Old Empire. Junker, in his analysis of the tombs of the Old Empire, demonstrated that the Butic ritual involved a boat trip, *totenfahrtz*, between Buto and other sacred cities of the Delta, mainly Sais and Heliopolis. Thus, the deceased king left Buto by boat, proceeded towards the cities of Sais and Heliopolis, and returned to Buto, where the final burial took place. According to the author, over time, the scenes of the Butic ritual were transformed and began to present new elements, especially associated with the cult of Osiris, which came to be represented within the Sacred District during the New Empire. Settgast, *Untersuchungen zu altägyptischnen Bestattungsdarstellungen*, 66–74; Junker, "Der Tanz der *Mww*," 38.

[14] Altenmüller suggests that the Muu were ritual agents who appeared at certain times throughout the ritual to greet the dead when transporting the boat to Sais and to receive the dead when the coffin was placed on the sled in the gates of Buto. In this sense, they would be boatmen who took care of the protection and transport of the deceased during the journey to Sais and Buto. See Hartwig Altenmüller, "Bestattungsritual," *LÄ* I, cols. 745–65.

[15] Junker, "Der Tanz der *Mww*," 30–32; Emma Brunner-Traut, *Der Tanz im alten Ägypten nachbildlichen und inschriftlichen Zeugnissen*, ÄgF 6 (Glückstadt-New York, 1958), 57.

[16] Junker suggests that the four individuals within the structure represent Buto's dead kings, the ancestral kings. Settgast, on the other hand, interprets the structure as the Great Gate of the Gods and individuals as guardians of the gate. A similar interpretation is given by Davies, who identifies the four individuals as demons who guard the gates of Paradise. See Junker, "Der Tanz der *Mww*," 32–37; Settgast,

building within the Sacred District. Unlike TT 123, where no entry to the building is shown, in TT 21 and TT 81, the building appears to have an entrance marked by the discontinuity of the external limits that may represent the entrance to the building.

In sequence, as in TT 53, there is another garden with palm trees and a fenced pond. In the upper portion, there is a senet game board, which is also present TT 100 and in Pahery's tomb in el-Kab. According to Hodel-Hoenes, senet in the funerary context represents the game that the dead man plays against the invisible, if he wins the match, he can be reborn.[17]

Proceeding to the right, the scene is divided into half registers where the divine chapels are located. In the upper register are nine chapels with closed doors. Junker[18] suggests that while in the Old Kingdom the chapels represented the royal cemetery of Buto, in the New Kingdom, they started to be reinterpreted as places of refuge for Osiris and his entourage. In the register below, six chapels appear and at least three gods can be seen. Settgast[19] identifies the gods as being the children of Horus, Hapi, Imsety, Duamutef, and Qebehsenuef.

In TT 123, the Four Pools shown to the right are represented as four rectangular structures connected by channels. These pools mark the end of the Sacred District. Two female figures with short hair and a headband kneel by the channel, holding spherical jars. Davies and Gardiner[20] suggested that they are performing a desert fertilization ritual to make it habitable for Osiris. Diamond suggested that the female figures represent the "bone collectors" (*dmḏ(y).t*), whose role was to collect the bones of the dead thus allowing the deceased to be reborn. [21] Other examples of this scene occur in TT 17, 21, 39, 81, 82, and 100.

After the Sacred District, there is a scene to the right that in TT 123 is poorly preserved due to fractures and voids in the wall, but that we can reconstruct based on similar scenes from other tombs, especially TT 53 (Amenemhet), 96B (Sennefer), 100 (Rekhmire), 125 (Duauneheh) and 179 (Nebamon). The scene shows two *Muu* dancers, or pseudo *Muu*, as Altenmüller suggests.[22] Further to the right, two priests appear, one holding a papyrus roll and the other presenting the *peseh-kef* to a chapel. In the tombs of Puimre, Amenemhet, Rekhmire, and Duauneheh, a similar chapel appears, but with a torch inside. In TT 123, the drawing is very faint, and it is impossible to verify the whether there was a torch inside the chapel.

Although in TT 123, we only have small strokes preserved, other tombs show the next scene consisted of a priest holding a sceptre behind a boat with a person sitting at the bow and the stern. In a similar scene in TT 100, the trip ends in front of the Goddess of the West, symbolizing the arrival of the dead in the Hereafter. According to Settgast,[23] there would be another boat that would symbolize the offerings for the crossing to the West to be successful, that is, the idea is that the delivery of offerings could allow safe passage. Finally, at the far right, is a building, of which in TT 123 we can see only a trace. However, in TT 100, the dead man, shown in smaller scale, appears with a hoe in his hand building a garden. As in TT 123, we have the outline of the celling and the space and proportions of the scene are similar, therefore we can assume that originally this scene was also present in TT 123.

Directly connected to the scene of the Sacred District is the scene of the journey to Sais. In TT 123, the journey is represented in the register above the Sacred District from the bottom up where we can observe the presence of a standing male figure with his arm extended (reconstruction shown in fig. 3, middle register). In the sequence, we have a small reed boat with at least three rowers, and a person standing at the stern holding the tiller for the steering oar. Next (to the left), we see a larger ceremonial papyrus boat. A female figure with short hair and a headband is seated at the bow. Behind her is a lector priest and a tall rectangular structure. To the left of the structure, we can observe a standing male figure and a female figure identical to the one at the bow of

---

Untersuchungen zu altägyptischnen Bestattungsdarstellungen, 51–52; Norman de Garis Davies, *The Tomb of Puyemre at Thebes, volume II, The Chapels of Hope,* PMMAR 2 (New York, 1923), 7, pl. XLVII.

[17] Sigrid Hode-Hoenes, *Life and Death in Ancient Egypt. Scenes from Private Tombs in New Kingdom Thebes* (Ithaca, 2000), 124.

[18] Junker, "Der Tanz der *Mww*," 30–32.

[19] Settgast, *Untersuchungen zu altägyptischnen Bestattungsdarstellungen,* 52–57.

[20] Davies, "The Tomb of Tetaky at Thebes," 52.

[21] Kelly-Anne Diamond, "*dmḏ(y)t: The 'Bone Collector.'*" *GM* 218 (2008), 24.

[22] Hartwig Altenmüller, "Zu Frage der *Mww*," *SAK* 2 (1975), 1.

[23] Settgast, *Untersuchungen zu altägyptischen Bestattungsdarstellungen,* 38–39.

the boat. The same scene can be seen in TT 53, 69, 92, 100, 112, 125, 127, 342, and in the tomb of Pahery. In TT 69, 92, 100, 112, and 127, as well as in Pahery, the beginning of the scene shows a priest (or the dead man), making an offering to the Anubis in his sanctuary (see fig. 3, middle right). While in TT 69, Anubis appears in his theriomorphic form, standing, holding a *wꜥs* sceptre with one hand and an ankh in the other, in Pahery's tomb, the god appears in the form of a jackal recumbent on a sanctuary. In TT 123 it is very likely, given the space and proportions of the scenes, that this image of Anubis was present, but given the fractures and voids in this location, it is impossible to attest to this with confidence. As demonstrated by Altenmüller,[24] inscriptions in these scenes identify the building as Sais. The rectangular structures that appear in the New Kingdom scenes are interpreted by Settgast[25] as the sarcophagus of the dead, an identification based on scenes from TT 69, 92, 100, 112, 127, and the tomb of Pahery, where a sarcophagus is carried by a group of men. According to Altenmüller, in some New Kingdom tombs, the scene of the journey to Sais is combined with those of the journey to Buto in the form of an extended seasonal trip (*Saisfahrt*).[26] As a result, even though the cities of Sais and Buto are relatively distant from each other, they are depicted side by side, or close together as in TT 123.

Crossing the Gates of *tꜣ-ḏsr:* Affecting and Being Affected

The big question is why Amenemhet chose to portray the Butic ritual. I think this choice has to do with how images were conceived in ancient Egypt. In Egyptology, the idea that images are mimetic or idealized representations of something, or someone is well accepted.[27] The idea that existences are manifest potential elements is one of the centers of ancient Egyptian ontology. In Egyptian cosmology, Atum, the creator god, becomes active when he differentiates himself from the primordial waters.[28] According to Egyptian cosmology, creation is not something that happens from nothing, but is a process of differentiation of everything that exists in a latent and potential state. Everything that exists in the Universe, including the Creator himself, exists in the form of a latent potentiality that inhabits an invisible, deep, dark, and eternal sphere. The transformation process is experienced as a process of differentiation where the being ceases to be an undifferentiated matter and becomes a distinct entity.[29] As Allen summarized, "darkness is light waiting to happen,"[30] just as "chaos is not chaos, but unstructured creative potentialities."[31] In this way, existence, in the ancient Egyptian conception, alternates latency and realization and happens from a continuous process of differentiation. In other words, existence is a continuous becoming that takes the form of a process of differentiation within a sea of potentialities. As a result of this process, beings become manifest.

According to Karenga, this idea that being is a latent potentiality amidst a sea of possibilities is not exclusive to the creator, but is inherent to all beings, including humans, both in terms of their capacity for development and of transcendence.[32] That is why the human being was thought to be in a continuous process of becoming. Death is life in another form since life continually moves between the spaces of latency and realization. According to the author, the ka, the ba, and the akh could be thought of as the manifestations of this transcendence. Nyord suggests, the "ka of a person is the undifferentiated potential of which the person is a manifestation, not

---

[24] Altenmuller, "Zu Frage der *Mww*," 6–7.

[25] Settgast, *Untersuchungen zu altägyptischnen Bestattungsdarstellungen*, 31.

[26] Altenmuller, "Zu Frage der *Mww*," 6–7.

[27] Rune Nyord, *Seeing Perfection: Ancient Egyptian Images beyond Representation, Elements in Ancient Egypt in Context* (Cambridge, 2020), 1; Nicola Harrington, *Living with the Dead: Ancestor Worship and Mortuary Ritual in Ancient Egypt* (Oxford, 2013), 46.

[28] See James Allen, *Genesis in Egypt: The Philosophy of Ancient Egyptian Creations Accounts*, YES *2* (New Haven, 1988), 34; Theophile Obenga, "African Philosophy of the Pharonic Period," in Ivan Van Sertima (ed.), *Egypt Revisited* (New Brunswick, 1989), 315; Maulana Karenga, *Maat, the Moral Ideal in Ancient Egypt: A Study in Classical African Ethics* (New York, 2004), 185–86; Ragnhild Finnestad, *Image of the World and Symbol of the Creator: On the Cosmological and Iconological Values of the Temple of Edfu* (Wiesbaden, 1985), 360–62; Ragnhild Finnestad, "On Transposing Soul and Body into a Monistic Conception of Being: An Example from Ancient Egypt," *Religion* 16 (1986), 363.

[29] Rune Nyord, *Seeing Perfection*, 6.

[30] James Allen, *Genesis in Egypt*, 34.

[31] Karenga, *Maat*, 186.

[32] Karenga, *Maat*, 185–87.

necessarily as a realization once and for all, but rather through a continuous process of updating."[33] That is, the ka would be an indeterminate potential that could be actualized as a living being, as a dead man's mummy, his sarcophagus, his statue or any other image or object. In this way the ka, ba, and ankh designate the human being as a perceived and complete form, and therefore we cannot think about them as parts of a human being, but as transcended vital totalities, that is, the ka, the ba, and the akh are alternative forms of human existence that can manifest themselves simultaneously. In the form of ka, ba or akh, the human being can move between states of existence without being confined to any one of them.[34]

I suggest that just as the ka, ba, and akh are alternative forms of existence that allow the dead to continue living in a transcendent way, images in tombs can be thought in the same way. Nyord, in his discussion of the ontological character of images in ancient Egypt, has shown that one of the ways the Egyptians used to refer to images was through the concept *nfrw*, which can have the meaning of limit or presence.[35] Although the term was mainly used to refer to divine images, this idea of presence could be extended to non-divine beings. In this way, images could be thought of as one of the means that the transcendent dead could continue to exist in a manifest way. The process of transcendence here would be enabled by specific rituals such as the Opening of the Mouth or even the delivery of daily offerings. This would allow the deceased, as a present and manifest being, to affect and be affected by other bodies.

Affect can be defined as an autonomous force between bodies that best expresses itself not in terms of emotions or experiences, but of intensities that increase or decrease the action potential of a body.[36] Affect, therefore, refers primarily to the reciprocal capacities of bodies to affect and be affected.[37] Bodies here are not just human bodies, but they cover all kinds of bodies that can affect and be affected, for example, an animal, a table, a book, or a tree.[38] Affection here is not a characteristic that pertains to an individual body but is a quality of the different kinds of relationships through which interrelated bodies are constituted, actualized, and constantly transformed. For Deleuze and Guattari,[39] an affective event is a meeting between the virtual and the real, a meeting of incorporeal concepts with the materiality of the world. Affect in this way is a relational process that makes us think of agency as the efficacy that is distributed between assemblages of human beings and not humans.

This is evident in the way in which the Egyptians created material-discursive strategies such as, for example, scenes to capture the attention of visitors, align the tomb so that the sun illuminates certain parts of the tomb and not others, leave express requests for visitors to make offerings, etc., that were intended to attract the visitor so that he would somehow take part in the funerary rituals when entering the tomb. Amenemhet, knew that the tomb would be visited—at least he expected it—and so he expected his images to affect people and people to affect his image allowing him to become manifest. Speech plays a key role in this process. As is well established, among Egyptians, speech did not only serve to structure the social image but also had a creative power. Among the Egyptians the word was regarded as a creative source. According to Meyer-Dietrich, the creative power of speech operated at different levels: operative (the transfiguration of objects and people, healing/cursing, curing or cursing); satisfaction (to calm and satisfy people), and identity (to reaffirm the identity and agency of individuals).[40] For example, to Assmann, during the process of embalming, even more important than the chemical or surgical treatment of the body was the verbal treatment that the deceased received, because it was through speech that the deceased was animated with conscience and physical strength.[41] Through the act of reciting, the incantations the body gained unity, and thus, one by one, every part of the body came to life. Speech in this sce-

33 Rune Nyord, "The Concept of *ka* between Egyptian and Egyptological Frameworks," in Rune Nyord (ed.), *Concepts in Middle Kingdom Funerary Culture: Proceedings of the Lady Wallis Budge Anniversary Symposium Held at Christ's College, Cambridge, 22 January 2016*, CHANE 102 (Leiden, 2019), 164.

34 Finnestad, "On Transposing Soul and Body," 362–63.

35 Nyord, *Seeing Perfection*, 16–21.

36 Gilles Deleuze and Felix Guattari, *A Thousand Plateaus: Capitalism and Schizophrenia* (Minneapolis, 1987), xvi.

37 Patricia Clough, "(De)coding the Subject-in-Affect," *Subjectivity* 23.1 (2008), 141.

38 C. Von Scheve, "A Social Relational Account of Affect," Working Paper SFB 1171 Affective Societies 03/16 (2016), 4–5.

39 Deleuze and Guattari, *A Thousand Plateaus*, 99.

40 Erika Meyer-Dietrich, "Recitation, Speech Acts, and Declamation," in Elizabeth Frood and Willeke Wendrich (eds.), *UCLA Encyclopedia of Egyptology* (Los Angeles, 2010), 4–5.

41 Jan Assmann, *Death and Salvation in Ancient Egypt* (Ithaca, 2005), 33.

nario has a clear ontological value, since according to the Memphite Theology, uttered by the demiurge, speech brings the world into existence.[42]

It is well established that the chapels of New Kingdom Theban tombs were open to the public. On certain occasions, such as the Beautiful Feast of Valley,[43] family members, friends, and visitors in general could enter and visit, fulfilling the functions of memory and worship, being linked to the idea of accessibility. As a public area, the chapel played a central role in the communication process between the living and the dead as the space where visitors interacted with the material-discursive[44] strategies proposed by the dead. For example, in some tombs, architectural elements such as pillars interact to the wall obstructing the view of the reliefs, capturing the attention and directing the visitor's body movement.[45] At the same time, decorative elements such as varnish were applied to certain scenes to highlight their significance and thus attract the visitor, as seen in TT 49, where some images of Neferhotep are covered with varnish creating a 3D effect.[46]

In this sense, the images are strategies that Amenemhet, the owner of TT 123, thought out and had created to affect people as a way to remain existing. The generated affects in these relationships and encounters allowed him to transcend to other forms of existence and thus guaranteed the continuity of his life. So, together with architects and artists, he thought about strategies which were intended to affect people and try to convince them to participate in his funeral rite,[47] such as the alignment of the tomb with the winter sunlight that illuminates the statues and hits the desert scenes first; the narrow passageway that encouraged walking, either into the tomb or out; the way in which the sound echoes more or less depending on where one is inside the tomb. Everything was designed to increase or decrease the ability of visitors to act. This also involved choosing and positioning the repertoire of scenes. In the passage corridor on the left there are scenes of the funerary procession, and on the right, there are scenes of hunting in the desert. The funerary scenes are directed to the west, that is, towards the funerary chamber. The desert scenes are directed to the east, to the tomb's entrance. Thus, the funerary scenes induce the visitor's way into the tomb, into the world of the dead, and the desert scenes take the visitor out into the world of the living.

The visitor here is not a mere spectator, he participates actively in all events alongside Amenemhet through the affective flows that were created during these encounters. In this way, the Sacred District is not just a representation or a discourse on ancestry, but it is an affective performance that truly allows Amenemhet to cross the boundaries between the world of the living and the world of the dead and to find his ancestors. This affective performance and the results that it will produce in the form of different actualizations of the existing potentialities depend on the visitors' affect and how they are affected by the images. Affecting and being affected by the place—by the images—sets in motion affective flows that will activate the *magic* of the place and only then Amenemhet will be able to continue meeting his ancestors.

Although Egyptologist usually think of the Sacred District as a representation of narratives about ancestry, I think that it is more than a narrative—the Sacred District is the very path that the dead takes in becoming manifest. If Nyord is correct in his interpretation that images in ancient Egypt vary ontologically depending on where they are and the role they play in each relationship,[48] we can suggest that the funeral procession scenes, as well as the Sacred District scenes, involve affective flows whose principle is to actualize the dead and thus make him manifest. This allows him to fulfil his destiny, meet his ancestors, and continue existing as a transcendent being through a continuous process of becoming.

---

[42] Obenga, "African Philosophy," 315.

[43] See for example, Alexis Doncker, "Theban Tomb Graffiti during the New Kingdom Research on the Reception of Ancient Egyptian Images by Ancient Egyptians," in Katalin Kóthay (ed.), *Art and Society Ancient and Modern Contexts of Egyptian Art* (Budapest, 2012), 25.

[44] Karen Barad, *Meeting the Universe Halfway: Quantum Physics and the Entanglement of Matter and Meaning*, 2nd ed. (Durham, NC, 2007), 146.

[45] See for example TT 96, Hode-Hoenes, *Life and Death in Ancient Egypt*, 112–39.

[46] Personal impression obtained during work at TT 49, from 2008 to 2012.

[47] José Pellini, "Dung on the Wall: Ontology and Relationality in Qurna; The Case of TT123," *Cambridge Archaeological Journal* (2021), 1–13.

[48] Nyord, *Seeing Perfection*, 25–28.

Some Ptolemaic and Roman Sites in the Central Eastern Desert

Steven E. Sidebotham
University of Delaware, USA

Hans Barnard
Cotsen Institute of Archaeology, UCLA, USA

Jennifer E. Gates-Foster
University of North Carolina at Chapel Hill, USA

Ronald E. Zitterkopf
Shawnee Mission, Kansas, USA

Abstract

The University of Delaware conducted numerous surveys in the Eastern Desert between 1987 and 2015. This contribution examines eight sites studied between 1990 and 1999 that lay east of the Nile city of Qena in Upper Egypt. They include mines, quarries, and road infrastructure (forts and accommodations for transport animals) that supported these mineral extraction activities. Sites throughout the region range from pre-historic to Islamic and modern, but this study focuses only on those from the Ptolemaic and Roman periods.

Examination of sites presented here expands our knowledge of the economic importance of this area of the Eastern Desert, dominated by mines and quarries and the infrastructure that facilitated exploitation of mineral resources and their transport to the Nile valley city of Qena.

الملخص

أجرت جامعة ديلاوير العديد من أعمال المسح الأثري في الصحراء الشرقية بين عامي 1987 و2015. تتناول هذه المقالة ثمانية مواقع تمت دراستها بين عامي 1990 و1999 وتقع شرق مدينة قنا في صعيد مصر. وهي تشمل المناجم والمحاجر والبنية التحتية للطرق (الحصون وأماكن إقامة الحيوانات التي كانت تستخدم للنقل) التي دعمت أنشطة استخراج المعادن. تتراوح المواقع في جميع أنحاء المنطقة من فترة ما قبل التاريخ إلى العصر الإسلامي والحديث، لكن هذه الدراسة تركز فقط على تلك التي تعود إلى الفترتين البطلمية والرومانية.

إن فحص المواقع المعروضة هنا يوسع معرفتنا بالأهمية الاقتصادية لهذه المنطقة من الصحراء الشرقية، والتي تسودها المناجم والمحاجر والبنية التحتية التي سهلت استغلال الموارد المعدنية ونقلها إلى مدينة قنا.

Introduction

Small teams under the aegis of the University of Delaware conducting archaeological surveys in the Eastern Desert between 1987 and 2015 recorded numerous examples of petroglyphs, cleared road sections, and graves and settlements from all periods with a special focus on the Ptolemaic and Roman eras. Time free for fieldwork, availability of suitable personnel, adequate funding, and requisite permits limited which areas could be exam-

Journal of the American Research Center in Egypt 58 (2022), 171–207
http://dx.doi.org/10.5913/jarce.58.2022.a010

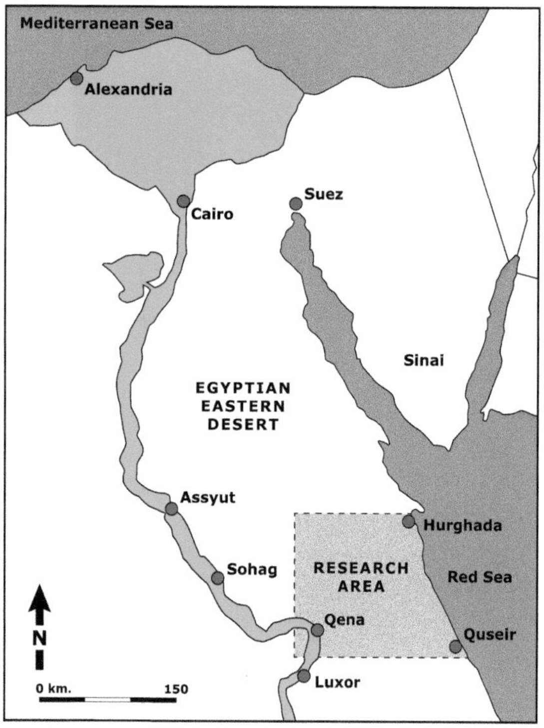

Fig. 1. Map locating survey area. Drawing by H. Barnard.

ined and in what detail they could be recorded during these nearly three decades. Surveys ranged as far north as GPS 28° 16.77' N/31° 53.96' E (an Early Roman and perhaps Early Islamic site at Umm Suwagi on the Via Nova Hadriana), as far south as 22° 34.07 N/35° 15.86' E. (a pre-dynastic animal cemetery at Bir Asele/ Esila), up to the Red Sea coast on the east and the Nile valley on the west. It is clear from discussions with Bedouin informants and guides that there are many more sites to be recorded.

This article presents eight sites documented between 1990 and 1999 during these surveys in the central part of the Eastern Desert east of the Nile city of Qena (ancient Kainopolis/Maximianopolis) in Upper Egypt.[1] This area of the desert witnessed extensive and intensive activity in the Ptolemaic and especially the Roman eras. The similarity of function and relative proximity of these sites to one another, and their reliance on Qena for logistical support warrants their separate study.

The sites examined included mines, quarries, and road stations supporting traffic between locations in the Eastern Desert and the Nile. All were interconnected

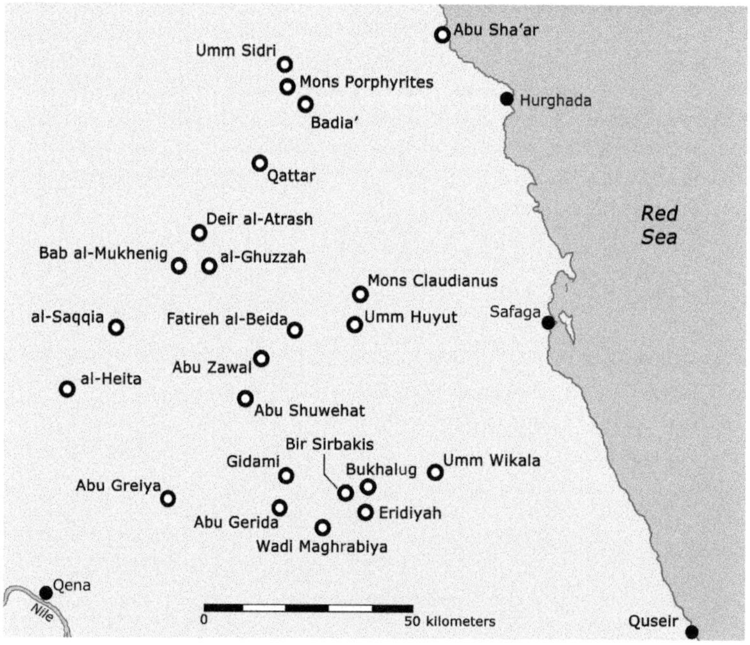

Fig. 2. Map locating sites mentioned in the text. Drawing by M. Hense.

[1] The authors thank J. Harrell for his useful comments on this manuscript and also thank the various offices and officers of the Egyptian Antiquities Organization (predecessor of the Supreme Council of Antiquities) for granting permits and assistance.

Site	DMS—Helmert 1906 geoid	UTM—WGS84 geoid
Abu Gerida - settlement	26°N 21'27.2"–33°E 17'13.9"	36R–528818E–2915326N
Abu Gerida - fort	26°N 21'16.7"–33°E 17'10.5"	36R–528723E–2915002N
Abu Greiya - East	26°N 22'15.2"–33°E 01'03.1"	36R–501912E–2916771N
Abu Greiya - animal lines	26°N 22'16.4"–33°E 01'00.1"	36R–501829E–2916808N
Abu Greiya - West	26°N 22'15.8"–33°E 00'42.7"	36R–501347E–2916789N
Bir Sirbakis - center	26°N 23'29.6"–33°E 27'01.9"	36R–545101E–2919139N
Bir Sirbakis - South	26°N 23'27.2"–33°E 27'04.9"	36R–545184E–2919065N
Bukhalug	26°N 24'10.4"–33°E 30'04.9"	36R–550166E–2920413N
Erediyah	26°N 21'05.6"–33°E 29'39.7"	36R–549490E–2914725N
Fatireh al-Beida	26°N 44'00.2"–33°E 19'18.7"	36R–532172E–2956959N
Gidami - settlement	26°N 25'21.2"–33°E 18'00.1"	36R–530081E–2922528N
Wadi Abu Shuwehat	26°N 35'09.2"–33°E 11'51.1"	36R–519832E–2940598N

Fig. 3. Coordinates of the sites under discussion.

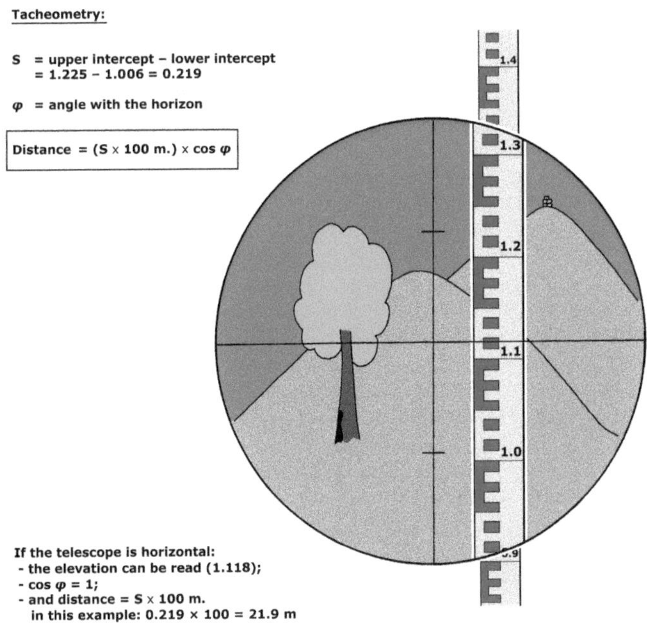

Fig. 4. Schematic overview of survey methods using polar coordinates (left) and tacheometry (right).

by roads, whose ultimate western terminus was Qena.[2] The sites presented are Fatireh al-Beida, (Wadi) Abu Shuwehat, (Wadi) Abu Greiya, Gidami, Abu Gerida, Bukhalug, (Bir) Sirbakis, and Eridiyah. Since the surveys took place, a team from the Mission archéologique française du désert Oriental (MAFDO) has recorded more accurately and partly excavated the Ptolemaic gold mining settlement and Roman fort at al-Ghuzzah.[3] As a result, discussion of that site is not included here although the Delaware teams originally surveyed it during the same period.

Saleh Ali Suelim, the project's Ma 'aza Bedouin guide, introduced the teams to all the sites and assisted with the work. The survey teams used tape measures, a hand-held compass, a Wild T2 theodolite, a stadia rod, and a Magellan NAV 1000 hand-held GPS receiver to plot sites and draw the plans. Until May 2000, GPS accuracy for civilian receivers was limited by the US Department of Defense Selective Availability Program to a resolution of around 100 m. As a result, the sites were relocated on Google Earth in late 2021 and the more accurate coordinates resulting from this are presented here.

Depending on the layout of extant structures, survey teams calculated dimensions either directly by measuring tape or measuring to a temporary baseline or established from observations taken with a theodolite and stadia-rod, a survey method known as tacheometry (fig. 4).

Sites Surveyed

Fatireh al-Beida

The survey visited Fatireh al-Beida in June 1993 and drew a plan in August 1997.[4] The site is about 200 m south of the modern al-Gesh-Safaga highway, which did not exist in 1997. Aside from relatively small-scale quarrying activities, Fatireh al-Beida may also have occasionally served as a stop linking quarrying operations at Mons Claudianus,—ca. 23.3 km away[5] towards the northeast via various wadis—with Qena.[6]

The maximum size of Fatireh al-Beida was ca. 85 m N-S x 135 m E-W with the densest concentration of structures in the center of the site measuring ca. 65 m N-S x 50 m E-W (fig. 5). Edifices at Fatireh al-Beida were primarily rectilinear in plan with walls ca. 0.6-0.9 m high x 0.4-0.6 m wide (figs. 6–7). There were at least three dif-

---

[2] L. Manière, M. Crépy, and B. Redon, "Building a Model to Reconstruct the Hellenistic and Roman Road Networks of the Eastern Desert of Egypt, a Semi-Empirical Approach Based on Modern Travelers' Itineraries," *Journal of Computer Applications in Archaeology*, 4.1 (2021), 20–46.

[3] The Delaware survey visited al-Ghuzzah in July 1992 and drew a plan in July 1996 published by H. Barnard, "Introduction to Part 2: The Last 2500 Years," in H. Barnard and K. Duistermaat (eds.), *The History of the Peoples of the Eastern Desert* (Los Angeles, 2012), 178; R. Klemm and D. Klemm, *Gold Mining in Ancient Egypt and Nubia. Geoarchaeology of the Ancient Gold Mining Sites in the Egyptian and Sudanese Eastern Deserts* (Berlin-Heidelberg, 2013), 68–70; B. de la Roque, "Voyage au Djebel Shaïb," *Bulletin de la Société royale de Géographie d'Égypte* 11 (1922), 119–22 for discussion and earlier sketches. J. Gates-Foster, I. Goncalves, B. Redon et al., "The Early Imperial Fortress of Berkou, Eastern Desert, Egypt," *Journal of Roman Archaeology* 34 (2021), 30–74; T. Faucher, B. Redon, A. Bülow-Jacobsen, M. Crépy et al., "Désert Oriental (2020)" *Bulletin archéologique des Écoles françaises à l'étranger, Égypt*, 30 May 2021, accessed 5 April 2022. URL: http://journals.openedition.org/baefe/2714; DOI: https://doi.org/10.4000/baefe.2714. The MAFDO 2022 excavations await publication.

[4] S. Sidebotham, M. Hense, and H. Nouwens, *The Red Land. The Illustrated Archaeology of Egypt's Eastern Desert* (Cairo-New York, 2008), 123 briefly describe this site; A. Weigall, *Travels in the Upper Egyptian Deserts* (Edinburgh-London, 1913), 131; D. Meredith and L. Tregenza, "Notes on Roman Roads and Stations in the Eastern Desert," *Bulletin of the Faculty of Arts, Fouad I (Cairo) University* 11.1 (1949), 100, 116; V. Brown and J. Harrell, "Topographical and Petrological Survey of Ancient Roman Quarries in the Eastern Desert of Egypt," in Y. Maniatis, N. Herz and Y. Basiakos (eds.), *Asmosia III Athens: Transactions of the 3rd International Symposium of the Association for the Study of Marble and Other Stones Used in Antiquity* (London, 1995), 221, 225 (Table 1 continued), 229 (fig. 6), 230; S. Sidebotham, "Map 78 Porphyrites et Claudianus Montes," in R. Talbert (ed.), *Barrington Atlas of the Greek and Roman World*, vol. 1 (Princeton, 2000); S. Sidebotham, "Map 78 Porphyrites et Claudianus Montes," in R. Talbert (ed.), *Barrington Atlas of the Greek and Roman World. Map-by-Map Directory*, vol. 2 (Princeton, 2000), 1159. See also https://desertnetworks.huma-num.fr/sites/DN_SIT0102.

[5] This measurement and others calculating distances between sites in this manuscript determined by using the path feature on Google Earth following wadis from one site to another.

[6] S. Sidebotham, R. Zitterkopf, and J. Riley, "Survey of the 'Abu Sha'ar-Nile Road," *AJA* 95.4 (1991), 571–622; D. Peacock, "Transportation and Routes to the Nile," in D. Peacock and V. Maxfield (eds.), *Survey and Excavations Mons Claudianus 1987–1993*, vol. 1, *Topography & Quarries*, FIFAO 37 (Cairo, 1997), 264–65; Sidebotham "Map 78," vol. 2, 1158–63; S. Sidebotham, *Berenike and the Ancient Maritime Spice Route* (Berkeley, 2011), 130–31 (Table 8–1, on 129–30).

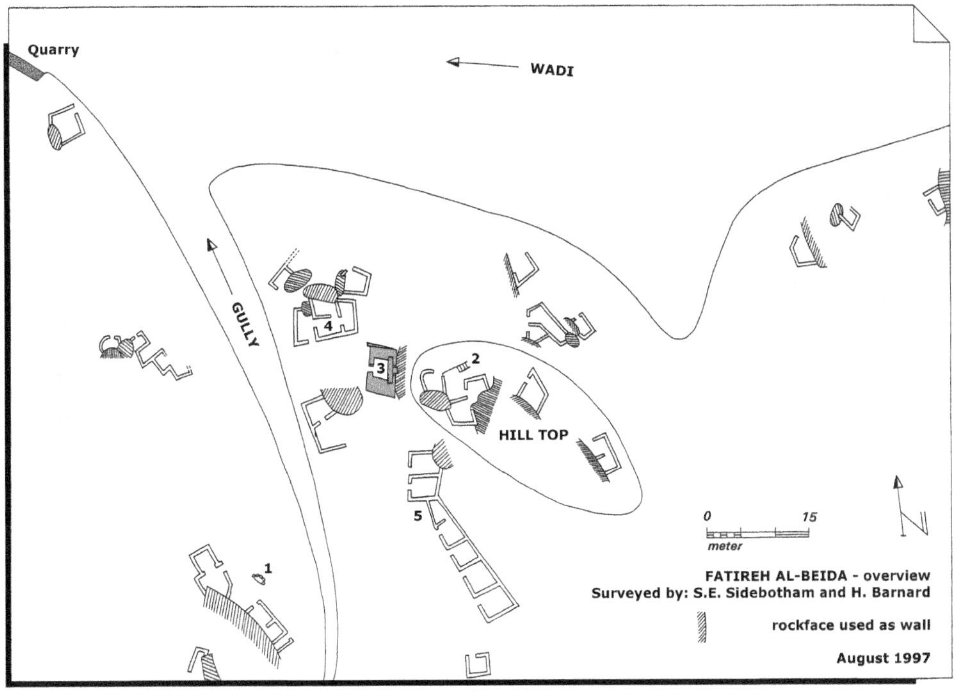

Fig. 5. Fatireh al-Beida plan. Drawing by H. Barnard.

Fig. 6. Fatireh al-Beida, detail of site. Photo by S. Sidebotham.

Fig. 7. Fatireh al-Beida, detail of site. Photo by S. Sidebotham.

ferent types of stone used in wall construction, which comprised stacked cobbles and boulders. While many extant buildings were free-standing, others used natural rock faces for one or more of their walls. There was a quarry ca. 80 m northwest of the center of the main settlement that provided some of the building stone used for constructing the temple/shrine (discussed below).

Structures throughout the site appeared to be roughly contemporary except for a semi-circle of stones (fig. 5.1) towards the southwestern side, which seemed to be a later addition. There was a staircase (fig. 5.2) leading to features on a hilltop in the center of the site, one of which may have been a watchtower. There was a putative temple/shrine immediately below and west of the hilltop with the staircase (fig. 5.3). The function of other structures could not be positively identified, but these likely included residential facilities, storage rooms and, just

Fig. 8. Fatireh al-Beida, temple. Photo by S. Sidebotham.

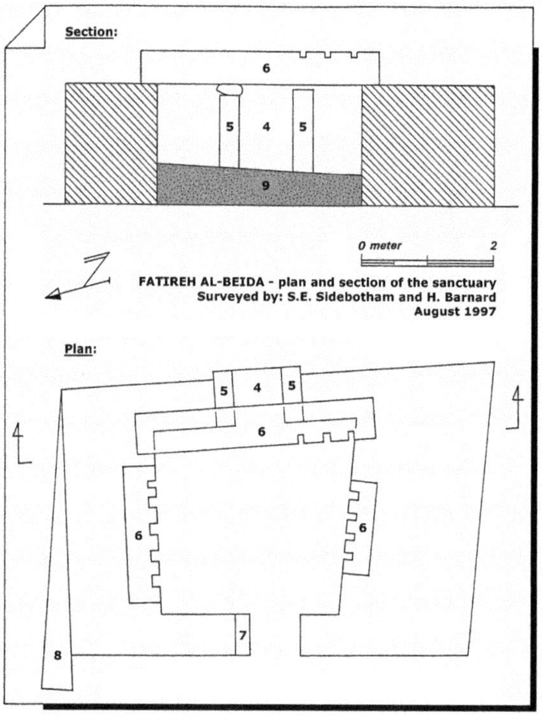

Fig. 9. Fatireh al-Beida, temple. Drawing by H. Barnard..

northwest of the temple/shrine (figs. 8–9), probably an administrative center (fig. 5.4), an identification based on its prominent location and multiple rooms.

The most noteworthy structure at Fatireh al-Beida was, likely, a temple/shrine built of locally quarried quartz diorite. Its overall dimensions were about 3.2 m N-S x ca. 3.5 m E-W x ca. 2.70 m high.[7] The outer walls comprised large boulders and cobbles. There was a niche at its eastern end (fig. 9.4) cut into the natural rock, which measured about 1.2 m wide x 0.8 m deep. Some roof slabs (fig. 9.6) from the nearby quarry remained *in situ* and preserved quarry wedge marks. Some of these blocks were quite large (2.9 m x 0.9 m). The single entrance on the western wall measured ca. 0.75–0.80 m wide and had been narrowed (fig. 9.7) on its northern side. On the external northern face of the temple wall was a triangular-shaped platform (fig. 9.8). There were two upright slabs of stone (fig. 9.5) flanking the niche on its northern and southern sides, which wind-blown sand partly covered (fig. 9.9). There was no evidence of who might have been venerated here.

The survey did not document any animal tethering lines at Fatireh al-Beida, which suggested that supporting logistical operations to and from Mons Claudianus was not an important function for this site. Surface sherds dated predominantly to the second half of the first to early second centuries AD with a small sampling dating from the fourth to fifth centuries AD.[8] If the dates of the sherds were an accurate reflection of periods of use, Fatireh al-Beida was a short-lived site.

Pottery

Fig. 10.1. Carinated dish with everted rim. Sandy purple-brown (10R 5/4) alluvial matrix, elsewhere orange (10R 6/6) throughout or internal margins and red-brown (10R 5/6) surfaces, part blackened on the underside. Dull matt wash or slip. Parallel: Imitation of ESA Hayes Form 34, mid-first century AD.

Fig. 10.2. Large hemispherical bowl with exterior groove below rim. Sandy marl with gray-green core and dull orange-red margins. Discolored surfaces. Parallel: Mons Claudianus bowl type 16, second century AD in

---

[7] D. Meredith and L. Tregenza, "Notes on Roman Roads and Stations in the Eastern Desert I, (a) From Qena to Bab el-Mukheiniq, (b) The Roman Station in W. Abu Zawal," *Bulletin of the Faculty of Arts, Fouad I University* 11.1 (1949), 4, 28–30; D. Meredith and L. Tregenza, "Mons Porphyrites: The North-west Village and Quarries," *Bulletin of the Faculty of Arts, Fouad I University* 12.1 (1950), 145.

[8] R. Tomber completed field recording of this material in 1997. Descriptions are based on her field notes and drawings.

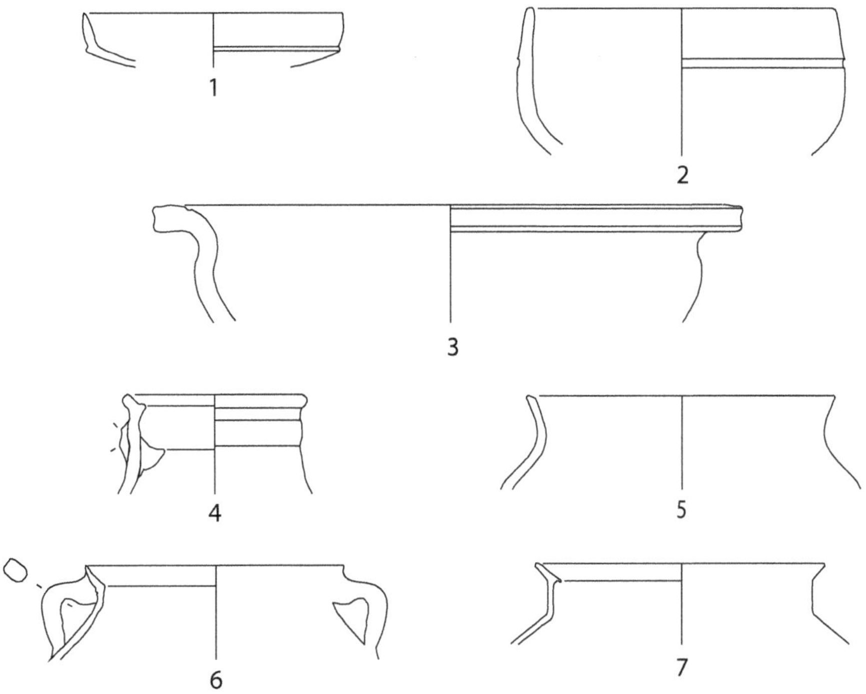

Fig. 10. Pottery from Fatireh al-Beida. Scale = 1:4. Drawings by J. Gates-Foster.

R. Tomber, "The Pottery," in V. Maxfield and D. Peacock (eds.), *Survey and Excavation Mons Claudianus 1987–1993*, vol. 3, *Ceramic Vessels and Related Objects*, FIFAO 54 (Cairo, 2006), fig. 1.39.
Fig. 10.3. Overhanging ledge-rim krater or basin. Sandy marl with pale green to gray core and dull pink margins. Characterized by poorly sorted clay, sometimes as lumps, common large quartz sand, and some lime and organics, particularly visible as white, flat plates. Red-brown surfaces, discolored. Parallel: Mons Claudianus jar type 90, first–second century AD, in Tomber, "The Pottery," fig. 1.36.
Fig. 10.4. Strainer jug with internal ledge and angled rim. Calcareous fabric. Dull brown margin with pink external lense and white slip outside and to base of rim inside. Parallel: al-Ghuzzah, late first century AD, in Gates-Foster et al., "Early Imperial fortress of Berkou," fig. 19.8.
Fig. 10.5. Wide-mouth cooking pot with slightly everted upper rim. Traces of square handle at shoulder and below rim (not illustrated). Orange-brown alluvial fabric with red-brown core and surfaces. Fine, with rare organic and limestone impurities. Parallel: Mons Claudianus cooking pot type 32, first-second century AD, in Tomber, "The Pottery," fig. 1.29.
Fig. 10.6. Wide-mouth cooking pot with squared-off handle joined to sharply everted rim. Brown alluvial fabric with pink core and red-brown surfaces. Slightly sandy. Parallel: Al-Ghuzzah, late first century AD, in Gates-Foster et al., "Early Imperial fortress of Berkou," fig. 17.13.
Fig. 10.7. Wide-mouth cooking pot with sharply everted broad, flat rim. Fine brown alluvial fabric with some visible inclusions. Brown with slightly red-brown external surface. Parallel: Mons Claudianus cookpot type 59, first-second century AD, in Tomber, "The Pottery," fig. 1.32.

From Fatireh al-Beida there were two options to reach the Nile. The shorter one—ca. 119 km long—left Fatireh al-Beida, headed southwest for ca. 31 km to the sizeable facilities at (Wadi) Abu Shuwehat and then ca. 47 km towards the south-southwest crossing the Naq' at-Ter (plain) to reach the station at Abu Greiya, discussed below, which is currently ca. 41 km from Qena via the modern highway. The sizeable distance between Abu

Site	DMS—Helmert 1906 geoid	UTM—WGS84 geoid
Abu Bokari	25°N 15'11.1"–33°E 45'18.3"	36R–576199E–2793196N
Abu Sha'ar	27°N 22'08.0"–33°E 40'52.3"	36R–567526E–3027491N
Abu Zawal	26°N 40'17.6"–33°E 14'20.5"	36R–523947E–2950093N
al-Heita - fort	26°N 36'30.8"–32E° 45'41.5"	36R–476422E–2943115N
al-Heita - waystation	26°N 36'26.0"–32°E 45'39.7"	36R–476372E–2942967N
al-Saqqia	26°N 44'03.8"–32°E 52'48.1"	36R–488232E–2957035N
Bab al-Mukhenig	26°N 52'06.2"–33°E 02'01.3"	36R–503510E–2971871N
al-Ghuzzah	26°N 52'08.0"–33°E 06'25.3"	36R–510794E–2971931N
Badia - animal lines	27°N 12'50.0"–33°E 20'36.7"	36R–534181E–3010185N
Bir Gidami - North	26°N 24'36.2"–33°E 24'10.3"	36R–540340E–2921172N
Bir Gidami - West	26°N 24'30.8"–33°E 24'05.5"	36R–540208E–2921005N
Bir Gidami - South	26°N 24'27.2"–33°E 24'06.7"	36R–540241E–2920895N
Bir Samut	24°N 48'35.1"–33°E 54'12.2"	36R–591466E–2744194N
Deir al-Atrash	26°N 56'07.4"–33°E 04'49.9"	36R–508157E–2979294N
Dunqash	24°N 56'20.3"–33°E 52'09.3"	36R–587926E–2758482N
Hangaliyah	24°N 50'34.5"–34°E 34'52.2"	36R–659935E–2748491N
Kab Marfu'a - shrine	24°N 32'39.4"–34°E 44'12.2"	36R–676076E–2715606N
Mons Porphyrites	27°N 15'02.4"–33°E 17'59.7"	36R–529855E–3014248N
Qattar - fort	27°N 05'20.6"–33°E 13'38.5"	36R–534181E–3010185N
Samut North	24°N 50'54.0"–33°E 54'50.0"	36R–592498E–2748473N
Sukkari	24°N 57'09.9"–34°E 42'34.9"	36R–672773E–2760814N
Umm Howeitat al-Qibli - North	25°N 26'39.9"–34°E 34'14.5"	36R–658101E–2815100N
Umm Howeitat al-Qibli - South	25°N 26'33.8"–34°E 34'09.5"	36R–657963E–2814911N
Umm Huyut - shrine	26°N 44'46.9"–33°E 28'04.1"	36R–546681E–2958441N
Umm Wikala - quarry	26°N 26'02.5"–33°E 39'46.0"	36R–566246E–2923933N
Wadi Ghadir	24°N 47'56.7"–34°E 50'07.9"	36R–685709E–2743959N
Wadi Maghrabiya	26°N 18'54.2"–33°E 23'26.5"	36R–539159E–2910647N

Fig. 11. Coordinates of selected sites mentioned in the text.

Shuwehat and Abu Greiya may suggest that there was an intermediate stop, which has never been located. Alternatively, the large animal accommodations at Abu Shuwehat may reflect intense efforts to water and feed animals prior to departing for the long journey to Abu Greiya and/or their feeding and watering after a lengthy and somewhat uphill trip from Abu Greiya.

A slightly longer route, totaling about 124 km, had stops better placed to accommodate traffic to and from Mons Porphyrites than that associated with Mons Claudianus. Nevertheless, a track from Fatireh al-Beida might also have used this route servicing traffic from Mons Porphyrites. It headed southwest and then west and northwest across the Naq' at-Ter to reach the station at al-Saqqia, about 49 km away. The great distance between Fatireh al-Beida and al-Saqqia suggests that there may have been an intermediate stop, but one has never been

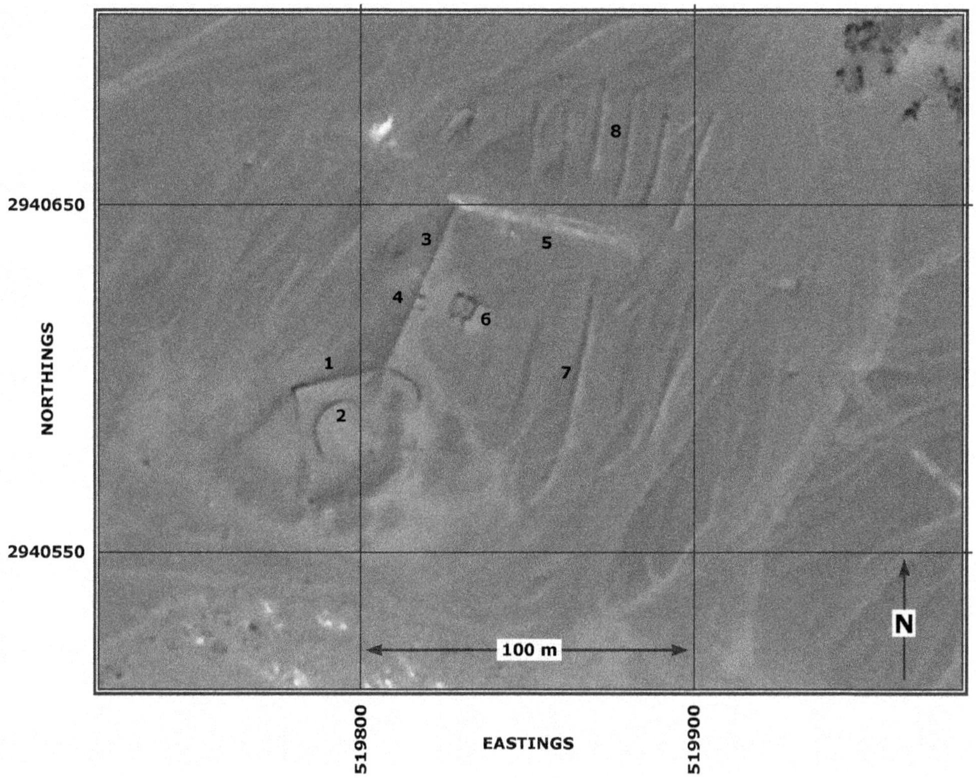

Fig. 12. (Wadi) Abu Shuwehat, Google Earth image. Enhanced by H. Barnard.

documented. From al-Saqqia, the route proceeded southwest and then south via Wadi Qena to the station at al-Heita, about 22 km away. The route from al-Heita to the next station at al- 'Aras (now destroyed) was about 29 km. From al- 'Aras it was only about 24 km to reach Qena.[9]

(Wadi) Abu Shuwehat

University of Delaware surveys visited the facilities in (Wadi) Abu Shuwehat in July 1990, late July 1992 and early June 1993.[10] The site primarily served traffic between Mons Claudianus and Qena. Additionally, this route had support facilities at Abu Zawal (also a gold mine) and (Wadi) Abu Greiya (see below), all of which provided protection and resting places to feed and water draft animals. Abu Shuwehat lay ca. 31 km southwest of Fatireh al-Beida and ca. 47 km northeast of the facilities at (Wadi) Abu Greiya.

The site at Abu Shuwehat is an important example of a Roman watering station in the Eastern Desert, but it seldom appears in the literature that discusses routes and stops in the region. T. Barron and W. Hume noted it.[11] D. Meredith and L. Tregenza suspected that there was a station in this general area between Abu Zawal and

[9] Sidebotham, Zitterkopf and Riley, "Survey of the 'Abu Sha'ar"; S. Sidebotham, "Map 78 Porphyrites et Claudianus Montes," vol. 1; S. Sidebotham, "Map 78 Porphyrites et Claudianus Montes," vol. 2, 1158–63; Sidebotham, *Berenike and the Ancient*, 130–31, table 8-1.

[10] Sidebotham, Hense, and Nouwens, *The Red Land*, 319–20 for brief description, photo and drawing; Klemm and Klemm, *Gold Mining*, 78–79 call it "Abu Shehat" and believe it (erroneously) to have been a Ptolemaic gold processing center; see H. Cuvigny, *Rome in Egypt's Eastern Desert*, vol. 1 (New York, 2021), 57, 259 and note 119. See also https://desertnetworks.huma-num.fr/sites/DN_SIT0029.

[11] T. Barron and W. Hume, *Topography and Geology of the Eastern Desert of Egypt, Central Portion*. Survey Department, Public Works Ministry, Geological Survey Report (Cairo, 1902), 41.

Fig. 13. (Wadi) Abu Shuwehat, detail of terracotta piping. Scale = 1 m. Photo by S. Sidebotham.

Fig. 14. (Wadi) Abu Shuwehat, water troughs along wall 5. Scale = 1 m (circled). Photo by S. Sidebotham.

Fig. 15. (Wadi) Abu Shuwehat, detail of water troughs on wall 5. Scale = 1 m. Photo by S. Sidebotham.

Abu Greiya,[12] which Tregenza eventually located.[13] R. Klemm and D. Klemm also reported the facilities here though they misunderstood their function and its date of operation.[14]

The station comprised extensive animal tethering lines, plastered water troughs, a walled water source and a terracotta pipeline to convey water from the well to the troughs. Yet, there were only two small permanent structures that humans could have used; to supplement these they may have erected temporary structures such as tents.

The overall dimensions were ca. 155 m N-S x ca. 115 m E-W. At the southwestern part of the site there was a large well surrounded by a rectilinear to ovoid-shaped wall of stones stacked without mortar (fig. 12.1), likely to keep animals out. This wall enclosing the well measured ca. 38 m N-S x 33.0 m E-W while within this area was an additional circular-shaped stone wall approximately 18.2 m in diameter x about 1 m high x ca. 0.9 m to

[12] Meredith and Tregenza, "Notes on Roman roads," 126; L. Tregenza, *The Red Sea Mountains of Egypt* (London-New York, 1955), 44.

[13] L. Tregenza, "Notes on a Recent Journey from Abu Zawal to the Greiya Station, II," *Bulletin of the Faculty of Arts, Fouad I (Cairo) University/Mağallat Kulliyyat al-Ādāb* 11.1 (1949), 130–33.

[14] See note 10.

1.8 m wide (fig. 12.2) to protect further the well from intrusive animals and encroaching sand. Stone wall 12.2 had an outer diameter of about 19.5 m x between 0.9-1.8 m wide x ca. 1 m high. It had an exterior opening on its southern side ca. 1.7 x 3.5 m, which likely provided another access to the well with, perhaps, stairs leading to the water. Mounds of sand on the eastern and southern sides were evidence of clearing to maintain access to the well after its original construction.

Between the northern side of the well and the outer wall was a rectangular accumulation of broken stone, possibly a platform, measuring ca. 3.7 m x 4.0 m. Perhaps it supported a water lifting device such as a *shadoof*.[15] This putative platform might also have accommodated a basin where water dumped by hand then flowed by gravity through the terracotta pipeline from the basin to the animal watering troughs.

Connected to this platform was a ca. 53 m-long base constructed of stones stacked without mortar extending to the north-northeast (fig. 12.3). This was a foundation for the terracotta pipeline set in mortar that ran its length. No sections of the pipeline at Abu Shuwehat survived *in situ* nor did the survey observe any complete circular sections of the pipe, though there were numerous pipe fragments that verified the existence of a pipeline. Pipe fragments had slight corrugations and inside diameters of ca. 110 mm and wall thicknesses of ca. 11 mm. Part way along base 12.3 and connected to it on its eastern side were the bare outlines of a room measuring 4.4 m x 3.75 m (fig. 12.4). This room appeared to have been built after the foundation for the pipeline; it may or may not have been used by quarry-related traffic using the facility. There was a similar pipeline supplying water to the late Roman Red Sea fort at Abu Sha'ar[16] and at the nearby *praesidium* at Abu Sha'ar al-Qibli, though the latter was not terracotta, but made of stones mortared together.[17]

The elevated pipeline at Abu Shuwehat emptied into plaster-lined troughs. No evidence of a transition structure was evident. These water troughs, running approximately north-northwest to east-southeast, were badly damaged at the two ends and the total length could not be determined, though 53 m were evident with a width of ca. 3.5 m. Fired bricks, varying in color from red to orange to light green, supported the troughs. At its inlet from the pipeline, the first trough had a single channel, but it then transitioned into two parallel channels each ca. 0.85 m wide. The divider wall was constructed of stones and the outer wall of the channels of fired brick. There were breaks in the divider wall to allow water to flow from one channel to the other and equalize the flow. Although the survey did not note this at Abu Shuwehat, D. Meredith mentioned that troughs at various animal tethering lines elsewhere in the region likely had plug holes at the bottom and overflow runnels at the top to regulate water flow.[18] This may have been the case at Abu Shuwehat as well.

Within the semi-enclosed area formed by the stone support for the pipeline and the water troughs, about 6.5–7.0 m east of the room along the N-S structure, was a two-roomed hut measuring 6.0 m N-S x and 6.9 m E-W (fig. 12.6). This may have monitored activities at five approximately north-south parallel animal tethering lines (fig. 12.7), the extant lengths of which varied from 25.2 to 56.4 m. North of the watering troughs (fig. 12.5) were six additional roughly parallel tethering lines (fig. 12.8) running approximately N-S. Flash floods had removed the northern ends of the four western-most lines. The extant remains of these northern lines varied in length from 20.0 to 35.7 m. The animal lines had a gravel base ranging from 1.0 to 2.4 m wide. Several of the animal tethers also had two parallel lines of boulders sitting atop the gravel bed. The animal lines were randomly laid out. The northern lines ranged from 8.1 m to 14.3 m apart and the southern ones 11.6 m to 28.1 m apart. Several of these lines were curved. Animals were tethered to these lines and brought to the water troughs in some organized fashion and then returned to their tethers.

The numbers and lengths of the tethering lines indicated that the facilities here accommodated large numbers of animals. The complex of animal tethering lines at Abu Shuwehat was substantially larger than those documented anywhere else in the Eastern Desert as figure 16 indicates.

---

15 See Sidebotham, Hense, and Nouwens, *The Red Land*, 320 (fig. 13.8).

16 S. Sidebotham, "University of Delaware Fieldwork in the Eastern Desert of Egypt, 1993," *Dumbarton Oaks Papers* 48 (1994), 267–68 and figs. 3, 13, 14 (between pp. 264–65).

17 Sidebotham, "University of Delaware," 266 and fig. 12 (between 264–65).

18 D. Meredith, "The Roman Remains in the Eastern Desert of Egypt," *JEA* 38 (1952), 96.

Site	Dimensions (approximate)	Area
Abu Shuwehat	155 m N-S x 115 m E-W	17,825 m^2
Badia[19]	65 m N-S x 46.0 E-W	2,990 m^2
Qattar[20]	66 m N-S x 46 m E-W	3,036 m^2
Deir al-Atrash[21]	57 m N-S x 37 m E-W	2,109 m^2
Bab al-Mukhenig[22]	21.5 m N-S x 34.5 m E-W	741.75 m^2
al-Saqqia[23]	55 m N-S x 42 m E-W	2,310 m^2
al-Heita[24]	43 m N-S x 61 m E-W	2,623 m^2
al-ʿAras[25]	Destroyed	---------
Mons Claudianus[26]	44.50 m N-S x 56 m E-W	2,492 m^2
(Wadi) Abu Greiya[27]	26/32 m N-S x 93/96 m E-W	2,418/3,072 m^2
Abu Zawal[28]	too damaged to measure	---------
Umm Sidri[29]	too damaged to measure	---------
Others	See text below for other examples on the Marsa Nakari-Edfu and Berenike-Nile roads	

Fig. 16. Sites with animal tethering lines in the central part of the Eastern Desert.[30]

There are animal tethering lines elsewhere in the Eastern Desert. Some of those recorded by the Delaware surveys farther south (e.g., at Rod Umm al-Farraj,[31] Rod al-Baram,[32] Bezah West[33]) were much smaller than those noted above and lacked enclosure walls. Two other sites are noteworthy. One at the juncture of Wadis Nuqrus/

---

[19] Sidebotham et al., "Survey of the ʿAbu Sha'ar," 579; V. Maxfield and Peacock, "Infrastructure," in V. Maxfield and D. Peacock (eds.), *The Roman Imperial Quarries Survey and Excavations at Mons Porphyrites 1994–1998.* Volume 1: *Topography and Quarries*, Sixty-Seventh Excavation Memoir (London, 2001), 225–29: record somewhat smaller dimensions of ca. 61.5 m N-S x 35 m E-W.

[20] Sidebotham et al., "Survey of the ʿAbu Sha'ar," 583.

[21] Sidebotham et al., "Survey of the ʿAbu Sha'ar," 587.

[22] Estimated from Google Earth imagery using the path feature.

[23] Sidebotham et al., "Survey of the ʿAbu Sha'ar," 590.

[24] Sidebotham et al., "Survey of the ʿAbu Sha'ar," 594.

[25] Sidebotham et al., "Survey of the ʿAbu Sha'ar," 595 and for earlier citations.

[26] Maxfield, "The Central Complex," 86.

[27] Estimated from Google Earth imagery using the path feature.

[28] Meredith and Tregenza, "Notes on Roman roads," 115–24; D. Meredith, "The Roman Remains in the Eastern Desert of Egypt (continued)," *JEA* 39 (1953), 95; Klemm and Klemm, *Gold Mining*, 70–78 also provide an alternate name for the site (Fatira) and indicate remains of the animal tethering lines north and northwest of the *praesidium.*

[29] For animal tethering lines at Umm Sidri, see Maxfield and Peacock "Infrastructure," 206–07.

[30] See V. Maxfield, "The Central Complex: A Description of the Visible Remains," in D. P. S. Peacock and V. A. Maxfield (eds.), *Survey and Excavations Mons Claudianus 1987-1993,* vol. I, *Topography & Quarries*, FIFAO 37 (Cairo, 1997), 91 (Fig. 2.55) for some of these sites.

[31] Ptolemaic-early Roman road station and animal tethering lines at Rod Umm al-Farraj (walled cistern at 25° 04.96' N/34°19.59' E) on the Marsa Nakari-Nile road, for which see S. Sidebotham, "The Survey of the Hinterland," in S. Sidebotham and W. Wendrich (eds.), *Berenike 1997. Report of the 1997 Excavations at Berenike and the Survey of the Egyptian Eastern Desert, including Excavations at Shenshef*, CNWS 4 (Leiden, 1999), 367 (364–68 for the road in general); animal lines were drawn in plan in summer 2000, but remain unpublished.

[32] Sidebotham, "Survey of the Hinterland," 366 (fig. 19-11), 367–68 (table 19-12); S. Sidebotham, H. Wright, J. Gates-Foster et al., "Gazetteer of Sites," in S. Sidebotham and J. Gates-Foster (eds.), *The Archaeological Survey of the Desert Roads between Berenike and the Nile Valley: Expeditions by the University of Michigan and the University of Delaware to the Eastern Desert of Egypt, 1988–2015*, American Schools of Oriental Research-Archaeological Reports 26 (Boston, 2019), 238–40 (fourth to second centuries BC and late first century BC). This site (GPS 25° 05.12' N/34° 08.20' E) served traffic on both the Marsa Nakari-Edfu and Berenike-Coptos roads.

[33] On the Marsa Nakari-Nile road at GPS 25° 04.97' N/34° 00.46' E; see Sidebotham, "Survey of the Hinterland," of unknown date: 366 (fig. 19-11), 367–68 (table 19-12). Future detailed publication is planned.

Sikait and Wadi Gimal had an enclosure wall, but lacked the actual lines inside, contrary to those noted farther north in the Eastern Desert.[34] There was another nearby at Wadi Gimal East[35] that resembled those at the juncture of Wadis Nuqrus/Sikait and Wadi Gimal, *viz.* there was an enclosure wall and water troughs, but no evident tethering lines inside the enclosure walls.

The substantial size and overall appearance of the Abu Shuwehat animal tethering lines and watering facilities compared to those found elsewhere in Eastern Desert are noteworthy. Figure 16 indicates that the facilities at Abu Shuwehat were almost six times larger than the next largest complexes at Wadi Abu Greiya and at Qattar. In addition to the massive size difference, the Abu Shuwehat facility also lacked an enclosure wall, which other animal tethering lines in the central Eastern Desert had, where they are well enough preserved to make that determination. The surface pottery collected and examined from Abu Shuwehat dated from the first to second centuries AD.[36]

There are several possible reasons for the unusual size and appearance of the Abu Shuwehat facilities. It may be that some animals passing in both directions (from Qena to Mons Claudianus and from Mons Claudianus to Qena) at the same time were held here until facilities at Mons Claudianus had sufficient room to handle inbound traffic. It might be, during peak periods of activity at Mons Porphyrites and Mons Claudianus in the first and second centuries, that Abu Shuwehat occasionally handled traffic between both sites and Qena, which would explain, at least in part, its massive size. The presence of the watering troughs (fig. 12.5) between two sets of lines (fig. 12.7 to the south and fig. 12.8 to the north) might indicate an administrative attempt to control traffic; one set of lines might have handled traffic to Mons Claudianus and the other set from Mons Claudianus.

The extant animal tethering lines at Mons Claudianus date no earlier than the reign of Antoninus Pius (AD 138–161)[37] and are likely later and not contemporary with the ones at Abu Shuwehat. Perhaps the earlier ones at Mons Claudianus, mentioned in several ostraca excavated at the site,[38] were larger.

Those animal tethering facilities with enclosure walls also had only single and relatively narrow entrances. This suggests that officials responsible for them limited access for administrative purposes to monitor and, perhaps, record what numbers and what kinds of animals were fed and watered. The lack of such an enclosure wall at Abu Shuwehat may indicate less emphasis on bureaucratic procedures and more concern with feeding and watering animals as quickly and efficiently as possible.

Abu Greiya

Abu Greiya is about 47 km southwest of the installation at (Wadi) Abu Shuwehat and ca. 41 km east of Qena via the modern asphalt highway. J. Wilkinson visited Abu Greiya in the early nineteenth century and drew a sketch plan of the installations. The Delaware survey visited in May 1992, June 1993, and in June 1999, and drew plans of the two *praesidia* and animal tethering lines.[39] It would be useful to compare the two sets of plans separated in time by approximately 170 years.

The eastern fort at Abu Greiya was rectilinear in plan with overall measurements of ca. 38–39 m N-S x 38–39 m E-W. Contrary to Wilkinson (fig. 17), the southern wall was not parallel with its northern counterpart (fig. 18), but headed slightly north of parallel to the northern wall so that the interior eastern end of the fort was narrower

34 Sidebotham, Wright, Gates-Foster et al., "Gazetteer," 111, likely Roman at 24° 34.49' N/34° 49.47' E.

35 Sidebotham, Wright, Gates-Foster et al., "Gazetteer," 112–15, 117: first to first half fourth century AD at least.

36 J. Riley examined surface pottery from Abu Shuwehat during field seasons in 1990, 1992, and 1993. His field notes offer only a brief statement of general dates for the collected sherds and no catalogue or drawings.

37 Cuvigny, *Rome in Egypt's Eastern Desert*, 186 (water for the guard of the stables), 188.

38 Cuvigny, *Rome in Egypt's Eastern Desert*, 186, 188 (Inv. 1538 + 2921) dated ca. 110 AD (= H. Cuvigny, "L'organigramme du personnel d'une carrière impériale d'après un ostracon du Mons Claudianus," *Chiron* 35 (2005), 309–53). H. Cuvigny reports (personal communication) that inv. 4155 is a small unpublished fragment that belongs to the same series as inv.1538 + 2921. A third unpublished Trajanic-era ostracon mentions a guardian of the stables (inv. 3069). The animal lines, in their present state, are built on *sebakh* containing ostraca dating to Antoninus Pius.

39 Meredith, "The Roman Remains, 1952," 102–03 (fig. 4) for Wilkinson's plan (now Ms. Wilkinson dep. D. 48), a brief description of the site (which he spells Ḳrēyah) and a list of earlier visitors.

than the western portion. The perimeter walls were about 2.0 m thick, but very damaged, making precise measurements impossible. Perimeter walls comprised stacked cobbles and boulders. Wilkinson drew no towers at this fort's corners, but identified two rounded ones at the fort's single entrance about midway along the western perimeter wall (fig. 17 compare with fig. 18.9). The interior preserved a modern circular well (fig. 18.1), constructed after Wilkinson's drawing of its ancient predecessor. Northwest of this well was an unfired mudbrick tower roughly square in plan with an entrance about 1 m wide on its southern side (fig. 18.2). Abutting the interior faces of the northeastern corner of the fort were barrel vaulted rooms measuring approximately 4 m x 8 m (fig. 18.3a), smaller versions of which were present along the interior face of the fort's eastern perimeter wall (fig. 18.3b). All were made of unfired mudbrick. Towards the southeastern corner of the fort interior was a 3 m x 3 m cistern with a pipeline running for about 6 m towards the northwest (fig. 18.4). On Wilkinson's plan, this pipeline terminated in a basin south of the well (fig. 18.1). Immediately east of the cistern (fig. 18.4) was a staircase abutting the southeastern corner of the fort interior (fig. 18.5) that led to the only putative tower noted by the Delaware survey; possibly square in plan and measuring 2.5 m x 2.5 m (fig. 18.6). Wilkinson indicated no external towers except, as noted above, flanking the single entrance (fig. 18.9) on the western perimeter wall. The Delaware survey estimated this portal to be ca. 2 m wide. There were two other rooms, one west of the cistern (fig. 18.7) measured about 3.0 m x 5.5 m with an entrance on its western wall. There was destruction from a bulldozer or front-end loader (fig. 18.14a) immediately west of this room and that separated it from another room (fig. 18.8), whose eastern end had been obliterated by some earth-moving machine. Wilkinson's plan indicated that this room had a narrow entrance about midway along its eastern wall (fig. 17). This latter room (fig. 18.8) abutted the southwestern corner of the fort interior.

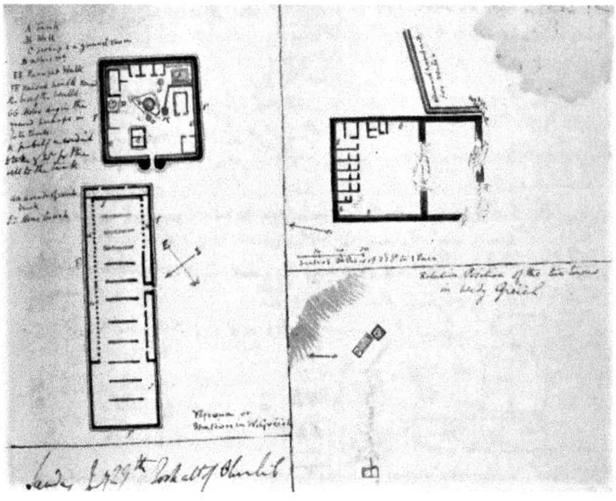

Fig. 17. Abu Greiya, plan by J.G. Wilkinson (Ms. Wilkinson dep. D. 48, courtesy of Bodleian Library, Oxford).

It is difficult to determine if the unfired mudbrick was contemporary with the stone architecture or formed a later addition. While unusual throughout much of the Eastern Desert, the use of unfired mudbrick to supplement stone architecture has been documented in other Roman-era fortifications in the central part of the desert. Examples include the fort at Abu Sha'ar, noted above.[40] Towers and internal wall sections of the installation at Deir al-Atrash, on the road linking Abu Sha'ar and Mons Porphyrites to the Nile, comprised large quantities of unfired mudbrick.[41] Both the upper and lower forts at al-Heita,[42] on the Abu Sha'ar/Mons Porphyrites-Nile road, also made extensive use of unfired mudbrick for walls and vaulted structures.

Approximately 8–9 m west and northwest of the eastern-most fort at Abu Greiya were extensive animal lines with overall measurements of ca. 26/32 m N-S x 93/96 m E-W.[43] The interior of the enclosure was wider towards the west and narrower towards the east (fig. 18), though Wilkinson did not note this (fig. 17). The enclosure walls were about 1.0 m thick. There was an entrance about midway along the southern wall that measured approximately 2.5 m wide (fig. 18.13). There was damage from a bulldozer or front-end loader (fig. 18.14b) towards the eastern end of the southern perimeter wall. Within the enclosure were eight or, possibly, nine low parallel

40 Especially S. Sidebotham, "University of Delaware Fieldwork," 268–69.

41 Sidebotham, Zitterkopf, and Riley, "Survey of the 'Abu Sha'ar," 584–87; Faucher, Redon, Bülow-Jacobsen et al., "Desert Oriental (2020)"; J. Marchand, J. Le Bomin, and A. Bülow-Jacobsen, "Signed by Valerius: An Early Imperial Wall Painting from the Fort of Deir el-Atrash in the Egyptian Eastern Desert," *Journal of Roman Archaeology* 35.2 (2022), 1–30, DOI: https://doi.org/10.1017/S1047759422000307.

42 Sidebotham, Zitterkopf, and Riley, "Survey of the 'Abu Sha'ar," 590–94.

43 Maxfield, "The Central Complex," 91 (fig. 2.55) = Maxfield and Peacock, "Infrastructure," 208 (fig. 5.26 bottom right for sketch of these animal tethering lines); in general: Sidebotham, Hense, and Nouwens, *The Red Land,* 88–89, 319; Sidebotham, *Berenike and the Ancient,* 118–22.

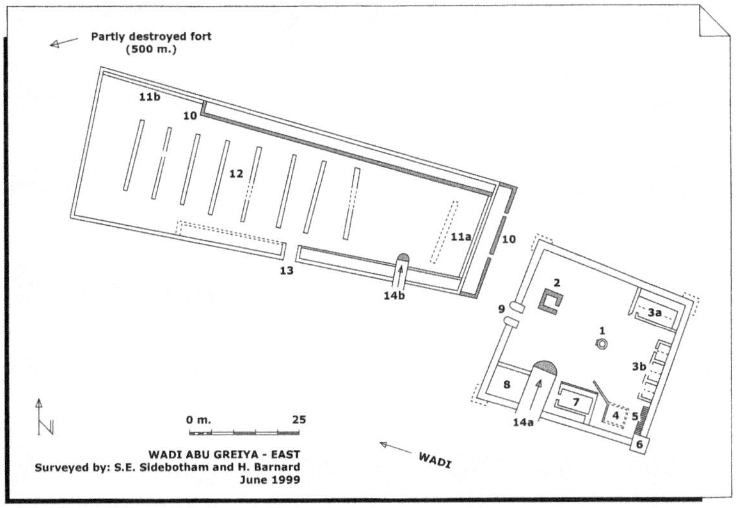

Fig. 18. Abu Greiya, animal tethering lines and eastern-most praesidium. Drawing by H. Barnard.

Fig. 19. Abu Greiya, animal tethering lines and eastern-most praesidium looking south. Scale = pickup truck (circled). Photo by S. Sidebotham.

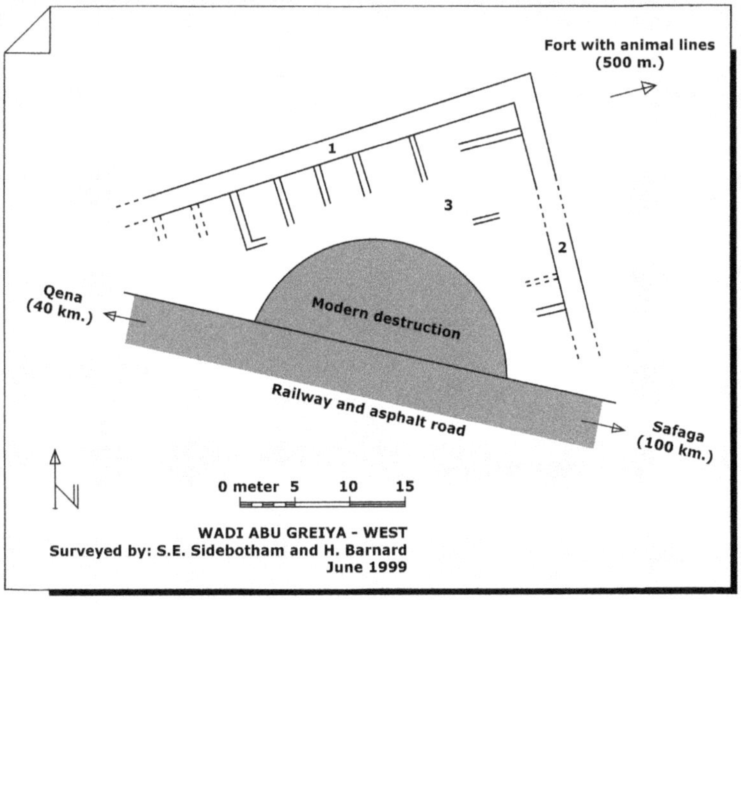

Fig. 20. Abu Greiya, western-most praesidium. Drawing by H. Barnard.

walls oriented roughly N-S (fig. 18.12) where animals could be tethered and from or near which they were then fed and watered. Wilkinson's plan indicated eight tethering lines with three additional lines in ruinous condition east of those visible to him. These varied in length from about 15 to 18 m. There were unfired mudbrick additions to the eastern exterior side of the animal tethering lines (fig. 18.10), which preserved two narrow entrances that did not lead to the animal lines themselves; there were also unfired mudbrick additions along the interior of the northern wall (fig. 18.10). There was shelving on the interior face of the eastern wall (fig. 18.11a) and along the interior of the northern wall towards its western end (fig. 18.11b).

The animal tethering lines at Abu Greiya were similar in appearance to those at Mons Claudianus,[44] Abu Zawal[45] and, leading to/from Mons Porphyrites, those at Umm Sidri,[46] Badia',[47] Qattar, where the tethering lines are now washed away,[48] Deir al-Atrash,[49] Bab al-Mukhenig,[50] al-Saqqia,[51] al-Heita,[52] and perhaps at al-'Aras[53] (fig. 16). Ostraca from Mons Claudianus also mention stables/animal tethering lines,[54] though it is uncertain if those are the ones currently extant, or an earlier set that is no longer visible (see above). The proximity of the animal tethering lines to the eastern-most fort at Abu Greiya, especially to that installation's western gate, is similar to that at Mons Claudianus though the animal lines at that large quarry site are somewhat southwest of the fort and its entrance.[55] This similarity between the two sites suggests that the initial installations at both Mons Claudianus and Abu Greiya may have been planned and built at the same time with the animal tethering lines at both locations probably constructed after their associated forts.

West of the animal tethering lines at Abu Greiya was another fort, now partly destroyed by construction of the asphalt road and a railway (fig. 20). Wilkinson's plan (fig. 17) indicated the layout of this installation. Its center lay approximately 440 m west of the southwestern-most corner of the animal tethering lines. Possibly as much as half or more of the southern end was missing in 1999. Surviving at the time of the 1999 survey were very ruinous eastern portions of the northern perimeter wall (fig. 20.1) (ca. 37.5-40.5 m long E-W x ca. 2 m wide) and the northern end of the eastern perimeter wall (fig. 20.2) (ca. 8–10.2 m. long N-S x ca. 2 m wide). Abutting the internal faces of the perimeter wall were rooms of varying dimensions (fig. 20.3).

Wilkinson's plan of this more westerly fort (fig. 17) indicated that the southern portion, which is now lost, once consisted of a large open area separated from the northern section by an east-west partition wall. Yet, even in Wilkinson's day that partition wall had been partially destroyed in the central area as had central portions of the southern perimeter wall and a section at the fort's southwestern corner. Wilkinson's plan also depicted a water conduit adjacent to and east of this western *praesidium*, but there is no indication from his plan that this pipeline entered the fort. There was no evidence for this hydraulic feature during the June 1999 survey. Sherds from both *praesidia* and animal tethering lines dated from the first to second centuries AD.[56]

These installations at Abu Greiya serviced traffic between Mons Claudianus and Qena and also provided an intermediate stop between the Nile and other desert settlements involved in mining and quarrying that lay to

---

44 Maxfield, "The Central Complex," 86–93.

45 Abu Zawal animal lines, west of *praesidium* and now mostly washed away; Tregenza, *The Red Sea Mountains*, 39–47 ("Abu Zawel:" not very informative); Sidebotham, Hense, and Nouwens, *The Red Land*, 321 briefly note it; Klemm and Klemm, *Gold Mining*, 70–78 date gold mining activities here to the New Kingdom, Ptolemaic, and Roman periods.

46 Sidebotham, Zitterkopf, and Riley, "Survey of the 'Abu Sha'ar," 575 only briefly; Maxfield and Peacock, "Infrastructure," 202–09.

47 Sidebotham, Zitterkopf and Riley, "Survey of the 'Abu Sha'ar," 578–80; Maxfield and Peacock, "Infrastructure," 225–29; Cuvigny, *Rome in Egypt's Eastern Desert*, 59.

48 Sidebotham, Zitterkopf, and Riley, "Survey of the 'Abu Sha'ar," 582–83; animal tethering lines survived west of the *praesidium* at the time of the survey in January 1989; Cuvigny, *Rome in Egypt's Eastern Desert*, 59.

49 Sidebotham, Zitterkopf, and Riley, "Survey of the 'Abu Sha'ar," 584–87; Sidebotham, Hense, and Nouwens, *The Red Land*, pls. 4.15-4.16; Faucher, Redon, Bülow-Jacobsen, Crépy et al., "Désert Oriental (2020)."

50 Sidebotham, Zitterkopf, and Riley, "Survey of the 'Abu Sha'ar," 587; Sidebotham, Hense, and Nouwens, *The Red Land*, pl. 13.6.

51 Sidebotham, Zitterkopf, and Riley, "Survey of the 'Abu Sha'ar," 588–91; Sidebotham, Hense, and Nouwens, *The Red Land*, pl. 13.5.

52 Sidebotham, Zitterkopf, and Riley, "Survey of the 'Abu Sha'ar," 590–94; Sidebotham, Hense, and Nouwens, *The Red Land*, pl. 4.17.

53 Sidebotham, Zitterkopf, and Riley, "Survey of the 'Abu Sha'ar," 595. Since the January 1989 survey this site has disappeared.

54 See note 38.

55 Maxfield, "The Central Complex," 21 (fig. 2.3).

56 J. Riley examined surface pottery from Abu Greiya during field seasons in 1992 and 1993. His field notes offer only a brief statement of general dates for the collected sherds but no catalogue or drawings.

the east, in an area south of Mons Claudianus. The latter probably included the quarries at Umm Wikala[57] and Wadi Maghrabiya[58] as well as others.

In general, the large-scale movement of draft and pack animals between major quarries in the Eastern Desert—and perhaps some mining sites—on the one hand and the Nile on the other, and the need to accommodate them during their journeys across the desert with installations specifically designed for their maintenance, seem to be a Roman innovation developed in the late first century BC and which blossomed in the first century AD and thereafter.[59] There is no conclusive evidence for such accommodations before this time or in the Islamic period.

Traffic between Mons Claudianus and the Nile might have occasionally stopped at Fatireh al-Beida and certainly at (Wadi) Abu Shuwehat, as noted above,[60] and then reached Abu Greiya before descending to Qena. Traffic between the Nile and Mons Claudianus might also have used several of the same stops with animal tethering lines from al-Saqqia westward and southward (al-Heita, al-'Aras) that accommodated traffic between Mons Porphyrites and the Nile.

Gidami

The survey first visited Gidami, in a wadi of the same name, in July 1993 and returned to draw a plan of the *praesidium* there in August 1997.[61] The *praesidium* at Gidami was quadrilateral, nearly rectangular, in shape. The remains of the fort consisted solely of perimeter walls with the eastern wall generally missing although all four corners of the fort could be identified. The interior lengths of the northern (fig. 21.1) and southern walls (fig. 21.3) were 37.2 m and 35.4 m respectively. The interior lengths of the eastern (fig. 21.2) and western walls (fig. 21.4) were 22.7 and 22.5 m respectively. The interior area of the fort was approximately 802 m^2.

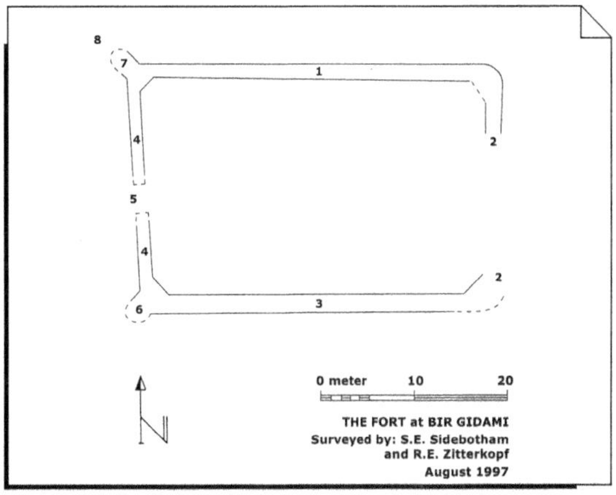

Fig. 21. Praesidium at Gidami. Drawing by R. Zitterkopf, digitized by H. Barnard.

The southwestern (fig. 21.6) and northwestern corner towers (fig. 21.7) were constructed contemporaneously with the perimeter walls as there were no construction joints visible. Instead, the exterior walls smoothly transitioned into the towers at a ca. 0.3 m radius and the two interior corners were skillfully shaped with an angular fill. Including this fill, the northwestern tower was ca. 3.5 m deep x 2.2 m wide. The southwestern tower was 2.4 m wide, but had collapsed and was missing stones from the exterior curve.

57 S. Sidebotham, H. Barnard, J. Harrell, and R. Tomber, "The Roman Quarry and Installations in Wadi Umm Wikala and Wadi Semna," *JEA* 87 (2001), 135–70; R. Klemm and D. Klemm, *Stones and Quarries in Ancient Egypt* (London, 2008), 291–94 (with some confusion between Wadi Semna and Wadi Umm Wikala).

58 S. Sidebotham, "Newly Discovered Sites in the Eastern Desert," *JEA* 82 (1996), 189–90; J. Harrell, V. Brown, and L. Lazzarini, "Two Newly Discovered Roman Quarries in the Eastern Desert of Egypt," in M. Schverer (ed.), *Actes de la IVe Conférence international ASMOSIA IV. France, Bordeaux-Talence, 9–13 octobre 1995. Université de Bordeaux 3/CNRS. Archéomateriaux Marbres et autres roches* (Bordeaux, 1999), 285–89; Klemm and Klemm, *Stones and Quarries*, 294.

59 See discussion of animal lines as a special feature of these installations, unique among Roman quarries, in A. Hirt, *Imperial Mines and Quarries in the Roman World. Organizational Aspects 27 BC – AD 235* (Oxford, 2010), 22, 24, 32.

60 Sidebotham, Hense, and Nouwens, *The Red Land*, 319–20 for brief description, photo and drawing. Klemm and Klemm, *Gold Mining*, 78–79 call it "Abu Shehat" and believe it (erroneously) to have been a "Ptolemaic processing plant."

61 For Gidami, see de la Roque, "Voyage," 136–37; G. Murray, "The Roman Roads and Stations in the Eastern Desert of Egypt," *JEA* 11 (1925), 146; Meredith, "The Roman Remains, 1952," 106; Meredith, "The Roman Remains, 1953," 95 (references to gold mines); Sidebotham "Map sheet 78," vol. 1; Sidebotham, "Map sheet 78," vol. 2, 1160.

Fig. 22. Praesidium at Gidami looking north. Photo by S. Sidebotham.

Fig. 23. Praesidium at Gidami looking west. Scale = Bedouin (circled). Photo by S. Sidebotham.

Fig. 24. Praesidium at Gidami, view of north wall and northwestern tower. Photo by S. Sidebotham.

Fig. 25. Praesidium at Gidami, view of northwestern tower and wall. Photo by S. Sidebotham.

The extant walls were substantial and relatively well preserved. They were constructed of two outer faces of large cobbles or boulders laid in horizontal lifts. The stones were usually roughly rectangular in shape; none appeared to be water-worn. Crumbled stone filled the interval between these facing stones, a common construction technique in the Eastern Desert.[62] The wall on the southern side was 2.5 m high and on the western side, 2.4 m high. The height of the northern wall near the northwest corner was 2.5 m x 1.3 m wide at the top. As the eastern wall was mostly missing, with only remnants at the corners extant, the survey took no measurements of wall heights there. The perimeter walls were generally ca. 1.5 to 1.7 m thick at the base and tapered to 1.3-1.5 m at the top. The front gate (fig. 21.5) was midway along the western wall; this was the obvious choice for an entrance as it faced upstream and the two corner towers flanked it. Due to wall collapse, the width of this opening was unclear, but was estimated as 2.7 m. There was no indication of parapets as the walls were relatively flat on top (fig. 23). There was a grayish water-consolidated material, probably lime mortar, used as binder in the middle of the wall on the western side of the *praesidium*. This binder was likely used in all the perimeter walls of the fort, but has since disappeared due to erosion.

The survey observed a scant amount of crumbled mortar, which may have come from a water basin. Some of the surface debris, appearing to be a gravel conglomerate, likely represented subsurface material suggesting that a well may have been dug here, although the survey observed no obvious surface evidence for one. Moreover, it is unknown whether this putative water supply was contemporaneous with the original construction. This facility at Gidami exhibited a better construction technique compared to most of the forts in the Eastern Desert observed by the University of Delaware surveys. However, the lack of any surface evidence of interior walls, the fact that some of the perimeter walls did not have their interior fill, and perhaps the missing eastern wall, suggested that this

[62] R. Zitterkopf, "Roman Construction Techniques in the Eastern Desert," in O. Kaper (ed.), *Life on the Fringe: Living in the Southern Egyptian Deserts during the Roman and early-Byzantine Periods, Proceedings of a Colloquium Held on the Occasion of the 25th Anniversary of the Netherlands Institute for Archaeology and Arabic Studies in Cairo, 9-12 December 1996* (Leiden, 1998), 279–80; S. Sidebotham, H. Barnard, and G. Pyke, "Five Enigmatic Late Roman Settlements in the Eastern Desert," *JEA* 88 (2002), 189; Sidebotham and Gates-Foster, *The Archaeological Survey of the Desert Roads*, 114–15.

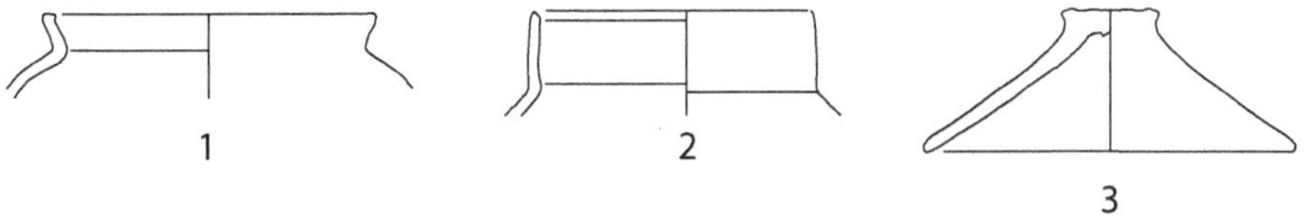

Fig. 26. Pottery from Gidami. Scale = 1:4. Drawings by J. Gates-Foster.

fort may not have been completed for its intended use. The atypically small number of sherds documented from this site date to the late first–second century AD, which suggests a relatively short period of use.[63]

Traffic from the *praesidium* headed east along Wadi Gidami for approximately 10.8 km where, in the later Roman period, travelers passed by the sizeable "enigmatic" community near Bir Gidami.[64] Thence, one followed the wadi towards the southeast for about 7.3 km to the settlement at (Bir) Sirbakis (discussed below), which would have been abandoned by the time of the construction and use of the fort at Gidami and the enigmatic settlement near Bir Gidami.

Pottery

Fig. 26.1. Small, wide-mouth cooking pot with low, everted lid-seat rim and slightly in-turned lip. Alluvial fabric with rare impurities, including limestone. Red-brown surfaces and margins with dull pink core. Parallel: al-Ghuzzah, late first century AD, in Gates-Foster et al., "Early Imperial fortress of Berkou," fig. 17.6.
Fig. 26.2. Wide-mouth, short-necked cooking pot with internal, beveled-edge rim. Alluvial fabric with dark gray core and red-brown margins and surfaces. Some black organic inclusions, although the clay is hard and well fired with smooth surfaces. Parallel: Mons Porphyrites, second century AD, in R. Tomber, "Pottery from the Excavated Deposits," in D. Peacock and V. Maxfield (eds), *The Roman Imperial Quarries: Survey and Excavation at Mons Porphyrites 1994–1998*, vol. 2. *The Excavations* (Cairo, 2007), fig. 6.7.50.
Fig. 26.3. Lid with poorly-made small knob handle. Tan-pink alluvial fabric with occasional limestone impurities. Soft and powdery.

A Rare Surface Find

One other noteworthy find was a Greek ostracon discovered on the surface near the northwestern tower (figs. 21.8 and 24). The sherd was broken at the top, left and perhaps at the bottom, and the ink was very worn and faint. Parts of twenty-five lines were preserved, but not well enough to give a good idea of the precise content. The text, perhaps a letter, was written in the first person and refers in several places to the goddess Aphrodite (lines 4, 12, 19, 23), more specifically to a possible shrine of Aphrodite (lines 11–12). An unusual feature of the text is the three numerals—4 (δ), 2 (β), and 2 (β)—which appear in oversized script in lines 7, 8, and 12, which lack clear referents.[65] After photography the survey buried the ostracon adjacent to the tower.

Abu Gerida

The survey first visited the site at Abu Gerida in July 1993 and returned to study it in more detail and draw plans in August 1997. There was another visit in June 1999.[66] The immediate environs preserved gold and iron mines

63 R. Tomber recorded this material in the field in 1997. Descriptions are based on her field notes and drawings.
64 Sidebotham, Barnard, and Pyke, "Five Enigmatic Late Roman Settlements," 198–201.
65 R. Ast (Heidelberg University) read, translated and commented on the ostracon based on photographs.
66 Sidebotham, Hense, and Nouwens, *The Red Land*, 223 for a brief description and photo (fig. 9.4).

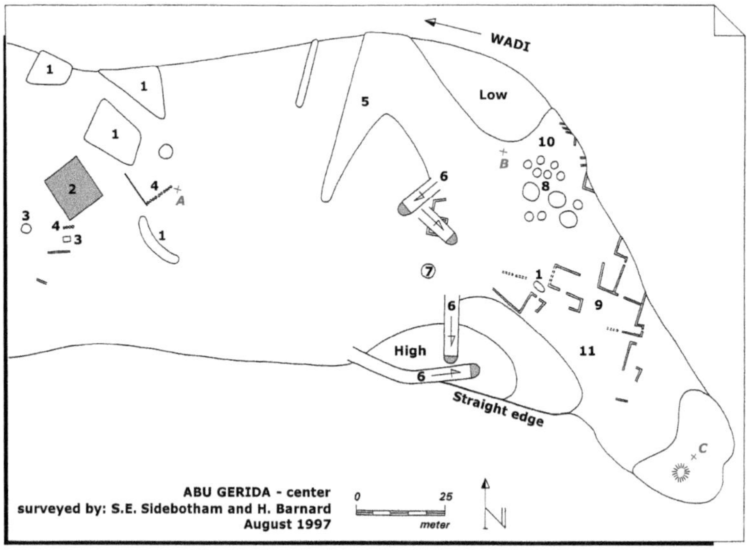

Fig. 27. Abu Gerida, central plan. Drawing by H. Barnard.

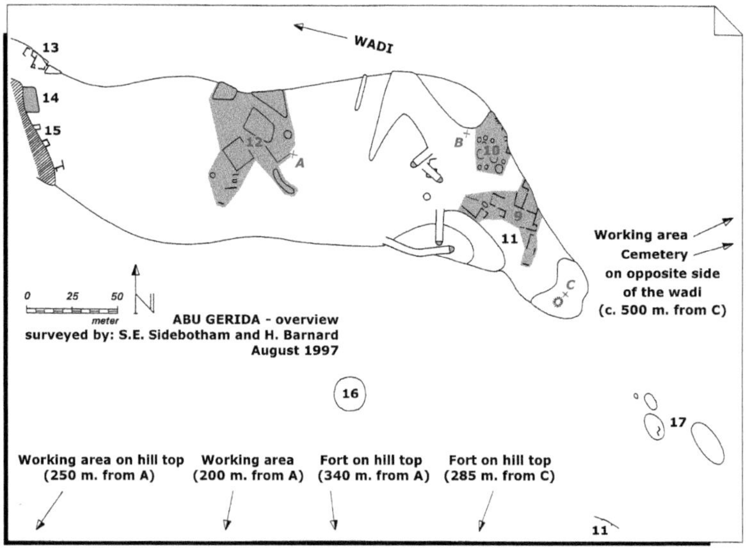

Fig. 28. Abu Gerida, overall plan. Drawing by H. Barnard.

and a rhyolite porphyry quarry.[67] There was also evidence of copper mining and smelting activities in the area.[68] Study of surface sherds (see below) indicated Ptolemaic and Early Roman activity. Not all the mineral wealth available here was, however, exploited throughout both periods of the site's occupation.

The main settlement in the wadi lay approximately 34 km west-southwest of (Bir) Sirbakis (discussed below), though the wadi system between Abu Gerida and Sirbakis would not have been convenient for regular commu-

[67] Meredith, "The Roman Remains, 1952," 106; J. Harrell, "*Porfido Rosso Laterizio* and the Discovery of its Source in Wadi Abu Gerida (Egypt)," *Marmora* 1 (2005), 37–48; Sidebotham, Hense, and Nouwens, *The Red Land*, 223; Klemm and Klemm, *Gold Mining*, 109, 110 (fig. 5.56); 110–15 (for Hamama).

[68] Y. Abd El-Rahman, A. Surour, A. El Manawi et al., "Ancient Mining and Smelting Activities in the Wadi Abu Gerida Area, Central Eastern Desert, Egypt: Preliminary Results," *Archaeometry* 55.6 (2013), 1067–87.

Fig. 29. Abu Gerida, hilltop enclosure looking west. Scales = person on hilltop and pickup truck below and to right (circled). Photo by S. Sidebotham.

Fig. 30. Abu Gerida wadi site looking north. Scale = pickup truck (circled). Photo by S. Sidebotham.

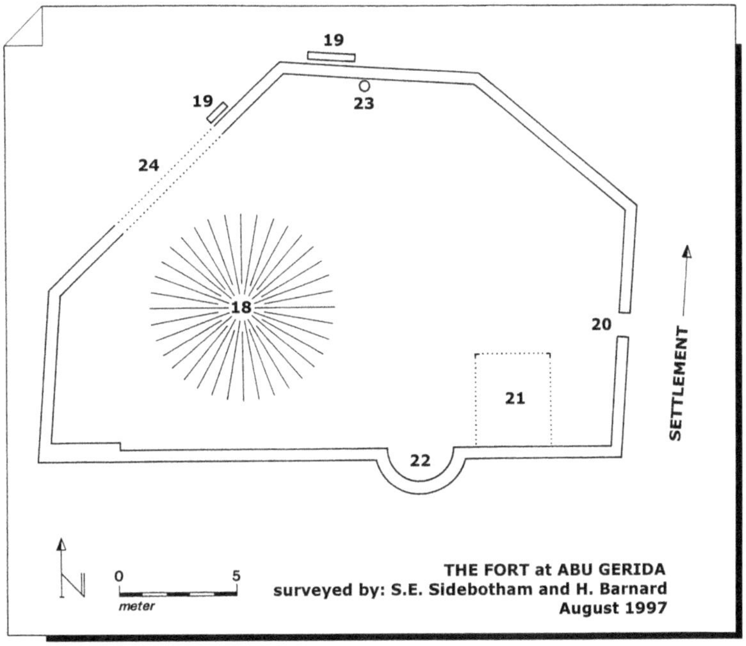

Fig. 31. Abu Gerida, hilltop enclosure. Drawing by H. Barnard.

nications between the two sites. An undetermined portion of the Abu Gerida wadi settlement had been washed away by floods over the centuries and it had also been badly looted, apparently in more recent times. In August 1997 the extant site in the wadi bottom measured ca. 350 m WNW-ESE x ca. 96 m N-S. Many of the walls of this main site comprised recycled ore grinding stones/querns made from locally available rhyolite porphyry from the nearby quarry.

The wadi settlement preserved mounds of debris (fig. 27.1) scattered around and in its center there was a spread of hydraulic plaster (fig. 27.2) indicating that a water tank or cistern originally lay in this area, undoubtedly for both domestic as well as industrial use. There were small, cleared work areas in the central portion of the extant site (fig. 27.3) and grinding stones nearby (fig. 27.4), south and east of the hydraulic plaster. The grinding stones were aligned in two separate groups suggesting that these arrangements had taken place relatively recently. A large area of grinding stone chips at the northern edge of the site suggested that some, likely final, phase of their manufacture took place there (fig. 27.5). These grinding stones for gold ore derived from the quarry ca. 500 m northwest of the wadi settlement. These were deep saddle querns similar to those found at other Ptolemaic-era gold mining sites in the Eastern Desert. There was relatively recent damage by a front-end loader or bulldozer at the southeastern and eastern parts of the main settlement (fig. 27.6). Between the two areas of destruction by modern earth-moving equipment was a small, heavily damaged structure of unknown function (fig. 27.7). There were mounds of iron slag at the northeastern edge of the site (fig. 27.8) and, adjacent to the immediate north, there was a metal working area (figs. 27.10 and 28.10). Stone molds found elsewhere in the area, discussed below, confirmed the repair or manufacture of metal tools.

A possible residential zone (figs. 27.9 and 28.9) lay south-southeast of the metal working area. It likely originally extended farther south and east. A large and relatively modern robber pit lay south of the putative residential area (figs. 27.11 and 28.11) and east of some of the damage inflicted by modern earth-moving equipment. Stone working concentrated west of the residential zone, in the approximate center of the site (fig. 28.12). Towards the northwestern edge of the site there was a large structure with remains of a tower in its southwestern corner and with a midden immediately to the east (fig. 28.13). South of 28.13 were mounds of debris (fig. 28.14) from which the survey recorded part of a statue, likely of a sphinx, discussed below. There were platforms of unknown function that survived immediately south of the mounds of debris (fig. 28.15). South of the extant main site, and separated from it by wadi wash, was another midden (fig. 28.16). East of that midden and southeast of the area marked "C" on the site plans were disturbed working areas (fig. 28.17).

Approximately 250 m southwest of the main settlement atop a hill was a working area. There was another such area and some petroglyphs at the edge of the wadi about 200 m south of the main settlement. About 500 m east-northeast of the settlement was another working area and a small cemetery.

Varying from ca. 285 to 340 m south of the wadi settlement and atop a nearby hill was a roughly hexagonally-shaped enclosure built of poorly erected low walls comprising stacked cobbles and boulders. Overall maximum measurements of this enclosure were 10 m N-S x 24.6 m E-W and it sloped from higher ground in the west to a lower point in the east. Maximum extant wall height was 1.47 m x ca. 0.40-0.75 m wide. The single entrance (fig. 31.20), ca. 1 m wide, lay midway along the eastern perimeter wall. There was a semi-circular-shaped niche or alcove along the southern wall (fig. 31.22), which measured about 3 m wide E-W x 1.2 m N-S deep, extending outward from the southern perimeter wall. There were few internal structures within the enclosure, though there was the rectilinear-shaped outline of a possible room ca. 3.9 m N-S x 3.30 m E-W (fig. 31.21) abutting the interior face of the southern wall towards its eastern end, not far from the single entrance (fig. 31.20) and just east of the niche (fig. 31.22). The interior of this walled hilltop structure preserved some evidence of robbing. There was a cairn ca. 0.50 m in diameter (fig. 31.23) inside this enclosed feature approximately midway along and very close to the enclosure's northern perimeter wall. There was also a knoll in the interior of the enclosure (fig. 31.18) towards the western and northwestern perimeter walls. Outside the northern and northwestern walls were remains of two stone-cut trenches (fig. 31.19). The trench parallel to the northern wall measured about 2.10 m long E-W x 0.20 m wide N-S, while that parallel to the exterior face of the northwestern wall measured about 1.10 m long SW-NE x 0.20 m wide SE-NW. An approximately 6.5 m-long portion of the northwestern circuit wall (fig. 31.24), starting just southwest of the smaller of the extramural cut trenches, was also badly dilapidated and missing in places. The perimeter walls of this large roughly hexagonally-shaped enclosure would have been ineffective for any defensive purposes; what function this feature served, aside from observation, remains unknown.

In addition to gold mining operations in the area, iron and copper mining also took place.[69] The main mining area lay ca. 5.8 km east-southeast of the wadi settlement.[70] Gold was probably no longer mined in the Early Roman period, but the quarry continued to produce stone at that time for use as smaller adornments or as small architectural elements. This stone has been identified in monuments from that period from elsewhere in the Mediterranean world.[71]

---

69 Harrell, "*Porfido Rosso*," 37–48; Abd el-Rahman, Surour, el Manawi et al., "Ancient Mining," 1067–87.

70 Measured by Harrell, "*Porfido Rosso*," 40 (fig. 3).

71 Harrell, "*Porfido Rosso*," 42, 46.

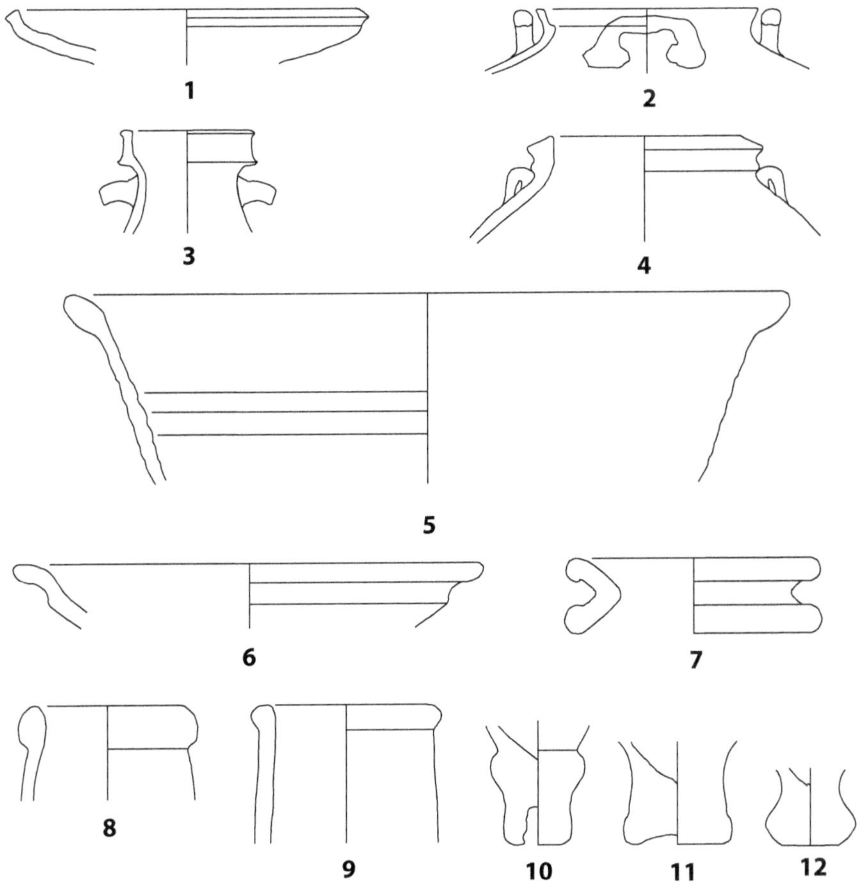

Fig. 32. Pottery from Abu Gerida. Scale = 1:4. Drawings by J. Gates-Foster.

The settlement in Wadi Abu Gerida lay about 30 km east of the two adjacent stations and large animal tethering lines at Abu Greiya, noted above. Abu Gerida's proximity to other mining and quarrying endeavors in the region, such as those at (Bir) Sirbakis (discussed below), Maghrabiya, about 19 km southeast of Abu Gerida, and al-Merkh, also suggested that it may have functioned as an administrative center for other mining and quarrying operations during some phase of its occupation.

Pottery

Study of surface sherds documented primarily from the wadi settlement[72] indicated occupation from the third to second centuries BC with a handful of sherds (not illustrated) dating to the Early Roman era, with, apparently, considerably less activity in the latter period.[73]

Fig. 32.1. Shallow bowl with beveled rim. Pale orange (2.5YR 7/6) with slightly darker (2.5YR 6/6) margins. Some limestone impurities, probably a calcareous fabric. Parallel: Karnak, second half of third-first half of second century BC in N. Licitra and R. David, "L'évolution des céramiques ptolémaïques à Karank d'apres la

[72] Which Abd El-Rahman, Surour, el Manawi et al., "Ancient Mining," 1069, refer to as Hamama.
[73] R. Tomber recorded this material in the field in 1997. Descriptions are based on her field notes and drawings.

documentation du Trésor de Chabaka," in R. David (ed.), *Céramiques ptolémaïques de la Région Thébain*, CCE 10 (2016), fig. 9.50.

Fig. 32.2. Cookpot with lid-seat rim and round, horizontal handle. Sandy alluvial fabric with sparse lime impurities. Orange-brown throughout, with original surfaces possibly wiped. Parallel: Tebtunis, second half of the third-early second century BC, in P. Ballet and A. Południkiewicz, *Tebtynis V. La céramique des époques hellénistique et impériale: Campagnes 1988–1993: Production, consommation et réception dans le Fayoum méridional*, FIFAO 68 (Cairo, 2012), pl. 23.257.

Fig. 32.3. Double-handled flagon or jar with flanged rim. Calcareous fabric discolored to muddy brown color, white surface outside. Handle section not provided. Parallel: al-Ghuzzah Ptolemaic village, second half of third-early second century BC.[74]

Fig. 32.4. Jar with collared rim and at least two handles. Calcareous fabric, overfired and discolored to brown-gray, with faint vestiges of a cream surface inside. Parallel: Karnak, second half of third century-first half of second century BC, in Licitra and David, "L'evolution des céramiques ptolémaïques," fig. 14.77.

Fig. 32.5. Large basin with everted, thickened rim and lightly ribbed walls. Hard and smooth. Fine, dense alluvial fabric with abundant small, well sorted inclusions. Dull gray-green (10YR 6/2) core with orange (2.5YR 6/6) margins and surfaces.

Fig. 32.6. Carinated dish with everted rim, but fairly large and crude. Coarse alluvial or mixed fabric with varied impurities. Dull gray core with pale red margins and slightly darker surfaces.

Fig. 32.7. Short open stand with thickened rims. Dense, vesicular alluvial fabric with some black organic inclusions, particularly on core which is dark to light gray. The break is brown and surfaces red-brown. Parallel: Coptos, early third to mid-second century BC, in S. Herbert and A. Berlin, "The excavation: occupation history and ceramic assemblages," in S. Herbert and A. Berlin (eds.), *Excavations at Coptos (Qift) in Upper Egypt, 1987–1992*, Journal of Roman Archaeology Supplementary Series 53 (Portsmouth, 2003), fig. 53.H2.52.

Fig. 32.8. Egyptian amphora (AE1) with prominent bead rim. Tan-brown (5YR 6/4) calcareous or mixed fabric with abundant limestone inclusions. Surface slightly abraded. See discussion of AE1-2.5 in D. Dixneuf, *Amphores égyptiennes. Production, typologie, contenu et diffusion (IIIe siècle avant J.-C.- IXe siècle après J.-C.), Études alexandrines* 22 (Alexandrie, 2011), 79-87, esp. fig. 56; and J. Gates-Foster, "Third Century BCE Supply Networks and Ptolemaic Transport Amphoras from 'Abbad and Bi'r Samut in Egypt's Eastern Desert," in B. Redon (ed.), *Networked Spaces: The Spatiality of Networks in the Red Sea and the Western Indian Ocean* (Lyon, 2022), 347–63.

Fig. 32.9. Egyptian amphora (AE1) with flatter bead. Handle scar indicates broad, strap-type handle. Pink-tan sandy fabric with no visible limestone, but slight vestiges of cream on the surfaces. Alluvial or mixed fabric.

Fig. 32.10. Banded amphora toe with central internal concavity. Sandy alluvial fabric, brown with a slightly pinker core. Parallel: See discussion of AE1-3.1 in Dixneuf, *Amphores égyptiennes*, 79–87, esp. fig. 57, and discussion of this type in the Eastern Desert in Gates-Foster, "Third Century BCE Supply Networks."

Fig. 32.11. Amphora toe with shallow underside concavity. Pitted and abraded alluvial fabric with sparse limestone impurities. Brown with purple tinge inside, outside red-brown. See discussion of AE1-3.3 in Dixneuf, *Amphores égyptiennes*, 79–87, esp. fig. 59.

Fig. 32.12. Amphora toe with rounded, solid spike. Pitted and abraded alluvial fabric with classic pale gray (or gray-green) (2.5YR 7/0) core and orange (2.5YR 6/6) inside to orange-red (2.5YR 5/4) outside, some limestone.

Other Small Finds

In addition to surface potsherds collected primarily from the wadi settlement, the survey recorded other small finds. These included, from the northwestern part of the site (fig. 28.14). a fragment of a crude representation of a human head, perhaps part of a sphinx, made of sandstone, a rock indigenous to the area (fig. 33).[75] It preserved the right side of the head, an ear, an eye, part of a nose and mouth, hair and a headdress. Its extant dimensions were 0.16 m high x 0.14 m wide x 0.065 m thick. From this same wadi settlement the survey also recorded a slab

[74] Semi-complete and restorable examples of this type were documented in the Ptolemaic village at al-Ghuzzah in abandonment deposits dating to the late third or early second centuries BC. These examples will be published by Gates-Foster as part of the MAFDO reports.

[75] Abd El-Rahman, Surour, el Manawi et al., "Ancient Mining," 1069.

of sandstone 0.24 m long x 0.26 m wide x 0.08 m thick, decorated with a motif that resembled the anchor of a ship. In the adjacent wadis the survey documented two stone molds for metal tool manufacture or repair.[76] The larger and more complete one had a preserved length of 0.15 m x preserved width 0.14 m x 0.09 m thick. The survey did not obtain measurements of the smaller broken stone mold. The survey left all finds on site. On the western side of the site, against a natural rock outcrop, the survey documented another irregularly shaped sandstone block measuring 0.275 m high x 0.24 m wide x 0.10 m thick and decorated with:

Γ •T

K•

Fig. 33. Abu Gerida, fragment of sandstone head (possibly of a sphinx). Scale = 20 cm. Photo by S. Sidebotham.

Bukhalug

The survey first visited Bukhalug[77] in July 1993 and drew a plan of the site in July 1996 and August 1997. Bukhalug lay in a narrow side wadi that stretched roughly west to east with buildings on both the northern and southern sides of the wadi and ascending the adjacent hills (figs. 34, 35). Structures were rectilinear to oval in plan and built of locally available cobbles and boulders. There was no extant evidence of binder in the walls. Walls varied from about 0.6-0.9 m high x 0.4-0.6 m wide. R. Klemm and D. Klemm briefly published the site and several others in the immediate environs, which they dated to the New Kingdom and Arab periods.[78] Bukhalug was about 6.65 km east–north-

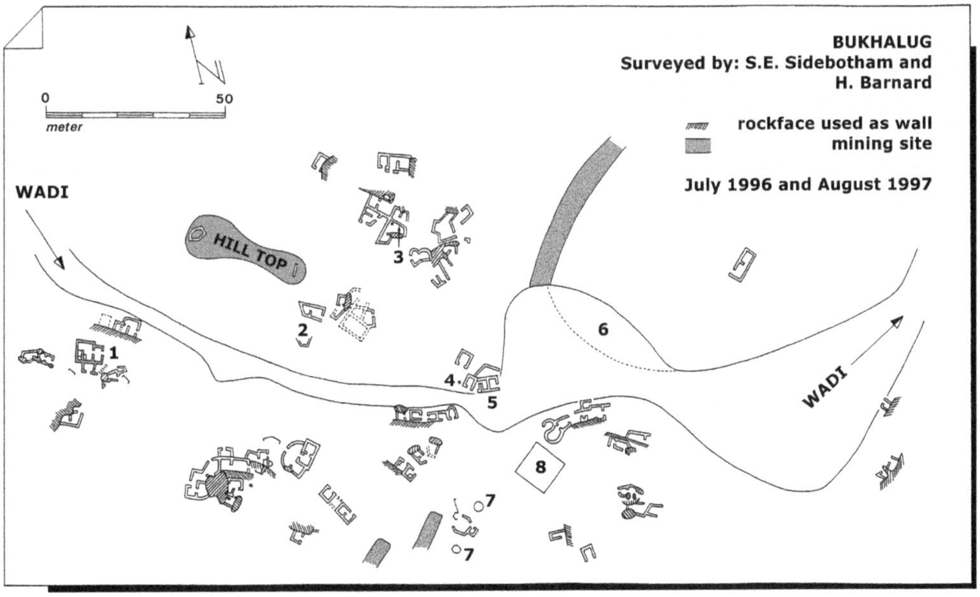

Fig. 34. Bukhalug. Drawing by H. Barnard.

[76] There is evidence for metal tool manufacture/repair elsewhere in the Eastern Desert, for example at Mons Claudianus: see Cuvigny, *Rome in Egypt's Eastern Desert*, 185–88; Hirt, *Imperial Mines and Quarries*, 212, and at Berenike: Sidebotham, *Berenike and the Ancient*, 116–17.

[77] Klemm and Klemm, *Gold Mining*, 100–101 refer to the site as Kab Amiri.

[78] Klemm and Klemm, *Gold Mining*, "Wadi Bahlog" 96–101. Their dates based on ceramics should be used with caution.

Fig. 35. Bukhalug. Photo by S. Sidebotham.

east of Bir Sirbakis via a convenient wadi. Communication between the two sites would have taken, at most, only a few hours on foot.

When the survey visited, Bukhalug comprised approximately 35 structures spread over an area about 120–130 m N-S x 250 m E-W; there were also mining shafts on both sides of the wadi and, although the surveys did not investigate this, likely elsewhere in the area.[79] While many structures were free-standing, a number used natural rock faces for one or more of their walls. Structures were rectilinear, polygonal and ovoid in plan. One building on the southern side of the wadi may have served some administrative function (fig. 34.1). On the northern side of the wadi was a platform (fig. 34.2), likely for working gold ore. A pentagonal-shaped structure atop a hill on the northern side of the wadi just northwest of figure 34.2 was probably a large watchtower. Also, on the northern side of the wadi was a naturally occurring doorway (fig. 34.3) into a polygonal-shaped room that was part of a larger complex. At the edge of the northern side of the wadi (fig. 34.4) the survey documented a faience scarab, described below. This find spot was adjacent to and immediately west of a structure with multiple rooms filled with debris (fig. 34.5) and with an ancient terracotta pipeline leading to it. Its central location on the site together with the pipeline suggested that it served a hydraulic function, likely for the storage and distribution of water to the settlement for domestic and industrial purposes.

On the northern side of the wadi, east of most buildings in the settlement and at the southern entrance of a large mining shaft, was an area covered by quartz chips, undoubtedly the by-product of gold mining operations (fig. 34.6). On the southern side of the wadi were cleared areas (fig. 34.7), perhaps for ore processing. Also, on the southern side of the wadi may be the remains of a dog or jackal cemetery (fig. 34.8) as the survey's Ma'aza Bedouin guide indicated, but that the survey could not independently confirm. The survey was less certain about the identifications of most other structures, but these would have included living accommodations, work and storage areas, and corrals or pens for keeping a few animals, likely goats.

Surface sherds collected throughout the site were almost entirely third-second centuries BC with a small number dating to the later Ptolemaic period (figs. 36.1 and 36.3) In 1993, J. Riley noted, but did not draw or otherwise describe, a small number of sherds which he dated first to second century AD, but later surveys did not find evidence of this phase.[80] Pottery from Bukhalug was quantitatively less than that recorded from (Bir) Sirbakis, but the cataloged sherds and bulk of the surface finds were, for the most part, contemporary with those from that site.

Pottery

Fig. 36.1. Carinated dish with splayed rim. Pale pink-tan calcareous or mixed fabric and surfaces with pale gray core. Occasional large quartz visible, but no limestone. Parallel: Karnak, first century BC, in Licitra and David, "L'evolution des céramiques ptolémaïques," fig. 29.152.

Fig. 36.2. Small jar with slightly everted rim and handle joined to upper surface of the rim. Pink-tan margins, medium gray core and surfaces mottled tan-pink to red-brown. Alluvial or mixed fabric, poorly-sorted with sand and some lime. Parallel: Karnak, second half of third century-first half of second century BC, in Licitra and David, "L'evolution des céramiques ptolémaïques," fig. 20.105.

Fig. 36.3. Jar with everted rim. Likely double-handled. Sandy, slightly green calcareous fabric with cream-pink margins and surfaces. Parallel: Tebtunis, first century BC–first century AD, in Ballet and Południkiewicz *Tebtynis V*, pl. 63.617.

[79] As indicated by Klemm and Klemm, *Gold Mining*, 96–101.

[80] R. Tomber recorded the material presented here in the field in 1996 and 1997. Descriptions are based on her field notes and drawings. She did not observe the Early Roman pottery recorded by Riley during the survey's earlier visit.

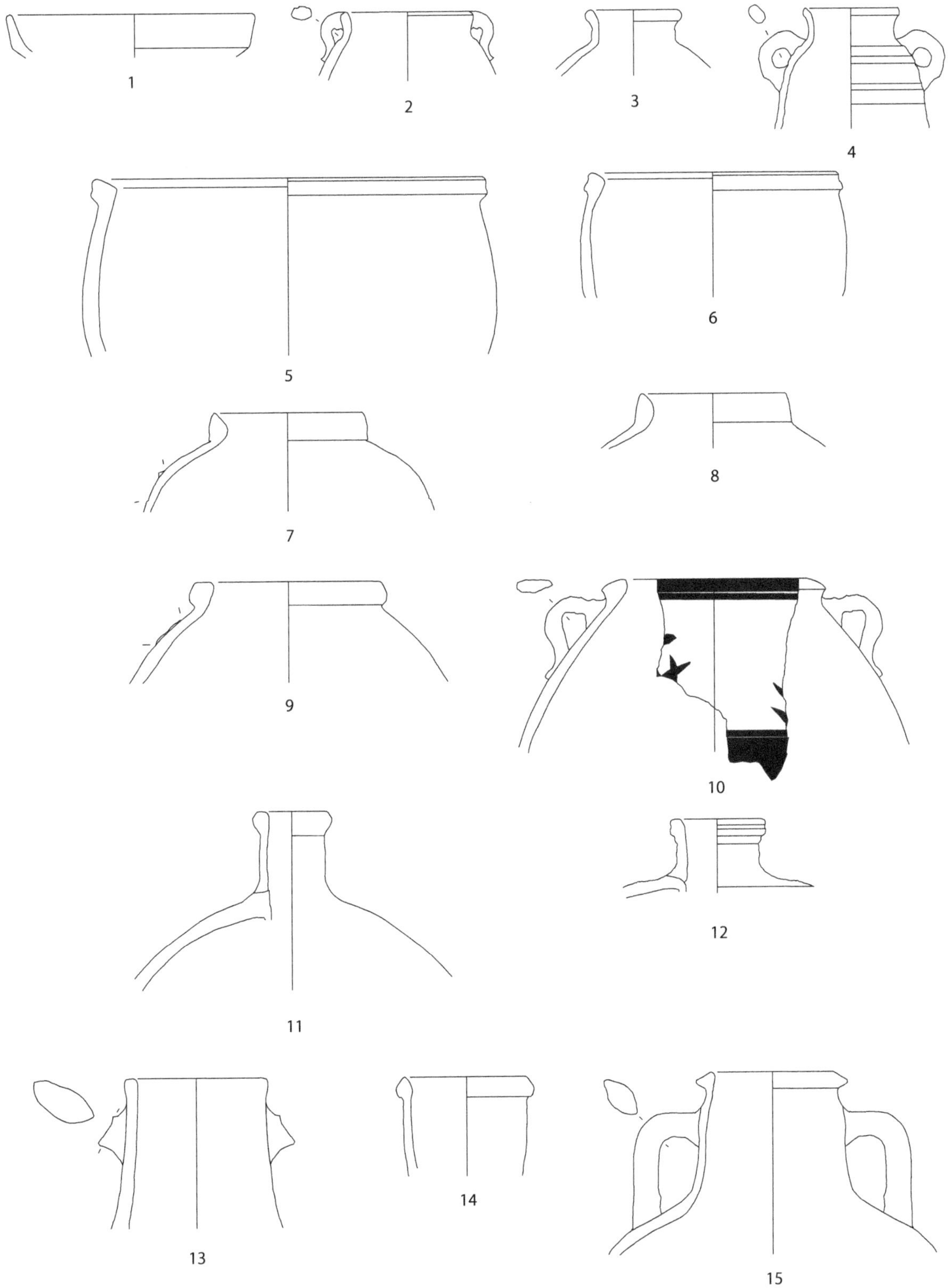

Fig. 36. Pottery from Bukhalug. Scale = 1:4. Drawings by J. Gates-Foster.

Fig. 36.4. Jar with everted rim, double handled (<50%), with ribbed belly, below handle. Dull brown calcareous fabric with cream surface outside.
Fig. 36.5. Large krater or basin with grooved, squared rim. Sandy, coarse poorly mixed calcareous or mixed fabric with common flat shell-like inclusions. Fabric has medium to dark gray core and pale pink margins. Surfaces discolored tan to pink to red-brown. Parallel: Elephantine, third century BC, in D. Aston, *Elephantine XIX: Pottery from the late New Kingdom to the Early Ptolemaic period.* AV 95 (Mainz, 1999), no. 2621.
Fig. 36.6. Large krater or basin with grooved, squared rim. Sandy, coarse poorly mixed calcareous or mixed fabric with common flat shell-like inclusions. Purple-pink core with red-brown margins and duller surfaces.
Fig. 36.7. Hole-mouth jar or amphora with slightly undulating walls. Single handle scar. Pale gray (N5/0) calcareous fabric with red-brown external margin and duller surface. Fine, slightly gritty fabric. Parallel: Imitation of Levantine amphora. Tebtunis, third century BC, in Ballet and Południkiewicz, *Tebtynis V*, pl. 75.681.
Fig. 36.8. Hole-mouth jar or amphora. Likely to be double-handled. Elegant, slightly curved everted rim of varying sizes. Hard-fired silt with gray core and dull brown-orange margins, in a smooth fabric similar. Orange surfaces.
Fig. 36.9. Large, likely double-handled jar or whole-mouth amphora with a more prominent, squared-off rim, and broad girth. Dark gray (N4/0) core with orange-brown (2.5YR 5/6) margins and surfaces, although the surfaces are light in part. Common limestone impurities and organics. Likely to be an alluvial or mixed fabric. Parallel: Tebtunis, third century BC, in Ballet and Południkiewicz, *Tebtynis V*, pl. 69.656.
Fig. 36.10. Double-handled jar. Hard, smooth and fine fabric with some visible alluvial inclusions and salt, with gray break and orange-red margins and surfaces. Black painted decoration. Parallel: Tebtunis, third century BC, in Ballet and Południkiewicz, *Tebtynis V*, pl. 65.631, unpainted.
Fig. 36.11. Keg with tall, narrow neck and bead rim. Overfired brown/purple with external orange-brown margins, red-brown surfaces and internal surface brown-gray.
Fig. 36.12. Keg with relatively wide diameter and double-lip rim. Distinctive orange (2.5YR 7/8) clay and brown-gray (2.5YR 4/2) external surface. Poorly mixed with common ill-sorted to 1.0 mm red argillaceous matter, sometimes angular. Aswan or oasis. Parallel: Elephantine, third century BC, in Aston, *Elephantine XIX*, no. 2754.
Fig. 36.13. Egyptian (AE1 variant) amphora with slightly thickened rim, slightly everted, and very broad, flat strap handle. Fine alluvial fabric with abundant sand. Pink-brown (2.5YR 6/6), with darkened surfaces (2.5YR 5/6).
Fig. 36.14. Egyptian (AE1) bead-rim amphora, fairly ovoid in section. Dull pale pink (2.5YR 6/4) with slightly darker margins and discolored surfaces mottled from pink to orange to red. Likely calcareous fabric. See discussion of AE1-2.5 in Dixneuf, *Amphores égyptiennes*, 79–87, esp. fig. 56, in Gates-Foster, "Third Century BCE Supply Networks," figs. 7–8.
Fig. 36.15. Egyptian amphora (AE1) with triangular rim, imitation of Rhodian or Cnidian import. Pale green calcareous fabric with sparse large quartz, dull pink external margin and brownish to pink surfaces where not concreted. See discussion of AE1-2.1, in Dixneuf, *Amphores égyptiennes*, 79–87, esp. fig. 52.

Another Surface Find

An important find was an intact faience scarab with a cartouche bearing the name *Nefer-ib-re*, "Beautiful is the heart of Re," which was the throne name of the 26th Dynasty pharaoh Psamtik II/Psammetichus II, who reigned 595–589 BC (fig. 37). This scarab measured 140 mm × 82 mm × 49 mm. While the surface sherds studied from Bukhalug did not indicate activi-

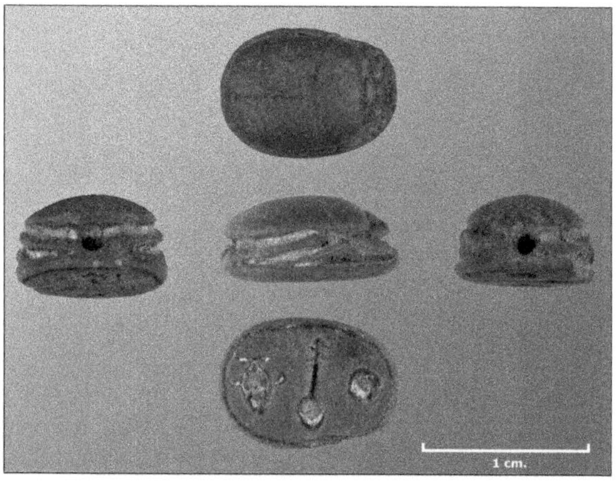

Fig. 37. Bukhalug, scarab with cartouche of Pharaoh Psamtik II/Psammetichus II (reigned 595–589 BC). Photos by H. Barnard.

ties here prior to the Ptolemaic era, the scarab might suggest otherwise. Equally, the scarab might have been an heirloom as the production of scarabs virtually ceased in the Ptolemaic era.[81]

(Bir) Sirbakis

The survey first visited (Bir) Sirbakis in July 1993 and returned in July 1996 and August 1997 to draw a plan of the site and collect additional potsherds for study.[82] Most of the ancient settlement lay at the northern edge of the juncture of three wadis (figs. 38–40), with a decreasing number of structures scattered towards the northwest. The survey identified a watchtower atop a mountain on the eastern side of the site from which excellent views of the settlement and beyond were possible. South of the largest concentration of structures, across the wadi, was a smaller cluster of buildings (figs. 38.6 and 39.6). Structures throughout the site varied in plan from rectilinear to oval with walls comprising stacked cobbles and boulders; there was no evidence of mud or clay binding material. Construction style and dimensions were typical of contemporary remains found elsewhere in the Eastern Desert.

Northwest of the main settlement were working/cleared areas (fig. 38.1). Also on the northern side of the wadi were graves, most of them circular in plan (figs. 38.2 and 38.8). Farther west were small dams across at least three gullies (fig. 39.9). These unusual features may have provided ephemeral, supplementary water supplies when it rained, or they may have been designed to catch water-borne soil to create plots for small gardens, as seen elsewhere in the Eastern Desert.[83] Northwest of the main settlement and east of the dammed gullies were

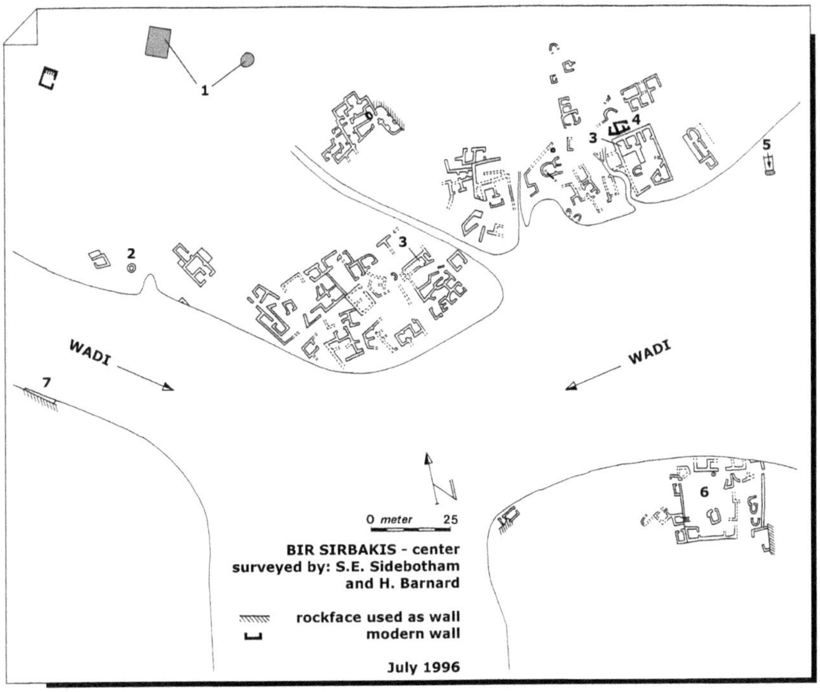

Fig. 38. Bir Sirbakis, central plan. Drawing by H. Barnard.

---

[81] See S. Sidebotham and I. Zych, "Berenike: Archaeological Fieldwork at a Ptolemaic-Roman Port on the Red Sea Coast of Egypt, 2011–2012," *Sahara* 23 (2012), 40. Information from E. Teeter, Oriental Institute, University of Chicago; Klemm and Klemm, *Gold Mining*, 96–101 dated activities here to the New Kingdom and Islamic periods.

[82] Brief preliminary publication in Sidebotham, "Newly Discovered," 182 (fig. 1), 190, pl. XIX.1.

[83] S. Sidebotham and J. Gates-Foster, "Introduction," in Sidebotham and Gates-Foster, *The Archaeological Survey of the Desert Roads*, 14, 16; Sidebotham, *Berenike and the Ancient*, 114–16. For gardens at Berenike in the Ptolemaic period, see M. Woźniak, S. Sidebotham, M. Osypińska et al., "Ptolemaic Berenike: Resources, Logistics, and Daily Life in a Hellenistic Fortress on the Red Sea Coast of Egypt," *AJA* 125.2 (2021), 264. For cultivation at Berenike and Shenshef in the Roman era, see R. Cappers, *Roman Foodprints at Berenike. Archaeobotanical Evidence of Subsis-*

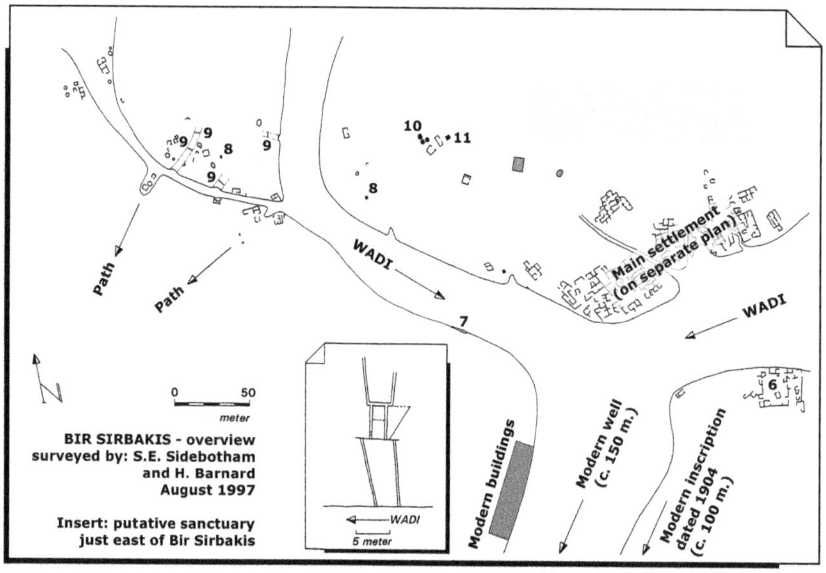

Fig. 39. Bir Sirbakis, overall plan. Drawing by H. Barnard.

Fig. 40. Bir Sirbakis, looking north. Scale = pickup truck (circled). Photo by S. Sidebotham.

Fig. 41. Bir Sirbakis, modern building wall incorporating ancient grinding stones. Photo by S. Sidebotham.

spoil heaps (fig. 39.10) and one or more damaged structures (fig. 39.11). Inside one oblong structure were raised areas (fig. 39.3), perhaps platforms for sleeping (*mastabas*). At the northeastern edge of the settlement was an ancient structure with modern repairs (fig. 39.4) perhaps associated with the reopening of the mines, apparently in the late nineteenth or early twentieth centuries. In the wadi entering the site from the northeast was modern damage made with a front-end loader or a bulldozer (fig. 39.5).

---

tence and Trade in the Eastern Desert of Egypt (Los Angeles, 2006), 156–67. For ʿAbabda gardens, see Cappers, *Roman Foodprints at Berenike*, 45–48; for gardens at Sikait, see S. Sidebotham, H. Nouwens, A. Hense, and J. Harrell, "Preliminary report on archaeological fieldwork at Sikait (Eastern Desert of Egypt), and environs 2002–2003," *Sahara* 15 (2004), 14–15, 16 (fig. 25), and Sidebotham, Hense, and Nouwens, *The Red Land*, 295–96. For gardens at ancient monasteries, see Sidebotham, Hense, and Nouwens, *The Red Land*, 324, also Palladius, *Historia Lausiaca* 7.4 (written in AD 419–420); for gardens at desert *praesidia*, see H. Cuvigny, "La société civile des *praesidia*," in H. Cuvigny (ed.), *La route de Myos Hormos. L'armée romaine dans le désert Oriental d'Égypte. Praesidia du désert de Bérénice*, FIFAO 48.2 (Cairo, 2003), 383.

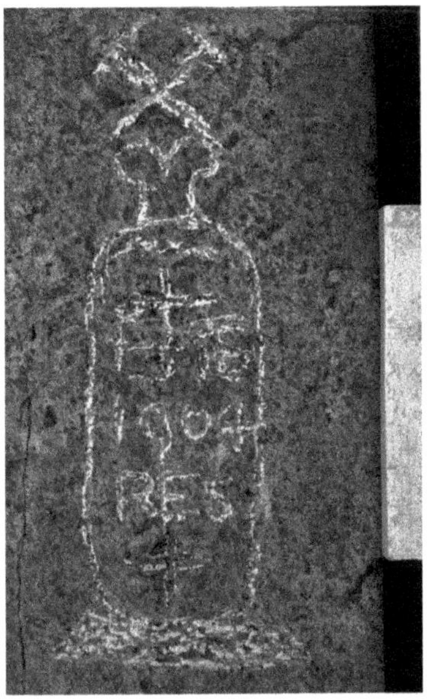

Fig. 42. Bir Sirbakis: Graffito/inscription. White increment on scale = 20 cm. Photo by S. Sidebotham.

Fig. 43. Bir Sirbakis, shrine looking north. Scale = Bedouin (circled). Photo by S. Sidebotham.

On the southern side of the wadi entering the site from the northeast was a major ancient structure (figs. 38.6 and 39.6). Its large open courtyard and associated rooms suggested an administrative function. Also west, south of the wadi entering from the northwest, was a platform cut into the natural rock face (figs. 38.7 and 39.7).

A modern well lay approximately 150 m south of the site in the bottom of a wadi. It may have been here or in the wadis entering the site from the northwest and northeast that ancient wells were located. If so, these have long since been filled in by wind-blown sand and floods, which occasionally pass through the area. Modern, but now abandoned, roofless and somewhat dilapidated, stone buildings lay on the hillside west of the well; the survey also noted ruins of modern structures north of the main site. Ancient grinding stones had been incorporated into some walls of these modern buildings (fig. 41). There was an elaborate graffito/inscription "RES 1904" carved into the natural rock face on the eastern side of the wadi, about 100 m south of the main site and 50 m north of the well (fig. 42). It was, very likely, related to gold mining operations that took place here and associated with the now abandoned modern structures found north and mainly south of the ancient site. This graffito had been looted and removed by persons unknown between the survey's visits in July 1996 and August 1997.

East of the main settlement were remains of what appeared to have been a shrine or a sanctuary that measured about 12.0 m N-S x 5.5 m E-W (fig. 43). It was similar in appearance to that documented at the Ptolemaic-early Roman amethyst mining settlement at Wadi Umm Diyeiba (in Wadi al-Gamashtat).[84] Another Delaware survey recorded a structure similar in appearance at Wadi Hatim/Hateem[85] just east of the major gold mining settlement at Sukkari.

There were structures that had or may have had religious functions at sites and settlements throughout the Eastern Desert.[86] One example, discussed above, was that at Fatireh al-Beida. Another may have been the el-

---

[84] J. Harrell, S. Sidebotham, R. Bagnall et al., "The Ptolemaic to Early Roman Amethyst Quarry at Abu Diyeiba in Egypt's Eastern Desert," *BIFAO* 106 (2006), 136–37.

[85] S. Sidebotham, R. Zitterkopf, R. Tomber, B. Cannon, and J. Harrell, *Survey of the Via Nova Hadriana in the Eastern Desert of Egypt*, in preparation.

[86] For example, S. Aufrère, "Prospects of the Mine in the Eastern Desert in Ptolemaic and Rome Times (= Autour de *L'Univers mineral* VIII)," in Kaper (ed.), *Life on the Fringe*, 5–19; G. Hölbl, *Altägypten im römischen Reich: Der römische Pharao und seine Tempel. 3. Heiligtümer und religiöses Leben in den ägyptischen Wüsten und Oasen* (Mainz am Rhein, 2005), 8–34; Sidebotham, Hense, and Nouwens, *The Red Land*, 111–50; A. Espinel,

evated structure accessed by two staircases at the quarry settlement at Umm Huyut,[87] while there was a temple erected on an artificial platform built part way up a mountainside at Kab Marfu'a.[88] Although uncertain of its function, Klemm and Klemm published a photograph of a structure at the gold mining settlement at Hamesh[89] that was also similar in appearance to the shrine at Bir Sirbakis. Much has been published about gods, religion, and shrines and temples in the Eastern Desert, in mining and quarrying settlements, and military installations in all historical periods.[90]

During the survey's work at the site, Ma'aza Bedouin men, women, and children herding numerous goats and donkeys visited the well. The survey team also sparingly used water from this well for bathing. The survey noted Bedouin children playing with toys and observed abandoned toys, evidence of longer-term occupation, or at least frequent visits to, and use of, the well here by these indigenous people.

Communications between (Bir) Sirbakis, and Bukhalug and the Nile would have headed west via the area of the later built *praesidium* at Gidami, about 17.5 km, partially through a winding wadi, west of Bir Sirbakis. From Gidami the route stretched westward and joined with one emanating from Mons Claudianus. West of Gidami, the route passed Abu Greiya, noted above, about 33 km (via the various wadis) west of Gidami, and westward, about 41 km from Qena (via the modern highway). This route eventually joined with that coming from Mons Porphyrites terminating at or near Qena.[91] It is evident that Roman-era routes made use of earlier Ptolemaic ones in this part of the central Eastern Desert, a practice that has been documented throughout this entire area between the Nile and the Red Sea over the millennia.[92]

Pottery

There was a relatively abundant scatter of surface sherds at (Bir) Sirbakis suggesting extensive activity predominantly in the third-second centuries BC with two sherds possibly dating to the mid-second to first centuries BC (figs. 44.8 and 44.17), and three sherds indicating later Roman activity, likely in the first–second centuries AD (figs. 44.1, 44.2, and 44.9).[93]

Fig. 44.1. Carinated cup with broad rim, sloping inwards. Alluvial fabric, possibly ERSB. Dull red matrix with common ill-sorted limestone impurities, and red-brown dull matt slip all over.
Fig. 44.2. Saucer with rounded rim. ERSA. Brown-yellow with pink-purple core, slightly sandy fabric. Good quality glossy red slip on the rim, same color wiped slipped surface elsewhere.
Fig. 44.3. Saucer with grooved rim. Fabric red-brown with a thin brown slightly pink core. Lime impurities, but likely to be alluvial fabric based on surface appearance. Red-slip surface on interior. Parallel: Tebtunis, third to second century BC, in Ballet and Południkiewicz, *Tebtynis V*, pl. 13.177.
Fig. 44.4. Black-glazed bowl with outturned rim, with double-rouletting on the floor. Pale orange (5YR 6/6) clean fabric with good quality black slip all over. Import. Parallel: Athens, third to second century BC, in S. Rotroff, *Hellenistic Pottery: Athenian and Imported Wheelmade Table Ware and Related Material. Athenian Agora*, vol. 29 (Princeton, 1997), figs. 59–60.
Fig. 44.5. Small shallow, flanged-rim bowl. Sandy coarse fabric with brown-pink core and red-brown margins. Cream-pink slip remains on the outside surface, below the flange and on the wall, but probably originally covered entire vessel.

"Gods in the Red Land: Development of Cults and Religious Activities in the Eastern Desert," 90–102; Sidebotham, Wright, Gates-Foster et al., "Gazetteer," 236 (shrine at Girf), 249–50 (shrine at Abu Qraya, with reference to others); Cuvigny, *Rome in Egypt's Eastern Desert*, 299–322.

87 Sidebotham, "Newly Discovered Sites," 186–89 for the site in general; Harrell, Brown and Lazzarini, "Two Newly Discovered," 289–92 for the quarry; Klemm and Klemm, *Stones and Quarries*, 291.

88 Sidebotham, Wright, Gates-Foster et al., "Gazetteer," 123–30 in general for Kab Marfu'a and Kab Marfu'a East.

89 Klemm and Klemm, *Gold Mining*, 265 (fig. 5.207).

90 Aufrère, "Prospects of the Mine," 5–19.

91 Sidebotham, Zitterkopf, and Riley, "Survey of the 'Abu Sha'ar"; Sidebotham, "Map sheet 78," vol. 1; Sidebotham, "Map sheet 78," vol. 2," 1158–63; Sidebotham, *Berenike and the Ancient*, 130–31 (table 8-1).

92 Sidebotham and Gates-Foster, "Introduction," 2–3 and note 7.

93 R. Tomber recorded this material in the field in 1996 and 1997. Descriptions are based on her field notes and drawings.

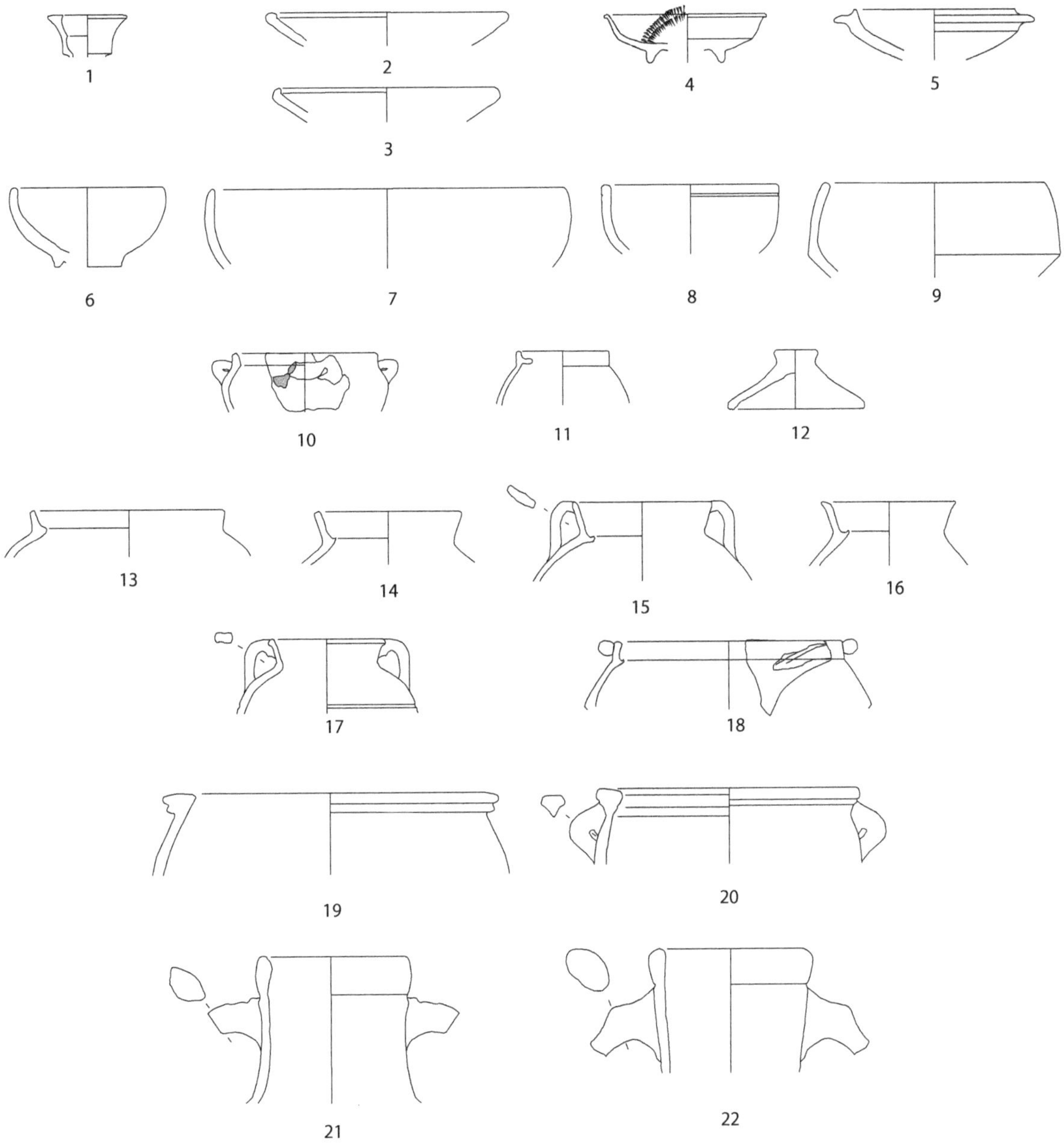

Fig. 44. Pottery from Bir Sirbakis. Scale = 1:4. Drawings by J. Gates-Foster.

Fig. 44.6. Hemispherical bowl with inturned rim. Red-brown with brown-purple core. Surfaces classic alluvial color, but fresh break has common large quartz and sparse limestone inclusions, suggesting mixed fabric. A general Hellenistic type, for discussion, see Ballet and Południkiewicz, *Tebtynis V*, 24–39.

Fig. 44.7. Large hemispherical bowl with inturned rim. Pink Aswan fabric with good quality red-brown slip outside, dull pink, but discolored in part inside.

Fig. 44.8. Hemispherical bowl with grooved rim. Brown calcareous fabric with pink margins and white surfaces. Parallel: Coptos, mid-second to mid-first century BC in Herbert and Berlin, "The excavation: occupation history and ceramic assemblages," fig. 66.H3.14.

Fig. 44.9. Carinated bowl with plain rim. Sandy dull red calcareous fabric with white surfaces. Parallel: al-Ghuzzah, second half of first century AD in Gates-Foster et al., "Early Imperial fortress of Berkou," fig. 14.11.
Fig. 44.10. "Koan-Cnidian" bowl. Applied horizontal handle, fine slightly sandy alluvial fabric, red brown throughout with wiped surfaces. Parallel: Coptos, third to mid-second century BC, in Herbert and Berlin, "The excavation: occupation history and ceramic assemblages," fig. 43.H2.15.
Fig. 44.11. Ptolemaic black ware (PBW) beaker. Discolored gray to pale brown alluvial fabric. Thick glossy black slip all over, vitrified to a near metallic state. For discussion of fabric and its dating, see J. Gill, "Ptolemaic 'Black Ware' from Mut el-Kharab," in C. Knoblauch and J. Gill (eds.), *Egyptology in Australia and New Zealand 2009: Proceedings of the Conference held in Melbourne, September 4th-6th,* BAR International Series 2355 (Oxford, 2012), 15–25.
Fig. 44.12. Lid with plain, slightly squared-off rim, and knob handle. Coarse sandy calcareous fabric with common impurities, including some limestone. Pale pink with dull orange margins and surfaces. Wire marks on handle.
Fig. 44.13. Cookpot with everted lid-seat rim. Gray-green (10YR6/1) with dull red to pink (10R5/6) margins and surfaces. Lime rich fabric, possibly a mix or marl.
Fig. 44.14. Cookpot with internal beveled lip and lid seat rim of moderate height. Pronounced interior flange. Dull pale red sandy calcareous or mixed fabric with pink core and surfaces.
Fig. 44.15. Cookpot with internal beveled lip and tall lid-seat rim. Double wide, flat vertical handles. Fine alluvial fabric with rare limestone impurities. Brown with pink core and discolored pink surfaces. Parallel: Karnak, second half of third-first half of second century BC, in Licitra and David "L'évolution des céramiques ptolémaïques," fig. 8.35.
Fig. 44.16. Cookpot with internal beveled lip and tall lid-seat rim. Sandy calcareous fabric with dull pink-brown core and darker margins and internal surface. The external surface has a thin, cream-colored skin.
Fig. 44.17 Globular, double-handled cookpot with everted rim. Shallow ribbing beginning just below the handle. Coarse, mottled alluvial fabric with brown break and orange to pink margins. Dull brown surface. Parallel: Coptos, third to mid-second century BC, in Herbert and Berlin, "The excavation: occupation history and ceramic assemblages," fig. 51.H2.39.
Fig. 44.18. Casserole with lid-seat, offset rim and applied, round horizontal handle. Alluvial fabric with rare large quartz. Red-brown with occasional gray-green core and red-brown surfaces, wiped. Parallel: Coptos, mid-second to mid-first century BC, in Herbert and Berlin, "The excavation: occupation history and ceramic assemblages," fig. 69.H3.35.
Fig. 44.19. Dinos with thickened, grooved rim. Red-brown (10R 5/6) throughout. Sparse large sand and common limestone inclusions. Probably an alluvial mixture. Parallel: Coptos, third to mid-second century BC, in Herbert and Berlin, "The excavation: occupation history and ceramic assemblages," fig. 46.H2.25.
Fig. 44.20. Dinos with thickened rim with a groove from finger wiping. Coarse sandy, poorly mixed calcareous clay. Dark purple with orange lenses and white surfaces.
Fig. 44.21. Egyptian amphora (AE1) with narrow bead rim and ovoid strap handle. Red-brown calcareous fabric with brown-gray external margin and white to green surface outside. Abundant limestone inclusions, small and well-sorted. See discussion of AE1-2.5 in Dixneuf, *Amphores égyptiennes*, 79–87, esp. fig. 56, and Gates-Foster, "Third Century BCE Supply Networks," figs. 7–8.
Fig. 44.22. Egyptian amphora (AE1) with narrow bead rim and ovoid strap handle. Red-brown silt throughout with some larger sand and lesser limestone inclusions. Darkened core near rim.

Eridiyah

There were few architectural remains visible at Eridiyah during the survey's visit in July 1993 (fig. 45).[94] The structures, mainly rectilinear in plan, comprised walls built of stacked stones. The survey did not plot these buildings and made no measurements of them. Among the structures, and to the south, were numerous, shallow,

[94] Meredith, "The Roman Remains, 1953," 95 mentions the site; see Klemm and Klemm, *Gold Mining*, 115–17 (Aradiya).

open pits, evidence of gold mining or prospecting efforts. Nearby was a cemetery, but the survey could not determine its age.

Eridiyah lay approximately 6.4 km southeast of (Bir) Sirbakis via a wide wadi. The distance between them required about a two-hour walk but, based on analysis of the surface sherds, these two sites were not contemporary. Any communication between Eridiyah and the Nile would then have used the same route as that from (Bir) Sirbakis via either Gidami or Abu Gerida westward.

The few permanent structures at Eridiyah suggested that operations here were neither large-scale nor perennial. Perhaps the area was exploratory with teams of prospectors sent from elsewhere as needed. Surface sherds dated to the second-third centuries and possibly fourth–fifth centuries AD.[95]

Fig. 45. Eridiyah, part of site. Photo by S. Sidebotham.

Conclusion

The results of the Delaware surveys indicated, unsurprisingly, that gold mining and stone quarrying occurred throughout the central Eastern Desert in Ptolemaic-Roman times. This report does not consider earlier or later efforts to extract and transport mineral wealth in the region, though these took place.[96] It is also evident that a single site, such as Abu Gerida, had multiple mining and quarrying functions and produced some of the tools, such as grinding stones and metal implements, used in those endeavors. It was likely also an administrative center for other activities in the region.

Gold ore grinding stones/querns made of rhyolite porphyry, very similar in appearance to those recorded at Abu Gerida, have been documented at other Ptolemaic-era mining facilities in the Eastern Desert. These include Wadi al-Naba and Umm Howeitat al-Qibli;[97] there may be others. There has been no chemical analysis conducted on these grinding stones to determine if they derived from the same quarry, i.e., that at Abu Gerida, and it is possible that they do not. However, if future analysis determines a common source for these grinding stones, then this may shed some light on Ptolemaic administrative control over aspects of gold mining operations at different sites in the Eastern Desert.

The appearance, numbers, sturdiness of construction and locations of the stone-built structures at sites examined here, except at Eridiyah, indicated that operations were, likely, conducted perennially, with, perhaps, some periods of reduced activities with populations probably increasing or decreasing throughout the year depending on a host of factors. This may not have been the case at Eridiyah, which preserved few extant stone structures. Operations here

---

[95] J. Riley examined surface pottery from Eridiyah during a field season in 1993. His field notes offer only a brief statement of general dates for the collected sherds and no catalogue or drawings.

[96] Klemm and Klemm, *Gold Mining*, and Klemm and Klemm, *Stones and Quarries*. Many of the dates they propose for activities at sites are inaccurate while others should be used with great caution. J. Harrell, *Archaeology and Geology of Ancient Egyptian Stones* (Toldeo, OH, forthcoming).

[97] Umm Howeitat al-Qibli: C. Alford, "Gold Mining in Egypt," *Transactions of the Institution of Mining and Metallurgy*, eleventh session: 10 (1901–1902), 12; S. Sidebotham and R. Zitterkopf, "Survey of the Via Hadriana by the University of Delaware: the 1996 Season," *BIFAO* 97 (1997), 224 (table "Umm Howeitat"), 233 fig. 5; Sidebotham, "Survey of the Hinterland," 368–69; H. Wright, "Archaeological survey in the Eastern Desert conducted by the University of Michigan and the University of Assiut: interim report," in Herbert and Berlin (eds.), *Kelsey Museum of the University of Michigan University of Assiut Excavations at Coptos (Qift)*, 228 (map: "Umm Howeytat"); Klemm and Klemm, *Gold Mining*, 153–58 (refer to it as Umm Rus with other remains in Wadi Mubarak, which is the Delaware survey's Umm Howeitat al-Qibli). Their pottery dates for the Wadi Mubarak site match those of the Delaware survey; Sidebotham, Zitterkopf, Tomber, Cannon, and Harrell, *Survey of the Via Nova Hadriana*, in preparation.

may have taken place only occasionally and not perennially. The scanty architectural remains suggested that few, if any personnel, stayed here throughout the year. They may have travelled here as needed. Of course, workers might have lived in tents or other structures that have left no trace in the archaeological record.

The state of preservation of stone structures at most sites examined here and dearth of wall tumble adjacent to them indicated that they were not much higher in antiquity. One must, therefore, conclude, as has been the case at other ancient sites throughout the Eastern Desert, that portions of upper walls, as well as any roofing, probably comprised perishable organic materials, such as wood and matting.[98]

There was little evidence for the presence of women and children as regular residents at any of these sites. Nor can it be determined if any of the population comprised servile or convict labor. Despite the well-known passage in Agatharchides', *On the Erythraean Sea* (copied in part, for example, by Diodorus Siculus and Photius) that discusses slave labor at Ptolemaic-era gold mines, including the abominable working and living conditions,[99] no archaeological evidence pointed conclusively to their presence or use—or that of convicts[100]—at any of the sites studied here. The surveys identified no fortifications at the mining and quarrying settlements. There were few watch towers and no facilities that appeared to have been places of confinement for slaves or convicts at any of the sites. The relative proximity of these settlements to the Nile would have allowed anybody who desired to escape to do so. Of course, this does not preclude the presence of slaves as private property in the study area.[101]

The relatively few graves recorded at the sites likely do not accurately reflect the numbers living in these settlements. This suggested that at least some of the deceased were returned from the desert to locations along the Nile for burial. While there is little or no evidence for this practice in the Ptolemaic era, it seems to have taken place at least in the early Roman period.[102] This Roman-era practice likely represented a long-standing Egyptian tradition.

Furthermore, the proximity of (Bir) Sirbakis to Bukhalug—no more than a few hours walk—and the contemporary pottery studied from those locations, suggested that there was probably regular official and unofficial communications between them. Fatireh al-Beida may have had multiple functions: as a quarry and potentially, though probably not officially, providing some very limited logistical support for teams moving between the Nile and Mons Claudianus. As Fatireh al-Beida was slightly off the main route between Mons Claudianus and the Nile and appeared to have been occupied only briefly in the Early and Late Roman periods, it would not have been a regular stop for this traffic.

---

98 See Sidebotham, Barnard, and Pyke, "Five Enigmatic Late Roman Settlements," 189; Sidebotham, Wright, Gates-Foster et al., "Gazetteer," 157 and note 68.

99 For example, Sidebotham, Hense, and Nouwens, *The Red Land*, 217–18, 220–21; Most recently H. Cuvigny, A. Bülow-Jacobsen, T. Faucher, and F. Téreygeol, "Agatharchide et les mines d'or du désert Oriental. Nouvelle traduction et commentaire des passages de Photius et Diodore," in B. Redon and T. Faucher (eds.), *Samut Nord. L'exploitation de l'or du désert Oriental à l'époque ptolémaïque*, FIFAO 83 (Cairo, 2020), 319–23.

100 See Cuvigny, *Rome in Egypt's Eastern Desert*, 608–10 for possible convicts.

101 Cuvigny, *Rome in Egypt's Eastern Desert*, 211 and note 96; however, see also p. 604.

102 Suggested by the Koptos Tariff of May 10, 90 AD: A. Bernand, *Les Portes du désert. Recueil des inscriptions grecques d'Antinooupolis, Tentyris, Koptos, Apollonopolis Parva et Apollonopolis Magna* (Paris, 1984), (no. 67), 201 line 31.

Emerging archaeological evidence from excavations at settlements such as Samut,[103] Samut North,[104] and al-Ghuzzah[105] and that from other sites, such as Abu Bokari,[106] Dunqash,[107] Hangaliya,[108] Sukkari,[109] Umm Howeitat al-Qibli,[110] Wadi Ghadir,[111] and yet others,[112] indicates that there was an uptick in gold mining activity in the Eastern Desert in the Ptolemaic period.[113] In some cases this took place at sites that had been previously exploited and in other instances these appear to have been areas only first mined in Ptolemaic times. These efforts resulted in the transformation of the desert landscape through the creation of a network of stations and transportation hubs designed to intensify exploitation across the entire region.[114] This appears to have been part of an overarching plan by the Ptolemaic state to augment its resources to support military and diplomatic efforts elsewhere in the Red Sea and throughout the Aegean/eastern Mediterranean regions, particularly during the third century BC when continual warfare and expansion strained the state's resources on many fronts.

Increased activities in the Eastern Desert in the Roman period beginning in the first century AD, especially in the central portion containing the sites under study, were most evident in the opening of massive quarrying operations at Mons Porphyrites, Mons Claudianus, and, to a lesser extent, at Umm Wikala. The recent French excavations at al-Ghuzzah documented an early Roman fortification located adjacent to a Ptolemaic village and mining complex where the older well and standing buildings were incorporated into the first century AD infrastructure of the Flavian fortification.[115] The elaborate logistical network of support facilities for these quarries and between them and the Nile further attested growing Roman interest in the region and the desire to return, where feasible, to older installations for further exploitation alongside new operations such as the imperial quarries.[116]

---

103 For example, J.-P. Brun, J-P. Deroin, T. Faucher, and B. Redon, "Les mines d'or ptolémaiques. Résultats des prospections dans le district minier de Samut (désert Oriental)," *BIFAO* 113 (2013), 111–42; B. Redon and T. Faucher, "Gold Mining in Early Ptolemaic Egypt," *EA* 46 (2015), 17–19; B. Redon and T. Faucher, "Rapport d'activité 2014-2015: Désert oriental," *Supplément au BIFAO* 115 (2015), 24–33; B. Redon, and T. Faucher, "Forts et mines d'or du désert Oriental d'Égypte: Découvertes récentes dans le district de Samut," *RA* 63 (2015–2016), 101–09; B. Redon and T. Faucher, "Samut North: 'Heavy Metal Processing Plants' are Mills," *EA* 48 (2016), 20–22; B. Redon and T. Faucher, "Rapport d'activité 2015–2016: Désert oriental," *Supplément au BIFAO* 116 (2016), 10–24; B. Redon and T. Faucher, "Forts et mines d'or du désert Oriental d'Égypte: découvertes récentes dans le district de Samut," *Revue archéologique* 1 (2017), 101–09; Sidebotham, Wright, Gates-Foster et al., "Gazetteer," 194–201.

104 Sidebotham, Wright, Gates-Foster et al., "Gazetteer," 201–07; Redon and Faucher, *Samud Nord.*

105 Gates-Foster, Goncalves, Redon et al., "The Early Imperial fortress."

106 Klemm and Klemm, *Gold Mining*, 179–90; J. Harrell, "Geology," in Sidebotham and Gates-Foster, *The Archaeological Survey of the Desert Roads*, 53.

107 Klemm and Klemm, *Gold Mining*, 228–35; Sidebotham, Wright, Gates-Foster et al., "Gazetteer," 211–14.

108 Klemm and Klemm, *Gold Mining*, 251–59; Sidebotham, Wright, Gates-Foster et al., "Gazetteer," 161–63.

109 Klemm and Klemm, *Gold Mining*, 212–19; S. Sidebotham, R. Zitterkopf, R. Tomber, Cannon, and J. Harrell, *Survey of the Via Nova Hadriana*, in preparation.

110 See note 97 above (on Umm Howeitat al-Qibli).

111 Klemm and Klemm, *Gold Mining*, 26–63; Harrell, "Geology," 70 (Table no. 17).

112 See Klemm and Klemm, *Gold Mining*, but many of their dates (based on ceramics) should be accepted with great caution.

113 Klemm and Klemm, *Gold Mining*, 12–15; Redon and Faucher, "Rapport d'activité 2014–2015"; T. Faucher, "Ptolemaic Gold: the Exploitation of Gold in the Eastern Desert," in J.-P. Brun, T. Faucher, B. Redon and S. Sidebotham (eds.), *The Eastern Desert of Egypt during the Greco-Roman Period: Archaeological Reports* (Paris, 2018) Online: Paris: Collège de France, 2018 (généré le 01 novembre 2018)

114 J. Gates-Foster, "The Eastern Desert in the Ptolemaic Period: A Developing Picture," in Barnard and Duistermaat (eds), *History of the Peoples*, 190–203; B. Redon, "The Control of the Eastern Desert by the Ptolemies: New Archaeological Data," in Brun, Faucher, Redon, and Sidebotham (eds.), *The Eastern Desert of Egypt.*

115 Gates-Foster, Goncalves, Redon et al., "The Early Imperial Fortress."

116 The exiguous pottery of fourth-fifth century date documented from Fatireh al-Beida and Eridiyah suggested some activity at that time as was also the case at Mons Porphyrites for which see D. P. S. Peacock, E. Peacock, and V. Maxfield, *The Roman Imperial Quarries: Survey and Excavation at Mons Porphyrites 1994–1998, vol. 2: The Excavations* (London, 2007).

The Hunters' Palette: A Novel Explanation of the Enigmatic Double Bull, an Image That Survived through the Millennia

Joe Smolik
Geneva, Switzerland

Abstract

This paper proposes that the enigmatic double bull on the Hunters' Palette, now at the British Museum and the Louvre, represents a rare type of mutant bovine, a conjoined twin of type ischiopagus. Although the incidence of this biological anomaly in cattle is low, it is likely that such creatures were observed from time to time in the Nile Valley. The case for a mutant bull is supported by pictures of modern ischiopagi, veterinary references, Nubian petroglyphs, and hieroglyphic signs. The portrayal of a mutant animal on predynastic palettes is not unprecedented.

Capart and Fischer suggested that the double bull was an early hieroglyph, but neither explained how or why it became a determinative in verbs meaning "to move back and forth." It is possible that it was inspired by the back and forth grazing movement of a real double bull. The proposal would seem consistent with Frankfort's observation about the profound influence of cattle on the ancient Egyptian language. The double bull hypothesis may also elucidate the puzzling association of such a creature with a canal in the Third Upper Nome of Egypt.

Other objects representing the double bull—amulets, seals, a macehead, etc.—are attested intermittently from the Predynastic to the Late Period when the amulet is rendered in the form of a "double Apis;" generally these objects have apotropaic connotations. Texts containing the double bull determinative exist more or less in parallel with the representational forms and maintain the same meaning throughout. The paper ends with a consideration of the Hunters' Palette as an exhibit of military power.

الملخص

تقترح هذه المقالة أن الثور المزدوج الغامض الموجود على لوحة الصيادين، الموجود الآن في المتحف البريطاني ومتحف اللوفر، يمثل نوعًا نادرًا من الأبقار المتحورة، وهو توأم ملتصق من نوع ischiopagus. على الرغم من أن نسبة حدوث هذا الشذوذ البيولوجي في الماشية منخفضة، فمن المحتمل أن هذه المخلوقات قد لوحظت من وقت لآخر في وادي النيل. يتم دعم وجود حالة الثور المتحور من خلال صور ischiopagus الحديث والمراجع البيطرية والنقوش النوبية والرموز الهيروغليفية. ان تصوير حيوان متحور على اللوحات ليس غير مسبوق.

اقترح كابارت وفيشر أن الثور المزدوج كان رمزاً من الرموز الهيروغليفية المبكرة، لكن لم يوضح أي منهما كيف أو لماذا أصبح خلال فترة الأسرات يرمز إلى الفعل الذي يعني «التحرك ذهابًا وإيابًا». من الممكن أن تكون مستوحاة من حركة الرعي (ذهابًا وإيابًا) لثور مزدوج حقيقي. قد يبدو الاقتراح متسقًا مع ملاحظة فرانكفورت حول التأثير العميق للماشية على اللغة المصرية القديمة. ثالثًا، قد توضح فرضية الثور المزدوج الارتباط المحير لمثل هذا المخلوق بقناة في الإقليم الثالث بمصر العليا.

توثق القطع الأخرى التي تمثل الثور المزدوج - التمائم، والأختام، ورأس الصولجان، وما إلى ذلك - بشكل متقطع من عصر ما قبل الأسرات إلى العصر المتأخر عندما يتم تقديم التميمة على شكل «أبيس مزدوج». توجد النصوص التي تحتوي على رمز الثور المزدوج بشكل أو بآخر بالتوازي مع الأشكال التمثيلية وتحافظ على نفس المعنى طوال الوقت.

Journal of the American Research Center in Egypt 58 (2022), 209–31
http://dx.doi.org/10.5913/jarce.58.2022.a011

The Double Bull: A Real or Composite Creature?

Since it came to light in the nineteenth century,[1] the Hunters' Palette (British Museum EA 20792; Louvre E.11254) has received considerable attention (fig. 1).[2] Nevertheless, the precise meaning of the complex scene—two rows of armed hunters herding a variety of desert animals—continues to be debated. This paper focuses on the enigmatic double bull carved on one of the "shoulders" of this large, possibly royal, ceremonial palette. The British Museum describes it as "a mythical beast consisting of the linked fore-parts of two buffalo;"[3] for Baines, it is "a motif of the fused forequarters of two bulls facing in opposite directions."[4] Others use similar formulations. The double bull and adjacent structure have generally been interpreted jointly. Heuzey thought that they might be emblematic.[5] Baines notes that "in late predynastic iconography the bull is a primarily royal symbol and this pair figure is likely to represent the king or kingship, or more broadly, royalty."[6] The building is also regarded as possibly religious because of the presence of the double bull.[7] Although infrequent, various interpretations of the scene on the Hunters' Palette specifically refer to the double bull. For example, Friedman observes "the hunters [controlling the animals] move towards the building defined by a double bull motif, probably signifying a religious structure for which and perhaps at which the action is taking place."[8] Patch describes the scene as one "where the animals are shown being brought under control before the gods or leaders, represented by the shrine and the double cow or bull."[9] While the remarks above describe the bull motif and seek to interpret the symbolism of the pair, they do not elucidate the nature of the creature itself.

Rather than a mythological animal, it is proposed that the double bull image represents a real bull, a rare type of conjoined twin with heads at both ends (ischiopagus). The notion that a mutant animal might be represented on a predynastic palette is not unprecedented. In fact, six cosmetic palettes depicting mutant creatures are known: three in the form of a double fish, one as two birds joined at their tails and two depicting dicephalous turtles.[10] Possibly the earliest palette, dated to Naqada IC, was described as a "turtle with heads at each end" by

---

[1] I extend great gratitude to R. Friedman for her early encouragement and commentary on the texts, to B. B. Williams for drawing my attention to the Abka and Mograkka rock drawings, to R. S. Bianchi, E. Wilkinson, and the late D. Huyge for suggesting relevant objects and references, to L. McNamara for the opportunity to study the macehead at the Ashmolean Museum, and to B. Monaghan for help in preparing the figures.

[2] https://www.britishmuseum.org/collection/object/Y_EA20792 (accessed December 31, 2020). https://collections.louvre.fr/ark:/53355/cl010007344 (accessed July 1, 2021). Both websites have selected bibliographies. Also see, for example, W. M. F. Petrie, *Ceremonial Slate Palettes*, BSAE 66 (London, 1953), 12–13; K. Cialowicz, *Les palettes Égyptiennes aux motifs zoomorphes et sans décoration: Études de l'art prédynastique* (Kraków, 1991); J. Baines, "Origins of Egyptian Kingship," in D. O'Connor and D. Silverman (eds.), *Ancient Egyptian Kingship*, PÄ 9 (Leiden-New York-Koln, 1995), 95–156; S. Hendrickx, "Bovines in Egyptian Predynastic and Early Dynastic Iconography," in F. Hassan (ed.), *Droughts, Food and Culture. Ecological Change and Food Security in Africa's Later Prehistory* (New York, 2002), 275–318; S. Hendrickx and M. Eyckerman, "Visual Representation and State Development in Egypt," *Archéo-Nil* 22 (2012), 23–72; D. Patch, "Early Dynastic Art," in D. Patch (ed.), *Dawn of Egyptian Art* (New York, 2012), 137–79; S. Hendrickx, F. Förster, K. Piquette et al., "A History of the Visualization of the Hunters' Palette and a Tentative Reconstruction of Its Missing Part," *Archéo-Nil* 30 (2020), 123–48.

[3] British Museum, curators' comments. The Louvre's website does not specifically comment on the double bull.

[4] Baines, "Origins of Egyptian Kingship," 112.

[5] L. Heuzey, "Égypte ou Chaldée," *Comptes rendus de l'Académie* Tirage à part 4 (1899), 64. Heuzey thought that the building resembled a tomb, which the Egyptians sometimes used to indicate the limit of the desert. See J. Capart, "Mélange 2: Remarques sur une des palettes archaïques du Musée Britannique," *RecTrav* 22 (1900), 108, https://digi.ub.uni-heidelberg.de/diglit/rectrav1900 (accessed June 19, 2020).

[6] Baines, "Origins of Egyptian Kingship," 112. Baines notes that the group of the building and double bull is a device that later disappears. See also Hendrickx, "Bovines in Egyptian Predynastic and Early Dynastic Iconography," 280.

[7] S. Hendrickx, " L'iconographie de la chasse dans le contexte social prédynastique,"*Archeo Nil*, 20 (2010), 130. R. Friedman, "Hierakonpolis," in Patch (ed.), *Dawn of Egyptian Art*, 85.

[8] Friedman, "Hierakonpolis," 85.

[9] Patch, "Early Dynastic Art," 143.

[10] J. Smolik, "Six Monstrous Zoomorphic Predynastic Palettes: Representations of Real Conjoined Twins?" *Archéo-Nil* 29 (2019), 179–93. The conjoined fish are possibly tilapia. The double fish palette at the Ashmolean Museum (1845.845) was found at Ballas in a tomb dated to Naqada IID2(?). The two other fish palettes, one in the Fitzwilliam Museum, Cambridge (1902.245), and the other in the Manchester Museum (9500), are of unknown provenance. Unfortunately, the latter also applies to the palettes in the form of twinned birds and a dicephalous turtle (side by side heads) in the Metropolitan Museum of Art (10.176.78 and 10.176.80).

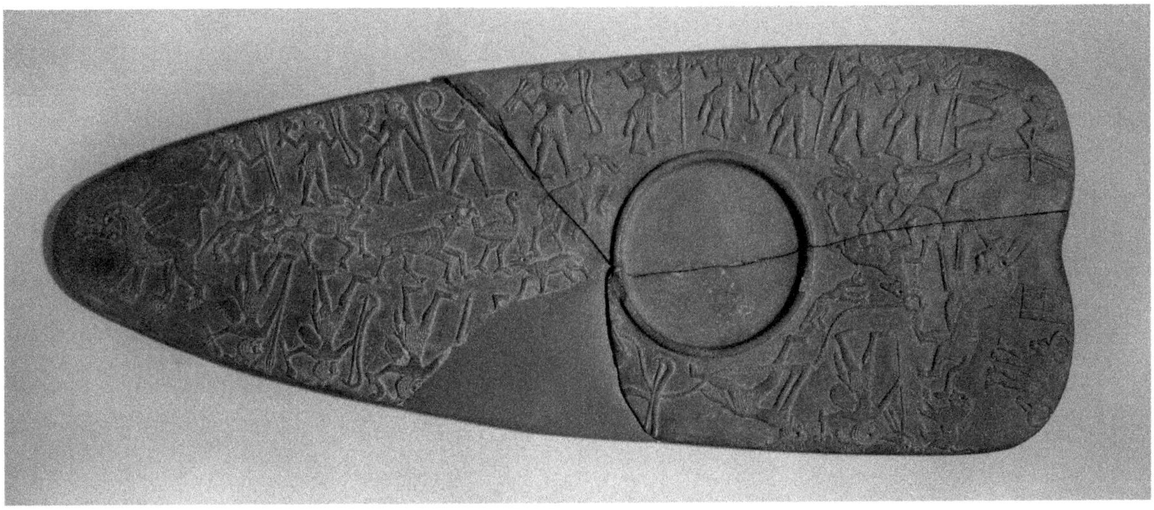

Fig. 1. The Hunters' Palette, Naqada III. Courtesy of the British Museum.

the excavators of el-Amrah.[11] That malformation is also of type ischiopagus. Interestingly, in this rather small sample, four variants of conjoined twinning are depicted; all represent a departure from well-known zoomorphic palettes of "normal animals." Presumably these creatures had some special, but unknown, meaning to the ancient Egyptians to merit memorialization.

The Case for a Mutant (ischiopagus) Bull

The double bull on the Hunters' Palette is highly stylized, but the muscles, tendons, hooves, and veins are rendered in considerable, if somewhat exaggerated, detail (fig. 2). Its impressive horns curve inward, but they may be idealized according to ancient Egyptian convention.[12] At the extremities, two heads stare in opposite directions. It is plausible that the image was inspired by a real bovine conjoined twin of type ischiopagus. An embalmed bovine with this malformation is on display at the Gregorio Aguilar Barea Archaeological Museum in Juigalpa in the heart of Nicaraguan cattle country (fig. 3).[13] Conjoined twinning (also known as congenital duplication) is a rare condition that afflicts humans and certain animal species, especially turtles, fish, and snakes. In cattle and sheep the anomaly is often manifested in the form of dual, side-by-side heads on a single torso (*dicephalus parapagus dipus*).[14] However, the incidence of ischiopagus in cattle is less common. It is characterized by the fusion of the two spines at a 180-degree angle in the lower pelvic region i.e., the spinal axis extends in a straight line. Ischiopagus is also characterized by one or more underdeveloped hind legs protruding from the torso.[15] In figure 3, two legs (there may be others) of the bovine are barely visible at the very back of the display case.

---

[11] D. Randall-McIver and A. Mace, *El Amrah and Abydos, 1899–1901*, EM 23 (London, 1902), 23, pl. 5.3. The present location of the ischiopagus turtle palette is unknown.

[12] Hendrickx has observed that although a great variability in shape is attested in archaeological finds, the rendering of bull's horns in predynastic and early dynastic art clearly became idealized and uniform. See Hendrickx, "Bovines in Egyptian Predynastic and Early Dynastic Iconography," 279.

[13] https://notesfromcamelidcountry.net/tag/two-headed-cow/.

[14] T. Hiraga and S. Dennis, "Congenital Duplication," *Veterinary Clinics of North America: Food Animal Practice* 9 (1993), 145–61. Almost all types of congenital duplications attested in humans are observed in food animals such as cattle. In cattle and humans, the anomaly occurs about once in 100,000 births.

[15] In addition to the two pairs of "normal" forelegs, ischiopagus bovines may have up to four additional, often incompletely developed, "hind" legs emanating from the torso (ischiopagus tetrapus). If the creature that inspired the double bull in figure 2 here also had "extra" (hind) legs, they were omitted from the image; either they were small and on the non-visible side of the animal, or they were omitted to suit Egyptian aesthetic tastes.

Fig. 2. The Hunters' Palette, double bull and "shrine." Courtesy of the British Museum.

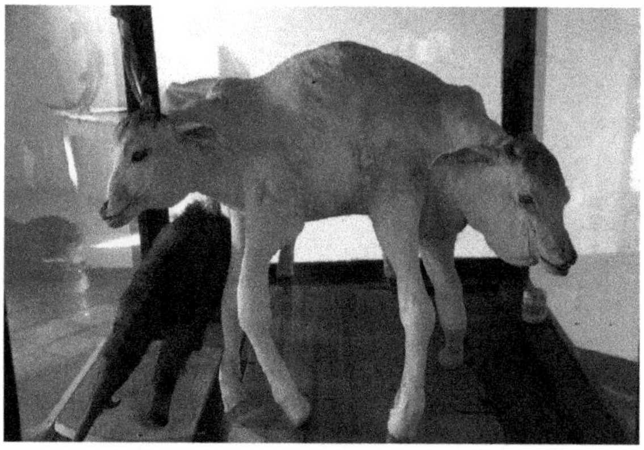

Fig. 3. Double bovine calf, Juigalpa, Nicaragua. Courtesy of Camelid Country.

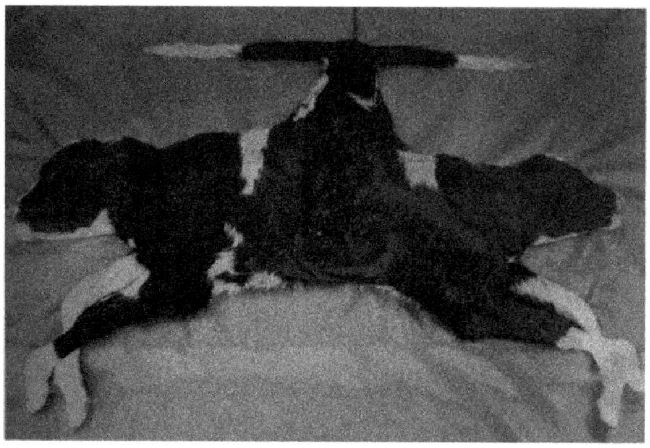

Fig. 4. Double bovine calf, veterinary reference, after Hiraga and Dennis, Congenital Duplication, *fig. 3.*

One or more appendages—generally a tail, rarely a penis—may hang from the abdomen.[16] Ischiopagus is a condition discussed in standard veterinary references such as Hiraga and Dennis.[17] The authors remark that the animal shown here in figure 4 had four underdeveloped hind legs that were amputated from the spinal area.[18] Presumably, the animal was considered viable.

Depending on the specific malformation, conjoined twins face various issues of survivability. Most are stillborn, or die soon after birth, often because of internal physical defects. Their viability depends on the normal functioning of the nervous system and internal organs (either shared or duplicated). Congenital duplication is a common cause of dystocia, i.e., difficult labor[19] that endangers both mother and calf. The chances of a live birth are improved by human intervention during calving (apparently herders often help to pull blocked fetuses[20]). A relief in the Dynasty 5 tomb of Ti at Saqqara shows a herdsman helping a cow with a delivery, overseen by a magician.[21] In a cattle culture, this practice probably had a long history. Nurturing by humans would also enhance the animal's chances of survival.[22] An

[16] What appears to be a penis or bull sheath on the double bull is more likely to be an abnormal tail, common in bovine ischiopagus (personal communication, L. Denholm GAICD, Principal Policy Analyst and Program Evaluator, Department of Premier and Cabinet, New South Wales, Australia). Denholm has published widely on the genetic defects, developmental duplication (DD) and conjoined twinning in cattle. I am thankful to him for multiple other comments as well. Interestingly, the male ischiopagus specimen examined by Pathan had three tails and no penis. See M. Pathan, U. Kumblar, and S. Dandopant, "Dicephalus tetrapus tetrabrachius tricaudatus ischiopagus: a conjoined twin calf," (2012): https://www.researchgate.net/figure/Ischiopagus-with-three-tails-two-are-completely-developed_fig1_230851401 (accessed December 21, 2020).

[17] Hiraga and Dennis, "Congenital Duplication," 146.

[18] Hiraga and Dennis, "Congenital Duplication," 147, fig. 3.

[19] Hiraga and Dennis, "Congenital Duplication," 145.

[20] E. Edwards and G. Balamayooran, *Necropsy Of Rare Bovine Conjoined Twins, Case Study* (2020) 1. https://tvmdl.tamu.edu/2020/02/24/necropsy-of-rare-bovine-conjoined-twins/ (accessed December 21, 2020).

[21] R. Ritner, *The Mechanics of Ancient Egyptian Magical Practice*, SAOC 54 (Chicago, 2008), 229 and fig. 22(b). The magician was present to boost the chances of a successful birth. According to Ritner, there was little or no difference between a magician and a doctor at the time.

[22] As an example, in Cajamarca, Peru, villagers bottle-fed a newly born dicephalous calf that was incapable of lifting its joined heads. https://www.dailymail.co.uk/news/article-3203487/TWO-HEADED-calf-born-Peru-villagers-split-s-evil-sign-gift-God.html (accessed January 25, 2021).

ischiopagus bovine faces greater challenges than normal animals do, in particular because restricted mobility makes it easier prey for predators. "Forward" movement requires the coordination of dual, independent brains to animate its two foreparts simultaneously in opposite directions; the two legs of one forepart must move "forward" while the other set of legs step "backwards." Consequently, the animal's normal movement would be largely linear, back and forth, suitable for grazing. However, rapid motion, whether linear or lateral, likely would be difficult. [23]

Already in the Predynastic Period, the ancient Egyptians were known to have kept food animals and wild beasts in captivity for sacrifice, prestige, displays of power, and to embellish elite burials. At Hierakonpolis, for example, an elephant, leopard, and baboons were brought from afar; they, and as well as local species—the hippo, domestic cattle, and others—were buried near members of the elite in cemetery HK6 as demonstrations of their power and prestige. In several cases, the animal remains indicate long periods of captivity.[24] A remarkable animal such as a conjoined twin bull could have been cared for and sheltered, perhaps in the adjacent shrine-like building (fig. 2), befitting an animal with possible religious connotations. Indeed, it would seem that such a creature would not be out of place in such a physical and ideological setting. The practice of royal menageries is also attested in the Dynastic Period when exotic beasts again served the leadership as status symbols and strong visual displays of power.[25]

Since the Neolithic Period, cattle occupied a central place in the social fabric of the ancient Nile Valley dwellers.[26] Cattle were of importance as an economic resource as well as for their symbolic and religious significance. In this context, the birth and survival of an actual double bull would have been a wondrous event,[27] the creature perhaps having been interpreted as the incarnation of divine power;[28] its duality and symmetry would also have appealed to the Egyptian mind. While religious practices in the Predynastic Period are open to question, it may be significant that the cult of the Apis bull, which involved the veneration of a creature selected on the basis of its distinctive appearance, is attested as early as the First Dynasty.[29] The idea of venerating a two-headed bull would not be entirely foreign to Egyptian thought, at least in later periods. A remarkable scene on an architec-

---

23 This particular animal could hardly be considered the powerful and raging (normal) bull occasionally portrayed in Pre-Early Dynastic iconography. See for, example the so-called Bull Palette (Louvre, E11255) and Narmer Palette (Cairo Museum, CG 14716).

24 Friedman, "Hierakonpolis," 87; M. V. Linseele, W. Van Neer, and R. Friedman, "Special Animals from a Special Place: The Fauna from HK9A at Predynastic Hierakonpolis," *JARCE* 45 (2009) 105–36; W. Van Neer, V. Linseele, and R. Friedman, "Animal Burials and Food Offerings at the Elite Cemetery HK6 of Hierakonpolis," in S. Hendrickx, R. Friedman, K.Cialowicz et al., (eds.), *Egypt at Its Origins: Studies in Memory of Barbara Adams, Proceedings of the International Conference 'Origin of the State in Early Dynastic Egypt,' Krakow, 28 August–1 September,* OLA 138 (Leuven 2004), 67–130; "Animals at Hierakonpolis Special," *Nekhen News* 33 (Winter, 2021).

25 Friedman, "Hierakonpolis," 88; R. Muller-Wöllerman, "'Zoologische Garten' als Mittel der Herrschaftslegitimation im alten Ägypten," *WO* 33 (2003), 31–43. In the present context, the so-called Botanical Garden built by Tuthmosis III at Karnak is noteworthy. One wall shows cattle with teratological anomalies, including those associated with conjoined twinning—one of the few post-Predynastic Period representations known of the condition. See N. Beaux, *Le cabinet de curiosités de Thoutmosis III : Plantes et animaux du «jardin botanique » de Karnak,* OLA 36 (Leuven, 1990), 275, fig. 1a-e; 279–83, pls. 34–41. One animal has three clearly carved horns (the probable three horns of the adjacent animals have been defaced fig. 1e) while another has a bifurcated tail (fig. 1b). Unfortunately, other relevant areas of the reliefs have been hammered or recut rendering identification of the beasts' anomalies uncertain. However, Beaux proposes that the face of one bovine is split ("epodyne") or that its two heads are partially merged ("rhinodyme," fig. 1c). Most of the upper register (fig. 1a) is missing, but one of the front legs of an animal appears to be duplicated ("melomélie") while a leg of the specimen in the center of the panel seems to be absent ("hémimélie"). These bovine anomalies are also discussed in Hiraga and Dennis "Congenital Duplication," 145–49.

26 H. Frankfort, *Kingship and the Gods: A Study of Ancient Near Eastern Religion as the Integration of Society & Nature* (Chicago, 1948), 162–80; D. Wengrow, "Rethinking 'Cattle Cults' in Early Egypt: Towards a Prehistoric Perspective on the Narmer Palette," *Cambridge Archaeological Journal* 11 (2001), 91–104; Hendrickx, "Bovines in Egyptian Predynastic and Early Dynastic Iconography," 275–76.

27 H. Frankfort, *Ancient Egyptian Religion, An Interpretation* (New York, 1948), 12–13, stressed what he thought was the ancient Egyptians' acute awareness of the special nature of animals, namely that all individuals of a species are nearly identical and that they never change in successive generations (unlike human beings). A real double bull would have departed from this reality and presumably made a powerful impression on the community.

28 For the community of Cajamarca mentioned above (note 22), the birth of a dicephalous calf had supernatural connotations, opinion being split as to whether the animal was an evil sign or a gift from God. For the religious and political significance that has, since antiquity, been attached to children born with malformations, see A. Leroi, *Mutants: On the Form, Variety and Errors of the Human Body* (London, 2005).

29 An inscription of a bowl naming Horus Aha alongside Apis seems bear out a statement of the Roman writer Aelian that the cult was founded by Menes (Narmer or Aha). A. Dodson, "Of Bulls and Princes: The Early Years of the Serapeum at Sakkara," *Kmt* 6.1 (Spring, 1995), 19–32. At least in later times, the Apis was considered physically unique, defined by the distinctive markings on the hide.

Fig. 5. Psamtek I before a "two headed bull god" (BM EA 20). Courtesy of the British Museum.

tural element carved several millennia later shows a "caped two headed bull god"[30] worshiped by Psamtek I, of Dynasty 26 (British Museum EA 20) (fig. 5). The relief recalls statuettes of Egyptian kings venerating the Apis bull. It is possible that this unusual deity on the slab was inspired by a real dicephalous cow, heads side by side, such as the Peruvian specimen mentioned in note 22 above; this particular variant of conjoined twinning is considerably more common than ischiopagus.[31]

Double Bulls in Nubia: A Record in Rock Art?

Supporting the possibility that ischiopagus-type bovines were observed in antiquity are three, perhaps four, rock drawings in Nubia. Those in the Abka region, near the Second Cataract of the Nile, are no longer visible due to the inundation of the area. Documented by the Scandinavian Joint Expedition, the area was characterized by black patinated stone outcrops richly decorated with drawings of animals, humans and various objects.[32] The presence of Neolithic, A, and C Group, and other cattle-breeding cultures is attested.[33] The three images were

---

[30] British Museum EA 20 found at el-Rashid (Rosetta) (https://www.britishmuseum.org/collection/object/Y_EA20). The description "caped two headed bull god" is from a museum gallery label (2015).

[31] Hiraga and Dennis, "Congenital Duplication," 145–46.

[32] P. Hellström, *The Rock Drawings*, Scandinavian Joint Expedition to Sudanese Nubia, vol. 1 (parts 1: Text, and 2: Plates) (Stockholm, 1970).

[33] Hellström, *The Rock Drawings*, vol. 1, part 1, 23.

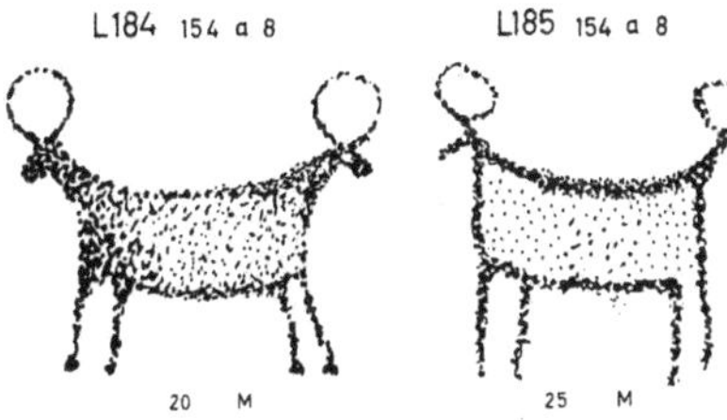

Fig. 6. Double bovine petroglyphs, Abka, Nubia, after Hellström, The Rock Drawings, *vol. 1, part 2, pl. Corpus 167–206.*

Fig. 7. Double bovine petroglyph, Mograkka, Nubia, after Vila, La Prospection Archéologique, *fig. 21.2.*

found in two separate areas, designated Stations 154a and 157m, which together host nearly 600 images of cattle, the most frequently portrayed animal.[34] It is thought that most of the cattle depicted here were domesticated.[35]

At Station 154a, two of the hammered representations of double bulls were designated as L185, described as possibly a "double headed ox or antelope," and L184, as "a double-headed quadruped" (fig. 6).[36] Both creatures are shown in profile, their (presumably stylized) horns forming closed circles, oriented toward the viewer. The relative size of the horns suggests that adults are portrayed. Whether or not the two images are contemporary or if they represent the same individual is open to question. The double bulls are separated by an apparently normal bovine with a curled tail (L186). The three are surrounded by a giraffe, antelope, and other easily identifiable animals, suggesting an unremarkable scene. Despite their exceptional physiology, the double bovines are treated as normal animals; they are not highlighted on the rock face by size, a preferential location, or framing of any type.

The third ischiopagus-type creature, C392, was portrayed on an outcrop at Station 157m. Described as an "ox [that] appears to have one head at each end, each with V-shaped horns." It is "probably the superposition of one ox on another."[37] However, there is no evidence on the drawing of "doubling" such as the presence of the extra legs of a second animal. It is noteworthy that no representations of mythical or composite creatures are attested in the region that might suggest a local population with an Egyptian-style imagination.[38]

The fourth possible example of a rock drawing of a double bovine is found south of Abka, in the archaeological area comprising Mograkka and Kosha where human habitation from the Neolithic to the Christian era is attested. The archaeological remains and petroglyphs were the subject of a joint French and Sudanese expedition

34 Hellström, *The Rock Drawings*, vol. 1, part 1, table 2, 52.

35 Hellström, *The Rock Drawings*, vol. 1, part 1, 29. The author believes that the majority of the drawings depict domesticated cattle, but that the possibility of some wild fauna among them cannot be excluded. However, Davis opines that it is impossible to tell the difference between domesticated and wild cattle from rock drawings: W. Davis, "The Earliest Art in the Nile Valley," in L. Krzyzaniak and M. Kobusiewicz (eds.), *Origin and Early Development of Food-Producing Cultures in the North East Nile Valley* (Poznan, 1984), 81–94. Whether an ischiopagus bovidae could survive in the wild would depend on its specific abnormalities and the habitat. Pictures have been posted by hunters online of double deer (ischiopagus), two adult deer joined at their heads and other cases of abnormal, wild bovidae, but these cases were not verified by medical experts.

36 Hellström, *The Rock Drawings*, vol. 1, part 1, 78 (site 154a.8). Drawings L184 and 185 are in vol. 1, part 2, pl. Corpus L167–206; a photograph of the rock surface showing the two bulls is in pl. 17.3. It is unlikely that image L185 portrays an antelope because it differs markedly from the animal figures identified as antelopes in Corpus L.

37 Hellström, *The Rock Drawings*, vol. 1, part 1, 114 (site 157m.183). Drawing C392 is in vol. 1, part 2, Corpus 375–409. Drawing C528 at site 359 is in part 2. Corpus 521–53 may also show another double bovine, but the details are unclear.

38 Signs of an Egyptian presence in the Abka area are negligible. Only one example of Predynastic Egyptian iconography—a boat carving—has been found between the First and Second Cataracts. See D. Wengrow, *The Archaeology of Early Egypt: Social Transformations in North-East Africa, 10,000 to 2650 BC* (Cambridge, 2006), 113. A few scattered hieroglyphs from the Middle Kingdom were found at Abka. See Hellström, *The Rock Drawings*, vol. 1, part 1, 234–35.

during the early 1970s.[39] Of specific interest here is Site 3-L-22B in Mograkka East on east bank of the Nile that is characterized by drawings of a large number of bovids. What Vila describes as a bovid with two heads is one of twenty images engraved on small granite outcrops along the river. Unfortunately, the image of the bovid was roughly hammered on an uneven surface (fig. 7).[40] Nevertheless, the dual foreparts can be clearly identified; the horns appear to be of the incurved type.

Due to the well-known difficulties of dating petroglyphs, it is doubtful that reliable dates can be attached to the double bull images. Hendrickx has noted that the plethora of rock art representing cattle in Upper Egypt and probably also in Nubia can be placed in the Naqada II and III periods.[41] Studies conducted at Abka attest to a longer time frame. Interestingly, one of the few excavations conducted in the area was at Abka Station 154a, below the two double bull images. It yielded dates ranging from around 4650 BC (corrected carbon C14 date) to the First Millennium AD,[42] but no finds at any strata could be reliably associated with the particular rock drawings above.

Other Early Objects Bearing Representations of the Double Bull

In addition to the image on the Hunters' Palette, several other early objects appear to take the form of an ischiopagus bull: three ivory amulets, a decoration surmounting a rhomboidal cosmetic palette, and a macehead (Table 1).[43] Aspects of the carving suggest they are products of craft specialization, a practice that tends to be associated with religious and/or ceremonial centers.[44] The three stylized ivory "double bull's head" amulets (fig. 8), in the Brussels Museum (E.3381a-c),[45] are presented in profile, with incurved horns, but without legs. Various features of the amulets suggest the work of a single artisan, or a single workshop: the torsos are nearly identical, although the proportions vary slightly; the pierced tenons and the delicate horns imply the careful removal of material; and the decorative lattices within the torso are carefully incised so as to retain a white substance. Due

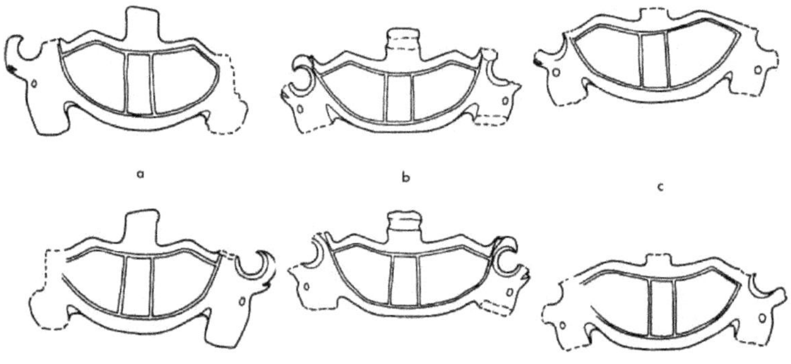

Fig. 8. Double Bull ivory amulets, after Hendrickx, "Bovines in Egyptian Predynastic and Early Dynastic Iconography," fig. 16.1.

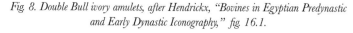

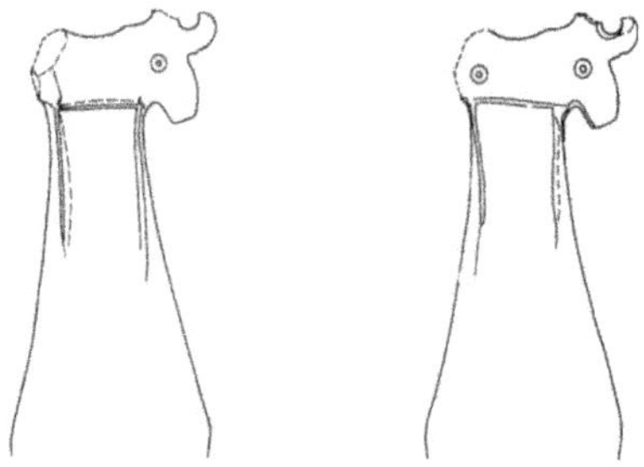

Fig. 9. Rhomboidal palette surmounted by a double bull, after Hendrickx, "Bovines in Egyptian Predynastic and Early Dynastic Iconography," fig. 16.10.

[39] A. Vila, *La Prospection Archéologique de la Valée du Nil Sud de la Cataracte de Dal (Nubie Soudanaise)* Fascicule 4 (Paris, 1976).

[40] Vila, *La Prospection Archéologique*, 52, fig. 21.2. The image is 30 cm long.

[41] Hendrickx, "Bovines in Egyptian Predynastic and Early Dynastic Iconography," 278.

[42] Hellström, *The Rock Drawings*, vol. 1, part 1, 27–29; Wengrow, *The Archaeology of Early Egypt*, 112.

[43] Hendrickx, "Bovines in Egyptian Predynastic and Early Dynastic Iconography," describes and places these objects in context. He applies the term "double bull" to the bovine on the Hunters' Palette (p. 280); a macehead is in the form of the "foreparts of two bulls" (p. 280); there are three amulets with a "double bull's head" (pp. 280–81, fig 16.1); and the rhomboid palette has "antithetical bull's heads" (pp. 292–93, fig. 16.10). Hendrickx considers the amulets to be related to the Hunters' Palette bull, but a possible relationship between all these objects is not specifically proposed.

[44] S. Hendrickx, "Crafts and Craft specialization," in E. Teeter (ed.), *Before the Pyramids*, OIMP 33 (Chicago 2011), 93–98.

[45] Hendrickx, "Bovines in Egyptian Predynastic and Early Dynastic Iconography," 280–81, fig. 16.1. Hilton Price, the buyer of the amulets, was told that they came from Abydos: H. Price, "Some Ivories from Abydos," *PSBA* 22 (1900), 160–61, figs. 1–3. His pictures reveal a white substance remaining in parts of the incised lattice.

Table 1. Representations of double bulls, object and script, and by period

Period	Object				Script	
	Type	**Museum / Location**	**Acc. No.**	**Material**	**Text**	**Material / Location**
Predynastic	Hunters' Palette, relief	BM; Louvre	EA 20790 E.11224	Mudstone	Hunter's Palette glyph?	Mudstone
	mace head	Ashmolean	E.134	Serpentine		
	amulets (3)	Brussels	E.3381a-c	ivory		
	rhomboid palette	Brussels	E.2182	mudstone		
	3 rock drawings (a)	Abka				
	rock drawing (a)	Mograkka				
Old Kingdom	Stamp seal	Berlin	23371	rock crystal	determinative	Unas Pyr.
	Stamp seal		na	gold	determinative	Pepi I Pyr.
	Cylinder seal		na	na		
Dynasty 11	Neferu wall relief	MMA	26.3.353a-b	limestone		
	Khety wall relief	MMA	26.3.354g2	limestone		
	Aashyt coffin frieze	EM	na	paint wood		
Middle Kingdom	"Assassif" tusk	EM	JE 56273	ivory		
	"Gourna" tusk	EM	JE 18640	ivory	Determinative Dynasty 13	Papyrus
	"Luxor" tusk 1	BM	EA 24426	ivory		
	"Luxor" tusk 2	MMA	19.2.18	ivory		
	Axe head (b)	MMA	21.2.7	bronze		
New Kingdom	Esna Amulet	Liverpool	25.11.05.163	Carnelian		
	"Apis" Amulet (c)	Private Coll		Carnelian		
	Amarna mold	na	na	Glaze?		
Dynasty 26	"Apis" Amulet	UCL	UC28168	Glaze		
	"Apis" Amulet	St.Peterburg	na	Glaze		
	"Apis" Amulet	Price Coll.	na	Glaze		
	"Apis" Amulet	Louvre	AF13553	Faience		
Ptolemaic Period					Petosiris Determinative	tomb wall
Period ?					Canal	3rd Nome

a: Dates of rock art are uncertain | na: not available

b: Date: Intermediate Period - New Kingdom, see text (c) Period uncertain

BM: British Musum; EA: Egyptian Museum; MMA: Metropolitan Museum of Art

UCL: University College London (Petrie) For references see text

to their size (ca. 10 x 5 cm), proportions, and the single suspension loop, it is doubtful that the amulets were practical and for daily adornment. The fact that there are three virtually identical examples points to some standardization of design and suggests that the motif enjoyed recognition beyond the owners. Price seems to imply that he purchased the three objects at the same time, so it is tempting to suppose that they were discovered in close proximity, perhaps even coming from a shrine or a workshop.

What appear to be the remains of an ischiopagus-type bull surmounts a unique rhomboidal cosmetic palette now at the Brussels Museum (E.2182) (fig. 9).[46] In this case as well, the creature is shown in profile with incurved horns. Unfortunately, one of the fore-parts is partially missing, but the Egyptians' stylistic preferences would argue for a symmetrical figure. This mudstone palette has been associated with comparable diamond-shaped palettes crowned by two different designs interpreted as bull's horns (Petrie's palette types 91 T-U).[47] Only a handful of this particular type of palette is of known provenance; the dates range from Naqada IC to (mostly) Naqada IIA–IIC.[48] The mounting of the double bull on a tip of a palette is reminiscent of single birds on two rhomboidal palettes now at the Cambridge Museum of Archaeology (Z 36229) and the Fitzwilliam Museum (E.16.1930). The latter was excavated by Brunton at Matmar and assigned sequence dates of SD 41–48[49] (Naqada IIA–IIC?), so it is possible that the double bull rhomboid was produced in that time frame as well.[50] Rhomboidal palettes, like other cosmetic palettes, were used to grind decorative minerals which, applied to the body, were thought to also provide protection to the owner.[51] All of the above are likely to have been elite goods produced by skillful craftsmen; the carving in stone of the fragile bulls' horns at an extremity of the rhomboid palette must have been challenging.

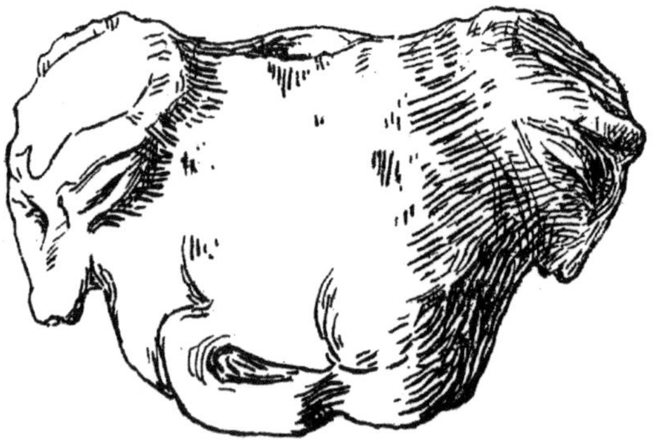

Fig. 10. Double bull mace head from Hierakonpolis (Ashmolean Museum E.134). After Adams, Ancient Hierakonpolis: Supplement, *12.*

The double bull motif also appears in the form of a double-ended, serpentine macehead now at the Ashmolean Museum (E.134) (fig. 10). Found in the Main Deposit at Hierakonpolis,[52] it is the only predynastic double bull object of known provenance (although probably not in its original location). In terms of size, it falls between most of the pear-shaped personal or votive maces[53] and the large, ceremonial Scorpion and Narmer maceheads

---

[46] Hendrickx, "Bovines in Egyptian Predynastic and Early Dynastic Iconography," 292–93, fig. 16.10.

[47] Hendrickx, "Bovines in Egyptian Predynastic and Early Dynastic Iconography," 292, after W. M. F. Petrie, *Prehistoric Egypt,* BSAE/ERA 31(London, 1920), pl. XLIV; W. M. F. Petrie, *Corpus of Prehistoric Pottery and Palettes*, BSAE/ERA 32 (London, 1921), pl. LVIII. The "horns" on type 91T are shaped as a continuous unbroken curve with tipped ends; palette type 91U horns are the incurved type.

[48] Hendrickx, "Bovines in Egyptian Predynastic and Early Dynastic Iconography," 313, Appendix K.

[49] G. Brunton, *Matmar*, British Museum Expedition to Middle Egypt 29 (London, 1948), pl.15, item #29.

[50] The dating question is revisited below. Ostriches, hippos, giraffes, and other quadrupeds have been carved in comparable style, topping the handles of early predynastic ivory and bone combs. See, for example, D. Patch, "From Land to Landscape" in Patch (ed.), *Dawn of Egyptian Art*, 57–59. The examples cited by Patch date mostly to Naqada late NI-NII (3700–3300).

[51] S. Hendrickx, "Decorated Palettes of a Different Type: Rhomboids from Hierakonpolis and Beyond," *Nekhen News* 30 (2018), 35–36. He notes that rhomboids are almost exclusively found in tombs, indicating private ownership.

[52] J. Quibell, *Hierakonpolis I,* ERA 4 (London, 1900), 8, pl. 19, item #3; pl. 25 (lower half). B. Adams, *Ancient Hierakonpolis: Supplement* (Warminster, 1974), 12. Quibell describes the serpentine mace as the foreparts of two bulls. The bovine identification has been largely accepted, see W. Needler, *Predynastic and Archaic Egypt in The Brooklyn Museum.* Wilbour Monographs 9 (Brooklyn, 1984), 261; Cialowicz, *Les palettes Égyptiennes aux motifs zoomorphes et sans décoration,* 45–46; Hendrickx "Bovines in Egyptian Predynastic and Early Dynastic Iconography," 280, among others. However, it has also been described as a "mace in shape of double ram's head" by J. Quibell and F. Green, *Hierakonpolis II,* ERA 5 (London, 1902), 30, 38, but also as a "double bull mace" on pl. XLVIIIa of the same volume, and as an antelope on a label accompanying the object on display at the Ashmolean Museum (July 2019). The mace is definitely of serpentine, not limestone as noted in Quibbell and Green, *Hierakonpolis II,* 38 and Adams, *Ancient Hierakonpolis Supplement* 12.

[53] The author measured the length as 13.1 cm, as opposed to c. 10.6 cm cited in Quibell and Green, *Hierakonpolis II*, pl. XLVIIIa; also

also found there. The speckled bichrome stone renders the recumbent creature's characteristics somewhat difficult to discern. However, the ears and horns are carved in relief, the latter curling backwards around the head (protruding horns being impractical on a stone macehead). Drilled almond-shaped holes, possibly originally encrusted, serve as eyes; one eye socket has been chipped off, and the top of the haft hole is damaged. The legs, also in relief, are folded beneath the torso, but they are missing on one side, as though sheared or ground off. The modern base permits upright display.

The macehead was found in a trench in the southwest verger of the Main Deposit. Within a distance of three meters lay other maceheads, various small objects, and a grouping that included the Two Dog Palette, now also at the Ashmolean Museum (1896.1908.E3924).[54] It is difficult to judge the importance of the double bull macehead in the context of those particular finds. However, it has been argued that the objects from the Main Deposit are associated with an area where festivals of kingship and royal power were celebrated, in particular the *sed*.[55] The objects are generally "royal in nature," many of them readily associated with kings, the ideology of kingship and power.[56] The presence of various carved ivories associated with royal cultic activity, e.g., curved staffs and scepters, is notable in this regard.[57] Most significant of the predynastic objects are the Narmer Palette and the Scorpion and Narmer Maceheads. Evidently, the double bull piece is not in the same class. However, it is distinguished as the only zoomorphic macehead discovered at the site, and by the serpentine stone and bovine attributes long associated with kingly power. These features also set it apart from the hundreds of other maces[58] and the numerous small, seemingly mundane, items—vases, bowls, and animal figurines.

The Main Deposit itself has been variously compared to a disposal pit for mainly discarded temple offerings or to a foundation deposit establishing the cultic significance of the site.[59] According to the latter view, certain objects selected for burial—ivories, weapons, and other symbols of power—were "decommissioned" so as to render them actually and symbolically powerless; the presence of stone maceheads is suggestive of such a process.[60] Interestingly, Green observed that the damage around the top of the haft hole of the double bull macehead could be explained by hammer strokes intended to remove the haft prior to burial,[61] actions that would support the "decommissioning" hypothesis. That someone would take the trouble to do so implies that the object and the removal of the haft was of some importance.

The Double Bull as an Emblem?

Taking account of the marked differences in representational forms, a broad similarity exists between the predynastic objects decorated with the double bull. That, and the rarity of the motif, raise questions whether these objects are somehow related, perhaps inspired by a common source in about the same time frame. Unfortunately, the lack of provenance rules out establishing reliable dates for any of these objects. The Naqada III Period is

---

Adams, *Ancient Hierakonpolis Supplement*, Appendix 3a (pl. 48a). The author weighed the mace, and at 441 grams, it is likely to be heavier than most maceheads.

[54] Quibell and Green, *Hierakonpolis II*, 31.

[55] L. McNamara, "The Revetted Mound at Hierakonpolis and Early Kingship: A Reinterpretation," in B. Midant-Reynes and Y. Tristant (eds.), *Egypt at its Origins 2. Proceedings of the International Conference 'Origin of the State, Predynastic and Early Dynastic Egypt,' Toulouse (France), 5th–8th September 2005*, OLA 172 (Leuven-Paris, 2008), 901–36.

[56] W. Fairservis, *The Hierakonpolis Project Season January to March 1978: Excavation of The Temple Area on The Kom El Gemuwia*, Occasional Papers in Anthropology (Poughkeepsie, 1983), 11; noted in McNamara, "The Revetted Mound at Hierakonpolis," 927.

[57] McNamara, "The Revetted Mound at Hierakonpolis," 929.

[58] Most of the numerous maceheads found in the Main Deposit are small, disc, or piriform in shape, the latter generally carved of limestone. Quibell and Green, *Hierakonpolis II*, 30–32, pls. XLVIIIa, b. For a compendium of those now at the Petrie Museum, see Adams, *Ancient Hierakonpolis*, xiii, 5–13. Several are only partially perforated indicating a purely votive function.

[59] Needler, *Predynastic and Archaic Egypt*, 259–60; Wengrow, *The Archaeology of Early Egypt*, 184, following H. Whitehouse, "A Decorated Knife Handle from the 'Main Deposit' at Hierakonpolis," *MDAIK* 58 (2002), 425–46.

[60] Wengrow, *The Archaeology of Early Egypt*, 184; Whitehouse, "A Decorated Knife Handle," 432.

[61] Adams, *Ancient Hierakonpolis Supplement*, 12, on the basis of F. Green's notes.

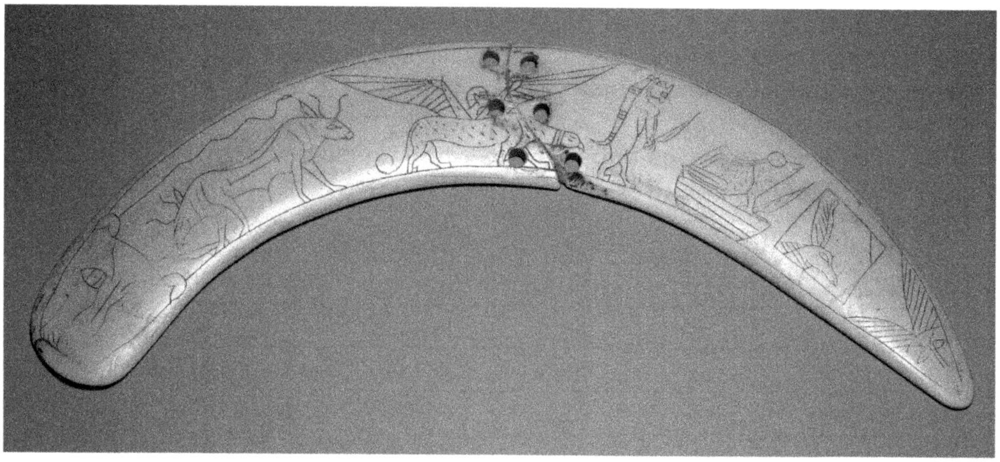

Fig. 11. Wand (tusk) with double bull, Middle Kingdom (BM EA 24426). Courtesy of the British Museum.

nastic Period are seen in the Dynastic Period as well, namely the migration of the double bull motif between different categories of objects and materials. Generally the renderings appear to have elite, or even royal, associations. Three seals bearing images of the double bull date to Dynasty 5.[78] They vary by type and material. A stamp seal of rock crystal is inscribed with a double bull centered on a "Hathor symbol," the latter framed by a facing lion pair and a recumbent Seth animal (?) (Berlin 23371). The same motif is inscribed on a cylinder seal. On a gold disk seal, two addorsed bovid foreparts are positioned under a recumbent Seth animal. The fact that there are three seals, whether intended for private or administrative use, suggests that the motif was commonly recognized, at least among the local elite, and, perhaps, that it had been known for some time.

Approximately three centuries elapse before the double bull is attested again, this time in Dynasty 11 funerary contexts with royal associations. At Deir el-Bahari, three similar motifs are dated to the reign of Mentuhotep II.[79] Only the one preserved in an object frieze inside the coffin of Aashyt, a queen consort,[80] shows the complete intended grouping—a double bull between two flails[81] inserted in ceremonial jars. This assemblage is flanked on both sides by rearing cobras and Wepwawet standards "collectively suggesting rights of kingship."[82] Only fragments of wall reliefs depicting a double bull and flails have survived in the tomb of Queen Neferu,[83] likely the first queen of Mentuhotep, and in the tomb of the treasurer, Khety.[84] The multiple examples of the double bull iconography in these elite contexts suggest that it was well established in this period. Probably somewhat later in date, but also from the Middle Kingdom, are four magic wands (also called tusks, or birthing tusks) each inscribed with a double bull.[85] Two are now in the Egyptian Museum, Cairo (JE 56273, JE 18640), and one each in the Metropolitan Museum of Art (MMA 19.2.18a, b) and the British Museum (EA 24426, fig. 11).[86] Three of them are said to have been purchased at Luxor; only JE 56273 in the Egyptian Museum was excavated, by the Metropolitan Museum at Asasif tomb 839.[87] The horns of the bulls on two wands are incurved while those on the other two are lyre-shaped. However, their stylized elongated bodies are similar, with interior lines follow-

[78] Quirke, *Birth Tusks*, 502 (fig. 5.110).

[79] Of the seven depictions of the double bull dating to the Middle Kingdom, at least six are associated with the Theban area.

[80] https://en.wikipedia.org/wiki/Ashayet (accessed January 10, 2021).

[81] The earliest representations of the flail make it one of the most ancient symbols of kingship and the ruler's coercive power. See T. Wilkinson, *Early Dynastic Egypt* (London-New York, 1999), 190.

[82] Quirke, *Birth Tusks*, 480.

[83] Quirke, *Birth Tusks*, 479–80.

[84] Metropolitan Museum of Art, 26.3.354g2 in Quirke, *Birth Tusks*, 480, (https://www.metmuseum.org/art/collection/search/565097) (accessed June 13, 2022).

[85] The double bull is not among the most represented motifs on the more than 150 known tusks.

[86] Quirke, *Birth Tusks*, 105 (fig. 2.9), 187 (fig. 2.83), 269 (fig. 3.47), 289 (fig. 3.65).

[87] Quirke, *Birth Tusks*, 105–6. Precise dates for the tusks are uncertain.

ing the curvature of the back, neck, and front leg attachment, and tails hang from the midsections. The wands are made of hippopotamus ivory, which, from earliest times, was believed to be magical, imbuing the user with the power of the beast.[88] Virtually all the wands are decorated with threatening animals, mythical monsters, and deities.[89] Most conveyed a negative connotation to the ancient Egyptians, but they were enlisted on the tusks against hostile real and supernatural powers. To that end, many figures, including the double bulls, brandish knives.

Fig. 12. Axe head with double bull, circa Middle Kingdom (MMA 21.2.7). Courtesy of the Metropolitan Museum.

A bronze parade axe in the Metropolitan Museum (MMA 21.2.7; fig. 12) has a double bull in openwork. It has been attributed to as early as the First Intermediate Period and as late as Dynasty 18.[90] The creature is shown in silhouette, its main features being clearly defined; the potentially important tail, discussed elsewhere in this paper, is as pronounced as on the Hunters' Palette and magical tusks. As a weapon, the axe conceptually recalls the predynastic double bull macehead (fig. 10), but it has been considered insufficiently sturdy for combat.[91] Hayes remarks that it is one of several such axes that are thought to have been given to officers of the armed forces as rewards for valor and were carried with them on state occasions. Given their prominent ceremonial role, it is likely that the bull image was well known at the time, at least among the elite, as were any magical powers attributed to it.

From the New Kingdom, three objects depicting the double bull are attested (Table 1). One of them is a mold for the manufacture of small double bull inlays or pendants unearthed at Tell el-Amarna.[92] Referring to a corpus of such objects from that site, Quirke notes that Akhetaten flourished not only during the period of the royal cult of Aten, but at least through the early years of Tutankhamun as well. This complicates the question whether some of deities represented in a host of recovered molds were worshipped during the period of the Aten cult or only afterwards;[93] this uncertainty applies to the double bull inlay as well. Of a different nature are two amulets carved in carnelian. The Liverpool World Museum notes that the example in its collection was found in a dated grave at Esna.[94] The upright bovine body is shown with a somewhat swayed, elongated back, reminiscent of the double bulls on the Middle Kingdom wands. The other carnelian example, a recumbent bull, was sold by the Zurqieh Company, an antiquities dealer, to a private buyer. In this case, the provenance is unspecified, or unknown, and the attribution to the New Kingdom is unexplained.[95] Interestingly, the dealer described it as a "double-sided Apis bull amulet." Its shape is comparable to that of the Louvre example (figs. 13a, b).

---

[88] For example, see G. Steindorff, "The Magical Knives of Ancient Egypt," *The Journal of the Walters Art Gallery* 9 (1946), 42.

[89] Steindorff, "The Magical Knives of Ancient Egypt," 48.

[90] In Quirke, *Birth Tusks*, 506, it is attributed to the First Intermediate Period-early Middle Kingdom. But see Metropolitan Museum https://www.metmuseum.org/art/collection/search/544818?searchField=AccessionNum&ft=21.2.7&offset=0&rpp=40&pos=1 (accessed March 19, 2022), for a Middle-early New Kingdom (Dynasty 12–18) date.

[91] W. Hayes, *Scepter of Egypt II: A Background for the Study of the Egyptian Antiquities in the Metropolitan Museum of Art: The Hyksos Period and the New Kingdom (1675–1080 B.C.)* (New York, 1959), 213 (fig. 126). Hayes proposes that in this particular setting, the double bull symbolized the "two-valved door of heaven and its Janus-like guardian."

[92] Quirke, *Birth Tusks*, 538 (fig. 5.156, (306m)), 539, citing W. F. M. Petrie, *Tell el Amarna* (London, 1894), pl. XVII, no. 306. The image was drawn from a recovered mold but apparently no pendant created from it was found. See Petrie, *Tell el-Amarna*, 28 and pl. XVII.

[93] Quirke, *Birth Tusks*, 537.

[94] National Museums Liverpool 25.11.05.163. The museum website describes it as "a finely carved carnelian double headed bull or calf amulet" found together with New Kingdom pottery in Esna grave 69E'05. The suspension loop is carved on the side of the creature rather than on its back. The dimensions are 30 l x 13 h x 8 w mm. https://www.liverpoolmuseums.org.uk/artifact/double-headed-bull-amulet (accessed March 18, 2022).

[95] Zurqieh Co, L.L.C., an internet antiquities dealer based in Dubai.

https://www.vcoins.com/fr/stores/zurqieh/171/product/ancient_egypt_carnelian_double_sided_apis_bull_amulet__new_kingdom_1400__1200_bc/1167407/Default.aspx (accessed April 3, 2022). The dimensions are given as 23 l x 18 h mm; copies of on-line photos are available from the author. The proposed New Kingdom date may have been arrived at by comparison to the Liverpool carnelian

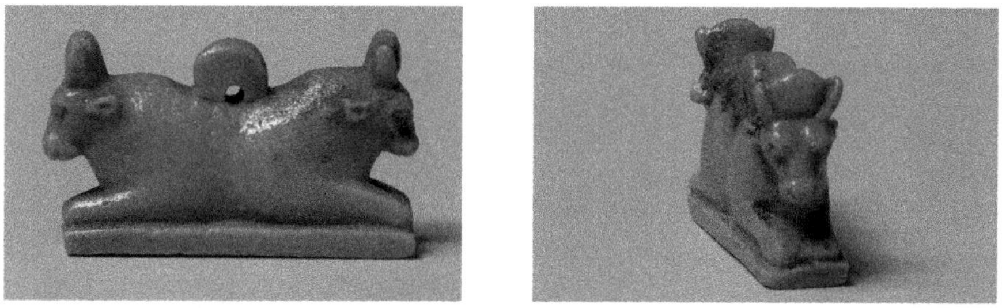

Fig. 13a–b. Two views of a double bull amulet, Late Period (Louvre AF 13553). Courtesy of the Louvre Museum.

Four amulets representing recumbent double bulls have been dated to the Late Period (Table 1). The aforementioned specimen, made of shiny blue-green faience (figs. 13a–b), is described by the Louvre as two antithetical bull protomes.[96] Petrie uses a similar formulation, labeling the three amulets as "two bulls, foreparts" shown only in profile (fig. 14).[97] He adds that this is a "very ancient combination, appearing on one of the predynastic slate palettes" (i.e., the Hunters' Palette) that had been discussed by Capart.[98] All three are thought to belong to Dynasty 26. The material is a glazed ceramic tinted in different shades of green; two of the amulets, 223a and b, were found at Hawara in the Fayyum. Although there are similarities among the amulets, the variations in modeling suggest the work of separate ateliers; the differences also imply that the basic motif was generally recognized, at least in a particular area.

As was noted, Zurqieh Co. labelled its amulet as a "double sided Apis bull." Each of the two heads is capped by a sun disc set between the horns, a symbol associated with the Apis. The uraeus, also linked to Apis, has been omitted.[99] The Apis identification receives support from the Walters Art Museum that interprets a two-sided pendant in its collection as formed by addorsed Apis and leonine foreparts.[100] As regards the Louvre pendant, a conservator mentions the discs, but not a possible relation to the Apis.[101] In these three cases, the solar discs are clearly identifiable in frontal views of the amulets, but in profile, they appear

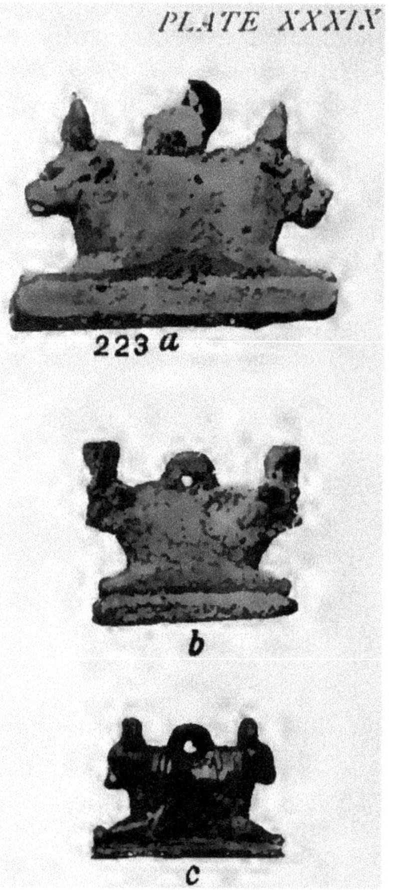

Fig. 14. Double bull ("Double Apis") amulets, Dynasty 26, after Petrie, Amulets, *pl. XXXIX.*

amulet (which however lacks the sun discs). Dodson remarks on the increase in evidence for the Apis cult in the New Kingdom, in particular the treatment of the animal after death: see Dodson, "Of Bulls and Princes," 19.

[96] The accession number of the Louvre pendant is AF 13553 and its dimensions are 3.25 l x 1.85 h x 0.8 w cm. https://collections.louvre.fr/recherche?q=AF+13553 (accessed March 21, 2022).

[97] Petrie, *Amulets*, 45 and pl. XXXIX, nos. 223a-c. Petrie notes that one is in the St. Petersburg collection and that another was in the Hilton Price collection. Amulet 223b, measuring about 2.5 l x 2 h cm is now in the Petrie Museum (LDUCE-UC28168). https://collections.ucl.ac.uk/Details/collect/42497 .

[98] Petrie, *Amulets,* 45; Capart, *Primitive Art*, fig. 170.

[99] On statues (or larger figurines) of the Apis, the upper head "assembly" consists of a sun disc between two horns, a uraeus abutting the front of the disc and ears below the horns (all of this is difficult to see in profile). Small amulets omit the uraeus, and often the ears as well. The Apis, associated with Memphis, is sometimes shown without the sun disc. The Mnevis bull, associated with Heliopolis, is also shown with a solar disc. Presumably identification of the intended bull on the amulets would be uncertain.

[100] The Walters Art Museum dates the amulet to the Late Period: https://art.thewalters.org/detail/5134/combined-fore-parts-of-lion-apis-bull/ (accessed March 18, 2022). Acc no. 48.1747, dimensions are 1.9 l x 0.96 h x 0.2 w cm.

[101] https://collections.louvre.fr/recherche?q=AF+13553 (accessed March 21, 2022).

only as vertical knobs (e.g., fig. 13a). The question arises whether Petrie's three double bull amulets—shown only in profile (fig. 14)—were also intended to depict the Apis. Petrie himself is silent on the issue; he also fails to mention the knobs (which almost certainly depict solar discs).[102] Elsewhere in the same volume, Petrie discusses "normal" Apis amulets, although his figures show them only in profile.[103] In fact, the knobbed heads of these Apis amulets are indistinguishable from those of the double bull amulets (fig. 14). It is very likely that the three double bull amulets represent what may be referred to more accurately as "double Apis" amulets.

If this identification is accepted, the five "double Apis" amulets could reflect the syncretism of two different iconographies, each with its own distinct symbolism. It is possible that in the Late Period (or even earlier), the ancient double bull motif merged with that of the then popular Apis bull image, the resulting creation retaining the double bull's important concepts of symmetry and duality. Symbolically, the new iconography incorporated the traditional protective aspect of the double bull (discussed below) and the religious potency of the Apis (as the herald of the creator god, Ptah). Consequently, the "double Apis" amulet could have been considered an exceptionally powerful symbol (to somewhat modify Huyge's terminology[104]). It may be recalled that the practice of creating symbolically extra powerful composite animals, by incorporating the particular potency of each creature, harkens back to the Predynastic Period.[105] Bearing in mind that the sample of Apis bull amulets is very small, it is nevertheless interesting that no double bull amulet without sun disc seems to be known after the New Kingdom. Is this an accident of discovery, or did the perceived symbolically superior power of the double Apis amulet become dominant, the way that market forces drive out old "inferior" products? Or did the ancient double bull image simply disappear because of the popularity of the "normal," perhaps better understood, Apis amulets?

Continuity, Change, and Chronological Gaps

The discussion of various representational objects bearing the double bull image reveals a more or less continuous record from the late Predynastic to the Late Period (Table 1). During this time, the bull image remains broadly unchanged:[106] the horns generally remain incurved, the proportions of the foreparts vary only modestly, and the creature is depicted upright or recumbent (or lacking legs). The identification is never in question. Continuity is also apparent in the apotropaic attributes of the double bull image. The protective nature of several predynastic objects has already been mentioned (for the Hunters' Palette, see below). The first attested Dynastic Period objects are the late Old Kingdom seals that are likely to be apotropaic as well as functional. However, the interpretation of the double bull images in the Dynasty 11 funerary context is uncertain. Due to their relative chronological proximity to the antecedent apotropaic seals, it is possible that those tableaux were intended to be protective as well, that is, the double bull safeguarded the deceased in the afterlife.[107] In the Middle Kingdom, magic tusks are known to have been employed to protect individuals and possibly places.[108] The impressive ceremonial axe bearing a double bull was likely to have been a symbol of power as well as protection through deterrence. In the New Kingdom and the Late Period, the double bull is attested in the form of ceramic, wearable amulets. Thus, while considerable changes occur in the types of objects represented, especially from the Predynastic to the Dynastic Period, a certain continuity is evident in the bull image as well as in the apotropaic

[102] The Petrie amulet at UCL is shown only in profile, without comment.

[103] Petrie, *Amulets*, 43–44, pls. XXXVII (207a-g), XLV (207h).

[104] Huyge used the term "double powerful": D. Huyge, "A Double Powerful Device for Regeneration: The Abu Zaidan Knife Handle Reconsidered," in Hendrickx, Friedman, Cialowicz et al. (eds.), *Egypt at Its Origins*, 823–36.

[105] Huyge, "A Double Powerful Device for Regeneration," and see also Hendrickx, "Composite Animal Palette," in Teeter, *Before the Pyramids*, 200–201, regarding OIM E11470, dated to Dynasty 1.

[106] Precise comparisons are complicated by differences in materials, art form, and mode of execution.

[107] This possible function of the double bull in the funerary tableau has not previously been proposed. The Metropolitan Museum interprets the assembly of the funerary ointment jars and flails as ritual objects symbolizing the purification of the deceased (https://www.metmuseum.org/art/collection/search/565097). In this context, the double bull may symbolize the setting and rising sun.

[108] For example, Metropolitan Museum of Art tusk 26.7.1288 is inscribed: "We have come in order to draw protection of life around the lady of the house, Merisenebes," in Quirke, *Birth Tusks*, 251.

qualities. The double bull motif enjoyed a remarkable lifetime, but in general it is represented on minor items. Apparently, it never entered the mainstream of Egyptian art in the form of statues and sizeable wall paintings.

Chronological gaps pervade the archaeological record of the double bull summarized in Table 1. Of course, they are to be expected given the vagaries of object survival and excavation, but political and religious developments may have played a role as well. As noted above, the disappearance of the double bull in the late Predynastic (or Early Dynastic) Period may have been a consequence of the unification of Egypt and the replacement of traditional (indigenous) art forms by "official" (formal) iconography. Fisher has suggested that in the Old Kingdom, traditional magical objects largely vanish due to constraints on the freedom of expression of popular superstition.[109] The reappearance of the double bull image in the Middle Kingdom is particularly interesting because of the possible parallels with the re-emergence of several fabulous predynastic creatures. The serpopard, griffin, and Seth animal, prominently portrayed on several predynastic ceremonial palettes, reappear in a host of Middle Kingdom contexts. According to one theory, temple furnishings and other offerings that had become redundant were consigned to the ground sometime during the Old Kingdom[110] only to be recovered during the temple renovations undertaken in the Middle Kingdom.[111] It is likely that the ancient Egyptians' reverence for antiquities explains the resurrection of old images and the discovery of new applications for them. A comparable scenario may apply to the double bull, supposing the recovery of the Hunters' Palette or other double bull objects.[112] Or perhaps the ancient finds in the Middle Kingdom merely revived the fortunes of a symbol that had largely fallen out of use.[113] Double bull objects are attested again during the New Kingdom and Late Period, but their absence during Second and Third Intermediate Periods could be due to the upheavals of those times, accidents of preservation, or simply temporary loss of popularity. Despite this, the record creates the impression that the bull image and its apotropaic symbolism never completely disappeared from public consciousness.

The Double Bull as a Predynastic Hieroglyph?

A number of scholars have considered the possibility that the double bull on the Hunters' Palette is an early hieroglyph. Capart, after rejecting several explanations for the image, concluded that it may have a phonetic value.[114] In support of this hypothesis (as he refers to it), he drew attention to the word  in the Pyramid Texts of Unis,[115] where the double bull 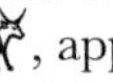, appears as a determinative. Capart adds that a variant of this word appears in the Dynasty 6 pyramid of Pepi I, the determinative, however, taking the form of two bulls' heads facing in opposite directions 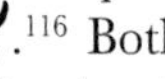.[116] Both variants have been interpreted by Gardiner as "referring to doors or a door, possibly such as could swing both forwards and backwards."[117] Many years later, Fischer

109 As evidence, Fischer cites the paucity of amulets found in the Old Kingdom cemeteries of Memphis. See H. Fischer, "The Ancient Egyptian Attitude Towards the Monstrous," in A. Farkas, P. Harper, and E. Harrison (eds.), *Monsters and Demons in the Ancient and Medieval World: Papers Presented in Honor of Edith Porada* (Mainz am Rhein, 1987), 13–23. Apparently greater freedom of expression during the Middle Kingdom gave, as he puts it, "monsters a new lease on life."

110 Wengrow, *The Archaeology of Early Egypt*, 184, after B. Kemp, "The Osiris Temple at Abydos," *MDAIK* 23 (1968), 138–55. At Elephantine, the site of the early shrine was simply filled in and paved over (Kemp, *Ancient Egypt*, 116).

111 Wahankh Intef II, the second king of the 11th (Theban) Dynasty initiated the renovation of several temples. See W. Grajetzki, *The Middle Kingdom of Ancient Egypt* (London, 2006), 14–15. Grajetzki's text indicates that Intef II's projects are the earliest known of the Middle Kingdom and would have preceded the reign of Mentuhotep II.

112 The provenance of the Hunters' Palette is unknown. Wilkinson thought it possible that the palette, and other large ceremonial palettes of the late Predynastic Period—the Battlefield, Libyan and Bull palettes—were found in the temple area of Abydos: Wilkinson, *Early Dynastic Egypt*, 314. Also see notes to https://collections.louvre.fr/ark:/53355/cl010007344; Hendrickx, Förster, Piquette et al., "A History of the Visualization of the Hunters' Palette," 124.

113 On the survival of pre-formal ("primitive") art alongside "official" art, see Kemp, *Ancient Egypt*, 134.

114 Capart, "Remarques sur une des palettes archaïques du Musée Britannique," 109–10.

115 The entry is now designated PT 275 (3). See J. Allen, *New Concordance of the Pyramid Texts, vol. 3, PT 247-421* (Providence 2013). https://oi-idb-static.uchicago.edu/multimedia/301965/PT%20III%20(247-421,%20Pyr%20257-751).pdf

116 Capart, "Remarques sur une des palettes archaïques du Musée Britannique," 109–10. The Pepi I texted is designated PT 534 (9). J. Allen, *New Concordance of the Pyramid Texts, vol. 4, PT 422–538* (Providence 2013): https://oi-idb-static.uchicago.edu/multimedia/301966/PT%20IV%20(422-538,%20Pyr%20752-1302).pdf.

117 A. Gardiner, "A Unique Funerary Liturgy," *JEA* 41 (1955), 13, n. 5. Found in a tomb below the Ramesseum, the Dynasty Thirteen

Fig. 15. Double bull determinative, Dynasty 13 text, after Gardiner, "A Unique Funerary Liturgy," pl. 13.

proposed that the predynastic double bull "may well be a purely hieroglyphic creation."[118] The hieroglyph appears in the verb *ḫns* in a funerary liturgy of Dynasty 13 (fig. 15). Fischer translated it as to "move back and forth" (or, to move one way and then another).[119] Figure 15 is a reproduction of a tracing showing the almost complete bull determinative.[120] It includes an appendage stemming from the midsection that is commented on later.

The double bull sign is also known from the tomb of Petosiris (4th century BC), where the "backwards and forwards" interpretation of the verb is also supported.[121] Finally, a canal in the Third Nome of Lower Egypt on the western edge of the Delta was named for, or associated with, the double bull ( ). Also see below.[122]

Fischer did not speculate on the possible origin of the double bull on the Hunters' Palette or the rationale for its apparent eventual adoption as a determinative. More generally it has been observed that "many aspects, such as the development of the early sign corpus and the thought process behind it, have received little attention."[123] It is proposed here that the observation of the grazing back and forth movement of a real double bull may have given rise to a verbal expression for the complex movement[124] and, perhaps, a name for the creature, "that which moves back and forth," in the vein of animals (or people) named after the way they habitually move, e.g., grass hopper, pointer (dog), and darter (fish).That an animal would have inspired a word, or phrase, in ancient Egypt would not have been unusual. Ikram has noted that animals provided the inspiration for much of the Egyptian script. By her calculation, "about 20 percent of hieroglyphic signs are derived from animals, and for their religious beliefs."[125] The coining of an expression, or name, as proposed for the double bull would seem consistent with Frankfort's view of the profound influence of cattle on the ancient Egyptian language. He noted that the animals played an "altogether extraordinary role in the consciousness of Egyptians. This led, on the one hand, to religious veneration, and, on the other hand, to the spontaneous production of cattle images and cattle similes whenever some unusual observation required figurative speech for an adequate expression."[126]

---

fragmentary papyrus scroll was photographed by Quibell soon after its unrolling in 1927. Gardiner, "A Unique Funerary Liturgy," 9. Gardiner cites Pyramid Texts 416a and 1266c, which correspond to Allen's PT 275 and PT534 and Capart's Unas 527 and Pepi I 496, respectively.

118 Initially, Fischer considered the possibility that the double bull on the Hunters' Palette depicted a real, monstrous animal, such as the dicephalous turtle represented in the form of a predynastic palette (see footnote 10). However, he rejected the monstrous animal hypothesis, proposing instead that the double bull was a hieroglyph, as used in the funerary liturgy document translated by Gardiner. It is likely that Fischer was independently aware of the two Pyramid Texts bearing the double bull determinative, although he does not mention it. See Fischer, "The Ancient Egyptian Attitude Towards the Monstrous," 15 and plate 1, fig. 3.

119 Fischer, "The Ancient Egyptian Attitude Towards the Monstrous," 15.

120 Gardiner, "A Unique Funerary Liturgy," 13, pl. III, cols. 48–49.

121 Gardiner, "A Unique Funerary Liturgy," Gardiner also mentions the presence of the double bull hieroglyph on stela C1 of the Louvre, 13, n. 5. The 4th century BC date for the tomb of Petosiris is according to the Landesmuseum in Hannover. https://www.tuna-el-gebel.com/en/tombs.html (accessed January 23, 2020).

122 H. Brugsch, *Dictionnaire Géographique d'Ancienne Égypte* (Leipzig, 1877–1881), 1022.

123 I. Regulski, *The Origins and Early Development of Writing in Egypt* (2016), 3 (https://www.oxfordhandbooks.com/view/10.1093/oxfordhb/9780199935413.001.0001/oxfordhb-9780199935413-e-61) (accessed January 23, 2021).

124 Importantly, this explanation of the verb's origin does not require the backward projection of the dynastic usage to the Predynastic Period. According to Gardiner, in , "the determinative suggests simultaneous movement in opposite directions." See Gardiner, "A Unique Funerary Liturgy," 13. Clearly this is physically impossible and does not accord with motion described by the phonetic component of the verb. However, if the double bull, the logographic component, is assumed to represent the abstract idea of backward and forward movement (as argued here), the determinative and the phonetic components become fully complementary.

125 S. Ikram, "Speculations on the Role of Animal Cults in the Economy of Ancient Egypt," in M. Massiera, B. Mathieu, and Fr. Rouffet (eds.), *Apprivoiser le sauvage/Taming the Wild*, CENIM 11 (Montpelier, 2015), 211.

126 Frankfort, *Kingship and the Gods*, 163. Frankfort also observes (p. 162): "Egyptian texts of the most varied nature abound in metaphors, appraisals, and other expressions which relate to cattle."

Interestingly, the representational forms of the double bull—amulets, seals, etc.—existed in parallel with script during two, possibly three, millennia (Table 1). It is difficult know if any interaction occurred between the two modes of communication. Both show continuity throughout that period: the objects tend to be consistently apotropaic (as noted above), while the meaning of the hieroglyphic verbs is unchanging. The latter is consistent with the general observation that once a hieroglyph was introduced, it tended to have the same meaning for thousands of years.

Did the Double Bull Represent a Real Animal? Some Last Thoughts

To return to the original question: was the Hunters' Palette double bull intended to represent a real conjoined twin bull or something else entirely? It has been described as a composite figure consisting of the addorsed protomes of two bulls, the fused forequarters of two bulls facing in opposite directions, or variations thereof. The description evokes the idea of a purely mechanical connection of two potentially stand-alone parts. However, the physiology of the double bull, including the tail, would seem to rule out such a hypothesis. A protome, or forepart, of an animal (or human) is considered, and generally shown, as a head on an upper torso only. However, the foreparts of the Hunters' Palette creature extend to the pelvic area from which stems a prominent appendage, probably a tail that was considered sufficiently important to be depicted on the Hunters' Palette, the Thirteenth Dynasty hieroglyph, the magic tusks and the metal ax.[127]

Alternatively, it has been proposed that the double bull is simply another mythical creature—a hybrid animal—in the vein of the serpopard, griffin, and Seth animal,[128] all well-known from the predynastic Two and Four Dog Palettes.[129] Probably of later dates are the ibex-tilapia and the elephant-vulture inscribed on the Abu Zaidan knife handle, and the bull-fish in the form of a cosmetic palette.[130] As the term implies, the hybrid creatures are composites of elements of different animal species (in a sense they do recall real animals because of their single heads, torsos with four legs and tails (or fins, depending on the creature). On the other hand, the double bull image on the Hunters' Palette is basically different, departing from the hybrid model in several respects: the two foreparts belong to the same species; and the back-to-back assembly creates an unusual two-headed physiology. The most important distinction, however, is that the double bull image mirrors a real creature, an ischiopagus bovine, documented by veterinary science (which also applies to the mutant creatures represented on several cosmetic palettes). The rock drawings at Abka and Mograkka could be explained by someone simply observing and hammering the image of a real animal into stone, without recourse to innovation. Therefore, rather than to compare the double bull relief to a fantastic, hybrid creature, it would seem more apt to compare it to the freak animals represented in the predynastic cosmetic palettes.[131] Those, too, are likely to have represented real animals that an artisan could simply observe and copy.

Although the incidence of ischiopagus in bovines is very low,[132] it is nevertheless likely that multiple viable specimens appeared in the Nile Valley throughout the ages. The rock drawings at Mograkka and Abka are possible records or their presence. At Abka, two nearly adjoining double bovines with circular horns pose questions whether they portray a single or different individuals and, if the latter, were they coterminous? The separate

[127] Assuming the appendage is a penis does not alter the argument.

[128] The hypothesis that these hybrids somehow served as models for the double bull would be difficult to verify, at least on the basis of available archaeological evidence.

[129] Both palettes may be earlier than the Hunters' Palette. According to Hendrickx, the decorated palettes are generally attributed to the end of Naqada II and the very beginning of Naqada III: Hendrickx, "Iconography of the Predynastic Period," 80.

[130] Huyge, "A Double Powerful Device for Regeneration," 831–33, discusses the ibex-tilapia and the elephant-vulture. The hybrid bull-fish palette, which Hendrickx has dated to Dynasty 1, is at the Oriental Institute Museum (OIM E11470). Hendrickx, "Composite Animal Palette," 200–201.

[131] See note 10, above.

[132] The malformation is thought to be a function of genetic and environmental factors that can vary between place and time. Regional data on bovid conjoined twinning is not systematically collected. However, in human populations, a relatively high incidence of the condition has been noted in Africa and India. See Y. Khan, "Ischiopagus Tripus Conjoined Twins," *APSP Journal of Case Reports* 2.1 (Jan-April, 2011), 5. (https://www.ncbi.nlm.nih.gov/pmc/articles/PMC3418005/) (accessed July 12, 2020). The apparent concentration of double bull rock art images in Nubia is noteworthy in the context of Khan's observation.

petroglyph of the double bovine with straight horns suggests the existence of a third individual in the area. A different animal may be assumed to have inspired the image on the Hunters' Palette, given its probable Upper Egyptian origin.[133] At least at Abka, evidence is lacking for artistic interchange that might explain the transmission of the image between the two venues. The historical association of a double bull with a canal in the Third Upper Nome of Egypt may provide another candidate for an individual specimen.[134] It would seem plausible that a cattle-herding community would name a geographical feature after a remarkable creature that had been present in the area. Whether any other ischiopagus bovines (or more generally, double bovidaes—sheep, goats, antelopes)[135] appeared during the Dynastic Period, perhaps explaining some of the "reappearances" of the image cited in Table 1, is difficult to know.

The Hunters' Palette as an Exhibit of Military Power: A Digression

Little is known of the historical context of the Hunters' Palette and the double bull related objects. Referring more broadly to predynastic low relief scenes in stone, Kemp notes the total absence "of many of the most distinctive features of the iconography of historic times. Almost the whole of the later iconography of kingship is missing" until the Scorpion Macehead and the Narmer Palette.[136] Hendrickx and Förster have made similar observations about the ceremonial palettes: "most of the stylistic characteristics of the Early Dynastic representations are not attested for the Predynastic period."[137] It is interesting to compare the iconography of the Hunters' Palette, dated broadly to Naqada III,[138] to certain rock tableau for which the dates are known with some confidence. Inscription 1, a tableau on the Gebel Tjauti rock formation, exhibits one of the earliest extensive corpuses of "early royal iconography that is paralleled in the art and inscriptions of the late Predynastic Period and Dynasty 0."[139] Those documents, together with the finds from Tomb U-j at Abydos, suggest that the tomb and the Gebel Tjauti inscription are contemporary, the authors proposing a date of Naqada IIIA1 (ca. 3200 BC).[140] The prominent early hieroglyphic inscriptions on the rock tableaux at el-Khawy,[141] also considered royal markers, belong to the tradition and time of the Tomb U-j as well.[142] Together, the Gebel Tjauti and el-Khawy tableaux suggest an iconographic thread that leads to the formal style.[143] However, significantly, the iconography of Hunters' Palette has little, if anything, in common with those two tableaux or the finds at Abydos or Hierakonpolis.[144] Yet Baines seems to have considered it among the artistically superior (and probably royal) of the

133 An unprovenanced double bovine-like palette, purchased by J. H. Breasted in Egypt in 1920, is now at the Oriental Institute Museum (E 11469). See Hendricks, "Iconography of the Predynastic and Early Dynastic Periods," 79–80, fig. 8.5. Hendrickx describes it as it having "double bovine heads and bird heads," and dates it to Naqada IIA-IIB. The museum's website (https://oi-idb.uchicago.edu/id/257a02ca-2e93-40a7-a2de-2e0cc4f95abb (accessed July 15, 2020), describes it as a "double hartebeest with head and horns," though that description predates Hendrickx's study of the piece. However, the object is ambiguous, combining elements of an ischiopagus with unrelated predynastic artistic conventions.

134 Brugsch, *Dictionnaire Géographique d'Ancienne Égypte*, 1022.

135 Insert new footnote here: Of interest in this context is the inspiration for a potmark of a double animal of unknown identity incised on a storage jar found in the C Group cemetery at HK 27C. See R. Friedman, "Animals Among the Nubian Residents at Hierakonpolis," in *Nekhen News* 33, 34–35. Given the long legs and backward sweeping horns, it may represent a type of antelope.

136 Kemp, *Ancient Egypt*, 92.

137 Hendrickx and Förster, "Early Dynastic art and iconography," 826–52.

138 As noted above, a time frame of 3300–3100 BC is cited for Naqada III, which would correspond from Naqada IIIA to roughly late Naqada IIIB, according to C. Köhler's chronology table in Teeter (ed.), *Before the Pyramids*, 8.

139 R. Friedman and S. Hendrickx, "Gebel Tjauti Rock Inscription 1," in J. Darnell, D. Darnell, R. Friedman et al., *Theban Desert Road Survey in the Egyptian Western Desert* I: *Gebel Tjauti Rock Inscriptions 1–45 and Wadi el-Hôl Rock Inscriptions 1–45*, OIP 119 (Chicago, 2002), 10–19.

140 Friedman and Hendrickx, "Gebel Tjauti Rock Inscription 1," 11.

141 J. Darnell, "The Early Hieroglyphic Inscription at el-Khawy," *Archéo-Nil* 27 (2017), 49–64, figs. 4–7.

142 Darnell, "The Early Hieroglyphic Inscription at el-Khawy," 49–64.

143 Perhaps significantly, representations of a stork (or storks) have been recovered at Gebel Tjauti, el-Khawy and on tags found in Tomb U-j, but the bird is absent on the Hunters' Palette. For tags with storks from Tomb U-j see G. Dreyer, "Tomb U-j: A Royal Burial of Dynasty 0 at Abydos," in Teeter (ed.), *Before the Pyramids*, 135 (fig. 14.18).

144 The exception may be the falcons on the standards carried by men leading the columns of hunters. At some time, the falcon becomes

decorated palettes.[145] A possible explanation is that the Hunters' Palette (and the three other bull-related objects) represent an alternative, but advanced, tradition of a chiefdom/proto-kingdom that existed roughly in parallel with the one responsible for the rock tableaux and that eventually prevailed in unifying the country.

Kemp has considered the political-military environment in which proto-states functioned, observing that the more successful "incipient city states had become engaged in more organized conflicts over territory."[146] The military challenges of the times may be a theme of the Hunters' Palette that has not received much attention; several aspects of the martial iconography stand out. First of all are the standards and the military-like order of the men positioned around the long edges of the palette. Second, most of the men carry weapons more suitable for combat than for capturing and controlling animals.[147] Seven men are armed with metal-headed spears (two men hold two spears) and an equal number hold bows (some with bunches of arrows), both instruments designed to kill.[148] Several men hold maces used in hand-to-hand combat or for dispatching prisoners (fit or wounded).[149] Throw sticks, traditionally associated with hunting, can be effective anti-personnel missiles as well; a number of throw sticks terminate in onion-shaped heads also rendering them dangerous as maces. Of course, a prudent hunting party would carry killing weapons, as the fallen lions attest. However, if the primary purpose is to capture sacrificial animals, the preponderance of heavy weapons would seem to be out of place: of a total of nineteen men, fourteen—nearly three-quarters—bear spears and bows. Only two men wield ropes, which also have military applications, including to bind captives. Lastly, it has been proposed that the oval shaped objects attached to the backs of certain men are backpacks, meant to extend the range of hunting in the desert;[150] they would be essential equipment for an expeditionary force as well. The ostentatious display of weapons may have been intended to show off the varied arsenal at the disposal of the group.[151] Virtually all the men menacingly brandish maces, double-ended axes or throw sticks as though prepared to smite enemies.[152] Perhaps most indicative of the intent to display weapons are the several archers who hold a bow in one hand and a mace in the other, ruling out the possibility of a bow shot.[153]

The Hunters' Palette has been interpreted using the ideas of Kemp[154] and Baines, namely that "the hunting and domination of wild animals probably symbolizes the maintenance of order and the containment of disorder."[155] These ideas are reflected in the probably earlier iconography of the Hierakonpolis (Two Dog)

---

recognized as a royal symbol, but in the context of the Hunters' Palette this aspect has not been argued. See, e.g., Hendrickx, Friedman, and Eyckerman, "Early Falcons," 138.

[145] Baines, "Origins of Egyptian Kingship," 112.

[146] Kemp, *Ancient Egypt*, 96–97. Kemp has pointed to documents depicting conflicts involving walled settlements. One of these is the Cities (Tjeheju) Palette at the Cairo Museum (JE27434) that he interprets as fortified towns being attacked by animals symbolizing the monarchy. The Battlefield Palette (British Museum (EA 20791)) also depicts scenes of human conflict. It has been proposed that the Gebel Tjauti Rock Inscription commemorates a military operation by Abydos in the early part of Naqada III, possibly against a target in the region of Naqada. See Friedman and Hendrickx, "Gebel Tjauti Rock Inscription 1," 17.

[147] Cialowicz has questioned the types of weapons portrayed: "the heavy equipment of the hunters is of little use hunting herbivores." Cialowicz, "Les palettes Égyptiennes aux motifs zoomorphes et sans décorations," 67. Except for the lions, live animals are portrayed in the center of the palette, implying capture by lasso and other non-lethal means, possibly by nets that are not shown.

[148] A recent reconstruction of the missing segment of the Hunters' Palette places a hunter holding two spears and a double-ended ax (or mace) behind the missing archer (only his bow survives); another spearman follows, holding a throw stick. The number of spears and bows cited in the above text also includes those in the reconstruction, including the spear reworked as a standard. Hendrickx, Förster, Piquette et al., "A History of the Visualization of the Hunters' Palette and a Tentative Reconstruction of its Missing Part," 141, 143.

[149] In a hunting mode, maces may have been used to stun netted creatures to bring them under control.

[150] Hendrickx, Förster, Piquette et al., "A History of the Visualization of the Hunters' Palette," 138.

[151] Elements of the scene—the uniformity of dress, the orderliness of the men, the display of weapons, and other features remind the author of modern, national day military parades favored by some countries. The display of military might a key objective.

[152] The variety of designs of spearheads, throw sticks, maceheads and double ended instruments is surprising for a group of limited size. See Legg's detailed drawings in Hendrickx, Förster, Piquette et al., "A History of the Visualization of the Hunters' Palette," 128, fig. 6.

[153] The portrayal of men with two weapons may stylistically hint at ancient fighting techniques. After a man had shot all his arrows, or thrown his spear, his mace, or throw stick (either initially hung from the waist) would become the primary weapon. Enemies at some distance may have been attacked first with throw sticks, spears coming into play in closer fighting. (No daggers are portrayed on the palette but they may have been carried as well.) The host of differentiated weapons suggests multiple combat scenarios.

[154] Kemp, *Ancient Egypt*, 92–97.

[155] Baines, "Origins of Egyptian Kingship," 111.

Palette where two hunting dogs frame varied creatures, thereby symbolizing the "containment of unrule in the universe."[156] Similarly, Hendrickx explains the canines on that palette as symbolizing the control of the chaotic forces represented by the encircled desert animals.[157] These ideas also play a role in the interpretation of the Hunters' Palette, the flanking dogs on the Two Dog (and Four Dog) palette having been replaced by two rows of hunters who drive a file of animals forward.[158] The Hunters' palette is also thought to express the significance of hunting in predynastic society. In the scene, returning elite hunters display captured animals and weapons, reinforcing their prestigious status. Their return is likely followed by the slaughter of the game and feasting by the elite that has ritualistic overtones.[159]

Kemp has noted that military conflict is among the sources of disorder in the late predynastic period.[160] The incorporation of a military theme in the Hunters' Palette—the demonstration of military might and the preparedness to respond to threats—may have been a response to more frequent conflict, or an actual existential threat to the proto-kingdom. In the context of ancient beliefs, the palette may have been intended to magically intimidate enemies, if not actually defeat them. The above multiple interpretations of the Hunters' Palette would seem compatible and complementary. However, taking note of its predominant share of the palette's surface, the demonstration military power may have been the principal message.

The apotropaic connotations that the double bull appears to have evoked raises the question whether the Hunters' Palette itself was considered an amuletic device in its time. As noted above, one interpretation of the palette centers on hunting and it's social/political role. However, hunting could be a dangerous activity, an issue that has been raised by several authors. Patch has suggested that the hazards may be symbolized on the palette by the hunter who has fallen victim to a lion. Perhaps not always fully appreciated is the potentially great personal risk implicit in the apparent practice of capturing animals alive. Even if the hunted quarry were bovidae (as opposed to ferocious, predatory animals), the hooves and horns of panicked, netted or lassoed, creatures could cause considerable harm, if not death. Periodic hippopotamus and crocodile hunts posed equal, if not greater dangers (although the objectives of these encounters were different, and these beasts are not represented on the Hunters' Palette). Undoubtedly, the horrors of military conflict were well understood by fighting men and were of equal, if not of greater concern. In each of these circumstances, whatever the particular challenges, it would seem likely that elite hunters or troop leaders—they probably were the same individuals—would have sought the protection of the supernatural, for example, through the enactment of pre-hunt or pre-combat rituals. As a part of these rites, the perceived powers of the Hunters' Palette may have been evoked, with the joint double bull-shrine possibly playing some role.

[156] Kemp, *Ancient Egypt,* 93–94, fig. 31.

[157] Hendrickx, " L'iconographie de la chasse dans le contexte social prédynastique," 129. Also, Hendrickx and F. Förster, "Early Dynastic art and iconography," 834–36.

[158] Hendrickx, " L'iconographie de la chasse dans le contexte social prédynastique," 130–31.

[159] Hendrickx, " L'iconographie de la chasse dans le contexte social prédynastique," 130–31. Hendrickx also draws attention to the close relationship between military/political power and hunting in the Naqadian culture, the hunt promoting skill with weapons and cooperation between men.

[160] Kemp, *Ancient Egypt,* 96.

Fourth Report on the Publication and Conservation of the Tomb of Ramesses III in the Valley of the Kings (KV 11)

ANKE WEBER
Humboldt-Universität zu Berlin, Germany

KLARA DIETZE
Universität Leipzig, Germany

LUTZ POPKO
Sächsische Akademie der Wissenschaften zu Leipzig, Germany

GARETH REES
Oxford Archaeology East, Cambridge, United Kingdom

SANDRO SCHWARZ
Staatliche Museen zu Berlin, Preußischer Kulturbesitz, Germany

Abstract

The following article presents preliminary results of a sondage in the burial chamber (hall J) and a visual survey in the areas H, I, J, Ja-Jd, K1, K2, and L during the 2019/2020 field season carried out by The Ramesses III (KV 11) Publication and Conservation Project in the tomb of pharaoh Ramesses III.[1] *The detailed description and interpretation of the initial excavation work were omitted from the Second Report*[2] *because it required more extensive discussion. The authors present their archaeological field work, their research, and the systematic examination of finds. Several unexpected finds shed new light on the use and reuse of KV 11. A sondage in the burial chamber provides insight into ancient and modern activities within the tomb. Additionally, more information is presented on photogrammetry in KV 11 as well as a provisional sketch of a site management plan centered on the digitization of a visitors' itinerary. The work was carried out under the supervision of the Egyptian Ministry of Tourism and Antiquities with support by Ahmed Hussein Youssef Mohamed and our Egyptian workmen.*

الملخص

يعرض المقال التالي النتائج الاولية للمجس في حجرة الدفن (حجرة J) والمسح البصري في المناطق H و I و J و Jd-Ja و K1 و K2 و L خلال الموسم الميداني 2020/2019 الذي نفذه مشروع رمسيس الثالث (KV11) للنشر والحفظ في مقبرة رمسيس الثالث.[3] تم حذف الوصف

[1] Website: www.ramesses-iii-project.com, accessed September 7, 2020.
[2] Anke Weber, Judith Bunbury, Klara Dietze et al., "Second Report on the Publication and Conservation of the Tomb of Ramesses III in the Valley of the Kings (KV 11)," *JARCE* 56 (2020), 213–44.
[3] www.ramesses-iii-project.com, تم زيارة الموقع في ٢٠٢٠-٩-٧

Journal of the American Research Center in Egypt 58 (2022), 233–65
http://dx.doi.org/10.5913/jarce.58.2022.a012

التفصيلي والتفسير لأعمال الحفر الأولية من التقرير الثاني[4] لأنها تتطلب مناقشة أكثر شمولاً. يقدم الباحثون عملهم الميداني الأثري، وأبحاثهم، والفحص المنهجي للاكتشافات. تلقي العديد من الاكتشافات الغير المتوقعة ضوءًا جديدًا على استخدام وإعادة استخدام مقبرة KV11. وفر المجس الذي تم في حجرة الدفن نظرة ثاقبة للأنشطة القديمة والحديثة داخل المقبرة. بالإضافة إلى ذلك، يتم تقديم المزيد من المعلومات حول القياس التصويري للمقبرة KV11 بالإضافة إلى رسم تخطيطي مؤقت لخطة إدارة الموقع التي تركز على رقمنة خط سير الزائر. تم تنفيذ العمل تحت إشراف وزارة السياحة والآثار المصرية بدعم من أحمد حسين يوسف محمد وعمالنا المصريين.

The tomb of pharaoh Ramesses III (KV 11) was subjected to flooding on a number of occasions, which caused sedimentation of fine-grained limestone particles, sand, and debris on the floor of the tomb's low-lying rear part.[5] One of the goals in the 2019/2020 field season was to collect information about the flood layers in the burial chamber and the surrounding rooms (H, I, Ja-Jd, K1-K2, L) in order to develop a plan for their systematic excavation. Accordingly, Anke Weber, and Klara Dietze focused on the tomb's rear part (see fig. 10). A sondage was cut into an already existing recent disturbance to reveal the chamber's floor level and to determine the height of each layer on top of it. An additional aim was to identify the highest flood water level in the burial chamber (hall J), which is the lowest part in the tomb, with a depression below the aisles of the cavetto cornice. A visual survey was therefore conducted. To this end, the hall was divided into digging squares which serve as a basic grid for documentation.[6] Small-scale clearances of significant parts of hall J were undertaken in squares V/VII, II, II/IV, XV, and X/XII as well as in room H (threshold between G and H) in order to investigate the *status quo* (height of debris, consistency of layer, etc.) for future excavation. The finds from the sondages were mainly processed by Anke Weber, Klara Dietze, Lutz Popko, and Sandro Schwarz. The most significant objects and the distribution of findings will be discussed below, together with a first attempt to contextualize them. Gareth Rees adds further notes on his photogrammetric work in the tomb, which will lead to an accurate 3D model of the entire site that can serve as a basis for conservation needs. Finally, the first steps toward the realization of a site management plan are presented by Anke Weber and Sandro Schwarz.

Excavation

The sondages in preparation for future excavation took place mainly in the burial chamber (hall J), while another one was conducted in room H. The area of a recent disturbance and some places close to it, as well as a part between pillars 1 and 3 were cleared of rubble and debris to reveal the floor level and to analyze the chronology of flooding events in KV 11. Several small finds were discovered during this work. Table 1 provides additional information about the dimensions and dating of finds as well as the corresponding plate numbers. To navigate through the table, readers are advised to use the numbers in brackets behind the description of objects.

The Recent Disturbance

An already existing pit lent itself for a sondage in order to draw up a chronology of the destruction of the rear area of the tomb. The pit had been dug into the sediment and sand layers in the southwestern corner of hall J, below the level of the cavetto cornice and in front of pillars 6 and 8. While no information is known about the origin of the pit, the date of its formation can at least be limited to a certain period of time. Hitherto, the photographs taken by Araldo de Luca in hall J in 2000[7] and an image of Matjaž Kačičnik from October 2005[8] served

[4] Weber et al., "Second Report, 213–44.

[5] Anke Weber, "First Report on the Publication and Conservation of the Tomb of Ramesses III in the Valley of the Kings (KV 11)," *JEA* 104.1 (2018), 62–65. Weber et al., "Second Report," 223 and fig. 15.

[6] Weber, "First Report," 68, fig. 9.

[7] Photograph nos. 30367-30368, cf. https://www.araldodeluca.com/de/bild/30367 and https://www.araldodeluca.com/de/bild/30368, accessed March 31, 2021.

[8] Image no. 20942: https://thebanmappingproject.com/images/20942jpg, accessed May 3, 2021. The TMP-website under supervision of the American Research Center in Egypt is continuously updated by our project with news and recent results.

Fig. 1. Excavation layers in the burial chamber. © The Ministry of Antiquities, The Ramesses III (KV 11) Publication and Conservation Project, 3D image: Willem Hovestreydt.

Fig. 2. Profile of layers of baked sediments (1), sandy mud (2), and fine quartz sand (3) within the recent disturbance. North–south view. © The Ministry of Antiquities, The Ramesses III (KV 11) Publication and Conservation Project, photo: Johannes Kramer.

as *termini post quem*, because the pit was not yet visible. A visit of the field director to the tomb's rear part in 2014[9] provided the *terminus ante quem* as the disturbance was already present at that time. Therefore, the disturbance

[9] The work was undertaken under the supervision of the Ministry of Tourism and Antiquities during Weber's Ph.D. thesis research.

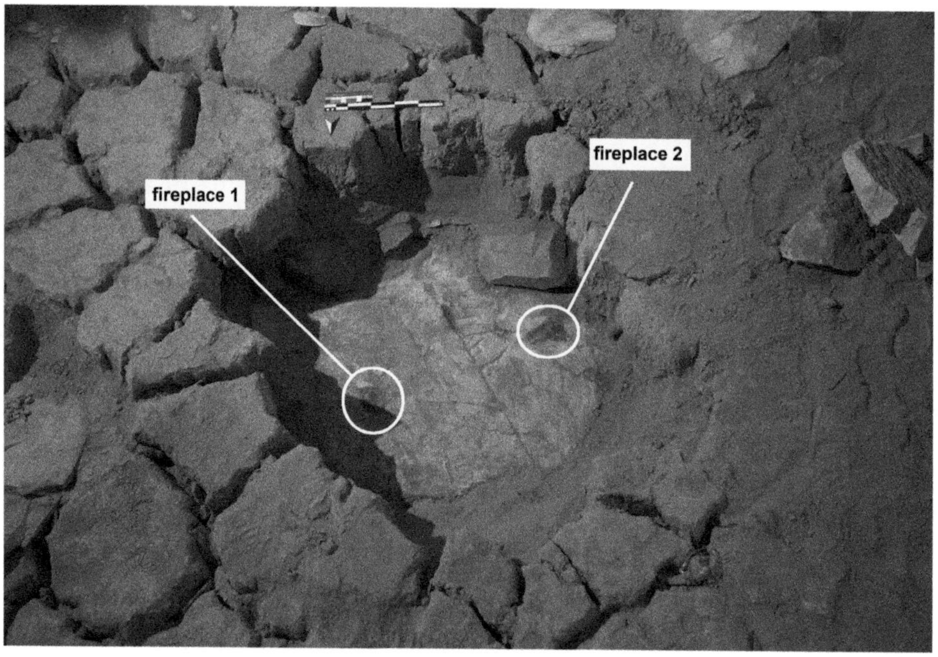

Fig. 3. Floor level of hall J with fireplaces inside the recent disturbance. © The Ministry of Antiquities, The Ramesses III (KV 11) Publication and Conservation Project, photo: Anke Weber.

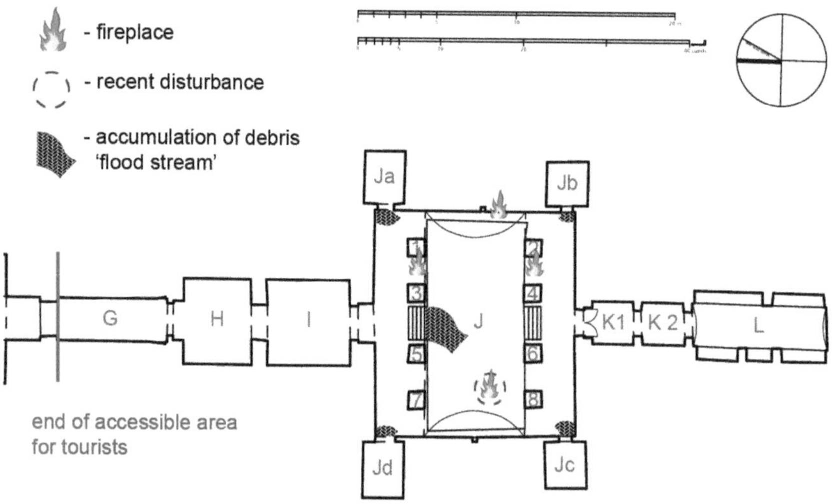

Fig. 4. Ground plan of the tomb's rear part including fireplaces found during the 2019 survey. Source: Theban Mapping Project.

must have been produced between 2005 and 2014. Around the pit, a fragment of a sarcophagus,[10] limestone fragments, a jar stopper (Table 1, #4), and mud clumps were arranged at the surface, making a provenance from the pit highly likely.

[10] See Weber et al., "Second Report," 239–43; Lea Rees and Helen Strudwick, "The Sarcophagus Ensemble of Ramesses III from KV 11: New Insights from Old Documents and Recent Finds," in Anke Weber, Martina Grünhagen, Lea Rees, and Jan Moje (eds.), *Akhet Neheh: Studies in Honour of Willem Hovestreydt on Occasion of His 75th Birthday*, GHP Egyptology 33 (London, 2020), 52, fig. 8.

The excavation of the sondage started in winter 2019/2020 by lifting the remaining sediment clumps from inside the pit. The baked sediments were carefully split to protect possible small finds within. However, only a few fragments of wood were discovered inside, the rest of the sediments consisting of loam only. The sediment clumps covered a ca. 30 cm deep compact sand layer of fine quartz and mica (figs. 1 and 2).[11] The sand will be properly examined, and its consistency analyzed by our petrologist, Judith Bunbury, as it seems likely that it was brought inside the tomb on purpose. This was suggested by the homogeneity of the small-grained sand, without contamination, the uniform height within the entire depression of hall J[12], and the consistent yellow color. More research is needed, however, and may shed new light on this question.

Several objects were discovered during the excavation of the sand, among them two fragments of red granite sarcophagi lids.[13] The objects were positioned directly on the floor level, covered by sand. According to the results of the survey conducted in hall J, the sand layer seems to be present in all parts of the burial chamber. In the sondage, only a very thin black layer of charcoal and ash separates the sandy layer from the original bottom of hall J. The origin of this layer is associated with two small-scale fireplaces that were observed on the floor (fig. 3). Further fireplaces were found during the survey all over the burial chamber (fig. 4).

Thus, the results from the sondage suggest the following destruction timeline of the rear part of the tomb: When hall J was accessible and its floor still visible, visitors probably came to the tomb and set up small fireplaces as a source of light. Whether or not the array of small finds, all found close to the floor level, is connected to these visits, remains a question for further studies. It is clear, however, that the majority of these finds have a secondary origin.[14] Some time afterward, the floor of hall J was (artificially?) covered with sand. Then, the tomb was flooded several times. The overlaying sediment clumps are again to be associated with flood waters that washed loam and debris into the rear part of KV 11.

Findings from the Recent Disturbance

In the following, the most important findings from the sondage will be introduced and discussed. As they are all from the same find spot, they are categorized according to their material. The three rose granite fragments from the recent disturbance have already been discussed in the project's Second Report.[15]

Plant Residues (fig. 13)

The remains of plants from the recent disturbance range from very tiny pieces of leaves and stems (Table 1, #3, 12, 54) to parts of fruits[16] (Table 1, #7, 8) and a date kernel (Table 1, #14). Although the discovered residues are relatively small in size, it became obvious that the high amount, especially from the sand layer and beneath, justifies a preliminary explanation as either visitors' remains or ancient burial gifts. It is likely that some were originally stored in one of the ceramic bowls of which we found several shattered pieces within the recent disturbance. Unfortunately, the pottery fragments were damaged so severely that only one sherd lends itself to further interpretation (see below). A date kernel (Table 1, #14) does not seem to be part of a funerary meal as one would expect the flesh of the fruit to have been preserved to some extent. However, the yellow layer surrounding the object reveals that it must have been within the tomb before the flooding events happened as the color was

---

11 For formation of the different layers see Weber et al., "Second Report," fig. 15.

12 The sand can be found everywhere in the burial chamber. Measurements were taken in several places in hall J. In the depression, the sand has a height of ca. 30 cm, while it is between 13 and 16 cm on the cavetto cornice.

13 On the fragments, see Weber et al., "Second Report," 239–42.

14 More evidence of this was found during our most recent work. For more information, see the Fifth Report planned for *JARCE* 59, 2023.

15 See note 10.

16 Most probably *Mimusops schimperi* or *Mandragora officinalis*. Both lead to the conclusion that they were parts of a funerary offering meal or a plant collar.

washed out from the linen shroud and attached to the kernel.[17] It may as well be a leftover from a visitors' snack in the 19th century. New finds around the pit will hopefully contribute to a clearer picture.

Pottery (fig. 16)

Some pottery from the well shaft of KV 11 was already excavated by David and Barbara Aston and Ted Brock in the 1990s.[18] Most of the discovered fragments consisted of mixed marl-silt clay and were originally parts of amphorae. Although one of the objects (no. 91) seems to be nearly complete, most of the finds are sherds, parts of which may have belonged to the original tomb equipment while others were washed inside KV 11 by flash floods from other areas of the wadi. The same interpretation seems likely for the findings from the recent disturbance (and other parts of the tomb's rear; see below), as the sherds belong to different vessels, and the fractures are in some cases eroded due to water. One significant find (Table 1, #10) was the partly damaged rim or upper neck of an open form Nile silt vessel containing an adhering piece of yellow linen and remains of a whitish substance on the inner surface.[19] It is unclear whether it was used as a container for mummified organic remains or just held the linen bandages which were left over after the mummification process. The linen can also be part of the vessel's sealing. Further investigation and excavation of the area around the recent disturbance will probably yield more pottery fragments.

Textiles (fig. 14)

In addition to the plant remains and the pottery finds, the linen fragments found thus far suggest that a burial was at least partly excavated from the pit at some point in time. The textiles (Table 1, #5, 9) were found within the sand layer in a highly fragmented condition. Some pieces of the same fabric (e.g., Table 1, #26) were discovered in the immediate vicinity to the recent disturbance, which makes it most likely that they originally came from the pit. Many of the shattered fragments show traces of burning, which confirm the assumption that small fires were lighted before the flooding. The sediment clumps that were lifted from the recent disturbance show traces of mud imprints underneath that reveal that linen bandages must have been placed below, as they show a textile pattern. This means that a mummy was probably embedded within the sand layer and may have been partly exposed. After the flooding event, the sediments settled and covered the exposed part. When drying out, the textile pattern of the linen shroud was impressed on the sediments, which then cracked and separated, leaving the present floor level on top of the original bottom.

Bone Fragments (fig. 14)

In addition to plant residues and textile pieces, some (probable) human bones were discovered in the sand layer of the recent disturbance, the most significant of which are presented in this section. A thorough analysis of these remains by osteologists will take place in one of our upcoming field campaigns and will be presented in future reports.

A long bone (Table 1, #11), probably a human tibia, with a partly preserved diaphysis and a mostly preserved epiphysis at one end was found broken along the longitudinal axis. The cortex is almost completely preserved, with the cancellous bone being visible at the fractures at both ends of the fragment.

Four adjacent vertebrae (Table 1, #15–18) were found while extracting the dry sediment clumps from the surface of area V. The cortex is mostly yellow and turns brown and grey in some parts, while the vertebral bodies are white in the anterior half of their lateral left side. The superior articular facets are partly preserved, but the spinous and transverse processes are damaged. Reassembled, the bones form a slight concave curvature. Remarkably, the vertebral body of no. 1 is slightly deformed, and the planned osteological examination will determine whether this shape is within the range of normal variety, by disease or, post-mortem, by the pressure

[17] For further information see below the description of limestones with adhering linen and plaster/cartonnage remains.

[18] David Aston, Barbara Aston, and Edwin C. Brock, "Pottery from the Valley of the Kings—Tombs of Merenptah, Ramesses III, Ramesses IV, Ramesses VI and Ramesses VII," *Ä&L* 8 (1998), 149 and 174–75.

[19] The consistency of this substance is going to be analyzed during one of our next field seasons.

of the sediment. Sometime after death, the joints between the vertebrae of the spine were artificially destroyed, as can be shown by a diagonal cut with a depth of 0.3 cm that runs from left to right at the dorsal half of the cancellous bone at the cranial transverse plane of vertebra no. 1. The circumstances of this cutting require further investigation, as well.

The bones under discussion reveal that at least one adult human or parts of a mummy were covered in the pit by the sand layer. Other findings close to the bones and the tomb's floor level, such as linen fragments, plant residues, and pottery with adhering textile, suggest a burial context.

Limestone Fragments with Adhering Linen and Plaster Remains

Within the recent disturbance and inside the sand layer, close to the chamber's floor level, several fairly large limestone fragments came to light. They were found with adhering layers of yellow sand, (burnt) textile fragments, and some brownish material that contains white chalky pieces. Some of the stone fragments were also covered with a white powdery layer which was partly preserved as remaining plaster. The latter indicates that these stones come from the original tomb decoration and were either moved intentionally to this place or fell from the ceiling. However, chisel marks commonly used for the preparation of the ceiling were not observed. Most likely, the stone fragments were transported to this area for a special purpose, probably in close connection with the find of human remains and linen fragments. The yellow color of the stones as well as the surrounding and adhering sand must come from the yellow-colored linen bandages in the recent disturbance. When the floodwater entered this area, the color must have been washed out from the cloth and penetrated the sand as well as objects nearby. For this reason, it is most likely that the mummy shroud was colored with safflower, as this natural plant color is water-soluble.[20]

Wooden Objects (fig. 15)

Wood was the material most frequently found, which is surprising as the burial chamber suffered repeated and severe flooding. Most likely, the well-preserved pieces were protected by the solid fine-grained sand layer in which they were found. Only a limited number of wooden pieces was discovered outside the recent disturbance, but it seems clear that those must have been placed within the burial chamber before the pit was excavated. Many wooden objects were found which may have belonged to sarcophagi or furniture, but most of them are too fragmentary to be certain and lack colors. Some still have wooden dowels or dowel holes, indicating that they were attached to another piece of wood. In the following, only relevant pieces that can be (roughly) identified will be discussed.

Ushabtis/Figurines (fig. 15)

During the excavation of the sand layer in the sondage in hall J, a fragment of the lower part of a wooden ushabti, ending in a sculptured, protruding foot, came to light (Table 1, #13). There is a horizontal broken edge on the upper side that shows traces of intense burning. On the underside, however, no traces of fire are visible. On all sides, the object has smoothed surfaces that are deformed—possibly because of water. On the right side of the base, a light blue pigment can be seen, suggesting that the object once was partly colored blue. Traces of potential further decoration are not preserved.

Another wooden fragment, possibly also from an ushabti, was discovered on the surface of the sediment layer in the neighboring area II of hall J (Table 1, #2). Since the fragment is small, it is not possible to identify it clearly. However, the protruding curved upper side with a straight base suggests it could be the foot of an ushabti. This is also suggested by the horizontal fracture edge, which is located at the point where the transition to the body would be expected. The fragment is also heavily charred, especially on the front side. The fact that the back side is comparatively less burnt might indicate that the fragment was exposed to fire while lying on its back. Conceivably, the object originally came from the recent disturbance.

[20] Renate Germer, *Flora des Pharaonischen Ägypten*, SDAIK 14 (Mainz, 1985), 173. Renate Germer, *Die Textilfärberei und die Verwendung gefärbter Textilien im Alten Ägypten*, ÄA 53 (Wiesbaden, 1992), 10–15.

While the charred wooden fragment (Table 1, #2) cannot be reliably assigned to any object group, the other one (Table 1, #13) can undoubtedly be identified as an ushabti and, therefore, it can most likely be considered a funerary object. It is highly doubtful, however, that it is an ushabti of Ramesses III himself. There is evidence of a wooden ushabti from the burial equipment of Ramesses III (cf. Louvre AF425), in addition to those made of calcite (cf. OIM E10755, BM EA 67816 with BM EA 8695), bronze (cf. BM EA 33938, Louvre N656A/BI and N656B,[21] Museo Egizio Torino 2507), and copper (Gulbenkian Museum Durham 1832 of EG 525). Louvre AF 425, however, has an engraved inscription extending to the base and appears to be of a much higher quality than the recent find—as far as its poor state of preservation allows a reconstruction. In view of the broad array of finds in the tombs of the Kings' Valley, it may well be an ushabti from another tomb that was secondarily brought to KV 11. When Giovanni Battista Belzoni discovered the tomb of Sety I (KV 17) in 1817, he observed an "immense quantity of small wooden figures of mummies."[22] Apparently, several of these resin-coated ushabtis were lit and used as a source of light by visitors to the tomb.[23] Concerning the burnt upper fracture, such a use might also be considered for the otherwise unburnt ushabti fragment (Table 1, #13).

Sediment Pieces with Color Imprints (fig. 17)

Several fragile sediment pieces in area V show multicolored, secondary imprints that derive from objects that fell onto the sediment when it was still humid. They appear to belong to two categories: imprints from plaster that presumably fell off the wall, and imprints from wooden objects.

Imprints from Plaster (fig. 17)

The most illustrative example of this group is one of eight sediment pieces (Table 1, #20) of different size that were found together as parts of the baked sediment layer on top of area V, with shared color selection and pattern. It is part of a sediment clump and shows its "surface" upside down relative to the floor level. It still bears some plaster remains, which are partly broken away on the larger part of the fragment and therefore reveal parts of the decoration that once were painted upon it and are now imprinted on the sediment: a green background with three rows of "U"-shaped black lines (line thickness: 0.3–0.5 cm) with additional blue ovals in the curvature. The "U"-shape in the middle row has a width of 2.6 cm and a height of 3.1 cm, with the blue oval having a height of 2.2 cm. The one preserved in the row above is slightly smaller: 2.6 cm × 2.8 cm (W × H), with the blue oval measuring only 1.2 cm. The same pattern is still discernible in two other samples of the find group. The other pieces of this group bear at least the same green and/or blue color but are too small to also preserve the "U"-shaped pattern. Two examples, moreover, bear not only one but two different layers of plaster, meaning that several fragments of plaster had fallen upon each other. Some of the pieces also show tiny black traces, the nature of which will require additional study. They slightly resemble the decayed wood on piece #22 in Table 1 (see below), but pigments or dirt cannot be excluded either.

The color pattern shown on these pieces resembles feathers and thus seems to belong to the body of the ram-headed vulture below the final panel of the Book of the Cavern on the west wall of hall J (fig. 5). Although the image has nowadays completely disappeared, it can be reconstructed by comparison with the decoration of the burial chambers in KV 8 (Merenptah) and KV 14 (Tawosret/Sethnakht). Despite their similarity with the plumage in the tombs of Merenptah and Tawosret/Sethnakht, the color pattern on our find (Table 1, #20) shows some variation, because the feathers are red and blue in KV 14, while they are green with blue dots in the tomb of Ramesses III.

Another piece of plaster (Table 1, #24) was found pressed onto the sediment, leaving some of its color pattern on it. This plaster fragment is different from the abovementioned group since it has a 3-dimensional structure and contains a right-angled recess (W × H: 6.1 cm × 3.4 cm) that is 0.2 cm deeper than the surrounding area. The framing surface bears yellow color traces, while the surface of the recess was largely blue, but also had some

[21] Cf. Aidan Dodson, *Ramesses III King of Egypt: His Life and Afterlife* (Cairo-New York, 2019), 117, fig. 113.

[22] Cf. https://egyptmanchester.wordpress.com/tag/valley-of-the-kings/, accessed March 29, 2021.

[23] Cf. https://egyptmanchester.wordpress.com/tag/valley-of-the-kings/, accessed March 29, 2021.

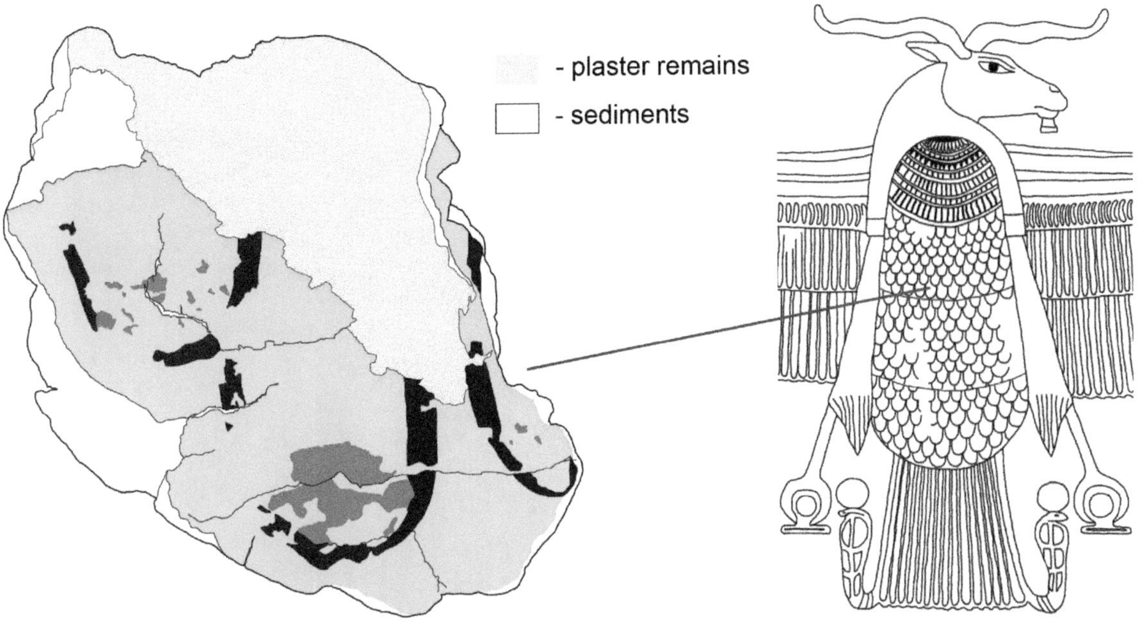

Fig. 5. Color imprint (Table 1, #20) showing parts of the feathers of the ram-headed vulture (cf. KV 14) from the "Schlussbild" of the Book of the Caverns. Drawings: Anke Weber.

yellow traces near the corner. The edge of the "relief" is mainly colored black but shows again some yellow traces in the left half (according to the orientation on fig. 17) of the lower edge. Future studies of the decoration of the west wall and its reconstruction will help to identify its original place.

A compact, light grey piece of sediment with two color imprints (Table 1, #19) shows a roughly oval shape (8.2 cm × 5.6 cm) on the upper side. Five parallel black stripes run in a slight curvature across a yellow-green background. The black stripes have a width of 0.5 cm, the yellow-green space between them measures 0.6 to 0.8 cm. A few centimeters below this striped pattern, a red-brown color imprint of irregular shape with a size of 6.0 cm × 1.2 cm is preserved. The combination of pattern and color is reminiscent of the kilts that are worn by the gods in the final tableau of the Book of the Caverns in KV 11 and—better preserved—in KV 14; the red-brown color imprint would fit the legs of the respective deities.[24] While these deities wear yellow kilts and green cuirasses in KV 14, they wear striped, green kilts and cuirasses in KV 11. The yellow-green pattern on the find, however, does not seem to fit to this scene, because the difference in the color scheme is too big and cannot be explained by fading, as the other sediment imprints with green patterns do not show a similar decrease in their coloring. Therefore, further research on the decoration of the western half of hall J is necessary to determine the possible origin of this imprint.

Imprint from a Painted Wooden Object(?) (fig. 17)

Fragment #22 in Table 1 has one smooth surface with yellow color imprints. Approximately in the middle of this surface, a rectangular shape (W × H: 6.8[+x] cm × 3.0 cm) is preserved, which is elevated by 0.1 cm over the surrounding surface. The outer frame of this rectangular elevation shows a blue color, while the inner part contains green traces; the border between the green inner part and the outer blue frame is still partly covered by a thin sediment layer that could not be removed without destroying the color imprints themselves. At the lower right corner and at the lower edge of the elevation, the blue color has vanished, and a substance resembling de-

[24] For the angle of the black stripes in relation to the presumed leg, see the detailed drawing of this tableau in KV 14 in Erik Hornung, *Tal der Könige: Die Ruhestätte der Pharaonen*, 3rd ed. (Augsburg, 1995), 109.

Fig. 6. North–south view of the "ramp" (white marks) leading from the entrance of the burial chamber (north) to the main hall (south). © The Ministry of Antiquities, The Ramesses III (KV 11) Publication and Conservation Project, photo: Johannes Kramer.

cayed wood is visible instead. This might give the impression that the entire elevation is made of painted wood. This impression cannot be confirmed, however, because a careful examination of the thin color layers in the upper edge did not reveal further wood traces beneath it. On the other hand, dark brown and dark grey traces are also preserved around the rectangle, which might be decayed wood as well, if they are not pigments. The upper edge of the sediment clump shows three further pieces of material, which are pressed on the surface, one of them with blue color traces beneath. More detailed studies and observations are necessary to determine the nature of this material.

The rectangular elevation and the wooden remains distinguish the fragment from the other sediment pieces. The elevation implies that the sediment was pressed on an object with a similarly shaped rectangular recess when still wet. The wood suggests, moreover, that this object was a piece of furniture. Another possibility is that the color layer and the wood are from two different objects: One can imagine a piece of plaster that fell on a wooden object, and both were later pressed together by the sediment. However, the observation that the blue color follows the edges of the elevation, points toward the first option.

Findings from the Top of J-VIII-1-c-s-01

For a small sondage, a place was chosen for its immediate vicinity to the recent disturbance. The area on top of J-VIII-1-c-s-01, a large limestone slab partly embedded into the mud from the ceiling above, connects the pit via a sloping stretch of ground (a "ramp") running diagonally through the burial chamber, to the entrance pathway between pillars 3 and 5. This "ramp" (fig. 6) is the remnant of a flood stream that provides a valuable insight into the number of flooding events and their chronology. In subsequent excavations, we aim to find out whether the "ramp" overlays the already dried out sediment crust which forms the uppermost layer on top of the burial chamber's floor level. If this proves to be the case, the "ramp" would provide evidence for minor flooding of the burial chamber after the whole area had dried up from the previous flooding.

Fig. 7. Sondage between pillars 1 and 3 revealing a fireplace and traces of burnt material. The dashed line shows the border between the mud that was washed inside the tomb by flooding and the lower, already existing sand layer. © The Ministry of Antiquities, The Ramesses III (KV 11) Publication and Conservation Project, photo: Anke Weber.

If the pit on the floor of hall J was indeed only recently excavated, i.e., after the mud had dried out, one would expect smaller finds on the surface of the baked mud. The sondage mentioned above actually proved this to be the case. Loose sediments on top of the mud yielded small linen pieces (Table 1, #26), part of a bone (Table 1, #27), pottery sherds, and pieces of burned wood. Judging by their type and characteristics, these finds most likely came from the recent disturbance. The traces of burning on the linen and pieces of wood strongly support this theory since they are similar to the findings from the lowest part of the pit, as was described above. Due to the distribution of loose finds, a path from the recent disturbance to the entrance of the burial chamber via the "ramp" can be traced.

Findings in Front of P6 and P8

To prepare area V for excavation, the surface of this area in front of pillars 6 and 8 (see fig. 10) was cleaned. Small finds like a bone (Table 1, #25) and a non-diagnostic sherd from Nile clay were discovered. While surrounding pieces of colored plaster elements were compacted inside the sediment layer, the finds remaining on top of the sediments were covered with a thin layer of dust. Therefore, they must have dislocated after the last flooding event. Since the recent disturbance is situated in the immediate vicinity of this area, and since the sherd has features similar to findings from the pit, it can be assumed that the objects originally derived from the same place.

Findings in Room H (threshold between G and H)

In order to detect the height of sediments to be excavated in room H for future fieldwork, a sondage was dug on the direct border between corridor G and the beginning of the tomb's rear part. The rectangular cut leading

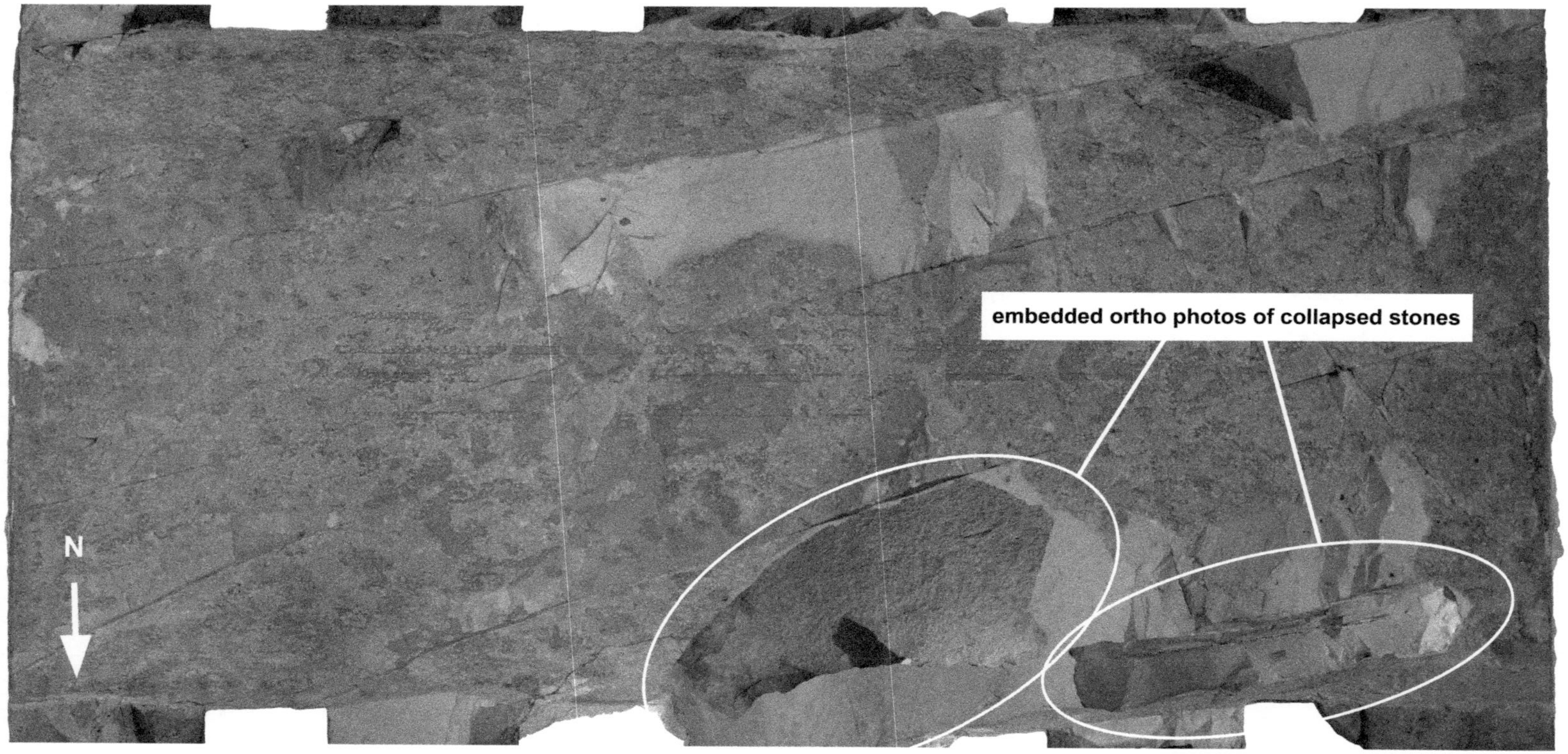

Fig. 8. Orthophoto of the ceiling in hall J including two large stones, which had collapsed and were virtually replaced in their original position.
© The Ministry of Antiquities, The Ramesses III (KV 11) Publication and Conservation Project, 3D models: Willem Hovestreydt.

over the threshold to room H revealed a couple of finds within a sand layer which seems to be similar to the sand layer of the excavated recent disturbance. Further investigation and comparison will show whether the sand consists of the same material and therefore was brought secondarily into the tomb, possibly covering the whole rear part. Apart from a number of obvious modern finds such as nails, paper, cigarette ends, a syringe, glass, wood splinters, and a Taiwanese 1 yuan coin (Table 1, #1), other finds included bone fragments, sherds, and plant residues. While the bones, pottery pieces, and plant residues may have been washed inside the tomb by flooding, the coin requires a different explanation. In 2014, a British penny from 2004 was spotted by the field director while crossing the area between rooms H and I. The coin had to remain in the tomb and was not properly registered because at that time the focus of the investigation was on the decoration of the rear part of the tomb. A 20 Swiss rappen coin from 1981 (see below, p. 247), was discovered during a visual survey in room H (Table 1, #62). These finds led to the conclusion that either visitors entered this part of the tomb and accidentally lost coins from their home countries, or they were intentionally thrown into the tomb's rear, in which case it was probably regarded as a sort of wishing well. The wishing coin has a long tradition among tourists all over the world and this area seems to fit well into this practice since it provides a barrier and mysterious darkness in a sacred environment. Further finds of this kind in our upcoming fieldwork will confirm or disprove this thesis.

The Visual Survey in the Rear Compartments of KV 11

During the fieldwork, a visual archaeological survey of the rear part (rooms H, I, Ja-Jd, K1-K2, L, and hall J) was conducted to get an overview of this area and to ascertain the maximum height of debris from the earlier flooding events. During this survey, some stray finds were discovered. In room H, we found modern coins, as described above.[25] Further modern surface finds were made in hall J and included cigarette packets, conservation material (wools, cords, worked cement, plastic pipes, etc.), water bottles, entry tickets to the Valley, newspapers, and a man's handkerchief made of textile (Table 1, #28). The latter was found below a layer of coarse-grained quartzite sand which must have been brought to the tomb in recent times since it covers parts of the fallen limestone pieces which were detached from the ceiling during or after the flooding events. The entry tickets for the Valley, which were found in room I and hall J, were of special interest since they provide an overview of modern disturbances of the rear part, which is currently closed for visitors. They date probably to the middle until the end of the 20th century and to the early 2000s, while the newspapers are from the beginning of the 1990s. The latter may have been brought to the tomb by conservators.[26]

The ancient surface finds consist of fragments of wall decoration (Table 1, #58–61), wooden furniture or coffin elements (Table 1, #55, 56), pottery sherds (Table 1, #57), and plant remains (Table 1, #54). The latter were found coated in sediment debris within a crack of pillar 4, at a height of 1.44 m. It proves that the plant remains were carried to this place by the flood water. In a crack of pillar 5, we even found a piece of wood at the height of 1.76 m, measured from top of the cavetto cornice. Adding this height to the 90 cm of depth of the depression in the middle of the burial chamber,[27] one can estimate the highest level of the flood water at probably more than 2.66 m[28] at some point between 1885/90 and 1914.[29] This was an enormous volume of water within the rear part and leaves no doubt that the side chambers Ja-Jd must have been flooded completely at least once. The standing waters were certainly soaked up by the friable limestone of Zone A in the lower area

[25] See the part concerning the finds in room H above.

[26] Kent Weeks (ed.), *Atlas of the Valley of the Kings* (Cairo, 2000), 156. The atlas does not mention when exactly the conservators worked here but it seems highly likely that it was at the beginning of the 90s because the newspapers were found in the direct vicinity of the conservation material and might have served this purpose, as well.

[27] The depth of the depression is the distance from the true floor level to the cavetto cornice. Currently the floor is covered by 60 cm of sand and sediment clumps. From the sediments to the cavetto cornice, it is a distance of 30 cm. In addition, this makes 90 cm from the floor to the cavetto cornice.

[28] From our most recent work, we know that the entire burial chamber was flooded almost completely at least once. For more information, see the upcoming Fifth Report that is planned for *JARCE* 59, 2023.

[29] Weber et al., "Third Report," *JEA* 107 (2021), table 2.

of the rear part.[30] The plant residues also show traces of burning and hence are comparable to similar-looking finds from all over the burial chamber. They presumably served as brushwood or firelighters because they are all burnt at the upper end only. Future investigation and the excavation of the entire burial chamber will hopefully bring light into the darkness.

By cleaning selected areas in the burial chamber (XI/IX [between pillars 1 and 3], XVI/XIV [between pillars 2 and 4], parts of the eastern and western cavetto cornice), several fireplaces with burnt material were identified (fig. 7), similar to those of the floor in the recent disturbance. All those fireplaces are in areas with higher elevation in hall J and therefore, they serve perfectly for the distribution of light from different sources.

For the time being, we regard these fireplaces as modern light sources that were used by visitors before the early 20th century to illuminate the chamber. A drawing from the Hay papers at the British Library, made by Joseph Bonomi, shows two men entering the burial chamber with a torch and another visitor sitting in front of at least one light source on the ground.[31] The drawing can be dated to the years 1832/33, when natural light sources were used for illumination.[32] In 1902, Howard Carter installed electric lighting in most of the tombs in the Valley.[33] By then, KV 11 had already been flooded at least once,[34] making the rear part of the tomb inaccessible to visitors, leaving that part without lighting. The feature of the fireplace between pillars 1 and 3 reveals another mystery in connection with Bonomi's drawing, which clearly shows that the cavetto cornice is still intact in that area. The fireplace must date after the drawing, but previous to the layer of fine-grained sand which covers the whole burial chamber up to 30 cm in height. If the sand was brought intentionally to the site (see above, p. 237) this must have happened between Bonomi's drawing and the flooding event that made the tomb's rear inaccessible. Therefore, the insertion of the sand can be dated between 1832/33 and 1890/1895.

Moreover, Bonomi's drawing points to an interesting fact about a large stone that fell from the ceiling and which nowadays lies almost in the center of hall J. Already in 1833, the object must have been in danger of collapse since the half-moon-shaped crack above the entrance to the hall is visible in the drawing.[35] Nevertheless, this event can only have taken place sometime after the disastrous flooding event in 1914, which submerged the entire rear part of the tomb.[36] Other stones which lay underneath the large stone and were easily removable do not show evidence of mud imprints below. This means that these stones fell prior to the large stone on the already dried-out sediment surface, making it unlikely that they were moved to this place by human activity. Furthermore, preliminary observations with an endoscope of the baked sediments below the large stone revealed that it fell on the already dried-out sediments on top of the floor. Using photogrammetry techniques and orthophotos of the ceiling as well as the collapsed, larger stones on the bottom, it is possible to fit the latter in their original position (fig. 8). In a later phase of the project, advice of a structural engineer and our conservators will help to assess whether a reconstruction of these parts of the ceiling will be able to bear heavy loads again. Such analyses are planned for the upcoming fieldwork.

While cleaning the areas between pillars 1 and 3, another discovery was made which provides information about the different layers of sand, mud, and baked sediments on top of the floor of the burial chamber. A sand layer of almost the same height everywhere (see fig. 7) covers the ground and seems to be comparable to the fine-grained sand which was found on top of the floor level inside the recent disturbance (see above, p. 237).

---

30 See Weber et al., "Second Report," 220–23.

31 See Weber et al., "Third Report," *JEA 107* (2021), fig. 14.

32 For the dating see Weber et al., "Third Report," *JEA 107* (2021), fn. 82.

33 Howard Carter, "Report on General Work done in the Southern Inspectorate," *ASAE* 4 (1903), 43. KV 11 was equipped with light and partly restored in 1902 and 1903 under the direction of the then chief inspector for the Upper Egyptian Antiquities Service, Howard Carter.

34 Weber et al., "Third Report," *JEA 107* (2021), table 2. Between ca. 1885/90 and 1895, a devastating flooding event must have occurred, so that the rear part of KV 11 was not accessible to visitors anymore.

35 Cf. Weber et al., "Third Report," *JEA* 107 (2021), fig. 14.

36 Weber et al., "Third Report," *JEA* 107 (2021), 99.

Finds from the Survey

The survey provided several important finds that can be used to date the deterioration of the tomb's rear part as well as the time periods of public access to it. Furthermore, we obtained an overview of the sort of artifacts to be expected in the future. A number of colorful plaster remains were found in front of the west wall of the burial chamber as well as in the western niche of room L (Table 1, #58–61). Due to their good state of preservation, they may be relocated by our conservators in the future. Another piece (Table 1, #6), e.g., is a part of the sandy path surrounding the "Schlussbild" of the Book of Caverns on the west wall of hall J, while other objects (e.g., Table 1, #60) confirm that offering tables were depicted in front of the deities in shrines in the niches of room L, as the front part of a lotus flower bud is shown.[37] However, the consistency of the plaster remains differs strongly. It is obvious that the plaster in hall J was mixed on a rougher and more coarse-grained basis, while the colored pieces from room L are from a finer quality, mainly consisting of a very pale gypsum-based mixture. The condition of these finds and their occurrence on the surface show that they collapsed after the flooding events. The color still remains, and the objects do not show any kind of damage by water.

A plant residue (Table 1, #54) in one of the cracks on the north side of pillar 4 which provides additional information on the flooding events was already discussed earlier in this article (see above p. 237).

Wood (fig. 15)

A polychrome decorated wooden fragment was recovered during the surface survey carried out in hall J (Table 1, #55). The fragment shows a smoothed face to which a thin layer of plaster has been applied. The coloring on it is divided into a light blue, a greenish/yellow and a yellow area, each separated from the other by a band of red shapes or slashes. The color application appears slightly washed out, which may be due to the effect of water. Although the small size prevents a clear attribution of the fragment, both the color combination and the stripe-like decoration are reminiscent of polychrome friezes that delimit image areas, for example on wooden ushabti boxes of the New Kingdom. Alternatively, it could also be a fragment of a wooden piece of furniture.

Modern Finds

While surveying the areas between rooms H and J, we found fifty-five modern objects (Table 1, #29-53). Most of these finds were tickets to the Valley of the Kings or for the mini train that takes tourists from the ticket office to the inner main wadi. The forty-three tickets in total were found in nine locations. Their running numbers reveal that the people who left them came either in groups of up to ten persons or a single person was carrying them in bunches, as most tickets that were found together were also bought at roughly the same time. The modern finds also include parts of food packaging,[38] pages from several Egyptian newspapers published in 1990,[39] an unused disposable flashbulb[40] (Table 1, #23), the above discussed Taiwanese 1 yuan coin from 1981 (Table 1, #1), as well as the Swiss 20 rappen (Table 1, #62) coin, also from 1981. The majority of these items have been left inside KV

[37] See the drawing of Francis Arundale, in Willem Hovestreydt, Lea Rees, and Anke Weber, "KV 11 revisited: Collecting Archive Material in Oxford and London Concerning the Tomb of Ramesses III," *EA* 58 (2021), 38–39.

[38] The food packaging consists of a water bottle label from 1986, an empty package of sugar from 1990 and two candy wrappers, one from 2003 and one from 2008.

[39] Find number M8 contains four pages of at least two newspapers from August and November 1990 according to the publishing date and a date given in an advertisement.

[40] The flashbulb (German "Blitzbirne") was part of photographic equipment. It is either an Osram Vacublitz XM1 or a Philips PF1. They were produced from the mid-50s until the late 70s. These flashbulbs were only used once and disposed of afterwards. This lightbulb nevertheless did not release a flash. Otherwise, the blue indicator dot still visible at the top of the bulb would have either turned pink or disappeared altogether. The authors would like to thank the project's photographer Johannes Kramer for the identification and dating of this object. For further reading on these flashbulbs see Helmut Stapf, *Fotografische Praxis* (Leipzig, 1955); Hans Leckscheid, "Vom Pulverblitz zum Elektronenblitzgerät," *Photographica Cabinett* 19/20 (2000), 32–59 and *Photographica Cabinett* 21 (2000), 15–24; and Michael Peres (ed.), *The Focal Encyclopedia of Photography* (Boston, 2013).

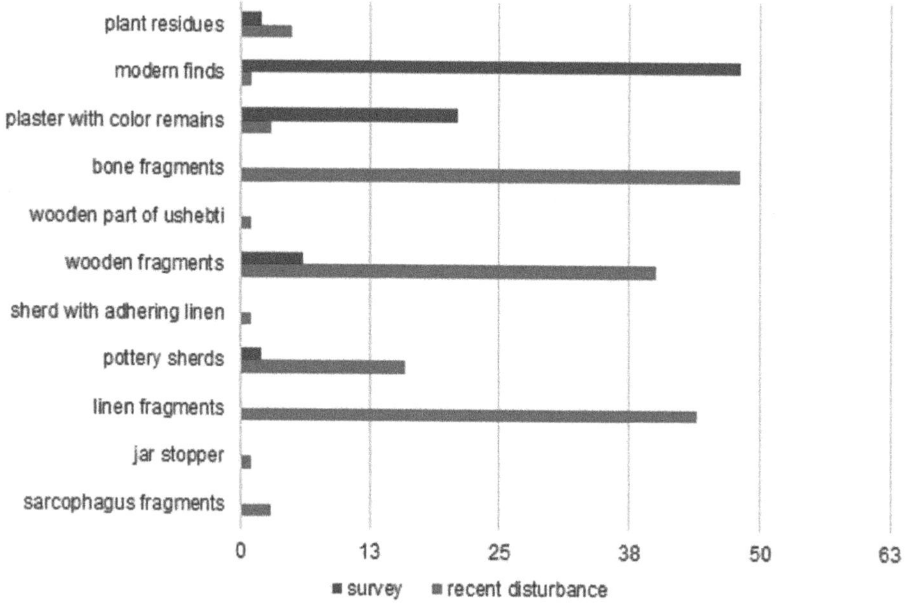

Fig. 9. Quantity of small finds from the recent disturbance (mainly from the sand layer on top of the floor) and the visual survey (on top of the sediment layer) in comparison.

11 between 1980 and the present day. It is worth noting that, while most modern objects came from chambers H and I, the finds that point to a longer stay, like the newspaper and datable candy wrappings, were found deeper inside the tomb, namely in chambers J and Jd.

Conclusions on the Distribution and Interpretation of Finds

Besides the already discussed sarcophagus fragments,[41] the excavation of the recent disturbance revealed several fragments of bones and a large amount of textile shreds inside and below the sand layer (fig. 14). The latter show traces of burning and are partly carbonized. Furthermore, burnt plant residues and wooden fragments came to light, among them fragments of the lower parts of wooden ushabtis with burn marks (Table 1, #13 and Table 1, #21[42]). Another entirely burnt fragment—probably also the lower part of a wooden ushabti—was found on the surface of the sediment layer close by (Table 1, #2). It may have been part of the content from the pit, or it belonged to the rubble that was removed from the recent disturbance. However, the traces of burning on most of the finds correlate with the fireplaces on the floor level within the pit. The fire must have been ignited before the homogeneous sand layer came into the tomb. Since the sand must have been deposited in hall J before the first flooding of the tomb occurred (see above, pp. 245–46), the described small finds cannot have been flushed into the tomb—at least not with the floods that caused the sedimentation layer on top of the sand.

Concerning the quantity of finds from inside the recent disturbance (fig. 9), it can be stated that the largest number of finds consists of pottery, wood, and bones, followed by textile, plant residues, and charcoal. A smaller amount of brushwood, modern finds, and wall fragments was found in the pit, which also included two rose granite fragments from a royal sarcophagus.

[41] Weber et al., "Second Report," 239–43.

[42] To date, it is unclear whether this fragment is part of the lower end of an ushabti, but the shape and material are heading in this direction. The object must have been extraordinarily large, although it is not unusual.

Close to the pit, plaster fragments from the wall paintings of the west wall were discovered. As the lower part of the west wall seemed to be lost forever, it was intriguing to find traces of color below the wall. These imprints resulted from the collapsing plaster, which fell on top of the wet mud, pressing its decorated part into the sediments. The undersides of the dried-out sediment clumps thus reveal in which colors the lower half of the west wall was once painted (Table 1, #20, cf. fig. 5). Hence, it will be important to keep and analyze sediment clumps with color impressions for future work, in order to reconstruct not only the decoration of walls, pillars, and ceiling, but their color pattern as well. Similar findings may be imprints from wooden objects (Table 1, #24), or may even contain pieces of wooden furniture itself (Table 1, #22).

Other imprints, for example, of linen garments, together with wooden furniture or sarcophagus pieces, bones, linen, pottery, and even the lower part of a wooden ushabti, seem to suggest a human burial including equipment. It seems that at least one coffin including an adult mummy (see bone, Table 1, #11), with additional (filled?) vessels and some ushabtis, was situated in this place. Whether the burial was positioned here in the 18th or 19th century to serve as fuel for the fireplace, or rather belongs to an ancient burial inside KV 11, will be part of our future investigation and can only be determined after excavating the whole burial chamber. Most of the objects from the recent disturbance show traces of burning that must be in close connection to the fireplaces from the floor level.

The modern finds from the visual survey are important for our ongoing work (fig. 9). They were used to date the visits of intruders during the last century. The largest number of finds consists of entry tickets to the Valley and tickets for the mini train ("taftaf"). Some of them contained a date while others could be dated at least approximately because of their lower prices compared to modern ones (ranging from 1 to 55 LE).[43] It can be assumed that the cheapest entry fee is the oldest while the higher price tickets which also show color prints are from more recent times. While the earlier tickets were found closer to the entrance of the burial chamber and in room I, the later tickets, as well as a bill for the mini train from 2013, were found much further in the rear. Some torn-off tickets are found in packages. A Cleopatra cigarette package was lying upon the eastern niche of room L that must have served as a resting place for somebody. Egyptian newspapers including dates from summer/fall 1990 (19 August, 03 November, and 07 November) might correlate with the finds of conservation equipment in and around the recent disturbance, as they were found in the small room Jd together with leftover cement powder and bags of sand.

Compared to the finds from the recent disturbance, the visual survey mainly provided finds of fragments from wall decoration, which are very promising for our future reconstruction work. With the result of this season, it is already possible to relocate colored plaster pieces from the west wall of hall J and from the western niche in room L, due to their findspots and their remaining decoration. The wooden parts of furniture and parts of the burial equipment found during the survey were located close to the recent disturbance. Most likely, they originate from inside the pit, as they show similarities (same wood, size, and presence of holes for wooden nails) to finds from inside it. Other surface finds like plant residues and pottery sherds show traces of a coating sediment layer and rounded corners which leads to the assumption that they were flushed inside the tomb by one of the flooding events, probably by the last one which was also one of the most destructive floods.

Photogrammetry

Work has continued on the processing of the 3D model of the tomb created with data derived from the 2019 photogrammetric survey of KV 11. The aim of the survey and subsequent processing was to capture data that would enable the creation of both a 3D model of the entire tomb, and high-resolution orthographic outputs of individual walls, pillars, and ceilings. Each of these desired outcomes is achievable using photogrammetry. However, the challenge of this project was to capture a dataset that would provide both simultaneously. To achieve this goal, several processes have been applied to the data. All the techniques described below are standard opera-

[43] The current (end of 2021) price is 240 LE for one person without a photo permission. Three tombs are included but Sety I, Ramesses V/VI, and Tutankhamun require an extra ticket.

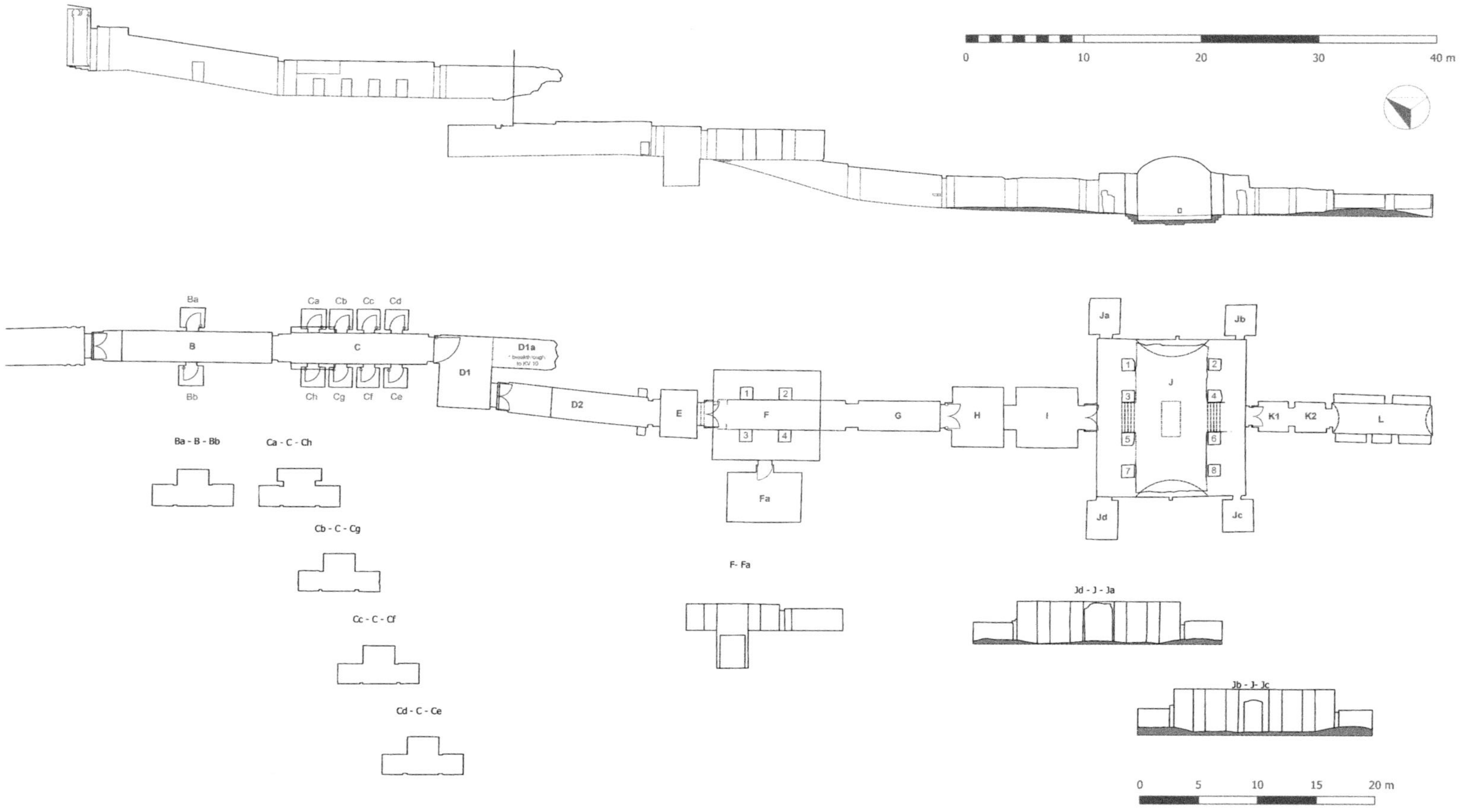

Fig. 10. Ground plan of KV 11 - state: 05/2021. © The Ramesses III (KV 11) Publication and Conservation Project, plan: Gareth Rees and Anke Weber.

tions for photogrammetry processing, following currently available guidelines for best practice,[44] but they are not always all necessary, and certain processes can negate or adversely affect others. For this reason, the workflow followed for this project with its specific aims, is outlined below.

Processing Steps

The initial analysis of the images took place during and immediately after the fieldwork, to check that image quality and overlap were sufficient for alignment of the photosets.[45] The next stage of processing involved improving accuracy and composite image quality for orthographic output. The initial alignment result was checked and filtered by "reprojection error," "reconstruction uncertainty," and "projection accuracy" to leave only high-quality points on which to build subsequent stages of the model.

Having separated the tomb into twenty-four zones for the practicality of the survey, each zone could be processed separately and exists as a stand-alone model. The benefit of this at the processing stage is that with smaller (i.e., lower mesh size) models higher resolutions can be obtained using limited computing power. The first stage of processing was to locate the georeferenced ground control targets in the photographs in which they appeared. Ground control was present in approximately one-third of the 40,660 photographs used for alignment. The overall accuracy of the model can be significantly improved by the addition of targets, the size and type of which can affect the accuracy.[46] Use of these targets also negates some of the systematic inaccuracies caused by taking photos at different focal lengths and varying distances.[47] Each of the 167 targets were either automatically or manually "pinned" to their location in each photo after which it was possible to adjust ("optimize") the location of the cameras in each zone to improve the positional accuracy of the model. The average error per target after adjustment was less than 4.2 mm which was within the acceptable margin of error.

The next stage of processing involved filtering photos by quality, another function partially automatized by the software. Given the high resolution needed for the final orthographic output, it was necessary to manually mask areas that were not correctly focused, badly lit, or contained elements not required in the final model, such as people and equipment. These anomalies were greatest at the transition between zones, where lighting and cables were located. In certain parts of the tomb, where the lighting was problematic, it was necessary to use either high ISOs or larger apertures to capture the required images; in these images, masking was often required to cover areas of blur on the edges of the photos whilst the subject area remained clear.

Using the masked, rectified, and filtered data, dense clouds of points were built for each zone ranging in size from 38 million to 288 million points. These points were again filtered to cut out any that were based on less than three images. The dense clouds were then trimmed, so that each zone overlapped exactly with the next, removing any unwanted features in the process. These trimmed and filtered dense point clouds were then used to build the 3D meshes of each part of the tomb on which orthophotos can be projected and extracted. Meshes range in size from 1.6–20 million faces with the possibility to increase this in some areas if greater detail is required.

Results

The first results to be produced were digital elevation models (DEMs) of the floors and ceilings in the rear part of the tomb. These were created for every room in the rear part of the tomb (rooms H–L) at a resolution of 1 mm per pixel (pp). Top-down orthophotos were then generated for the same zones, also at a resolution of 1mm pp;

[44] Jon Bedford, *Photogrammetric Applications for Cultural Heritage. Guidance for Good Practice;* Historic England (Swindon, 2017); Sébastien Lachambre, Sébastien Lagarde, and Cyril Jover, *Unity: Photogrammetry Workflow* (2017), accessed January 1, 2020 via https://unity.com/solutions/photogrammetry; AgiSoft (ed.), *Agisoft Metashape user manual: Professional edition, Version 1.7* (2021), accessed June 2, 2021, https://www.agisoft.com/pdf/metashape-pro_1_7_en.pdf.

[45] Weber et al., "Second Report," 229-31.

[46] See Miroslav Krajňák, Katarína Pukanská, and Karol Bartoš, "Application of digital photogrammetry in the process of documentation of archaeological artefacts," *Ročník* 16 (2011), 340.

[47] Lachambre, Lagarde, and Jover, "Photogrammetric Applications," 21.

the maximum quality available of 0.2–0.3 mm pp was not required for these areas. An even greater resolution is available for the walls of the tomb, where higher resolution images were taken to fully document reliefs and paintings.

Results from the mesh creation so far have been individual models of each column in the tomb chamber along with orthographic images of each face that have been used to aid our ongoing conservation work.

Combining the model created from the total station survey and a combined 3D model of all twenty-four zones allowed a new plan of the tomb to be drawn to a level of detail previously not possible.[48] Along with an updated plan view of KV 11, cross-sections were created of the entire eastern elevation, corridors B-C, rooms F-Fa, and rooms Jd-J-Ja as well as Jb-J-Jc. Work on creating orthographic images of individual walls continues. The existing tomb plan made by the Theban Mapping Project was revised with the new detailed information (fig. 10). Some changes were added: The direction of door openings in the chambers Ba and Ca to Cd was changed due to the position of remaining pivot holes in their ceilings. A dashed line in front of D1a shows now that the room was originally covered by a decorated wall. Pivot holes identified in front of rooms H and J are indicative of double-winged doors in these locations. The stairs from the burial chamber were exchanged with dashed lines since they are currently not visible, and it is unclear how many steps are remaining. A depression for the sarcophagus was added; its measurements were based on those taken from our 3D models of the coffer and the lid, now in the Musée du Louvre and the Fitzwilliam Museum in Cambridge, respectively. The orientation of the sarcophagus is still questionable and will be discussed in another article. Finally, the floor levels of corridors and rooms with wooden walkways are presented with a dashed line as we were not able to survey on the original surface. There remain areas of this preliminary tomb plan that require clarification, and we aim to provide more information and updated plans during our ongoing fieldwork.

Site Management

Site management plays a key role in the project's plan for the opening of the site, its publication, and conservation. It establishes a direct link between visitors, researchers, and a sustainable and safe future for the tomb. Therefore, the following sketch is based on the already existing site management strategy for the Valley of the Kings that was developed by Kent Weeks and the Theban Mapping Project.[49] In the following, we present some ideas that will be elaborated on in upcoming reports.

Visitors' Guidance and Additional Information

KV 11 is one of the most frequently visited tombs in the Valley of the Kings because it is close to the modern rest house, free of additional entrance fees, and very well preserved—at least in the officially accessible front part. Therefore, tour guides always recommend its visit. During the winter season 2019/2020, the longest time needed to leave the tomb from corridor G to B took almost half an hour, which was caused by the masses of tourists entering and leaving the site, taking pictures, and lingering in certain areas. The situation is not only uncomfortable for the visitors, but also for the project members, and it damages the tomb itself. Climate measurements

[48] Thanks to Kent Weeks and the Theban Mapping Project (TMP) who previously surveyed the tomb and provided the locations of their survey points on which the new model is georeferenced. The level of detail in the photogrammetry model allows the possibility to slice through the tomb at different locations both vertically and horizontally. For example, the shape of the pillars will vary in plan depending on the level at which they are cut. This is a great benefit for conservation allowing the creation of models at specific height zones related to past flooding events. It should be noted that in the elevation illustrated here, the level of rubble and the ceiling height in the rear part of the tomb will also change depending on where the model is cut. Except for two points where the surface floor level has been exposed by excavation, the true floor level was not surveyed, either due to modern wooden flooring covering it or due to rubble collapse. Thanks also to Walton Chan of the TMP who provided useful information on the original survey methods used in the 1980s, and through close comparison of the TMP's plan and our new plan of the tomb was able to add valuable insights into some of the architectural detail.

[49] Kent Weeks and Nigel Hetherington, *The Valley of the Kings: A Site Management Handbook* (Cairo, 2014). The field director is currently working on a similar site management plan for KV 11 to provide a basis for other single sites in the wadi.

(fig. 11) taken during one of the crowded days show that temperature and humidity increase between room D1 and corridor G, while the entrance and the inaccessible rear part show the same temperature throughout the day, illustrating that the hot and humid air accumulates in the middle of the tomb where no fresh air can reach and the tourists tend to linger. The latter is caused by the increasingly narrow space in the tomb[50] and the fence in front of corridor G where visitors are abruptly stopped and have less space to move around. The high humidity, heavy temperature fluctuation, and (deliberate or accidental) touching of walls by visitors trying to make their way through the site, cause major damage to the tomb and will contribute to its deterioration.

The site may be considered an indoor museum (the tomb) inside an open-air museum (the wadi). Accordingly, the situation will remain manageable by providing the type of clear visitor guidance and entry restrictions that have become the rule in modern museums. Many of the information panels that are currently attached to the glass in front of the walls are too small for the large amount of information they display, which forces the visitors to pause a long time in front of them. Solutions are needed to provide additional information and guide visitors through the tomb in an efficient and organized manner, that will be sustainable, affordable, and future-oriented at the same time. One such solution is a museum-based strategy for visitor guidance, utilizing educational applications that include 3D visualizations, virtual reality (VR), and augmented reality (AR) content. With these aims in mind, preliminary tests were made with Raspberry Pi computers (mini single board computers) to build a localized Wi-Fi network that will provide the necessary data. These computers are made for difficult environments, such as we have to deal with in the Valley. They are small, flexible all-in-one PCs without a fan, monitor, or any other peripheral. Only a power connection is necessary for their operation. The CPU is cooled passively with a heat sink. There are no mechanical moving parts that would be susceptible to wear and tear from the dusty conditions in the Valley of the Kings. This makes the proposed setup extremely resistant and durable.

The necessary infrastructure inside the tomb is limited to only a few Raspberry Pi's. They will function both as access points inside a mesh network as well as web servers. When a visitor logs into the Wi-Fi, the browser will be automatically routed to our future web app that is stored and provided by the Raspberry Pi. With this strategy we will neither need an internet connection through land lines nor a valid data plan on the smartphones.

To evaluate how many minicomputers would be needed and in what position they should be installed to get full coverage in KV 11, we set up a single Raspberry Pi with a power bank and located it either on the side of the wooden floor or, alternatively, on top of the posts that hold the glass to protect the reliefs. We tested eight positions in total with a standard mobile phone to produce a Wi-Fi heat map (fig. 12). Measurements that reach values between -30 to -67 dBm designate areas where the app would run without any losses in service quality. The heat maps show that three of the tested positions on top of the posts had enough overlapping coverage to offer an uninterrupted service throughout the tomb. To send the signal from this position we will add external antennas to the setup. The Raspberry Pi's can be placed out of sight. Only a small cable will run up the back of the post to reach an antenna positioned on top.

The strategy for an intuitive visitors' itinerary includes restrictions on the accessibility of the tomb. This can be realized easily by keeping single groups outside of the tomb while other groups are inside. It is planned to install one of the most attractive 3D tools in the space under a shelter in front of the entrance, which provides an ideal place for an additional information panel. Benches can be used for resting. By scanning a QR code with their own mobile device, tourists can view 3D models of objects found in KV 11 from museums around the world as well as being provided with additional information about their purpose. This feature will enable an intuitive visitors' itinerary right at the beginning of the site visit. Afterwards, the tourists may enter the tomb via corridor A and follow clearly visible arrows on the bottom of the wooden walkways. The circuit inside the tomb will start on the left side, while the visitors will be guided outside on the right. This follows the ancient Egyptian ordering with the beginning of the Litany of Re on the east wall of corridor B and its end on the west wall. The walk corresponds with the media content, which will be provided by QR codes on the glass panels in front of the corridor and room walls. The codes will provide short additional information about the scene content via

[50] Figure 11 does not show that well chamber E and hall F are not fully accessible. Room E is spanned with a bridge which has hardly the dimensions of the width of corridor D2, and hall F only provides space in the middle (steps leading to corridor G), while the aisles behind the pillars and room Fa are inaccessible for tourists most of the time.

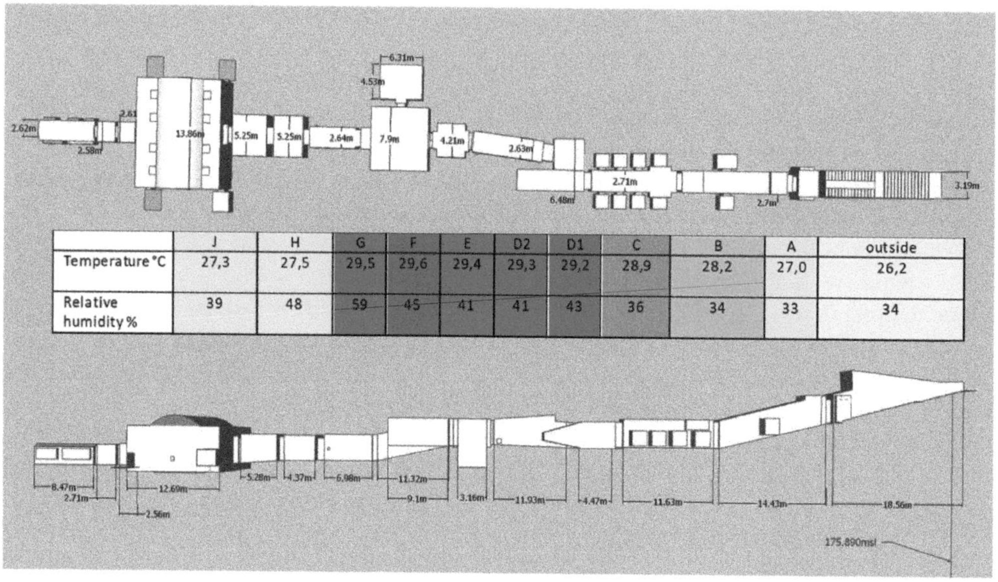

	J	H	G	F	E	D2	D1	C	B	A	outside
Temperature °C	27,3	27,5	29,5	29,6	29,4	29,3	29,2	28,9	28,2	27,0	26,2
Relative humidity %	39	48	59	45	41	41	43	36	34	33	34

Fig. 11. Climate measurements on December 1, 2019 (9:50-10:13 A.M.). Source: The Theban Mapping Project.

Fig. 12. Heat map (left) and position of Raspberry Pi in room D1 (right) to cover the area from the entrance up to hall F. © The Ministry of Antiquities, The Ramesses III (KV 11) Publication and Conservation Project, photo: Sandro Schwarz.

AR in three different languages (English, Arabic, German). Furthermore, they remind the visitor to move along inside the tomb to avoid traffic jams. The codes will be placed in corridor B, room D1, room E and (if accessible) room Fa. A last feature will be shown at the end of the tomb's accessible part, right in front of corridor G. From this area, one has a perfect view into the burial chamber which is still filled with rubble and debris. By scanning a last QR code, the tourists will be able to see the 3D model of the sarcophagus and its lid, which are currently exhibited in Paris and Cambridge, via VR. A short lifting of the mobile phone will reveal what the view inside the burial chamber once looked like in comparison to today. For the future, when the burial chamber is fully accessible to tourists, it is planned to incorporate archive material, like drawings and old pictures to show the original wall decoration of this now heavily destroyed part of the tomb.[51]

Acknowledgements

We are grateful to the Egyptian Ministry of Tourism and Antiquities (MoTA), the Minister of Antiquities His Excellency Dr. Khaled el-Enany, SCA secretary general Dr. Mostafa Waziri, the director of Foreign Missions Affairs, Dr. Nashwa Gaber, and the Permanent Committee for their ongoing support of our work in KV 11. Furthermore, for local administrative support we would like to thank: Fathy Yassin, General Director of the Western Inspectorate at Luxor, Ramadan Ahmed Ali, Director of Missions and Excavations at Luxor's west bank, Ali Redda, Director of the Valley of the Kings, Hussein Fawzy, Chief Inspector of the Valley of the Kings, and our inspectors during the mission's fieldwork. We are also very grateful to Prof. Dr. Frank Kammerzell and Prof. Dr. Silvia Kutscher as well as Karin Lippold and Dr. Christoph Raiser (all of Humboldt-Universität zu Berlin) for their administrative support. Additional thanks go to our scientific advisory board, J. Brett McClain for reviewing this article, and Nigel Strudwick for constantly supporting our work. Our deepest gratitude goes to our Egyptian workmen and Ahmed Hussein Youssef Mohamed who tirelessly worked to make this season a full success.

Addenda

Concerning the "Second Report on the Publication and Conservation of the Tomb of Ramesses III in the Valley of the Kings (KV 11)," *JARCE* 56 (2020), 213–44, we want to add some corrections. Notes 39–43 on page 234 are missing. The following notes were originally submitted:

[39] Stimulating remarks on the heuristic value of models and reconstructions are offered by Bernard Frischer, "Introduction: From Digital Illustration to Digital Heuristics," in Bernard Frischer and Anastasia Dakouri-Hild (eds.), *Beyond Illustration: 2D and 3D Digital Technologies as Tools for Discovery in Archaeology* (Oxford, 2008), v–xxiv.

[40] Apart from the article by Mauric-Barberio cited in note 36, see Wolfgang Waitkus, "Zur Deutung einiger apotropäischer Götter in den Gräbern im Tal der Königinnen und im Grabe Ramses III," *GM* 99 (1987), 51–82.

[41] See the contribution of Judith Bunbury concerning the geology.

[42] Cf. https://www.getty.edu/conservation/publications_resources/pdf_publications/pdf/qv_vol2.pdf, 24, last accessed October 19, 2022.

[43] Large areas, like the big breakout on the east wall in hall J, were covered by a wall construction consisting of limestone pieces and mortar. See Weber, "First Report," fig. 2.

[51] For more information about our archive research, see Hovestreydt et al., "KV 11 revisited," 36–41; and Weber et al., "Third Report," 79–104.

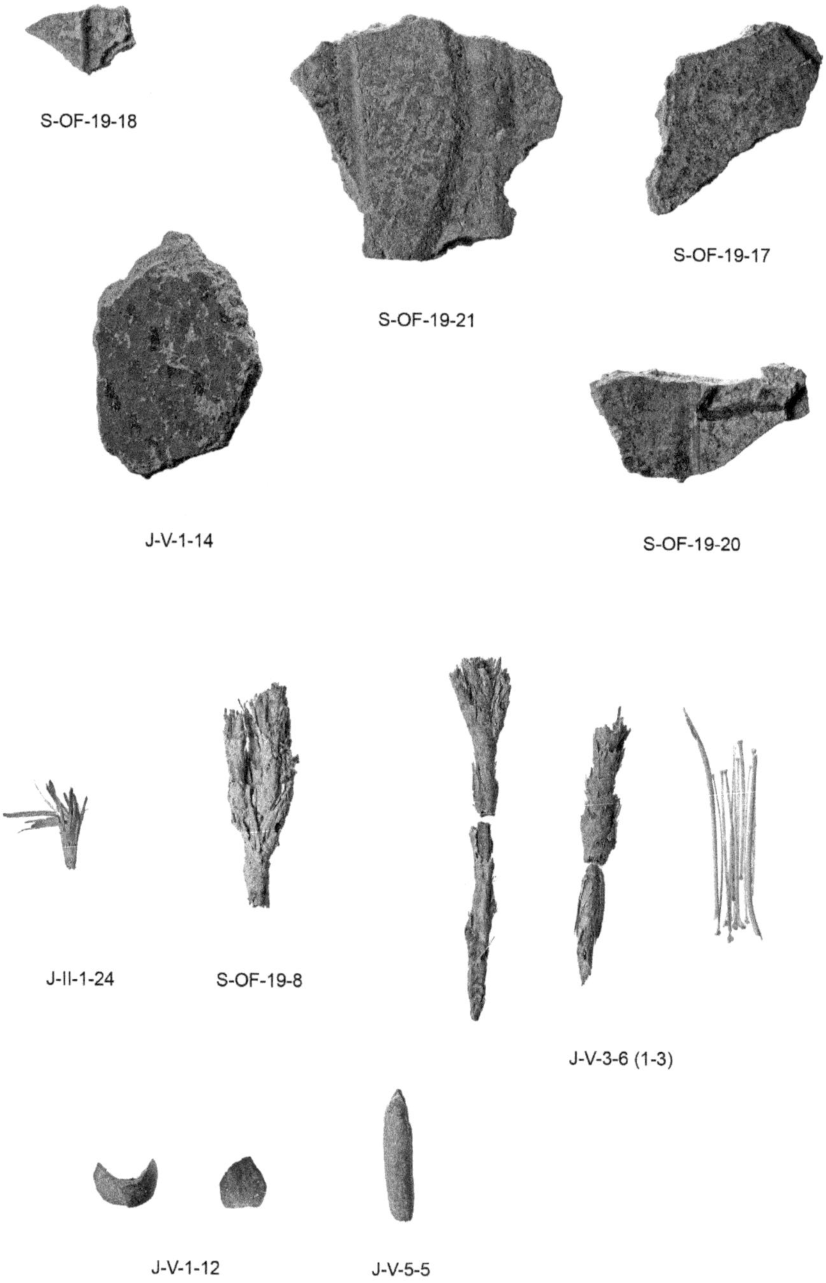

Fig. 13. Plaster fragments and plant residues. © The Ministry of Antiquities, The Ramesses III (KV 11) Publication and Conservation Project, photos: Johannes Kramer.

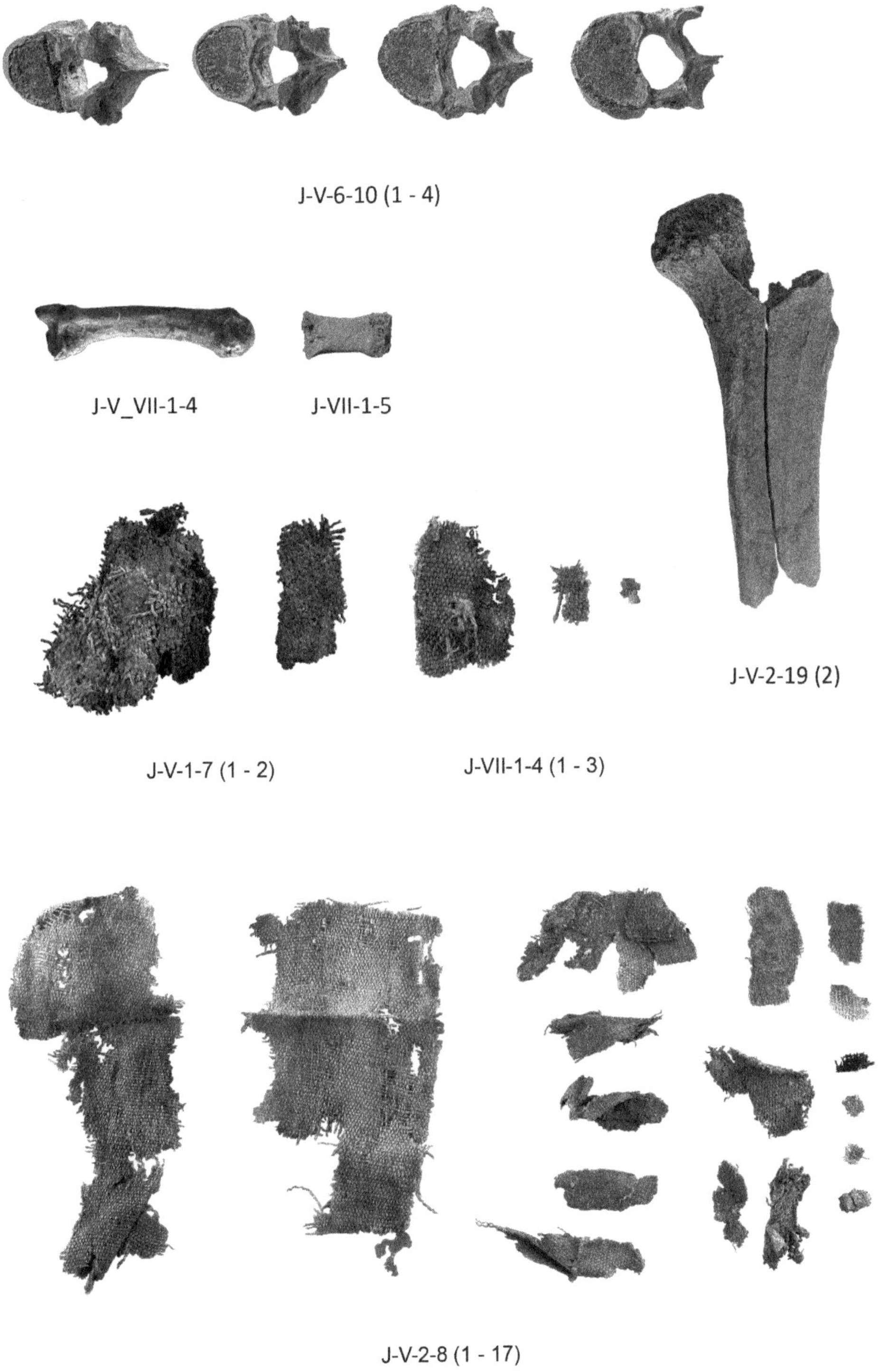

Fig. 14. Bones and linen fragments. © The Ministry of Antiquities, The Ramesses III (KV 11) Publication and Conservation Project, photos: Johannes Kramer, Anke Weber.

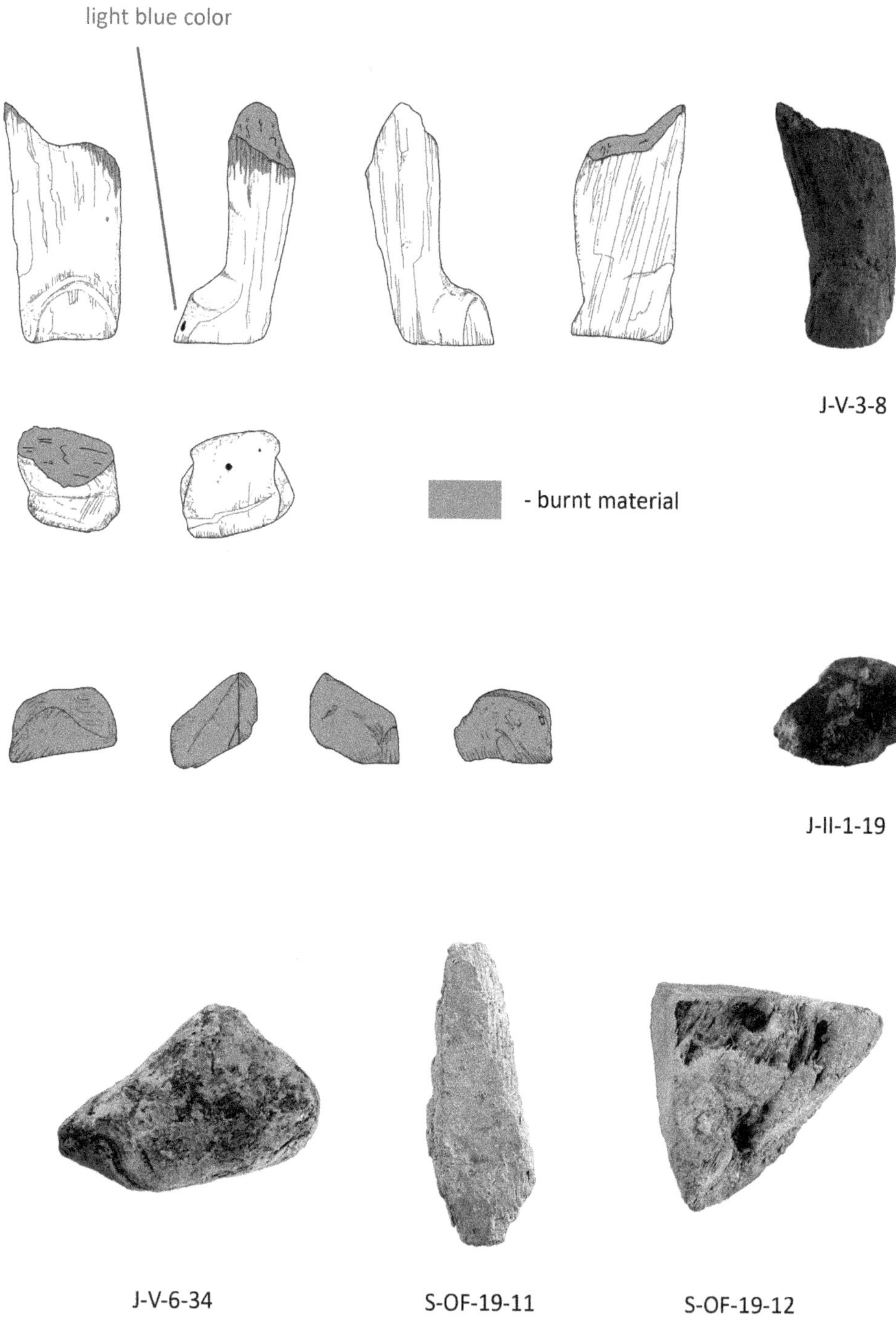

Fig. 15. Wooden finds. © The Ministry of Antiquities, The Ramesses III (KV 11) Publication and Conservation Project, photos: Johannes Kramer, Anke Weber, drawings: Anke Weber.

J-V-2-10

S-OF-19-14

J-V-1-2

Fig. 16. Sherds and jar stopper. © The Ministry of Antiquities, The Ramesses III (KV 11) Publication and Conservation Project, photos: Johannes Kramer, Anke Weber.

Fig. 17. Color imprints from decoration of the burial chamber and wood imprint probably from furniture. © The Ministry of Antiquities, The Ramesses III (KV 11) Publication and Conservation Project, photos: Johannes Kramer, Anke Weber.

Table 1. Discussed finds from the 2019/2020 field season.

No.	Find No.	Category	Material	Height in cm	Width in cm	Depth in cm	Remarks	Dating	Figure
1	H-1-7	coin	metal	2	2	0.15	Taiwanese one yuan coin	1981	
2	J-II-1-19	foot of an ushabti (?)	wood	2.8	2.2	1.4	completely burnt		15
3	J-II-1-24	plant residue	organic	1.5	1.9	0.1			13
4	J-V-1-2	jar stopper	clay mixture	7.6	12.2	-	part of embalming vessel (?)	probably New Kingdom or later	16
5	J-V-1-7 (1)	linen fragment	textile	2	3.5	0.2	mummy shroud?		14
6	J-V-1-14	wall fragment	paint on plaster	7.4	2.5	2.7	sand way, west wall hall J	Ramesses III	13
7	J-V-1-12 (1)	plant residue	organic	0.7	1.2	0.1	Persea?		13
8	J-V-1-12 (2)	plant residue	organic	1.0	1.0	0.1	Persea?		13
9	J-V-2-8 (1-17)	linen fragments	textile	(too fragile and too small to be measured)			mummy shroud?		14
10	J-V-2-10	vessel fragment	pottery	4.3	5.3	1.2	sherd with adhering linen		16
11	J-V-2-19 (2)	bone fragment	bone	14.2	6.6	3.0	human, adult		14
12	J-V-3-6 (2)	plant residue	organic	7.4	1.4	0.3			13
13	J-V-3-8	foot of an ushabti	wood	5.3	2.7	2.3	partly burnt		15
14	J-V-5-5	date kernel	organic	2.7	0.7	0.7		modern?	13
15	J-V-6-10 (1)	bone fragment	bone	3.9	1.9	2.4	vertebra		14
16	J-V-6-10 (2)	bone fragment	bone	3.8	1.9	2.4	vertebra		14
17	J-V-6-10 (3)	bone fragment	bone	3.9	2.1	2.3	vertebra		14
18	J-V-6-10 (4)	bone fragment	bone	4.2	2.5	2.5	vertebra		14

No.	*Find No.*	*Category*	*Material*	*Height in cm*	*Width in cm*	*Depth in cm*	*Remarks*	*Dating*	*Figure*
19	J-V-6-25	color imprint	sediment	16.0	12.9	21.0	painting from west wall or pillar (?)	Ramesses III	17
20	J-V-6-27 (2)	color imprint	sediment	9.4	7.6	-	ram-headed vulture, west wall hall J (?)	Ramesses III	17
21	J-V-6-34	foot of an ushabti?	wood	6.8	4.8	2.1			15
22	J-V-6-37	color imprint	sediment	12.0	18.8	11.0	rest of painted wooden object?	Ramesses III	17
23	J-V-6-44	flashbulb	glass	4.2	1.6	1.6		1950s–1970s	
24	J-V-6-53 (2)	color imprint	sediment, plaster	8.1	7.4	2.2	rest of hieroglyph from wall or column (?)	Ramesses III	17
25	J-V_VII-1-4	bone fragment	bone	5.9	0.8-1.2		human?		14
26	J-VII-1-4 (1)	linen fragment	textile	2.3	2.7	0.1	mummy shroud?		14
27	J-VII-1-5	bone fragment	bone	2.5	1.0	0.9	human?		14
28	J-IX_XI-1-7	handkerchief	textile	26.0	26.0	-		modern	
29	M1 (1)	ticket to Valley of the Kings, 3 tombs	paper				I; ticket price 55 EGP; colored SCA logo; No. 054636	modern	
30	M1 (2-4)	tickets to Valley of the Kings	paper				I; ticket price 5 EGP; SCA logo; Nos. 342412, 342428, 342429	modern	
31	M1 (5)	ticket to Valley of the Kings, 3 tombs	paper				I; ticket price 10 EGP; EAO logo; No. 439626	modern	
32	M2 (1-2)	tickets mini train	paper				J; ticket price 100 p.; Nos. 17574, 17575	modern	

No.	*Find No.*	*Category*	*Material*	*Height in cm*	*Width in cm*	*Depth in cm*	*Remarks*	*Dating*	*Figure*
33	M4 (1-10)	tickets to Valley of the Kings	paper				Jd; ticket price 1 EGP; EAO logo; Nos. 129466, 129467, 129468, 129469, 129484, 129490, 129491, 129492, 129493, 129494	modern	
34	M4 (11-14)	tickets to Valley of the Kings	paper				Jd; ticket price 5 EGP; SCA logo; Nos. 338977, 338980, 454185, 454192	modern	
35	M5 (1-5)	tickets to Valley of the Kings, 3 tombs	paper				I; ticket price 10 EGP; EAO logo; numbers torn off	modern	
36	M5 (6)	ticket to Valley of the Kings, 3 tombs	paper				I; ticket price 55 EGP; SCA logo; No. 054471	modern	
37	M5 (7)	ticket to Luxor Temple (by day)	paper				I; ticket price 20 EGP; SCA logo; No. 993317	modern	
38	M5 (8)	water bottle label	paper				I; brand name Vittel	1986	
39	M6 (1-6)	tickets to Valley of the Kings	paper				I; ticket price 1 EGP; EAO logo; numbers torn off	modern	
40	M6 (7)	ticket to Valley of the Kings	paper				I; ticket price 1 EGP; EAO logo; No. 831910	modern	
41	M7 (1)	ticket to Valley of the Kings	paper				I; ticket price 5 EGP; SCA logo; number torn off	modern	

No.	*Find No.*	*Category*	*Material*	*Height in cm*	*Width in cm*	*Depth in cm*	*Remarks*	*Dating*	*Figure*
42	M7 (2)	ticket to Valley of the Kings, 3 tombs	paper				I; ticket price 55 EGP; colored SCA logo; No. 1054461	modern	
43	M7 (3)	ticket to Valley of the Kings	paper				I; ticket price 5 EGP; SCA logo; No. 420219	modern	
44	M7 (4)	sugar packaging	plastic				I; "سكر مستورد" (Eng: imported sugar)	1990	
45	M8 (1)	newspaper page	paper				Jd	Aug. 19, 1990	
46	M8 (2-3)	newspaper pages	paper				Jd	Nov. 3, 1990	
47	M8 (4)	newspaper page	paper				Jd; includes an add with the date of Nov. 7, 1990	Nov. 1990	
48	M9	ticket to Valley of the Kings, 3 tombs	paper				Ja; ticket price 1 EGP; SCA logo; number torn off	modern	
49	M10	ticket mini train	paper				I; ticket price 4 EGP; No. 168	Mar. 11, 2013	
50	M11	food packaging of chocolate wafer	metalized plastic				I; brand and product name Candy Makers – Tito	production date Jan. 1, 2008; expiration date Sep. 31, 2009	
51	M12 (1-3)	tickets to Valley of the Kings	paper				I; ticket price torn off; EAO logo; Nos. 292473, 292475; 292476; found on a modern restoration	modern	
52	M13 (1-2)	newspaper pages	paper				I	modern	

No.	*Find No.*	*Category*	*Material*	*Height in cm*	*Width in cm*	*Depth in cm*	*Remarks*	*Dating*	*Figure*
53	M13 (3)	candy packaging	paper				I, product name Deemah Juice	production date: Dec. 1, 2003; expiration date Dec. 31, 2004	
54	S-OF-19-8	plant residue	organic	5.9	1.5	0.4			13
55	S-OF-19-11	piece of furniture/ coffin?	wood with painting layer	6.7	2.3	0.9	ushabti box (?) or coffin (?)		15
56	S-OF-19-12	piece of furniture/ coffin?	wood	8.6	7.4	3.7			15
57	S-OF-19-14	vessel fragment	pottery	8.0	9.9	0.6	sherd of an amphora	New Kingdom	16
58	S-OF-19-17	wall fragment	paint on plaster	6.2	6.9	0.8	decoration, room L, niche west wall	Ramesses III	13
59	S-OF-19-18	wall fragment	paint on plaster	2.4	4.3	1.1	decoration, room L, niche west wall	Ramesses III	13
60	S-OF-19-20	wall fragment	paint on plaster	5.6	9.4	1.2	decoration, room L, niche west wall	Ramesses III	13
61	S-OF-19-21	wall fragment	paint on plaster	11.0	9.7	3.4	decoration, room L, niche west wall	Ramesses III	13
62	S-OF-19-31	coin	metal	2.1	2.1	0.15	Swiss 20 rappen coin	1981	

A Basinophorous Statue for Meryptah and Ruiu in Glencairn Museum

Jennifer Houser Wegner
Egyptian Section, University of Pennsylvania Museum of Archaeology and Antropology, USA

Abstract

Statues comprised of an individual kneeling at the edge of an offering basin make their appearance as early as the Middle Kingdom. This is a relatively rare type of statuary with only several dozen examples known. These basinophorous statues promised their owners eternal refreshment. A previously unpublished example is presented here. A chantress of Amun named Ruiu and her husband Meryptah, who held a series of high-status offices during the reign of Amenhotep III, are the dedicants of this basin. This article suggests that the Meryptah mentioned on this basin may be the same as the Meryptah attested on other monuments from Amenhotep III's reign.

الملخص

تظهر التماثيل المكونة من فرد راكع على حافة حوض قرابين من فترة الدولة الوسطى بمصر القديمة. إن هذا نوع نادر نسبيًا من التماثيل، مع وجود عشرات الأمثلة المعروفة فقط. وقد ضمنت هذه التماثيل لأصحابها القرابين الأبدية. يتم تقديم مثال غير منشور سابقًا هنا من هذا النوع من التماثيل. ان هذا التمثال يمثل منشدة للإله آمون تُدعى رويو وزوجها مريبتاح، اللذان كانا يشغلان سلسلة من المناصب الرفيعة المستوى في عهد أمنحتب الثالث. يقترح هذا المقال أن مريبتاح المذكور في هذا التمثال قد يكون هو نفسه مريبتاح الذي يمثل على آثار أخرى من عهد أمنحتب الثالث.

History of the Glencairn Basin

Glencairn Museum in Bryn Athyn, Pennsylvania has a small, but chronologically and typologically representative collection of ancient Egyptian objects. Glencairn, a medieval Romanesque castle-style ninety-room mansion was the private home of Raymond Pitcairn and his wife, Mildred Glenn Pitcairn. Raymond Pitcairn was the eldest son of John Pitcairn, Jr., a wealthy industrialist who worked in both the oil and natural gas industries and was a founder of the Pittsburgh Plate Glass Company. John Pitcairn amassed one of the largest fortunes in the United States by the time of his death in 1916, and his son Raymond followed in his father's footsteps. Raymond was a lawyer and a businessman by profession, but he was also an amateur architect and was responsible for the design of Glencairn. The building was intended to be the family's private residence as well as a repository for their art collection. The Pitcairn family—Raymond, his wife Mildred, and their children—moved into Glencairn in 1939. The building served as their private home until Mildred died in 1979; Raymond had predeceased her in 1966.

In 1980, Glencairn and its contents, including the art collection, were given to the Academy of the New Church, the alma mater of both Raymond and Mildred Pitcairn. The collections of the Academy's museum moved to Glencairn and merged with the Pitcairn collections to create what is today known as Glencairn Mu-

Journal of the American Research Center in Egypt 58 (2022), 267–83
http://dx.doi.org/10.5913/jarce.58.2022.a013

Fig. 1. View of Glencairn Museum in Bryn Athyn, PA. Photo courtesy of Glencairn Museum.

seum, an institution with a focus on religious art and history (fig. 1). The museum's collections include materials from ancient Egypt, the Near East, and the Classical World, as well as Asian Art, tapestries, and a world-renowned collection of medieval stained glass and statuary.[1] Glencairn's Egyptian collection is displayed chronologically and thematically on the fourth floor of the museum in a dedicated gallery space. However, one Egyptian object—an impressive granodiorite offering basin (E1178)—is housed on the museum's first floor in a room designed with an arched niche decorated with a beautiful cut-glass mosaic of a large white peacock (figs. 2, 3).[2] Raymond Pitcairn designed this space specifically for the purpose of displaying the offering basin.[3]

Both Raymond Pitcairn and his brother Theodore Pitcairn had an interest in ancient art, and they frequented dealers, principally in New York City, making many significant art purchases in the 1920s. This basin was purchased by Raymond Pitcairn on behalf of his brother Theodore from the dealers George and Lucien Demotte in 1923. The archives at Glencairn Museum preserve correspondence about the acquisition of the piece. Raymond wrote in a letter to Theodore: "It is a very good and rare piece in my estimation. I felt this on seeing it

[1] Built between 1928–1939, Glencairn takes its name from a combination of Raymond and Mildred's surnames. For a discussion of Glencairn Museum and its collections see E. Bruce Glenn et al., *Glencairn: the Story of a Home* (Bryn Athyn, 1990); Ed Gyllenhaal, "From parlor to castle: the Egyptian collection at Glencairn Museum," in Zahi Hawass and Jennifer Houser Wegner (eds.), *Millions of Jubilees: Studies in Honor of David P. Silverman*, vol. 1 (Cairo, 2010), 175–203, and Ed Gyllenhaal and Kirsten Hansen Gyllenhaal, *The Bryn Athyn Historic District* (Charleston, 2011). I am grateful to the following individuals for their assistance during the research of the Glencairn basin: Bret Bostock (Assistant Director, Glencairn Museum), Kevin Cahail (Penn Museum), Ed Gyllenhaal (Curator, Glencairn Museum), Kirsten Gyllenhaal (Museum Researcher, Glencairn Museum), Brian Henderson (Director, Glencairn Museum), Drew Nehlig, (Historic Buildings Project Manager, Glencairn Museum), and Joe Wegner (Penn Museum). A preliminary study of this object was presented at the ARCE 68th Annual Meeting in Kansas City, MO in 2017. See also https://glencairnmuseum.org/newsletter/2017/7/19/egyptian-libation-bowl-at-glencairn-museum

[2] This room is referred to as the Bird Room due to the preponderance of avian motifs on the walls and ceiling.

[3] Throughout the years the family lived in the home this niche was a favorite place to photograph important guests who came to visit and to take family photos. The basin itself was a favorite object of the Pitcairns, and the Pitcairn children used to raise baby turtles in it.

Fig. 2. The basin of Meryptah and Ruiu (E1178) on display in the so-called Bird Room. Photo courtesy of Glencairn Museum.

Fig. 3. Top and side view of the basin of Meryptah and Ruiu. Photo © Jennifer Houser Wegner.

several times at Demotte's and this view was confirmed by a very good letter from the director of the Egyptian Department at the Metropolitan shown to me by Demotte."[4] Raymond further assured his brother that if he wasn't happy with the purchase: "I like it sufficiently well to be ready at any time to take it off your hands if you do not care to have it."[5] Ultimately, Raymond Pitcairn's wife, Mildred Pitcairn, was so fond of the dark stone basin with the small kneeling figure that her brother-in-law gave the basin to her as a gift, and in 1939, it was permanently installed in Glencairn, the family's home.

Basinophorous Statues

Raymond Pitcairn was quite correct in his estimation of the piece as a significant work of art.[6] Examples of Egyptian statuary consisting of a human figure kneeling while supporting or presenting an object such as a stela, shrine, sistrum, or divine image are well known from the Middle Kingdom through the Late Period.[7] Statues of figures with an accompanying circular or rectangular basin, however, are considerably less common. Characteristically, one individual is present, but a few examples are known with multiple figures—either a pair of figures,[8] or in one case, a group of three individuals.[9] Variations in the posture of the figures occur. Most of the figures

[4] Letter dated 2/2/1923 (Glencairn curatorial records).

[5] Letter dated 2/2/1923 (Glencairn curatorial records).

[6] In the years following the basin's acquisition, Raymond Pitcairn reached out to several scholars for their opinions on the basin and translations of the texts, but none of these preliminary examinations were ever published. The archives at Glencairn contain copies of these early translations including those of R. W. Brown (1927), Battiscombe Gunn (n.d.), and John D. Cooney (1948).

[7] For a discussion of the increased popularity of this statue type in the Eighteenth Dynasty, see Edith Bernhauer, *Innovationen in der Privatplastik: Die 18. Dynastie un ihre Entwicklung* (Wiesbaden, 2010).

[8] There are six examples of basinophorous statuary which include two figures: the Late Period example inscribed with an offering formula to Taweret and Hathor (British Museum EA1258); the basin of Heka-maat-re-nakht and his wife Ujai (Vienna, Kunsthistorisches Museum, Ägyptisch-Orientalische Sammlung 50); the statue of Osiris with two kneeling figures and basin (Marseille, Château Borély 211); the seated statue of Osiris with two kneeling figures and basin (Cairo CG 38411); the basin of Hyhy and his wife Nena (Boston, Museum of Fine Arts Exp. No. 26-1-495). See Kirsten Konrad, "Ein weiterer Basinophor: Zur Deutung der Sitzstatue eines Schreibers namens Eje (Ijj)," *SAK* 42 (2013), 183, n. 20.

[9] BM EA465 is a fragmentary libation basin with three figures. See Morris L. Bierbrier, *Hieroglyphic Texts from Egyptian Stelae, etc., in the British Museum, Part 10* (London, 1982), 38 and pl. 87.

appear in a kneeling position, but some examples show the individual in a cross-legged seated position. The position of the figure's arms and hands also varies. Most have their hands resting atop the rim of the basin, but some individuals hug, hold, or offer the water receptacle held in their arms.[10] Often, an inscription in the form of a *ḥtp-di-nswt* offering prayer decorates the rim or exterior faces of the basin. The Glencairn libation basin is among the best preserved of this category of artifacts and it is certainly one of the finest surviving examples of this genre of sculpture.[11]

Although previously known to scholars of Egyptian sculpture, detailed discussion of objects of this type began in 1985 when Dietrich Wildung published a "Kniefigur am Opferbecken" statue belonging to a man by the name of Ptahankh.[12] Dating to the reign of Amenhotep III, Wildung identified this statue as a rare type, and he documented thirteen parallels ranging in date from the New Kingdom to the Late Period.[13] Wildung proposed that the appearance of this new form of statuary in the mid-Eighteenth Dynasty was an expression of a changed relationship between an individual and the divine that would further develop into the "personal piety" seen in the Ramesside Period.[14] As these statues incorporate both a representation of an individual (or individuals) as well as a basin for liquids, Wildung suggested that by drinking from the basin, the figure—shown in the midst of this action—would, therefore (eternally) share in offerings to the gods, and be able to commune with the divine.[15]

In 2004, Kirsten Konrad expanded on the analysis of one of the statues previously identified by Wildung: a uniquely designed rectangular basin decorated with architectural motifs and a figure of a scribe by the name of Amenemhet.[16] This object was discovered in the sanctuary of the small temple of Ramses II in the southwest corner of the enclosure of the Great Temple of Ptah at Memphis.[17] In her study of the piece, Konrad proposed the use of the term "basinophorous" statue[18] to describe statuary of this type and concurred with Wildung's previous interpretation that these basinophorous statues were an overt expression of an individual's personal piety in an era when religious practices increasingly expanded modes of divine interaction. In the case of Amenemhat's statue, a close association with the Memphite creator god Ptah is emphasized. She posits that the sculpture represented Amenemhet's private cosmos and would provide for his enduring maintenance.[19]

In a second article focusing on basinophorous statues, Konrad argued in favor of further expanding the original corpus to include a total of thirty-five examples,[20] contending that the origins of this statue type can be identified as early as the Middle Kingdom.[21] She did, however, observe that the New Kingdom was the main period of production of basinophorous statues, while the sculptural type persisted into later eras and several additional examples date to the Late Period.[22] A distinct subset of the corpus of basinophorous statues consists of those with a large round basin and associated figure(s). This group consists of ten examples, six dating to the

---

[10] Note for example the arm position of the figure on the basin of Ptahankh (Antikenmuseum und Sammlung Ludwig in Basel, inventory number BSAe 1031) and that of the anonymous figure in Cairo (JE 45636). See Dietrich Wildung, "Die Kniefigur am Opferbecken: Überlegungen zur Funktion altägyptischer Plastik," *Münchner Jahrbuch der bildenden Kunst. Dritte Folge* 36 (1985), 14–15 and figs. 1–4.

[11] The Glencairn basin is also quite unusual as it is the only known basinophorous statue with a single female figure represented.

[12] Wildung, "Die Kniefigur am Opferbecken," 17–38.

[13] Wildung, "Die Kniefigur am Opferbecken," 19–33.

[14] Wildung, "Die Kniefigur am Opferbecken," 36.

[15] Wildung, "Die Kniefigur am Opferbecken," 33.

[16] Kirsten Konrad, "Der Ptah des Amenemhet: zur theologischen Konzeption einer Kniefigur am Opferbecken," *SAK* 32 (2004), 255–74.

[17] For the history of the publication of this statue, see Konrad, "Der Ptah des Amenemhet," 255–56, nn. 2–5.

[18] This term is a counterpart to previously accepted descriptive terms for statuary such as "naophorous," "stelaphorous" and "sistophorous" wherein individuals are depicted holding or presenting such attributes, see Konrad, "Der Ptah des Amenemhet," 257–58.

[19] Konrad, "Der Ptah des Amenemhet," 273–74.

[20] Konrad, "Ein weiterer Basinophor," 181–92. It should be noted that after the publication of this article, another New Kingdom example was excavated at the Mut complex in Luxor by the Brooklyn Museum in 2010. See https://www.brooklynmuseum.org/community/blogosphere/2010/01/22/were-up-and-running/ and https://d1lfxha3ugu3d4.cloudfront.net/features/docs/Preliminary_Report_2010.pdf.

[21] Konrad cites two documents dating to this time, the statue of *Shebnu* from Elephantine (Aswan Museum, Magazine) and the miniature example in the Metropolitan Museum Art (15.3.591.2). See Konrad, "Ein weiterer Basinophor," 192.

[22] Five basinophorous statues are known from the Late Period. All of them are designed with (a) kneeling figure(s) and a large circular basin. See British Museum EA1258; British Museum EA 1292; Statue of Peftjawnawyaset (Copenhagen Thorvaldsend Museum H357); statue of Wahibre (Christie's, New York, Antiquities, 08.06.2001, 81: Lot 114); statue fragment of Horwedja (Bonhams, London, Antiquities,

New Kingdom and four to the Late Period. As we shall discuss in detail below, the Glencairn basin, dating to the reign of Amenhotep III, is amongst the earliest of the group.[23]

The ritual and religious function of the basinophorous statues clearly lies in the sphere of libations. Liquid offerings were an essential part of Egyptian cult practices, both in tomb and temple settings.[24] Konrad observed that the round basins resemble the form of Gardiner N41 symbolizing a spring filled with water, while the rectangular examples have the form of Gardiner W10 and at the same time are also reminiscent of the lake or canal hieroglyph (Gardiner N36 and N37). This connection with various water features also recalls the Nile floodwaters. As such, the associated figure(s) can be envisioned as drinking the life-giving waters of the Nile and participating in the annual regeneration of the whole country.[25] Wildung drew a parallel between basinophorous statues where the individual kneels in a respectful pose before an empty basin hoping and expecting that the gods will provide the life-giving water, and the Ramesside tomb scenes which depict deceased individuals alongside their ba, drinking from pools often before a water-bearing tree goddess.[26]

A similarity can also be seen between these statues and contemporary texts that express a desire to receive water in the afterlife. In the Amarna tomb of Pentu, we see the wish: "May you grant that I rest in my place of continuity that I be enclosed in the cavern of eternity; that I may go forth and enter into my tomb without my Ba's being restrained from what it wishes; that I might stride to the place of my heart's determining, in the groves which I made on earth; that I might drink water at the edge of my pool every day without cease."[27] Similar wishes can be found on Eighteenth Dynasty stelae, for example: "May they (i.e., the gods) grant (to me) to be an Akh in heaven, powerful on earth, justified in the god's domain, to enter my tomb and to come out of it, to refresh myself in its shadow and to drink water from my pool every day"[28] and "… when thy name is invoked at the table of offering every time the rite is performed, may thy Ba cry aloud so that it may be heard. (Thus) it shall not be kept back from the great place, and thou wilt partake of the offerings brought forward and drink water at the edge of the pool."[29] An additional explanation for the function of these basinophorous statues can be seen on an inscription on one of the Late Period examples which states that "the deceased may be refreshed by

---

30.10.2003, 13: Lot 23). If one also includes the Thirtieth Dynasty healing statue of Djedhor (Cairo Museum, JE46341), that brings the total to six. Konrad, "Ein weiterer Basinophor," 183.

[23] These round basins are as follows: (1) basin of Ruiu and Meryptah (Glencairn Museum E1178), Eighteenth Dynasty, temp. Amenhotep III; (2) basin of Huy (Berlin, Ägyptisches Museum 19900), Eighteenth Dynasty (temp. Tutankhamun?); (3) basin of Heka-maat-re-nakht and Ujai (Vienna, Kunsthistorisches Museum, Ägyptisch-Orientalische Sammlung, INV 50), Eighteenth-Nineteenth Dynasty; (4) fragment of basin (Brooklyn Museum Mut Temple excavations (24ME.3), Eighteenth-Nineteenth Dynasty; (5) basin with two figures (British Museum EA 1258), Nineteenth Dynasty; (6) basin of Hormin (British Museum EA 465); (7) basin of Montuemhet (British Museum EA 1292), Twenty-Sixth Dynasty; (8) statue fragment of Horwedja (Bonhams, London, Antiquities, 30.10.2003, 13: Lot 23), Twenty-Sixth Dynasty (9) statue of Peftjawnawyaset (Copenhagen Thorvaldsend Museum H357), Twenty-sixth Dynasty and (10) statue of Wahibre, (Christie's, New York, Antiquities, 08.06.2001, 81: Lot 114). For the relevant bibliography, see Wildung, "Die Kniefigur am Opferbecken," 29–30; Konrad, "Der Ptah des Amenemhet," 256–57, n. 9, and Konrad, "Ein weiterer Basinophor," 182, n. 5. It is also interesting to note that when the statues with rectangular basins are compared with the round exemplars, none of the rectangular basins bear Hathoric imagery, while most of the round ones do.

[24] Basins for liquid offerings have been found in Old Kingdom tombs and offering tables with receptacles for liquid are known from tombs dating to the Middle Kingdom (1980–1630 BCE) through the Greco-Roman Period (332 BCE and later). Water is also ubiquitous in temple cult rituals, used for purification and as a liquid offering, see Joris F. Borghouts, 1980. "Libation," in *LÄ* 3, cols. 1014–15. It should be noted that healing statues such as that of Djedhor (Cairo Museum, JE46341) also make use of water receptacles, see Pierre Lacau, *Les Statues "guérisseuses" dans L'ancienne Égypte* (Paris, 1922), 191–93.

[25] Konrad, "Der Ptah des Amenemhet," 259. Further, drinking the water activates the formula on the side of the pool, see Erika Meyer-Dietrich, *Auditive Räume des alten Ägypten: Die Umgestaltung einer Hörkultur in der Amarnazeit* (Leiden; Boston, 2017), 105–06.

[26] Wildung, "Die Kniefigur am Opferbecken," 34–36.

[27] For this translation, see William J. Murnane and Edmund S Meltzer, *Texts from the Amarna Period in Egypt* (Atlanta, 1995), 181 (80.3). For this text in the tomb of Pentu, see Norman de Garis, *The Rock Tombs of El-'Amarna, part IV. The Tombs of Penthu, Mahu & Others* (London, 1906), 30 and pl. 4.

[28] From Louvre C55, the stela of Nakhtmin. See Alfred Hermann, *Die Stelen Der Thebanischen Felsgräber Der 18. Dynastie* (Glückstadt, 1940), 52*. Translation from Louis V. Žabkar, *A Study of the Ba Concept in Ancient Egyptian Texts,* SAOC 34 (Chicago, 1968), 138.

[29] From the stela in tomb C1 at Gurna (Amenhotep). See Victor Loret, "Le Tombeau de l'am-xent Amen-hotep," *MMAF* 1.1 (1889), 25, and Hermann, *Die Stelen Der Thebanischen Felsgräber*, 48*, and Žabkar, *A Study of the Ba Concept*, 139.

means of it," i.e., the contents of the bowl.[30] Based on these textual sources, basinophorous statues might be viewed as three-dimensional, sculptural versions of the scene described in the texts. The statues emphasize the eternal presence of the individuals poised to receive the liquid refreshment that the basins contain.

Concerning the original location of these objects, unfortunately, many of the basinophorous statues have no provenience (as is also the case for the Glencairn basin). While Wildung has argued that many of the unprovenanced examples likely have a Memphite origin,[31] excavated examples have come from a wide geographical range including not only Memphis, [32] but also Abusir,[33] Hermopolis,[34] Deir el Bahri,[35] and Luxor Temple.[36] As for the specific architectural setting (i.e., a tomb versus temple context) where these objects were originally installed, a relief now in the collection of the Petrie Museum, University College London, perhaps of Memphite origin, may provide some insight (fig. 4). The scene depicts a man and a woman kneeling at the edge of a water container into which liquid is flowing from an offering table adjacent to the basin.[37] It is interesting to note that the position of the man and woman's heads and hands on the rim of the basin is exactly the same as what we see on most of the basinophorous statues, and the profile of the basin takes the shape of Gardiner W10. The appearance of colossal statuary and columns surrounding the pair and the basin suggest that the locale depicted is a temple.[38] We will return to this issue of the possible context of the Glencairn basinophorous statue after examining the date and ownership of the object.

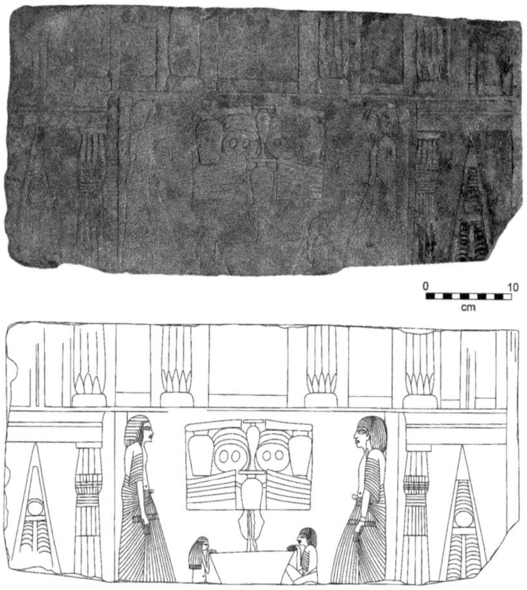

Fig. 4. Fragment of raised limestone relief (UC 408) depicting a man and woman kneeling by a basin surrounded by architectural features. Image courtesy of The Petrie Museum of Egyptian Archaeology UCL.

---

30 See https://www.bonhams.com/auctions/10370/lot/23/?category=list&length=10&page=3 for a translation of the text on the basin of Horwedja.

31 Wildung, "Kniefigur am Opferbecken," 33.

32 The basin of Amenemhet, see *PM* 3², 845; Rudolf Anthes, *Mit Rahineh 1956* (Philadelphia, 1965), 73–75, pls. 24–25; Jean Jacquet, "Un bassin de libation du Nouvel Empire dédié à Ptah. Première partie: l'architecture," *MDAIK* 16 (1958), 161–67; Helen Wall-Gordon, " A New Kingdom libation basin dedicated to Ptah: second part. The inscriptions," *MDAIK* 16 (1958), 168–75; Wildung, "Kniefigur am Opferbecken," 29.

33 The basin of Huy, Berlin, Ägyptisches Museum 19900. *PM* 3², 334; Ludwig Borchardt, *Das Grabdenkmal des Königs Sahure* I (Leipzig, 1910), 120–21, fig. 164; Bodil Hornemann, *Types of Ancient Egyptian Statuary* III (Copenhagen, 1957), pl. 636; Wildung, "Kniefigur am Opferbecken," 29 and fig. 21.

34 The basin of Nehemawai, see Günther Roeder, *Hermopolis 1929–1939* (Hildesheim 1959), pl. 73a, and Wildung, "Kniefigur am Opferbecken," 28 and fig. 18.

35 The basin of Amenmose, Rome, Museo Egizio Vaticano 142, see Rudolf Anthes, "Das Opferbecken des Wesiers Amenmose im Museo Egizio Vaticano," in Anonymous (ed.), *Miscellanea Gregoriana: raccolta di scritti pubblicati nel I centenario dalla fondazione del Pont. Museo Egizio (1839–1939)* (Rome, 1941), 1–7, and Wildung, "Kniefigur am Opferbecken," 29.

36 A fragment of a basinophorous statue from the Brooklyn Museum's Mut Temple excavations (24ME.3). See note 20 above.

37 For this relief, see Jean Capart, *Recueil de monuments égyptiens: cinquante planches phototypiques avec texte explicatif* (Bruxelles, 1902), pl. 42; Harry Milne Stewart, *Egyptian Stelae, Reliefs and Paintings from the Petrie Collection: Part 1. The New Kingdom* (Warminster, 1976), 55, and pl. 53; Geoffrey Thorndike Martin, *The Hidden Tombs of Memphis: New Discoveries from the Time of Tutankhamun and Ramesses the Great* (New York, 1991), 205, and pl. 126; and Alain Charron and Christophe Barbotin (eds.), *Savoir et Pouvoir. À l'Époque de Ramses II. Khaemouaset. Le Prince Archaéologue* (Arles, 2016), 63.

38 For a review of the debate of temple versus tomb setting, see Eric P. Uphill, "A New Kingdom Relief from Memphis," *JEA* 48 (1962), 162–63. See also Wildung, "Die Kniefigur am Opferbecken," 33–34, fig. 26. He observes that the standing pose of the figures and the position of the hands of the statues in a prayerful gesture is more typical of what one would expect to find in a temple forecourt rather than in a

Description of the Glencairn Basin

The Glencairn basin is carved from a single block of granodiorite and measures 65 centimeters in diameter. The object is in an excellent state of preservation with little damage to its sculptural components and only minor losses to the inscriptions that decorate the rim of the bowl.[39] The bowl itself has a rounded bottom, carinated sides, and a recurved upper body. The area on which the figure sits projects from the exterior wall of the basin in a trapezoidal form (figs. 5, 6). Atop this projection, a beautifully carved small female figure perches with her chin and hands resting on the basin's edge. Her head is finely detailed, but her body is less distinct. It has a gumdrop-like shape. Her lower extremities are merely suggested under her garment and her feet are not visible. A decorative feature on the figure's proper right arm represents the pleating on the sleeve of her gown. Her hands rest atop a carved depiction of an offering table decorated with offerings of meats, loaves, and vessels. The table takes the shape of a *hetep* sign, the "loaf" of which projects slightly into the bowl.

She wears a large and elaborate long wig with two significant features: a distinctive type of braid and a noticeable depiction of her hairline (fig. 7). Her heavy wig is embellished with a triple braid that runs down the center

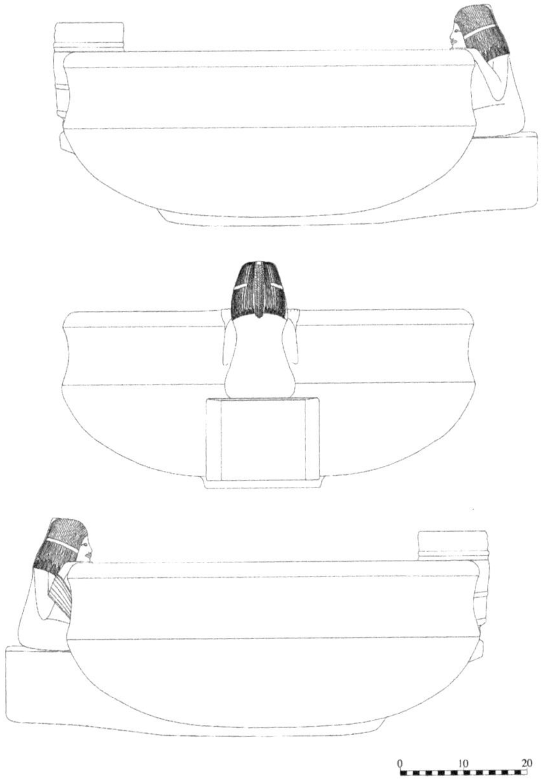

Fig. 5. Drawing of the profile of the basin of Meryptah and Ruiu. Drawing © Josef Wegner.

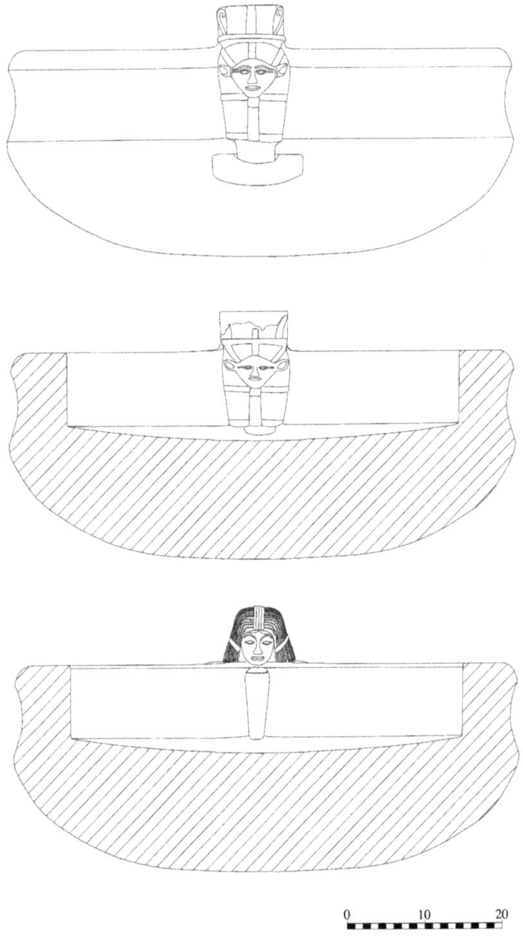

Fig. 6. Drawing of the profile and cross section of the basin of Meryptah and Ruiu. Drawing © Josef Wegner.

New Kingdom tomb setting where the tomb owner is almost always shown seated. Martin, however, describes this scene as that of an offering chapel of a private tomb with colossal statues of the tomb owner. See Martin, *The Hidden Tombs of Memphis*, 205 and pl. 126.

39 The basin underwent a conservation condition survey in March 2019 (Glencairn Museum curatorial records).

Fig. 7. Views of the female figure's distinctive hairstyle featuring a triple braid (left, center) and her natural hairline under her wig (right). Photo © Jennifer Houser Wegner.

of the back of her head. In her study of Egyptian hairstyles, Joann Fletcher has noted that this plaited element first appears during the reign of Tuthmosis IV and is often found on depictions in statuary and paintings of women who hold the title Priestess of Hathor.[40] Another striking element of the figure's wig is the appearance of her natural hairline at the top of her forehead peeking out slightly from beneath her full wig. This feature frequently occurs in women's hairstyles of the Old Kingdom but became less popular during the Middle through New Kingdoms. This type of coiffure seems to have been revived, perhaps as a conscious archaizing style during the reign of Amenhotep III, when several images of his wife, Queen Tiye, depict her natural hairline visible under a large and elaborate wig.[41] This hairstyle can also be seen on the figure of Menana from the pair statue depicting her together with her husband Khaemwaset, similarly dated to the reign of Amenhotep III.[42]

While the figure's chin is set directly on the rim of the basin, her gaze is directed slightly downwards into the vessel, as if she is meant to be looking at the liquid within the bowl. Facing her on the opposite side of the basin is a protome featuring the head of the goddess Hathor carved in high relief (fig. 8). Hathor wears her typically heavy wig banded by a series of ribbons. Atop her head is a crown that takes the form of the *bḫn*, a pylon-like structure framed by two tall tendrils—a feature often seen decorating sistrum sound boxes. The Hathor decoration on the interior wall of the basin is balanced on the vessel's exterior with a similar image of this goddess with comparable attributes. Here the form of Hathor depicted may be the syncretic version of this goddess, Hathor-Nebet-Hetepet, as the adjacent texts and her naos-shaped crown suggests.[43]

[40] Joann Fletcher, *Ancient Egyptian Hair: A Study in Style, Form and Function* (Ph.D. dissertation, University of Manchester, 1995), 69. Lady Ruiu does not hold this title. However, a particular devotion to the goddess Hathor is suggested by the appearance of the two Hathor protomes, as well as the invocation to Hathor-Nebet-Hetepet in the offering formula.

[41] Fletcher, *Ancient Egyptian Hair*, 20. For examples of Queen Tiye with this hairline, see Louvre E25493 (https://collections.louvre.fr/en/ark:/53355/cl010002360) and a statue now in an English private collection, see Arielle P. Kozloff, Betsy M. Bryan, and Lawrence M. Berman (eds.), *Egypt's Dazzling Sun: Amenhotep III and His World* (Cleveland, 1992), 170–71.

[42] Cairo Museum JE 87911, see Mohamed Saleh and Hourig Sourouzian, *The Egyptian Museum, Cairo: Official Catalogue* (Cairo, 1987), no. 152.

[43] The identification of the goddess is slightly confounding as there are two possibilities for her identity. We either have a depiction of the goddess Hathor, here given the epithet *nb.t ḥtp.t*, "lady of offerings" (or lady of the vulva) or we have an image of the syncretic goddess, Hathor-Nebet-Hetepet. For *nb.t ḥtp.t* as an epithet of Hathor, see Christian Leitz et al., *Lexikon der Ägyptischen Götter und Götterbezeichnungen* 3, OLA 112 (Leuven, 2002), 111. The independent goddess Nebet-Hetep is often conflated with Hathor and they share certain epithets such as "the hand of Atum." (The role of the "hand of Atum" is later reinterpreted as expressing the female creative principle which is embodied in Hathor-Nebet-Hetepet. See Geraldine Pinch, "Offerings to Hathor," *Folklore* 93.2 [1982], 146 and Hosam Hosam, "Nebet-Hetepet, Iusas und Temet: Die weiblichen Komplemente des Atum," *GM* 181 [2001], 89–94.) For a discussion of the goddess (Hathor) Nebet-Hetepet, see Jacques Vandier, "Iousaas et (Hathor) Nebet-Hetepet," *RdE* 16 (1964), 55–146; Jacques Vandier, "Iousaas et (Hathor) Nebet-Hetepet," *RdE* 17 (1965), 89–176 and Jacques Vandier, "Iousaas et (Hathor) Nebet-Hetepet," *RdE* 18 (1966), 67–142. Hathor-Nebet-Hetepet is often

Fig. 8. Views of the Hathor protomes on the basin's exterior (left) and interior (right). Photo © Jennifer Houser Wegner.

Fig. 9. RTI image of the slightly raised rectangular area on the rim showing the abraded area of the inscription that contains the cartouche of Nebmaatre. Photo © Jennifer Houser Wegner.

Atop the Hathor heads, in a slightly raised rectangular area on the rim, is a short two-column inscription that has suffered some damage, particularly in the area of the cartouche (fig. 9). The inscription reads: *nswt bity* [/////////] *di ꜥnḫ mry Ḥw.t-Ḥr-Nbt-Ḥtpt* "The king of Upper and Lower Egypt [/////////] given life, the beloved of Hathor-Nebet-Hetepet." The damage to the king's name and its encircling cartouche is severe. Reflective Transformation Imaging photography (RTI) was carried out in an attempt to read more of the signs, but it seems the inscription is truly lost.[44] The only sign within the cartouche which seems visible is a circular sign reading *Rꜥ* (Re). Unfortunately, as prenomina as a rule include the *Rꜥ* (Re) element, the appearance of this sign doesn't help to determine with any certainty which king is named. The name Neb-Maat-Re, would certainly fit the available space.

When one combines Ruiu's distinctive hairstyle, the figure's almond-shaped eyes and plastic eyebrows, and the likely reading of the name of Amenhotep III on the basin's inscriptions, there is no doubt that this libation basin was created during that king's reign. Further support for this date comes from the identification of the individuals named in the dedication inscription as we now discuss.

The Dedication Inscription

The flat rim of the basin is inscribed with two symmetrically placed texts that begin at the rectangular raised panel containing the royal name and read towards the female figure.

These inscriptions contain offering formulae that mention the goddess Hathor-Nebet-Hetepet, and name the dedicants of the basin, a man named Meryptah[45] and his wife, Ruiu.[46] The inscriptions read as follows:

---

connected with the naos sistrum, a version of which we see atop each of the "Hathor" heads on this bowl, See Wilfried Gutekunst, "Nebet-hetepet," *LÄ* 3, col. 362. With regard to a connection between Amenhotep III and Hathor-Nebet-Hetepet, Vandier notes two scarabs with this king's name reading "Nebmaatre, beloved of Hathor-Nebet-Hetepet," see Vandier, "Iousaas et (Hathor) Nebet-Hetepet," *RdE* 16, 80 and W. M. Flinders Petrie, *Scarabs and Cylinders with Names: Illustrated by the Egyptian Collection in University College, London* (London, 1917), pl. 33, nos. 39–40. For the association between Queen Tiye and Hathor-Nebet-Hetepet, see Anna Stevens, "The Amarna Royal Women as Images of Fertility: Perspectives on a Royal Cult," *Journal of Ancient Near Eastern Religions* 4.1 (2004), 117, n. 29.

[44] The RTI was carried out by Joe Wegner and Kevin Cahail in March of 2017.

[45] For the name Meryptah, see Ranke, *PN I*, 160.14.

[46] For the name Ruiu, see Ranke, *PN I*, 221.5 and Ranke, *PN II*, 373. The name Ruiu comes into use in the New Kingdom. Its origin may be Nubian as there are several Nubian chiefs with this name early in the New Kingdom. See *PM* 8, 79 and *PM* 8, 128; W. Vivian Davies, "Egypt and Nubia: Conflict with the Kingdom of Kush," in Catharine H. Roehrig (ed.), *Hatshepsut: From Queen to Pharaoh* (New York, 2005),

Left side: *ḥtp dꞽ nswt Ḥwt-Ḥr nb[.t] ḥtpt n (sꞽś) nb[.t] pt ḥnw.t nṯr.w dꞽ.s ʿnḫ wḏꜣ snb n kꜣ n ḥsy n nṯr nfr sš nswt sš nfr.w Mry-Ptḥ sn[.t].f mr[.t].f nb.t pr šmʿ.yt n ꞽImn Rwꞽw.*

An offering which the king gives and which Hathor-Nebet-hetepet, Lady of Heaven, Mistress of the Gods, gives that she may give life, prosperity, and health to the ka of the one praised of the great god, the Royal Scribe, the Scribe of Recruits/elite Forces Meryptah (and) his wife, his beloved, the Lady of the House, the Chantress of Amun, Ruiu.

Right side: *ḥtp dꞽ nswt Ḥwt-Ḥr nb.t ḥtpt nb.t pt ḥnw.t n nṯr.w dꞽ.s ḥsw m-bꜣḥ nswt*[47] *n kꜣ n sš nswt ꞽmy-r ip.t-nswt ꞽmy-r pr Mry-Ptḥ sn.t.f nb.t pr šmʿ.yt n ꞽImn Rwꞽw.*

An offering which the king gives and which Hathor-Nebet-hetepet, Lady of Heaven, Mistress of the Gods gives that she may give praise before the king for the ka of the royal scribe, the Overseer of the Royal Harem, the Steward, Meryptah (and) his wife, the Lady of the House, the Chantress of Amun, Ruiu.

The Identity of Meryptah and Ruiu

The titles held by Meryptah indicate his high status during the reign of Amenhotep III. Meryptah was a Royal Scribe (*sš nswt*), [48] a Scribe of Recruits/elite Forces (*sš nfr.w*),[49] an Overseer of the Royal Apartment (*ꞽmy-r ip.t-nswt*) [50] and a Steward (*ꞽmy-r pr*). [51] While the title of Royal Scribe (*sš nswt*) is quite common, Meryptah's other titles are considerably less frequent and have the potential to offer insights and some of the unique aspects of his career and possibly his familial associations. The title Scribe of Recruits/elite Forces (*sš nfr.w*) is attested for very few individuals in the Eighteenth Dynasty, the period in which this title first appears.[52] It has been suggested

54. As a female name, in addition to the citations listed in Ranke, *PN*, there is a woman named Ruiu who was buried in the tomb of her father, Neferkhawet. This family tomb was excavated by the Metropolitan Museum of Art in 1935. Burials for ten individuals were identified including those of Neferkhawet and his wife Rennefer, their son Amenemhat, their daughter Ruiu, and her husband Baki. As for a date for these individuals, it appears that the tomb's above-ground offering chapel was razed to make way for a building project carried out by Thutmose III, sometime before the end of his reign in 1425 BCE. For this tomb and its associated materials, see *PM* 1², 621; *PM* 1², 782; Manfred Cassirer, "A Granite Group of the Eighteenth Dynasty," *JEA* 41 (1955), 72–74, pl. XIX, and Betsy Bryan, "An Early Eighteenth Dynasty Group Statue," *BES* 10 (1989) 27–28. The mother of Kheruef, the steward of Queen Tiye, was named Ruiu. She held the titles of Royal Ornament, Chantress of Isis, the God's Mother, and Chantress of Amun. See *PM* 1², 298. A stela that was in the Hilton Price Collection records the names of Simut and his wife, Ruiu. See F. G. Hilton Price, *A Catalogue of the Egyptian Antiquities in the Possession of F.G. Hilton Price* 1 (London, 1897), 211, no. 2007; *PM* 1², 812. The whereabouts of this stela is currently unknown. Another attestation of a woman named Ruiu can be found on a black granite statue of a seated man in a private collection in Philadelphia. The statue is described as having a "strange style and curious often garbled hieroglyphs inscribed: ... *n kꜣ n Kꜣ-ms .... in mwt.f sʿnḫ rn.f rwꞽw nb.t imꜣḫ*" (Glencairn Museum archival records, no photograph was available). None of these women seem to have any connection to the Ruiu on the Glencairn basin.

47 This area of the basin is very eroded. The traces of visible signs support the reading *nswt*. For similar phrasing, see Winfried Barta, *Aufbau und Bedeutung der altägyptische Opferformel* (Glückstadt, 1968), 167 (Bitte 122).

48 Abdul Rahman Al-Ayedi, *Index of Egyptian Administrative, Religious and Military Titles of the New Kingdom* (Ismailia, 2006), 537–44 [1816]. The title of *sš nswt* may be distinct from *sš nswt mꜣʿ* (True Royal Scribe) that is held by fewer individuals during the New Kingdom. For *sš nswt mꜣʿ*, see Al-Ayedi, *Index of Egyptian Administrative, Religious and Military Titles*, 547–49 [1823]. See also Jeannette Anne Taylor, *An Index of Male Non-Royal Egyptian Titles, Epithets & Phrases of the 18th Dynasty* (London, 2001), 212–13.

49 Al-Ayedi, *Index of Egyptian Administrative, Religious and Military Titles*, 533–34 [1804]. See also Taylor, *Index of Male Non-Royal Egyptian Titles*, 212.

50 Al-Ayedi, *Index of Egyptian Administrative, Religious and Military Titles*, 8–9 [27]. See also Taylor, *Index of Male Non-Royal Egyptian Titles*, 11. For a recent discussion of the *ꞽmy-rꜣ ip.t nswt* and relevant bibliography, see Dana Bělohoubková, "*Jmy-rꜣ jp.t nsw* at the end of the 18th dynasty: an iconographical study," in Marta Arranz Cárcamo, Raúl Sánchez Casado, Albert Planelles Orozco et al. (eds.), *Current Research in Egyptology 2019: Proceedings of the Twentieth Annual Symposium, University of Alcalá, 17–21 June 2019* (Oxford, 2021), 130–41.

51 Al-Ayedi, *Index of Egyptian Administrative, Religious and Military Titles*, 26–27 [89]. See also Taylor, *Index of Male Non-Royal Egyptian Titles*, 19.

52 For a discussion of the title Scribe of Recruits, see Wolfgang Helck, *Der Einfluss der Militärführer* (Leipzig, 1939), 15–17; Raymond O. Faulkner, "Egyptian Military Organization," *JEA* 39 (1953), 45; Alan Schulman, "The Egyptian Chariotry: a Reexamination," *JARCE* 2 (1963), 76, n. 4; Alan Schulman, *Military Rank, Title and Organization in the Egyptian New Kingdom* (Berlin, 1964), 20–21, 63–64, 159–160; Ahmed Kadry, "The Social Status and Education of Military Scribes in Egypt during the 18th Dynasty," *Oikumene* 5 (1986), 155–62. In addition to

that the title originated at this time as a result of the intensification of Egyptian military operations during this period of expansion of the empire.[53] However, the exact nature of the *nfr.w* has been debated. The term has been translated variously as "recruits" or "elite forces"—two groups of military men with obviously opposing levels of experience. The category of recruits should refer to young men freshly enlisted into the military, while the term "elite forces" would suggest well-trained and experienced soldiers.[54] It is possible that by the time of the reign of Amenhotep III, the *nfr.w* would have been harnessed to undertake operations of a non-military nature, such as building projects or other activities that would support the kingdom's internal infrastructure.[55] One of the well-known holders of this title is the official, Amenhotep son of Hapu. A description of the type of work encompassed by the scribe of recruits can be found in a text on one of his monuments which states:

> ... he put all the people subject to me, and the listing of their number under my control, as superior king's-scribe over recruits. I levied the (military) classes of my lord, my pen reckoned the numbers of millions; I put them in [classes (?)] in the place of their [elders (?)]; the staff of old age as his beloved son. I taxed the houses with the numbers belonging thereto, I divided the troops (of workmen) and their houses, I filled out the subjects with the best of the captivity, which his majesty had captured on the battlefield. I appointed all their troops, I levied -------. I placed troops at the heads of the way(s) to turn back the foreigners in their places.[56]

As Meryptah held the title *sš nfr.w* like Amenhotep son of Hapu, we may perhaps see evidence for comparable paths of ascension through the ranks of royal administration. His role as *sš nfr.w* may have occurred as part of a long career which saw him rise to a position of considerable status within the royal and religious administration during the reign of Amenhotep III, a career path reflected in his other titles.

As noted above, on the Glencairn basin Meryptah also held the title Overseer of the Royal Apartment (*imy-r ip.t-nswt*), a comparatively uncommon position attested during the Eighteenth Dynasty for only a handful of officials including the mayor of Thebes, Sennefer (TT 96); Userhat (TT 47); the Royal Tutor, Hekareshu (TT 226); Mery-re II, at el-Amarna (Tomb 2); Huya, at el-Amarna (Tomb 1); and Ptahmose (British Museum EA160).[57]

Meryptah, nineteen known individuals held this title from the reign of Tuthmosis III through the end of the Eighteenth Dynasty. These individuals are as follows: (1) Abkauser, temp. Tuthmosis III; (2) Intef, temp. Tuthmosis III; (3) Minhotep, temp. Amenhotep II; (4) Horemheb, temp. Tuthmosis IV; (5) Amenhotep (called Huy) temp. Amenhotep III; (6) Amenhotep son of Hapu temp. Amenhotep III; (7) Men, temp. Amenhotep III; (8) Sa-aset, temp. Amenhotep III; (9) Sennu, temp. Amenhotep III; (10) Tjanuny, temp. Amenhotep III; (11) Tjena, temp. Amenhotep III; (12) Huy, son of Aper-el, temp. Akhenaten; (13) May, temp. Akhenaten; (14) Horemheb (future king), temp. Akhenaten; (15) Ramose, temp. Akhenaten; (16) Iy, Eighteenth Dynasty (Louvre Statue C76); (17) Raya, Eighteenth Dynasty; (18) Ti, late Dynasty 18; (19) Ranero, Eighteenth Dynasty. (The sides of the base of a sphinx of Tuthmosis IV were reworked to replace the original royal inscription with that of the scribe of recruits, Ranero, see Betsy M. Bryan, *The Reign of Tuthmosis IV* [Ph.D. dissertation, Yale University, 1980], 362–65.) For relevant bibliography on these individuals, see Schulman, *Military Rank, Title and Organization*, 159–60; Pierre-Marie Chevereau, *Prosopographie des cadres militaire égyptiens du Nouvel Empire* (Paris, 2003), 216–19 and Alain Zivie, *Découverte à Saqqarah: Le Vizir Oublié* (Paris, 1990), 61 for a discussion of Huy, son of Aper-el who does not appear in Chevereau's list of scribes of recruits.

[53] The path for career advancement seems to have been that scribes of the army were sometimes promoted to Chief of Military Scribes, then to the rank Scribe of Recruits, and ultimately to General. All of the generals immediately before and during the Amarna Period bore the title of Scribe of Recruits before being promoted to General. These Generals would have been the direct subordinate of the Crown Prince. These Crown Princes would have been taught by royal tutors who more often than not bore military titles. See Kadry, "The Social status and Education of Military Scribes, 155–62. There is no indication that Meryptah ever attained the rank of General.

[54] See Helck, *Der Einfluss der Militärführer*, 20 and Schulman, *Military Rank, Title and Organization*, 20–21 for opposing views on the proper translation of the term *nfr.w*.

[55] See William J. Murnane, "The Organization of Government under Amenhotep III," in David O'Connor and Eric H. Cline (eds.), *Amenhotep III: Perspectives on His Reign* (Ann Arbor, MI, 1998), 198, and JJ Shirley, "What's in a Title? Military and Civil Officials in the Egyptian 18th Dynasty Military Sphere," in S. Bar, D. Kahn, and JJ Shirley (eds.), *Egypt, Canaan and Israel: History, Imperialism, Ideology and Literature. Proceedings of a Conference at the University of Haifa, 3–7 May 2009* (Leiden, 2011), 297–98.

[56] Statue E (CG 583 + CG 835 [frag.]) from Karnak, James H. Breasted *Ancient Records of Egypt: Historical Documents from the Earliest Times to the Persian Conquest* 2 (Chicago, 1906–7), §916, from the third statue of Amenhotep at Karnak, see Auguste Mariette, *Karnak* (Leipzig, 1875), 36–37. See also Alexandre Varille, *Inscriptions concernant l'architecte Amenhotep, fils de Hapou*, BdÉ 44 (Cairo, 1968) and Eleanor Beth Simmance, *Amenhotep Son of Hapu: Self-Presentation through Statues and Their Texts in Pursuit of Semi-Divine Intermediary Status* (M.Res., University of Birmingham, 2014).

[57] See Bělohoubková, "*Jmy-r3 jp.t nsw* at the End of the 18th Dynasty," 130–41.

This title indicates that Meryptah would have been one of the rare officials granted close access to the royal household as a high-ranking member of the palace staff. Meryptah's final title, Steward (*imy-r pr*), although common in other periods is relatively rare during the late Eighteenth Dynasty.[58] As we examine in detail below, it is possible the writing of this title on the Glencairn basin may be a shortened version of a title identifying Meryptah as the steward of a specific royal foundation.

Meryptah's wife, Ruiu, is identified in the dedicatory inscription with only two titles: Lady of the House (*nb.t pr*) and Chantress of Amun (*šmꜥ.yt n Ỉmn*).[59] Ruiu is a previously unrecognized Chantress of Amun. Her identification during the reign of Amenhotep III adds to the comparatively small number of chantresses dating to this king's reign. Suzanne Onstine has noted that during this period, women who hold the title of Chantress derive predominantly from the upper echelon of society. [60] Unfortunately, there appear to exist no other inscriptional or monumental remains that commemorate this lady Ruiu and her familial background remains unknown. However, her position as Meryptah's wife confirmed on this basin provides a useful source of evidence on the particular identity of Meryptah himself as we consider below.

The high-status titles of Meryptah, suggest that Meryptah and his wife were certainly well-connected individuals. Their social status is reflected in the extremely high quality of craftsmanship of the basinophorous statue. Indeed, in view of the sculptural quality of the object, the inclusion of the name of the king (with little doubt Nebmaatre-Amenhotep III) and sculptural details such as the hairstyle of Ruiu echoing that of Queen Tiye, we may wonder whether this object derives from a royal workshop. It may well have been a piece commissioned by the owners themselves, but access to its manufacture likely reflects the position held by Meryptah and his relationship to the royal establishment. Who was this particular Meryptah? We turn now to examine the identity of the Meryptah commemorated alongside his wife Ruiu on the Glencairn basin.

The Identity of Meryptah on the Glencairn Basin

There are several attestations of officials with the name Meryptah during the reign of Amenhotep III and many of these individuals held high-ranking administrative positions (fig. 10). Can we say with any certainty that all or some of these texts refer to the same person? It is certainly possible that we may be witnessing two, or more, different officials with the same name. However, there is also the intriguing possibility that the multiple appearances of the name Meryptah during the reign of Amenhotep III allude to the same individual. In the following overview we will explore the set of evidence that may shed light on Meryptah.

On the Glencairn basinophorous statue, we have seen that the titles listed for Meryptah are as follows: Royal Scribe (*sš nsw*), Scribe of Recruits (*sš nfr.w*), Overseer of the Royal Apartment (*imy-r ipt nsw*), and Steward (*imy-r pr*) of an unnamed establishment. An object that shows the closest correlation in titles with the Glencairn basin is a ceremonial schist cubit rod dated to the late Eighteenth Dynasty for an official named Meryptah now in a private collection.[61] On this rod, the owner, Meryptah, is identified as a Royal Scribe (*sš nswt*), a True Royal Scribe (*sš nswt mꜣꜥ*), and a Steward (*imy-r pr*) of an unspecified establishment. Given the two shared titles on this rod and the Glencairn basin, and the absence of any other official named Meryptah who shared these two titles, these two objects may reference the same Meryptah.

---

[58] See Al-Ayedi, *Index of Egyptian Administrative, Religious and Military Titles*, 26–27 [89] and Taylor, *Index of Male Non-Royal Titles*, 19.

[59] See Suzanne L. Onstine, *The Role of the Chantress (šmꜥ.yt) in Ancient Egypt* (Oxford, 2005), 139–40 for the function of the *šmꜥ.yt*.

[60] See Onstine, *Role of the Chantress*, 7, 93, and 96 for the elite status of the husband of a *šmꜥ.yt*.

[61] This cubit rod sold at a Sotheby's auction in 2010, for which see: https://www.sothebys.com/en/auctions/ecatalogue/2010/egyptian-classical-and-western-asiatic-antiquities-n08688/lot.65.html. Cubit rods such as this were grave goods presented as royal gifts to loyal officials. Several dozen examples of such rods are known. See Nora E. Scott, "Egyptian Cubit Rods," *MMA Bull.* 1.1 (1942–1943), 70–75. For another late Eighteenth Dynasty green schist votive cubit rod with an offering formula, likely from the area of Memphis, see the example inscribed for Ptahmose, High Priest of Ptah, in the Rijksmuseum van Oudheden in Leiden (inv. no. AD 54) in Eva Eggebrecht and Arne Eggebrecht, *Ägyptens Aufstieg zur Weltmacht* (Mainz am Rhein, 1987), 141, no. 52. See also the inscribed green schist cubit rod found together with a wooden example in the late Eighteenth Dynasty tomb of Aper-el at Saqqara in Alain Zivie, *Découverte à Saqqarah: Le Vizir Oublié* (Paris, 1990), 136, and Zahi A. Hawass, *Hidden Treasures of the Egyptian Museum* (Cairo, 2002), 46.

BASIN OF RUIU and MERYPTAH (Glencairn E1178)	*sš nswt sš nfrw ỉmy-r ỉpt nswt ỉmy-r pr*
Cubit Rod of Meryptah (Sotheby's, Private Collection)	*sš nswt sš nswt mꜣꜥ ỉmy-r pr*
Stela of Meryptah and Ptahmose (Leiden V14/Petrie UC14463)	*ḥm-nṯr ỉmy-r pr* (abbr =) *ỉmy-r pr n tꜣ ḥwt Nb-mꜣꜥt-rꜥ*
Meryptah, Malqata Sealings (Amenhotep III, Years 30-37)	*ḥm-nṯr ỉmy-r n tꜣ ḥwt pr-ꜥꜣ*
Funerary Cone of Meryptah (Davies and MacAdam 412) **Stamped Brick, Medinet Habu** (Teeter and Wilfong 290)	*sm m pr Ptḥ wr ḫrp ḥmwt m Ỉwnw Šmꜥw ḥm-nṯr m ḥwt Nb-mꜣꜥt-rꜥ*
Figure Label of Meryptah (Tomb of Ramose, TT55)	*sm m tꜣ [ḥwt Nb-mꜣꜥt-rꜥ] ỉmy-r pr*
Kneeling Statue of Meryptah (Durham EG4006)	*ḥry-tp ꜥꜣ m pr-nswt ỉmy-r ḥmw-nṯr nṯrw nbw ḫtmty-bỉty ḥm-nṯr tpy n Ỉmn*
Stamped Bricks of Meryptah (Berlin and MMA)	*ḥm-nṯr tpy n Ỉmn*
Meryptah on Statue of Nebnefer (Brussels E1103) (Amenhotep III, Year 20)	*ḥm-nṯr tpy n Ỉmn*
Block Statue of Meryptah (Chicago, OIN E10796)	*ḫtmty-bỉty ḥm-nṯr tpy n Ỉmn*
Meryptah on Hieratic Stela (British Museum, EA 138) (21st Dynasty copy of text Amenhotep III, Year 31)	*ỉmy-r pr nbw*

Fig. 10. Inscribed materials associated with Meryptah dating to the reign of Amenhotep III.

The third attestation of a man named Meryptah who lived during the reign of Amenhotep III appears on the well-known family stela of Meryptah and Ptahmose.[62] This monument commemorates members of an important Memphite family including a vizier by the name of Thutmose, his wife Tawy, and their two sons. One son is Ptahmose, a High Priest of Ptah at Memphis and the other is a man named Meryptah who is a Prophet (*ḥm-nṯr*) and a Steward of the Mansion of Nebmaatre (*ỉmy-r pr n tꜣ ḥwt Nb-mꜣꜥt-rꜥ*). A fifth individual also appears, another High Priest of Ptah—also named Ptahmose—who is the son of a Prophet named Menkheper. Two details on this monument are of note. In the horizontal inscription above the cavetto cornice, Meryptah's full title of Steward of the Mansion of Nebmaatre is abbreviated to simply Steward (*ỉmy-r pr*), a title we have encountered on both the Glencairn basinophorous statue and the cubit rod of Meryptah. Secondly, not only do

[62] See Kate Bosse-Griffiths, "The Memphite stela of Merptaḥ and Ptaḥmosĕ," *JEA* 41 (1955), 56–63. This monument is split between two collections: Leiden Inventory number: AP 11 https://www.rmo.nl/collectie/collectiezoeker/collectiestuk/?object=22634; UCL Inventory number: UC14463 https://petriecat.museums.ucl.ac.uk/detail.aspx?parentpriref=#. See Stewart, *Egyptian Stelae, Reliefs and Paintings*, 26, pl. 16.

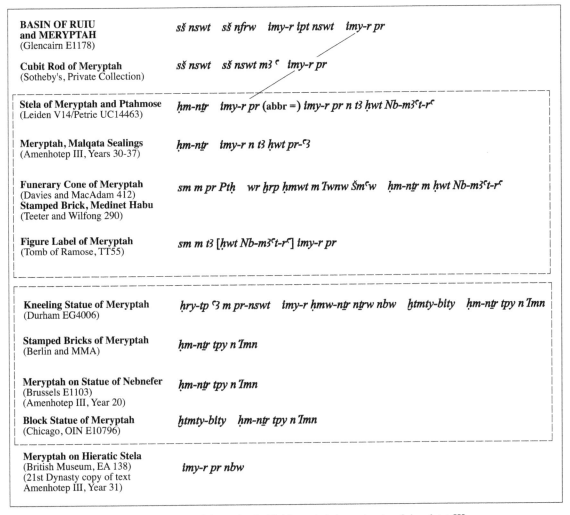

the two named High Priests of Ptah wear the special jackal collar normally worn exclusively by holders of that office, but so too does Meryptah, although he is not assigned this sacerdotal title in the texts on this monument.[63]

Hieratic labels on sealings from Malkata dating to Years 30 through 37 of the reign of Amenhotep III likewise mention an individual named Meryptah who bore the titles Prophet (*ḥm-nṯr*) and Steward of the Mansion of Pharaoh (*ỉmy-r n tꜣ ḥwt pr-ꜥꜣ*).[64] In his publication of these dockets, William Hayes has suggested that this person is the same as the Meryptah mentioned on the London-Leiden stela and that the *tꜣ ḥwt pr-ꜥꜣ* seen on the dockets is the same institution as the *tꜣ ḥwt Nb-mꜣꜥt-rꜥ* referred to on the stela.[65] Nevertheless, a question remains as to which temple of Amenhotep III is being referenced here. Hayes believed that the Steward Meryptah mentioned on the Malkata labels held office and probably resided in northern Egypt.[66]

Hayes stated that the word *ḥwt* in the New Kingdom was used in reference to mortuary temples but recognized that the term also can be used in a broader frame of reference to denote the "domain" or "foundation" that supported such temples. He went on to say that labels 3 and 58 (q) tell us that the domain in question was that of the temple [of Amenhotep III] at Memphis. The labels in question read: "Year 26 wine of /// *ḥwt* of /// l.p.h. in Memphis" (label 3) and "Year 37 wine of the *ḥwt* /// in Memphis of the vineyard master (*ḥry kꜣmw*) /// (label 58). Another docket (label 6) makes mention of "Year 1 wine of the vineyard master (*ḥry kꜣ*[*mw*]) of the *ḥwt* of Nebmaatre." This leaves us with the fact that there is a *ḥwt* associated with Amenhotep III (although the king is not explicitly named in label 3 or 58) at Memphis and there is a *ḥwt* of Nebmaatre (without a specific geographical location given).[67] This raises the question: must the *ḥwt* in Memphis be the same establishment as the *ḥwt* of Nebmaatre? There is after all a temple at Memphis which is known as "Amenhotep III-united-with-Ptah"[68] and there is, of course, his funerary temple at Kom el Heitan. Perhaps both of these foundations are represented in the Malkata dockets and the *ḥwt* of Nebmaatre mentioned in the Malkata dockets is the king's mortuary temple in Thebes rather than a Memphite establishment. This temple may be the same as the *tꜣ ḥwt pr-ꜥꜣ* mentioned on the London Leiden stela.

Another attestation of a Meryptah associated with the reign of Amenhotep III occurs on a funerary cone from the Theban necropolis.[69] This cone is inscribed for the *sem*-priest in the Temple of Ptah (*sm m pr Ptḥ*), the Great Director of Craftsmen in the Southern Heliopolis (*wr ḫrp ḥmwt m ʾIwnw Šmꜥw*); i.e., the High Priest of Ptah at Thebes, and the Prophet in the Temple of Nebmaatre (*ḥm-nṯr m ḥwt Nb-mꜣꜥt-Rꜥ*), Meryptah. The mention of the *ḥwt Nb-mꜣꜥt-Rꜥ* suggests that this individual may be the same Meryptah referenced in the Malqata sealings. Furthermore, the appearance of the title *wr ḫrp ḥmwt m ʾIwnw Šmꜥw* on this cone may help to explain why the Meryptah depicted on the Memphite family stela wears the accoutrements of a High Priest of Ptah despite not being listed with that title on that monument. It appears viable that Meryptah of the Memphite stela

---

63 For a discussion of the jackal collar worn by the Memphite high priest of Ptah, see Darya V. Vanyukova, "Ожерелье верховных жрецов Птаха: семантика изображения," in Andrey Bolshakov (ed.), *Петербургские Египтологические Чтения 2009–2010: доклады, памяти Светланы Измайловны Ходжаш [и] Александра Серафимовича Четверухина* (St. Petersburg, 2011), 46–55.

64 William C. Hayes, "Inscriptions from the Palace of Amenhotep III," *JNES* 10.2 (1951), 82–112. Hayes records (fig. 19) that Meryptah appears on twenty-four examples of dockets representing eight different label types (34, 38, 59, 103, 109, 158, 188 and 241). However, the transcriptions for docket type 103 and 158 in William C. Hayes, "Inscriptions from the Palace of Amenhotep III," *JNES* 10.1 (1951), figs. 7 and 12 do not support that, as his name does not appear those transcriptions. See also M. A. Leahy, *Excavations at Malkata and the Birket Habu 1971–74: The Inscriptions* (Warminster, 1978), 7, and Federico Rocchi, "The First Prophet of Amenhotep IV/Akhenaten," in A. K. Eyma and C. J. Bennett (eds.), *A Delta-man in Yebu* (Boca Raton, 2003), 46.

65 Hayes, "Inscriptions from the Palace," *JNES* 10.2, 98–99. The current author believes Meryptah may have resided in Thebes, while members of this family were prominent Memphite officials.

66 See Hayes, "Inscriptions from the Palace," *JNES* 10.2, 90.

67 See Hayes, "Inscriptions from the Palace," *JNES* 10.2, 98–99.

68 See Robert Morkot, "*Nb-mꜣꜥt-Rꜥ*-United-with-Ptah," *JNES* 49.4 (1990), 323–37.

69 Davies and Macadam, no. 412, see Norman de Garis Davies and M. F. Laming Macadam, *A Corpus of Inscribed Funerary Cones* (Oxford, 1957); Kento Zenihiro, *The Complete Funerary Cones* (Tokyo, 2009), 171, and Gary Dibley and Bron Lipkin, *A Compendium of Egyptian Funerary Cones* (London, 2009), 134–253. A brick from Medinet Habu excavated by the Oriental Institute of the University of Chicago is impressed with the same seal as the funerary cone, see Emily Teeter and Terry Wilfong, *Scarabs, Scaraboids, Seals and Seal Impressions from Medinet Habu*, OIP 118 (Chicago, 2003), 179, no. 290 and pl. 94. Note that the translation "domain of Seth" seen in Davies and Macadam and Teeter and Wilfong should be read "temple of Nebmaatre." Rocchi ("First Prophet of Amenhotep IV," 45) notes that this is a misreading of the rebus form of the king's name.

and Meryptah named on this cone are the same individual; the cone could reflect the fact that Meryptah served as the southern counterpart to the office of Memphite High Priest of Ptah, an office in fact held contemporaneously by his brother Ptahmose.[70]

A man named Meryptah also appears in the tomb of Ramose (TT 55) and may be related to the family of the vizier. Various individuals and family members of Ramose are depicted in his tomb and one of these men is labeled as a *sm m t3* [*ḥwt Nb-m3ʿt-Rʿ*] and a Steward (*ỉmy-r pr*) of an unspecified establishment.[71] This combination of titles is similar to those just discussed for the Meryptah of the funerary cone and Malkata dockets. In an article on the first prophet of Amenhotep IV/Akhenaten, Federico Rocchi makes special note of an official named Meryptah[72] and suggests the Memphite family stela, the Malqata sealings, the funerary cone, and the figure in the tomb of Ramose all commemorate the same individual. If that is the case, it then offers the possibility that the Glencairn basin and Sotheby's cubit rod also belong to the same Meryptah. Another intriguing suggestion that Rocchi makes is that this Meryptah may be the same man as the one mentioned on the statue of Nebnefer now in Brussels.[73] This statue dates to Year 20 of Amenhotep III and in the inscription, a man named Meryptah is referred to as the High Priest of Amun (*ḥm-nṯr tpy n ỉmn*).[74] There are only two First Prophets of Amun attested during the reign of Amenhotep III, a man named Meryptah and a Ptahmose.[75] Rocchi further proposed that a connection between the High Priest of Amun and the king's mortuary temple may be seen in that, he argues, until a king dies, the First Prophet of Amun may have been the principal official responsible for the operations of a king's completed mortuary temple.[76]

If we accept that the Meryptah on the Nebnefer statue is the same as the other Meryptah(s), we are then able to connect another series of monuments belonging to the *ḥm-nṯr tpy n ỉmn* Meryptah. These objects include a stelaphorous statue of this individual inscribed with a sun hymn, now in Durham, upon which he holds the titles Great Chief in the Palace (*ḥry-tp ʿ3 m pr-nswt*), Overseer of Priests of All the Gods (*ỉmy-r ḥmw-ntr nṯrw nbw*), Royal Seal Bearer (*ḫtmty-bity*), and High Priest of Amun (*ḥm-nṯr tpy n ỉmn*).[77] This statue was found in a pit at Gurna behind "Yanni's house" which was built above TT 52. [78] Also found were several other associated objects including stamped bricks for the *ḥm-nṯr tpy n ỉmn* Meryptah.[79] Work on the nearby Theban tomb of Paenkhemenu (TT 68) has revealed that this tomb was initially made for the *ḥm-nṯr tpy n ỉmn* Meryptah, but that

70 See William J. Murnane, "Too Many High Priests? Once again the Ptahmoses of Ancient Memphis," in David P. Silverman (ed.), *For his Ka: Essays Offered in Memory of Klaus Baer*, SAOC 55 (Chicago, 1994), 190–91.

71 See Norman de Garis Davies, *The Tomb of the Vizier Ramose* (London, 1941), pl. ix; *Urk.* IV, 1787 who restores the name as Meryptah. Rocchi suggests that it would be preferable to restore the text as *sem*-priest in the temple of [Ptah] as seen on the funerary cone, see Rocchi, "First Prophet of Amenhotep IV," 45.

72 Rocchi, "First Prophet of Amenhotep IV," 45–47.

73 Statue of Nebnefer (Brussels E1103) See Rocchi, "First Prophet of Amenhotep IV," 46, and also see for example, Louis Speleers, *Recueil des inscriptions égyptiennes des Musées Royaux du Cinquantenaire à Bruxelles* (Bruxelles, 1923), 60, nº 250; *Urk.* IV, 1885; Baudouin van de Walle, "La publication des textes des Musées: Bruxelles (Musées royaux d'Art et d'Histoire)," in Serge Sauneron, *Textes et languages de l'Égypte pharaonique. Hommage à Jean-François Champollion*, BdÉ 64.3 (Cairo, 1974), 174; B. G. Davies, *Historical Records of the Late Eighteenth Dynasty*, fas. 6 (Warminster, 1995), 44–45 and Arielle Kozloff, *Amenhotep III: Egypt's Radiant Pharaoh* (Cambridge, 2012), 110–11.

74 Rocchi ("First Prophet of Amenhotep IV," 46) notes "The first four monuments clearly refer to the same person, Meryptah, *sem*-priest in the temple of Ptah and prophet in the temple of Nebmaatra, who lived during the reign of Amenhotep III. Whether the fifth monument mentions the same Meryptah is not fully certain, seeing the difference in titles, but it seems likely."

75 Aldred states that the holders of the four main priestly offices of Amun are known from an inscription dated to Amenhotep III's regnal year 20. The men are: Meryptah, Anen, Amenemhat, and Si-Mut. This Meryptah seems to have succeeded Ptahmose as High Priest of Amun (*ḥm-nṯr tpy n ỉmn*) in year 20 (or a little earlier) and appears to have served in that role until the death of Amenhotep III as there are no other High Priests known from his reign. See Cyril Aldred, "Two Theban Notables during the Later Reign of Amenophis III," *JNES* 18.2 (1959), 113–20.

76 Rocchi, "First Prophet of Amenhotep IV," 37.

77 Durham EG4006 (http://discover.durham.ac.uk/permalink/f/1sbb0j7/44DUR_ADLIB_DS3915); Aldred, "Two Theban Notables," 113.

78 See Morris L. Bierbrier, *Who Was Who in Egyptology*, fourth edition (London, 2012), 28, and Kees van der Spek, *The Modern Neighbors of Tutankhamun: History, Life, and Work in the Villages of the Theban West Bank* (Cairo, 2011), 219–20.

79 See *PM* 1^2, 670–71. Several of these bricks are in the Metropolitan Museum of Art (11.155.4, 14.1.424, 14.1.423) and in Berlin (1575-7, 1583). See also Karl-Joachim Seyfried, *Das Grab des Paenkhemenu (TT 68) und die Anlage TT 227* (Mainz, 1991), 117 for a discussion of stamped bricks from the tomb of Meryptah.

little remains of this original phase of the tomb.[80] This tomb (TT 68) is located not far from the area where the tomb goods inscribed for Meryptah were found. Another significant monument for a *ḥm-nṯr tpy n Ỉmn* named Meryptah is a block statue now in the Oriental Institute that has been dated to the reign of Amenhotep III.[81] Here Meryptah is given the titles royal seal bearer (*ḫtmty-bity*) and high priest of Amun (*ḥm-nṯr tpy n Ỉmn*)—two of the titles also seen on the stelaphorous statue in Durham.

A final mention of a man named Meryptah dating to the reign of Amenhotep III can be found on a hieratic stela now in the British Museum.[82] This stela was inscribed during the Twenty-first Dynasty but records a royal decree dating to year 31 of the reign of Amenhotep III. The witnesses for this decree included the vizier Amenhotep and a man named Meryptah who has the unusual title of Overseer of the House of Gold (*imy-r pr nbw*).[83] William Murnane noted that the combination of name and title was curious as there are no actual attestations of this person during the reign of Amenhotep III. He proposed that the steward of Amenhotep's funerary temple may have also been responsible for carrying out this fiscal role.[84] Earlier, Varille had stated that this *imy-r pr nbw* Meryptah was the same person as the *ḥm-nṯr tpy n Ỉmn* Meryptah who would have also carried out duties related to the treasury.[85]

Might it not be the case that the Meryptah who was the Steward of Amenhotep's funerary temple and the Meryptah who was the High Priest of Amun were the same person?[86] This would leave us with one man named Meryptah who held a series of important positions during his long career, which lasted from at least year 20 through year 37 of Amenhotep III, and who possessed the following titles: (honorific): *ḥ3ty-ʿ, ḥry-tp ʿ3 m pr-nswt, iry pʿt*; (administrative): *imy-r ipt nsw, imy-r pr n t3 ḥwt pr-ʿ3/ imy-r pr n t3 ḥwt Nb-m3ʿt-Rʿ, imy-r pr, imy-r pr nbw, ḫtmty-bity*; (priestly): *ḥm-nṯr, ḥm-nṯr m ḥwt Nb-m3ʿt-Rʿ, ḥm-nṯr tpy n Ỉmn, imy-r ḥmw-nṯr nṯrw nbw, sm m pr Ptḥ, sm m t3* [*ḥwt Nb-m3ʿt-Rʿ*], *wr ḫrp ḥmwt m Ỉwnw Šmʿw*; (scribal): *sš nswt, sš nswt m3ʿ, sš nfr.w*. Following this line of reasoning, rather than a group of different men named Meryptah with a variety of complementary and overlapping titles, it appears possible that we have a set of inscribed evidence reflecting the evolving career of one of the important officials of Amenhotep III's reign. Like the better-known Amenhotep son of Hapu, Meryptah may have been a man entrusted over a long timeframe with a series of significant religious and administrative functions.

If this is the case, the Meryptah commemorated alongside his wife Ruiu on the Glencairn basin was a part of an important Memphite family.[87] While his family members served in the north as vizier and high priest of Ptah,

---

[80] Seyfried, *Das Grab des Paenkhemenu*, 116–17. No texts or scenes remain from this first phase of tomb use except for some mud-brick architecture and some stamped bricks.

[81] Chicago OIM E10796. See Regine Schulz, *Die Entwicklung und Bedeutung des Kuboiden Statuentypus: Eine Untersuchung zu den Sogenannten "würfelhockern,"* HÄB 33 (Hildesheim, 1992), 123.

[82] EA138. See Alexandre Varille, *Inscriptions concernant l'architecte Amenhotep fils de Hapu,* BdÉ 14 (Cairo 1944), 67–85, and T. G. H. James, *An Introduction to Ancient Egypt* (London, 1979), 90.

[83] For this title in the Eighteenth Dynasty, see Taylor, *Index of Male Non-Royal Egyptian Titles*, 17. Another holder of this title can be found in TT A24, the tomb of Si-mut, an official of the reign of Amenhotep III. In his tomb this title reads in full, *imy-r pr nbw imy-r r pr.wy ḥḏ*. See Lise Manniche, *Lost Tombs: a Study of Certain Eighteenth Dynasty Monuments in the Theban Necropolis* (London, 1988), 96.

[84] Murnane, "The Organization of Government under Amenhotep III," 220.

[85] Aldred, "Two Theban Notables," 118, who cites Alexandre Varille, "Une statue de Ptahmôse, grand prêtre d'Amon sous Aménophis III," *ASAE* 40 (1940), 647.

[86] Kozloff, *Amenhotep III*, 93 notes that during the reign of Amenhotep III, the High Priest of Amun and the chief of his mortuary temple were both named Meryptah and may have been the same person.

[87] For a discussion of the rising importance of Memphite families during the reign of Amenhotep III, see Murnane, "The Organization of Government under Amenhotep III," 210. He states, "not only was Meriptah in charge of the king's mansion of millions of years on the west of Thebes, but he was also *Sem* in the house of Ptah and chief of the master craftsmen in Southern Heliopolis—in other words, the high priest of the Theban cult of Ptah and a perfect foil for his relatives who exercised the superior office in Memphis." Also note JJ Shirley, "Crisis and restructuring of the state: from the Second Intermediate Period to the advent of the Ramesses [sic]," in Juan Carlos Moreno García (ed.), *Ancient Egyptian Administration* (Leiden, 2013), 593–94. This family may have had blood ties to the king. If Meryptah's mother Tawy is the same as the Tawy who was a (half-) sibling of the king, this possibility would make Meryptah the (half-) nephew of Amenhotep III—an intriguing suggestion, but currently one that is impossible to prove. See Kozloff, *Amenhotep III*, 25 and 93. Kozloff, *Amenhotep III*, 180 further observes that the family of Meryptah and Ptahmose had control over the major priesthoods at this time as Ptahmose served as High Priest of Ptah at Memphis and Meryptah became Steward of Amenhotep's mortuary temple after being High Priest of Ptah at Thebes. Here again she notes that he "may also have been the same Meryptah who was High Priest of Amun at Karnak in Year 20."

Meryptah was based in the south at Thebes and performed his duties for Amenhotep III from that southern base.[88] He was granted a tomb in Thebes (while being commemorated in the north on a family monument at Saqqara) and was ultimately buried at Gurna during the last few years of the reign of Amenhotep III.[89]

Questions of Commemoration and Context

In the final section of our analysis of the basinophorous statue of Ruiu and Meryptah we turn to consider the possible dedicatory context and provenance of the object. Although no final answers can be provided on these issues there are several observations that we can make. One of the striking sculptural aspects of the basin is that while the texts commemorate both Meryptah and Ruiu, it is only the figure of Ruiu who appears sculpted, sitting at the rim of the basin. Given the status of Meryptah as a high-ranking royal official, we may question: why is it that Meryptah was not depicted on this basin alongside his wife? Several examples of basinophorous statues that we have mentioned above include multiple figures and dual depiction of husband and wife together appears to have been a desirable feature of these ritual objects. As Ruiu is depicted here alone, this suggests the basin might not have been a singular object, but rather belonged to a set, possibly a pair, one that depicted Meryptah and one depicting Ruiu but with dedicatory texts commemorating the two together. These objects may have been dedicated in the same context, possibly a temple setting relevant to the careers of both husband and wife. If we accept the Theban associations of Meryptah's career discussed above, combined with the status of Ruiu as Chantress of Amun, this suggests that the Glencairn basin (and a possible companion object depicting Meryptah) once stood in a Theban context, conceivably the Temple of Amun at Karnak, or some other Theban shrine, possibly in the area where Meryptah and Ruiu were ultimately buried. Meryptah's evident role in royal administration of Amenhotep III, and his title of *imy-r pr* (Steward), possibly a shortened form for *imy-r pr n tꜣ ḥwt Nb-mꜣʿt-Rʿ*, as we have discussed above, also raises the possibility that basinophorous statues of Meryptah and Ruiu were set up in one of the royal monuments of Amenemhat III on the West Bank. One wonders if Meryptah had a major role in administering the royal mortuary temple, might these basins have once been dedicated within the Kom el-Heitan itself or some neighboring structure?

While the possibility of two complementary basinophorous statues established in a single context appears attractive, however, we cannot exclude the scenario of a separate dedication of a basin commemorating Ruiu in one location and one depicting Meryptah in some other location. The couple's independent roles and Ruiu's status as Chantress of Amun might equally well have determined the location in which the Glencairn basin once stood.

Finally, in considering the provenance of the piece, although a Theban origin appears more probable, we cannot conclusively exclude the possibility it once stood at some other location in Egypt. Given the evidence summarized above indicating that Meryptah derived from a Memphite family and he may be the figure commemorated alongside his brother Ptahmose on the Leiden-London family stela, we also have the possibility that Meryptah and his wife were commemorated in a Memphite temple. Here again the presence of the temple Amenhotep III-united-with-Ptah in Memphis discussed above might offer another viable setting for this basin. Clearly, no final answer can be provided on the basis of the Glencairn basin alone. However, the object serves to further highlight the fascinating issues of identity surrounding the figure of Meryptah during the reign of Amenhotep III. It is remarkable that amongst all the surviving evidence mentioning one (or more) high officials named Meryptah no mention occurs of Meryptah's wife. The Glencairn basin is the only surviving monument to commemorate Meryptah's wife Ruiu. This remarkably fine example of a basinophorous statue of Amenhotep III's reign provides a glimpse into a man and wife who were members of the upper echelons of royal society at that stage in the late Eighteenth Dynasty. Now, properly attributed, the Glencairn basin of Ruiu and Meryptah forms a major addition to the sculptural traditions of the reign of Amenhotep III.

---

[88] It may also be of note that his wife Ruiu served as a Chantress of Amun whose major cult center was based at Thebes.

[89] Concerning the materials recovered from the pit "behind Yanni's house," Aldred ("Two Theban Notables," 113) states that their condition—without any evidence of deliberate destruction—suggests that "Meryptah had died and been buried in the odor of sanctity, presumably just before the end of the reign of Amenophis III."

Book Reviews

Louise Blanke, *An Archaeology of Egyptian Monasticism: Settlement, Economy and Daily Life at the White Monastery Federation*. Yale Egyptological Publications 2. New Haven, Yale University Press, 2019. ISBN 9781950343003. Pp. 245, 99 figures (including maps, tables, site plans). $40.

The monastic federation named after the famed abbot Shenoute of Atripe (also known as the White Monastery Federation) was incontrovertibly one of the largest and most important monasteries in Egypt. Extensive archaeological remains survive for both the women's and men's communities, as does a large corpus of letters, sermons, monastic rules, and other Coptic texts from late antiquity. The White Monastery (named for its large basilica built of white stone) was the central administrative settlement, with a smaller men's monastery in the north (the Red Monastery) and a women's monastery to the south in Atripe. Scholarship in the past two decades has increased our understanding of the site from multiple perspectives. Publications of Shenoute's writings, historical and literary analyses of these texts, digital publications of primary sources, restorations and analyses of the extensive painting programs in the churches, and renewed archaeological excavations have illuminated multiple aspects of the Federation's history, particularly in late antiquity.[1] *An Archaeology of Egyptian Monasticism* builds on this work and also fills a critical gap. This impressive monograph sheds new light on daily life in the White Monastery Federation through an archaeological examination of all three settlements in the Federation. It is a revision of Blanke's Yale dissertation and results from extensive fieldwork as a member of the Yale Monastic Archaeology Project. This detailed and well-documented book also contains nintynine photographs, tables, site plans, and other illustrations.

Chapter One presents a survey of Egyptian monasticism. Blanke steers clear of a "great men" approach to history in her summary of the main types of monasticism (urban, desert, coenobitic, i.e., community). She mentions the well-known Antony, Pachomius, and Shenoute but does not frame the monastic enterprise through their stories. Instead, the chapter surveys the monastic economy, emphasizing the diversity of economic contexts. Some monasteries banned private property while in others some monks designated heirs for their property. A brief deep dive into the known monasteries in and around Akhmim reminds readers that the White Monastery, while influential, was but one of many monastic settlements in the area. The chapter ends with a helpful digest of buildings and spaces typically found in late antique Egyptian monasteries.

Blanke writes a critical historical survey and historiography in Chapter 2, "Framing the White Monastery." The story begins with "The White Monastery before the Monks," where Blanke argues for likely human settlement in the Neolithic period. She then summarizes the pharaonic activity. The early history of the monastery is told through the lens of the first five abbots (Pcol, Ebonh, Shenoute, Besa, and Zenobios) and highlights building construction and key events in the growth of the federation. From the sixth to the sixteenth centuries, textual sources grow sparser, but Blanke nonetheless provides a mostly comprehensive account of continuous settlement, including its engagement with the patriarchs in Alexandria, the cult of the saints, and manuscript production. Especially of note is the Armenian community during the twelfth and thirteenth centuries. The section on Western "discovery" applies an appropriately critical eye to the orientalist and orientalizing narratives by American and European visitors who disparaged the local Christians living in the monastery's church. The chapter concludes with judicious analysis of archaeological campaigns from Wm. Flinders Petrie to the present. Photographs, site plans, and a table of key historical moments illustrate the chapter. There are two absences of note (in an otherwise exemplary study). The Table overview omits nineteenth and early twentieth century publications of White Monastery texts by Johannes Leipoldt, Georg Zoega,

[1] Of note are Elizabeth S. Bolman, *The Red Monastery Church: Beauty and Asceticism in Upper Egypt* (Yale University Press, 2016); David Brakke and Andrew Crislip, trans. *Selected Discourses of Shenoute the Great: Community, Theology, and Social Conflict in Late Antique Egypt* (New York, 2015); Darlene Brooks Hedstrom, *The Monastic Landscape of Late Antique Egypt* (Cambridge, 2017); Rebecca Krawiec, *Shenoute and the Women of the White Monastery* (New York, 2002); Bentley Layton, *The Canons of Our Fathers: Monastic Rules of Shenoute* (Oxford, 2014); Dana Robinson, *Food, Virtue, and the Shaping of Early Christianity* (Cambridge, 2020); Caroline T. Schroeder, *Children and Family in Late Antique Egyptian Monasticism* (Cambridge, 2021) and *Monastic Bodies: Discipline and Salvation in Shenoute of Atripe* (Philadelphia, 2007).

Journal of the American Research Center in Egypt 58 (2022), 285–87
http://dx.doi.org/10.5913/jarce.58.2022.rev001

and others (although it mentions a still unfinished twenty-first century publication project). Additionally, the corpus of writings by Apa John the Archimandrite of the White Monastery (likely from the sixth or seventh centuries) should have been included.[2]

Chapter 3 presents a comprehensive archaeological history of the White Monastery site. Blanke partitions the site into smaller segments and provides not only her interpretations of the archaeology and surveys of each area, but she also summarizes and assesses centuries of surveys, visitors' observations, and excavations at the White Monastery. A four-page table in an Appendix summarizes the features in each zone and subsection. Over fifty maps and photographs document the site's features. The chapter draws substantially from previously unpublished field reports from the Yale project. Thus, the chapter provides an up-to-date authoritative survey of the monastery. Throughout, the author signals where her analysis departs from previous research (particularly Peter Grossmann's, which until recently has been the authoritative work on the site).[3] Anyone working on the White Monastery (from any discipline) should consult the relevant sections in this chapter. One book review cannot do justice to the meticulous detail and copious information presented. This chapter illuminates the structures of daily life in the late antique community—the refectory, streets, wells, kitchens, to name a few—and also later use. What emerges is a bustling monastic village, evolving over time, waning in use in by monastics after the ninth century, with a revival in the twelfth and thirteenth centuries, and then transforming into a primarily lay settlement in the nineteenth and twentieth centuries until the Coptic Orthodox Church reestablished it as an active monastery.

Blanke then thematically analyzes all of this evidence in Chapter 4, which concerns settlement, economy, and visitors. Blanke begins with the basic architectural structure, "built environment," and size of the monastery, demonstrating that this one residence in the larger Federation was one of the largest monasteries in Egypt at 77,500 square meters. Blanke describes streets ranging from smaller arteries to wide thoroughfares. A large courtyard with several entry-points, flanked by a large two-story administrative building, functioned as a major center of activity in late antiquity. Blanke also analyzes the water supply system, including wells, methods for retrieving water from wells, pipelines, and storage. Her descriptions paint vivid pictures of ancient and medieval labor and infrastructure. Her examination reminds historians such as myself that this infrastructure "was clearly an integral part of the design of the monastic space and of the construction of individual buildings" including the great basilica (p. 130).

Blanke treats the monastic economy next. This section also discusses discoveries (such as coin hoards) that are not well published, and draws on Shenoute's writings to his monks to supplement the archaeological evidence. (As the author notes, we have little documentary evidence from the White Monastery Federation, and the bulk of our literary sources date to the fifth century). Once again the water system proved essential for pottery, food, and textile production as well as building projects (of which there were many). The size and quantity of vats for crushing olives suggest the monastery may have sold or traded olive oil not used in the community. A millstone and ovens were used for baking bread (the primary food staple). Book production certainly occurred on site, and Blanke explores the possibility that book commissions may have contributed to the monastic economy. Gold coin hoards, individual copper coins, and a mold for producing imitation copper coins "reveal a scale of wealth that emphasizes the economic importance of the White Monastery" (p. 143). The final section of the chapter examines the history of visitors, especially to the White Monastery church. Pilgrimage seems to have developed in earnest at the end of late antiquity, and there is some evidence of relics as well as a robust liturgical calendar that may have drawn pilgrims and other visitors. Of the three monastic settlements in the Federation, only the White Monastery church had a baptism, and Blanke explores the possibility of pilgrim baptisms, since the phenomenon is attested elsewhere in Egypt and the Mediterranean.

The men's community at the Red Monastery to the north and the women's community in Atripe to the south receive attention in Chapter 5. Blanke examines the settlements at each site as well as the overall federation's economic interdependence. Remains at the Red Monastery site are fewer and less studied than at the White, but Blanke nonetheless finds evidence for a substantial water system, food production areas (including oil, flour, and bread), and storage. Although monastic settlements (and literary texts about them) often attest to craft production, Blanke finds none surviving here. The community was active through at least the thirteenth century, with its most robust period likely in the fifth through seventh centuries (as deduced from ceramics, the decorative program in the church, and other factors).

In Atripe to the south, we find remarkable evidence for a women's monastic community and their reuse of pharaonic structures (notably a substantial Ptolemaic temple). Blanke here relies on previously published material from four cycles of excavation, providing her own interpretations of the evidence and providing a detailed account of the site few outside of late antique Egyptian archaeology would

[2] See Diliana Atanassova's digital editions published in the Coptic Old Testament project website (http://coptot.manuscriptroom.com/web/apa-johannes), some of which have been annotated and republished in searchable formats at the Coptic SCRIPTORIUM project site (http://data.copticscriptorium.org/urn:cts:copticLit:johannes.canons.)

[3] Peter Grossman's oeuvre is too extensive to cite here; see for example his *Christliche Architektur in Ägypten* (Leiden, 2002).

have already known.[4] A substantial refectory with circular benches survives, from which Blanke deduces the population was 200–300 monks.[5] Blanke then uses this data along with size of the water system to extrapolate to the populations of the White Monastery—up to 600 monks—and the Red Monastery—perhaps as many as 300. These estimates contrast with the *Life of Shenoute*, which assuredly exaggerates in its assertion that the Federation housed thousands of women and men. A kitchen and food production space were in the remains of the temple, and three dye shops for coloring textiles have also been found, although no evidence for weaving has yet been discovered. The Atripe community provided the wider federation with fabric and clothing, while they in turn received other goods and supplies from the White Monastery. Blanke proposes that the women's monastery died out by the eighth century. Inscriptions and dipinti have been found *in situ*, but had not yet been published at the time of the book's release; readers should see recent publications by Stephen Davis and the Yale Monastic Archaeology Project about these finds, which include the names of some of the late antique women monastics.[6]

The conclusion presents the federation as a complex human and economic system much like the other landed estates of late antique and medieval Egypt.[7] They produced food, books, olive oil, and garments for their own use and may have sold some of these goods in the wider region. Likewise, pilgrims and other visitors contributed to the Federation's economy. Blanke discusses many political, religious, and economic factors leading to the Federation's contraction in the medieval period—taxes, the changing religious demographics of Egypt, and violent regional conflicts all contributed.

In sum, *An Archaeology of Egyptian Monasticism* proves itself already to be a contemporary classic, a must-read for scholars of multiple disciplines and methodologies. Blanke provides essential updates to older theories of the sites, particularly to the heretofore authoritative work by Grossmann. The extensive maps, photographs, tables, and other illustrations are important complements to Blanke's narrative analysis. The photographs also function as an important tool of preservation, recording the state of the remains at certain moments in time on sites that are heavily traveled and, in the case of the men's monasteries, face continued modern construction. Additionally, Blanke's prose is quite accessible to archaeologists and non-archaeologists alike, presenting in clear language a complex analysis that draws on multiple streams of evidence. This important volume should find a place in most scholarly libraries, and in mine I suspect it will quickly become well-worn from much use.

Caroline Schroeder
University of Oklahoma

[4] See for example Rafed el-Sayed, Yahya el-Masry, and Victoria Altmann, *Athribis I. General Site Survey 2003–2007. Archaeological & Conservation Studies. The Gate of Ptolemy IX. Architecture and Inscriptions*, Athribis 1.1 (Cairo, 2012); Christian Leitz, Daniela Mendel, and Yahya el-Masry, *Athribis II. Die Inschriften des Tempels Ptolemaios XII.: Die Opfersäle, der Umgang und die Sanktuarräume*, 3 volumes, Athribis 2 (Cairo, 2010); Christian Leitz and Daniela Mendel, *Athribis III. Die östlichen Zugangsräume und Seitenkapellen sowie die Treppe zum Dach und die rückwärtigen Räume des Tempels Ptolemaios XII*, 2 volumes, Athirbis 3 (Cairo, 2017) and also *Athribis IV. Der Umgang L 1 bis L 3*, 2 volumes, Athribis 4 (Cairo, 2017).

[5] I follow Krawiec's work (AU: provide citation) in using the terminology of monk for both male and female monastics in the White Monastery Federation.

[6] Stephen J. Davis, "Anastasia, Thecla, and Friends," *Le Muséon*, no. 3 (2020), 259–87. https://doi.org/10.2143/MUS.133.3.3288869.

[7] See also the literary analysis of the federation as an estate in the conclusion of my *Children and Family in Late Antique Egyptian Monasticism.*

Journal of the American Research Center in Egypt 58 (2022), 287–89
http://dx.doi.org/10.5913/jarce.58.2022.rev002

Aidan Dodson, *Nefertiti: Queen and Pharaoh of Egypt. Her Life and Afterlife.* Cairo: AUC Press, 2020. ISBN 978-9774169908. Pp. 184 with 137 color photographs and black and white illustrations. $35.00.

Any student or scholar of the Amarna Period knows that this era in Egyptian history is often riddled with more questions than answers; in particular, research on the prominent historical figures of this period are some of the most contested within the Egyptological community. Such is the case with Nefertiti, whose influential role during the reign of her husband, Akhenaten, is the subject of numerous studies.[1] New to this corpus of Amarna-themed books is Aidan Dodson's *Nefertiti: Queen and Pharaoh of Egypt. Her Life and Afterlife*. Dodson's reason for writing another book on Nefertiti is to give a "fresh holistic view" of this famous queen, and to provide readers with an account of the Amarna interlude based on his own working hypotheses for this period (pp. x–xi). The book not only covers the life of the famous queen during Dynasty 18, but also the rediscovery of Nefertiti, the ongoing search for her burial and mummy, and the ways in which her icon and image "overshadow the woman herself" in more recent times (pp. 1–2).

Chapter 1 discusses what (little) is known about Nefertiti before the Amarna Period. Nefertiti's origins before she married Amenhotep IV/Akhenaten are obscure, since our earliest historical record of Nefertiti comes from blocks from the *Gem-Pa-Aten* temple at Karnak that show the prominence of Nefertiti from early in Amenhotep IV/

[1] As of December 15, 2021, a search on the *Online Egyptological Bibliography* (http://oeb.griffith.ox.ac.uk) produces 701 search results for the term "Nefertiti" that represent only those sources entered into the database.

Akhenaten's reign (p. 8). The second part of this chapter is a summation by Dodson of his hypothesis as to who the parents of Nefertiti were, his suggestion being Ay as her father, with either Iuy or Tey as her mother (pp. 18–20). The end of the chapter summarizes the recent DNA analysis of several royal mummies, including the Younger Lady from KV35—the purported mother of Tutankhamun. Dodson believes that the Younger Lady represents the mummified remains of Nefertiti herself, and to genetically make the link to Tutankhamun, he proposes that Nefertiti was the third in a series of first cousin marriages (pp. 20–22).[2]

The subject of Chapter 2 is Nefertiti's role as queen of Egypt. The chapter covers several topics, including the official titles she held, her epithets, and the evolution of the way her name was written over time (pp. 23–27); her iconography and artistic depictions during the period (pp. 26–30 and 55–59); the royal family (pp. 30–31, 46–50, and 50–52); and the founding of Akhetaten (Amarna) as a capital city, its accompanying royal necropolis (pp. 32–46), and the establishment of the Aten cult (pp. 52–55). Here Dodson further elaborates on his hypothesis that Nefertiti is the likely candidate for Tutankhaten's birth mother (as opposed to being his step-mother), based on evidence from Amarna monuments as well as DNA analysis (p. 50). One should note here that the transliteration of consonants only throughout the book for ancient Egyptian names and titles proves to be cumbersome for readers who are unfamiliar with the unvoweled reading of such texts (for example: pp. 13, 23–25), though the transliteration is ideal for scholarly research.

Dodson writes about the available evidence to show Nefertiti's transition from Great Royal Wife to Pharaoh in Chapter 3. The beginning section lays out the series of deaths in the royal family and the rise of Smenkhkare as a co-regent with Akhenaten (pp. 63–72). Dodson suggests that Smenkhkare was a younger brother of Akhenaten, based on his long-standing hypothesis that the KV55 burial in the Valley of the Kings was made for Smenkhkare,[3] rather than Akhenaten (pp. 69–70). It continues with a discussion of Nefertiti's ascension to kingship as Neferneferuaten, first as a co-regent with Akhenaten, and subsequently as a three-year regent to Tutankhaten (pp. 72–83). The chapter ends with a discussion of Neferneferuaten's death and the subsequent reuse of much of her funerary equipment for the burial of Tutankhamun (pp. 88–95). Dodson reiterates his hypothesis that the Younger Lady from KV35 is the mummy of Nefertiti, and here proposes that her untimely death was because of murder (pp. 94–95).

A number of theories regarding the potential burial place (or places) of several Amarna royal family members within the Valley of the Kings is the topic of Chapter 4, including the burial of Nefertiti/Neferneferuaten (pp. 97–102). Dodson's discussion suggests that the central area of the King's Valley, near the tombs of Tutankhamun (KV62), the "Amarna Cache" (KV55), and the cache of Amarna-era embalming materials (KV63), would be the most viable candidate for the undiscovered burial place of Nefertiti/Nefernefruaten and/or the burials of several members of the Amarna royal family. Dodson writes that "Certainly, there is enough space in the part of this area *that remains unexcavated* to accommodate such a sepulcher" (p. 99; emphasis by author). The reader should note, however, that this area of the Valley of the Kings has been almost entirely excavated by several different groups over time, including the Davis/Ayrton excavations in 1907, the Amarna Royal Tombs Project from 1999–2000, the Supreme Council of Antiquities between 2008 to 2009, and finally the ongoing KV10/KV63 Amenmesse Project.[4] Dodson does not fully endorse, nor refute, Reeves' theory that KV62 was the original burial place of Nefertiti/Neferneferuaten,[5] but provides alternative ideas as to how the tomb may have functioned for her burial before Tutankhamun's death (p. 101).

Lastly, Chapter 5 deals with the story of Nefertiti in more recent history, and the effect she has had on popular interest in Egyptology. The chapter summarizes the rediscovery of Nefertiti in the historical records during the nineteenth and twentieth centuries (pp. 107–15); this discussion is particularly strong in bringing together many obscure and complicated sources into one cohesive narrative. A brief synopsis of the excavation history of Amarna is given, including the discovery of the iconic Nefertiti bust and its subsequent removal to Berlin (pp. 115–20), as well as its display history in Germany and the debate between Egyptian and German authorities about its return to Egypt (pp. 123–28). Note that the text for figure 120 (p. 116) erroneously states that Nefertiti's painted bust was found in Amarna house O47.20 while her quartzite head was from P47.2. These house numbers should be reversed for the caption, but are correctly stated within the text (pp. 117–18). The debate about the sex of Neferneferuaten, and whether Smenkhkare and Neferneferuaten were two separate individuals or one person is summarized (pp. 128–29);[6] this is followed by an overview

[2] For an accessible summation on the pros and cons of ancient DNA studies, see: Jo Marchant, *The Shadow King* (Boston, 2013), 197–211.

[3] Aidan Dodson, *Amarna Sunset: Nefertiti, Tutankhamun, Ay, Horemheb and the Egyptian Counter-Reformation* (Cairo, 2009), 40–42.

[4] Stephen W. Cross, "The Workmen's Huts and Stratigraphy in the Valley of the Kings," *JEA* 100 (2014), 138–41.

[5] Nicholas Reeves, "The Burial of Nefertiti?," *Amarna Royal Tombs Project, Occasional Paper* No. 1 (2015), 1–16.

[6] Aidan Dodson, James Allen, and Nozomu Kawai all view Smenkhkare and Neferneferuaten as two separate kings: James Allen, "The Amarna Succession," in Peter Brand and Louise Cooper (eds.), *Causing His Name to Live: Studies in Egyptian History and Epigraphy in Memory of William J. Murnane* (Leiden, 2009), 9–20; Nozomu Kawai, "King Neferneferuaten from the Tomb of Tutankhamun Revisited" (in press). Kara Cooney and Nicholas Reeves view the two kings as one and the same person: Kara Cooney, *When Women*

of the recent investigations to identify the mummified remains of Nefertiti, including ancient DNA analysis (pp. 129–31). The chapter ends with a brief overview of Nefertiti's "afterlife," and how her icon and image became her defining characteristic in the modern world (pp. 131–32). One should note in figure 130's caption that El-Zeft's "Nefertiti" was installed on Mohammed Mahmoud street in September 2012, rather than at the start of the Egyptian revolution in 2011. It is commendable that Dodson briefly mentions Nefertiti's influence in modern Egypt (p. 132), though a more in-depth discussion would have helped to shift the conversation away from a Western-focused perspective of Nefertiti's modern influence.[7]

Dodson's *Nefertiti* proves itself to be a prime example of meticulous and thorough scholarship, which brings together a wide variety of academic sources into one coherent narrative. This book will surely be useful as a scholarly reference for professionals in the field, but also as an accessible read for the general public or students of ancient Egyptian history and the Amarna Period. In addition to the written content, the number of color figures and illustrations throughout the book helps the reader visualize all of the available pieces of evidence within one source. The affordable cost of the book will make it available for anyone to add to their personal or institutional libraries.

Nicholas Brown
University of California, Los Angeles

Richard A. Fazzini and Betsy M. Bryan, *The Precinct of Mut at South Karnak: An Archaeological Guide*. Cairo: AUC Press, 2021. ISBN: 9774169735. Pp. 94, 106 color illustrations. Pbk $19.65.

The *Precinct of Mut at South Karnak: An Archaeological Guide* by Richard Fazzini and Betsy Bryan is a very useful summary of the archaeological remains of the remarkable Precinct of Mut that sits approximately 100 meters south of the Amun Precinct of Karnak. Although the book is short, it is packed with photos and plans that are very helpful in elucidating the many layers of this site.

The book consists of nine chapters (with a chronology of the dynasties, glossary, further reading section, acknowledgements, photography credits, and index). The first chapter of the guide provides a brief synopsis of what is known about the goddess Mut, including a discussion on the Eye of Re goddesses and how they overlap and interact, the mythological stories involving Sekhmet, and the larger context of the Sekhmet statues, for which this temple is so well-known. The second chapter is a review of the archaeological history of the site: beginning with the first western records of the site from the *Description de l'Egypte* and the publications of Lepsius and Mariette in the early-mid 1800s. The earliest scientific excavations were begun in the late 1800s by British scholars Margaret Benson and Jane Gourlay. In the 1920s Maurice Pillet, then Director of Works for the Egyptian Antiquities Service at Karnak,[1] carried out further work at the site, followed in the 1970s by a team from the Brooklyn Museum (with assistance from the Detroit Institute of Art).[2] The Johns Hopkins University team began a separate but collaborative set of projects at the temple precinct in 2001. As the excavation history of this temple is not as well-known as that of many of the other temples in Luxor, this section is illuminating, and the added contextualization of some of the earliest work (along with the selection of historical photos) clearly contributes to the understanding of the site.

The remaining seven chapters (chapters 3–9) are each based on the different areas of the Precinct. Thus, the first of these chapters covers the entrance; the second covers the many elements of the Mut Temple proper (including the porches, Hut-ka chapel of Nesptah, Taharqa rams, pylons, courts, Sekhmet statues, rear of the temple, contra-temple, open air museum, and the temple in Dynasty 25); the third covers Temple A (including the courts, pylons, rear of the temple, and central sanctuary); the fourth covers Chapel B; the fifth covers the Northwest Quadrant (including the Taharqa gate and the Ptolemaic chapel); the sixth covers the temple of Ramesses III; and finally the seventh covers the Sacred Lake and the south half of the precinct. Each chapter outlines the most pertinent archaeological information for the area, with notes on the chronology and any objects uncovered during excavation. In addition, each chapter

Ruled the World (Washington D.C., 2018), 195–97; Nicholas Reeves, "The Burial of Nefertiti?" and also "Tutankhamun's Mask Reconsidered," *Bulletin of the Egyptological Seminar* 19 (2015), 511–26. Some scholars, however, propose that Meritaten, the eldest daughter of Akhenaten and Nefertiti, is a viable candidate for Neferneferuaten; e.g., Marc Gabolde, *D'Akhenaton à Tout-ânkhamon* (Lyon, 1998), 178–83; Tarek Tawfik, Susanna Thomas, and Ina Hegenbarth-Reichardt, "New evidence for Tutankhamun's parents. Revelations from the Grand Egyptian Museum," *MDAIK* 74 (2018), 177–92.

[7] For more on the influence of Nefertiti's icon and image in modern Egypt, see: Nicholas Brown, "The Beautiful One Returns: the Altered Identities of the Nefertiti Bust," in Fayza Haikal, Mervat Abdel-Nasser, Yasmin El-Shazly, Ehaab D. Abdou and Fatma Keshk (eds.), *Egyptians' Representations and Perceptions of Ancient Egypt: Towards an Antiquity Transmission and Reception Theory* (Cairo, in press).

[1] As he is identified in Morris Bierbrier, *Who Was Who in Egyptology*, Fifth revised edition (London: The Egypt Exploration Society, 2019), 369.

[2] Perhaps due to the brevity of the engagement (1985 and 1986), the book omits the explorations of the site by the All Women's Archaeological Research Expedition, or AWARE, sponsored by the then Museum of Archaeology in Fort Lauderdale, FL, and the Egyptian Antiquities Organization (https://www.nytimes.com/1985/05/12/magazine/the-new-women-of-karnak.html).

Journal of the American Research Center in Egypt 58 (2022), 289–90
doi: http://dx.doi.org/10.5913/jarce.58.2022.rev003

contains a floor plan for the structure under discussion and numerous color photos, often with internal labels to indicate any noteworthy features. These labels are tremendously helpful, as the remains of many of the structures can be difficult to distinguish (see, for example, on pp. 23–24—in the section on the Horwedja Chapel—where the photos have labels indicating the *in situ* location of some reused blocks). The information provided here is invaluable for anyone interested in visiting the site, or in using the complex for comparative work.

This admirable volume could have been improved by the inclusion of captions for each figure. Although the images are referenced in the surrounding text, their content is sometimes difficult to understand without explanatory captions. That being said, the book is well organized, and the number and variety of photographs and plans are notable assets. Additionally, the "Further Reading" section is comprehensive and will be useful for anyone interested in the Mut complex.

Overall, this book is an excellent resource, as beneficial for a layperson looking to visit the site, as for an Egyptologist looking to better understand the larger historical context of the temple compound and the complex interplay of layers and chronology.

Ariel Singer
University of Chicago

Ellen Morris, *The Architecture of Imperialism: Military Bases and the Evolution of Foreign Policy in Egypt's New Kingdom*. Leiden: Brill, 2005. Probleme der Ägyptologie 22. ISBN 90-04-1406-0. Pp ix + 891, 63 black and white illustrations. $451.00.

Ellen Morris, *Ancient Egyptian Imperialism*. Hoboken, NJ: Wiley Blackwell, 2018. ISBN_9781405136785. Pp xi + 320, numerous black and white illustrations. $99.95; Pbk $39.95.

Ancient Egypt provides an early example of imperial expansion and domination, a facet of Egyptian civilization that a number of scholars have explored. Although one must be cautious in adopting modern terminology for ancient phenomena, Egypt's northward and southward conquests and occupation meet modern definitions of imperialism, settler colonialism, and even a similar post-colonial dynamic, particularly in Nubia, although of course there are points of comparison and contrast. Ellen Morris's work on ancient Egyptian imperialism is important in recognizing the complex dynamics of ancient imperialism while providing a useful set of comparisons and contrasts with examples from various times and places. Through a happy accident, I was sent both her older book, published through Brill, and the more recent volume from Blackwell. I begin with a short consideration of her earlier *The Architecture of Imperialism*, before returning to a more extended review of her recent new book, *Ancient Egyptian Imperialism*.

Although published some time ago, *The Architecture of Imperialism* remains an impressive *tour de force* review of military installations during the New Kingdom, ancient Egypt's most expansive period. Although new discoveries need to be considered since the volume was published in 2005, it remains a valuable resource and starting point for any study of the mechanics of Egypt's New Kingdom empire. An adaptation of her dissertation, the volume is organized into sections covering the Early, Mid, and Late Eighteenth Dynasty, and the Nineteenth and Twentieth Dynasties. Each section presents a historical summary of ancient Egypt's expansion into Syria-Palestine and Nubia, with the Libyan Desert added for the later dynasties. Each regional section summarizes the textual and archaeological evidence for Egyptian military/imperial installations. Each chronological part concludes with a cross-frontier comparison and contrast of the larger implications of this patterning for imperial policy. Both this study and the newer volume are remarkable for the balance between north and south—typically research on Egyptian imperialism focuses on one or the other region. As a result, it also represents a massive effort in compiling information about Egyptian imperial installations, making it an essential starting point for anyone studying the subject. Although heavy on the particular, Morris nevertheless provides a number of important insights into the organization of empire north and south (again, the combination of both is both highly unusual and valuable). However, because of the volume's massive size and level of detail, it remains more of a reference for the specialist interested in the New Kingdom empire than a resource for general reading about this important aspect of ancient Egyptian civilization.

Morris's new book, *Ancient Egyptian Imperialism*, covers similar ground but in a more accessible and synthetic way that will appeal to a broad audience crossing disciplinary boundaries, as well as the interested public. She also increases the time frame, which now runs from the emergence of the Egyptian state, where she sees an imperial dynamic playing an important role, through the New Kingdom. This study is more analytical and theoretically informed, and provides updates from more recent archaeological work, especially in Sudanese Nubia. Instead of being organized by period and region, this new volume explores various overlapping themes within a broadly chronological and regional organization. She begins by drawing comparisons between later empire and the initial consolidation and expansion of the Egyptian state, centered around the acquisition of exotica in a political economy that expressed and enhanced elite power. This discussion provides a welcome focus on the exploitative and extractive nature of Egyptian imperialism—a feature of empires worldwide.

Journal of the American Research Center in Egypt 58 (2022), 290–94
doi: http://dx.doi.org/10.5913/jarce.58.2022.rev004

Chapter 2 focuses on settler colonialism in the oases and Lower Nubia during the Old Kingdom, a theme that continues in Chapter 3 (and 4), where she traces the shift from military occupation to settler colonialism in Lower Nubia through the Middle Kingdom, noting the increasing entanglements between Egyptian colonists and the local population over the course of imperial shifts from garrisons to militarized communities. Based on archaeological and textual evidence, I would place that transition slightly earlier in the late Twelfth Dynasty and the later shift to Kushite control somewhat later at the very end of the Thirteenth Dynasty,[1] but these are minor points.

The discussion of the oases in Chapter 2 is fascinating and highlights the critical role that the western desert played in diplomacy and trade, often neglected in Egyptology. Dakhla in particular was an important link in the desert roads exploited by Harkhuf and other trade and diplomatic expedition leaders, with a surprising degree of continuity across the First Intermediate Period and on into the Middle Kingdom (and likely beyond). I was happy to see that Morris correctly locates Yam to the west. Contrasting with its usual placement by Egyptologists along the Nile at Kerma, this new interpretation is consistent with the recently discovered Middle Kingdom graffito at Uweinat in northwestern Sudan that mentions a meeting between emissaries of Yam and Montuhotep II. The route extending from Dakhla to Abu Ballas through the Gilf Kebir and Uweinat makes little sense if Kerma was the goal, but would make perfect sense if the destination lay to the southwest, either Chad's Ennedi Mountains and/or Darfur in far western Sudan.[2] As Morris points out, Yam was likely in close contact with both Kerma and Egypt, part of a network of northeast African polities that engaged in long distance exchange across what is too often seen as impassible desert, but was navigable via donkey caravan by experienced expedition leaders like Harkhuf with the help of the kind of desert infrastructure and residual settlement revealed in older and more recent deep Saharan surveys.[3] Her focus on the desert serves to highlight the importance of the oases in Egypt's larger imperial policy and serves as a reminder of their importance throughout Egyptian history as well as ancient Egypt's extensive interconnections with other parts of Africa.

Chapter 4 explores intercultural interactions in Nubia through the lens of transculturation—the combination of cultural features in the context of empire and intercultural interaction. Identity became more entangled over time with the shifts from Egyptian to Kushite and back to Egyptian control from the Middle through New Kingdom, especially with the emergence of bicultural families in the colonial centers. This perspective goes against older ideas of Egyptian withdrawal, native "squatters," and reconquest and "Egyptianization," instead providing a welcome focus on how strategies by settlers and indigenous communities and everyday decisions shaped the course of intercultural interaction. However, I would argue that the spread of Egyptian material culture from the Second Intermediate Period into the New Kingdom, while dramatic, was not quite as complete as she suggests. Nubian handmade ceramic and other material culture traditions and practices were muted, but never disappeared, even at the colonial centers.[4] Having said that, Morris rightly points out that the presence of an Egyptian ceramic industry and cultural features like supine, coffined burials reflects a major shift towards Egyptian practices, even though the continuing presence of flexed burial and other Nubian traditions produced complex and highly variable outcomes both regionally and individually, something she emphasizes throughout the book.

Chapters 5 and 6 pivot to Egypt's expansion into Syria-Palestine at the beginning of the New Kingdom, focusing on the intersection of military power, colonial infrastructure, and diplomatic influence that incentivized collaboration but led to an inherently unstable imperial strategy. Her description of the thin line walked by Levantine rulers, negotiating their way between local and imperial interests is compelling and I appreciate the focus it brings to the role of imperial subjects in the empire. For example, rather than seeing the Amarna Letters as a sign of imperial weakness, Morris provides insights into what they reflect about the interplay between imperial power, local resistance, and manipulation for advantage among competing vassals.

Chapters 7 and 8 round out the volume, shifting to the Ramesside Period with a focus on Syria-Palestine and Nubia, respectively. She begins in the north by looking at the interplay of rulers, populace, and imperial interests in Syria-Palestine. A heavier profile of empire in the Levant produced a stronger archaeological signature with evidence for Egyptian outposts with transplanted ceramic industries, foodways, and religious institutions. This expansion was followed by contraction in the later Twentieth Dynasty, with Egypt's sphere of influence waning and foreign mercenaries replacing Egyptian garrisons in areas still under imperial control. In contrast, Egypt's heavier imperial footprint in Nubia was renewed and expanded dramatically during the New Kingdom. Morris explores how the shift in strategy from fortresses to temple towns served to encourage an Egyptian pattern of life as settler colonialism and a temple dominated economy mirroring Egypt's expanded upstream

[1] Stuart Tyson Smith, *Askut in Nubia: The Economics and Ideology of Egyptian Imperialism in the Second Millennium BC* (London, 1995), 53–80.

[2] Julien Cooper, "Reconsidering the Location of Yam," *JARCE* 48 (2012), 1–21.

[3] Stefan Kröpelin and Rudolph Kuper, "More Corridors to Africa," *CRIPEL* 26 (2006–2007), 219–29.

[4] Stuart Tyson Smith, "The Nubian Experience of Egyptian Domination During the New Kingdom," in Geoff Emberling and Bruce Beyer Williams (eds.), *The Oxford Handbook of Ancient Nubia* (Oxford, 2020), 369–94.

past the second cataract. She also argues that these new lightly fortified settlements transformed a Nubian pastoral society into an agrarian one, but the Kerma-based Kushite state was already characterized by settled life, having relied heavily on agriculture since the formative pre-Kerma phase.[5] At the same time, she is right about the continuing value and symbolic importance of cattle, which as she notes looms large in imperial accounts.

In a shift from her earlier book, Morris rightly pushes back against the notion of decline and depopulation in Nubia during the Ramesside Period, in contrast to the pattern in the Levant, which was wracked by the collapse of the Mediterranean Bronze Age. She rightly notes the problems in archaeological visibility, including an early bias against settlement archaeology, poor coverage in Upper Nubia, and the simplification in burial practices that tend to make Ramesside tombs more difficult to identify chronologically. I would add that excavation has sometimes simply failed to reach the right strata or locations to identify New Kingdom settlements associated with large temple complexes, including Kawa and Tabo in Upper Nubia. The recent identification of settlement areas at other sites, especially at Napata, have the potential to change this picture as new work proceeds. As she notes, recent excavation at colonial sites that were once thought to be abandoned in the late New Kingdom, including Amara West and Sesebi, have now identified continuity across the end of the empire. Ongoing excavations at Tombos document an occupation across the New Kingdom into the Napatan period. Through Strontium Isotope Analysis, we have also documented a continuing flow of colonists arriving from Egypt as late as the Ramesside Period, along with the continued construction of monumental tombs in the cemetery.[6] In contrast to the Levant, the contraction of the New Kingdom's southern empire was not a withdrawal of Egyptian resources and personal from Nubia, as she notes at one point, but rather a Nubian withdrawal from Egyptian control. Morris generally acknowledges this distinction in an in-depth discussion of the career of Panehesy, the last Viceroy of Kush, and his struggle for power and potential contribution to the end of the New Kingdom.

Chapter 8 ends with an exploration of how the deeper engagement between Egypt and Nubia in the New Kingdom led to a truly post-colonial era with important implications for the rise of the Kushite (Twenty-fifth) Dynasty. The usual model of reversion to older practices and fragmentation into a series of competing "chiefdoms," reforming into a powerful "Egyptianized" state with renewed Egyptian influence, has been increasingly rejected in Nubian Studies, although the notion still has traction. Morris notes that local leaders, whether ultimately of Egyptian, Nubian, or mixed ancestry, had increasingly taken responsibility for managing the colony. Although she briefly alludes to a withdrawal of resources and personnel, this idea seems unlikely given how embedded members of colonial communities had become in local social, economic, and power structures. As she discusses, Panehesy himself retreated south after his failed attempt at seizing the throne and survived to be buried in grand style at Aniba, the colonial capital. Thus, the colonial infrastructure, temple economies, and other extractive industries that had profited Egypt under the empire did not cease, but could continue, managed for Nubian rather than Egyptian interests. Morris astutely observes that Panehesy's interest in Thebes and conflict with the Theban high priest of Amun foreshadows Piankhi's later preoccupation with a "restoration" of the proper cult of the god, who by this time had been syncretized with a Kushite deity associated with rams, lending Amun his later ram manifestation.

Along with the discussion in Chapter 4, this section deftly explores the complexities of identity in the context of empire, with a vibrant and diverse interweaving of different cultural features as the former colony moved into a truly post-colonial era. Rather than seeing this phenomenon as an "Egyptianization" followed by Nubian revival or the creation of a generalized hybrid blending the two, she rightly argues for variability between sites and even among individuals, who interwove Nubian and Egyptian cultural features in ways that became naturalized. The fusion of Kushite ram symbolism connected with the cult of Amun and the theological importance of the mountain of Gebel Barkal as Amun's birthplace provides a good example of this kind of internalization, as well as a dynamic of mutual influence. In this case, one of Egypt's most important gods was transformed and "Nubianized," playing as central a role, if not more, in Kushite religion as he did in Egypt.[7] Morris perceptively notes that this may have helped pave the way for the later Kushite assumption of Egyptian kingship during the Twenty-fifth Dynasty, giving Kushite kings considerable appeal as rulers in Egypt, especially at Thebes. Here I see a lost opportunity to consider the Kushite kings not so much as foreign or "Egyptianized" invaders, but rather through a post-colonial lens as forging a new double kingdom with its own imperial dynamic, including a struggle over the southern Levant with the rising power of Assyria. It is important to recognize that Piankhi's famous campaign in c. 727 BCE was not an invasion, but rather the suppression of a northern revolt against the authority of the Kushite Dynasty. I

[5] Elisabeth Anne Hildebrand and Timothy M. Schilling, "Storage amidst early agriculture along the Nile: Perspectives from Sai Island, Sudan," *Quaternary International* 412 (2000), 81–95.

[6] Michele R. Buzon, Stuart Tyson Smith, and Antonio Simonetti, "Entanglement and the Formation of the Ancient Nubian Napatan State," *American Anthropologist* 118 (2016), 284–300.

[7] Luc Gabolde, "Insight into the Perception of Royal and Divine Powers among Kushites and Egyptians," in Matthieu Honegger (ed.), *Nubian Archaeology in the XXIst Century. Proceedings of the Thirteenth International Conference for Nubian Studies, Neuchâtel, 1st-6th September 2014* (Leuven, 2018), 91–103.

would argue that this political expansion was facilitated decades before by their close ties with Thebes rather than military conquest, consistent with Morris's observations on the post-colonial dynamic surrounding the cult of Amun-Re.

In an epilogue, she deconstructs representations of the Presentation of *Inu* ceremony as a clever metaphor about the goals and limitations of empire and colonial power. She begins by emphasizing the event's outward emphasis on foreign luxuries for the prestige economy as well as the mobilization of staple goods, an outward show of how the empire benefited Egyptians, collaborators among conquered peoples, and fueled international diplomacy. She then moves on to a perceptive analysis of the subtext of the Presentation Ceremonies, reinforcing royal ideological, economic, and political power. In line with anthropological studies of similar events, this kind of political theater reflects a more fragile hold on power than the picture the carefully choreographed events conveyed. Appealing to Said's idea of "discrepant experience," she disagrees with my conclusion that Nubian princes like Hekanefer of Miam, shown in the Viceroy Amenhotep Huy's tomb in full Nubian regalia, might have been annoyed at having to present themselves as the pacified "other." In contrast, she argues for a variable experience, including the possibility that they wore these costumes in "defiant pride," as some scholars have argued. While I do not disagree with Edward Said's notion of the "massively knotted and complex histories of special but nevertheless overlapping and interconnected experiences" that characterize empires, I note that he also points out that the concept is not intended to circumvent the imperial dynamics of ideology and power.[8] Defiance would be expressed by throwing off the trappings of alterity that reinforced what Antonio Loprieno has characterized as the *ausländer topos*.[9] This is exactly what the Maharaja Sayaji Rao did in the context of the 1911 British Imperial Durbar, an event that provides some interesting comparisons and contrasts with the presentation ceremony. During this coronation ceremony installing the British monarch as Emperor of India, he departed from the carefully arranged script when he threw off his "native" and imperial regalia and casually approached the British King/Emperor, giving only a perfunctory obeisance, walking stick in hand. As one of the most important Indian rulers, his act disordered the carefully constructed picture of imperial self and Indian other that legitimated British royal authority, as well as blurring carefully drawn cultural lines with the adoption of a walking stick, a marker of elite English society. The Nubian princes may have appreciated the benefits that collaboration conveyed and like the other Maharajas have complied with the humiliating subordination to imperial rule—a central theme and one of the strengths in Morris's book, but Rao's comment "it would have been all right if we had not to act in it like animals in a circus" seems like a more likely reaction from the princes than feelings of ethnic pride that are completely absent from self-representation in their tombs, where, as Morris acknowledges, they appear as Egyptian officials.[10] I would argue that real defiance resided in individual choices like the women at Tombos (and the families who buried them), who were positioned in Kushite style in a way that would have dramatically signaled their alterity in a context where conformity would have been expected, as opposed to the Prince's celebrating an alterity that they did not otherwise express in a context where it was demanded. As with the colonial Durbars, there would be little room for expression outside of the carefully choreographed presentation. James Scott points out any departure from events like these that would undermine the ideological message would provoke a strong reaction.[11] This was the case with Sayaji Rao, whose position was threatened by official and public outrage in the aftermath of his defiance. Morris takes a similar position elsewhere, pointing out that grand displays mask insecurity, and I would add that any acts that might crack the façade of royal ideology would be seen as a direct threat to royal authority.

In sum, the two studies by Morris complement one another and provide essential reading for those interested in ancient Egyptian imperialism as well as empires worldwide. *The Architecture of Imperialism* presents a rich data set describing Egypt's imperial footprint that is still useful for the specialist and is remarkable for its in-depth discussion of both the northern and southern empires. *Ancient Egyptian Imperialism* moves forward from this foundation in a greater engagement with theory and cross-cultural comparison that gives it considerable appeal to general Egyptology and a more popular audience, updating and probing how different groups and individuals within conquered societies negotiated their way in the context of colonialism, which is refreshing given the tendency to homogenize empires and focus on the metropole. Both volumes are remarkable in adopting a multi-scalar approach with a strong focus on the variable strategies taken in Egypt's western, northern, and southern empires. Her integration of comparative examples from more recent imperial episodes provides insights that might otherwise be missed, including perceptive allusions to Machiavelli and classic analyses of other empires like Luttwak on Roman imperial strategy, Wells on the complexities of intercultural interaction in the similar

[8] Edward Said, *Culture and Imperialism* (New York, 1993), 32–33.

[9] Antonio Loprieno, *Topos und Mimesis*, ÄGAB 48 (Wiesbaden, 1988), 22–34.

[10] Stuart Tyson Smith, "Colonial Gatherings: The Presentation of Inu in New Kingdom Egypt and the British Imperial Durbar, a Comparison," in Fiona Belgane (ed.), *Gatherings: Past and Present. Proceedings from the 2013 Archaeology of Gatherings International Conference at IT, Sligo, Ireland* (Oxford, 2017), 102–12.

[11] James C. Scott, *Domination and the Arts of Resistance: Hidden Transcripts* (New Haven, 1990), 17–19, 77–90, and 202–28.

Roman contexts, and other imperial ventures and occupations worldwide, including China, Spain in the New World, and more recently in Iraq and Afghanistan. This emphasis on individual agency and how it helps drive imperial outcomes aligns this study with the latest approaches to ancient imperialism. Her interpretations are situated solidly within anthropological and archaeological theory relating to empires, making the volume stronger as a result and broadening the volume's impact within and outside the field. All too often, Egyptology focuses on the particular without a consideration of broader context, among other ancient societies and especially issues relevant to modern life. Morris's work is exemplary in framing issues surrounding within a larger scholarly and theoretical context with the result that her scholarship makes an important contribution to the archaeology and history of ancient Egyptian imperialism as well as empires more generally.

Stuart Tyson Smith
University of California, Santa Barbara

Jennifer Taylor Westerfeld, *Egyptian Hieroglyphs in the Late Antique Imagination*. Philadelphia: University of Pennsylvania Press, 2019. ISBN 978-0-8122-5157-9. Pp. xiv + 242, 15 black and white illustrations. $32.37.

The year 2022 marks the bicentenary of Champollion's decipherment of the hieroglyphic script, marking the start of the modern study of the ancient Egyptian language, as well as its public reception. Yet interest in and engagement with hieroglyphs is not a modern phenomenon, and this volume aims to address a gap both in the history of their study and the reception of pharaonic history. Drawing upon classical (i.e., Greek and Roman) writers and early Christian authors, Westerfeld explores different ways that hieroglyphs were interpreted, reinterpreted, and utilised in late antiquity.

The first chapter primarily consists of background information for readers unfamiliar with the hieroglyphic writing system, as well as questions of literacy, status, priesthood, multilingualism, and script obsolescence.[1] The treatment of the late antique sources starts in the following chapter. Here, two main points are tackled: classical and late antique authors' understandings of the invention of the hieroglyphic script and Egyptian history writing practices. The role accredited to Thoth (and the syncretic Thoth-Hermes-Mercury) in the invention of writing is discussed. A key feature that Westerfeld returns to throughout this volume is how the Christian sources came to terms with earlier discourses and the strategies that different individuals had for dealing with them. In this case, Thoth is reduced to a man, not a god. For example, for Clement of Alexandria (second–third century CE theologian) Hermes was a priest, while for Augustine (fourth–fifth century CE) Mercury was a human cultural hero. Augustine also offers an alternative tradition in which Isis (the deified version of a human queen, Io) is accredited as the inventor of writing. These authors faced an additional issue in dealing with the Egyptian historical tradition and their use of it in the establishment of a universal chronology. On one hand, the Egyptian records provided Christians with a claim to greater antiquity than the Greeks, but the length of Egyptian chronologies also provided a conundrum with how to align such histories with the stricter Biblical genealogies and not assign them greater antiquity than the Hebrew prophets.

Moving from the invention of hieroglyphs and the Egyptian historical tradition, Chapter 3 examines how the script itself was understood. The general attitude found across the sources is that hieroglyphs were symbolic in nature, designed to conceal priestly wisdom. While highlighting this general misunderstanding of the script, Westerfeld also notes the Egyptian use of cryptographic scripts (such as that of the hymn to Khnum at Esna, which consists of variations of ram and crocodile signs), which provide a precedent for the actual use of hieroglyphs to conceal knowledge. As the hymn is largely contemporaneous with the early classical authors (including the first century BCE historian Diodorus Siculus), how much it establishes such a precedent is somewhat questionable. A pragmatic point is also raised here, but is not developed, namely how low literacy levels concealed the meaning of hieroglyphs to the majority of the population. The focus on mythic secrecy therefore somewhat obscures how the knowledge contained within the hieroglyphic script (let alone cryptographic scripts) was inaccessible to almost everybody who encountered them. Moving from classical to Christian authors, another source of tension is encountered in the figure of Moses. His Egyptian education cannot be denied, but it can be problematized. Augustine, for example, condemns Egyptian pride in their wisdom tradition as foolish and vainglorious; after all, Moses beat the Egyptians at their own game, demonstrating the superiority of divine intervention. Late antiquity also saw the emergence of other sources of intellectual authority, principally monasticism, and in particular the trope of the uneducated monk. This topic is introduced but not further developed.[2]

This mention of monks transitions the discussion to one of the most important figures of Egyptian monasticism, Shenoute of Atripe (late fourth and fifth century CE).

[1] On script change during this period, see now Edward O. D. Love, *Script Switching in Roman Egypt Case Studies in Script Conventions, Domains, Shift, and Obsolescence from Hieroglyphic, Hieratic, Demotic, and Old Coptic Manuscripts* (Berlin, 2021).

[2] On this trope and more generally monastic education, see now the collected articles in Lillian Larsen and Samuel Rubenson (eds.), *Monastic Education in Late Antiquity. The Transformation of Classical* Paideia (Cambridge-New York, 2018).

Journal of the American Research Center in Egypt 58 (2022), 294–96
doi: http://dx.doi.org/10.5913/jarce.58.2022.rev005

Shenoute was a prolific writer, and this chapter focuses on his work known as *Acephalous work 6*, which contains an invective against hieroglyphs. Westerfeld not only discusses the local, Egyptian element (attitudes towards hieroglyphs) of this passage but also the wider tropes in Christian literature on which it draws (the conversion of temples to churches). On one hand, Shenoute presents a realistic description of hieroglyphs, but he characterises them as a locus of spiritual danger, of idolatry, animal worship, and blood sacrifice. Each of these accusations is situated within the broader literary tradition, drawing upon Biblical parallels in particular. Westerfeld notes that Shenoute's recognition of the power of hieroglyphs is "not out of keeping" (p. 113) with beliefs from earlier periods. However, while recognising an inherent power in the signs, Shenoute's reasoning is very different and the attempt to connect late antique responses to their ancient predecessors seems to this reviewer a bit of a reach. Furthermore, Shenoute's strategy is to undermine the power of the signs by emphasising that they are the works of human hands, and as such are open to ridicule (a rhetorical practice witnessed in other examples presented throughout this study), which diminishes their threat.

The final chapter turns to the problem of translating hieroglyphs and the use of hieroglyphs in constructing authority in late antiquity. Three main case studies are provided: obelisks in Rome, the destruction of the Serapeum in Alexandria during the reign of Theodosius I (c. 391 CE), and a literary episode involving the patriarch Theophilus of Alexandria. In the first of these examples, the focus is on the translation accredited to Hermapion of Rameses II's obelisk that today stands in the Piazza del Popolo in Rome, particularly Hermapion's translation choices, through a comparison with the actual text. While the newly carved obelisk of Domitian in Piazza Navona is mentioned, such obelisks produced and inscribed in Rome during the imperial period are not discussed in any detail. An opportunity has therefore been lost to examine translation *into* Egyptian during this period and the range of questions that it raises concerning knowledge of hieroglyphs outside of Egypt at this time, which itself would also further the discussion about classical understanding of hieroglyphs.[3] The other two case studies focus rather on the (re-)interpretation of certain signs. The ankh sign, as seen in the Serapeum, provides the opportunity for an excursus on the use of the ankh in late-antique Egypt, for example, in reliefs and on textiles. In the second case, Theophilus interprets the meaning of three thetas on a temple relief, but what he reads as the Greek letter θ is probably the sun disk with uraeai on either side. In this instance, the hieroglyphic signs are converted into Christian messages, the understanding of which is only possible through inspiration of the holy spirit. Westerfeld argues that such readings are examples of the Christian exertion of authority over the signs being translated.

In addition to drawing together the main arguments from across the five chapters, Westerfeld also uses the relatively short conclusion to propose two avenues for future research. The first of these is to bridge the gap between the late-antique Christian treatment of hieroglyphs to that in the early medieval Islamic sources, to examine whether and how Arabic authors were in dialogue with earlier works. The second avenue is to focus not on the discourse surrounding hieroglyphs but the material aspects of late-antique responses to inscriptions. Westerfeld in part already demonstrates the potential for reinterpreting spaces in her brief discussion of the graffito of the monk Jacob in KV2 (the tomb of Rameses IV), in which she addresses the uncritical comments of previous scholarship.[4] The practice of transforming temples and tombs into villages, churches, and monastic complexes throughout this period offers considerable case studies and potential for such a study.

There are many points to recommend this volume. Throughout, Westerfeld draws upon a broad range of sources, in terms of both genre (primarily literary texts, but also documents and the epigraphic record) and languages (Demotic, Coptic, Greek, Latin), and manages to present the diverse material and arguments in a clear and engaging writing style. In so doing, she challenges previous scholarship that has tended to oversimplify the attitudes of late antique authors towards the pharaonic past. However, one critique of the volume is that it is not always clear who the intended audience is. While one of Westerfeld's main goals is to address a significant gap in the reception of pharaonic Egypt, the presentation of the material seems to be directed mainly at classicists and late-antique scholars who will be familiar already with many of the sources. Readers without this background may get lost in the array of authors and works discussed, most of whom are given only very brief introductions. This audience may also be more confident with how select words and phrases from the original text (mainly Greek, but on occasion Egyptian in transliteration and Latin) are interspersed within the provided translations. The utility of such inclusions, rather than the entire original passage, which appear with irregular frequency across the relevant extracts is also questionable: those who can read the original may prefer the entire passage, while those who cannot read the original may find their presence distracting from the translation. One possible suggestion for the future, based on the wealth of sources included throughout this

[3] On other monuments carved during the reign of Domitian, the twin obelisks of Benevento, see Luigi Prada, "'To Isis the Great, Lady of Benevento': Privately Dedicated Egyptian Obelisks in Imperial Rome and the Twin Obelisks of Benevento Reedited," in Jeffrey Spier and Sara E. Cole (eds.), *Egypt and the Classical World: Cross-Cultural Encounters in Antiquity* (Los Angeles, 2022).

[4] A color image of this graffito, as well as others written throughout KV2, are available to view on the Theban Mapping Project website (https://thebanmappingproject.com).

volume, is a sourcebook that brings together the relevant passages, together with contextual information and commentary, such that audiences with diverse backgrounds, but all interested in the history of the reception of pharaonic history, can confidently access the material.

Ultimately, this desire for more information is testament to the possibilities that Westerfeld highlights in her monograph, and how she has paved the way for further enquiry. *Egyptian Hieroglyphs in the Late Antique Imagination* is an important addition to the reception of hieroglyphs and of pharaonic culture. Westerfeld provides a nuanced treatment of the classical and Christian works, understanding them on their own merit and within their own context, demonstrating that their responses to hieroglyphs were more complex than has often been portrayed. Westerfeld highlights what can be achieved through exploration of these sources and opens up exciting new routes of further enquiry.

Jennifer Cromwell
Manchester Metropolitan University
Manchester, UK